*Seasonal Affective Disorders
and Phototherapy*

Seasonal Affective Disorders and Phototherapy

Edited by
Norman E. Rosenthal
Mary C. Blehar
National Institute of Mental Health

THE GUILFORD PRESS
New York   London

The opinions expressed herein are the views of the individual authors and do not
necessarily reflect the official position of the National Institute of Mental Health or any
other part of the U.S. Department of Health and Human Services.

The chapters in this volume emanated from a 1987 workshop on seasonal affective
disorders sponsored by the National Institute of Mental Health. Unless attributed to a
previously published report, all material contained herein is in the public domain and may
be used without permission from the Institute or the author. Citation of the source is
appreciated.

Published 1989 by The Guilford Press
A Division of Guilford Publications, Inc.
72 Spring Street, New York, N.Y. 10012

Printed in the United States of America

Last digit is print number: 9 8 7 6 5 4 3 2 1

Library of Congress Cataloging-in-Publication Data

Seasonal affective disorders and phototherapy / edited by Norman E.
    Rosenthal and Mary C. Blehar.
        p. cm.
    Includes bibliographies and index.
    ISBN 0-89862-741-9
    1. Seasonal affective disorder—
Treatment. 2. Phototherapy.
    I. Rosenthal, Norman E. II. Blehar, Mary.
    [DNLM: 1. Affective Disorders—therapy. 2. Phototherapy.
    3. Seasons. WM 171 S439]
    RC545.S43 1989
    616.85′27—dc19
    DNLM/DLC
    for Library of Congress   88-24402
                                                        CIP

Contributors

Barbara Ainsworth, PhD, Departments of Physiology and Epidemiology, School of Medicine, University of Minnesota, Minneapolis, Minnesota

Paul Arbisi, BS, Department of Psychology, University of Minnesota, Minneapolis, Minnesota

Mary C. Blehar, PhD, Mood, Anxiety, and Personality Disorders Research Branch, National Institute of Mental Health, Rockville, Maryland

Richard A. Depue, PhD, Department of Psychology, University of Minnesota, Minneapolis, Minnesota

Connie C. Duncan, PhD, Laboratory of Psychology and Psychopathology, National Institute of Mental Health, Bethesda, Maryland

Paul A. Gaist, BA, Clinical Psychobiology Branch, National Institute of Mental Health, Bethesda, Maryland

Holly Giesen, BA, Clinical Psychobiology Branch, National Institute of Mental Health, Bethesda, Maryland

J. C. Gillin, MD, San Diego Veterans Administration Medical Center, San Diego, California; Department of Psychiatry, University of California at San Diego, La Jolla, California

Carla Hellekson, MD, Department of Psychiatry and Behavioral Sciences, University of Washington Medical School, Seattle, Washington; Fairbanks Psychiatric and Neurologic Clinic, Fairbanks, Alaska

Tana M. Hoban, PhD, Departments of Psychiatry, Ophthalmology, and Pharmacology, Sleep and Mood Disorders Laboratory, Oregon Health Sciences University, Portland, Oregon; current address: Department of Animal Physiology, University of California at Davis, Davis, California

Frederick M. Jacobsen, MD, MPH, Clinical Psychobiology Branch and Laboratory of Clinical Science, National Institute of Mental Health, Bethesda, Maryland

Jean R. Joseph-Vanderpool, MD, Clinical Psychobiology Branch, National Institute of Mental Health, Bethesda, Maryland

Siegfried Kasper, MD, Clinical Psychobiology Branch, National Institute of Mental Health, Bethesda, Maryland

Karen A. Kelly, MD, Clinical Psychobiology Branch, National Institute of Mental Health, Bethesda, Maryland

D. F. Kripke, MD, San Diego Veterans Administration Medical Center, San Diego, California; Department of Psychiatry, University of California at San Diego, La Jolla, California

Verena Lacoste, PhD, Psychiatric University Clinic, CH-4025 Basel, Switzerland

Arthur Leon, MD, Departments of Physiology and Epidemiology, School of Medicine, University of Minnesota, Minneapolis, Minnesota

Alfred J. Lewy, MD, PhD, Departments of Psychiatry, Ophthalmology, and Pharmacology, Sleep and Mood Disorders Laboratory, Oregon Health Sciences University, Portland, Oregon

N. Mrosovsky, PhD, Departments of Zoology and Psychology, University of Toronto, Toronto, Ontario, Canada

D. J. Mullaney, MS, San Diego Veterans Administration Medical Center, San Diego, California; Department of Psychiatry, University of California at San Diego, La Jolla, California

Dennis L. Murphy, MD, Laboratory of Clinical Science, National Institute of Mental Health, Bethesda, Maryland

Colin S. Pittendrigh, PhD, Hopkins Marine Station, Stanford University, Stanford California

Susan L. B. Rogers, RN, Clinical Psychobiology Branch, National Institute of Mental Health, Bethesda, Maryland

Norman E. Rosenthal, MD, Clinical Psychobiology Branch, National Institute of Mental Health, Bethesda, Maryland

David A. Sack, MD, Clinical Psychobiology Branch, National Institute of Mental Health, Bethesda, Maryland

Robert L. Sack, MD, Departments of Psychiatry, Ophthalmology, and Pharmacology, Sleep and Mood Disorders Laboratory, Oregon Health Sciences University, Portland, Oregon

T. J. Savides, MD, San Diego Veterans Administration Medical Center, San Diego, California; Department of Psychiatry, University of California at San Diego, La Jolla, California

Patricia M. Schulz, MSW, Clinical Psychobiology Branch, National Institute of Mental Health, Bethesda, Maryland

Clifford M. Singer, MD, Departments of Psychiatry, Ophthalmology, and Pharmacology, Sleep and Mood Disorders Laboratory, Oregon Health Sciences University, Portland, Oregon

Robert G. Skwerer, MD, Clinical Psychobiology Branch, National Institute of Mental Health, Bethesda, Maryland

William A. Sonis, MD, Philadelphia Child Guidance Clinic, Division of Child and Adolescent Psychiatry, University of Pennsylvania, Philadelphia, Pennsylvania

Robert L. Spitzer, MD, Department of Psychiatry, Columbia University College of Physicians and Surgeons, New York, New York

Michele R. Spoont, BA, Department of Psychology, University of Minnesota, Minneapolis, Minnesota

Lawrence Tamarkin, PhD, Clinical Psychobiology Branch, National Institute of Mental Health, Bethesda, Maryland

Michael Terman, PhD, New York State Psychiatric Institute, New York, New York; Department of Psychiatry, Columbia University, New York, New York

Michael E. Thase, MD, Department of Psychiatry, University of Pittsburgh School of Medicine, Pittsburgh, Pennsylvania; Western Psychiatric Institute and Clinic, Pittsburgh, Pennsylvania

George N. Wade, PhD, Department of Psychology and Neuroscience and Behavior Program, University of Massachusetts, Amherst, Massachusetts

Thomas A. Wehr, MD, Clinical Psychobiology Branch, National Institute of Mental Health, Bethesda, Maryland

David M. White, PhD, Departments of Psychiatry, Ophthalmology, and Pharmacology, Sleep and Mood Disorders Laboratory, Oregon Health Sciences University, Portland, Oregon; current address: Psychology Laboratory, Harborview Medical Center, Seattle, Washington

Janet B. W. Williams, DSW, Department of Psychiatry, Columbia University College of Physicians and Surgeons, New York, New York

Anna Wirz-Justice, PhD, Psychiatric University Clinic, CH-4025 Basel, Switzerland

Angela Yancey, PhD, Clinical Psychobiology Branch, National Institute of Mental Health, Bethesda, Maryland

Irving Zucker, PhD, Department of Psychology, University of California, Berkeley, California

Contents

1. **Introduction and Overview**   **1**
   Mary C. Blehar and Norman E. Rosenthal

I. **Clinical Aspects of Seasonal Affective Disorders**

2. **Seasonal Affective Disorders: A Historical Overview**   **11**
   Thomas A. Wehr

3. **Phenomenology of Seasonal Affective Disorder:**
   An Alaskan Perspective   **33**
   Carla Hellekson

4. **Seasonal Affective Disorder of Childhood and Adolescence:**
   A Review   **46**
   William A. Sonis

5. **Summer Depression: Description of the Syndrome and**
   Comparison with Winter Depression   **55**
   Thomas A. Wehr, Holly Giesen, Patricia M. Schulz,
   Jean R. Joseph-Vanderpool, Siegfried Kasper, Karen A. Kelly,
   and Norman E. Rosenthal

6. **Comparison between Seasonal Affective Disorder and**
   Other Forms of Recurrent Depression   **64**
   Michael E. Thase

7. **The Validity of Seasonal Affective Disorder**   **79**
   Robert L. Spitzer and Janet B. W. Williams

II. **A Search for Animal Models of Seasonal Affective Disorders**

8. **The Photoperiodic Phenomena: Seasonal Modulation**
   of the "Day Within"   **87**
   Colin S. Pittendrigh

9. *Seasonal Variations in Body Weight and Metabolism in Hamsters*   **105**
   George N. Wade

10. *Seasonal Affective Disorder, Hibernation, and Annual*
    Cycles in Animals: Chipmunks in the Sky   **127**
    N. Mrosovsky

11. *Seasonal Affective Disorders: Animal Models Non Fingo*   **149**
    Irving Zucker

III. **Seasonal Changes in the Normal Population**

12. *Seasonal Variation in Normal Subjects: An Update of Variables*
    Current in Depression Research   **167**
    Verena Lacoste and Anna Wirz-Justice

13. *Dopamine Functioning in the Behavioral Facilitation System and*
    Seasonal Variation in Behavior: Normal Population and
    Clinical Studies   **230**
    Richard A. Depue, Paul Arbisi, Michele R. Spoont,
    Arthur Leon, and Barbara Ainsworth

14. *Psychological Effects of Light Therapy in Normals*   **260**
    Siegfried Kasper, Susan L. B. Rogers, Angela Yancey,
    Robert G. Skwerer, Patricia M. Schulz, and
    Norman E. Rosenthal

IV. **Phototherapy for Winter Seasonal Affective**
    Disorder and Nonseasonal Depression:
    Clinical and Theoretical Considerations

15. *Phototherapy for Seasonal Affective Disorder*   **273**
    Norman E. Rosenthal, David A. Sack, Robert G. Skwerer,
    Frederick M. Jacobsen, and Thomas A. Wehr

16. *Winter Depression and the Phase-Shift Hypothesis for*
    Bright Light's Therapeutic Effects: History, Theory, and
    Experimental Evidence   **295**
    Alfred J. Lewy, Robert L. Sack, Clifford M. Singer,
    David M. White, and Tana M. Hoban

17. *Neurobiology of Seasonal Affective Disorder and Phototherapy*   **311**
    Robert G. Skwerer, Frederick M. Jacobsen, Connie C. Duncan,
    Karen A. Kelly, David A. Sack, Lawrence Tamarkin,
    Paul A. Gaist, Siegfried Kasper, and Norman E. Rosenthal

18. *The Role of Serotonin in Seasonal Affective Disorder
    and the Antidepressant Response to Phototherapy*   333
    Frederick M. Jacobsen, Dennis L. Murphy, and
    Norman E. Rosenthal

19. *Phototherapy for Nonseasonal Major Depressive Disorders*   342
    D. F. Kripke, D. J. Mullaney, T. J. Savides, and J. C. Gillin

20. *On the Question of Mechanism in Phototherapy for Seasonal
    Affective Disorder: Considerations of Clinical Efficacy
    and Epidemiology*   357
    Michael Terman

Index   377

*Seasonal Affective Disorders
and Phototherapy*

Introduction and Overview

Mary C. Blehar and Norman E. Rosenthal

In the past 10 years interest in seasonal affective disorder (SAD) has grown dramatically. The disorder, also known as winter depression, has a recurrent pattern of fall–winter onset and spring remission. Since the beginning of contemporary investigations into SAD, its etiology has been compellingly related to seasonal changes in ambient light. An abundance of animal models of seasonal change exist which have provided a source of mechanistic hypotheses to be investigated in humans. The signal work of Lewy *et al.* (1980), demonstrating that melatonin secretion could be suppressed by bright light in humans, underscored the continuity between human and animal physiology with regard to responsiveness to environmental factors.

Wehr (see Chapter 2, this volume) reviews the history of the association between seasonality and affective episodes which dates at least from the time of Hippocrates. Wehr points out that prominent 19th-century psychiatrists recognized the existence of patients whose depressions recurred regularly during a given season. Nonetheless, it is only relatively recently that many in the clinical research community have taken seriously the idea that seasonality may characterize some types of mood disorders. As Wehr notes, modern medical researchers are unused to thinking in terms of cyclical influences on health and illness, not only because they are by and large shielded from dramatic changes in environment, but more importantly because their training typically fails to acquaint them with a variety of historic ideas in medicine. Consequently, it is understandable that early reports of seasonality in mood disorders were received with considerable skepticism.

That scientific attitudes concerning SAD have changed significantly is a result of a number of factors. The recognition that melatonin could be suppressed by bright light (Lewy *et al.*, 1980), the delineation of SAD as a syndrome with distinct clinical and therapeutic implications (Rosenthal *et al.*, 1984), and the efficacy of bright light in the treatment of this condition (Lewy *et al.*,

Mary C. Blehar. Mood, Anxiety, and Personality Disorders Research Branch, National Institute of Mental Health, Rockville, Maryland.

Norman E. Rosenthal. Clinical Psychobiology Branch, National Institute of Mental Health, Bethesda, Maryland.

1982, Chapter 16, this volume; Rosenthal *et al.*, 1984, Chapter 15, this volume), were all important steps in this regard. The therapeutic value of bright light in SAD closely aligns the biology of the disorder with its treatment and introduces into psychiatry an exciting new therapeutic modality. In the past decade, there has been considerable progress in the development of sensitive bioassays to measure hormones and peptides, some of which have been shown to respond to changes in environmental light with changes in circadian phase and amplitude of secretion. Chapters in this volume by Skwerer *et al.* (see Chapter 17), Lewy *et al.* (see Chapter 16), and Jacobsen *et al.* (see Chapter 18) discuss some of these recent findings.

The clinical picture of winter depression also has appeal to the popular mind, since many individuals experience some degree of mood, sleep, and weight variations which they attribute to winter. Patients with SAD have been found in large numbers in many different countries on at least three continents, and it seems clear that the disorder is not so rare as it was initially thought to be.

The revised third edition of the *Diagnostic and Statistical Manual of Mental Disorders* (DSM-III-R; American Psychiatric Association, 1987) included "seasonal pattern" as a descriptor of recurrent major depression and bipolar disorder. The inclusion itself will no doubt serve as a significant stimulus for research in this area.

Despite the above developments and the increased research activity into the disorder, a number of fundamental issues remain unresolved. For example, although there is consensus regarding the efficacy of bright light in SAD, neither the pathophysiology of SAD nor the therapeutic mechanism of bright light is understood. Despite the existence of numerous animal models of photoperiodic behavior and physiological change, the animal literature has yielded few clues to explain these human phenomena. Relatively little is known about seasonality in normal human behavior and physiology and its relationship to psychopathological seasonality. Although there is considerable agreement about clinical issues pertaining to SAD, comparatively little work in epidemiology has been done as yet to establish the public health significance of SAD.

This volume was planned in order to address many of the areas in which work on SAD and phototherapy have been done with animals and humans. It covers four major areas of interest in SAD—namely, clinical, diagnostic, and epidemiological issues; animal models of seasonality and their applicability to humans; normal human seasonality and its relationship to seasonal disorders; and light treatment and its neurobiology.

Clinical, Diagnostic, and Epidemiological Issues

Although many of the contributions to this volume touch upon aspects of phenomenology, diagnosis, and epidemiology of SAD, six chapters in Section I deal directly with these topics. Wehr's chapter on conceptual trends in the study of SAD places the role of seasonality in health and illness in historical perspective.

Hellekson (see Chapter 3) and Thase (see Chapter 6) describe the phenomenology of SAD. Clinical features of winter depression are fairly consistent across series of patients. Most researchers report a clinical picture of hyperphagia, hypersomnia, and weight gain, in addition to depression and social withdrawal. Similar to other forms of mood disorder, winter depression is a disorder predominantly affecting women, but even more so. Patients are female by a ratio of 4:1, as compared to ratios of 2:1 typically reported in general surveys of depression. By and large, the disorder tends not to be as severe as some other forms of major depression, since those suffering from it rarely require hospitalization, become psychotic, or are serious risks for suicide.

The least settled questions about the clinical picture of SAD at this time pertain to the polarity of seasonal patients. The contributors to this volume differ among themselves in reporting predominantly bipolar or unipolar patients from their samples. Although such differences in course may stem from random variations in patient characteristics across series, it is more likely that some differences in interpretation of clinical criteria are involved in light of the striking similarities in the other clinical features among populations. Hypomania is known to be one of the most difficult diagnoses to make, especially if lifetime diagnosis is sought. Furthermore, patient self-reports of exuberance may be made in comparison to those of the depressed state, but such mood states may not deviate from population norms.

In light of this continuing controversy, it is of note that the DSM-III-R criteria allow for the characterization of both bipolar disorders and depressive disorders as seasonal. Despite such controversy and although validation work on the disorder is still under way, Spitzer and Williams (see Chapter 7) find the evidence for the validity of SAD to be more compelling than the evidence available for other widely made and clinically important diagnoses such as melancholia and dysthymia. Nonetheless, the diagnostic criteria formulated in DSM-III-R are provisional and are meant to stimulate further research on validation and clinical characteristics rather than to reify a syndrome at this point. Seasonality per se is considered by most of the contributors to the volume to be the sole clear defining feature of the syndrome to be established currently. It remains to be determined which other clinical characteristics, if any, are core and which ones are frequently associated with the disorder, but do not define it.

In Chapter 5 Wehr *et al.*'s reports of summer depression and even summer and winter depression in the same individual introduce the possibility, at once perplexing and exciting, that winter depression represents only one kind of seasonal pattern, and that seasonality may have diverse manifestations and etiologies. The clinical picture of summer depression is more ''endogenous'' than that of winter depression and usually involves weight loss, insomnia, and decreased appetite. Although Wehr *et al.* have reported inducing remission of symptoms by cooling the environment in some patients with summer SAD, the specificity of this effect, as well as its potency, has yet to be properly evaluated.

Mrosovsky (see Chapter 10) cautions the reader against uncritical acceptance of the reality of SAD. The often used strategy of recruiting patients for studies through the media may result in the appearance of symptom clustering when, in fact, what is reflected is ascertainment bias. On the other hand, Thase's report suggests not only that mood disorders meeting seasonal criteria occur with a higher than expected frequency in clinic samples not selected for their seasonality, but also that clinic patients with recurrent depressions show seasonal patterns in their episodes.

Sonis (see Chapter 4) describes findings of seasonality and SAD in children and adolescents. Although the clinical picture of childhood SAD that he reports differs in minor aspects from the one of adults, the childhood version of the disorder also responds to light therapy. Sonis distinguishes between winter depression in children and hyperactivity with secondary dysphoria which may become more problematic in the winter when classroom demands are made upon such children.

This volume contains several reports of the prevalence of SAD (see Chapters 4, 6, 13, and 20) which suggest that it may occur in approximately 5% of the population and that subclinical dysfunctional changes may occur in yet more individuals. For example, Terman (see Chapter 20) finds that approximately 14% of persons responding to a survey in the New York metropolitan area reported some difficulties during the winter, and a total of 25% complained of being affected adversely by either winter, summer, or both.

Animal Models of Human Seasonality

The second section of the volume contains four chapters from researchers working in comparative psychology or biology. Animal models have been particularly appealing in the study of winter depression since a variety of mammals respond to changes in the photoperiod with changes in physiology and behavior. Recent discussions of SAD in the popular media have drawn comparisons between hibernation and the disorder. However, animal models have not proven directly applicable to understanding the pathophysiology of SAD. The authors in this section are unanimous in urging caution in extrapolating from animal behavior and physiology to a clinical condition in humans. In Chapter 10 Mrosovsky discounts hibernation as an appropriate model for SAD since hibernation is not found in large mammals (such as humans) who are able to store fat faster than it is metabolized. He stresses that different strategies have been adopted by different species to cope with seasonal changes. Therefore it is likely that the most productive comparisons between species are those made in terms of discrete behaviors rather than more extensive coordinated responses to the seasons.

Wade (see Chapter 9) reviews the literature on seasonal fluctuations in body weight, reproduction, and metabolism in a number of small mammals. He notes that the systems controlling changes are separate and independent, although typically synchronized. By analogy, the same complexity in mechanisms is likely to underlie the cluster of symptoms characteristic of SAD.

Zucker underscores this complexity of mechanisms in Chapter 11, which reminds the reader that even within a single species different members of the species may use different physiological strategies to accomplish the same type of seasonal behavioral change.

Pittendrigh (see Chapter 8) explores the explanatory power of photoperiodism in SAD. His review also highlights the complexity of mechanisms that may serve the same functional goals. He notes that a critical issue in photoperiod control across species of both plants and animals is the extent to which light coincides with specific phases of the subjective night of the circadian cycle. He states that findings of the efficacy of either morning or evening light in treating SAD can be encompassed by circadian theory, but that midday light efficacy cannot be assimilated into an explanatory theory based exclusively on even broad circadian principles.

Seasonal Changes in the Normal Population

Chapters in Section III further develop the notion of continuity between animals and humans and between normal and pathological responses to the seasons. Depue et al. (see Chapter 13) present a neurobiological theory of basic systems involved in mobilizing behavior and engaging the organism with its environment. This theory, in which the dopaminergic system figures prominently, is applied both to seasonal changes in normal motivated behavior and to SAD. In Chapter 12 Lacoste and Wirz-Justice systematically review a vast literature on seasonality in normal human behavior and in those aspects of physiology (e.g., thyroid, norepinephrine, serotonin function) which have been theorized to underlie the pathophysiological changes found in winter depression. Similar to Depue et al., Lacoste and Wirz-Justice conclude that the mood and related personality changes observed in SAD probably represent extremes of normal human seasonality, and that the disorder's pathophysiology is on a continuum with a range of physiological, biochemical, and neurobiological seasonal changes found in the general population.

Kasper et al. (see Chapter 14) provide evidence for the pervasiveness of human seasonality. Having obtained a sample of persons who reported themselves as adversely seasonal but who did not meet diagnostic criteria for depression (subsyndromal SAD), they found that such individuals responded to phototherapy with mood elevations. If, as Terman reports from a survey of the

New York metropolitan area (see Chapter 20), there are generally a significant number of such winter complainers, then the ramifications of winter light deprivation may be more widespread than previously thought. If these milder dysphorias respond well to alterations in environmental light, then one can readily envision such considerations of ambient light being routinely incorporated into design of indoor environments.

Phototherapy: Controversy and Consensus

The final section of this book offers the reader thorough and broad reports on findings to date concerning light therapy. One of the most controversial areas of research into SAD involves its treatment. As Rosenthal *et al.* note in Chapter 15, by mid-1987 at least 24 controlled phototherapy trials comparing two different types of light treatment had been carried out at several centers. Most of these studies had reported significant differences between control (typically dim light) and active treatments. This chapter highlights a variety of remaining controversies including assessment of placebo effect, choice of placebo control, and the importance of the timing of light treatment to its antidepressant effect.

While bright light's antidepressant effects are disputed by few, more controversy is centered around explanations of the mechanism of action. In Chapter 16 Lewy *et al.* present a theory of winter depression that explains its pathophysiology in terms of a phase delay in circadian rhythms and the therapeutic effect of light in terms of its ability to phase advance patients when administered in the morning.

This circadian phase-shift theory is currently highly controversial and is the topic of active research into the mechanism of action of phototherapy. Findings of the efficacy of evening and even midday light (reviewed by Rosenthal *et al.* and by Terman) require some modifications of the theory. Nonetheless, in a cross-center analysis of published findings, Terman finds evidence for the superiority of morning light over light administered at other times, as well as some evidence for the efficacy of evening light relative to placebo dim-light control.

Several chapters in this section present a variety of evidence for and against the circadian phase-shift theory and other theories of SAD that have been developed. A variety of biological findings in SAD are given in the reports of Lewy *et al.*, Jacobsen *et al.*, and Skwerer *et al.*

Skwerer *et al.* (see Chapter 17) review the evidence for and against a "melatonin hypothesis," originally advanced by the National Institute of Mental Health (NIMH) group, which had proposed that antidepressant response to phototherapy was mediated by changes in melatonin secretion. Skwerer *et al.* also report on the results of some recent biological measurements made at the NIMH on SAD subjects, indicating changes following successful phototherapy in neurotransmitter levels, electroencephalographic measures of visual attention results, and immune response. In Chapter 18 Jacobsen *et al.* raise the possibility that the abnormalities of the serotonergic system are involved in SAD.

In Chapter 19 Kripke *et al.* raise the question of the specificity of phototherapy to the treatment of SAD. They report finding a striking antidepressant effect of bright light in the treatment of nonseasonal depression.

In summary, there is agreement among clinical researchers that SAD is a common condition and that in a large percentage of cases the symptoms of winter depression respond well to treatment with bright environmental light. These symptoms are often of an "atypical" vegetative pattern. Beyond these fundamental points of agreement, many other aspects of this area remain controversial. Most notable among these is the mechanism of action of bright light. The chapters in this book provide a comprehensive picture of the different sides involved in these controversies. They represent the the latest developments in this rapidly growing field. However, we eagerly look forward to the inevitable shifts and changes in our current view of this research area which will accompany new findings from researchers, many of whom are among the contributors to this book.

References

American Psychiatric Association (1987) *Diagnostic and Statistical Manual of Mental Disorders,* 3rd ed., rev., American Psychiatric Association, Washington, DC.

Lewy, A. J., H. A. Kern, N. E. Rosenthal, and T. A. Wehr (1982) Bright artificial light treatment of a manic–depressive patient with a seasonal mood cycle. Amer. J. Psychiat. *139:* 1496–1498.

Lewy, A. J., T. A. Wehr, F. K. Goodwin, D. A. Newsome, and S. P. Markey (1980) Light suppresses melatonin secretion in humans. Science *210:* 1267–1269.

Rosenthal, N. E., D. A. Sack, J. C. Gillin, A. J. Lewy, F. K. Goodwin, Y. Davenport, D. A. Newsome, and T. A. Wehr (1984) Seasonal affective disorder: A description of the syndrome and preliminary findings with light therapy. Arch. Gen. Psychiat. *4:* 72–80.

Clinical Aspects of Seasonal Affective Disorders

Seasonal Affective Disorders: A Historical Overview

Thomas A. Wehr

The influence of seasons on patients with affective illness has been an enduring theme of writings on depression and mania for over 2000 years. In this chapter, I review the extensive history of this subject.

Two Opposite Seasonal Patterns of Affective Illness

In considering the historical writings, it is useful to keep in mind that there appear to be mainly two opposite seasonal influences on affective illness—one beginning in spring and peaking in summer, the other beginning in fall and peaking in winter (see Fig. 2-1). Thus, affective episodes are more likely to begin in the spring or in the fall than at other times of year (Leuthold, 1940; Angst *et al.*, 1969; Faust and Sarreither, 1975; Payk, 1976; Eastwood and Stiasny, 1978; Frangos *et al.*, 1980; Rihmer, 1980; Aschoff, 1981; Parker and Walter, 1982; Rosenthal *et al.*, 1983; Wehr and Rosenthal, submitted). In many cases episodes recur irregularly, but in some cases they recur regularly on an annual or semiannual basis, producing patterns of recurrent winter depression, recurrent summer depression, or recurrent summer and winter depression (Rosenthal *et al.*, 1984; Wehr *et al.*, 1987b; Boyce and Parker, 1988; Rosenthal *et al.*, Chapter 15, this volume; Terman, Chapter 20, this volume; Kasper *et al.*, in press; Wehr, Giesen, Schulz, Joseph-Vanderpool, Kelly, Kasper, and Rosenthal, submitted; Wehr and Rosenthal, submitted). It is also useful to keep in mind that the sensitivity of affective illness to seasonal and environmental influences is important because it implies that episodes of the illness can be precipitated and terminated by changes in the physical environment. On the basis of ample experimental evidence, there is reason to believe that recurrent winter depressions are precipitated by the seasonal decline in natural light in

Thomas A. Wehr. Clinical Psychobiology Branch, National Institute of Mental Health, Bethesda, Maryland.

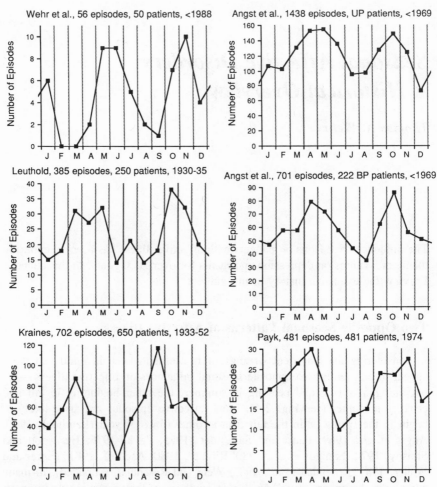

FIGURE 2-1. Similar seasonal patterns of onset of depressive episodes in a series of patients with regularly recurring annual depressions (top left diagram) and in general populations of patients with affective illness not specifically identified as seasonal (all other diagrams.). Onsets are more likely to occur in the spring and fall than at other times of year. Patients with annual recurrences (top left) had summer depression ($n=20$), winter depression ($n=24$), or combined summer and winter depressions ($n=6$). The data are from Wehr and Rosenthal (in press), Leuthold (1940), Kraines (1957), Angst *et al.* (1969), and Payk (1976). UP, unipolar; BP, bipolar.

the winter (see Rosenthal *et al.*, Chapter 15, this volume, and Terman, Chapter 20, this volume). Whether summer depressions are precipitated by heat or by some other factor is currently being investigated (see Wehr *et al.*, Chapter 5, this volume).

 The observation that affective illness is sensitive to seasonal and environmental influences was central to ancient theories about the etiology of disease (see Fig. 2-2) (Jackson, 1986). Hippocrates (460–370 B.C.) taught that "it is chiefly the changes of seasons which produce diseases, and in the seasons the great changes from cold or heat" (1923–1931, p. 123). In the *Nature of Man*, he wrote:

> In the body are many constituents, which, by heating, by cooling, by drying, or by wetting one another contrary to nature, engender diseases. . . . The body of man has in itself blood, phlegm, yellow bile and black bile. . . . Phlegm increases in winter; for phlegm being the coldest constituent of the body, is closest akin to winter. . . . The blood accordingly increases through the showers and the hot days. For these conditions of the year are most akin to the nature of blood, spring being moist and warm. And in summer blood is still strong, and bile rises in the body and extends until autumn. When winter comes on . . . phlegm increases because of the abundance of rain and the length of the nights. . . . As the year goes round they become now greater and now less, each in turn and according to its nature. . . .
>
> Such diseases as increase in the winter ought to cease in the summer, and such as increase in the summer ought to cease in the winter. . . . The physician too must treat disease with the conviction that each of them is powerful in the body according to the season which is most conformable to it. (1923–1931, pp. 7–27)

With regard to affective illness, Posidonius summarized the views of many ancient physicians when he noted in the 4th century A.D. that mania is "an

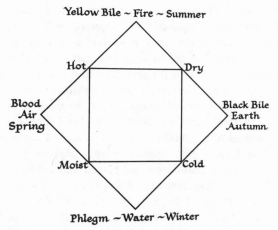

FIGURE 2-2. Relationships among humors, their qualities, and the seasons, according to the ancient humoral theory of disease. Mania (atrabilia) was considered to result from a hot and dry condition of the brain and a predominance of the yellow bile, and to occur in summer; depression (melancholia) was considered to result from a cold and dry condition of the brain and a predominance of the black bile, and to occur in autumn. Lethargus, a state characterized by anergia and somnolence, was considered to result form a cold and moist condition of the brain and a predominance of phlegm, and to occur in winter. From Jackson (1986); reprinted from H. E. Sigerist (1961) by permission of Oxford University Press.

intermittent disease, which proceeds through a periodical circuit. . . . It repeats itself once a year or more often. . . .[M]elancholy occurs in autumn whereas mania [occurs] in summer" (quoted in Roccatagliata, 1986, p. 143). They also believed that this pattern was produced by seasonal changes in temperature acting on body humors. As Aristotle (384–322 b.c.) explained, "black bile . . . when it is overheated . . . produces cheerfulness accompanied by song and frenzy. . . .[I]f it be cold beyond due measure, it produces groundless despondency; hence suicide by hanging occurs" (Aristotle, 1953, p. 954).

The idea that different individuals might react in opposite ways to the seasons was discussed in a general way by Hippocrates, who made the observation that "of constitutions some are well or ill adapted to summer, others are well or ill adapted to winter" (1923–1931, p. 47). Pinel (1806; see below) recorded examples of patients who experienced recurrent mania each summer and others who experienced recurrent mania each winter. Pinel's protégé, Esquirol (1845; see also below), delineated two opposite patterns of affective recurrence, noting that "there are individuals who pass the summer in a state of prostration or agitation; whilst in the winter they are in an opposite condition" (p. 32).

To my knowledge, the earliest examples of individuals with the two opposite seasonal patterns of affective recurrence are from the 17th century. Ann Grenville (1642–1691), an English noblewoman, appears to have suffered for many years from regularly recurring winter depressions and summer manias (Dewhurst, 1962). Her physician wrote that "there are twin symptoms, which are her constant companions, mania and melancholy, and they succeed each other in a double and alternate act. . . . Mania breaks all bonds . . . each year during the dog days" (quoted in Dewhurst, 1962, p. 121). The English poet John Milton (1608–1674) may have had a type of regularly recurring summer depression. He confided to an acquaintance "that his vein never happily flowed but from the autumnal equinoctial to the vernal, and that whatever he attempted [in summer] was never to his satisfaction . . . so that all the years he was about this poem *[Paradise Lost]*, he may be said to have spent but half his time therein" (Philips, 1694, quoted in Patterson, 1957, p. xli).

The development of psychiatry as a subspecialty of medicine can be traced to the late 18th and early 19th centuries, when asylums for the insane were transformed into medical institutions and placed under the supervision of physicians. One of the first psychiatrists of this era was Pinel (1745–1826) (Fig. 2-3), who became director of the Becetre and Salpêtrière Hospitals during the French Revolution. Pinel wrote about seasonal influences in his *Treatise on Insanity,* one of the first textbooks of psychiatry (Pinel, 1806). He adopted a rather modern scientific attitude in his observations and in his treatment of the subject. When he became director of the Bicetre he "resolved to . . . notice successively every fact, without any object than that of collecting materials for future use" (p. 2). He ensured that "all our new cases were entered at great length upon the journals of the house. Due attention was paid to the changes

FIGURE 2-3. Philippe Pinel (1745–1826).

of the seasons and the weather, and their respective influences upon the patients were minutely noticed'' (p. 3). Pinel described opposite seasonal influences on excited states. He wrote about recurrent summer mania:

> It is curious to trace the effects of solar influence upon the return and progress of maniacal paroxysms. They generally begin immediately after the summer solstice, are continued with more or less violence during the heat of summer, and commonly terminate towards the decline of autumn. Their duration is limited within the space of three, four or five months, according to differences of individual sensibility, and according as the season happens to be earlier, later, or unsettled as to its temperature. Maniacs of all descriptions are subject to a kind of effervescence or tumultuous agitation, upon the approach either of stormy or very warm weather . . . (p. 10)

He also described recurrent winter mania:

> We must not, however, extend this law of solar influence beyond its natural boundary, nor conclude that the return of maniacal paroxysms is universally dependent upon a high temperature of the atmosphere. I have seen three cases in which the paroxysms returned upon the approach of winter, i.e., when the cold weather of December and January set in; and their remis-

sion and exacerbation corresponded with the changes of the temperature of the atmosphere from mildness to severe cold. (p. 11)

Moreover, he mentioned two patients who experienced summer recurrences every few years, then switched to a pattern of winter recurrences.

Although Pinel wrote about seasonal influences on mania, primarily it appears that patients who became manic during one season were also subject to depressions during other seasons, like modern patients with one type or the other of seasonal affective disorder (SAD):

> Paroxysms of insanity, which continue with more or less violence during the whole of summer and the greatest part of autumn, seldom fail to induce a considerable degree of exhaustion. The high excitement, so lately characteristic of active mania, is now exchanged for a languor approaching to syncope, a general sense of lassitude, extreme confusion of ideas, and in some instances a state of stupor and insensibility, or rather a gloomy moroseness, accompanied by a most profound melancholy. (pp. 261–265)

Pinel's protégé, Esquirol (1772–1840) (Fig. 2-4), made many contributions to modern research on the seasonality of affective illness (Esquirol, 1845). He published epidemiological data on seasonal variation in the occurrence of affective episodes, and he also described individuals with regular, seasonal pat-

FIGURE 2-4. Julien Esquirol (1772–1840).

terns of recurrence. Like Hippocrates, he recognized that changes in the physical environment might precipitate affective episodes, and he experimented with environmental manipulations as treatments. Esquirol described several examples of patients with recurrent summer depression and winter mania. For example, he gave the following account of

> a young man from the South, 25 years old, with an exceedingly nervous disposition, [who] at the approach of winter, for three years, is seized with great excitation. Then he is very active, always moving, talks a great deal, believes himself to be of remarkable intelligence, begins a thousand projects, spends a lot of money, buys, borrows, without worrying about paying; very irritable, everyone offends him, stirs up his wrath and fury; he no longer responds to the affection of his parents, he doesn't even heed the voice of his father.
>
> As soon as spring makes its influence felt, the young man becomes more calm; little by little he is less active, talks less, is less responsive; as the temperature rises, his physical and intellectual forces seem to leave him, he subsides into inaction, apathy, reproaches himself for all the excesses to which he abandoned himself during the phase of excitation; he ends up totally anergic, wishing to kill himself, and finally makes suicide attempts. (p. 31)

He described a similar case,

> remarkable for the alternate recurrence of excitement and composure. . . . Mad'e de R . . . passes a very active winter, occupied with her affairs, enjoying society, seeking the world one more, and taking much exercise. . . . In the spring, and during the summer, she is composed, more sedentary and indolent, living alone, taking no care of her fortune, and deciding upon nothing. . . . These conditions . . . are renewed alternately for several years. . . .
>
> [Later] She is talking incessantly, even during the night. . . . Winter passes in this state of excitement. . . . In the spring, she becomes more peaceful . . . is less active, walks less, and says little. She also sleeps more. . . . After eight years, passed in alternate seasons of excitement and repose, she becomes habitually more peaceful. (p. 33)

Esquirol also provided an account of a patient with recurrent winter depressions:

> M . . . forty-two years of age . . . consults me at the close of the winter of 1825 . . . "Three years since, I experienced a trifling vexation. It was at the beginning of autumn, and I became sad, gloomy and susceptible. By degress I neglected my business, and deserted my house to avoid my uneasiness. I felt feeble . . . I became irritable . . . I suffered also from insomnia and inappetence. . . . At length I fell into a profound apathy, incapable of every thing, except drinking and grieving.
>
> "At the approach of spring I felt my affections revive. I recovered all my intellectual activity, and all my ardor for business. I was very well all the ensuing summer, but from the commencement of the damp and cold weather of autumn, there was a return of sadness, uneasiness. . . . During the last autumn and present winter, I have experienced for the third time the same phenomena." (pp. 226–227)

Esquirol noted that SAD might also occur in a subsyndromal form. Of one of his patients, he wrote that "It was necessary to live on terms of intimacy with her, in order to perceive the change . . . which took place during summer and winter" (p. 328)

Griesinger (1855/1882) described circular forms of affective illness with "transformations into mania, and the passage from this again into melancholia" (p. 163), and he noted seasonal patterns of recurrence: "Other observers, including myself, have seen cases where regularly at one particular season—for example, in winter—a profound melancholia has supervened, which in spring passes into mania, which again in autumn gradually gives way to melancholia" (p. 163).

Baillarger (1854) and Pilcz (1901) also published histories of patients with recurrent winter depressions and recurrent summer depressions (Figs. 2-5 and 2-6). Like Pinel, Pilcz observed a case in which the course of illness shifted from recurrent summer depression to recurrent winter depression (Fig. 2-6).

Early in this century, Kraepelin (1921) (Fig. 2-7) described patients with recurrent winter depressions. He wrote that he

repeatedly . . . saw in these cases moodiness set in in autumn and pass over in spring, when the sap shoots in the trees, to excitement, corresponding in a certain sense to the emotional changes which come over even healthy individuals at the changes of the seasons. As a rule [these might represent cases] with a very slight course, hypomania and simple inhibition. (p. 139)

In 1957, Kraines wrote that

cyclic (circular, alternating, cyclothymic) attacks are characterized by continuous changes from manic to depressive phases. In the typical cyclic case, there are two attacks in each year, one manic and one depressive, each lasting from four to eight months and with almost no free or normal interval between attacks. . . . [T]he onset of one phase tends to occur in the spring, and the opposite phase in the fall. (pp. 78, 97)

Like Pinel and Pilcz, Kraines noted that patients sometimes switched from one seasonal pattern to an opposite one during the course of their illness (see Fig. 2-6): "As a rule, patients whose cyclic attacks begin before the age of 35 have manic swings in the fall and depressive ones in the spring. These same patients after 50, as a rule, change to the usual pattern of depressive onset in the fall of the year" (p. 100). Kraines gave several examples, one of which is illustrated in Figure 2-6.

Seasonal patterns of recurrence can also be detected in records of the longitudinal course of recurrent affective illness published by various investigators who did not comment on seasonality. For example, patients with recurrent summer depression and recurrent winter depression can be found among subjects whose histories were charted by Baastrup and Schou (1967), Arnold and Kryspin-Exner (1965) (see Figs. 2-5 and 2-8), and Kukopulos and Reginaldi (1973) (see Fig. 2-9).

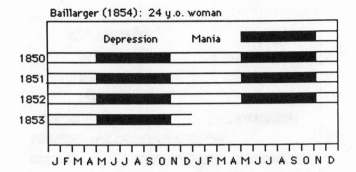

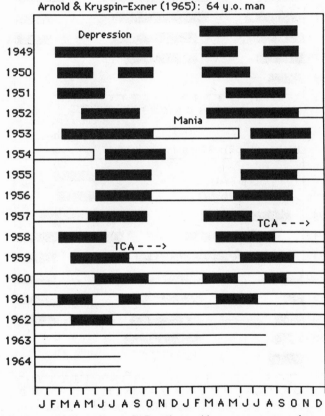

FIGURE 2-5. Course of illness in two SAD patients with recurrent summer depression. Data are plotted in a raster format with consecutive years of data plotted beneath one another. The data are double-plotted to the right to facilitate visual inspection. Depression episodes are indicated by black horizontal bars. The data are from Baillarger (1854) and Arnold and Kryspin-Exner (1965). TCA, tricyclic antidepressant. The antidepressant appears to have induced manic episodes, which altered the course of the patient's illness.

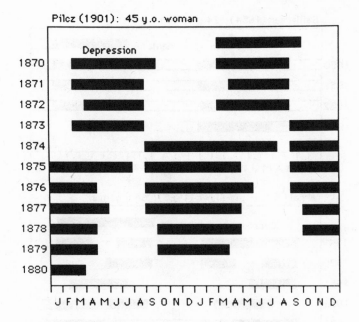

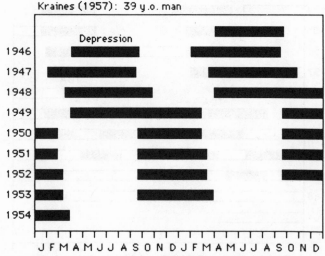

FIGURE 2-6. Patients with SAD whose course of illness shifted from a pattern of recurrent summer depression to an opposite one of recurrent winter depression. Raster plot shows months of occurrence of depressive episodes for each year. The data are double-plotted to the right. The data are from Pilcz (1901) and Kraines (1957).

FIGURE 2-7. Emil Kraepelin (1856–1927).

In 1981–1982, our research group at the National Institute of Mental Health (NIMH) systematically investigated a series of patients with winter depression and delineated the clinical features of the syndrome (Rosenthal *et al.*, 1984). We developed operational criteria for the diagnosis of SAD and presented evidence for its validity based on a distinctive course, clinical and demographic features, and response to a specific treatment (phototherapy). This evidence has been replicated in its essentials by several other groups (Wirz-Justice *et al.*, 1986; Boyce and Parker, 1988; Garvey *et. al.*, 1988; Thompson and Isaacs, 1988). Recently, my colleagues and I have described a series of patients with summer depression and patients who had a combination of the two seasonal patterns with two depressions per year, one in the winter and one in the summer (Wehr *et al.*, 1987b). Although these recent contributions might be viewed as extensions of earlier work by Pinel, Esquirol, and others, they also represent a departure from the teachings of such eminent 20th-century psychiatrists as Kraepelin and Lewis, who believed that attempts to classify subtypes of affective illness on the basis of their course "must of necessity wreck on the irregularity of the disease" (Kraepelin, 1921, p. 139).

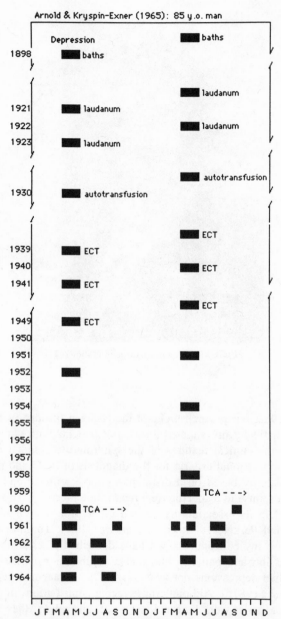

FIGURE 2-8. Course of illness in SAD patient with recurrent spring-onset depressions. Raster plot as in Figure 2-5. The data are from Arnold and Kryspin-Exner (1965). ECT, electroconvulsive therapy, TCA, tricyclic antidepressant. The antidepressant appears to have increased the frequency of episodes and altered the course of the patient's illness.

SAD with Fall-Winter Depression

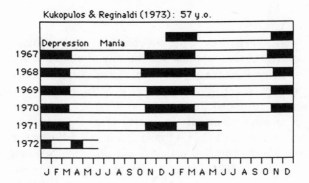

SAD with Spring-Summer Depression

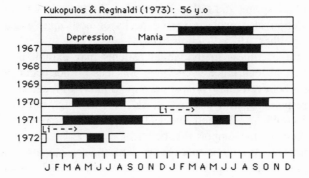

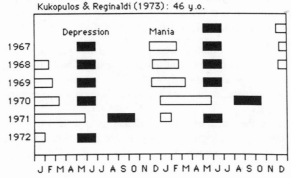

FIGURE 2-9. Course of illness in SAD patients with recurrent winter depression and summer mania (top) and recurrent summer depression and winter mania (middle and bottom). Li, lithium carbonate. The data are from Kukopulos and Reginaldi (1973).

Sensitivity to Season and Latitude in Affective Illness in General

Sensitivity to seasonal changes in the environment may be a fundamental characteristic of affective illness, not just a peculiarity of cases labeled "seasonal." Records of the natural course of affective illness obtained before the era of modern drug therapy reveal robust seasonal patterns in the onset of episodes, and these patterns are remarkably similar to those seen in patients with regularly recurring seasonal forms of the illness (Fig. 2-1). In separate studies, Leuthold (1940) and Kraines (1957) found spring and fall peaks in the onset of 1087 depressive episodes in 900 patients, and this same seasonal pattern has been reported more recently by several other investigators (Angst et al., 1969; Payk, 1976; Eastwood and Stiasny, 1978; Frangos et al., 1980; Rihmer, 1980; Parker and Walter, 1982; see also Rosenthal et al., 1983, and Wehr and Rosenthal, submitted). Summer depressions and winter depressions similarly have their onsets in the spring and fall, respectively. The frequency of suicide in the general population also exhibits spring peaks or both spring and fall peaks (Faust and Sarreither, 1975; Aschoff, 1981).

The course of illness in individual patients may exhibit a characteristic seasonal pattern of recurrence even when episodes do not occur on an annual basis. Esquirol believed that "relapses are most likely to recur at the season of the year corresponding with the first attack . . . although after an interval of many years" (1845, p. 32), and Slater (1938) published evidence drawn from Kraepelin's patients that support this belief.

Environmental conditions that change with the seasons also vary with latitude, and many writers in previous centuries expressed views about the influence of latitude on mood and temperament. Some of these views have become cultural stereotypes that are familiar to the modern reader. Robert Burton, in the *Anatomy of Melancholy* (1621/1961), wrote that

> hot countries are most troubled with . . . great numbers of madmen, insomuch that they are compelled in all cities of note, to build peculiar hospitals for them. . . . They are ordinarily so choleric in their speeches, that scarce two words pass without railing or chiding in common talk, and often quarreling in their streets. . . .
>
> Cold air in the other extreme is almost as bad as hot. . . . In those northern countries, the people are therefore generally dull, heavy, and many witches, which [various authors] . . . ascribe to melancholy. (pp. 237–239)

Implications for Treatment

Observations that season and latitude can influence the course of affective illness have two important implications: First, changes in the physical environment may precipitate affective episodes; second, modifications of the physical environment may be used to treat affective episodes. In previous eras many physicians recognized these implications and devised environmental treatments for their patients. One approach was climatotherapy—treatment by traveling to a different latitude and climate. For example, Esquirol (1845, p. 227) advised a patient with winter depression to "be in Italy before the close of October, from whence you must not return until the month of May." Subsequently, the patient "escaped a fourth attack by withdrawing himself from the coldness and moisture of autumn . . . [and returned] to Paris in the month of May in the enjoyment of excellent health." Hellpach (1911) described similar responses to changes in latitude and climate.

Manipulation of Temperature

From the beginning, physicians attempted to identify specific environmental factors, such as light or temperature, that might be responsible for seasonal patterns of recurrence of affective episodes. By manipulating such factors they hoped to be able to treat the illness, "by opposing opposites [to] prepare for the change from summer to winter," as Hippocrates said (1923–1931, p. 47). Most focused on temperature, and most believed, like Aristotle (see above), that heat elevates mood. For example, Esquirol (1845) wrote that "heat, like cold, acts upon the insane, with this difference, that the continuance of warmth augments the excitement, while cold prolongs the depression" (p. 31). In discussing the effects of temperature on mood and energy, Galen (129–200 A.D.) may have been the first to invoke hibernation as an animal model of winter lethargy in human beings. He wrote:

> Lethargicus: . . . the diathesis is generally cold. . . . Great heat leads to sleeplessness, whereas cooling results in somnolence. And, indeed, the warm and biliary diseases seem to cause a lack of sleep, dilirium and phrenitis. In contrast to these, phlegmatic and cold [diseases] induce torpor and sinking spells. . . . One can see that cold weakens the mental activities. This is evident in animals which are forced by the frost to hibernate. (Galen, 1976, p. 81)

There was a second, opposite opinion about the effects of temperature on mood. Soranus and other physicians of the "solidist" school argued that "mania is aggravated and intensified . . . by cooling remedies" (Soranus, 1967, p. 29). Some modern writers agreed. Pinel (1806) was cautious in his conclusions, believing that "the real utility of bathing in maniacal disorders, remains yet to be ascertained" (p. 264), but he recorded that he was "led to suppose that the warm bath may be resorted to with more probability of success, as a preventative of approaching maniacal paroxysms" (p. 264), and he described a patient whose mania was aggravated by cold baths. Kraepelin claimed that "in severe excitement, prolonged warm baths give excellent results" and that "in the depressed states . . . evening baths with cold effusions . . . may be used with great benefit" (Defendorf, 1902, pp. 313–314). In a pilot study, my colleagues and I reported that exposure to cold improved summer depression in some patients (Wehr *et al.*, 1987b, 1988).

Manipulation of Light and Darkness

The idea that light and darkness can influence depression also has ancient origins. To begin with, Greek and Roman physicians conceived of depression as a kind of internal darkness (Jackson, 1986). Galen, citing Hippocrates, wrote that "the color of the black humor induces fear when its darkness throws a shadow over the area of thought . . . as external darkness renders almost all persons fearful" (quoted by Jackson, 1986, p. 93). This idea was still in vogue 1400 years later, when Thomas Willis (1621–1675) wrote that the animal spirits "become in melancholy obscure, thick, and dark, so that they represent the images of things, as it were, in a shadow or covered with darkness" (quoted by Jackson, 1986, p. 111).

Remarkably, light was used to treat depression and lethargy nearly 2000 years ago. Aretaeus (2nd century A.D.) wrote that "lethargics are to be laid in the light, and exposed to the rays of the sun (for the disease is gloom)" (1856, p. 387), and Caelius Aurelianus (250–320 A.D.) specified that the light must be applied to the eyes to be effective (as we recently confirmed in an experiment; Wehr *et al.*, 1987a). "This light," Caelius Aurelianus said, "may be a lamplight or daylight but should be skillfully arranged, so that . . . it will cover only the patient's face. . . . In this way the spread of mental derangement will be allayed . . . for . . . light is a relaxing agent by reason of the color by which it is seen" (1950, p. 41).

In the modern era, journeys to polar regions led to new insights about light and depression. Frederick Cook, a ship's physician, recorded that members of an 1898 antarctic expedition were afflicted with "langour" during the winter darkness, and that "bright artificial lights relieve this to some extent" (cited in Cameron, 1974, and quoted by Jefferson, 1986, p. 261). To my knowledge, the first report in a medical journal of phototherapy of winter depression is that of Marx, who in 1946 described episodes of recurrent winter depression among soldiers in northern Scandinavia, and reported that he successfully treated them with light. He speculated that the condition was due to hypophyseal insufficiency caused by light deprivation, and that the therapeutic effects of light were mediated by retinohypophyseal pathways.

Herbert Kern, a research scientist who suffered from regularly recurring winter depressions, played an important role as a catalyst of modern phototherapy research. He thought that seasonal changes in light might be responsible for his mood swings. He became a charter member of the American Society for Photobiology and attended scientific meetings on this subject. He corresponded with Wurtman, Czeisler, and other investigators in this field. When he learned of our NIMH group's research on light and human melatonin (Lewy *et al.*, 1980), he contacted us to discuss his illness and his idea about light. Animal researchers had previously demonstrated that light triggers seasonal changes in reproduction, and that its effects are mediated by suppression of pineal melatonin secretion (Gwinner, 1981; Hoffman, 1981; Goldman and Darrow, 1983). Since we had recently shown that human melatonin secretion could be suppressed by bright light (Lewy *et al.*, 1980), and since we had speculated that light acting on seasonal photoperiodic mechanisms might have antidepressant effects (Wehr and Goodwin, 1981; see also Kripke *et al.*, 1978), we were receptive to Kern's suggestion that bright light might be used to treat his winter depressions. We treated Kern with light in the winter of 1980–1981, and he improved (Lewy *et al.*, 1982). In that same winter, Mueller, a psychiatrist with whom Kern had previously discussed his ideas, also successfully treated a patient with light (Mueller and Allen, 1984; Rosenthal *et al.*, 1984).

The following year, our group (Rosenthal *et al.*, 1984) conducted controlled trials of phototherapy of winter depression with sham treatments, blind raters, and balanced randomization crossover designs, and showed that bright light was an effective antidepressant in most patients.

Comparisons with Rhythms in Animals

The symptoms and seasonal patterns of SAD invite obvious comparisons with hibernation and other types of seasonal rhythms in animals. As mentioned before, this connection was already apparent to Galen, who considered hibernation in animals and winter lethargy in human beings both to result from cooling of the brain. Sixty years ago, Lange (1928) argued that the only cyclical processes in nature with amplitudes similar in magnitude to manic–depressive cycles were daily, monthly, and annual biological rhythms, such as the sleep–wake, menstrual, and hibernation cycles, and he suggested that further research on these normal processes might provide insights into the nature of manic–depressive illness. Although comparisons with animals should not be taken too literally (see Mrosovsky, Chapter 10, this volume), they led us to propose that affective illness might be a disorder of environmental physiology and of mechanisms that regulate the energy economy of the organism (Rosenthal *et al.*, 1985; Wehr *et al.*, 1988, submitted; Wehr and Rosenthal, in press).

Modern Lack of Interest in Seasonality

Modern psychiatrists seem to have been much less aware than their predecessors of the seasonality of affective illness and its implications about environmental causes. Ironically, Item 17 of a widely used version of the Hamilton

Rating Scale for Depression contains instructions to rate patients as lacking insight into their illness if they attribute depression to climate; such patients are given a rating of 1 on the item, as opposed to 0 for full acknowledgment of depression and 2 for total denial (Hedlung and Vieweg, 1979). Of 29 modern English-language textbooks of psychiatry that I have reviewed, only 1 mentions SAD (Meyer-Gross *et al.*, 1960).

Modern psychiatrists' lack of interest in seasonality can be attributed to several factors:

1. The history of medicine is seldom taught to physicians during their medical training.
2. Theories play an important role in medicine, and the ancient humoral theory, which emphasized seasonal influences on disease, fell into disfavor.
3. Meanwhile, psychological and biological theories, which emphasized internal mental and biochemical processes, respectively, have dominated psychiatric thinking for most of this century.
4. Modern psychiatrists in developed countries are less exposed to seasonal changes in their own environment, and therefore may be less apt to think of seasonal influences on their patients.
5. There has been a cultural shift away from a cyclical to a linear perception of time (Gould, 1987), so that psychiatrists and patients may be more likely to perceive affective recurrences as a succession of separate events than as a seasonal cycle of events.
6. Modern nosology has emphasized cross-sectional features and neglected longitudinal features of psychiatric illness, following Kraepe-

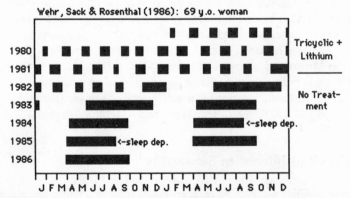

FIGURE 2-10. Course of illness in patient who exhibited rapid cycling depressive episodes during continuous treatment with tricyclic antidepressant and lithium carbonate and recurrent summer depressive episodes during a period without drugs. The data are from Wehr, Sack, and Rosenthal (unpublished).

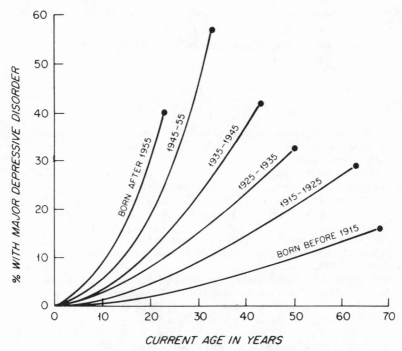

FIGURE 2-11. Prevalence of depression appears to be increasing in susceptible individuals during the 20th century. From Klerman (1988). Reprinted by permission of the *British Journal of Psychiatry*.

lin's (1921) dictum (cited above) that efforts at classification based on course of illness "must of necessity wreck on the irregularity of the disease" (p. 139).

7. Modern treatments of affective illness may have altered its course, thereby obscuring seasonal influences (Arnold and Kryspin-Exner, 1965; Wehr and Goodwin, 1987). This last possibility is suggested by case histories described by Arnold and Kryspin-Exner (1965) and Wehr (unpublished data) (see Figs. 2-8 and 2-10).

To the modern psychiatrist, recent reports about the influence of seasons and the physical environment on affective illness may appear novel and relevant only to a few unusual patients. However, for over 2000 years seasonal and environmental influences were enduring themes in writing on depression and mania, and they played a significant role in theories about pathogenesis. This historical record is surprisingly consistent with modern observations about seasonality, and it suggests that seasonal and environmental influences may be of more general relevance to the problem of affective illness. Environmental influences on affective illness may be particularly important in modern times. During the second half of this century, the prevalence of depression has increased among those at risk for the disease (see Fig. 2-11), and environmental factors ("agent blue") have been invoked as possible causes of this increase (Klerman, 1988). Perhaps future research on environmental influences, which were of such interest to ancient physicians, may help to identify these factors.

References

Angst, J., P. Grof, H. Hippius, and W. Poldinger (1969) Verlaufsgesetzlichkeiten depressiver Syndrome. In *Das Depressive Syndrom*, H. Hippius and H. Selbach, eds., pp. 93–100, G. Fischer Verlag, Stuttgart.

Aretaeus (1856) On the therapeutics of acute diseases. In *The Extant Works of Aretaeus, the Cappadocian*, F. Adams, ed., p. 387, London, Sydenham Society.

Aristotle (1953) Problemata, Book XXX, Problem 1. In *The Works of Aristotle Translated into English*, Vol. 7, W. D. Ross, ed., E. S. Forster, trans., p. 954, Oxford University Press, Oxford.

Arnold, O. H., and K. Kryspin-Exner (1965) Zur Frage der Beeinflußung des Verlaufes des manisch–depressiven Krankheitsgeschehens durch Antidepressiva. Wien. Med. Wochenschr. *45/46:* 929–934.

Aschoff, J. (1981) Annual rhythms in man. In *Handbook of Behavioral Neurobiology*, Vol. 4, *Biological Rhythms*, J. Ashoff, ed., pp. 475–487, Plenum, New York.

Baastrup, C. P., and M. Schou (1967) Lithium as a prophylactic agent: Its effect against recurrent depression and manic–depressive psychosis. Arch. Gen. Psychiat. *16:* 162–172.

Baillarger, J. (1854) Note sur une genre de folie dont les accès sont caractérisés par deux périodes régulières, l'une de dépression et l'autre d'excitation. Gaz. Heb. Med. Chir. *132:* 263–265.

Boyce, P., and G. Parker (1988) Seasonal affective disorder in the Southern Hemisphere. Amer. J. Psychiat. *145:* 97–99.

Burton, R. (1961) *The Anatomy of Melancholy*, J. M. Dent & Sons, London. (Original work published 1621).

Caelius Aurelianus (1950) *On Acute Diseases and on Chronic Diseases*, E. I. Drabkin, ed. and trans., University of Chicago Press, Chicago.

Cameron, I. (1974) *Antarctica: The Last Continent*, Little Brown, Boston.

Defendorf, A. R. (1902) *Clinical Psychiatry: A Text-Book Abstracted and Adapted from the Sixth German Edition of Kraepelin's "Lehrbuch der Psychiatrie*, Macmillan, New York.

Dewhurst, K. (1962) A seventeenth-century symposium on manic–depressive psychosis. Brit. J. Med. Psychol. *35:* 113–125.

Eastwood, M. R., and S. Stiasny (1978) Psychiatric disorder, hospital admission and season. Arch. Gen. Psychiat. *35:* 769–771.

Esquirol, J. E. D. (1845) *Mental Maladies: Treatise on Insanity*, E. K. Hunt, trans., Lea & Blanchard, Philadelphia.

Faust, V., and P. Sarreither (1975) Jahreszeit und psychiatrische Krankheit. Med. Klin. *70:* 467–473.

Frangos, E., G. Athanassenas, and S. Tsitourides (1980) Seasonality of the episodes of recurrent affective psychoses: Possible prophylactic interventions. J. Affect. Dis. *2:* 239–247.

Galen (1976) *On the affected parts*, R. E. Siegel, ed. and trans., S. Karger, New York.

Garvey, M. J., R. Wesner, and M. Godes (1988) Comparison of seasonal and nonseasonal affective disorders. Amer. J. Psychiat. *145:* 100–102.

Goldman, B., and J. Darrow (1983) The pineal gland and mammalian photoperiodism. Neuroendocrinology *37:* 386–396.

Gould, S. J. (1987) *Time's Cycle and Time's Arrow: Myth and Metaphor in the Discovery of Geological Time*, Harvard University Press, Cambridge, MA.

Griesinger, W. (1882) *Mental Pathology and Therapeutics,* J. Rutherford, ed., C. L. Robertson, trans., William Wood, New York. (Original work published 1855)

Gwinner, E. (1981) Annual rhythms: Perspective. In J. Aschoff, ed., *Handbook of Behavioral Neurobiology,* Vol. 4, *Biological Rhythms,* pp. 381–389, Plenum, New York.

Hedlung J. L., and B. W. Vieweg (1979) The Hamilton Rating Scale for Depression. J. Oper. Psychiat. *10*(2): 164.

Hellpach, W. (1911) *Die geopsychischen Erscheinungen: Wetter, Klima und Landschaft in ihrem Einfluss auf das Seelenleben,* Engelmann Verlag, Leipzig.

Hippocrates (1923–1931) *Works of Hippocrates,* W. H. S. Jones and E. T. Withington, eds. and trans., Harvard University Press, Cambridge, MA.

Hoffman, K. (1981) Photoperiodism in vertebrates. In *Handbook of Behavioral Neurobiology,* Vol. 4, *Biological Rhythms,* J. Aschoff, ed., pp. 449–473, Plenum, New York.

Jackson, S. W. (1986) *Melancholia and Depression from Hippocratic Times to Modern Times,* Yale University Press, New Haven, CT.

Jefferson, J. W. (1986). An early study of seasonal depression (Letter to the editor). Amer. J. Psychiat. *143:* 261–262.

Kasper, S., T. A. Wehr, J. Bartko, P. A. Gaist, and N. E. Rosenthal (in press) Epidemiological findings of seasonal changes in mood and behavior: A telephone survey of Montgomery County, Maryland. Arch. Gen. Psychiat.

Klerman, G. L. (1988) The current age of youthful melancholia: Evidence for increase in depression among adolescents and young adults. Brit. J. Psychiat. *152:* 4–14.

Kraepelin, E. (1921) *Manic–Depressive Insanity and Paranoia,* G. M. Robertson, ed., R. M. Barclay, trans., E. & S. Livingstone, Edinburgh.

Kraines, S. (1957) *Mental Depressions and Their Treatment,* Macmillan, New York.

Kripke, D. F., D. J. Mullaney M. Atkinson, and S. Wolf (1978) Circadian rhythm disorders in manic–depressives. Biol. Psychiat. *13:* 335–350.

Kukopulos, A., and D. Reginaldi (1973) Does lithium prevent depressions by suppressing manias? Int. Pharmacopsychiat. *8:* 152–158.

Lange J. (1928) Die endogenen und reaktiven Gemütserkrankungen. In *Handbuch der Geisteskrankheiten,* Vol. 6, O. Bumke, ed., pp. 211–231, Springer-Verlag, Berlin.

Leuthold, G. H. (1940) Jahreszeit und Phasenbeginn manisach–depressiver Psychosen. Arch. Psychiat. *111:* 55–61.

Lewy, A. J., H. A. Kern, N. E. Rosenthal, and T. A. Wehr (1982) Bright artificial light treatment of a manic–depressive patient with a seasonal mood cycle. Amer. J. Psychiat. *139:* 1496–1498.

Lewy, A. J., T. A. Wehr, F. K. Goodwin, P. A. Newsome, and S. P. Markey (1980) Light suppresses melatonin secretion in humans. Science *210:* 1267–1269.

Marx, H. (1946) "Hypophysäre Insuffizienz" bei Lichtmangel. Klin. Wochenschr. *24/25:* 18–21.

Meyer-Gross, W., E. Slater, and M. Roth (1960) *Clinical Psychiatry,* Cassell, London.

Mueller, P. S., and N. G. Allen (1984) Diagnosis and treatment of severe light-sensitive seasonal energy syndrome (SES) and its relationship to melatonin anabolism. Fair Oaks Hosp. Psychiat. Lett. *2:* 1–5.

Parker, G., and S. Walter (1982) Seasonal variation in depressive disorders and suicidal deaths in New South Wales. Brit. J. Psychiat. *140:* 626–632.

Patterson, F. A. (1957) *The Student's Milton,* Appleton-Century-Crofts, New York.

Payk, T. R. (1976) Zur jahreszeitlicher Bindung neurologischer und psychiatrischer Erkrankungen. Münchner Med. Wochenschr. *118:* 1669–1670.

Pilcz, A. (1901) *Die Periodischen Geistesstörungen.* G. Fischer Verlag, Jena.

Pinel, P. (1806) *A Treatise on Insanity,* D. D. Davis trans., Cadell & Davies, London.

Rihmer, Z. (1980) Season of birth and season of hospital admissions in bipolar depressed female patients. Psychiat. Res. *3:* 247–251.

Roccatagliata, G. (1986) *A History of Ancient Psychiatry,* Greenwood Press, New York.

Rosenthal, N. E., D. A. Sack, C. J. Carpenter, B. L. Parry, W. B. Mendelson, and T. A Wehr

(1985) Antidepressant effects of light in seasonal affective disorder. Amer. J. Psychiat. *142:* 163–170.

Rosenthal, N. E., D. A. Sack, J. C. Gillin, A. J. Lewy, F. K. Goodwin, Y. Davenport, P. S. Mueller, D. A. Newsome, and T. A. Wehr (1984) Seasonal affective disorder: A description of the syndrome and preliminary findings with light treatment. Arch. Gen. Psychiat. *41:* 72–80.

Rosenthal, N. E., D. A. Sack, and T. A. Wehr (1983) Seasonal variation in affective disorders. In *Circadian Rhythms in Psychiatry,* T. A. Wehr and F. K. Goodwin, eds., pp. 185–210, Boxwood Press, Pacific Grove, CA.

Sigerist, H. E. (1961) *A History of Medicine,* Vol. 2, p. 323, Oxford University Press, New York.

Slater, E. (1938) zur Periodik des manisch–depressiven Irreseins. Neurol. Psychiat. *162:* 794–801.

Soranus (1967) *Documentary History of Psychiatry,* C. E. Goshen, ed., Philosophical Library, New York.

Thompson, C., and G. Isaacs (1988) Seasonal affective disorder—a British sample: Symptomatology in relation to mode of referral and diagnostic subtype. J. Affect. Dis. *14:* 1–11.

Wehr, T. A., and F. K. Goodwin (1981) Biological rhythms and psychiatry. In *American Handbook of Psychiatry,* Vol. 7, S. Arieti and H. K. H. Brodie, eds., pp. 46–74, Basic Books, New York.

Wehr, T. A., and F. K. Goodwin (1987) Can antidepressants cause mania and worsen the course of affective illness? Amer. J. Psychiat. *144:* 1403–1411.

Wehr, T. A., and N. E. Rosenthal (in press) The seasonality of affective illness. Amer. J. Psychiat.

Wehr, T. A., D. A. Sack, and N. E. Rosenthal (1987b) Seasonal affective disorder with summer depression and winter hypomania. Amer. J. Psychiat. *144:* 1602–1603.

Wehr, T. A., D. A. Sack, and N. E. Rosenthal (1988) Environmental and behavioral influences on affective illness. Acta Psychiat. Scand. Suppl. *77:* 44–52.

Wehr, T. A., R. G. Skwerer, F. M. Jacobsen, D. A. Sack, and N. E. Rosenthal (1987a) Eye versus skin phototherapy of seasonal affective disorder. Amer. J. Psychiat. *144:* 753–757.

Wirz-Justice, A., C. Buchelli, P. Graw, P. Kielholz, H.-U. Fisch, and B. Woggon (1986) Light treatment of seasonal affective disorder in Switzerland. Acta Psychiat. Scand. *74:* 193–204.

3

Phenomenology of Seasonal Affective Disorder: An Alaskan Perspective

Carla Hellekson

Seasonal variations in mood, energy, appetite, weight, libido, and other psychophysiological functions may be manifested as affective illnesses in individuals with increased sensitivity to environmental cues. Seasonal affective disorder (SAD), as recently described by Rosenthal *et al.* (1984), may represent represent a dysfunctional portion of a large spectrum of behavioral changes that affect high-latitude residents, who frequently complain of late winter "cabin fever." Such seasonal behavior changes may also occur at temperate latitudes. Seasonal changes in normal individuals, patients with affective illness, patients with SAD, and suicides are described, and results of a survey of seven centers engaged in SAD research are presented.

Seasonal Changes in Normal Individuals

An early polar explorer, Dr. Frederick Cook, after 9 years at 78°N on the northwest coast of Greenland, described the effects of annual light changes on his crew as follows: "The light of the Arctic summer is . . . an efficient tonic to the mind and body; but before the night begins the stimulation is replaced by a progressive depression. The darkness, cold, and isolation then drive the mental faculties on to melancholy" (Cook, 1897, quoted by Simpson & Bohlen, 1973, pp. 112–113). It is reported that Dr. Cook used bright artificial lights to increase the well-being of his ship's crew while trapped in Antarctica's ice pack in 1898 (Jefferson, 1986). More recently, Paterson (1975) reported a reduced amount of slow-wave sleep, among coastal station workers in Antarctica's continuous winter darkness. Seasonal changes in sleep among shift workers in the Arctic, reported by Anderson *et al.* (1984), showed less restful sleep in the autumn and winter than in spring and summer. However, Weitzman *et*

Carla Hellekson. Department of Psychiatry and Behavioral Sciences, University of Washington Medical School, Seattle, Washington; Fairbanks Psychiatric and Neurologic Clinic, Fairbanks, Alaska.

al. (1975) did not find seasonal changes in sleep structure in an earlier study of seven male subjects in Tromsø, Norway. Lingjaerde *et al.* (1985) described a condition of midwinter insomnia occurring during the "dark period" in northern Norway, which appeared not to be associated with other psychiatric complaints of mood or anxiety problems. Jacobsen *et al.* (1987) reported a preliminary survey from the Washington DC area, in which approximately 20% of normal individuals complained of marked seasonal changes in mood and energy. From Ontario, Eastwood *et al.* (1985) compared daily self-reports of mood, sleep, energy, and other variables in 30 patients with affective disorder and 34 normal controls, and found that the majority (81%) of both groups had infradian rhythms in affective symptoms, with the distribution skewed toward cycles; the principal difference between groups was a higher amplitude of the cycles in the group with affective disorder.

Seasonal Variation in Affective Illness and Suicide

The seasonal nature of depressive illness in general has been noted since antiquity. Hippocrates (circa 400 B.C.) noted that "melancholia occurs in the spring." In a review by Rosenthal *et al.* (1983), hospital admissions for unipolar affective disorder were noted to peak in the spring; for bipolar affective disorder, there was a major spring peak and a minor fall peak. Admissions for manic illness have been highest in the summer (Symonds and Williams, 1976; Walter, 1977) with a shorter latency from onset of symptoms to admission (Rosenthal *et al.*, 1983). Alcoholism has been the only other major psychiatric disorder to show a seasonal variation, with a spring predominance (Symonds and Williams, 1976). Studies have not supported the widespread belief that holidays exacerbate depression (Phillips and Liu, 1980; Hillard *et al.*, 1981). Similar seasonal variations in affective disorders in the Southern Hemisphere have pointed to the underlying importance of geographic and climatic variables (Parker and Walter, 1982).

Aschoff (1981) reported a consistent May–June peak of suicide over a 100-year period in several European countries and Japan. The amplitude of this curve was above 25% during the second half of the last century, and the subsequent decline in the amplitude of the curve suggested a decrease in the influence of seasonal factors with increased control over our living environment. The acrophase or peak of the suicide rhythm was independent of latitude, but the amplitude reached maximal values at about 40°N, the latitude at which the seasonal rhythms of monthly ambient temperature and monthly duration of sunshine also reach a maximum (Aschoff, 1981).

Seasonal Affective Disorder

The syndrome of SAD was defined by Rosenthal *et al.* (1984) as follows: (1) a history of major affective disorder, according to Research Diagnostic Criteria

(RDC; Spitzer *et al.*, 1978); (2) at least 2 consecutive years of fall–winter depressions that remitted the following spring–summer; (3) absence of any other *Diagnostic and Statistical Manual of Mental Disorders,* third edition (DSM-III) Axis I psychiatric disorder (American Psychiatric Association, 1980); and (4) absence of seasonal psychosocial stressors. The consistent recurrence of seasonal depression and the reactivity of the symptoms to either temporary or permanent changes in latitude and environmental light exposure have suggested that SAD may be a distinct subgroup of depressive illness. Although no formal epidemiological studies of SAD have as yet been performed, Thase (1986) reported that 15.6% of a large clinic population ($n = 115$) with recurrent depressive disorders met the criteria for SAD, as defined above.

Survey and Review of the Literature

For this chapter, I surveyed several centers where data on patients with SAD have been collected systematically. A structured questionnaire was sent to the various research centers, and the data provided are shown in Tables 3-1 through 3-5. Survey results and pertinent reports from the literature concerning the phenomenology of SAD are presented here.

PATIENT POPULATION

Most centers relied primarily on volunteers who responded to newspaper and other media requests (Table 3-1). Selection bias is inherent in this kind of approach. The expectation of a nondrug approach such as light therapy provided a major incentive for many volunteers. In Alaska, the high prevalence of shiftwork and complicated commuting arrangements to distant work sites eliminated several excellent volunteers. Factors intrinsic to the depressed state in SAD, such as daytime sleepiness, hypersomnia, and social withdrawal, limited participation of some volunteers with more severe SAD. The seasonal group ($n = 18$) reported by Thase (1986) came from a clinical research population ($n = 115$) selected for inclusion in a study of unipolar depression in which phototherapy was not an option.

DEMOGRAPHIC CHARACTERISTICS

In the seven centers surveyed here (Table 3-1), most volunteers presented for studies in middle age (mean ages reported varied from 30 to 44 years). Retrospective estimate of age of onset was early adulthood in most cases. The report of SAD in seven children and adolescents points out childhood manifestations of the disorder (Rosenthal *et al.*, 1986). The striking predominance of female volunteers (sites reported 74–94% female subjects) was higher than the 2:1 ratio estimated for other affective disorders (Weissman and Klerman, 1977).

TABLE 3-1. Survey Results

Site[a]	Latitude	No. years research in progress	n	Primary source of volunteers	Mean age (years)	Mean age at onset (years)	Percentage female
MD	39°N	7	246	Media/referrals	38	22	82
CH	47°N	3	63	Media/referrals	44	32	78
OR	45°N	3	40	Media	40	~25	85
MN	45°N	3	50	Media	~30	~20	~80
NY	41°N	2	112	Media/referrals	40	19	83
PA	40°N	2	18	Clinical research	44	23	78
AK	64°N	3	17	Media/referrals	38	25	94

[a]Sites: MD, National Institute of Mental Health, Bethesda, MD (Rosenthal, personal communication, 1987); CH, Psychiatric University Clinic, Basel, Switzerland (Wirz-Justice, personal communication, 1987); OR, Oregon Health Sciences University, Portland, OR (Lewy, personal communication, 1987); MN, University of Minnesota, Minneapolis, MN (Depue, personal communication, 1987); NY, New York State Psychiatric Institute, New York, NY (Terman, personal communication, 1987); PA, Western Psychiatric Institute, Pittsburgh, PA (Thase, personal communication, 1987); AK, Fairbanks Psychiatric and Neurologic Clinic, Fairbanks, AK (Hellekson, unpublished data).

TABLE 3-2. Symptoms Reported by SAD Patients during Winter at Two Sites

		Percentage of patients	
Variables	Symptoms reported	MD[a] (n = 246)	CH[a] (n = 63)
Activity	Decreased	95	98
Affect	Sadness	96	92
	Irritability	86	73
	Anxiety	87	85
Appetite	Increase	71	45
	Decrease	18	32
	Mixed	1	2
	No change	11	21
	Carbohydrate craving	72	73
Weight	Increase	76	52
	Decrease	10	21
	Mixed	1	0
	No change	13	25
Libido	Decrease	59	—
Sleep	Increased duration	83	64
	Earlier onset	69	—
	Change in quality	64	79
	Daytime drowsiness	73	—
Other	Symptoms milder near equator	89 (n = 100)	—
	Menstrual difficulties	58 (n = 185)	—
	Work difficulties	86	95
	Interpersonal difficulties	93	84

[a]For clarification of sites, see Table 3-1.

WINTER SYMPTOM SPECTRUM

The winter symptoms (Table 3-2) frequently included decreased activity with affective complaints of sadness, irritability, and/or anxiety. Weight gain and carbohydrate craving were more common than the more classic depressive complaints of decreased appetite and weight loss. Other winter complaints included decreased libido, hypersomnia, daytime drowsiness, interpersonal difficulties, and work difficulties.

Most of the sites surveyed assessed severity of depression with the 21-item Hamilton Depression Rating Scale (HDRS; Hamilton, 1967), whereas Thase (personal communication, 1987) used the original 17-item HDRS (Hamilton, 1960). The HDRS focuses on factors typical of classical depressive symptomatology, such as insomnia and weight loss. A supplementary rating scale to assess the winter complaints characteristic of the "atypical" depression (Liebowitz et al., 1984), such as increased duration of sleep, weight gain, carbohydrate craving, and social withdrawal, has been developed (Rosenthal and Hefferman, 1986). Thase (1986) noted an increase in the "reversed neurovegetative symptoms'' in the seasonal compared to the nonseasonal depressives, but not to the degree noted by Jacobsen *et al.* (1987).

Decreased libido and increased complaints of menstrually related difficulties were reported in more than half of the National Institute of Mental Health (NIMH) subjects (Table 3-2). Depue (personal communication, 1987) noted fewer menstrual complaints than were described by NIMH. Preliminary observations by NIMH (Jacobsen *et al.*, 1987) and Wirz-Justice *et. al.* (1986) suggest that SAD patients have a skewed circannual monthly birthrate, with children of SAD patients tending to be born between January and June, reflecting a decreased rate of conception between November and March.

In the winter, volunteers with SAD complained of daytime sleepiness, prolonged sleep length with earlier bedtimes, and difficulty arising in the morning. Winter and summer polysomnography of SAD patients confirmed significantly increased average sleep length (17%) and decreased average delta sleep (46%) in the winter; however, rapid eye movement (REM) latency was not shortened as in other types of depression (Rosenthal *et al.*, 1984).

Dexamethasone suppressed the hypothalamic–pituitary–adrenal axis in a normal manner (James *et al.*, 1986). Various metabolic parameters such as thyroid and glucose tolerance appeared to be normal in SAD (Jacobsen *et al.*, 1987).

The NIMH reported that most patients began to complain of SAD in November (Jacobsen and Rosenthal, 1988), whereas Alaskan volunteers complained of symptom onset in late August, with a full syndrome developing by October or early November. The mean durations of depressive episodes were as follows: Maryland, 5.2 ± 1.3 months ($n = 245$) (Rosenthal, personal communication, 1987); Switzerland, 5.2 ± 1.2 months ($n = 63$) (Wirz-Justice, personal communication, 1987); and Alaska, 5.7 ± 1.7 months ($n = 17$) (Hellekson, unpublished data).

SUMMER SYMPTOM SPECTRUM

The original retrospective questionnaire survey of SAD complaints by NIMH in 1981 (Rosenthal *et al.*, 1983) found that all but 1 of 42 subjects had a prior history of hypomania or mania. Subsequent reports from NIMH and Alaska continued to find retrospective reports of hypomania to be common (Hellekson *et al.*, 1986; Woodward, 1987; Jacobson and Rosenthal, 1988). However, summer follow-up of SAD study volunteers at two centers found hypomanic complaints to be rare (Lewy, personal communication, 1987; Wirz-Justice, personal communication, 1987). Depue (personal communication, 1987) required the presence of hypomania for inclusion. In the studies of Terman and colleagues ($n = 112$), the following summer symptoms were described: hypomania, 25.9%; weight loss, 12.5%; hyposomnia, 19.6%; and increased energy, 38.4% (Terman, personal communication, 1987).

COURSE

The duration and severity of the winter syndrome in SAD may show individual variation from year to year and at different latitudes and climes. A write-in survey of *USA Today* readers (Potkin *et al.*, 1986) showed a 10-fold increase in the prevalence of SAD complaints from south to north (in 32 of the "lower 48" states). A factor to be considered in incidence and prevalence studies of SAD would be the self-selection involved in who chooses to live in different climates and latitudes. The mean length of residence in Alaska SAD studies ($n = 17$) was 12.2 ± 8.5 years (Hellekson, unpublished data).

Wirz-Justice *et al.* (1986) reported that in 20 of 22 SAD patients, symptoms changed over time, with 13 reporting an increase in severity. SAD improved with moves to lower latitudes, and pattern reversals occurred with moves to the Southern Hemisphere (Rosenthal *et al.*, 1984; Wirz-Justice *et al.*, 1986). For example, a Native Alaskan (Athabascan) woman with many years of SAD reported 3 years of robust, vital well-being while living in Panama (latitude 9°N). Similarly, mood improvement occured in 83% of an SAD patient sample with vacations to lower latitudes (Rosenthal *et al.*, 1984). As in the response to phototherapy, a lag of approximately 4 days is generally seen both for the symptomatic improvement on arriving at the vacation site, and for recurrence of symptoms following return to the north (Rosenthal *et al.*, 1984). Changes in environmental exposure to light in the winter, either by increased artificial illumination or by physical moves to south-facing locations with improved natural illumination have improved winter complaints of SAD patients.

FAMILY HISTORY

A family history of a first-degree relative with affective disorder was seen in more than half of patients with SAD in the four centers reporting this information (Table 3-3). This is higher than expected for other affective disorders (Winokur and Morrison, 1973). A family history of SAD and alcoholism was also common. In a report of SAD in seven children and adolescents (Rosenthal

TABLE 3-3. Family History Data from Four Sites

Family history[a]	MD[b] ($n = 246$)	CH[b] ($n = 59$)	AK[b] ($n = 17$)	OR[b] ($n = 40$)
Affective disorder	55%	58%	57%	53%
SAD	15% ($n = 220$)	15%	15%	28%
Alcoholism	36%	17%	42%	33%

[a] At least one affected first-degree relative.
[b] For clarification of sites, see Table 3-1.

et al., 1986), the finding that five had a parent with the condition awaits further
clarification through epidemiological studies.

TREATMENT HISTORY

Between 25% and 43% of the volunteers for SAD studies surveyed had not
received antidepressant pharmacotherapy for depression (at sites supplying this
information; see Table 3-4). In contrast to other sites, phototherapy was not an
option for Thase's (1986) seasonal group, where the treatment outcome of conventional pharmacotherapy and supportive psychotherapy was identical for both
the seasonal and nonseasonal groups.

RISK FACTORS

Suicidal ideation in the depressed phase of SAD was not uncommon, but actual
suicide attempts, during a course of phototherapy treatment, have not yet been
reported. In two instances in the Alaskan sample, the relapse into depression
upon light withdrawal was more severe than at baseline and coincided with
rapidly shortening days (Woodward, 1987). At the other extreme, phototherapy
appeared to precipitate a manic episode in one Alaskan subject.

DIAGNOSES OF VOLUNTEERS

Marked differences in the diagnoses assigned (Table 3-5) to SAD volunteers
were noted among the different sites. An RDC diagnosis of bipolar II requires
episodes of depression and hypomania, in contrast to a diagnosis of bipolar I,
which requires episodes of depression and mania. The Maryland, Switzerland,
and Alaska studies found bipolar II to be most common. By study criteria,
100% of the Minnesota group were diagnosed as having bipolar II. In contrast,
the Oregon, New York, and Pennsylvania studies diagnosed major depressive
disorder in a majority of instances. This describes episodes of winter depres-

TABLE 3-4. Previous Treatment Received by Patients at Four Sites

Previous treatment	MD[a] (n = 246)	CH[a] (n = 62)	AK[a] (n = 17)	OR[a] (n = 40)
None	26%	26%	43%	25%
Antidepressants	42%	—	33%	50%
Lithium	10%	—	—	17%
Antidepressants/lithium	—	66%	—	—
Hospitalization	11%	6%	8%	—

[a]For clarification of sites, see Table 3-1.

TABLE 3-5. Diagnoses Assigned to Subjects at All Sites

Psychiatric diagnosis (RDC)	MD[a] (n = 246)	CH[a] (n = 39)	OR[a] (n = 40)	NY[a] (n = 112)	MN[a] (n = 50)	PA[a] (n = 18)	AK[a] (n = 17)
Major depressive disorder	12%	46%	88%	50%	—	83%	18%
Minor depressive disorder	—	44%	—	16%	—	—	—
Bipolar I	7%	0%	3%	2%	—	—	—
Bipolar II	81%	8%	5%	26%	100%	17%	82%
Intermittent depression	—	—	—	6%	—	—	—
Other	—	2%	4%	—	—	—	—

[a]For clarification of sites, see Table 3-1.

sions with return to normal baseline mood at other times of year. Differing interpretation among centers as to whether the spring–summer energy component of the SAD syndrome constituted hypomania with dysfunction at home or at work accounted in part for this discrepancy in psychiatric diagnoses of study volunteers.

Phototherapy in Alaska

The merits of phototherapy have been addressed elsewhere in this volume. Briefly, the Alaskan experience in the first two winters' studies of SAD volunteers showed that 2 hr of phototherapy a day for 1 week improved mood, and that the time of day at which a total of 2 hr of light therapy was administered (i.e., morning, evening, etc.) did not influence the antidepressant response (Hellekson et al., 1986; Hellekson and Rosenthal, 1986). In the third winter's project, the duration of light therapy, in a small (n = 5) group of phototherapy responders, showed 0.5 hr of light to be effective in only one subject, whereas 1 hr and 2 hr of phototherapy were equally effective in all five responders (Woodward, 1987). Examination of phototherapy treatment failures in the three Alaskan projects suggest that 2 hr of phototherapy may be inadequate for more severe seasonal depression and for subjects around the time of the winter solstice.

Is Seasonal Affective Disorder a Valid Diagnostic Entity?

Since the initial case history by Lewy et al. (1982) and the description of SAD by Rosenthal et al. (1984), a distinct seasonal subgroup of depressives has been the focus of research at centers worldwide. Seven centers have been surveyed here. Subjects have been females in a ratio of at least 4:1. Complaints of seasonal mood problems, including sadness, irritability, and anxiety, may begin as early as childhood. The "atypical" symptom pattern of increased appetite, weight gain, carbohydrate craving, and increased sleep time has been commonly reported, although the classical depressive picture with decreased appetite, weight loss, and insomnia has also been noted. Although the revision of DSM-III (DSM-III-R; American Psychiatric Association, 1987) continues to group both the classical and "atypical" pattern under major depressive syndrome by allowing either weight gain or loss, and insomnia or hypersomnia, SAD research would benefit by continuing to discriminate between these two separate symptom complexes until it is determined whether a differential treatment response is present to phototherapy and/or antidepressant pharmacotherapy.

This survey found less agreement among centers in regard to the spring–summer energy syndrome as a characteristic of SAD. Jacobsen and Rosenthal (1988) have described the improved sense of well-being, and decreases in appetite, weight, and sleep sometimes seen in SAD, as hypomania. Other centers, inclined toward viewing hypomania as dysfunctional, have not reported this finding. The most recent diagnostic classification, DSM-III-R (American Psychiatric Association, 1987), differentiates hypomania from mania in that, in hypomania, "the disturbance is not severe enough to cause marked impairment in social or occupational functioning or to require hospitalization" (p. 218). The difficulty in differentiating hypomania from euthymia or normal mood rests in whether hypomania requires an impairment in social or occupational functioning. To resolve this dilemma, the term "hyperthymia" has been suggested at the workshop from which this volume has been compiled to describe a robust sense of well-being with less need for sleep, decreased appetite, increased energy, and increased creativeness, yet without impairment in social or occupational functioning. Hypomania would be reserved for the elevated mood state associated with mild but not marked impairment in functioning. Revisions of hypomania rating scales to include hyperthymia should improve diagnostic reliability between centers involved in research on SAD (Williams, Link, Rosenthal, and Terman, personal communication, 1988).

The predictable recurrence of symptoms from year to year and the improvement of symptoms with permanent or transient moves to more southern latitudes are unique features of this syndrome and point toward an underlying climatic factor. Future SAD research should look for factors that result in increased susceptibility to environmental cues. Although the focus has been on the annual variation in environmental light, other factors, such as temperature, global radiation, precipitation, humidity, auroral electromagnetic activity, and seasonally determined psychosocial variations, need to be examined as causal factors in SAD.

Initial criteria for SAD required the "absence of any clear-cut seasonally changing psychosocial variables that would account for the seasonal variability in mood and behavior" (Rosenthal et al., 1984, p. 79). However, it should be noted that the winter experience in high-latitude locations is a complex "biopsychosocial'' stressor that affects all inhabitants. The preliminary finding of a correlation of the increased incidence of SAD with increased latitude needs further epidemiological investigation (Potkin *et al.,* 1986).

The female predominance, common menstrually related complaints, skewed seasonal fertility pattern, and prompt reactivity (in a matter of days) to changes in environment (either through phototherapy or relocation to lower latitudes) all suggest a distinct depressive subgroup with an underlying neuroendocrine mechanism.

Modifications of the diagnostic criteria for SAD are suggested, based on the ''seasonal pattern'' as outlined in DSM-III-R (American Psychiatric Association, 1987, p. 224). These modifications include (1) deleting the note regarding seasonal psychosocial stressors as an exclusionary criterion, and (2) adding hyperthymia to section B. The modified criteria for SAD would be as follows:

A. There has been a regular temporal relationship between the onset of an episode of Bipolar Disorder (including Bipolar Disorder NOS [Not Otherwise Specified]) or Recurrent Major Depression (including Depressive Disorder NOS) and a particular 60-day period of the year (e.g., regular appearance of depression between the beginning of October and the end of November).

B. Full remissions to euthymia (or a change from depression to mania, hypomania, or hyperthymia) also occurred within a particular 60-day period of the year (e.g., depression disappears from mid-February to mid-April).

C. There have been at least three episodes of mood disturbance in three separate years that demonstrate the temporal seasonal relationship defined in A and B; at least two of the years were consecutive.

D. Seasonal episodes of mood disturbance, as described above, outnumbered any nonseasonal episodes of such disturbance that may have occurred by more than three to one.

Preliminary studies over the past 7 years have delineated a seasonal subgroup of depressive illness with unique characteristics and treatment response patterns. Following the original description of SAD by Rosenthal *et al.* (1984), diagnostic criteria for a seasonal pattern have been added to the DSM-III-R (American Psychiatric Association, 1987). With the modifications suggested above, this will serve as a useful basis for further work in this area. The use of standardized diagnostic interview schedules, depression and hypomania/hyperthymia rating scales, and criteria for assessing treatment response will help further the understanding of this unique subtype of affective illness.

Acknowledgments

I wish to express appreciation to N. E. Rosenthal, A. Wirz-Justice, A. J. Lewy, M. E. Thase, R. A. Depue, and M. Terman for survey participation. I also thank Marianna Woodward, WAMI Program, University of Washington School of Medicine, for assistance in the preparation of the manuscript.

References

American Psychiatric Association (1980) *Diagnostic and Statistical Manual of Mental Disorders,* 3rd ed., American Psychiatric Association, Washington, DC.

American Psychiatric Association (1987) *Diagnostic and Statistical Manual of Mental Disorders,* 3rd ed., rev., American Psychiatric Association, Washington, DC.

Anderson, H., M. C. Chamber, G. Myhre, A. N. Nicolson, and B. M. Stone (1984) Sleep of shiftworkers within the Arctic Circle. Aviat. Space and Environ. Med. *55:* 1026–1030.

Aschoff, J. (1981) Annual rhythms in man. In *Handbook of Behavioral Neurobiology,* Vol. 4, *Biological Rhythms,* J. Aschoff, ed., pp. 475–487, Plenum, New York.

Eastwood, M. R., J. L. Whitton, P. M. Kramer, and A. M. Peter (1985) Infradian rhythms: A comparison of affective disorders and normal persons. Arch. Gen. Psychiat. *42:* 295–299.

Hamilton, M. (1960) A rating scale for depression. J. Neurol. Neurosurg. Psychiat. *23:* 56–62.

Hamilton, M. (1967) Development of a rating scale for primary depressive illness. Brit. J. Soc. Clin. Psychol. *6:* 278–296.

Hellekson, C. J., J. A. Kline, and N. E. Rosenthal (1986) Phototherapy for seasonal affective disorder in Alaska. Amer. J. Psychiat. *143:* 1035–1037.

Hellekson, C. J., and N. E. Rosenthal (1986) New light on Alaskan "cabin fever." In *Continuing Medical Education Syllabus and Scientific Proceedings,* p. 67, American Psychiatric Association, Washington, DC.

Hillard, J. R., J. M. Holland, and D. Ramm (1981) Christmas and psychopathology: Data from a psychiatric emergency room population. Arch. Gen. Psychiat. *38:* 1377–1381.

Hippocrates (1846) *Oeuvres Complètes d'Hippocrate,* Littre, ed. J. B. Bailliere, London.

Jacobsen, F. M., and N. E. Rosenthal (1988) Seasonal affective disorder. In *Depression and Mania: A Comparative Textbook,* A. Georgotas and R. Cancro, eds., pp. 104–116, Elsevier, New York.

Jacobsen, F. M., T. A. Wehr, D. A. Sack, S. D. James, and N. E. Rosenthal (1987) Seasonal affective disorder: A review of the syndrome and its public health implications. Amer. J. Pub. Health *77:* 57–60.

James, S. P., T. A. Wehr, D. A. Sack, B. L. Parry, S. Rogers, and N. E. Rosenthal (1986) The dexamethasone suppression test in seasonal affective disorder. Psychiatry *27:* 224–226.

Jefferson, J. W. (1986) An early "study" of seasonal depression (Letter to the editor). Amer. J. Psychiat. *143:* 261–262.

Lewy, A. J., H. A. Kern, N. E. Rosenthal, and T. A. Wehr (1982) Bright artificial light treatment of a manic–depressive patient with a seasonal mood cycle. Amer. J. Psychiat. *139:* 1496–1498.

Liebowitz, M. R., F. M. Quitkin, J. W. Stewart, P. J. McGrath, J. Rabkin, E. Tricamo, J. S. Markowitz, and D. F. Klein (1984) Phenelzine vs. imipramine in atypical depression. Arch. Gen. Psychiat. *41:* 667–669.

Lingjaerde, O., T. Bratlid, and T. Hansen (1985) Insomnia during the "dark period" in northern Norway. Acta Psychiat. Scand. *71:* 506–512.

Parker, G., and S. Walter (1982) Seasonal variation in depressive disorders and suicidal deaths in New South Wales. Brit. J. Psychiat. *140:* 626–632.

Paterson, R. A. H. (1975) Seasonal reduction of slow-wave sleep at an Antarctic coastal station. Lancet *i:* 468–469.

Phillips, D. P., and J. Liu (1980) The frequency of suicides around major public holidays: Some surprising findings. Suicide and Life-Threat. Behav. *10:* 41–50.

Potkin, S. G., M. Zetin, V. Stamenkovic, D. F. Kripke, and W. E. Bunney (1986) Seasonal affective disorder: Prevalence varies with latitude and climate. Clin. Neuropharmacol. *9* (Suppl. 4): 181–183.

Rosenthal, N. E., C. J. Carpenter, S. P. James, B. L. Parry, S. L. B. Rogers, and T. A. Wehr

(1986) Seasonal affective disorder in children and adolescents. Amer. J. Psychiat. *143:* 356–358.

Rosenthal, N. E., and M. M. Heffernan (1986) Bulimia, carbohydrate craving, and depression: A central connection? In *Nutrition and the Brain,* Vol. 7, R. J. Wurtman and J. J. Wurtman, eds., pp. 139–166, Raven Press, New York.

Rosenthal, N. E., D. A. Sack, J. C. Gillin, A. J. Lewy, F. K. Goodwin, P. S. Mueller, D. A. Newsome, and T. A. Wehr (1984) Seasonal affective disorder: A description of the syndrome and preliminary findings with light therapy. Arch. Gen. Psychiat. *41:* 72–80.

Rosenthal, N. E., D. A. Sack, and T. A. Wehr (1983) Seasonal variation in affective disorders. In *Circadian Rhythms in Psychiatry,* T. A. Wehr and F. K. Goodwin, eds., pp. 185–201, Boxwood Press, Pacific Grove, CA.

Simpson, H. W., and J. G. Bohen (1973) Latitude and the human circadian system. In *Biologic Aspects of Circadian Rhythms,* J. N. Mils, ed., pp. 112–113, Plenum, New York.

Spitzer, R. L., J. Endicott, and E. Robins (1978) Research Diagnostic Criteria. Arch. Gen. Psychiat. *35:* 773–782.

Symonds, R. L., and P. Williams (1976) Seasonal variation in the incidence of mania. Brit. J. Psychiat. *129:* 45–48.

Thase, M. (1986) Interview: Defining and treating seasonal affective disorder. Psychiat. Ann. *16:* 733–737.

Walter, S. D. (1977) Seasonality of mania: A reappraisal. Brit. J. Psychiat. *131:* 345–350.

Weissman, M. M., and G. L. Klerman (1977) Sex differences in the epidemiology of depression. Arch. Gen. Psychiat. *34:* 98–111.

Weitzman, E. D., A. S. de Graff, J. F. Sassin, T. Hansen, O. B. Godtilbsen, M. Perlow, and L. Hellman (1975) Seasonal patterns of sleep states and secretion of cortisol and growth hormone during 24 hours periods in northern Norway. Acta Endocrinol. *78:* 65–75.

Winokur, G., and J. Morrison (1973) The Iowa 500: Followup of 225 depressives. Brit. J. Psychiat. *123:* 543–548.

Wirz-Justice, A., C. Bucheli, P. Graw, P. Kielholz, H.-U. Fisch, and B. Woggon (1986) Light treatment of seasonal affective disorder in Switzerland. Acta Psychiatr. Scand. *74:* 193–204.

Woodward, M. B. (1987) *The 1986 Fairbanks Study of Light Therapy for Seasonal Affective Disorder,* student research thesis, University of Washington Medical School.

4

Seasonal Affective Disorder of Childhood and Adolescence: A Review

William A. Sonis

There's a certain slant of light
On winter afternoons,
That oppresses, like the weight
Of cathedral tunes.

Heavenly hurt it gives us;
We can find no scar,
But internal difference
Where the meanings are.
          —Emily Dickinson

Etiology and Phenomenology

Recently, systematic observations and investigations have delineated a group of patients who repeatedly become depressed in the winter and euthymic or hyperthymic in summer. This pattern of mood disturbance has become known as seasonal affective disorder (SAD), and etiological theories have tended to invoke a chronobiological disturbance. Although SAD has been investigated primarily in adults (Rosenthal *et al.*, 1984, 1985a,b; Lewy and Sack, 1986), Rosenthal *et al.* (1986) found that one-third of their adult subjects reported symptom onset in adolescence and childhood. Evidence is accumulating that many subtypes of mood disorder, including bipolar disorder and cyclothymia (Klein *et al.*, 1985), may have an early onset. Despite the increased interest in the diagnosis and treatment of mood disorders in children and adolescents, there is a paucity of information about their etiology and course, and still less is known about chronobiological disturbances in children and adolescents.

Occasionally, clinical reports on the topic of chronobiological disturbances

William A. Sonis. Philadelphia Child Guidance Clinic, Division of Child and Adolescent Psychiatry, University of Pennsylvania, Philadelphia, Pennsylvania.

in children and adolescents have been published. These include a report of a seasonal pattern of depression and mania in an 11-year-old girl with manic–depressive illness (Carlson, 1983); abnormalities of the rest–activity cycle in a 17-year-old school refuser (Chiba, 1984); cycles of disruptive behaviors among 12 children in residential placement (Taylor, 1982); and two recent studies describing SAD in children and adolescents (Rosenthal *et al.*, 1986; Sonis *et al.*, 1987).

Rosenthal *et al.* (1986) studied 6 subjects with SAD of childhood and adolescence (SAD-CA) in an open study of phototherapy, whereas our group (Sonis *et al.*, 1987) compared 5 subjects with SAD-CA to 15 subjects without SAD (patients with nonseasonal major depression, patients with attention deficit disorder, and symptomatic normals) in a randomly assigned single-blind crossover study comparing phototherapy with relaxation treatment. Table 4-1 compares the two studies. Although the number of reported subjects with SAD-CA treated with phototherapy is small ($n = 12$), this chapter highlights the preliminary knowledge about the phenomenology of SAD-CA.

Virtually nothing is known about the biology of the syndrome in children and adolescents, although it is not unreasonable to think that the underlying mechanism is similar to adult SAD. Likewise, little can be said about the prevalence of SAD-CA, although despite wide media coverage in newspaper articles and television news stories in the greater Minneapolis area, only 30 self-referred subjects in 2 years met criteria for SAD-CA in a population base of approximately 500,000 children and adolescents. Rosenthal *et al.* (1986) recruited 7 subjects over a similar time span in a similar population base, many of whom were the children of adults with SAD.

There is more information available about the diagnostic and clinical picture of SAD-CA. Information about the clinical picture of subjects with SAD-CA is derived from Rosenthal *et al.*'s (1986) open study of phototherapy, and our study comparing evening phototherapy with systematic relaxation (Sonis *et al.*, 1987). In our study, we compared the efficacy of 2 hr of light (2500 lux) in the evening to a similar duration of systematic relaxation in 20 children and adolescents (5 had SAD-CA, 5 had nonseasonal major depressive disorder, 5 had attention deficit disorder, and 5 subjects had no diagnosis). Both Rosenthal *et al.*'s study and our own used the same diagnostic criteria for children

TABLE 4-1. Studies of SAD-CA

Authors and date	*n*	Design	Placebo	Comparison treatment	Standard measures
Rosenthal *et al.* (1986)	7	Open	No	No	No
Sonis *et al.* (1987)	5	Single-blind	No	Yes	Yes

and adolescents as used for adults. That is, the individual had to meet *Diagnostic and Statistical Manual of Mental Disorders,* third edition (DSM-III; American Psychiatric Association, 1980) criteria for a major depressive disorder and to have experienced at least 2 consecutive years of winter depression with resolution of depressive symptoms in the summer. In both studies, the male-to-female ratio in SAD-CA was closer to 1:1, rather than 1:4, as described in the adult literature (Rosenthal *et al.,* 1984); this may represent a developmental difference in sex ratio. Four out of five subjects in our study reported the onset of their symptoms before age 11. Their average age at the time of presentation was 16.2 years (± 2.6). The average number of cycles was 6.0 (± 3.5). No subject had previously been treated for depression. All subjects met Diagnostic Interview for Children and Adolescents (DICA) criteria (Herjanic and Campbell, 1977) for unipolar depression. One patient subsequently had a hypomanic episode. The diagnosis of unipolar depression in SAD-CA subjects is consistent with the findings of Quitkin *et al.* (1986), a majority of whose adult SAD patients had a unipolar diagnosis, but differs from the results of Rosenthal *et al.* (1984), who diagnosed 83% of their adult SAD patients as having a bipolar II disorder.

The symptoms of SAD-CA are generally similar to symptoms of SAD. Three-quarters of the parents of the SAD-CA subjects reported that their children experienced fatigue, irritability, sadness, decreased concentration, crying, worrying, and decreased activity during the months of November to March. This was not true of subjects with nonseasonal unipolar depression. These key symptoms waned during the summer. Hypersomnia and hyperphagia were not central features, as described in the adult literature on SAD, but anergia was. All of the parents of SAD-CA subjects reported increased periods of energy and talkativeness during the summer. The onset and offset of symptoms in children and adolescents were similar to those seen in adults; that is, symptoms began to emerge in October, peaked in December and January, and began to wane toward the end of February. SAD-CA subjects scored significantly higher ($p < 0.05$) than all other subjects on the Seasonal Symptom Checklist for Children (SSCL-C), a self-report questionnaire of seasonal variation in depressive symptoms (Sonis *et al.,* 1986a). The average SSCL-C score of the SAD-CA subjects was 35.7 ± 5.7, compared to 23.0 ± 8.8 for subjects with nonseasonal depression, 11.7 ± 10.2 for subjects with attention deficit disorder, and 24.0 ± 18.5 for the subjects with no diagnosis (Sonis *et al.,* 1986a). To date, there is no information about biological markers in SAD-CA.

As a follow-up to our initial study, we reviewed the symptom profile of 60 children and adolescents who reported recurrent winter depression. Thirty subjects (20 females and 10 males) met DSM-III criteria for major depressive episode, recurrent; scored in the depressed range (≥ 40) on the Children's Depression Rating Scale (CDRS; Poznanski *et al.,* 1984); exhibited extreme seasonal variation in symptoms (SSCL-C score ≥ 26); and reported moderate interference with psychosocial function during their depressed phase for at least 2 years (criteria for SAD-CA).

We compared the symptom profiles of these subjects with the symptom profiles of adults with SAD (Rosenthal *et al.*, 1985b). Over 70% of the SAD-CA subjects reported sadness, fatigue, poor-quality sleep, irritability, anhedonia, anxiety, and difficulty with concentration and school work. Compared to adults with SAD (Rosenthal *et al.*, 1985b), significantly fewer ($p < 0.05$) SAD-CA subjects reported changes in activity and sadness, while significantly more ($p < 0.05$) subjects with SAD-CA reported decreased sleep. Fewer SAD-CA subjects than adults with SAD reported anxiety and increased appetite, while more SAD-CA subjects than adults reported irritability; these differences approached but did not reach significance.

Differential Diagnosis and Treatment

The symptoms of SAD-CA can overlap with those of several other disorders, although several features differentiate nonseasonal major depressive disorder, attention deficit disorder (with or without hyperactivity), and symptomatic normal mood and energy variation from SAD-CA. By definition, children with major depressive disorder without seasonal variation do not have the typical waxing and waning of symptoms with the seasons. Nonseasonal depression persists for an average of 8 months (Kovacs *et al.*, 1984), compared to an average of 5 months in our subjects. Nonseasonal depressives may report an exacerbation of symptoms in the winter, but the symptoms fail to remit in spring and summer. No consistent monthly symptom peak is reported. Individuals with attention deficit disorder can present with seasonal dysphoria, but do not have the constellation of depressive symptoms, particularly anergia, reported in SAD-CA. Parents of subjects with attention deficit disorder did not report the seasonal peak of symptoms endorsed by the SAD-CA parents in our study. Finally, "normal" children or adolescents may experience a seasonal pattern of energy variation and mild dysphoria, without the severity reported in subjects with SAD-CA (Sonis *et al.*, 1986a). In many ways, our normal subjects presented with a picture more consistent with adult SAD than did our subjects with SAD-CA; 75% of the parents of symptomatic normals reported hypersomnia and carbohydrate craving in their children during winter. The normal subjects failed to meet diagnostic criteria for dysthymic disorder because of the persistent rather than intermittent dysphoria and the absence of symptoms for more than 2 months.

Children and adolescents with SAD also respond to phototherapy. Children and adolescents with SAD improve on both morning and evening (Rosenthal *et al.*, 1986) or evening phototherapy alone (Sonis *et. al.*, 1986a). Our subjects with SAD-CA experienced a 20.2-point drop (32% improvement over

TABLE 4-2. Children's Depression Rating Scale Scores

Group	Baseline[a]		Light[b]		Washout		Relaxation	
	$\bar{x}$	(SD)	$\bar{x}$	(SD)	$\bar{x}$	(SD)	$\bar{x}$	(SD)
SAD-CA	62.6	(16.3)	42.4	(11.4)	53.0	(17.6)[c]	57.4	(15.2)[c]
Major depression	59.9	(4.9)	52.3	(10.4)	38.3	(5.9)[c]	34.3	(4.5)
Attention deficit disorder	33.6	(6.2)	22.6	(5.0)	24.8	(8.0)	24.4	(8.5)
No diagnosis	30.6	(4.8)	20.6	(1.3)	19.2	(5.9)	20.8	(4.3)

Note. Multivariate analysis of covariance: $F (6, 26) = 3.07, p < 0.02$.
[a] Initial and pretreatment combined.
[b] Analysis of covariance: $F (3, 13) = 8.81, p < 0.002$.
[c] Studentized maximum modulus: $df = 13, p < 0.05$.

baseline) in their mean CDRS scores during light treatment (2500 lux for 2 hr at dusk), whereas subjects with nonseasonal major depressive disorder only demonstrated a 7.6-point drop (12% improvement) (see Table 4-2). Subjects with SAD-CA demonstrated virtually no improvement on relaxation treatment, whereas subjects with major depression reported a 43% improvement in the same condition. SAD-CA subjects reported improvement primarily in neuro-vegatative symptoms of depression with phototherapy, whereas subjects with major depression reported an improvement in the cognitive symptoms of depression during relaxation treatment. These results were significant ($p < 0.01$). There was a similar pattern of improvement on a self-report measure of depression, although the results were not statistically significant.

Normal Mood and Energy Variation

One of the possible variations of SAD-CA is extreme normal variation in mood and energy. In an attempt to explore the complex relationship between seasonal mood variation and depressive feelings, we screened 900 high school students during the winter of 1985–1986 for extreme nonpathological seasonal mood variation and depression (Sonis et al., 1986b). To do this, we developed the SSCL-C (Sonis et al., 1985), a self-report scale inquiring about seasonal variation in depressive symptoms such as irritability, sleep, and energy. The 13 items on the SSCL-C were derived from clinical samples of children and adolescents with SAD. In completing the SSCL-C, subjects are asked to rate the degree to which the listed symptoms vary with the season. Subjects may rate the change in symptoms from "not at all" (0) to "extreme" (4). The SSCL-C is scored by summing all 13 items. Subjects are also asked to report the degree to which these fluctuations interfere with their activities (severity) and the number of years they have experienced the seasonal variations (duration).

The final sample in our study consisted of 355 boys and 424 girls. Their ages varied between 14 and 18 years ($\bar{x} = 16.4 \pm 1.1$ years). The mean SSCL-C score ($\pm SD$) for the total sample was 10 ± 7.9. Because scores tended to pile up toward the low end of the scoring range and were not normally distributed, we defined individuals who scored greater than the third quartile (Q3) as high scorers. The Q3 was 13 for the boys, but 17 for the girls. There were both sex and age effects for the total SSCL-C score; 16-year-old girls scored significantly higher than all other age and sex combinations. Post hoc tests ($p < 0.001$) revealed that five items (fatigue, headaches, craves sweets, crying, and worrying) accounted for the significant differences (see Table 4-3).

We classified 51 students (6.4% of the total sample) as "highly seasonal"; that is, they scored above the Q3 on the total SSCL-C and experienced marked interference (score ≥ 3) with activities for more than 2 years. Of the adolescents who reported themselves to be highly seasonal, 29% also scored in the severely depressed range (≥ 24) (Kaplan *et al.*, 1984) on the Beck Depression Inventory (BDI). This group (highly seasonal/severely depressed) represented 1% of the total sample. Table 4-4 compares the highly seasonal and the highly seasonal/severely depressed groups. The sensitivity of the SSCL-C in predicting depres-

TABLE 4-3. Sex Differences in Individual Items on the Seasonal Symptom Checklist for Children

	Boys ($n = 355$)			Girls ($n = 424$)				
	Q3	n	Percentage >Q3	Q3	n	Percentage >Q3	df	F
Total score	13	355	22.8	17	424	22.9	1, 176	26.30
Individual items								
Irritability	1	64	18.0	1	101	23.8	1, 163	2.30
Fatigue	1	83	23.4	2	63	14.9	1, 144	97.65*
Energy	2	38	10.7	2	53	12.5	1, 089	0.62
Sad	1	28	7.9	1	80	19.3	1, 108	0.03
Sleep	2	69	19.4	2	87	20.5	1, 154	0.07
Headache	0	69	19.4	1	74	17.5	1, 141	57.06*
Appetite	1	50	14.1	1	104	24.5	1, 152	0.43
Activity	2	54	15.2	2	72	17.7	1, 727	1.80
Sweets	0	77	21.7	1	45	10.6	1, 120	39.46*
Cry	0	20	5.6	1	42	9.9	1, 060	11.83*
Worry	1	68	19.2	2	44	10.4	1, 110	29.86*
Social withdrawal	1	82	24.0	1	102	24.0	1, 182	0.08
Tantrum	0	57	16.1	0	91	21.5	1, 146	0.09
Interference	2	32	9.5	2	42	10.3	1, 072	1.32

*$p < 0.001$.

TABLE 4-4. Comparison of Highly Seasonal and Highly Seasonal/Severely Depressed Groups

Class			SSCL-C		BDI	
Highly seasonal	Severely depressed	n	$\bar{x}$	(SD)	$\bar{x}$	(SD)
Yes	No	15[a]	20.3	(4.1)	10.2	(5.4)
Yes	Yes	15	27.6	(8.1)[b]	26.9	(4.0)

[a] Matched to highly seasonal/severely depressed subjects by age/sex.
[b] t test: $df = 28$, $t = 3.1$, $p < 0.004$.

sion was 55%; its relative specificity was 97%. Individuals who reported themselves as highly seasonal were eight times more likely to report depression than other individuals. Thus, highly seasonal changes in mood symptoms may be a marker for a depressive diasthesis.

Highly seasonal behavior and depression in children and adolescents provide insight into one aspect of pathological seasonal mood variation. Additional epidemiological data about the seasonal aspects of mood can be obtained by analysis of suicides and psychiatric admissions. Analysis of suicide (which is considered to be an indirect marker of depression) has demonstrated both winter and early spring peaks for teenage suicides, as well as fall peaks, in contrast to the spring and early summer peaks reported for adults (Kevan, 1980). There are no published data on the seasonality of psychiatric admissions or outpatient visits in children and adolescents, as there are for adults. Preliminary analysis of psychiatric admissions and outpatient visits over a 5-year period at the Division of Child Psychiatry, University of Minnesota, revealed that there was an increase in the percentage of children with the diagnosis of major depressive disorder in the spring and fall. Thus, although the data are sparse, there is emerging epidemiological evidence in support of a seasonal rhythm in the presentation of prepubertal and pubertal mood disorders.

Summary

What are the conclusions of this review and the implication for future research? First, there is a small group of children and adolescents who do meet criteria for SAD and experience clinically significant winter depression. These children and adolescents are more likely than their adult counterparts to present with decreased sleep and increased irritability, and less likely to present with changed activity, sadness, anxiety, and hyperphagia. Although no precise figures are available, SAD-CA appears to be rare within the general population. We also lack information about its prevalence in the psychiatrically ill child and adolescent populations. Second, individuals with SAD-CA experience a decrease in symptoms in response to phototherapy. Our study (Sonis et al., 1987) found that 2500 lux of supplemental evening illumination was sufficient to induce remission of symptoms within 1 week. Finally, there is evidence that children and adolescents may experience significant nonclinical seasonal fluctuations in mood, affect, and energy; these may constitute a risk factor for depression.

Additional research is needed to further define the syndrome of SAD in children and adolescents. Specific areas for research include the following: isolation of normal and pathological infradian rhythms of mood variation in children and adolescents from environmental factors, such as the school year; differentiation of SAD-CA from other forms of recurrent depression; identification of chronobiological correlates of SAD-CA (such as changes in dim-light melatonin onset); and additional studies of phototherapy, using more stringent methodology (placebo exclusion and placebo controls), to determine the efficacy and specificity of phototherapy in SAD-CA.

Research programs in these areas will enable us to develop strategies for early recognition and intervention in order to minimize the psychiatric, educational, and social morbidity of this disorder. Research programs will also enable us to design intervention strategies to aid less severely affected children and adolescents, who do not meet formal criteria for SAD-CA but nonetheless experience repeated winter depression.

References

American Psychiatric Association (1980) *Diagnostic and Statistical Manual of Mental Disorders,* 3rd ed., American Psychiatric Association, Washington, DC.

Carlson, G. A. (1983) Bipolar disorders. In *Affective Disorders in Childhood and Adolescence,* D. P. Cantwell and G. A. Carlson, eds., pp. 3–18, Spectrum, New York.

Chiba, Y. (1984). A school refuser: His best activity rhythm involved multiple circadian components. Chronobiologia *11:* 21–27.

Herjanic, B., and W. Campbell (1977) Differentiating psychiatrically disturbed children on the basis of a structured interview. J. Abnorm. Child Psychol. *5:* 127–136.

Kaplan, S. L., G. K. Hong, and C. Weinhold (1984) Epidemiology of depressive symptomatology in adolescents. J. Amer. Acad. Child Psychiat. *23:* 91–98.

Kevan, S. M. (1980) Perspectives on season of suicide: A review. Soc. Sci. Med. *14:* 369–378.

Klein, D. N., R. A. Depue, and J. F. Slater (1985) Cyclothymia in the adolescent offspring of parents with bipolar affective disorder. J. Abnorm. Psychol. *94:* 25–127.

Kovacs, M., T. L. Feinberg, M. A. Crouse-Novak, S. L. Paulaskas, and R. Finkelstein (1984) Depressive disorders in childhood: II. A longitudinal study of the risks of subsequent major depression. Arch. Gen. Psychiat. *41:* 643–649.

Lewy, A. L., and R. L. Sack (1986) Light therapy and psychiatry. Proc. Soc. Exp. Biol. Med. *183:* 11–18.

Poznanski, E. O., J. A. Crossman, Y. Bachbum, M. Barnegas, L. Freeman, and R. Gibbon (1984) Preliminary studies of reliability and validity of the Children's Depression Rating Scale. J. Amer. Acad. Child Psychiat. *23:* 191–197.

Quitkin, F., M. Terman, J. Terman, P. McGrath, and J. Stewart (1986) Light treatment of seasonal affective disorder. Paper presented at the 25th annual meeting of the American College of Neuropsychopharmacology, Washington, DC, December 8–12.

Rosenthal, N. E., C. J. Carpenter, S. P. James, B. L. Parry, S. L. B. Rogers, and T. A. Wehr

(1986) Seasonal affective disorder in children and adolescents. Amer. J. Psychiat. *143:* 356–358.

Rosenthal, N. E., D. A. Sack, C. J. Carpenter, B. L. Parry, W. B. Mendelson, and T. A. Wehr (1985a) Antidepressant effects of light in seasonal affective disorder. Amer. J. Psychiat. *142:* 163–170.

Rosenthal, N. E., D. A. Sack, C. J. Gillin, A. J. Lewy, F. K. Goodwin, Y. Davenport, P. S. Mueller, D. A. Newsome, and T. A. Wehr (1984) Seasonal affective disorder: A description of the syndrome and preliminary findings with light treatment. Arch. Gen. Psychiat. *41:* 72–80.

Rosenthal, N. E., D. A. Sack, S. P. James, B. L. Parry, W. B. Mendelson, L. Tamarkin, and T. A. Wehr (1985b) Seasonal affective disorder and phototherapy. Ann. NY Acad. Sci. *453:* 260–269.

Sonis, W. A., A. M. Yellin, B. D. Garfinkel, and H. H. Hoberman (1986a) Seasonal affective disorder of childhood and adolescence: Response to light treatment. Paper presented at the 33rd annual meeting of the American Academy of Child and Adolescent Psychiatry, Los Angeles, October.

Sonis, W. A., A. M. Yellin, M. Rennie, and B. D. Garfinkel (1986b) Seasonal mood variation in adolescence: Normal and pathologic. Paper presented at the 33rd annual meeting of the American Academy of Child and Adolescent Psychiatry, Los Angeles, October.

Sonis, W. A., A. M. Yellin, B. D. Garfinkel, and H. H. Hoberman (1987) The antidepressant effect of light in seasonal affective disorder of childhood and adolescence. Psychopharmacol. Bull. *23* (3): 360–363.

Taylor, W. M. (1982) Several day cycles in disturbed children's behavior. Chronobiologia *9:* 329–331.

5

Summer Depression: Description of the Syndrome and Comparison with Winter Depression

Thomas A. Wehr, Holly Giesen, Patricia M. Schulz,
Jean R. Joseph-Vanderpool, Siegfried Kasper,
Karen A. Kelly, and Norman E. Rosenthal

Background

Some patients with seasonal affective disorder (SAD) have recurrent summer depressions (Wehr *et al.*, 1987; Boyce and Parker, 1988; Wehr, Giesen, Schulz, Joseph-Vanderpool, Kelly, Kasper, and Rosenthal, submitted)—a pattern opposite to that of most patients described in this volume. We first became aware of summer depression when individuals affected with this condition learned of our seasonal depression research program at the National Institute of Mental Health (NIMH) and wrote to us to describe the problem. Publicity about our program focused on recurrent winter depression, and thousands of patients with SAD wrote for information about the syndrome. However, about 5% of the letters began with a disclaimer that the individual's seasonal pattern of illness was opposite to that described in the publicity about winter depression. This was such a recurring theme in the letters that we decided to investigate a group of these patients.

We were also stimulated to look into the problem further by two patients who presented themselves for treatment of summer depression. One was a middle-aged man who had suffered from recurrent summer depressions since childhood. An interesting feature of this patient's history was that he had lived in several different parts of the world (in the Middle East, Europe, and the United States), and found that his depressive symptoms were highly dependent on

Thomas A. Wehr, Holly Giesen, Patricia M. Schulz, Jean R. Joseph-Vanderpool, Seigfried Kasper, Karen A. Kelly, and Norman E. Rosenthal. Clinical Psychobiology Branch, National Institute of Mental Health, Bethesda, Maryland.

climate and latitude—more severe at low latitudes, less severe at high latitudes. He sometimes experienced complete remissions after traveling north in the summer. He responded to treatment with a tricyclic antidepressant. The second patient was a retired secretary who had suffered from recurrent summer depressions since her 20s. At the time of her first consultation in June 1986, she gave a 20-year history of recurrent summer depressions that usually began in April and ended in September each year. She was apologetic because her depression had spontaneously remitted a day or two before the consultation. Just before she remitted an unusual cold front had moved through the area, reducing Washington's summer temperature to an uncharacteristic 4°C. Of course, the association between these two events might have been coincidental, but it piqued our curiosity about summer depression and its possible sensitivity to changes in physical environment. We were further interested when this patient appeared to improve after several days of a treatment that consisted of confinement to an air-conditioned house and repeated cold showers (Wehr et al., 1987). This type of treatment was impractical, however, so we administered a monoamine oxidase inhibitor (MAOI), and she responded.

Ultimately, we recruited a series of patients from our referral network and through media publicity, delineated clinical features of the syndrome, and investigated the responsivity of the syndrome to manipulations of environmental temperature and light.

As so often happens, when we looked into the older psychiatric literature, we discovered that we were not the first to describe summer depression. As early as 1838, Esquirol described a number of cases (Esquirol, 1845), and subsequently other psychiatrists made similar observations (Pilcz, 1901; Kraines, 1957). Cases of summer depression can also be detected in data on recurrent affective illness published by 20th-century authors (Arnold and Kryspin-Exner, 1965; Kukopulos and Reginaldi, 1973). As mentioned in Chapter 2 of this volume, the English poet John Milton (1608–1674) may be the earliest individual recorded to have suffered from a type of summer depression (Philip, 1694, cited in Patterson, 1957). Up to the beginning of this century, seasonal influences on affective illness were thought to depend on changes in temperature and humidity, and therefore summer depression was attributed to heat (Esquirol, 1845).

Contrasts between Summer and Winter Depression

Our investigations revealed some interesting contrasts between summer depression and winter depression (Wehr et al., submitted): Summer depression is more likely to have endogenous features, whereas winter depression is more likely to have atypical features. We compared 20 patients with each type of depression (total, 40 patients). There were several sources of information for this comparison. Each patient completed the Seasonal Pattern Assessment

Questionnaire (SPAQ), a self-administered inventory of information about seasonal changes in a variety of psychological and physical factors and sensitivity to various types of changes in the physical environment (Rosenthal *et al.*, 1988). Each patient also completed the Seasonal Symptom Questionnaire (SSQ), a self-administered instrument designed to elicit information about symptoms and course of seasonal mood disorders (Rosenthal, Hardin, and Wehr, unpublished). Patients were evaluated with structured diagnostic interviews, including the Structured Clinical Interview for the DSM-III-R (SCID; Spitzer *et al.*, 1986). In addition, each patient was prospectively observed to become depressed during the season of risk, and was evaluated at that time with the Hamilton Depression Rating Scale (HDRS; Hamilton, 1967).

There were approximately equal numbers of patients with unipolar and bipolar illness in each group. However, summer depressives were distinguished by often having coexisting anxiety disorders (25% vs. 0%). As noted previously by Rosenthal *et al.* (1984) and others (Mueller and Allen, 1984; Wirz-Justice *et al.*, 1986; Boyce and Parker, 1988; Garvey *et al.*, 1988; Thompson and Isaacs, 1988), patients with winter depression were more likely to have atypical depressive symptoms, such as anergia, fatigue, increased appetite, carbohydrate craving, weight gain, and hypersomnia. They were also more likely to have decreased interest in sex. Opposite changes were found in summer depression (see Tables 5-1, 5-2, and 5-3). Patients with summer depression were more likely to have endogenous depressive symptoms, such as agitation, loss of appetite, weight loss, and insomnia. More patients with summer depression reported suicidal thoughts and first-degree relatives who had attempted

TABLE 5-1. Contrasting Symptoms of Summer and Winter Depressions (Selected Items from the SSQ and SPAQ)

Feature	Percentage with summer depression ($n = 20$)	Percentage with winter depression ($n = 20$)
Sleep		
Decreased sleep	40	15
Increased sleep	35	85**
Appetite and weight		
Decreased appetite	40**	0
Weight loss	25*	0
Increased appetite	35	100***
Carbohydrate craving	20	75***
Weight gain	50	75
Beliefs about environmental influences		
Influenced more by temperature	95***	15
Influenced more by light	0	75***

$*p < 0.05$; $**p < 0.01$; $***p < 0.001$ (χ^2 for all comparisons).

TABLE 5-2. Contrasting Symptoms of Summer and Winter Depressions
(Selected HDRS Item Scores)

	Mean ± SD	
Feature	Summer depression (n = 20)	Winter depression (n = 20)
Sleep		
Early insomnia	0.80 ± 0.89 **	0.20 ± 0.52
Middle insomnia	0.90 ± 0.97	0.70 ± 0.86
Late insomnia	1.00 ± 0.92	0.50 ± 0.76
Psychomotor symptoms		
Retardation	0.85 ± 0.49	1.25 ± 0.71 *
Agitation	0.55 ± 0.89	0.25 ± 0.44
Genital symptoms	0.53 ± 0.77	1.05 ± 0.85 *
Total HDRS score	19.95 ± 4.38	19.65 ± 5.23

$*p < 0.05$; $**p < 0.01$ (independent t test for all comparisons).

suicide, but this difference was not statistically significant. In general, these findings are consistent with trends reported previously by Boyce and Parker (1988) in the only other study that contrasts winter and summer depression.

The contrasts between summer and winter depression resemble contrasts previously described for other dichotomous subtypes of depression, such as endogenous and reactive, psychotic and neurotic (Carney *et al.*, 1965; Kiloh *et al.*, 1972; Kendell, 1976; Paykel, 1977; Akiskal, 1983), unipolar I and unipolar II (Kupfer *et al.*, 1975), typical and atypical (V-type) (Liebowitz and Klein, 1979; Quitkin *et al.*, 1979; Klein *et al.*, 1980; Sovner, 1981; Davidson *et al.*,

TABLE 5-3. Contrasting Symptoms of Summer and Winter Depressions
(Selected Supplemental Rating Scale Item Scores)

	Mean ± SD	
Feature	Summer depression (n = 20)	Winter depression (n = 20)
Sleep		
Hypersomnia	0.40 ± 0.99	1.60 ± 0.88 ***
Appetite and weight		
Increased appetite	0.60 ± 1.14	1.80 ± 1.36 **
Increased eating	0.40 ± 0.99	1.80 ± 1.24 ***
Carbohydrate craving	0.80 ± 1.24	2.25 ± 0.85 ***
Weight gain	0.35 ± 0.75	0.90 ± 0.85 *

$*p < 0.05$; $**p < 0.01$; $***p < 0.001$ (independent t test for all comparisons).

1982; Beeber and Pies, 1983; Paykel *et al.*, 1983; Liebowitz *et al.*, 1984; Davidson and Pelton, 1986), and unipolar and bipolar (Detre *et al.*, 1972; Kupfer *et al.*, 1975). In light of the present findings, it would be interesting to know whether any of these subtypes exhibits seasonal patterns of occurrence, and if so, whether the patterns are consistent with those found by Boyce and Parker (1988) and our group for summer and winter depression. To our knowledge, only one study has addressed this issue. Eastwood and Stiasny (1978) examined seasonal patterns of hospital admissions in Canada for endogenous and neurotic depressions and found spring peaks and winter troughs for the former and fall peaks and summer troughs for the latter—a pattern that may be consistent with our findings.

The opposite seasonal patterns of the two types of depression may be clues to their nature. As we discuss below, endogenous and atypical depressions may be exaggerated expressions of normal behavioral and physiological adaptations to environmental conditions that prevail in summer and winter, respectively.

It could be argued (see Mrosovsky, Chapter 10, this volume) that the bimodal seasonal patterns of winter and summer depression are artifacts of recruitment methods in which the two types of depression were advertised and sought. According to this interpretation, new categories of depression might be found for every season, if media publicity were tailored to achieve this result. This is a reasonable and serious criticism, which can only be answered with epidemiological studies with appropriate sampling methods. However, some epidemiological evidence discussed below bears on this issue, and it does tend to support the concept that there are primarily two opposite seasonal influences on depression.

The majority of studies of the seasonal distribution of onsets of depressive episodes show that there are two peaks, one in the spring and one in the fall (Leuthold, 1940; Kraines, 1957; Angst *et al.*, 1969; Payk, 1976; Frangos *et al.*, 1980; Rihmer, 1980) (see Wehr, Chapter 2, Fig. 2-1, this volume). A similar pattern obtains in most studies of suicide (Faust and Sarreither, 1975). These patterns are congruent with those of recurrent summer depression and winter depression, which begin in the spring and the fall, respectively. Seasonal patterns of annually recurring depressions have been investigated in four different survey studies. We (Kasper, Bartko, Wehr, and Rosenthal, submitted) conducted structured interviews with over 400 residents of Montgomery County, Maryland, selected by randomly dialed telephone numbers, with over 90% responding. Terman and colleagues (see Terman, Chapter 20, this volume) used a questionnaire to conduct a survey by mail of over 400 randomly selected residents of Manhattan, with over 60% responding. Boyce and Parker (1988) solicited responses to a questionnaire from readers of a women's magazine in Australia, and Rosen, Rosenthal, Targum, *et al.* (unpublished) solicited responses to a questionnaire from patients visiting doctors' offices in cities at three different latitudes in the eastern United States. The results of all four studies were similar in showing that respondents who experienced seasonal changes in mood and energy exhibited primarily two seasonal patterns: either recurrent summer depression or recurrent winter depression.

Possible Environmental Factors in Summer Depression

Environmental factors that might trigger summer depressions have not yet been clearly identified. Most patients believe that their summer depressions are triggered by heat, and a few patients have improved after being isolated from heat and exposed to cold in uncontrolled studies (Wehr *et al.,* 1987). In order to investigate the hypothesis that summer depression is caused either by heat or by light, we conducted a balanced randomization crossover study in which we treated summer depressives by (1) isolating them from heat and exposing them to cold, or (2) isolating them from light and exposing them to dark (Wehr *et al.,* submitted).

The treatments were carried out during two different 5-day periods on a research wards at NIMH. During one 5-day period (the ''cold treatment''), they were isolated from heat by being confined to the air-conditioned ward, and they were exposed to cold by being asked to lie between two 5°C hypothermia blankets for 20 min four times a day. They were also asked to sit in front of a window with a southern exposure for 20 min four times a day so that they would not be totally deprived of exposure to sunlight. During the other 5-day period (the ''dark treatment''), they were isolated from bright light by being confined to the ward and by wearing goggles that filtered out 70% of the ambient light, and they were exposed to dark for 20 min four times a day. They were also asked to go out of doors, while wearing the goggles, for 20 min four times a day, so that they would not be totally deprived of exposure to heat. The two treatments were administered in a balanced randomization crossover design, with at least 7 days between treatment periods to allow for relapse before the second treatment. Raters blind to treatment conditions used the HDRS (Hamilton, 1967) and supplemental items (Rosenthal and Hefferman, 1988) to assess patients' clincal state before treatment, at the end of treatment, and 7 days after withdrawal from treatment. Results were evaluated with a two-way analysis of variance.

Six patients completed both phases of the study. They improved after both types of treatment, and there was no significant interaction between response to treatment and type of treatment. There are several possible explanations for these results: (1) Both cold and dark are antidepressant, and both heat and light are depressogenic. (2) Only cold or dark is antidepressant, but the two modalities were confounded in the experimental conditions. (3) Some other aspect of the treatments, not specifically related to cold or dark, was responsible for the improvements. No specific interpretation is possible. We suspect that the second explanation is the most likely because patients were largely isolated from both light and heat during each phase of the experiment.

The most interesting findings to emerge from these studies are the contrasts between the symptoms of summer depression and winter depression, which are rather consistent in our study and that of Boyce and Parker (1988). It is as though the seasons are separating two subtypes of depression, like a chromatograph, on the basis of differences in their sensitivities to physical forces in the environment. What are these physical forces? The case with winter depression seems clear; apparently seasonal changes in environmental light trigger and terminate the depression (see Rosenthal *et al.*, Chapter 15, this volume, and Terman, Chapter 20, this volume). The case with summer depression is less clear and requires further investigation.

Seasonal Patterns in Endogenous and Atypical Depressions

The seasonal patterns of occurrence of endogenous and atypical depressions may be clues to their nature. The sensitivity of each type of depression to changes in the physical environment, and the occurence together of characteristic groups of symptoms in each types of depression, may have their basis in mechanisms of environmental physiology. Endogenous (summer-type) depressions and atypical (winter-type) depression may be exaggerated expressions of normal adaptations to environmental conditions that prevail in summer and winter, respectively (Wehr and Rosenthal, in press).

References

Akiskal, H. S. (1983) Diagnosis and classification of affective disorders: New insights from clinical and laboratory approaches. Psychiat. Dev. *2:* 123–160.

Angst, J., P. Grof, H. Hippius, and W. Pöldinger (1969) Verlaufsgesetzlichkeiten depressiver Syndrom. In *Das Depressive Syndrom,* H. Hippius and H. Selbach, eds., pp. 93–100, G. Fischer Verlag, Stuttgart.

Arnold, O. H. and K. Kryspin-Exner (1965) Zur Frage der Beeinflussung des Verlaufes des manisch–depressiven Krankheitsgeschehens durch Antidepressiva. Wien Med. Wochenschr. *45/46:* 929–934.

Beeber, A. R. and R. W. Pies (1983) The nonmelancholic syndromes: An alternate approach to classifacation. J. Nerv. Ment. Dis. *171:* 3–9.

Boyce, P., and G. Parker (1988) Seasonal affective disorder in the Southern Hemisphere. Am. J. Psychiat. *145:* 97–99.

Carney, M. W. P., M. Roth, and R. F. Garside (1965) The diagnosis of depressive syndromes and the prediction of E. C. T. response. Brit. J. Psychiat. *111:* 659–674.

Davidson, J. R. T. and S. Pelton (1986) Forms of atypical depression and their response to antidepressant drugs. Psychiat. Res. *17:* 87–95.

Davidson, J. R. T., R. D. Miller, C. D. Turnbull, and J. L. Sullivan (1982) Atypical depression. Arch. Gen. Psychiat. *39:* 527–534.

Detre, T. P., H. Himmelhoch, M. Swartzburg, C. M. Andersen, R. Byck, and D. J. Kupfer (1972) Hypersomnia and manic–depressive disease. Amer. J. Psychiat. *128:* 1303–1305.

Eastwood, M. R., and S. Stiasny (1978) Psychiatric disorder, hospital admission and season. Arch. Gen. Psychiat. 35: 769–771.

Esquirol, J. E. D. (1845) Mental Maladies: Treatise on Insanity, E. K. Hunt, trans., Lea & Blanchard, Philadelphia.

Faust, V., and P. Sarreither (1975) Jahrezeit und psychiatrische Krankheit. Med. Klin. 70: 467–473.

Frangos, E., G. Athanassenas, and S. Tsitourides (1980) Seasonality of the episodes of recurrent affective psychoses: Possible prophylactic interventions. J. Affect. Dis. 2: 239–247.

Garvey, M. J., R. Wesner, and M. Godes (1988) Comparison of seasonal and nonseasonal affective disorders. Amer. J. Psychiat. 145: 100–102.

Hamilton, M. (1967) Development of a rating scale for primary depressive illness. Brit. J. Soc. Clin. Psychol. 6: 278–296.

Kendell, R. E. (1976) The classifacation of depressions: A review of contemporary confusion. Brit. J. Psychiat. 129: 15–28.

Kiloh, L. G., G. Andrews, M. Neilson, and G. N. Bianchi (1972) The relationship of the syndromes called endogenous and neurotic depression. Brit. J. Psychiat. 121: 183–196.

Klein, D. F., R. Gittelman, and F. Quitkin (1980) Diagnosis and Drug Treatment of Psychiatric Disorders: Adults and Children, Williams & Wilkins, Baltimore.

Kraines, S. (1957) Mental Depressions and Their Treatment, Macmillan, New York.

Kukopulos, A., and D. Reginaldi (1973) Does lithium prevent depressions by suppressing manias? Int. Pharmacopsychiat. 8: 152–158.

Kupfer, D. J., F. G. Foster, T. P. Detre, and J. Himmelhoch (1975) Sleep EEG and motor activity as indicators in affective states. Neuropsychobiology 1: 296–303.

Leuthold, G. H. (1940) Jahreszeit and Phasenbeginn manisch–depressiver Psychosen. Arch. Psychiat. 111: 55–61.

Liebowitz, M. R., and D. F. Klein (1979) Hysteroid dysphoria. Psychiat. Clin. N. Amer. 2: 555–575.

Liebowitz, M. R., F. M. Quitkin, J. W. Steward, P. J. McGrath, W. Harrison, J. G. Rabkin, E. Tricamo, J. S. Markowitz, and D. F. Klein (1984) Psychopharmacologic validation of atypical depression. J. Clin. Psychiat. 45: 22–25.

Mueller, P. S., and N. G. Allen (1984) Diagnosis and treatment of severe light-sensitive seasonal energy syndrome (SES) and its relationship to melatonin anabolism. Fair Oaks Hosp. Psychiat. Lett. 2: 1–5.

Patterson, F. A., ed. (1957) The Student's Milton, Appleton-Century-Crofts, New York.

Payk, T. R. (1976) Zur jahreszeitlicher Bindung neurologisher und psychiatrischer Erkrankungen. Munchner Med. Wochenschr. 118: 1669–1670.

Paykel, E. S. (1977) Depression and appetite. J. Psychosom. Res. 21: 401–407.

Paykel, E. S., R. R. Parker, P. R. Rowan, B. M. Rao, and C. N. Taylor (1983) Nosology of atypical depression. Psychol. Med. 13: 131–139.

Pilcz, A. (1901) Die periodischen Geistesstörungen, G. Fischer Verlag, Jena.

Quitkin, F., A. Rifkin, and D. F. Klein (1979) Monoamine oxidase inhibitors: A review of antidepressant effectiveness. Arch. Gen. Psychiat. 36: 749–760.

Rihmer, Z. (1980) Season of birth and season of hospital admissions in bipolar depressed female patients. Psychiat. Res. 3: 247–251.

Rosenthal, N. E. M. Genhart, D. A. Sack, R. G. Skwerer, and T. A. Wehr (1988) Seasonal affective disorder and its relevance for the understanding and treatment of bulimia. In Psychobiology of Bulimia, J. I. Hudson and H. G. Pope, Jr., eds., pp. 205–228, American Psychiatric Press, Washington, DC.

Rosenthal, N. E., and M. Hefferman (1988) Bulemia, carbohydrate craving and depression: A central connection? Nutrition and the Brain, 7: 139–166.

Rosenthal, N. E., D. A. Sack, J. C. Gillin, A. J. Lewy, F. K. Goodwin, Y. Davenport, P. S. Mueller, D. A. Newsome, and T. A. Wehr (1984) Seasonal affective disorder: A description of the syndrome and preliminary findings with light treatment. Arch. Gen. Psychiat. *41:* 72–80.

Sovner, R. (1981) The clinical characteristics and treatment of atypical depression. J. Clin. Psychiat. *46:* 285–289.

Spitzer, R. L., J. B. W. Williams, and M. Gibbon (1986) *Structured Clinical Interview for DSM-III-R,* Biometrics Research Department, New York State Psychiatric Institute, New York.

Thompson, C. and G. Isaacs (1988) Seasonal affective disorder—A British sample: Symptomatology in relation to mode of referral and diagnostic subtype. J. Affect. Dis. *14:* 1–11.

Wehr, T. A. and N. E. Rosenthal (in press) The seasonality of affective illness. Amer. J. Psychiat.

Wehr, T. A., D. A. Sack, and N. E. Rosenthal (1987) Seasonal affective disorder with summer depression and winter hypomania. Amer. J. Psychiat. *144:* 1602–1603.

Wirz-Justice, A., C. Buchelli, P. Graw, P. Kielholz, H. U. Fisch, and B. Woggon (1986) Light treatment of seasonal affective disorder in Switzerland. Acta Psychiat. Scand. *74:* 193–204.

6

Comparison between Seasonal Affective Disorder and Other Forms of Recurrent Depression

Michael E. Thase

Classification in medicine serves two main purposes: communication and prediction. Seasonal affective disorder (SAD) is a recently proposed classification to describe patients who experience the predictable occurrence of episodes of depression in the fall and winter. Although optimum criteria for definition of cases of SAD remain open for empirical study, most investigators currently classify SAD according to the framework developed by Rosenthal *et al.*, (1984) at the National Institute of Mental Health (NIMH). Briefly, these provisional criteria include (1) at least one lifetime episode of major depression; (2) history of recurrent episodes of depression (major or minor episodes occurring in at least two consecutive winters) with onset in fall or winter and recovery by spring or summer; and (3) an absence of any other major psychiatric disorder. Thus, patients considered to have SAD would be classified in the current nomenclature as suffering from either a bipolar disorder (typical or atypical) or a recurrent major depressive disorder. Therefore, it is pertinent to examine SAD in comparison to other forms of recurrent major affective disorder. This chapter addresses the issue of the uniqueness of SAD within the broader spectrum of recurrent affective illness. Evidence to be considered is drawn from the traditional domains suggested by the St. Louis group (e.g., Goodwin and Guze, 1979): phenomenology, epidemiology, natural history, treatment response, family history, and laboratory studies. Review of data from these areas of investigation may help support the validity of SAD as a distinct form of recurrent affective illness, or, conversely, may suggest that it is a curious variant of already known conditions.

Michael E. Thase. Department of Psychiatry, University of Pittsburgh School of Medicine, Pittsburgh, Pennsylvania; Western Psychiatric Institute and Clinic, Pittsburgh, Pennsylvania.

Phenomenology

The phenomenology of SAD is reviewed in detail elsewhere in this volume (see Hellekson, Chapter 3). To briefly summarize, the work of the NIMH group (Rosenthal et al., 1984, 1985; Rosenthal and Wehr, 1987) provides support for the uniqueness of SAD by documenting a high frequency of so-called atypical symptoms of depression. For example, in the most recent series of 220 SAD cases (Rosenthal and Wehr, 1987) increased appetite (70%), carbohydrate craving (75%), increased weight (75%), and increased duration of sleep (83%) were all substantially overrepresented. Wirz-Justice et al., (1986) similarly reported increased frequencies of carbohydrate craving (77%), weight gain (55%), and hypersomnia (82%) in a survey of 22 Swiss-German patients with SAD. It should be noted, however, that the results of Wirz-Justice et al. do not represent a truly independent replication, since these investigators employed a definition of SAD stipulating that patients must manifest at least three of the high-frequency symptoms reported by Rosenthal et al. (1984). Although Yerevanian et al. (1986) did not report specific symptom counts in their sample of nine SAD patients, only one (11%) met Research Diagnostic Criteria (RDC; Spitzer et al., 1978) for definite endogenous depression, and 44% (four out of nine) of the sample were described as hypersomnic.

Such high frequencies of reversed neurovegetative symptoms would not be encountered in an unselected series of depressed outpatients, as features such as increased appetite, weight gain, and hypersomnia routinely are reported in only 15–30% of cases (Himmelhoch and Thase, in press). Moreover, hypersomnia and increased appetite or weight generally are only weakly correlated in unselected series of outpatient depressives (e.g., Paykel et al., 1983). Thus, the apparently close association of these features in SAD patients might suggest the existence of a unique affective syndrome. However, a majority of the SAD cases described by the NIMH group (Rosenthal et al., 1984; Rosenthal and Wehr, 1987) and Wirz-Justice et al. (1986) show phenomenological similarity to the conditions Himmelhoch et al. (1982) have called "anergic" depression and Davidson et al. (1982) have termed "V-type" atypical depression. It may be of some interest that a great majority of the patients in the NIMH and Swiss series have bipolar depression (predominantly type II), as do the anergic depression patients described by our group in Pittsburgh (Himmelhoch et al., 1982; Himmelhoch and Thase, in press). Indeed, the frequencies of symptoms such as decreased activity, increased appetite or weight gain, decreased energy, daytime sleepiness, and hypersomnia reported in our ongoing study of anergic bipolar depression (Himmelhoch and Thase, in press) correspond closely to the values reported for SAD by the NIMH (e.g., Rosenthal and Wehr, 1987) and Swiss (Wirz-Justice et al., 1986) groups (see Table 6-1).

Not all patients meeting provisional criteria for SAD manifest reversed neurovegetative symptoms. For example, Bick (1986) described four cases (two

TABLE 6-1. Comparison of Selected Symptoms in SAD and Anergic
Bipolar Depression

Symptom	SAD, NIMH[a] (n = 220)	SAD, Swiss[b] (n = 22)	Anergic bipolar depression[c] (n = 49)
Sad affect	95	91	98
Decreased activity	94	100	96
Increased appetite	70	45	51
Increased weight	75	55	39
Increased sleep time	83	82	67
Decreased libido	55	77	89
Daytime sleepiness	71	—	67

[a]Rosenthal and Wehr (1987).
[b]Wirz-Justice et al. (1986).
[c]Himmelhoch and Thase (in press).

bipolar, two unipolar) who met criteria for SAD but whose depressions were marked by more typical endogenomorphic symptomatology. Similarly, roughly 30% of the cases studied by NIMH (Rosenthal et al., 1984, 1985; Rosenthal and Wehr, 1987) have endogenous features. In our own preliminary series of 18 cases of SAD drawn from a sample of 115 patients treated in a research clinic for recurrent major depression (see Thase, 1986), only 6 patients (33%) had a reversed neurovegetative symptom profile characterized by increased appetite, weight gain, and/or hypersomnia. The remaining 12 patients in this series met RDC for definite endogenous subtype. Furthermore, the seasonal and nonseasonal groups did not differ with respect to frequency of hypersomnia, increased appetite, and weight gain. The groups did, however, significantly differ on five symptoms (middle insomnia, appetite loss, inability to sit still, pacing, and diurnal mood variation). In each case, the SAD group showed less "endogenomorphic" disturbance than the nonseasonal recurrent depressives. The results of the Pittsburgh survey thus provide weak support for the uniqueness of SAD compared to nonseasonal recurrent depression.

Results of studies examining phenomenology of SAD certainly indicate that, in most series, patients with recurrent fall–winter depressions are disproportionately likely to manifest nonendogenous depressions characterized by reversed neurovegetative features. Sampling techniques may influence such observations, as reflected by the Pittsburgh study of SAD. As described above, the Pittsburgh SAD sample was drawn from a research clinic that primarily treats unipolar depressions. If reversed neurovegetative symptoms are indeed linked to the bipolar spectrum (e.g., Davidson et al., 1982; Himmelhoch and Thase, in press), then it should not be surprising that fewer "atypical" symptoms were observed in a predominantly unipolar sample. Nevertheless, the symptomatology of SAD should not be considered to be unique, in that it is similar to other proposed "atypical" subforms of depression (i.e., Davidson *et al.* 1982; Himmelhock *et al.*, 1982). It will be informative to re-evaluate patients classified as having anergic or "V-type" depressions to ascertain what proportion also meet criteria for SAD. Future investigations also should address the personal phenomenology of seasonal rhythms in mood, to ascertain whether the subjective awareness of mood alterations differentiates SAD from other major affective disorders.

Epidemiology

The prevalence of SAD in community samples is not known. However, a diagnosis of SAD requires sufficient depressive symptoms to warrant RDC diagnoses of intermittent minor depression, cyclothymia, major depression, or bipolar disorder, it must be assumed that, to date, epidemiological surveys have grouped SAD patients within other diagnostic categories.

Several crude estimates of treatment prevalence are available from inpatient and outpatient sources. Kraepelin (1921) recognized a pattern of recurrent fall–winter depressions, characterized by anergia and social withdrawal, in about 4% of the patients evaluated by his group. This may be taken as a minimum estimate of the institutional treatment prevalence of SAD circa 1910, since Kraepelin's work was based in an inpatient setting. In an outpatient sample of 220 patients treated in the Depression Prevention Program, a specialty clinic for individuals with a history of three or more episodes of depression, there was clear seasonality noted with respects to months of depression when data were collected retrospectively (Fig. 6-1) and prospectively (Fig. 6-2). Moreover, 16.1% (18/112) of a subsample of those patients met criteria for SAD (Thase, 1986). This prevalence rate is significantly greater than a chance expectancy of 6%, calculated from the independent probabilities (for this subsample) of meeting the three major criteria for SAD simultaneously ($\chi^2 = 5.45$, $df = 1$, $p < 0.01$). Since roughly one-half of all diagnosed depressions can be assumed to be recurrent, a maximum estimate of the outpatient treatment prevalence of SAD (based on the 16% Pittsburgh prevalence rate) is 8%. This figure is inflated by the fact that patients with chronic, unremitted depressions or complicated affective syndromes were excluded from the Pittsburgh series. Therefore, a conservative estimate of treatment prevalence of 4–6% may be more accurate. Conversely, these factors may be offset by the fact that the Pittsburgh series was predominantly unipolar.

Evidence collected by Rosenthal and Wehr (1987) and Wirz-Justice *et al.* (1986) suggest that accurate rates for SAD cannot be derived from treatment settings, since a majority of patients in each series had never been hospitalized and many were not currently in outpatient treatment. Such patients often seek psychiatric attention for fall or winter depressions only after reading about work on phototherapy and SAD in the newspaper. Therefore, an undetermined pro-

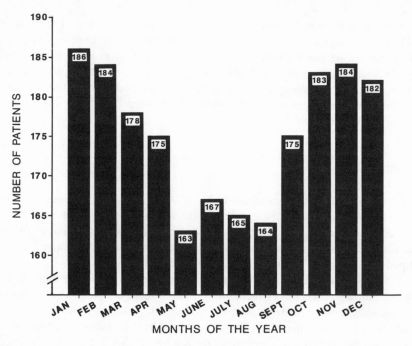

FIGURE 6-1. Reported months of depression during the index episode of Depression Prevention Program (DPP) patients with recurrent major depressive disorder ($n = 220$).

portion of untreated depressives identified in community surveys would also meet criteria for SAD. There is a clear need for a careful epidemiological survey to establish the prevalence of SAD. However, such a labor-intensive study should wait for the establishment of widely accepted and validated criteria for SAD.

Natural History

The NIMH group's (Rosenthal *et al.*, 1984, 1985, 1986; Rosenthal and Wehr, 1987) studies of the natural history of SAD suggest a unique clinical course. In addition to the aforementioned history of recurrent fall–winter depressions with spontaneous remission by spring or summer, the NIMH group described an accompanying constellation of historical features that do not typically characterize recurrent depression. First, an unusually high proportion (89%) of patients reported a history of mild hypomanic episodes regularly occurring in the spring or early summer. Conversely, a history of full-blown manic episodes was quite uncommon in this sample (6%), indicating that bipolar II disorder was significantly overrepresented in the NIMH sample. Wirz-Justice *et al.* (1986) similarly reported an extraordinarily high frequency of bipolar II disorder in their sample: 17 definite and 4 probable cases among a 22-patient sample. The frequency of unipolar depression was considerably higher in our own series (15/18, or 83%), as well as in small series collected in Rochester, New York (8/9, or 89%; Yerevanian *et al.*, 1986) and Alaska (9/10, or 90%; Hellekson *et al.*, 1986). It remains to be seen whether these striking differences in the frequency of a history of hypomanic episodes are due to climatic or geographic variation, subject selection factors, or differential sensitivity for diagnosing bipolar II disorder. Nevertheless, it also will be important to evaluate seasonality patterns in samples with clear-cut bipolar I affective disorder.

Second, the NIMH group has reported patient observations about changes in environment or exposure to sunlight that provide independent support for the validity of the SAD diagnosis. For example, 88% (79/90) of patients surveyed by Rosenthal and Wehr (1987) reported improvement in mood associated with winter travel to areas closer to the equator. Similar perceptions were described by an unspecified number of patients studied by Wirz-Justice *et al.* (1986); three patients in the Swiss series reported definite worsening of fall–winter depressions following their return to Switzerland from sunnier locales. A critical test of the potential utility of such information for diagnosis of SAD will necessitate asking these questions to nonseasonal depressives. We have recently initiated such a project in Pittsburgh.

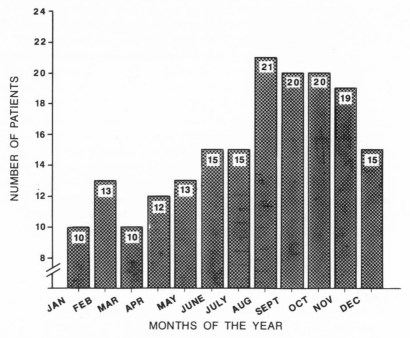

FIGURE 6-2. Prospectively observed months of depression following recurrence of depression in DPP patients with recurrent major depression.

Third, nearly one-half of SAD patients report the onset of seasonal mood swings in adolescence or even childhood (Rosenthal et al., 1984; Wirz-Justice et al., 1986; Rosenthal and Wehr, 1987). Although there is increasing recognition that recurrent affective disorder can begin before adulthood, demonstration of a 50% early-onset rate is well beyond what would be expected in an unselected adult population. Indeed, the NIMH group has reported on a small series of children and adolescents with histories of SAD (Rosenthal et al., 1986).

Despite the apparent calendar-wise regularity of mood changes reported by some patients, others report more pronounced year-to-year variations in SAD. In one of the initial case presentations describing phototherapy of SAD, Lewy et al. (1982) described a patient whose mood cycle, at one point, included a 1-year-long episode of major depression. Varying numbers of SAD patients in the NIMH (Rosenthal et al., 1985) and Swiss series (Wirz-Justice et al., 1986) reported fluctuations in cycle length and severity of depressions. Somewhat surprisingly, Wirz-Justice et al. (1986) found no evidence of hypomania in 15 patients from their sample when these were followed prospectively into the spring or summer. In our own series (Thase, 1986), six patients (33%) originally classified as SAD no longer met criteria for this disorder when re-evaluated 1 year later. Among these patients, three patients reported different onset–offset dates for episodes of depression; two had failed to recover throughout the summer following their index episode; and one patient developed a recurrence of major depression during the summer. By contrast, 98% (92/94) of the cases originally classified as nonseasonal continued to be excluded by the SAD criteria; only 2 of these patients reported revised onset or offset dates to warrant reclassification. Although these longitudinal data may suggest an unacceptably high rate of false-positive diagnoses, it should be noted that tricyclic treatment (as received by all patients in the Pittsburgh series) may alter seasonality cycles in patients with recurrent affective disorder (H. S. Akiskal, personal communication, 1986). It should also be noted that patient and clinician opinions regarding the presence or absence of SAD were not determined in the original Pittsburgh survey, and, hence, it seems likely that some patients were included because of coincidental history of an annual cycle of affective disorder. It may be useful to identify and validate a criterion dealing with awareness of seasonal variation as part of the definition of SAD. Indeed, such a criterion is implicitly part of any study of SAD that recruits patients following media presentation of a research project.

Treatment Response

The critical issues pertaining to treatment response as an external validator of a diagnosis are these: (1) the specific efficacy of a particular treatment for patients with the proposed disorder but not for patients with other conditions; and (2) the efficacy of well-established conventional treatments for the proposed disorder as compared to other conditions. With respect to SAD, evidence is growing to address the first issue, and some preliminary data are available concerning the second. These data are reviewed here.

The apparent effectiveness of treatment with 2–6 hr a day of bright white light (i.e., 2000–2500 lux) in SAD has been repeatedly demonstrated in open and controlled investigations (Rosenthal *et al.*, 1984, 1985, 1986; James *et al.*, 1985; Hellekson *et al.*, 1986; Wehr *et al.*, 1986; Yerevanian *et al.*, 1986; Rosenthal and Wehr, 1987). Indeed, overall results published to date indicate that approximately 80% of patients with SAD respond to phototherapy and that, when phototherapy is effective, clinical change usually is apparent within 1 week of initiating treatment (see Rosenthal and Wehr, 1987). One group evaluating phototherapy of SAD has failed to find a statistically significant difference between bright light and a dim-light comparison condition (Wirz-Justice *et al.*, 1986). It should be noted that in the Wirz-Justice *et al.* report, a small sample size, high attrition rate, and high response rate to the comparison intervention may have obscured detection of a clinically significant effect. Furthermore, relapse following premature discontinuation of phototherapy—namely, before the expected remission of winter depression—helps to confirm the effectiveness of the experimental treatment (Rosenthal *et al.*, 1985; Wirz-Justice *et al.*, 1986). Neither the efficacy rate nor the rapidity of response observed for phototherapy is characteristic of a "true response" to antidepressant medication (e.g., Quitkin *et al.*, 1984), which provides additional indirect evidence that either SAD or phototherapy, or both, may involve some unique mechanism.

It remains to be seen, however, whether phototherapy is specifically effective in SAD as compared to other forms of recurrent depression. Preliminary evidence by several groups suggests that treatment with bright white light may not be a clincally effective treatment for hospitalized depressed patients who do not have a history of recurrent fall–winter depressions (Kripke, 1985; Yerevanian *et al.*, 1986). For example, Yerevanian *et al.* (1986) reported that none of their sample of severely (nonseasonally) endogenously depressed inpatients responded to 1- or 2-week open trials of phototherapy. By contrast, all nine SAD patients in this series responded, including one patient with RDC endogenous depression and all three patients who presented with early-morning awakening. Although Yerevanian *et al.*'s open study certainly warrants replication, their findings do suggest that phototherapy may be relatively ineffective in nonseasonal endogenous depression. Moreover, it also appears that at least some SAD patients who do not have the characteristic clinical presentation described in the NIMH series (i.e., nonendogenous bipolar II depression with hypersomnia) can also benefit from phototherapy.

Less is known regarding the effectiveness of conventional antidepressant treatment in patients with SAD. Several of the initial reports describing phototherapy might be interpreted as supporting the conclusion that SAD patients do not do well with conventional treatment: A majority of patients described past treatment with tricyclics, monoamine oxidase inhibitors (MAOIs), and/or lithium, but few had remained on these medications (Rosenthal *et al.*, 1984; Wirz-Justice *et al.*, 1986). Although consumer satisfaction can indeed provide an index of treatment efficacy, it should not replace the results of comparative outcome trials. Unfortunately, no controlled studies have been published to date comparing the efficacy of conventional treatment in SAD and nonseasonal depressions. In the Pittsburgh series (Thase, 1986), we were able to compare the response to 16 weeks of open treatment with the combination of imipramine and interpersonal psychotherapy in recurrent depressions defined as either seasonal ($n = 18$) or nonseasonal ($n = 73$) according to the criteria of Rosenthal *et al.* (1984). Although the response rates were virtually identical after 16 weeks of treatment (SAD, 72%; non-SAD, 71%), there was a trend suggesting more rapid response to conventional treatment in SAD. For example, 61% (11/18) of SAD patients were fully remitted within 8 weeks of conventional treatment, compared to only 33% (24/73) of non-SAD patients ($\chi^2 = 4.86$, $p < 0.05$). Thus, the predominantly unipolar SAD patients in this series responded quite well to conventional treatment.

We had the opportunity to explore further the possible relationships between and among clinical features, length of episode, and treatment response in the Pittsburgh series. Among the seven SAD patients who did not show a rapid response to treatment, five (71%) were found to manifest a reversed neurovegetative pattern. By comparison, only one (9%) of the SAD patients who had recovered after 8 weeks of conventional treatment had a reversed neurovegetative profile. This difference in response rates was statistically significant (Fisher's exact test, $p = 0.05$), despite the small sample size. Furthermore, the length of the current episode was *inversely* related to favorable outcome in the SAD group ($r = -0.52$, $p = 0.02$), but not in the non-SAD group ($r = 0.03$). This unexpected finding indicated that the apparent favorable response to conventional treatment in SAD was not due to an artifact created by spontaneous remission of naturally occurring short episodes. Rather, it suggests that tricyclic treatment near the expected end of an episode of SAD actually might prolong the length of the depression!

In summary, there is strong evidence to support the hypothesis that phototherapy is effective in SAD. This hypothesis must now be tested more rigorously. In future studies of phototherapy of nonseasonal depressions, it will be crucial to include patients with acute, good-prognosis disorders *and* patients with reversed neurovegetative features and/or bipolar II disorders, since both groups of patients have been overrepresented in most series studying SAD. By contrast, in our experience, it appears that unipolar SAD patients also may be effectively treated with conventional strategies. Taken together, these observations provide limited support for validity of SAD as a unique form of recurrent depression.

Family History

Only a very limited amount of data is available on family history in patients with SAD. Rosenthal and Wehr (1987) report that 55% of their sample of 220 SAD patients had at least one first-degree relative with a major affective disorder, whereas Wirz-Justice et al. (1986) found a history of affective disorder in 67% (12/18) of their sample. These values, apparently collected using the family history method, are comparable to other investigators' findings in unselected samples of bipolar II (Dunner et al., 1982) or cyclothymic (Akiskal et al., 1977) patients. As might be expected, the proportion of affected families reported for SAD is somewhat lower than that observed in contemporary studies utilizing the more sensitive family study method to investigate unipolar, bipolar I, and bipolar II families (e.g., Gershon et al., 1982; Coryell et al., 1985; Endicott et al., 1985), although such a difference is probably a result of method variance. Both Rosenthal and Wehr (1987) and Wirz-Justice et al. (1986) report relatively high rates of familial alcoholism in their samples (34% and 28%, respectively), although such values are not markedly greater than those detected in other studies of bipolar and unipolar depression (e.g., Endicott et al., 1985). Interestingly, familial SAD has been described by both the NIMH (38%; Rosenthal et al., 1985) and Swiss (15%; Wirz-Justice et al., 1986) groups.

The uniqueness of SAD, at least from a family history perspective, may indeed be best supported by evidence of the disorder "breeding true" within families of SAD probands but not in the families of patients with other forms of recurrent affective illness. Such a study undoubtedly will need to be done using the expensive and time-consuming family study method; evidence from this line of inquiry is unlikely to be available in the foreseeable future unless studies already under way can be modified or utilized for this purpose.

Laboratory Studies

The final type of external validating criterion to be considered in this chapter is derived from biological studies of affective disorders. Here, again, results are relatively meager, and conclusions must be tempered by the small samples from which they are drawn.

Rosenthal et al. (1985) briefly described preliminary results of ongoing studies utilizing three common biological tests in depressed patients: electroencephalographic (EEG) sleep studies, the thyrotropin-releasing hormone (TRH) stimulation test, and the dexamethasone suppression test (DST). All-night sleep studies were completed in a series of 17 SAD patients, during both summer remissions and winter depressions. They noted that during winter depression, total sleep time increased (consistent with clinical reports of hypersomnia), delta sleep time decreased, and rapid eye movement (REM) density increased. The latter two characteristics are well-described features of EEG sleep in primary depression (Kupfer and Thase, 1983). Of note is the finding that REM latency, perhaps the best-studied EEG sleep correlate of endogenous depression (Kupfer and Thase, 1983), was not reduced during winter depression. With respect to neuroendocrine profiles, TRH stimulation tests were completed during both summer remissions and winter depressions in seven patients and were not found to be abnormal. James et al. (1986) also found a very low (10%) DST non-suppression rate in 10 patients with SAD. Lower rates of DST abnormality in fall and winter depressions (as compared to spring and summer rates) have also been reported by Arato et al. (1986) in an inpatient study. When taken together, these findings suggest that few SAD patients manifest the characteristic neuroendocrine and EEG sleep features of endogenous depression—a suggestion circularly linked to the observation that few patients in the NIMH series had clinical diagnoses of endogenous depression.

In the Pittsburgh series, EEG sleep profiles were compared in 16 SAD patients and 91 nonseasonal recurrent depressives (see Table 6-2). Contrary to expectation, SAD patients had significantly longer sleep latency ($p = 0.04$) and poorer sleep efficiency ($p = 0.05$). Slow-wave sleep time and REM density did not differ between these groups, with both SAD and nonseasonal patients manifesting significantly greater disturbance than seen in normal controls. Consistent with the earlier report by Rosenthal et al. (1985), mean REM latency was not reduced in SAD (mean = 79.3 min), with marked variability across individuals (standard deviation = 64.0 min). The corresponding values for nonseasonal cases were 62.7 min ± 32.2 min. Only 6 SAD (37.5%) cases had mean REM latency values of less than 60 min, compared with 54% (49/91) of the nonseasonal patients. Despite these apparent differences, neither mean nor categorically defined REM latency values significantly differed between SAD and nonseasonal groups.

Although several groups have reported low plasma or urinary levels of

TABLE 6-2. Selected EEG Sleep Variables in SAD and Nonseasonal Recurrent Depression

Variable	Seasonal ($n = 16$)		Nonseasonal ($n = 91$)		t
Sleep latency (min)	32.9	(30.6)[a]	21.8	(16.6)	2.12[a]**
Awakenings	4.4	(3.7)	5.8	(3.5)	1.37
Sleep efficiency (%)	80.2	(13.7)	86.6	(11.5)	1.99[a]*
Delta (%)	6.2	(8.9)	7.7	(8.3)	0.67
REM (min)	76.3	(30.0)	83.9	(25.5)	1.08
REM density (units)	1.25	(0.28)	1.22	(0.38)	0.40
REM latency (min)	79.3	(64.0)[a]	62.7	(32.2)	1.38

[a]Denotes unequal variances.
*$p = 0.05$.
**$p = 0.04$.

melatonin or its metabolite in depression (Mendlewicz *et al.*, 1980; Beck-Friis *et al.*, 1984; Brown *et al.*, 1985), decreased melatonin levels have not been demonstrated in SAD (Rosenthal *et al.*, 1985; Wehr *et al.*, 1986). Furthermore, patients with reduced melatonin levels in other studies have tended to be older and endogenously depressed (Beck-Friis *et al.*, 1985; Brown *et al.*, 1985). Lewy *et al.* (1987) have described a phase delay of melatonin circadian rhythm in a small sample of SAD patients, although corresponding studies of nonseasonal depressives in winter have not been completed. However, recent work by Wehr *et al.*, (1986) suggests that effective treatment of SAD with phototherapy may not be dependent on altering melatonin secretion. No studies have yet been published that directly compare melatonin secretory rhythm in SAD and nonseasonal depressive disorders.

The research reviewed above suggests that the comparability of patients with SAD or nonseasonal recurrent depression on conventional biological measures may be directly related to the clinical characteristics of the samples studied. Preliminary results from the NIMH group point to a relative absence of conventional ''markers'' of endogenous depression in SAD. However, such a finding is not necessarily unique, in that it would also be true for other nonendogenous depression samples. For example, we have recently documented increased sleep time, increased REM indices, normal REM latency, and low (13%) DST nonsuppression rates in a study of anergic bipolar depressives recruited without regard to seasonality (Himmelhoch and Thase, in press). The results of the Pittsburgh study indicate that seasonality is not associated with a particular pattern of EEG sleep characteristics when compared to a nonseasonal group of equivalent severity and endogeneity.

Where, then, do these findings lead? Investigations of mechanisms more intimately linked to proposed pathophysiological alterations in SAD would be a high priority. Several such investigations are already under way, including research concerning possible circadian phase disturbances (both phase advances and phase delays) in depression (Lewy *et al.*, 1985b, 1987) and studies of the relationship of melatonin patterns and response to phototherapy (Lewy *et al.*, 1985b; Wehr *et al.*, 1986). Of particular interest, Lewy *et al.* (1981, 1985a) have reported that most bipolar patients show a supersensitivity to light-suppressant effects on melatonin secretion, both during depression (1981) and during remission (1985a). Such sensitivity to light may predispose patients to develop circadian phase abnormalities. It remains to be seen whether light supersensitivity is a common feature of unipolar depression *and* whether patients with SAD show this abnormality.

Conclusions and Recommendations

A review of the evidence concerning the validity of the diagnosis of SAD points to several conclusions. First, with respect to phenomenology, patients with a SAD pattern of recurrent depression seem to be more likely to manifest reversed neurovegetative features and to experience hypomanic episodes than patients typically seen in unselected samples. The clinical profile identified by the NIMH group and subsequently replicated by Wirz-Justice et al. (1986) closely overlaps with types of depression described by other investigators (i.e., "V-type" atypical depression and "anergic" bipolar depression), and it will be useful to examine the question of seasonality in these samples. The reversed neurovegetative profile in SAD has not been observed by all investigators, and sampling differences need to be addressed. Some consensus should be reached concerning the possible use of reversed neurovegetative symptomatology as a diagnostic criterion for SAD. Furthermore, given the well-known problems with the reliability of diagnosis of bipolar II disorder (Coryell et al., 1985), longitudinal confirmation of the association of lengthening days in springtime and development of hypomania is in order.

Second, in addition to the frequently reported hypomanic episodes in SAD, these patients often describe a natural history of predictable modulation of moods associated with travel to more or less sunny locales. Mood variation between sunny and overcast days is also described. Such a history could prove to be a powerful discriminator between truly seasonal depressions and recurrent affective disorders that, for a period, happen to cycle on a seasonal basis. The potential utility of routinely assessing patients' awareness of mood changes associated with seasonal patterns or sunlight exposure should be carefully evaluated. As briefly discussed earlier, it is recommended that further research on methods of optimally categorizing SAD be completed before epidemiological studies of this disorder are pursued.

Finally, definitive demonstration of a specific effect for phototherapy in SAD and not in other forms of recurrent depression would greatly facilitate research on classification. Relevant comparison populations include patients with unipolar and bipolar II major depressions who present for treatment in the winter but who do not report a history of clear seasonality. It will be interesting to see whether most patients with reversed neurovegetative symptoms respond to phototherapy, independently of a history of SAD. If phototherapy is indeed a relatively specific intervention, then results of a trial of light therapy can be used, retrospectively and prospectively, to identify those historical, demographic, and phenomenological correlates that can be used to discriminate SAD from other forms of recurrent depression. Studies integrating response to phototherapy with effects on biological parameters similarly will prove quite informative, particular with respect to Lewy et al.'s (1985b, 1987) suggestion that SAD may present with either circadian phase advances or phase delays.

Acknowledgments

The research reported here was supported in part by Grant Nos. MH-37266 and MH-30915 from the National Institute of Mental Health. The support, collaboration, and assistance of Henry Lahmayer, MD, Ms. Nancy Karwowski, and David J. Kupfer, MD, in the preparation of the manuscript are greatly appreciated.

References

Akiskal, H. S., A. H. Djenderedjian, R. H. Rosenthal, and M. K. Khani (1977) Cyclothymic disorder: Validity criteria for inclusion in the bipolar affective group. Amer. J. Psychiat. *134:* 1227–1233.

Arato, M., Z. Rihmer, and E. Szadoczky (1986) Seasonal influence on the dexamethasone suppression test results in unipolar depression. Arch. Gen. Psychiat. *43:* 813.

Beck-Friis, J., D. Van Rosen, B. F. Kjellman, J. G. Ljunggren, and L. Wetterberg (1984) Melatonin in relation to body measures, sex, age, season, and the use of drugs in patients with major affective disorders and healthy subjects. Psychoneuroendocrinology *9:* 261–277.

Bick, P. A. (1986) Seasonal major affective disorder. Amer. J. Psychiat. *143:* 90–91.

Brown, R., J. H. Kocsis, S. Caroff, J. Amsterdam, A. Winokur, P. E. Stokes, and A. Frazer (1985) Differences in nocturnal melatonin secretion between melancholic depressed patients and control subjects. Amer. J. Psychiat. *142:* 811–816.

Coryell, W., J. Endicott, N. Andreasen, and M. B. Keller (1985) Bipolar I, bipolar II, and non-bipolar major depression among the relatives of affectively ill probands. Amer. J. Psychiat. *142:* 817–821.

Davidson, J. R. T., R. D. Miller, C. D. Turnbull, and J. L. Sullivan (1982) Atypical depression. Arch. Gen. Psychiat. *39:* 527–534.

Dunner, D. L., F. D. Russek, B. Russek, and R. R. Fieve (1982) Classification of bipolar affective disorder subtypes. Comp. Psychiat. *23:* 186–189.

Endicott, J., J. Nee, N. Andreasen, P. Clayton, M. Keller, and W. Coryell (1985) Bipolar II: Combine or keep separate? J. Affect. Dis. *8:* 17–28.

Gershon, E. S., J. Hamovit, J. J. Guroff, E. Dribble, J. F. Lackman, W. Sceery, S. D. Targum, J. L. Nurenberger, R. R. Goldin, and W. E. Bunney (1982) A family study of schizoaffective, bipolar I, bipolar II, unipolar, and normal control probands. Arch. Gen. Psychiat. *39:* 1157–1167.

Goodwin, D. W., and S. B. Guze (1979) *Psychiatric Diagnosis,* Oxford University Press, New York.

Hellekson, C. J., J. A. Kline, and N. E. Rosenthal (1986) Phototherapy for seasonal affective disorder in Alaska. Amer. J. Psychiat. *143:* 1035–1037.

Himmelhoch, J. M., C. Z. Fuchs, and B. J. Symons (1982) A double-blind study of tranylcypromine treatment of major anergic depression. J. Nerv. Ment. Dis. *170:* 628–634.

Himmelhoch, J. M., and M. E. Thase (in press) Atypical depressive syndromes. In *Modern Perspectives in the Psychiatry of Depression,* J. G. Howells, ed., Brunner/Mazel, New York.

James, S. P., T. A. Wehr, D. A. Sack, B. L. Parry, S. L. B. Rogers, and N. E. Rosenthal (1986) The dexamethasone suppression test in seasonal affective disorder. Comp. Psychiat. *27:* 224–226.

James, S. P., T. A. Wehr, D. A. Sack, B. L. Parry, and N. E. Rosenthal (1985) Evening light treatment of seasonal affective disorder. Brit. J. Psychiat. *147:* 424–428.

Kraepelin, E. (1921) *Manic–Depressive Illness and Paranoia,* R. M. Barclay, trans., G. M. Robertson, ed., E & S Livingstone, Edinburgh.

Kripke, D. F. (1985) Therapeutic effects of bright light in depressed patients. Ann. NY Acad. Sci. *453:* 270–281.

Kupfer, D. J., and M. E. Thase (1983) The use of the sleep laboratory in the diagnosis of affective disorders. Psychiatr. Clin. N. Amer. *6:* 3–25.

Lewy, A. J., H. A. Kern, N. E. Rosenthal, and T. A. Wehr (1982) Bright artificial light treatment of a manic–depressive patient with a seasonal mood cycle. Amer. J. Psychiat. *139:* 1496–1498.

Lewy, A. J., J. I. Nurenberger, T. A. Wehr, D. Pack, L. E. Becker, R. Powell, and D. A. Newsome (1985a) Supersensitivity to light: Possible trait marker for manic–depressive illness. Amer. J. Psychiat. *142:* 725–727.

Lewy, A. J., R. L. Sack, S. Miller, and T. M. Hoban (1987) Antidepressant and circadian phase-shifting effects of light. Science *235:* 352–354.

Lewy, A. J., R. L. Sack, and C. M. Singer (1985b) Bright light, melatonin and biological rhythms: Implications for the affective disorders. Pharmacol. Bull. *21:* 368–372.

Lewy, A. J., T. A. Wehr, F. K. Goodwin, D. A. Newsome, and N. E. Rosenthal (1981) Manic–depressive patients may be supersensitive to light (Letter to the editor). Lancet *i:* 383–384.

Mendlewicz, J. L., L. Branchey, U. Weinberg, M. Branchey, P. Linkowski, and E. D. Weitzman (1980) The 24-hour profile of plasma melatonin in depressed patients before and after treatment. Psychopharmacology *4:* 49–55.

Paykel E. S., P. R. Rowan, B. M. Rao, and A. Bhat (1983) Atypical depression: nosology and response to antidepressants. In *Treatment of Depression: Old Controversies and New Approaches,* P. J. Clayton and J. E. Barrett, eds., pp. 237–250, Raven Press, New York.

Quitkin, F. M., J. G. Rabkin, D. Ross, and P. J. McGrath (1984) Duration of antidepressant drug treatment. Arch. Gen. Psychiat. *41:* 238–245.

Rosenthal, N. E., C. J. Carpenter, S. P. James, B. L. Parry, S. L. B. Rogers, and T. A. Wehr (1986) Seasonal affective disorder in children and adolescents. Amer. J. Psychiat. *143:* 356–358.

Rosenthal, N. E., D. A. Sack, J. C. Gillin, A. J. Lewy, F. K. Goodwin, Y. Davenport, P. S. Mueller, D. A. Newsome, and T. A. Wehr (1984) Seasonal affective disorder: A description of the syndrome and preliminary findings with light therapy. Arch. Gen. Psychiat. *41:* 72–80.

Rosenthal, N. E., D. A. Sack, S. P. James, B. L. Parry, W. B. Mendelson, L. Tamarkin, and T. A. Wehr (1985) Seasonal affective disorder and phototherapy. Ann. NY Acad. Sci. *453:* 260–269.

Rosenthal, N. E., and T. A. Wehr (1987) Seasonal affective disorders. Psychiat. Ann. *17:* 670–674.

Spitzer, R. L., J. Endicott, and E. Robins Research Diagnostic Criteria. Arch. Gen. Psychiat. *35:* 773–782.

Thase, M. E. (1986) Interview: Defining and treating seasonal affectional disorder. Psychiat. Ann. *16:* 733–737.

Wehr, T. A., F. M. Jacobsen, D. A. Sack, J. Arendt, L. Tamarkin, and N. E. Rosenthal (1986) Phototherapy in seasonal affective disorder: Time of day and suppression of melatonin are not critical for antidepressant effects. Arch. Gen. Psychiat. *43:* 870–875.

Wirz-Justice, A., C. Bucheli, P. Graw, P. Kielholz, H.-V. Fisch, and B. Woggon (1986) Light treatment of seasonal affective disorder in Switzerland. Acta Psychiat. Scand. *74:* 193–204.

Yerevanian, B. I., J. L. Anderson, L. J. Grota, and M. Bray (1986) Effects of bright incandescent light on seasonal and nonseasonal major depressive disorder. Psychiat. Res. *18:* 355–364.

7

The Validity of Seasonal Affective Disorder

Robert L. Spitzer and Janet B. W. Williams

One purpose of the conference that was the basis of this book was to examine the validity of a new diagnosis: seasonal affective disorder (SAD). This chapter begins with a review of the different kinds of diagnostic validity. Following this is a discussion of the process of revising the *Diagnostic and Statistical Manual of Mental Disorders,* third edition (DSM-III), with the final addition of the concept of "seasonal pattern."

As recently as 10 years ago, there were only a few types of affective disorders that were considered valid because of their clinical utility: manic–depressive illness, psychotic depressive reaction, depressive neurosis, and involutional melancholia. Manic–depressive illness was a useful and frequently diagnosed category. However, it was defined somewhat differently from the way we now define it because it included unipolar depression.

Psychotic depressive reaction was another category that resulted from a distinction made at that time between endogenous and reactive illnesses. Eventually that distinction was recognized as an unreliable one; in addition, there was a lack of evidence demonstrating that once a depression had developed, its course and response to treatment were affected by whether or not its onset was precipitated by psychosocial stress.

Depressive neurosis, another unreliable diagnosis, was actually a combination of many different concepts, including chronicity, mild severity, and an etiology of intrapsychic conflict (Klerman *et al.,* 1979). Since there has been no consensus as to how to define this concept, and a generally atheoretical approach has been taken in the DSM-III and DSM-III, revised (DSM-III-R) classifications, depressive neurosis is not included as a separate category.

Finally, involutional melancholia was, at the time, an exciting concept because it embodied the notion of a process—the idea that there was some particular phase of the life cycle that was associated with a particular clinical

Robert L. Spitzer and Janet B. W. Williams. Department of Psychiatry, Columbia University College of Physicians and Surgeons, New York, New York.

picture. It also had important treatment implications: the need for electrocon-vulsive therapy or another form of somatic therapy. However, numerous stud-ies have since shown that there is no peak of depression in the involutional period, so this concept is no longer embraced by our standard nomenclatures (Weissman, 1979).

By the time DSM-III was in development, the only seemingly valid dis-tinctions that could be made in the classification of affective disorders were the unipolar–bipolar distinction, the concept of melancholia or an endogenous sub-type of depression, and the concept of dysthymia. The unipolar–bipolar dis-tinction still seems to be a valid one, and is the major distinction in the DSM-III-R classification of mood disorders. In the years since the publication of DSM-III, however, the validity of melancholia has been tested using accepted indicators of validity, such as family history and treatment response (Zimmer-man and Spitzer, 1989). The conclusion had to be drawn that validity evidence for the subtype was lacking. Therefore, the DSM-III-R Mood Disorders Advis-ory Committee considered replacing melancholia with a severity continuum model. However, in the end that approach was deemed premature, so melan-cholia was retained in DSM-III-R, although somewhat redefined. Clearly, the data that are presented in this volume and that have appeared in the literature would indicate that there is more unequivocal evidence for the diagnostic valid-ity of SAD than for melancholia.

Diagnostic Validity

Elsewhere, we have fully discussed different kinds of diagnostic validity (Spitzer and Williams, 1980). The following is a review of types of diagnostic validity that are often described, from a psychometric point of view. The first, "face validity," is related to the degree to which people who are expert in the area in question think a concept is an important distinction. This can sometimes be measured (albeit somewhat humorously) as the proportion of people who smile and nod when one describes the concept.

Moving beyond face validity is "descriptive validity," an important but often overlooked concept. Descriptive validity is the extent to which the defin-ing or associated features of an illness are unique to that illness—that is, not also seen in other disorders. Thase, in Chapter 6 of this volume, raises the issue of whether the "atypical" symptoms that are said to characterize seasonal depression are, in fact, more common in SAD patients than in non-SAD pa-tients. The extent to which these symptoms are as common in cases of nonsea-sonal depression represents a limitation of the descriptive validity of the symp-tom picture seen in seasonal depression. Ideally, symptoms that occur *only* in seasonal depression, and not in cases of nonseasonal depression, would be identified, indicating good descriptive validity of the concept. One must also consider the extent to which seasonality is specific to mood disorders as compared to nonmood disorders. With the possible exception of alcoholism, seasonality has not been reported in nonmood disorders to anywhere near the extent that it exists in some subgroups of patients with mood disorders. This suggests that the central concept of SAD—that there is a relationship between the onset and offset of the disorder and the season of the year—does have a fair degree of descriptive validity.

Descriptive validity, like all other kinds of validity, is not merely either "present" or "absent," but exists to different degrees. Therefore, even if borderline cases are encountered in the search for a purely defined "seasonality" group, the concept may still have considerable descriptive validity. The field will have to determine how stringent the criteria will be that determine what degree of this type of validity must be demonstrated in order for the concept to be accepted.

"Predictive validity" is what clinicians are most concerned about, since it deals with the issue of treatment specificity. If a diagnosis has high predictive validity, it is useful for predicting the natural history and treatment response of a person with the disorder. There seems to be compelling evidence that light therapy is effective in a large proportion of SAD cases and is not effective for nonseasonal depression, indicating a degree of specificity of this treatment, and thus evidence for its predictive validity (see Rosenthal et al., Chapter 15, this volume).

Finally, "construct validity" refers to the kind of evidence that suggests that we have some understanding about the etiology or pathophysiological mechanism of a disorder. Evidence for construct validity includes demonstration of a biological mechanism, biological abnormality, and association with environmental variables. In a way, the most exciting aspect of SAD is that we have knowledge both of the defining feature of the disorder (i.e., its seasonality) and the evidence for a specific treatment. This suggests some basis for understanding the underlying mechanism of the disorder. This evidence is lacking for nonseasonal depression, since we know that tricyclic antidepressants and monoamine oxidase inhibitors are certainly not specific to depression (they are effective also, for example, in the treatment of panic disorder).

The Revision of the DSM-III Affective Disorders

A Work Group to Revise DSM-III was appointed by the American Psychiatric Association in 1983. A Mood Disorders Advisory Committee to the Work Group was appointed and met very early in the revision process to discuss needed changes in the affective disorders section of DSM-III. One obvious change recommended by this committee was changing the name of the class of disorders to "mood disorders," as a more accurate term.

For most of the mood disorders, the changes that were recommended were relatively minor. The most major change was in the basic organization of the classification, abandoning the division into "major" and "minor" disorders, and instead dividing the categories into "bipolar" and "depressive" disorders. The bipolar disorders include bipolar disorder and cyclothymia, and the depressive disorders include major depression and dysthymia. Both groups also have a residual category (bipolar disorder not otherwise specified [NOS], and depressive disorder NOS).

The issue of including SAD in DSM-III-R was never discussed by the full Mood Disorders Advisory Committee. This was because the committee met so early in the process of revising DSM-III, holding most of its meetings in 1984 or 1985. Had these meetings been held 2 years later, undoubtedly the category would have been discussed. In any case, relatively late in the process of the revision, it occurred to us that the categories of melancholia and dysthymia were being retained in the revision, despite their uncertain validity; yet SAD, which in many aspects had more demonstrated diagnostic validity, had not even been considered for inclusion. In response to this realization, and ad hoc advisory group was quickly established, consisting of ourselves, Norman Rosenthal, and Michael Terman, to consider whether and how the concept could be brought into DSM-III-R.

At first glance, it would seem that the most logical approach would have been to add a new category of "seasonal mood disorder." However, that would have meant that everything else would have had to be defined as nonseasonal mood disorders, with both of these categories then being divided into bipolar and depressive types. This approach seemed to place *too* much emphasis on this still-new concept. Therefore, the group took another tack, and decided that the concept of seasonality should be incorporated as a "pattern" of mood disturbance. This pattern could then apply to bipolar disorder and recurrent major depression, as well as to the two residual categories, for cases in which the mood disturbance was relatively short-lived or milder than the full mood syndrome. This added specification meant that a clinician could indicate "seasonal pattern" after one of these mood disorder diagnoses.

The next challenge was to develop a definition for this "seasonal pattern." (For the final DSM-III-R version, see American Psychiatric Association, 1987, p. 224.) Using Rosenthal's basic definition as a starting place, the ad hoc committee held numerous discussions in an effort to operationalize the criteria as much as possible. The main problem was to define what was meant by a "regular temporal relationship" between the onset of one of the mood disorders and the time of the year. For example, if someone gets depressed in October of one year and January of the next, should that be considered the "same" time of the year? Initially the phrase was changed to "same season," but it quickly became clear that a "season" is too long a period of time, and not sufficiently restrictive to identify cases that were truly ones of SAD. Therefore, the definition was finally restricted to a 60-day window, meaning that the disorder had to reappear within a 60-day period each year (e.g., between the beginning of October and the end of November). Cases in which there is an obvious effect of seasonally related psychosocial stresses every winter are excluded in this definition. At the meeting that was the basis of this volume, there was criticism of this criterion—mainly, that it introduces an issue that practically never actually arises in the clinical evaluation of patients with possible seasonal pattern to a mood disturbance.

It should be noted that this definition does not require that the depression be in the winter; the "regular temporal relationship" criterion could apply as well to summer depressions. The purpose of this lack of restriction was to allow the diagnosis of summer depressions, which have recently been identified and are just beginning to become the focus of study (Wehr et al., 1987).

The next issue dealt with how much a person has to recover in between episodes in order for the pattern to be considered truly "seasonal." The committee decided to keep this criterion fairly strict and require a *full* remission between episodes. However, the criterion does not exclude cases involving a change from depression to mania or hypomania. Thus the criterion would exclude cases of major depression that had only a partial remission into dysthymia.

How many episodes does a person have to have had before the illness can be said to have a seasonal pattern? Rosenthal's criteria originally required two episodes. However, in order to further reduce the possibility of misdiagnosis because of the chance occurrence of two sequential but unrelated depressions, DSM-III-R requires three episodes, at least two of which have to be consecutive. Related to this is the issue of how many *non*seasonal episodes one could have and still be said to have a "seasonal pattern." This consideration led to a decision based on clinical experience to require a ratio of at least 3:1 of seasonal to nonseasonal affective episodes.

These criteria were added at the last minute to DSM-III-R, after the approval (by mail vote) of the full Mood Disorders Advisory Committee. Ideally, a full subcommittee would have been formed to discuss the issue and to give a larger number of people input into the criteria. However, because of the timing this was not possible, and these criteria should be regarded as only a beginning attempt to specify SAD in our standard manual of mental disorder definitions. It is hoped that this definition will be studied by clinicians and researchers in this area, and specific suggestions will emerge for improvements that can be incorporated into DSM-IV.

References

American Psychiatric Association (1987) *Diagnostic and Statistical Manual of Mental Disorders,* 3rd ed., rev., American Psychiatric Association, Washington, DC.

Klerman, G. L., J. Endicott, R. L. Spitzer, and R. M. A. Hirschfeld (1979) Neurotic depression: A systematic analysis of multiple criteria and multiple meanings. Amer. J. Psychiat. *136:* 57–61.

Spitzer, R. L., and J. B. W. Williams (1980) Classification of mental disorders and DSM-III. In *Comprehensive Textbook of Psychiatry,* 3rd ed., Vol. 1, H. Kaplan, A. Freedman, and B. Sadock, eds., pp. 1035–1072, Williams & Wilkins, Baltimore.

Wehr, T. A., D. A. Sack, and N. E. Rosenthal (1987) Seasonal affective disorder with summer depression and winter hypomania. Amer. J. Psychiat. *144:* 1602–1603.

Weissman, M. M. (1979). The myth of involutional melancholia. J. Amer. Med. Assoc. *242:* 742–744.

Zimmerman, M., and R. L. Spitzer (1989) Melancholia: From DSM-III to DSM-III-R. Amer. J. Psychiat. 146: 20–28.

A Search for Animal Models of Seasonal Affective Disorders

The Photoperiodic Phenomena: Seasonal Modulation of the "Day Within"

Colin S. Pittendrigh

My task in this chapter is to outline for colleagues in psychiatry what little the biologist currently understands about photoperiodism in animals—indeed, in eukaryotes more generally. Are there general principles underlying the photoperiodic phenomena that will facilitate better understanding and treatment of seasonal affective disorders (SAD)? Is there any justification for the assumption that SAD is a "true" photoperiodic disorder of humans? There are such generalizations about photoperiodic phenomena, but they do not at present involve concrete molecular mechanisms: There is no evidence, for example, that rhodopsin or melatonin is involved in the flowering response of duckweed to daylength, nor that phytochrome plays any role in the mammalian system! It is not even clear that rhodopsin mediates all the daylength responses of vertebrates, or phytochrome those of flowering plants. Nevertheless, duckweeds, fruitflies, sparrows, and hamsters have been shown to share some common "mechanisms"—all of them at higher levels of organization and relevant, I think, to the psychiatric issues we are addressing here.

The history of life, as is usual in biological analysis, offers some useful perspectives. There has been immense impact on that history from the ubiquitous environmental cycles that result from the motions of the earth about the sun and the moon about the earth. Daily, lunar–tidal, and annual periodicity in the conditions of life present, on the one hand, major challenges, as in the heat of the desert midday or the chill of Arctic winter. And on the other hand, the unparalleled predictability of these cycles has provided natural selection with an opportunity—seized again and again in life's history—to develop an innate temporal program of biological function that appropriately matches the periodicity of environmental change. There is, in Fritz Buhnemann's happy phrase, a "day within" in the life of organisms that matches and copes with the "day outside."

Colin S. Pittendrigh. Hopkins Marine Station, Stanford University, Stanford, California.

The ubiquity and significance of this inborn temporal programming are still poorly appreciated, and the more dramatic aspects are commonly doubted. The photosynthetic system of those plants that have been adequately studied exhibits a remarkable persisting rhythmicity whose period is close to 24 hr (i.e., circadian) even in an environment of constant light, constant CO_2 tension, and constant temperature: The photosystems in the chloroplasts are somehow switched off for about 12 hr of what is, to the cell, its "subjective night" when, in nature, the opportunity to reduce CO_2 is predictably not there. And in many xerophytic plants there is a programmed separation in time of CO_2 uptake (at night) and its later photoreduction (in the day) that permits them to exploit the driest environments, where stomatal opening (to capture CO_2) by day is extremely hazardous. In nocturnal rodents, feeding activity is programmed into the early hours of the "subjective night," when darkness provides *some* screen against predators, and the enzymatic machinery of gut and liver necessary to process the food is appropriately mobilized in time just ahead of its programmed intake. Sometimes there seems to be very little in the life of such well-studied animals that is not, to some extent, under the influence of a "circadian program." It is surely only the convenience of its assay that makes "running-wheel activity" (Fig. 8-1) the principal object of the older literature; the timing of a daily somatostatin pulse in cerebrospinal fluid (CSF) is just as thoroughly programmed but more troublesome to monitor routinely. Figure 8-2 summarizes observations (principally from Halberg's laboratory) that document the extent to which the physiology of, for example, a mammal is subject to such control. Wilhelm Hüfeland put it succinctly over 200 years ago: *"Die 24-Stundige Periode . . . sie ist gleichsam die Einheit unserer natur-lichen Chronologie."*

Although the daily case has understandably received the bulk of attention so far, we should not lose sight of the lunar–tidal programming so important in the life of marine organisms (see Neumann, 1981), nor of the truly remarkable and surprising demonstrations (see Gwinner, 1981) of annual programming that have special relevance to the central theme of this issue. Gwinner's brilliant studies of the annual cycle in passerine birds show that virtually every aspect of the bird's year is anticipated in an inherited program: the times of moulting; of gonadal growth and reproductive activity more generally; and of migratory activity, including its duration and flight path relative (presumably) to the earth's magnetic field.

None of this programming would, of course, serve any useful purpose without provision for its appropriate phasing relative to the periodicities of the outside world. And herein lies the answer to a question often raised: Why has natural selection used a self-sustaining oscillation in cells as the temporal framework of these programs? Why not some simpler "hourglass" (i.e., nonperiodic) timer? The innate pacemaking oscillation responsible for circadian, circatidal, or circannual rhythms is susceptible, like all self-sustaining oscillations, to "entrainment" by some external periodicity to which it can be cou-

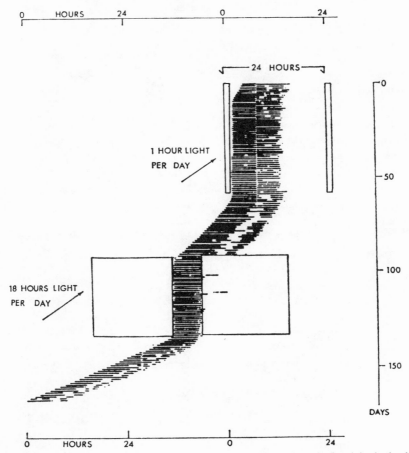

FIGURE 8-1. Entrained and free-running circadian rhythms of running-wheel activity in the deer mouse, *Peromyscus leucopus*. The animal used a running wheel during its nightly activity period, which lasted about 10 hr and is recorded as a heavy black line. Successive days are plotted beneath each other. The observation lasted 6 months. On the 10th day of the experiment, the animal had locked onto (was entrained by) the daily light pulse (1-hr duration). On the 60th day, the light was discontinued; the rhythm persisted with a circadian period (τ) of 23.6 hr. On the 90th day, it was again entrained by a 24-hr light cycle in which the light pulse lasted 18 hr. On the 140th day, the light was discontinued, and the rhythm again ran free with a circadian period of 23.0 hr. The value of τ shows an "aftereffect" of the prior light pulse.

pled—coupled in the sense of permitting a periodic energy input from the external cycle, which in the biological literature is referred to as the "zeitgeber." In the daily case the principal and universal zeitgeber is the light–dark cycle, although the "noisier" temperature cycle does make some contribution (still poorly analyzed) to entrainment of the innate circadian program of some organisms. In the tidal case, the periodicity of mechanical vibration (wave action)

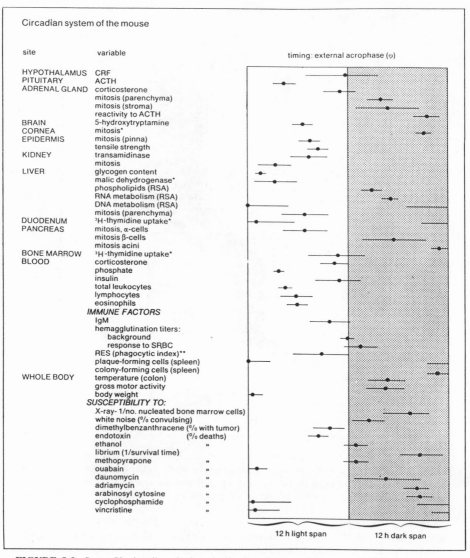

FIGURE 8-2. Some 50 circadian rhythms in the house mouse *(Mus musculus)*. Points are the estimated times of the maximum in each of the rhythms, with ± *SEM* indicated by bars. From Szabo *et al.* (1978). Reprinted by permission.

has been shown to be the zeitgeber (Neumann, 1981). But in spite of suggestive observations implicating the annual cycle of photoperiod as their zeitgeber, the entrainment of circannual programs remains the least well understood of all.

In this chapter we are, however, more concerned with an alternative strategy that natural selection has pursued in coping with the yearly cycle of seasonal change. Animals and plants of all longevities, lasting weeks or years, very commonly use photoperiod (or daylength) as a cue to season. More strictly, as we shall see, they use the duration of darkness at night (not the duration of sunlight) as a signal or "releaser" of seasonally appropriate metabolic pathways and behavioral repertoires. Hibernation or diapause and the development of low temperature tolerance are all, for example, initiated by a photoperiod signal (long night) that heralds the approach of winter. The range of phenomena influenced by photoperiod is remarkable and probably still underestimated. The first example was a reported only about 70 years ago, when Garner and Allard (1920) showed that flowering time was determined photoperiodically. And as the field has subsequently developed, investigators have, for obvious reasons, focused attention on easily assayed (all-or-nothing) responses, just as the circadian field focused for so long on "running-wheel activities" and the like. But it becomes increasingly clear that every aspect of the metabolic and nervous systems of animals that can be adjusted to some seasonal challenge is liable to be controlled by the signal of nightlength. The photoperiodic control of cold-hardiness in insects, for example, sometimes involves the induction of specific antifreeze proteins. And the extent to which we are currently underestimating the pervasiveness of such control has recently been emphasized in the finding (Randall, 1981) that the size of the receptive field for a scratch reflex in cats is photoperiodically regulated! We will do well to suspect that those phenomena currently known to be controlled in this way are only the tip of an iceberg.

What concerns us here is the way photoperiod is sensed: Are there general rules? And how does circadian rhythmicity relate to the organism's use of "daylength–nightlength" as a seasonal cue? It is worth recording even in this written account of the SAD symposium's transactions that some of the discussion reflected misunderstanding of the issues at stake here. Namely, it was said that there were *two* ways of rationalizing the phototherapeutic programs currently used in the treatment of SAD; one of these was a "circadian approach" and the other was the "photoperiodic approach." As I see it, that distinction lacks meaning: The photoperiodic responses of virtually every organism tested, with the exceptions of Lees's (1973) aphid and Underwood's (1978) lizard, are mediated by the circadian system, as Erwin Bünning was the first to suggest as long ago as 1936. When we speak of light's effect on the photoperiodic system, we necessarily refer to its effect on the circadian system. And we should, accordingly, first become clear on how the daily cycle of light and darkness acts as zeitgeber of the "day within."

Figure 8-3 gives a phase response curve (PRC) for the circadian pacemaker that, in *Drosophila pseudoobscura,* indirectly dictates the time of day at which the insect emerges from its pupal case. Exotic as this particular case may seem in the context of human behavior, one should emphasize the essential universality of PRC shape. Figure 8-4 documents this with PRCs from a wide array of animals. The PRC for *D. pseudoobscura* in this figure plots the phase-shift response of the pacemaking oscillation (in the fly's brain) to a brief

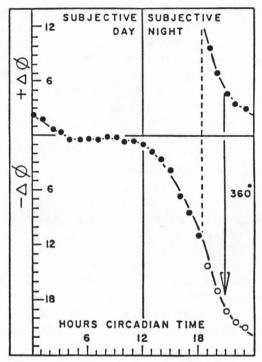

FIGURE 8-3. The response to short (15-min) light pulses of the circadian oscillation that drives the eclosion gating system in *D. pseudoobscura*. This phase response curve (PRC) plots the steady-state phase delays ($-\Delta\Phi$) and phase advances ($+\Delta\Phi$) caused by pulses applied at 24 different phases (circadian times, or ct) of the oscillation. The phase shift induced is dependent on the phase pulsed. When $+\Delta\Phi$ values are displaced 360°, one obtains a monotonic curve.

(15-min) light pulse applied at different phases of the oscillator's cycle. During the part of the cycle that coincides with sunlight in nature, the phase-shifting response ($\Delta\Phi_n$) to light signals is minimal; but during the half-cycle that coincides with darkness each night, it is pronounced. A moment's thought shows this to be, of course, an analytic necessity: In the steady-state phase relationship of pacemaker to light cycle, the part of the circadian program that coincides with light is the least affected by it, in terms of phase shifting. It is this part of the temporal program that is commonly called the "subjective day." On the other hand, that part of the program called the "subjective night" *is* very responsive to light (which immediately phase-shifts it) and consequently coincides with darkness in the entrained steady state. In the beginning of the "subjective night," the phase-shift responses are delays, replaced by advances in the later subjective night.

Each of the several PRCs in Figure 8-5 is characteristic of a particular light pulse. The shift caused by a light pulse is a function of the "strength" (intensity × duration) of that pulse. As a result, the PRC for a "weak" pulse has a lower amplitude than that for a "stronger" pulse. Figure 8-6 gives the PRCs for two geographic races of a Japanese fruit fly, *Drosophila auraria*. In both cases (Miyake from ~33°N and Hokkaido from ~43°N), the experimental light pulse used in assaying the PRC was the same—namely, 1 hr of ~50-lux white light. The difference in the amplitude of the two PRCs means that the Hokkaido pacemaker "sees" less of the light than does that of Miyake: It is more weakly coupled to the zeitgeber than that of Miyake (Takamura and Pittendrigh, unpublished data). It is as though natural selection had inserted a neutral density filter in the pathway of light to the Hokkaido pacemaker. Circadian pacemakers may differ in the strength of their coupling to the light cycle, but the topology of their PRCs is essentially invariant.

Equally remarkable are the kinetics of light-induced pacemaker phase shifts.

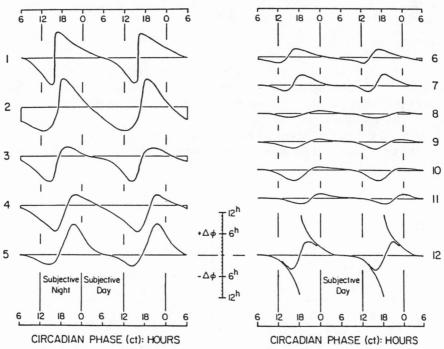

FIGURE 8-4. PRCs for light pulses from a diversity of organisms, unicellular, plant, insect, and vertebrate. Based on data from various sources. (1) *Sarcophaga* (fly); pulse = 3 hr, 100 lux; (2) *Coleus* (Green plant); pulse = 4 hr, 13,000 lux; (3) *Leucophaea* (cockroach); pulse = 6 hr, 50,000 lux; (4) *Euglena* (unicellular); pulse = 4 hr, 1000 lux; (5) *Gonyaulax* (unicellular); pulse = 3 hr, ? intensity; (6) *Anopheles* (mosquito); pulse = 1 hr, 70 lux; (7) *Mesocricetus* (hamster); pulse = 0.25 hr, 100 lux; (8) *Peromyscus leucopus* (deer mouse); pulse = 0.25 hr, 100 lux; (9) *Peromyscus maniculatus* (deer mouse); pulse = 0.25 hr, 100 lux; (10) *Mus musculus* (house mouse); pulse = 0.25 hr, 100 lux; (11) *Taphozous* (bat); pulse = 0.25 hr, 100 lux; and (12) *Drosophila pseudoobscura* (fruit fly); pulse = 0.25 hr (Type 0 PRC) and 1 msec (Type 1 PRC).

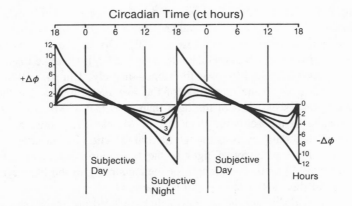

Pulse strengths: 1<2<3<4

FIGURE 8-5. A family of PRCs (based on experiments with *Drosophila pseudoobscura*) for 15-min light pulses of four different intensities: 1 < 2 < 3 < 4. See text.

In *D. pseudoobscura,* a shift of ~12 hr (or 180°) is effected nearly "instanta-neously," as shown by the two-pulse experiments in Figure 8-7. Each of the points plotted in that figure records the supplementary phase shift caused by a second (or test) pulse given at some interval after a first pulse. The responses to such test pulses are fully predicted by assuming that the phrase shift caused by the first pulse is immediate (cf. Pittendrigh, 1974, 1981a). Comparable

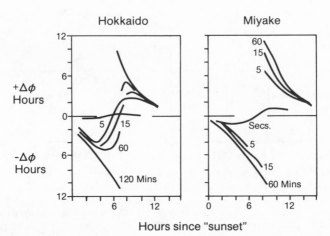

Hours since "sunset"

FIGURE 8-6. PRCs for two latitudinal strains of *Drosophila auraria.* Miyake is southern at 34.2°N; Hokkaido is northern at 42.9°N. At each phase in the cycle (hours since sunset) the Hokkaido phase-shift response to any pulse duration (viz., 5 min, 15 min, 60 min) is lower than that of Miyake.

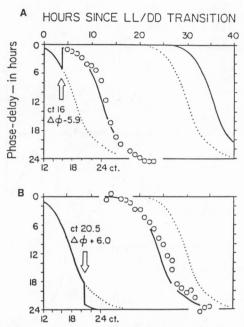

FIGURE 8-7. The "instantaneous" nature of *D. pseudoobscura*'s pacemaker phase shifts. (A) A "first" pulse (open arrow) is given at ct 16; second "test" pulses are used to track the time course of the pacemaker after the first pulse. It is well predicted by the assumption (solid curve) of an instantaneous 6-hr delay of the PRC. (B) The same protocol shows that a pulse at ct 20.5 causes an instantaneous 6-hr advance. LL, constant light; DD, constant darkness.

demonstrations have now been made using mammals (Elliot and Pittendrigh, unpublished data).

These remarkable kinetics account for the utility of PRCs in explaining the entrainment of circadian systems by the light–dark cycle. When the pacemaking oscillation (with period τ hr) entrains to a light cycle (with period T hr), the action of the light in each cycle is to cause a phase shift that is equal to $\tau - T$. This is illustrated by the two cases in Figure 8-8 where the pacemaker of *D. pseudoobscura*'s emergence rhythm ($\tau \simeq 24$ hr) is entrained to experimental light cycles whose periods (T) are 21 and 27 hours. In both cases the light pulse in each cycle has the same strength (0.25 hr at ~50 lux) as that used in deriving the PRC. When T = 21 hr, the pulse in each cycle has to cause a 3-hr phase advance (τ of $24 - T$ of $21 = +3$ hr). When T = 27 hr, the steady-state phase shift is a 3-hr delay. The steady-state phase relationship (Ψ_{PL}) of pacemaker (P) to light (L) pulse is, then, readily predicted from the appropriate PRC: The light pulse falls at that pacemaker phase in each cycle where the magnitude and sign of the resultant phase shift is equal to $\tau - T$.

Ψ_{PL} is the interval (in hours) between arbitrarily chosen phase reference

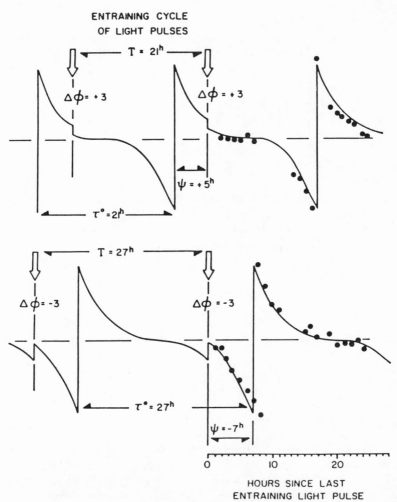

FIGURE 8-8. The steady states in *Drosophila pseudoobscura* created by light cycles (15-min pulses) with T = 21 and T = 27 hr. In T 21, the pulse falls at ct 23.4, causing a 3-hr advance in each cycle; in T 27, it falls at ct 14.3, causing a 3-hr delay. The predicted phase relation of pacemaker to light cycle is tested by measuring the phase of the PRC after release from entrainment.

points in pacemaker (P) and light (L) cycle. For convenience, one usually chooses the midpoint of the photoperiod and the middle of the subjective night as phase references for zeitgeber and pacemaker, respectively. Figure 8-9 illustrates how Ψ_{PL} is dependent on the strength of coupling between pacemaker and light cycle. If we decrease the light intensity of the 15-min pulse, the appropriate PRC has a lower amplitude; that is, the pulse produces a smaller phase shift no matter where it falls. If we now entrain the pacemaker using the lower-intensity pulse when $T = 21$ hr the light pulse in each cycle must fall at an earlier phase in the late subjective night to cause the necessary phase advance of 3 hr, and when $T = 27$ it must fall later in the early subjective night. In the one case ($T = 21$ and is smaller than $\tau = 24$), Ψ_{PL} gets larger as coupling strength (intensity of the light) decreases; in the other case ($T = 27$ and is larger than $\tau = 24$), it gets smaller.

The generalization is given, schematically, in Figure 8-10, which shows the dependence of Ψ on C (coupling strength) and ρ (the ratio τ/T). It plots Ψ as a function of ρ for seven increasingly strong coupling strengths (in this case, represented by increasing photoperiod length). The biological interest in that family of curves, which is great, derives from the node, at $\rho = 1.0$, which the curves go through. When ρ is less than 1.0, Ψ gets smaller as coupling strength is weakened, but it gets larger when ρ is greater than 1.0. These complexities are readily understood from the details of Figure 8-9; and I have introduced them in this sketch of entrainment phonomena because of their bearing on the biology of photoperiod.

When photoperiod—the duration of the daily light pulse—is changed seasonally, it amounts to a change in the strength of coupling between a circadian pacemaker and its zeitgeber. The coupling gets progressively stronger in the spring as photoperiod lengthens and weaker in the fall as it shortens. The family of curves given in Figure 8-10 now takes on its biological importance. It clarifies not only the significance of τ being only *circa* T, but the otherwise perplexing generalization in "Aschoff's rule" that τ is typically shorter than 24 hr (i.e., shorter than T) in night-active organisms, but longer than 24 hr in

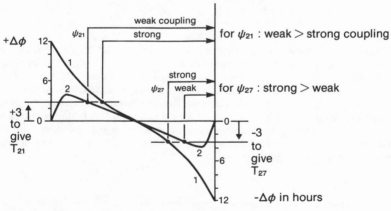

FIGURE 8-9. Response curves or light pulses of two different intensities $(1 > 2)$, which constitute two different strengths of coupling between light cycle and circadian pacemaker. The figure considers entrainment to light cycles of 21- and 27-hr periods, and two intensities of light for each period. When $\rho < 1$ (viz., T of 27), the phase relation (Ψ_{27}) of pacemaker to light cycle is more negative for the *strong* pulse; but when $\rho > 1$ (T of 21), that phase relation (Ψ_{21}) is more negative for the *weak* pulse.

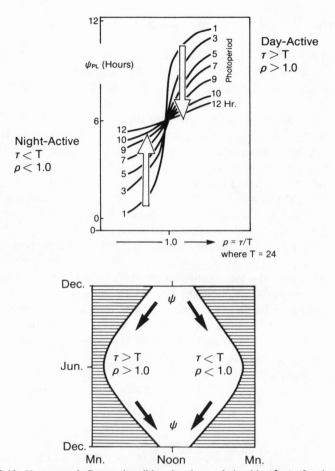

FIGURE 8-10. *Upper panel:* Curves describing the phase relationship (Ψ_{PL}) of a circadian pace-maker (P) to the light cycle (L) that entrains it. The abscissa is $\rho = \tau/T$ where τ is the period of pacemaker (22 . . . 26 hr), and T is the period (24 hr) of the light cycle. The seven curves are for light cycles with period (T = 24 hr) and light-pulse durations (or photoperiods) of 1, 3, 5, . . . 12 hr. As photoperiod increases, coupling between light and pacemaker increases; Ψ_{PL} becomes *more* negative when $\rho < 1.0$, but *less* negative when $\rho > 1.0$. *Lower panel:* This means that when $\rho < 1.0$ (as in night-active organisms), the onset of the circadian program gets *later* in the spring as daylength increases; but when $\rho > 1.0$ (as in day-active species), the onset of the program gets *earlier* in the spring as daylength increases.

day-active animals. This translates to ρ (τ/T) being less than 1.0 in nocturnal species but greater than 1.0 in day-active forms. The consequence is clear: Sunrise gets earlier in the spring as photoperiod lengthens, and the phase of the circadian program in day-active forms (τ and $\rho > 1.0$) also advances; the onset of the "day within" tracks the advancing onset of the "day outside." And, similarly, onset of the program for nocturnal species gets later each day in the spring, *because* in these forms $\tau > 24$ and hence ρ is less than 1.0.

There is much more to the biological importance of changing photoperiod than these aspects of phase control, especially in its potential relationship to SAD; however, I must first review the evidence that entrainment of the circadian system does indeed underlie the seasonal adjustment of program that we call "photoperiodism."

Figures 8-11 and 8-12 illustrate two of the most powerful experimental protocols that yield evidence of the circadian system's involvement. Both involve entrainment by exotic light cycles and are part of a recent study by myself and Takamura using *Drosophila auraria*. The outcome of the experiments summarized in Figure 8-11 leaves no doubt (1) that the duration of uninterrupted darkness (nightlength, not photoperiod) is crucial, and (2) that the circadian system (in its entrainment behavior) is responsible for measuring that dark period. It is the "clock" at the heart of the photoperiod phenomena. The experiments employ an exotic light–dark cycle that includes two long dark periods (one of 10 hr, the other of 12 hr) separated by 1-hr light pulses (two per cycle). In entraining to this zeitgeber, the *Drosophila* pacemaker can assume either of two stable phase relationships (designated Ψ_{14} or Ψ_{12}) to the light pulses (see Pittendrigh and Minis, 1971). These differ only in the duration of the dark period (10 or 12 hr for Ψ_{14} and Ψ_{12}, respectively) that embraces the circadian pacemaker's "subjective night."

The steady state realized (Ψ_{14} and Ψ_{12}) in any given test is fully determined by the initial conditions at the onset of entrainment. The relevant conditions are (1) the duration of the first dark period (10 or 12 hr), and (2) the phase of the pacemaker illuminated by the first light pulse. Figure 8-11 in an earlier paper (Pittendrigh and Minis, 1971) elaborates the detail involved. Using the information in that figure, we have recently made 12 tests in each of which half the flies *(D. auraria)* were entrained to Ψ_{14} and half to Ψ_{12}. In each of the 12 tests there was more reproductive diapause (winter metabolic state) in those females entrained to Ψ_{12} (long "winter" night) than in their sisters

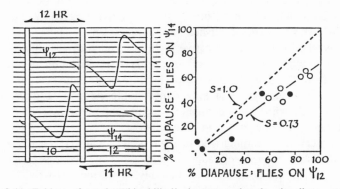

FIGURE 8-11. Evidence from the "bistability" phenomena that the circadian system assesses nightlength (duration of darkness). Left: The two steady-state phase relations of pacemaker to light cycle. Right: Solid points = Miyake, open points = Hokkaido. See text.

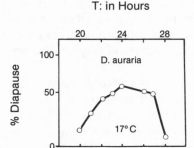

FIGURE 8-12. The incidence of reproductive diapause in *Drosophila auraria* females when entrained to cycles of white light (each with 1-hr, 50-lux pulses) whose periods (T) range from 20 to 28 hr.

entrained to Ψ_{14} (short "summer" night). The overall response level varied in the 12 experiments, due principally to strain and temperature differences; however, in each experiment, the incidence of diapause among flies whose "subjective night" fell in the shorter dark interval was only 76% of that among their sisters whose "circadian night" experienced longer darkness. Nightlength is appraised by the extent to which light invades the half of the circadian program ("subjective night") that in the entrained steady state is, for the most part, not illuminated.

The crucial role of light's invasion of this "subjective" night is underscored again by the so-called T experiments, illustrated in Figure 8-12, which compare the photoperiodic effectiveness of a wide range of light–dark cycles whose period (T) is different from but close to 24 hr. The photoperiod in each cycle is short (i.e., 1 hr), and T is varied by differences in the duration of darkness (e.g., 20, 21, . . . 26 hr of dark). In none of these cycles, therefore, does the duration of light (1 hr) or of darkness (20–26 hr) bear any relation to the comparable durations encountered in nature. The utility of these exotic cycles emerges from the analysis of entrainment developed earlier. We can predict what phase of the circadian cycle (in terms of its PRC) will be illuminated by the 1-hr pulse in each cycle. As T gets further away from (smaller or larger than) $\tau \simeq 24$ hours, light must invade the subjective night further to elicit the phase-shift response that establishes the entrained steady state. And as Figure 8-12 shows, the further the subjective night is invaded by the light, the greater is the "long-day" (short-night, summer) response. Different as these exotic cycles are from the daily light–dark cycles in nature, their bearing in the natural case is clear enough: The longer the photoperiod, the further does light overlap (coincide with) some phases in the circadian program's subjective night (Takamura and Pittendrigh, unpublished data).

The observations summarized in Figures 8-11 and 8-12 clearly establish a close relationship between circadian organization and those seasonally meaningful changes in metabolic behavior that daylength (more strictly, nightlength) elicits. And there is a sense in which, given the history of life, such a relationship seems almost inevitable, not just plausible. Natural selection has had to evolve a "day within" that not only changes its phase relationship to the day outside as dawn or dusk shifts with the season, but, just as importantly, changes in its *pattern*. An inflexible temporal program may be appropriate at one season, but without modification will be at least somewhat inappropriate at others. In short, the fine texture of the "day within" must respond to signals cuing seasonal change, and *nightlength* is such a cue.

Unfortunately, it is not easy to develop this aspect of photoperiodism, which is our real concern, much further, because we still lack any detailed knowledge of how the sequence of events in a circadian program is actually timed by the pacemaker. Nevertheless, what little we do know does provide for adjustment with change in nightlength. There is now increasing evidence that the circadian system of an animal comprises a multiplicity of oscillators—even several that are independently coupled to the light cycle. This is clearly the case in saturnid moths, whose brain and prothoracic glands both contain pacemakers coupled separately to the light–dark cycle (Mizoguchi and Ishizaki, 1982). It is also true of sparrows, where Takahashi and Menaker (1982) have demonstrated that a host of light-coupled oscillators exists in addition to that in the pineal. Daan and I (Pittendrigh, 1974; Pittendrigh & Daan, 1976) have given strong evidence that in hamsters (and in other mammals) there are two oscillators, separately coupled to sunset and dawn, that control its daily activity pattern. The independent couplings to the onset and end of the night guarantee a seasonal adjustment to changing daylength.

I have also suggested (Pittendrigh, 1981b) how a complex circadian program could be constructed on the basis of relatively few (perhaps even one) light-coupled pacemakers that themselves function as drivers—or zeitgebers, if you will—for a population of slave oscillations in peripheral organs. Such a pacemaker–slave architecture to the program has the attractive feature of permitting selection to adjust the daily timing of one function (controlled by one slave oscillation) without interfering with others. That adjustment would be effected by a change in the individual slave oscillation's free-running period, or the strength of its coupling to the system pacemaker (which in higher vertebrates is evidently located in the pineal gland or the suprachiasmatic nuclei of the hypothalamus). The importance of all these conceptualizations of a circadian program—of the "day within"—lies in their multioscillator foundation and the associated assumption that the constituent oscillators (either as pacemakers or slaves) differ in their intrinsic periods (frequencies) and coupling, directly or indirectly, to the light cycle. It follows that the temporal fine structure of any such daily program will change seasonally as photoperiod (and hence the coupling strength of zeitgeber to pacemaker) changes.

The importance of stressing this very general conclusion—which is all that current knowledge warrants—is its independence of mechanism detail. Whether one is discussing the photoperiodism of duckweeds, flies, or humans, the one sure way to effect seasonal change in the "day within" is to manipulate the duration of darkness at night. What this does, either directly or indirectly, is to change the mutual phase relationship of the several oscillations that constitute the program. All this reduces to saying that if the psychiatrist is correct in diagnosing SAD as a photoperiodic disorder—as a pathological caricature of the brain's winter state—then the phototherapist is on firm ground in reducing the duration of nightly darkness by light supplements at either the beginning or end of the day. And the current evidence that shortening the night by supplementary light in the morning (advancing dawn) is more effective than evening supplements is also compatible with current views of the entrainment of day-active animals, such as humans (see Pittendrigh, 1981b).

Closing Comments

Both Mrosovsky (Chapter 10, this volume) and Zucker (Chapter 11, this volume) have properly emphasized the limited utility of animal models in the study of SAD. There is, of course, great diversity in the neuroendocrine basis of seasonal change in animals—differences not only between species, but between different responses in the same individual. How, in such diversity, is one to recognize a reliable model of seasonality in human emotional states (if, indeed, it exists at all)?

On the other hand, animal studies have clear utility in evaluating and developing the widespread assumption that SAD and its phototherapy have a circadian basis. The most significant feature of SAD is its seasonality: The winter state of the circadian system, induced by natural short photoperiods, is abnormal in SAD patients, but its summer state, induced by longer natural daylengths, is essentially normal in the same individuals. Phototherapy, in extending the short winter day, returns the patient's circadian system to its essentially normal summer state.

Two aspects of this view of SAD should, I think, be emphasized in closing. First, there is no meaning to the distinction—circadian versus photoperiodic—that was implicit in several of the SAD symposium's discussions: Photoperiodic effects have a circadian basis, and the only seasonal variations in circadian organization we know of are elicited by either photoperiodic or thermoperiodic change. (The possible role of thermoperiod as an agent of SAD's seasonality has received very little attention except from Wehr and colleagues.)

Second, the circadian–photoperiodic rationale for phototherapy does imply that the *timing* of light supplements is important (indeed, crucial). The difference between summer and winter states of the circadian system, as animal models show, is the extent to which the lengthened photoperiod of summer illuminates phases of the oscillating system that see no light in winter. When the phototherapist's light *extends* the natural photoperiod, it simulates summer, but that is not the case if (as Wehr and colleagues have done) the supplement is given at midday. The report (Wehr et al., 1986) that midday light is beneficial is troublesome for the circadian hypothesis, and collection of stronger data on this point is an urgent task in its evaluation.

Another approach to this issue would be use of the so-called T experiment, such as that illustrated in Figure 8-12, which used *Drosophila auraria*. If successful phototherapy of SAD does indeed have the same circadian foundation as other "true" photoperiodic effects, it should be possible to lower the Hamilton Depression Rating Scale scores of patients by exposing them to 23- or 22-hr light–dark cycles in which the photoperiod itself is short and winter-like—say, 6 or 8 hr. Indeed, the therapeutic effect should increase as T (light cycle period) is shortened and the light pulse advances further into the patients' subjective night.

Acknowledgments

This chapter originally appeared in *Journal of Biological Rhythms,* Volume 3, Number 2, 1988, pp. 173–188, 1988. Reprinted by permission of The Guilford Press.

References

Garner, W. H., and H. A. Allared (1920) Effect of the relative length of day and night and other factors of the environment on growth and reproduction in plants. J. Agr. Res. *27:* 553–606.

Gwinner, E. (1981) Circannual systems. In *Handbook of Behavioral Neurobiology,* Vol. 4, *Biological Rhythms,* J. Aschoff, ed., pp. 351–381, Plenum Press, New York.

Lees, A. D. (1973) Photoperiodic time measurement in the aphid *Megoura viciae.* J. Insect Physiol. *19:* 2279–2316.

Mizoguchi, A., and H. Ishizaki (1982) Prothoracic glands of the saturnid moth *Samia cynthia ricini* possess a circadian clock controlling gut-purge timing. Proc. Natl. Acad. Sci. USA *79:* 2726–2730.

Neumann, D. (1981). Tidal and lunar rhythms. In *Handbook of Behavioral Neurobiology,* Vol. 4, *Biological Rhythms,* J. Aschoff, ed., pp. 351–381, Plenum Press, New York.

Pittendrigh, C. S. (1974) Circadian oscillations in cells and the circadian organization of multicellular systems. In *The Neurosciences: Third Study Program,* F. O. Schmitt and F. G. Wordon, eds., pp. 435–458, MIT Press, Cambridge, MA.

Pittendrigh, C. S. (1981a) Circadian systems: Entrainment. In *Handbook of Behavioral Neurobiology,* Vol. 4, *Biological Rhythms,* J. Aschoff, ed., pp. 95–124, Plenum Press, New York.

Pittendrigh, C. S. (1981b) Circadian organization and the photoperiodic phenomena. In *Biological Clocks in Seasonal Reproductive Cycles,* B. K. Follett and D. E. Follett, eds., pp. 1–34, John Wright and Sons, Bristol, England.

Pittendrigh, C. S., and S. Daan (1976) A functional analysis of circadian pacemakers in nocturnal rodents: V. Pacemaker structure: A clock for all seasons. J. Comp. Physiol. *106:* 333–355.

Pittendrigh, C. S., and D. H. Minis (1971) The photoperiodic time measurement in *Pectinophora gossypiella* and its relation to the circadian system in that species. In *Biochronometry,* M. Menaker, ed., pp. 212–250, National Academy of Sciences, Washington, DC.

Randall, W. (1981) A complex seasonal rhythm controlled by photoperiod. J. Comp. Physiol. *142:* 227–235.

Szabo, I., T. G. Kovats, and F. Halberg (1978) Circadian rhythm in murine reticuloendothelial function. Chronobiologia 5: 137–143.

Takahashi, J., and M. Menaker (1982) Entrainment of the circadian system of the house sparrow: A population of oscillators in pinealectomized birds. J. Comp. Physiol. 146: 245–253.

Underwood, H. (1978) Photoperiodic time-measurement in the male lizard Anolis carolinensis. J. Comp. Physiol. 125: 143–150.

Wehr, T. A., F. M. Jacobsen, D. A. Sack, J. Arendt, L. Tamarkin, and N. E. Rosenthal (1986) Phototherapy in seasonal affective disorder: Time of day and suppression of melatonin are not critical for antidepressant effects. Arch. Gen. Psychiat. 43: 870–875.

9

Seasonal Variations in Body Weight and Metabolism in Hamsters

George N. Wade

Temperate-zone mammals often exhibit dramatic seasonal fluctuations in a wide variety of behaviors and physiological processes, including reproduction, body growth and fat storage, thermoregulation, and metabolic and endocrine functions (Bittman, 1984; Bartness and Wade, 1985; Bronson, 1985; Dark and Zucker, 1985; Mrosovsky, 1985). These changes allow the animals to adjust their activities, particularly production of offspring, in anticipation of seasonal variations in food supplies and metabolic demands. The ability to anticipate these climatic changes, rather than simply to react to them, would seem to be advantageous.

Seasonal rhythms have been documented in human beings, too (Aschoff, 1981). Some examples include conception rates, mortality, growth rate, endocrine activities, and emotional states. There has been a recent surge of interest in seasonality in human beings, due to the discovery of a form of recurrent depression, seasonal affective disorder (SAD; Rosenthal *et al.*, 1984). SAD patients exhibit periods of depression in the autumn and winter, interspersed with nondepressed periods in the spring and summer. These winter depressions are accompanied by a number of physical and behavioral changes that include overeating, carbohydrate craving, and body weight gains (Rosenthal *et al.*, 1987). It appears as though the winter depression and other changes in SAD patients may be responses to changes in environmental illumination, because exposure to intense artificial light reverses many of the symptoms (Rosenthal *et al.*, 1984, 1987; Lewy *et al.*, 1987). In light-treated SAD patients, some, but not all, of these symptoms are reinstated by administration of the pineal gland hormone, melatonin (Rosenthal *et al.*, 1987).

It has been suggested that the seasonal cycles exhibited by SAD patients are simply exaggerated versions of those seen in the general population (Rosenthal *et al.*, 1987). There is certainly ample evidence for seasonal cycles in body weight and fatness in human beings. In both adults and children, weight gains

George N. Wade. Department of Psychology and Neuroscience and Behavior Program, University of Massachusetts, Amherst, Massachusetts.

(as opposed to linear growth) are reported to be greatest in autumn and winter and lowest in spring and summer (e.g., Marshall, 1937; Reynolds and Sontag, 1944; Shull *et al.*, 1978; VanStaveren *et al.*, 1986). The prevalence of obesity is generally highest in autumn or winter and lowest in summer (Johnson *et al.*, 1956; Dietz and Gortmaker, 1984). Finally, in obese women, weight loss treatments have been reported to be most effective in the spring and least effective in winter (Zahorska-Markiewicz, 1980). These seasonal weight fluctuations seem to occur in the absence of any changes in total caloric intake (VanStaveren *et al.*, 1986), suggesting that there are probably important seasonal variations in energy *expenditure*. The environmental signals for these seasonal weight cycles are not known, but the recent work with SAD patients suggests that light is probably an important cue (Rosenthal *et al.*, 1987).

One goal of this section of the present volume is to determine whether or not there are appropriate animal models for SAD and its associated phenomena, such as body weight change. There is certainly no shortage of species that exhibit seasonal fluctuations in energy metabolism and regulation of body weight and fatness. They include marmots, ground squirrels, Syrian hamsters, Djungarian hamsters, European hamsters, meadow voles, pine voles, prairie voles, dormice, rats, cattle, and sheep, to name a few (e.g., Davis, 1976; Nelson and Zucker, 1981; Tucker and Ringer, 1982; Steinlechner *et al.*, 1983; Bartness and Wade, 1985; Dark and Zucker, 1983, 1985; Mrosovsky, 1985; Nelson *et al.*, 1985; Vernon *et al.*, 1986). Of these, the most frequently studied species are probably marmots, ground squirrels, Syrian hamsters, meadow voles, and Djungarian hamsters.

Upon superficial inspection of these species Syrian (golden) hamsters *(Mesocricetus auratus)* appear to be most similar to human beings in terms of seasonal body weight change. Although marmots and ground squirrels fatten in the autumn, as SAD patients may do, they do not seem to be photoperiodic. Instead, their body weight cycles are due to endogenous, circannual rhythms for which the zeitgeber is not known (Davis, 1976; Mrosovsky, 1985; Zucker and Dark, 1986). Thus, although we can learn a great deal about the physiological bases of seasonal weight change from studying these animals, they are less than ideal subjects if one is interested in how photoperiodic cues are translated into neuroendocrine signals for body weight change. On the other hand, most hamsters and voles are photoperiodic; their seasonal cycles of reproduction and body weight are driven by daylength. However, of the more commonly studied species, only Syrian hamsters fatten in the autumn (in short days), as human beings are thought to do (Steinlechner *et al.*, 1983; Bartness and Wade, 1985; Dark and Zucker, 1985; Rosenthal *et al.*, 1987). Meadow voles and Djungarian hamsters actually lose weight in preparation for winter (in short photoperiods or during melatonin treatment).

The discussion that follows focuses largely on data from work using Syrian hamsters, although the reasons for doing so are superficial and, perhaps, inappropriate. I draw upon data from other species as necessary either to reinforce or to qualify my conclusions.

Seasonal Reproduction in Syrian Hamsters

Although the focus of this chapter is on seasonal changes in body weight and metabolism, the vast majority of the work on mammalian photoperiodism has examined reproductive function rather than energy balance. The work on seasonal weight cycles has simply used the methods and concepts from the reproduction studies and looked at different endpoints. Thus, before discussing seasonal body weight cycles in hamsters, I briefly summarize some of the principles derived from research on seasonal breeding. A number of excellent reviews of this are are available (e.g., Elliott and Goldman, 1981; Goldman, 1983; Bittman, 1984; Stetson and Watson-Whitmyre, 1984, 1986).

Syrian hamsters are long-day breeders; they will remain reproductively active as long as the daylength exceeds 12.5 hr per day. When daylength falls below this critical value, as in the autumn, circulating follicle-stimulating hormone and prolactin levels decline, the ovaries and testes become inactive, and reproductive activity ceases. After 4–5 months in short photoperiods, the hamsters become photorefractory, and there is a spontaneous recovery of reproductive function despite the fact that daylength has not yet reached 12.5 hr. This spontaneous recovery assures that the animals will be reproductively competent as soon as conditions are favorable in the spring. Prolonged exposure (>11 weeks) to long days during the summer then restores photosensitivity, so that reproduction will be arrested when daylength decreases the following autumn.

The effects of photoperiod on hamster reproduction are mediated by the pineal gland and its hormone, melatonin. Pinealectomized (PINX) Syrian hamsters remain reproductively active regardless of the photoperiod. The pineal gland secretes melatonin almost solely at night, and the duration of the nocturnal melatonin pulse is inversely related to daylength (Stetson and Watson-Whitmyre, 1986). Experiments in which PINX sheep or Djungarian hamsters were infused with physiological amounts of melatonin in different temporal patterns suggest that it is the *duration* of the melatonin secretion that conveys daylength information to the reproductive system (Carter and Goldman, 1983; Bittman, 1984; cf. Stetson and Watson-Whitmyre, 1986). A long-duration melatonin pulse mimicks short days and inhibits reproductive activity in Djungarian hamsters. Comparable melatonin infusion experiments have not yet been done in PINX Syrian hamsters because of the difficulty in maintaining long-term infusions in this species. However, exogenous injections of melatonin suppress gonadal function in long-day-housed Syrian hamsters only when given at times that would appear to extend the duration of the endogenous nocturnal melatonin pulse (Tamarkin *et al.*, 1976; Stetson and Tay, 1983). Thus, Syrian hamsters, too, may be responding to the duration of melatonin secretion. A long melatonin pulse signals short days and inhibits reproduction in hamsters.

Seasonal Body Weight Change in Syrian Hamsters

Syrian hamsters gain weight when exposed to short photoperiods or when housed in long days and given melatonin treatments that inhibit reproductive activity (Hoffman *et al.*, 1982; Campbell *et al.*, 1983; Wade, 1983; Bartness and Wade, 1984; Wade and Bartness, 1984b; McElroy and Wade, 1986; Wade *et al.*, 1986; Bartness *et al.*, 1987) (Fig. 9-1). Most of this weight gain is due to enhanced deposition of triglycerides in white adipose tissue storage depots, as reflected in fat pad weights and total carcass lipid content (Fig. 9-2).

This enhanced energy storage often occurs without any increase in food intake (Fig. 9-1), indicating that exposure to short photoperiods or treatment with melatonin decreases energy expenditure. The fact that melatonin-treated hamsters have a lowered metabolic rate (Viswanathan *et al.*, 1986a,b) supports

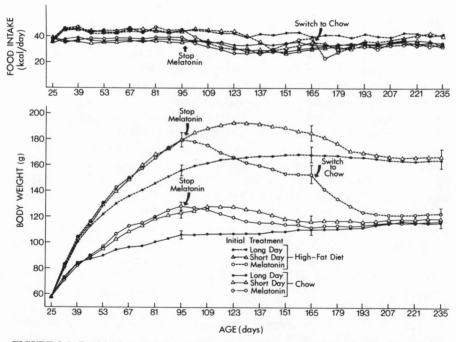

FIGURE 9-1. Food intake and body weight of female Syrian hamsters housed in long (LD 16:8) or short (LD 8:16) photoperiods. Animals housed in long photoperiods were treated with melatonin (25 μg/day, 3 hr before lights-off) or saline vehicle for 10 weeks. Animals were fed Purina chow or a high-fat diet.

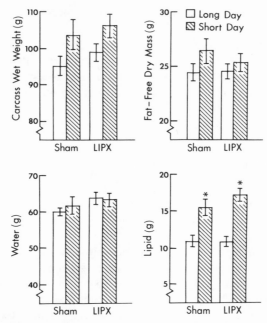

FIGURE 9-2. Carcass composition of female Syrian hamsters. Animals were sham-operated or lipectomized (LIPX) (parametrial, retroperitoneal, and inguinal fat pads removed—35–40% of total carcass lipid) prior to being placed in long (LD 16:8) or short (LD 8:16) photoperiods for 12 weeks. *$p < 0.01$.

this conclusion. Although total intake of a composite commercial chow is often unaffected by photoperiod, there may be changes in other food-related behaviors. Indeed, hoarding of food is enhanced in hamsters housed in short days (Fleming *et al.,* 1986). It is possible that other measures such as macronutrient preferences or "hunger motivation" could be affected, too.

The changes in body fat content seem to be a *regulated* response to photoperiod. If female hamsters are lipectomized (35–40% of total body lipid is excised surgically), they are able to restore their body fat completely and accurately to control levels. In addition, these lipectomized hamsters fatten to an appropriate degree when exposed to short photoperiods (Fig. 9-2). This restoration of total body fat content occurs despite the fact that the excised fat pads (parametrial, retroperitoneal, and inguinal) do not rengenerate completely. That is, the compensation takes place at other, as yet undefined, loci (Hamilton and Wade, 1988). This work replicates previous findings in ground squirrels. Lipectomized ground squirrels restore excised body fat and make seasonally appropriate adjustments in their fat stores (Dark *et al.,* 1985; Forger *et al.,* 1986). These findings are consistent with the possibility that body fat content is accurately regulated and that this regulation is particularly important in species exhibiting seasonal cycles in fatness.

Characteristics of Seasonal Body Weight Changes

Over the past few years, several lines of research have been directed at further describing and characterizing photoperiod- and melatonin-induced body weight changes in Syrian hamsters, with an eye toward comparisons with reproductive function when possible. This work is summarized below.

Reversibility

If these are indeed seasonal changes we are seeing in body weight and fatness, then they should be completely reversible. This is in fact the case (Fig. 9-1). When melatonin injections are withdrawn, hamsters promptly lose weight until they do not differ from long-day-housed, placebo-treated controls. If hamsters are kept in short photoperiods for an extended period of time (>20 weeks), they initially fatten, but then they spontaneously lose this extra weight (Figs. 9-1 and 9-3), just as gonadal function spontaneously recovers (Wade and Bartness, 1984b; Wade *et al.*, 1986). After this spontaneous recovery occurs, the hamsters are refractory both to short photoperiods and to melatonin treatment (Wade *et al.*, 1986), as is the case with reproductive function. Carcass analyses indicate that the effects of photoperiod and melatonin treatment on body fat content are completely reversible (Wade and Bartness, 1984b).

Effects of Diet

All of the actions of short photoperiods or melatonin treatments on energy balance are mimicked by feeding Syrian hamsters a high-fat diet (Wade, 1982, 1983; Bartness and Wade, 1984; Wade and Bartness, 1984b; Hamilton *et al.*,

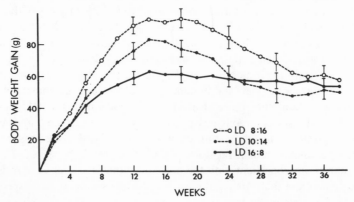

FIGURE 9-3. Body weights of female Syrian hamsters housed in three different photoperiods (LD 16:8, LD 10:14, or LD 8:16). Baseline body weight = 108 g.

1986). In addition, the weight gains induced by short photoperiods are exaggerated in the fat-fed hamsters when compared with chow-fed controls. These diet-induced increases in body weight and fatness are reversible simply by returning the hamsters to the chow diet (Fig. 9-1).

These interactions between diet and photoperiod have led us to speculate that the macronutrient composition of the diet may play a significant role in seasonal changes in energy balance in Syrian hamsters (Wade, 1982, 1983; Bartness and Wade, 1984, 1985; Wade and Bartness, 1984b; Hamilton *et al.*, 1986). One can imagine that even a modest shift in diet from primarily grasses (a low-fat diet) to more seeds and nuts (a higher-fat diet) in the autumn would promote fattening, particularly when coupled with decreasing daylength. This sort of shift in diet composition could be due to an increasing availability of seeds and nuts (preferred foods for hamsters) in the late summer and autumn or to an increasing preference for high-fat diets, as in dormice and squirrels and, perhaps, in human beings (Sherman, personal communication, 1982; VanStaveren *et al.*, 1986; Mrosovsky, Chapter 10, this volume). Unfortunately, virtually nothing is known about the food habits of Syrian hamsters in the wild. It would seem to be worthwhile to examine the effects of photoperiod on the macronutrient preferences of hamsters.

Sex Differences

Both male and female hamsters fatten when housed in short photoperiods or treated with melatonin, but females gain significantly more weight than males (Bartness and Wade, 1984). Female hamsters also fatten more than males when fed high-fat diets (Wade, 1983). These findings are not particularly surprising, given that there are sexual dimorphisms in a number of experimental rodent obesities (Cox *et al.*, 1969; Kemnitz *et al.*, 1977; Berdanier *et al.*, 1979; Bonnevie-Nielsen, 1980). (Typically females become fatter than males, but this is not always the case. For example, male golden-mantled ground squirrels fatten more than females in preparation for winter; Zucker and Boshes, 1982.) Syrian hamsters might be an ideal species in which to examine the sexual differentiation of photoperiod- or diet-induced obesity.

It is interesting to note that the vast majority of SAD patients are women (Rosenthal *et al.*, 1984, 1987). In the general population, obesity is certainly more common among women than men (Stuart and Jacobson, 1979; Hoyenga and Hoyenga, 1982), but I am not aware of any reports of sex differences in seasonal body weight change in human beings.

Timing of the Melatonin Signal

It has been noted that in Syrian hamsters exogenous melatonin injections suppress reproductive function only when given at times which extend the endogenous nocturnal melatonin peak. The same appears to be true of body weight changes. Melatonin injections given just before lights-off increase body weight of female hamsters, but injections at midday are ineffective (Wade and Bartness, 1984b).

Recent work in which PINX Djungarian hamsters were infused with melatonin in various temporal patterns clearly indicates that it is the *duration* of the melatonin pulse that signals the seasonal body weight changes in this species (Bartness and Goldman, 1986). Comparable infusion experiments have yet to be done in Syrian hamsters. The fact that adipose tissues respond to melatonin treatments with a relatively short latency (<2 weeks; see below) indicates that infusion experiments should be feasible in Syrian hamsters.

Graded Responses to Melatonin or Photoperiod

Body weight responses to short photoperiods or melatonin treatments are graded, rather than all-or-none. For example, a low dose of melatonin (2.5 μg/day) caused weight gains that were more modest than those produced by higher doses (10 or 25 μg/day). The noteworthy feature of this particular experiment is that the low dose of melatonin induced a significant increase in body weight and fatness without suppressing reproductive function (Wade and Bartness, 1984b). This is one of a number of findings (see below) indicating that the various responses to photoperiod can be independent of one another.

The graded body weight responses to various photoperiods are illustrated in Figure 9-3. Syrian hamsters exposed to 8-hr days exhibit greater weight gains that begin earlier and last longer than hamsters housed in 10-hr days (Wade *et al.*, 1986). The obvious implication of this finding is that hamsters are able to adjust their metabolic responses to different latitudes. Since the winter solstice precedes the most severe climatic conditions, hamsters at more northerly latitudes could conceivably use this daylength information to make appropriate adjustments in the magnitude and duration of their metabolic responses.

Latency of Melatonin Effects

Typically, Syrian hamsters must be treated with melatonin for several weeks before there are observable changes in reproductive function (e.g., decreased testis weights, interruption of estrous cycles (Tamarkin *et al.*, 1976; Stetson & Tay, 1983). On the other hand, melatonin effects on body weight and adipose tissues are evident within 2 weeks (Wade and Bartness, 1984; Wade *et al.*, 1986; Wade and Hamilton, unpublished data). Two weeks of melatonin treatment significantly increased the rate of weight gain, carcass lipid content (Fig. 9-4), weights of individual fat pads, and adipose tissue enzyme activities (see

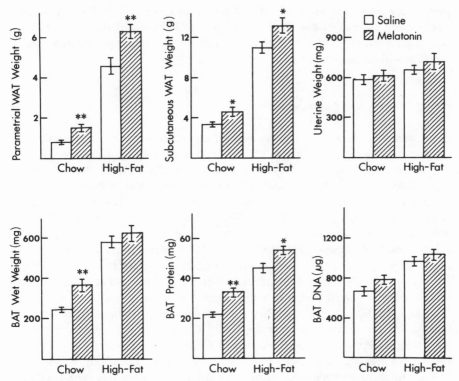

FIGURE 9-4. Tissue weights of female Syrian hamsters treated with melatonin (10 μg/day, 3 hr before lights-off) or saline vehicle for 2 weeks. Animals were fed Purina chow or a high-fat diet. BAT, brown adipose tissue; WAT, white adipose tissue. $*p < 0.05$; $**p < 0.01$.

below) in female Syrian hamsters. In these same melatonin-treated hamsters, there was no effect on estrous cyclicity or uterine weight (Wade and Hamilton, unpublished data). Thus, once again, we have dissociated the effects of melatonin on reproduction and energy balance.

Circadian Timing Mechanisms

There is now a vast literature indicating that in their seasonal reproductive cycles hamsters use circadian timing mechanisms to measure daylength (see, e.g., Elliott and Goldman, 1981, for review). That is, they respond to the relative timing of dawn and dusk, rather than to the absolute amounts of light or darkness. The same appears to be the case for body weight changes. When exposed to skeleton photoperiods (constant darkness interrupted by two 1-hr light pulses per 24 hr to simulate dawn and dusk), hamsters fatten in a skeleton 10-hr day, but not in a skeleton 16-hr day (Wade *et al.*, 1986). Thus, body weight seems to respond to the relative timing of dawn and dusk (a circadian mechanism), instead of the absolute amounts of light and darkness (an hourglass mechanism). Additional experiments utilizing resonance photoperiods and T-cycles will be necessary to confirm this conclusion.

Pineal-Independent Mechanisms

In hamsters, the effects of photoperiod on reproduction (and other functions) are mediated by the pineal gland; PINX hamsters do not respond to changes in the photoperiod (e.g., Elliott and Goldman, 1981; Goldman, 1983; Vriend, 1983; Bittman, 1984; Stetson and Watson-Whitmyre, 1984, 1986). It has become widely assumed that *all* physiological responses to photoperiod are dependent on an intact pineal gland. However, there are some responses, including changes in body weight, which also appear to be affected by pineal-independent mechanisms. Hoffman *et al.* (1982) reported that PINX male Syrian hamsters gained weight in short photoperiods. Subsequently, we replicated this finding in PINX female hamsters; when exposed to a short photoperiod, PINX hamsters gained as much body weight and fat as pineal-intact animals (Fig. 9-5). In this experiment, PINX prevented the suppression of reproductive function by the short photoperiod (Fig. 9-5), dissociating the reproductive and body weight responses again (Bartness and Wade, 1984). More recently, PINX Djungarian hamsters have been found to exhibit appropriate body weight responses to short photoperiods, albeit with a longer latency than pineal-intact hamsters (Holtorf *et al.*, 1985).

Therefore, in addition to the pineal/melatonin-mediated actions of photoperiod on body weight in Syrian and Djungarian hamsters, there seem to be additional pineal-independent mechanisms. The nature of these pineal-independent mechanisms is unclear. They may be somewhat difficult to study, because they are not always evident. We have looked for short-photoperiod-induced weight gains in PINX Syrian hamsters four times. Twice the animals gained weight, and twice they did not (Bartness, Alexander, and Wade, unpublished data). Thus, before we can study the pineal-independent effects of photoperiod on body weight, we need to determine the circumstances under which they are expressed.

Finally, pineal/melatonin-independent responses to photoperiod are not restricted to hamster body weight change. In female, but not male, Syrian hamsters, photoperiodic effects on pituitary prolactin cell activity are at least partially pineal-independent (Blask *et al.*, 1986). Of course, in human beings, some SAD-associated symptoms do not appear to be influenced by melatonin (Rosenthal *et al.*, 1987). Therefore, contrary to the prevailing opinion, pineal-independent responses to photoperiod could be fairly widespread. However, these may be fairly subtle responses and may be expressed only under certain (as yet undefined) circumstances.

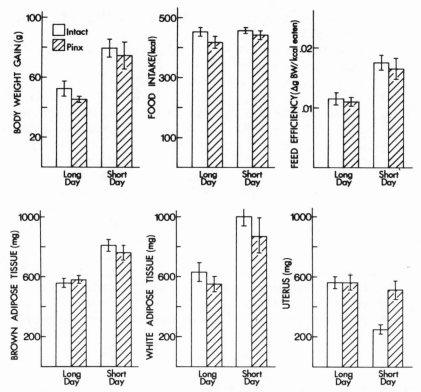

FIGURE 9-5. Body weight, food intake, and organ weights of pinealectomized (Pinx) or intact female Syrian hamsters housed in long (LD 16:8) or short (LD 8:16) photoperiods for 14 weeks. Baseline body weights = 101–108 g.

Seasonal Changes in Brown and White Adipose Tissues

Brown Adipose Tissue

The fact that Syrian hamsters housed in a short photoperiod or treated with melatonin can fatten without increasing their food intake (Fig. 9-1) suggests that these treatments reduce energy expenditure. In fact, resting metabolic rate is significantly reduced in melatonin-treated hamsters (Viswanathan *et al.*, 1986a,b). These findings raise the question of what tissues are responsible for these energy savings. Brown adipose tissue (BAT) is one obvious candidate. BAT is a major heat-producing tissue in small rodents and contains specialized mitochondria that are capable of oxidizing metabolic fuels without generating adenosine triphosphate (Nicholls and Locke, 1984). In addition to its thermoregulatory functions, BAT is thought to play a significant role in regulation of energy balance in rodents, and some obesities may be caused in part by defects in BAT thermogenesis (Girardier and Stock, 1983; Himms-Hagen, 1985; Tray-hurn and Nicholls, 1986).

However, short-photoperiod-induced changes in BAT cannot account for the decreased energy expenditure seen in Syrian hamsters. In fact, short photoperiods or melatonin treatments actually *stimulate* BAT growth and thermogenesis in both Syrian and Djungarian hamsters (Fig. 9-6) (Heldmaier and Hoffman, 1974; Heldmaier *et al.*, 1981; Bartness and Wade, 1984; McElroy *et al.*, 1986; McElroy and Wade, 1986; Viswanathan *et al.*, 1986b). Note that in Syrian hamsters this growth and increased thermogenic activity in BAT is achieved without a change in sympathetic nervous system activity (Fig. 9-6) (McElroy and Wade, 1986; Viswanathan *et al.*, 1986b). These results are consistent with earlier work on diet-induced BAT growth in Syrian hamsters (Hamilton *et al.*, 1986) and contrast with the findings in rats and mice, where sympathetic nerves play an extremely important role in BAT function (e.g., Landsberg and Young, 1983; Himms-Hagen, 1985).

Thus, melatonin-treated Syrian hamsters exhibit decreased metabolic rates and increased energy storage despite increases in BAT energy expenditure. This means that the substantial energy savings are occurring elsewhere in the body. Other than the fact that they do not seem to involve BAT, we have no evidence as to how the savings are achieved. Possibilities include decreases in futile

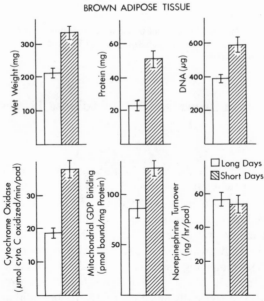

FIGURE 9-6. Brown adipose tissue weight, cytochrome oxidase activity, mitochondrial guanosine diphosphate (GDP) binding, and norepinephrine turnover in female Syrian hamsters housed in long (LD 16:8) or short (LD 8:16) photoperiods for 11 weeks.

metabolic cycles and sodium pumping in tissues such as liver or skeletal muscle. Photoperiod- or melatonin-induced decreases in voluntary exercise (Widmaier and Campbell, 1980; Ellis and Turek, 1983) would conserve energy but cannot account for the reductions in resting metabolic rate (Viswanathan *et al.*, 1986a,b). Decreases in heat loss certainly contribute to the energy savings. Heat conservation may be accomplished via changes in pelage, distribution of body fat, and thermoregulatory behaviors (Heldmaier and Steinlechner, 1981; Dark and Zucker, 1983, 1985; Wade and Bartness, 1984a).

Finally, although changes in BAT do not contribute to the observed energy savings, they almost certainly play an important role in thermoregulation. That is, photoperiod-induced BAT growth is associated with an increase in thermogenic capacity in hamsters (e.g., Bartness and Wade, 1984; Heldmaier *et al.*, 1982) and other species.

White Adipose Tissue

Given the dramatic effects of photoperiod or melatonin treatments on white adipose tissue mass in hamsters, it is somewhat surprising that we know rather little about how these changes are accomplished. For example, we do not even know whether the seasonal cycles in fatness are due to changes in the filling of existing adipocytes or to changes in cell number. Since the changes in fatness are completely reversible (Wade and Bartness, 1984b; Wade *et al.*, 1986), it seems likely that they are the result of changes in cell size, rather than number. It would not appear to make sense to add fat cells in the autumn, particularly if they could not be shed the following spring. Indeed, at least in woodchucks, the seasonal weight gains are due to lipid deposition in existing adipocytes, rather than to an increase in the number of fat cells (Young *et al.*, 1982).

Recent work has begun to describe some of the metabolic changes in hamster white adipose tissue. In Syrian hamsters, treatment with melatonin for 2 weeks significantly increases white adipose tissue lipoprotein lipase activity (Fig. 9-7) (Wade and Hamilton, unpublished data). Therefore, the increases in body fat content in these animals (Fig. 9-4) are due in part to enhanced uptake of circulating chylomicron- or very-low-density-lipoprotein-derived fatty acids by adipose tissues. In Djungarian hamsters, photoperiod-induced changes in fatness are accompanied by changes in both lipoprotein lipase activity and in *de novo* lipogenesis (tritium incorporation into newly synthesized fatty acids from tritiated water) (Bartness, Wade, and Hamilton, unpublished data). It is likely that future work will reveal that in both species of hamsters, seasonal changes in body lipid stores are due to coordinated changes in several metabolic processes in adipocytes (e.g., lipoprotein lipase activity, *in situ* lipogenesis, and hormone-sensitive lipase activity).

As noted above, these seasonal changes in total body fat stores seem to be rather precisely regulated (e.g., Dark *et al.*, 1985; Forger *et al.*, 1986;

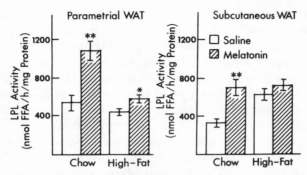

FIGURE 9-7. White adipose tissue (WAT) lipoprotein lipase activity in female Syrian hamsters treated with melatonin (10 μg/day, 3 hr before lights-off) or saline vehicle for 2 weeks. Animals were fed Purina chow or a high-fat diet. $*p < 0.05$; $**p < 0.01$.

Hamilton and Wade, 1988). Although there seems to be no shortage of hypotheses as to how this sort of regulation might be achieved, the experimental evidence is less than conclusive.

Physiological Signals for Changes in Energy Balance

A major remaining question is this: What are the neuroendocrine signals to the adipose tissues and other organs that exhibit seasonal change? Once photoperiodic information is received, any number of efferent pathways could be activated. They involve both neural and endocrine outputs.

The autonomic nervous system could play a role. The paraventricular nucleus of the hypothalamus (PVN) receives photoperiod information via the retinohypothalamic tract and the suprachiasmatic nuclei (Klein *et al.*, 1983; Lehman *et al.*, 1984). The PVN influences both autonomic activity (including pineal function) and regulatory behaviors (Leibowitz *et al.*, 1981; Klein *et al.*, 1983; Lehman *et al.*, 1984; Luiten *et al.*, 1985), providing potential neural mechanisms for both pineal-dependent and -independent control of energy balance.

Although sympathetic activity (norepinephrine turnover) in BAT is not affected by daylength, melatonin treatment and exposure to a short photoperiod have been reported to suppress cardiac norepinephrine turnover in Syrian hamsters (Viswanathan *et al.*, 1986a,b; but cf. McElroy and Wade, 1986). Because a suppression of sympathetic activity would be expected to facilitate fattening, it would be worthwhile to determine how widespread and reproducible this phenomenon is. One could also examine the effects of sympathectomy on seasonal body weight changes. Parasympathetic nerves may not be crucial for the expression of seasonal weight change. Vagotomized ground squirrels continued to show normal circannual body weight cycles (Powley and Fox, 1986), but this finding certainly does not preclude any role for parasympathetic nerves.

A wide variety of possible photoperiod-induced hormonal signals could influence energy balance. The most obvious is melatonin. Melatonin could affect energy balance directly, or it could do so by altering the secretion of other hormones. Target sites for melatonin action have not yet been identified conclusively, but melatonin receptors have been described in the brain (e.g., Niles *et al.*, 1979; Duncan *et al.*, 1986). Intrahypothalamic melatonin injections have been reported to affect reproduction in white-footed mice (Glass and Lynch, 1982) and body weight in Syrian hamsters (Bartness and Wade, 1985). In addition to possible neural sites of action, melatonin could act concurrently in peripheral tissues, as other hormones do (Wade, 1986).

Other potential hormonal mediators of photoperiodic actions on energy balance include gonadotropins, prolactin, gonadal steroids, thyroid hormones, glucocorticoids, and insulin. These hormonal signals are probably driven by melatonin, but at least some of them might be influenced by extrapineal mechanisms, too.

Several lines of evidence indicate that changes in gonadotropins, gonadal steroids, and prolactin are not required in order to see photoperiod-induced body weight fluctuations in Syrian hamsters: (1) Ovariectomized hamsters fatten when housed in short photoperiods, indicating that the weight gains are not simply due to a photic castration (Bartness and Wade, 1984). (2) Low doses of melatonin (2.5 μg/day) induce fattening in Syrian hamsters without interrupting estrous cycles or affecting uterine weights (Wade and Bartness, 1984b). (3) Exposure to short photoperiods can cause fattening in PINX female hamsters without suppressing reproductive function (Bartness and Wade, 1984). (4) Relatively brief treatments with melatonin (2 weeks) affect adipose tissues without affecting estrous cycles or uterine weights (Figs. 9-4 and 9-7) (Wade and Hamilton, unpublished data). (5) Experimental manipulations of circulating prolactin levels within the physiological range do not affect body weight responses to photoperiod in either Syrian or Djungarian hamsters (Bartness *et al.*, 1987). Thus, although a photic suppression of gonadal steroid production probably contributes to short-photoperiod-induced weight gains in Syrian hamsters (Bartness and Wade, 1984, 1985), changes in reproductive hormones are not required for the seasonal weight changes.

Exposure to short photoperiods decreases circulating titers of thyroid hormones in several species, including Syrian hamsters (see Vriend, 1983, for review). This decrease in thyroid activity could help to account for the reduced metabolic rate, enhanced energy savings, and increased lipid storage that are seen in melatonin-treated or short-photoperiod-housed hamsters. However, the fact that suppression of thyroid activity with propylthiouracil does not cause body weight gains in Syrian hamsters (Morin *et al.*, 1986) would seem to suggest that reduced thyroid hormone section is not sufficient to account for the photoperiod-induced weight changes. As in the case of gonadal steroids, this sort of evidence does not rule out the possibility that changes in thyroid activity could participate as one of several endocrine changes influencing seasonal cycles in body weight and metabolism.

Adrenal glucocorticoids also seem to play a role in body weight regulation

(Dallman, 1984); in rats and mice, several experimental obesities are prevented by adrenalectomy (e.g., Debons *et al.*, 1982; King and Smith, 1985). Not much is known about the effects of photoperiod on adrenocortical activity in hamsters, although the amplitude of the daily rhythm in circulating cortisol levels may be reduced in short photoperiods (T. J. Bartness, personal communication, 1987). It would be interesting to see whether the fattening induced by short photoperiods or melatonin treatments is prevented by adrenalectomy, as some other experimental obesities are. It may be noteworthy that the effects of high-fat diets on energy balance (Wade, 1982, 1983; Bartness and Wade, 1984; Wade and Bartness, 1984b; Hamilton *et al.*, 1986) are not blocked by adrenalectomy in Syrian hamsters (McElroy and Wade, unpublished data).

The possibility that insulin plays an important role in seasonal body weight cycles has received a great deal of attention, particularly among investigators studying hibernators (see, e.g., Florant and Bauman, 1985; Mrosovsky, 1985). Seasonal changes in carbohydrate metabolism, insulin levels, insulin sensitivity, insulin binding, and so on have been reported in marmots, dormice, and ground squirrels. Unfortunately, in a system as complicated as this one, it is difficult to discern the direction of causality. In hamsters, perhaps the first step should be to make animals severely diabetic, replace insulin in sufficient levels to prevent glycosuria, and then see whether photoperiod affects energy balance. If animals with clamped insulin levels still show appropriate body weight changes in various photoperiods, one could then look for changes in insulin sensitivity (tissue insulin binding). This might be the most direct way to investigate the role (if any) of insulin in hamster seasonal weight cycles.

To summarize, there are quite a few neural and endocrine pathways that could participate in photoperiodic control of body weight and metabolism. Although a number of these candidates do not seem to be required for the expression of seasonal body weight changes (e.g., gonadal steroids, prolactin, the vagi), none has been ruled out as a contributor. It is not unlikely that seasonal metabolic changes are mediated by multiple, redundant mechanisms, just as gonadal effects on energy balance seem to be (Wade, 1986). Thus, no single mechanism would be essential, because the others would be capable of compensating for its absence. It makes sense to design an animal this way, but it is not particularly convenient for those of us trying to determine the physiological bases of seasonal body weight cycles.

Conclusions and Future Directions

A number of mammalian species exhibit dramatic seasonal fluctuations in reproduction, body weight regulation, and thermoregulation. Although these functions typically cycle in synchrony with one another across the seasons, they appear to be separate and independent responses. Within a species, they can be dissociated by appropriate experimental manipulations. For example, we have separated seasonal changes in reproduction and energy balance in several ways. Comparisons across species also reveal a variety of patterns of seasonal change: short-day versus long-day breeders (e.g., sheep vs. hamsters); short-day versus long-day fatteners (e.g., Syrian hamsters vs. Djungarian hamsters); and species that show seasonal weight cycles but are not seasonal breeders (e.g., rats, cattle, and perhaps human beings). The only consistencies across these species seems to be that reproduction is timed so that the young are born in the spring and that thermoregulatory adjustments are made prior to winter.

The fact that the various responses to photoperiod are independent of one another is not without implications for the study of SAD. SAD patients appear to exhibit a wide variety of change in behaviors and physiological functions, and there is no reason to assume that all of these changes are inextricably linked to one another. For example, we have already seen that some components respond to melatonin treatment, whereas others do not. Thus, if one is interested in understanding the depression seen in SAD patients, an important step would be to determine just which aspects of the syndrome are consistently linked with the depression and which ones are not. In that way, it would be possible to narrow the focus of the work on physiological mechanisms of the depression.

Most responses to photoperiod seem to be mediated by the pineal gland and its hormone, melatonin. How the melatonin signal is translated into metabolic change is not known. Timed melatonin infusions in PINX Djungarian hamsters and sheep indicate that these species are responding to the duration of the nocturnal melatonin pulse, but comparable work has not been done yet in Syrian hamsters. The tissues detecting the melatonin signal have not been unambiguously defined, although hypothalamic sites (including the PVN) are among the leading candidates. Progress in elucidating sites and mechanisms of melatonin action awaits the development of reliable melatonin receptor assays.

Once the melatonin signal is generated by the pineal and detected by the various target tissues, it must be translated into neuroendocrine signals to the tissues processing and storing energy (e.g., adipose tissues). Again, there is no shortage of candidates, and the animals may use multiple, redundant pathways and mechanisms to make seasonally appropriate metabolic responses.

There is also evidence for pineal-independent responses to daylength, including body weight change in Syrian and Djungarian hamsters. One challenge will be to define the exact circumstances under which the pineal-independent metabolic responses are expressed, because in our hands PINX Syrian hamsters do not always gain weight in short photoperiods. There may be some particular genetic or environmental factors that predispose animals to exhibit pineal-independent responses. Once we can elicit body weight responses reliably in PINX hamsters, we can go on to compare and contrast pineal-dependent and -independent mechanisms.

One important question is this: Do the two kinds of mechanisms influence metabolism and body weight via the same neuroendocrine pathways? An interesting possibility is that some hypothalamic site(s) that have direct access to photoperiodic information, such as the PVN or suprachiasmatic nuclei, could also be melatonin target tissues. These structures then could be activated directly by neural inputs (via the retinohypothalamic tract) or indirectly by melatonin. This is just one of several testable hypotheses as to how photic information could be transmitted to central and peripheral tissues.

Acknowledgments

Preparation of this chapter was supported by Research Grant Nos. DK 32976-04 and NS 10873-15 from the National Institutes of Health and by Research Scientist Development Award No. MH 00321-07 from the National Institute of Mental Health. I am grateful to Anita Bhatia, Jill Schneider, and Irving Zucker for helpful advice and discussions. I am also greatly indebted to Jan Alexander, Tim Bartness, Joan Hamilton, and John McElroy, who actually performed much of the work described in this chapter.

References

Aschoff, J. (1981) Annual rhythms in man. In *Handbook of Behavioral Neurobiology,* Vol. 4, *Biological Rhythms,* J. Aschoff, ed., pp. 475–487, Plenum, New York.

Bartness, T. J., and B. D. Goldman (1986) Timed melatonin infusions in adult Siberian hamsters: Effects on body weight, body fat, lipid metabolism and gonadal activity. Soc. Neurosci. Abstr. *12:* 843.

Bartness, T. J., and G. N. Wade (1984) Photoperiodic control of body weight and energy metabolism in Syrian hamsters *(Mesocricetus auratus):* Role of pineal gland, melatonin, gonads, and diet. Endocrinology *114:* 492–498.

Bartness, T. J., and G. N. Wade (1985) Photoperiodic control of seasonal body weight cycles in hamsters. Neurosci. Biobehav. Rev. *9:* 599–612.

Bartness, T. J., G. N. Wade, and B. D. Goldman (1987) Are short-photoperiod-induced decreases in serum prolactin responsible for seasonal changes in energy balance in Syrian and Siberian hamsters? J. Exp. Zool. *244:* 437–454.

Berdanier, C. D., R. D. Tobin, V. DeVore, and L. Cook (1979) Effect of sex on the strain differences in hepatic metabolism of starved and nonstarved rats. J. Nutr. *109:* 272–280.

Bittman, E. L. (1984) Melatonin and photoperiodic time measurement: Evidence from rodents and ruminants. In *The Pineal Gland,* R. J. Reiter, ed., pp. 155–192, Raven Press, New York.

Blask, D. E., C. A. Leadem, K. M. Orstead, and B. R. Larsen (1986) Prolactin cell activity in female and male Syrian hamsters: An apparent sexually dimorphic response to light deprivation and pinealectomy. Neuroendocrinology *42:* 15–20.

Bonnevie-Nielsen, V. (1980) Experimental diets affect pancreatic insulin and glucagon differently in male and female mice. Metabolism *29:* 386–391.

Bronson, F. H. (1985) Mammalian reproduction: An ecological perspective. Biol.Reprod. *32:* 1–26.

Campbell, C. S., J. Tabor, and J. D. Davis (1983) Small effect of brown adipose tissue and major effect of photoperiod on body weight in hamsters *(Mesocricetus auratus).* Physiol. Behav. *30:* 349–352.

Carter, D. S., and B. D. Goldman (1983) Antigonadal effects of timed melatonin infusion in pinealectomized Djungarian hamsters *(Phodopus sungorus sungorus):* Duration is the critical parameter. Endocrinology *113:* 1261–1267.

Cox, V. C., J. W. Kakolewski, and E. S. Valenstein (1969) Ventromedial hypothalamus lesions and changes in body weight and food consumption in male and female rats. J. Comp. Physiol. Psychol. *67:* 320–326.

Dallman, M. F. (1984) Viewing the ventromedial hypothalamus from the adrenal gland. Amer. J. Physiol. *248:* R1–R12.

Dark, J., N. G. Forger, J. S. Stern, and I. Zucker (1985) Recovery of lipid mass after removal of adipose tissue in ground squirrels. Amer. J. Physiol. *249:* R73–R78.

Dark, J., and I. Zucker (1983) Short photoperiods reduce winter energy requirements of the meadow vole, *Microtus pennsylvanicus.* Physiol. Behav. *31:* 699–702.

Dark, J., and I. Zucker (1985) Seasonal cycles in energy balance: Regulation by light. Ann. NY Acad. Sci. *453:* 170–181.

Davis, D. E. (1976) Hibernation and circannual rhythms of food consumption in marmots and ground squirrels. Quart. Rev. Biol. *51:* 477–514.

Debons, A. F., E. Siclari, K. C. Das, and B. Fuhr (1982) Gold thioglucose-induced hypothalamic damage, hyperphagia, and obesity: Dependence on the adrenal gland. Endocrinology *110:* 2024–2029.

Dietz, W. H., Jr. and S. L. Gortmaker (1984) Factors within the physical environment associated with childhood obesity. Amer. J. Clin. Nutr. *39:* 619–624.

Duncan, M. J., J. S. Takahasi, and M. L. Dubocovich (1986) Binding characteristics of 2-[^{125}I]-iodomelatonin in hamster brain membranes. Soc Neurosci. Abstr. *12:* 994.

Elliott, J. A., and B. D. Goldman (1981) Seasonal reproduction: Photoperiodism and biological clocks. In *Neuroendocrinology of Reproduction,* N. T. Adler, ed., pp. 377–423, Plenum, New York.

Ellis, G. B., and F. W. Turek (1983) Testosterone and photoperiod interact to regulate locomotor activity in male hamsters. Physiol. Behav. *17:* 66–75.

Fleming, A. S., D. S. Scardicchio, and L. G. Scardicchio (1986) Photoperiodic and pineal effects on food intake, food retrieval, and body weight in female hamsters, J. Biol. Rhythms *1:* 285–302.

Florant, G. A., and W. A. Bauman (1985) Seasonal variations in carbohydrate metabolism in mammalian hibernators: Insulin and body weight changes. In *Recent Advances in Obesity Research IV,* J. Hirsch and T. B. Vanltallie, eds., pp. 57–64, John Libbey, London.

Forger, N. G., J. Dark, and I. Zucker (1986) Recovery of white adipose tissue after lipectomy in female ground squirrels. Can. J. Zool. *64:* 128–131.

Girardier, L., and M. J. Stock, eds. (1983) *Mammalian Thermogenesis,* Chapman & Hall, London.

Glass, J. D., and G. R. Lynch (1982) Diurnal rhythm of response to chronic intrahypothalamic melatonin injections in the white-footed mouse, *Peromyscus leucopus.* Neuroendocrinology *35:* 117–122.

Goldman, B. D. (1983) The physiology of melatonin in mammals. In *Pineal Research Review,* Vol. 1, R. J. Reiter, ed., pp. 145–182, Alan R. Liss, New York.

Hamilton, J. M., P. W. Mason, J. F. McElroy, and G. N. Wade (1986) Dissociation of sympathetic and thermogenic activity in brown fat of Syrian hamsters. Amer. J. Physiol. *250:* R389–R395.

Hamilton, J. M., and G. N. Wade (1988) Lipectomy does not impair fattening induced by short photoperiods or high-fat diets in female Syrian hamsters. Physiol. Bchav. *43:* 85–92.

Heldmaier, G., and K. Hoffmann (1974) Melatonin stimulates growth of brown adipose tissue. Nature *247:* 224–225.

Heldmaier, G., and S. Steinlechner (1981) Seasonal control of energy requirements for thermoregulation in the Djungarian hamster *(Phodopus sungorus)* living in natural photoperiod. J. Comp. Physiol. B. *142:* 429–437.

Heldmaier, G., S. Steinlechner, and J. Rafael (1982) Nonshivering thermogenesis and cold resistance during seasonal acclimation in the Djungarian hamster. J. Comp. Physiol. B *149:* 1–9.

Heldmaier, G., S. Steinlechner, J. Rafael, and P. Vsiansky (1981) Photoperiodic control and effects of melatonin on non-shivering thermogenesis and brown adipose tissue. Science *212:* 917–919.

Himms-Hagen, J. (1985) Brown adipose tissue metabolism and thermogenesis. An. Rev. Nutr. *5:* 69–94.

Hoffman, R. A., K. Davidson, and K. Steinberg (1982) Influence of photoperiod and temperature on weight gain, food consumption, fat pads and thyroxine in male golden hamsters. Growth *46:* 150–162.

Holtorf, A. P., G. Heldmaier, G. Thiele, and S. Steinlechner (1985) Diurnal changes in sensitivity to melatonin in intact and pinealectomized Djungarian hamsters: Effects on thermogenesis, cold tolerance, and gonads. J. Pineal Res. *2:* 393–403.

Hoyenga, K. B., and K. T. Hoyenga (1982) Gender and energy balance: Sex differences in adaptations for feast and famine. Physiol. Behav. *28:* 545–563.

Johnson, M. L., B. S. Burke, and J. Mayer (1956) The prevalence and incidence of obesity in a cross-section of elementary and secondary school children. Amer. J. Clin. Nutr. *4:* 231–238.

Kemnitz, J. W., R. W. Goy, and R. E. Keesey (1977) Effects of gonadectomy on hypothalamic obesity in male and female rats. Int. J. Obesity *1:* 259–270.

King, B. M., and R. L. Smith (1985) Hypothalamic obesity after hypophysectomy or adrenalectomy: Dependence on corticosterone. Am. J. Physiol. *249:* R522–R526.

Klein, D. C., R. Smoot, J. L. Weller, S. Higa, A. P. Markey, G. J. Creed, and D. M. Jacobowitz (1983) Lesions of the paraventricular nucleus area of the hypothalamus disrupt the suprachiasmatic–spinal cord circuit in the melatonin rhythm generating system. Brain Res. Bull. *10:* 647–652.

Landsberg, L., and J. B. Young (1983) Autonomic regulation of thermogenesis. In *Mammalian Thermogenesis,* L. Girardier and M. J. Stock, eds., pp. 99–140, Chapman & Hall, London.

Lehman, M. N., E. L. Bittman, and S. W. Newman (1984) Role of the hypothalamic paraventricular nucleus in neuroendocrine responses to daylength in the golden hamster. Brain Res. *308:* 28–32.

Leibowitz, S. F., N. J. Hammer, and K. Chang (1981) Hypothalamic paraventricular nucleus lesions produce overeating and obesity in the rat. Physiol. Behav. *27:* 1031–1040.

Lewy, A. J., R. L. Sack, S. Miller, and T. M. Hoban (1987) Antidepressant and circadian phase-shifting effects of light. Science *235:* 352–354.

Luiten, P. G. M., G. J. terHorst, and A. B. Steffens (1985) The course of paraventricular hypothalamic efferents to autonomic structures in medulla and spinal cord. Brain Res. *329:* 374–378.

Marshall, E. L. (1937) A review of American research on seasonal variation in stature and body weight. J. Pediatr. *10:* 819–829.

McElroy, J. F., P. W. Mason, J. M. Hamilton, and G. N. Wade (1986) Effect of diet and photoperiod on NE turnover and GDP binding in Siberian hamster brown adipose tissue. Amer. J. Physiol. *250:* R383–R388.

McElroy, J. F., and G. N. Wade (1986) Short photoperiod stimulates brown adipose tissue growth and thermogenesis but not norepinephrine turnover in Syrian hamsters. Physiol. Behav. *37:* 307–311.

Morin, L. P., M. L. Gavin, and J. E. Ottenweller (1986) Proplythiouracil causes phase delays and circadian period lengthening in male and female hamsters. Amer. J. Physiol. *250:* R151–R160.

Mrosovsky, N. (1985) Cyclical obesity in hibernators: The search for the adjustable regulator. In *Recent Advances in Obesity Research IV,* J. Hirsch and T. B. Vanltallie, eds., pp. 45–56, John Libbey, London.

Nelson, R. J., A. S. Fleming, C. J. Wysocki, T. W. Shinder, and I. Zucker (1985) Chemosensory and neural influences on photoperiodic responsiveness of laboratory rats. Neuroendocrinology *40:* 285–290.

Nelson, R. J., and I. Zucker (1981) Photoperiodic control of reproduction in olfactory-bulbectomized rats. Neuroendocrinology 32: 266–271.

Nicholls, D. G., and R. Locke (1984) Thermogenic mechanisms in brown fat. Physiol. Rev. 64: 1–64.

Niles, L. P., Y.-W. Wong, R. K. Mishra, and G. M. Brown (1979) Melatonin receptors in brain. Eur. J. Pharmacol. 55: 219–220.

Powley, T. L., and E. A. Fox (1986) Vagotomy does not alter circannual body weight cycles in the hibernator Citellus lateralis. Brain Res. 364: 159–161.

Reynolds, E. L., and L. W. Sontag (1944) Seasonal variationa in weight, height, and appearance of ossification centers. J. Pediatr. 24: 524–535.

Rosenthal, N. E., M. Genhart, F. M. Jacobsen, R. G. Skwerer, and T. A. Wehr (1987) Disturbances of appetite and weight regulation in seasonal affective disorder. Ann. NY Acad. Sci. 499: 216–230.

Rosenthal, N. E., D. A. Sack, C. Gillin, A. J. Lewy, F. K. Goodwin, Y. Davenport, P. S. Mueller, D. A. Newsome, and T. A. Wehr (1984) Seasonal affective disorder: A description of the syndrome and preliminary findings with light therapy. Arch Gen. Psychiat. 41: 72–80.

Shull, M., I. Valadian, R. B. Reed, R. Palombo, H. Thorne, and J. Dwyer (1978) Seasonal variations in preschool vegetarian children's growth velocities. Amer. J. Clin. Nutr. 31: 1–2.

Steinlechner, S., G. Heldmaier, and H. Becker (1983) The seasonal cycle of body weight in the Djungarian hamster: Photoperiodic control and the influence of starvation and melatonin. Oecologia 60: 401–405.

Stetson, M. H., and D. E. Tay (1983) Time-course of sensitivity of golden hamsters to melatonin injections throughout the day. Biol. Reprod. 29: 432–438.

Stetson, M. H., and M. Watson-Whitmyre (1984) Physiology of the pineal and its hormone melatonin in annual reproduction in rodents. In The Pineal Gland, R. J. Reiter, ed., pp. 109–153, Raven Press, New York.

Stetson, M. H., and M. Watson-Whitmyre (1986) Effects of exogenous and endogenous melatonin on gonadal function in hamsters. J. Neural Trans. (Suppl. 21): 55–80.

Stuart, R. B., and B. Jackson (1979) Sex differences in obesity. In Gender and Disordered Behavior, E. S. Gomberg and V. Franks, eds., pp. 241–256, Brunner/Mazel, New York.

Tamarkin, L., W. K. Westrom, A. I. Hamill, and B. D. Goldman (1976) Effect of melatonin on the reproductive systems of male and female Syrian hamsters: A diurnal rhythm in sensitivity to melatonin. Endocrinology 99: 1534–1541.

Trayhurn, P., and D. G. Nicholls (1986) Brown Adipose Tissue, Edward Arnold, Baltimore.

Tucker, H. A., and R. K. Ringer (1982) Controlled photoperiodic environments for food animals. Science 216: 1381–1386.

VanStaveren, W. A., P. Deurenberg, J. Burema, L. C. P. G. M. DeGroot, and J. G. A. J. Hautvast (1986) Seasonal variation in food intake, pattern of physical activity and change in body weight in a group of young adult Dutch women consuming self-selected diets. Int. J. Obesity 10: 133–145.

Vernon, R. G., R. A. Clegg, and D. J. Flint (1986) Adipose tissue metabolism in sheep: Response to season and its modulation by reproductive state. Horm. Metab. Res. 18: 308–312.

Viswanathan, M., R. Hissa, and J. C. George (1986a) Suppression of sympathetic nervous system by short photoperiod and melatonin in the Syrian hamster. Life Sci. 38: 73–79.

Viswanathan, M., R. Hissa, and J. C. George (1986b) Effects of short photoperiod and melatonin treatment on thermogenesis in the Syrian hamster. J. Pineal Res. 3: 311–321.

Vriend, J. (1983) Evidence for pineal gland modulation of the neuroendocrine–thyroid axis. Neuroendocrinology 36: 68–78.

Wade, G. N. (1982) Obesity without overeating in golden hamsters. Physiol. Behav. 29: 701–707.

Wade, G. N. (1983) Dietary obesity in golden hamsters: Reversibility and effects of sex and photoperiod. Physiol. Behav. 30: 131–137.

Wade, G. N. (1986) Sex steroids and energy balance: Sites and mechanisms of action. Ann. NY Acad. Sci. *474:* 389–399.

Wade, G. N., and T. J. Bartness (1984a) Effects of photoperiod and gonadectomy on food intake, body weight, and body composition in Siberian hamsters. Amer. J. Physiol. *246:* R26–R30.

Wade, G. N., and T. J. Bartness (1984b) Seasonal obesity in Syrian hamsters: Effects of age, diet, photoperiod and melatonin. Amer. J. Physiol. *247:* R328–R334.

Wade, G. N., T. J. Bartness, and J. R. Alexander (1986) Photoperiod and body weight in female Syrian hamsters: Skeleton photoperiods, response magnitude, and development of photorefractoriness. Physiol. Behav. *37:* 863–868.

Widmaier, E. P., and C. S. Campbell (1980) Interaction of estradiol and photoperiod on activity patterns in the female hamster. Physiol. Behav. *24:* 923–930.

Young, R. A., L. B. Salans, and E. A. H. Sims (1982) Adipose tissue cellularity in woodchucks: Effects of season and captivity at an early age. J. Lipid Res. *23:* 887–892.

Zahorska-Markiewicz, B. (1980) Weight reduction and seasonal variation. Int. J. Obesity *4:* 139–143.

Zucker, I., and M. Boshes (1982) Circannual body weight rhythms of ground squirrels: Role of gonadal hormones. Amer. J. Physiol. *243:* R546–R551.

Zucker, I., and J. Dark (1986) Neuroendocrine substrates of circannual rhythms in ground squirrels. In *Living in the Cold: Physiological and Biochemical Adaptations,* H. C. Heller, X. J. Musacchia, and L. C. H. Wang, eds., pp. 351–358, Elsevier, New York.

10

Seasonal Affective Disorder, Hibernation, and Annual Cycles in Animals: Chipmunks in the Sky

N. Mrosovsky

It is remarkable that psychiatrists should be interested in hibernation, because hibernation is unlikely to have evolved in man; there is no need for it. It has long been known that hibernation is absent or minimal in large mammals (Morrison, 1960). The reason is that metabolic rate per gram of tissue is proportional to body weight$^{0.75}$ (or some similar exponent). As French (1986) has reaffirmed,

> When mammals are compared under similar environmental conditions and with similar percentages of their masses as body fat, then energy stores scale directly with mass (M)[1] whereas the rate that energy is used during euthermia scales approximately with mass$^{3/4}$ at temperatures within thermal neutrality. . . . Therefore, as body size increases, the ability to store fat increases faster than the rate of fat metabolization. Small species will deplete their fat reserves in only a few days unless they become torpid, but large species potentially can remain euthermic for many months without eating. In fact, no mammal over approximately 5 kg in mass has evolved the capacity to reduce its body temperature more than a few degrees even though many of them, such as bears [Hock, 1960], have long dormant (inactive) seasons.

Even the few degrees Centigrade of hypothermia sometimes seen in bears (Hock, 1960; see also Morrison, 1960) are unlikely to occur in people over the winter because they do not become anorexic. If anything, they may eat more (see below).

The essential general points about the selective pressures for hibernation and their relationship to size have been made by Bartholomew (1986):

> [T]he evolutionary forces . . . that have produced and now sustain hibernation and other types of temporal heterothermy are not primarily related to

N. Mrosovsky. Departments of Zoology and Psychology, University of Toronto, Toronto, Ontario, Canada.

thermoregulation *per se*, but to the temporal scheduling of the rates at which
energy transactions take place. . . .

The inverse relationship between body mass and the advantages of seasonal dormancy are obvious and can be adduced without reference to specific
taxon or special ecological circumstances.

Despite such considerations, there have been repeated proposals that hibernation may be a useful model for depression. Two different aspects of depression
have interested psychiatrists in hibernation: the apparently withdrawn state and
the periodicity of its manifestations. Although not mutually exclusive, these are
sometimes confused in animal models, and must be distinguished.

Torpor as a Model for the Depressed State

A number of recent investigators have been impressed by similarities between
hibernation and depression. Feierman *et al.* (1978) indicated that hibernation
might be a model for depression, in that the antidepressant imipramine reduced
the amount of torpor in ground squirrels. Wirz-Justice *et al.* (1986) have written that the parallel between depression and hibernation "is a potential neurobiological model for SAD." Kripke (1981) says that "perhaps depression in
humans is to some extent analogous to animal hibernation, while mania may
resemble a rutting response." Zvolsky *et al.* (1981), working with golden hamsters, also found that imipramine reduced the amount of torpor; they remarked
on the "striking analogies and similarities between hibernation and depression."

Notwithstanding the distinguished ancestry of such ideas (Lange, 1928),
the similarities between these two states have never been apparent to me. I
suspect that they are little more than anthropomorphic projections based on the
curled-up posture and inertness of hibernation. Of course, at 5°C the mammalian motor system lacks agility, but hibernating animals are capable of vocal-
izing (Strumwasser, 1959), of reacting in other ways to mechanical and thermal
stimuli (Leucke and South, 1972) and of arousing themselves if these stimuli
persist. As soon as reasonably coordinated movement is possible, ground squirrels will bar-press to obtain rewarding brain stimulation (Mrosovsky, 1966).
The torpid hibernator, in its own cold way, is trying to react appropriately to
circumstances.

Hibernation as a Model for Periodic Events

It has also been suggested that hibernation can be used as "an animal model
of periodic events" (Zvolsky *et al.*, 1981). This is the idea informing recent
studies showing that lithium reduced hibernation in Turkish hamsters (Giedke
and Pohl, 1985). Used in this way, it is not evident that hibernation is superior

to other periodic events as an index of clock-related processes. In some ways it is probably a poor choice, in that it can be readily influenced by nonspecific factors such as noise or other disturbances.

Hibernation itself, at least in laboratory conditions, is only an optional part of the endogenous circannual cycle in ground squirrels. In a room sufficiently warm to permit only shallow sporadic hibernation, rhythms of body weight, reproductive state, and molt still persist (Joy and Mrosovsky, 1982). Even in a cold room, there are often one or two individuals out of a larger group that do not become torpid, yet still show seasonal changes in weight (Mrosovsky, 1971). Body weight cycles in ground squirrels are extremely robust. A variety of brain lesions, including the ablation of the pineal or suprachiasmatic nuclei, fail to abolish these cycles (for reviews, see Mrosovsky, 1985; Zucker and Dark, 1986).

In the experiments cited with imipramine and lithium, there was no evidence that temporal processes were altered. The drugs might just as well have disrupted the expression of hibernation. For instance, lithium has diuretic effects. Other diuretics, such as potassium or urea (Fisher, 1964; Fisher and Mrosovsky, 1970), arouse animals from hibernation. Because the kidney is incapable of full functioning in the hypothermic state, arousals may be necessary to eliminate metabolic end products or other substances that threaten homeostasis (for review, see Mrosovsky, 1971).

Seasonal Affective Disorder and Animal Models

A particular form of recurrent depression, seasonal affective disorder (SAD), has boosted hopes that animal models may be of help in understanding mood disturbances. Let us accept for the moment that the data base for SAD and related phenomena is solid. Let us then address the question of whether there are similarities between the constellation of symptoms that appear in SAD (weight gain, carbohydrate craving, hypersomnia, depression, inactivity, etc.) and seasonally occurring changes in animals, especially mammalian hibernators. It has been suggested that the symptoms in SAD "may be coordinated by neurophysiological systems that vary seasonally in an interrelated way" (Rosenthal et al., 1987a). "It is conceivable that SAD may be a pathologic manifestation of an atavistic seasonal rhythm" (Rosenthal et al., 1984). Because weight gain and inactivity are features of cycles in hibernators, the implication is that such animals may be useful for modeling both the specific symptoms of SAD and their periodic occurrence. To quote Wehr et al. (1987):

> At the most primitive level, depression may represent an exaggeration of behaviors and physiological changes related to energy conservation. . . . Obvious animal models . . . of seasonal affective disorder are hibernation and estivation. These states occur at opposite times of year but are physiologically indistinguishable. In this regard they can be compared with spring–summer

and fall–winter depression, which occur at opposite times of year but have similar symptoms.

Paradoxically, the inability to study mood in animals is not necessarily a major obstacle to drawing comparisons between SAD and animals. There is no particular evidence that mood changes in SAD patients are primary to their other problems. Alterations in sleep patterns, eating, and activity levels might impair the ability to function effectively in society. Reaction to these inadequacies might then give rise to depression.

Are there, then, seasonal rhythms that have adaptive value for animals, and may have had adaptive value for our ancestors too, but whose expression in people today detracts from their functioning in contemporary society and is accompanied by depression? The idea of neurophysiological coordination of a group of changes varying in an interrelated way suggests that it might be possible to activate these symptoms in some relatively simple way by tapping into this coordinating system. But it is soon apparent that the idea of a coordinated seasonal system that may be activated in different circumstances is not viable. There are simply too many differences between SAD and seasonality in animals, and between seasonality in different animals. Rosenthal and his colleagues are aware of many of the problems, but it is necessary for the subsequent argument in this chapter to recapitulate and augment the list.

Dissimilarities between SAD and Hibernation

Reproduction

Periods of reproductive quiescence are a prominent feature of many speices whose physiologies vary seasonally. Kayser (1961), in his book on hibernation, gives the absence of reproduction in the winter as one of the ways to characterize a species as a hibernator. Annual rhythms for the frequency of birth do exist in many societies, but it is a moot point whether these reflect diminished physiological prowess or social constraints and family planning. Sack, Rosenthal, Hobbs, and Wehr (unpublished observations) also found large-amplitude birth rhythms in their sample of offspring ($n = 219$) of SAD patients. Minimal conception rates occurred in August and November, with September a close second. This would mean decreased conception over the winter, as also found by Wirz-Justice et al. (1986) with a smaller sample ($n = 35$). Of SAD patients, 69% report decreased libido (Rosenthal et al., 1984). Nevertheless, this is vastly different from the total physiological shutdown in seasonal breeders. Further work is needed to show that there are more than superficial similarities between seasonal breeders and SAD patients.

Sex Differences

In Rosenthal *et al.*'s (1984) sample, 85% of the patients were female. This may point to a sociocultural as much as to a biological factor. There are some sex differences in body weight and the degree of fattening prior to hibernation (Smale *et al.* 1986), but winter is winter; on the whole it affects both sexes alike.

Sleep and Temperature

During episodes of seasonal depression, people sleep less deeply, and there is no evidence for dramatic changes in temperature. In this respect, SAD differs from hibernation (Rosenthal *et al.*, 1984). It should be added that hibernation is now considered to be an extension of slow-wave sleep. In deep hibernation, the amplitude of the EEG is too low to recognize bouts of rapid eye movement (REM) and slow-wave sleep, but during entry to hibernation or in shallow torpor (about 27.0°C), the proportion of slow-wave sleep increases (Heller and Glotzbach, 1977; Walker *et al.*, 1979). In contrast, seasonally depressed people, although they sleep more in the winter, spend a smaller proportion of this time in the slow-wave state (Rosenthal *et al.*, 1984).

When ground squirrels are kept continuously at 22°C, hibernation during the winter is reduced to short bouts of shallow torpor. The animals spend more time sleeping at normothermic body temperatures (34–37°C), but the proportion of total sleep that is REM remains constant at about 20% throughout the year (Walker *et al.*, 1980).

Carbohydrate Craving

Little is known about changes in food preferences as a function of seasonal cycles of fattening and weight loss in hibernators. There are at least some indications that fat, rather than carbohydrate, is selected more during phases of weight gain. Garden dormice, given a choice of chopped beef, peanuts, and strawberry jam, went for the fatty peanuts more when they were gaining weight in preparation for hibernation (Haberey *et al.*, 1966). Protein intake remained fairly constant. On the other hand, warblers (nonhibernators) eat relatively more *Tenebrio* larvae than berries when they fatten before migration (Berthold, 1976).

Phase Relationships between Weight Gain, Hibernation, and Reproduction

Weight gain precedes torpor in hibernators. This may not be as damaging as it seems to an analogy between SAD and cycles in hibernators. At least in ground squirrels and dormice, activity measured by running wheels decreases well before the attainment of peak body weights (Pengelley and Fisher, 1966; Mrosovsky *et al.*, 1980; Fig. 10-1). Inactivity and weight gain go together at this time.

The relationship between food intake and body weight is also relevant here. Intakes begin to decrease as early as halfway through the phase of weight gain (Fig. 10-2), suggesting that decreased energy expenditure and increased food utilization efficiency contribute to fattening.

In ground squirrels and a variety of other hibernators, gonad size and steroid levels decline at the start of the weight gain phase (see Mrosovsky, 1971; Licht *et al.*, 1982). In other species, such as the Djungarian hamster, gonad size is greatest during the weight gain phase (Hoffmann, 1973).

In SAD, increased eating, weight gain, and decreased libido appear to go together. More detailed description of the time course of these changes is needed before valid comparisons to hibernators can be made.

Diversity of Synchronizing Agents in Hibernators

The idea of light therapy for SAD derives from the assumption that photoperiod is vital in the seasonality of the symptoms. Among hibernators, golden hamsters and some other species of hamsters do indeed depend on changes in daylength. In these cases, the seasonal changes are directly driven by the changes in photoperiod; if the days do not become short, the testes do not regress.

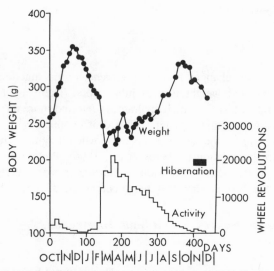

FIGURE 10-1. Running-wheel activity (histogram) and body weight (line) of a golden-mantled ground squirrel kept at 21°C on an LD 12:12 schedule. Horizontal bar shows period over which hibernation occurred. The data are from Pengelley and Fisher (1966).

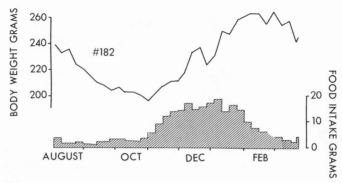

FIGURE 10-2. Relationship between food intake of Purina chow and body weight in a golden-mantled ground squirrel kept at 22°C on an LD 12:12 schedule.

In other hibernators, the mechanism for seasonality is different. Ground squirrels and woodchucks possess an endogenous seasonal cycle that continues through all its phases, despite constancy in lighting and temperature. Periodicity in such constant conditions is circannual, not annual. After a few years in captivity, preparation for hibernation is advanced to spring or earlier. In natural conditions, the endogenous circannual cycles must be synchronized to the solar year. Temperature and photoperiod are obvious candidates for such synchronizers or zeitgebers. The action of photoperiod in synchronizing an endogenous circannual cycle that persists anyway can be distinguished from that of photoperiod in driving a cycle that would not persist without this input. In fact, there is little to suggest that photoperiod is an important zeitgeber for endogenous circannual cycles in hibernators, although this action may be present in some other mammals and birds (see Gwinner, 1986, for a review). Some work on Californian ground squirrels (Davis and Swade, 1983), claiming to implicate photoperiod as an influence on circannual rhythms, lacks adequate statistical support.

In contrast, there are a growing number of experiments showing that the circannual cycles of ground squirrels can be affected by temperature (see Mrosovsky, 1986, for a review; Ambid and Berges, 1986). In particular, keeping animals in the cold for several months over the spring phase of low weight and reproductive activity delays the cycle, compared to that of animals kept continuously in a warm room (Fig. 10-3). Whether temperature synchronizes a self-sustaining endogenous cycle or acts in some other way is discussed elsewhere (Mrosovsky, 1986). The point noted here is that there is species diversity in hibernators with respect to the temporal control of their cycles. Although further tests with photoperiodic stimuli should be made, in some species cold has important effects.

So "the hibernator" is an abstraction; there are different species of hibernators responding differently to environmental signals and behaving differently

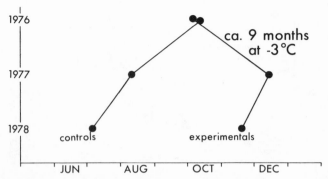

FIGURE 10-3. Phase delay in cycles of golden-mantled ground squirrels produced by a $-3°C$ cold pulse lasting approximately from mid-December 1976 to early September 1977. At other times the experimental group was at 21°C. The control group was at 21°C throughout. Dots show median times of peak body weights. The data are from Mrosovsky (1986).

in numerous other ways. Those seeking to model SAD must take their pick among the different hibernators—or perhaps among nonhibernating animals.

Species Diversity of Seasonal Strategies

It has been argued that superficial similarities between torpor and depression have been overinterpreted and that such comparisons between SAD and hibernators as can be based on data are not encouraging. But, of course, numerous other animals exhibit seasonal changes almost as dramatic as those of hibernators. Perhaps some of these would provide more appropriate models.

Many species fatten before winter without hibernating afterwards. A recently studied example is the Svalbard ptarmigan, a bird that neither hibernates nor migrates but survives the winter in its northern home by laying down large fat reserves in advance (Mortensen and Blix, 1985). Other species, such as voles, lose weight before the winter. This has also been considered as an adaptation to seasonal scarcity, in that the reduced metabolic mass requires less maintenance (Dark and Zucker, 1983). This is not contested, though it leads to an unsatisfactory theoretical position: Both gaining and losing weight in the autumn can be explained as adaptive, but there are no grounds for deciding what determines the choice between these two strategies.

Phasing of reproduction also varies with respect to season. Emperor penguins breed in the middle of the Antarctic winter. Some species, small rodents in particular, stop breeding in short days. In contrast, ungulates with long gestation times become sexually active in the fall.

Some species migrate; others pass much of the winter within protected places, like beavers in their lodges. Home ranges alter and activity levels change in various ways. One could fill a book illustrating the point that different species meet the challenge of winter in different ways (Rosenthal *et al.*, 1987b). What implications does this diversity have for animal models of SAD?

Strategies for Selecting Animal Models for SAD

One response to this heterogeneity of animal seasonality would be to search for the species showing the profile of winter changes closest to the constellation of symptoms seen in people, and then study this animal intensively. If the species were a primate rather than a ptarmigan it would be rather more convincing.

Such a search through the phylogenetic supermarket of animal diversity is the wrong approach. The variety of seasonal mechanisms shows that a large number of processes change seasonally. Just as a composer selects different instrumental combinations for a symphony, so evolution assembles seasonal processes in different combinations in different species, according to the particular challenges they face and the historical constraints on their plasticity. My contention is that comparisons between man and animals will be more fruitful at the level of the instrument than at the level of the physiological orchestra playing in unison.

If we concentrate on particular processes such as weight gain, reproductive quiescence, lethargy, and so on, then knowledge of seasonal changes in animals may indeed be helpful in understanding SAD. Some examples are now presented of how analyses of particular processes, using animal preparations, can generate suggestions for investigations in a clinical setting.

Sensitivity Changes to Negative Feedback from Gonadal Steroids

To discover whether SAD patients exhibit a mild version of annual reproductive quiescence in animals, it may be profitable to look for gonadostat resetting. During appropriate photoperiods, circulating gonadal steroids in hamsters (Sisk and Turek, 1983) and sheep (Lincoln and Short, 1980; Karsch and Foster, 1981) become more effective in the negative feedback loop. Even low levels are capable of inhibiting the production of gonadotropic hormones.

Seasonal gonadostat resetting during short photoperiods is an adjustment in a particular regulatory system, rather than a widespread shift in steroid dynamics. Steroids become less effective in initiating mating behavior (Raeside and McDonald, 1959; Morin and Zucker, 1978) at the same time as they become more effective in inhibiting the production of luteinizing hormone.

Climbing and Sliding Set Points for Body Weight

When animals fatten before hibernation, they do not do so at the maximal rates possible; instead they follow a programmed weight gain. It is as if a set point

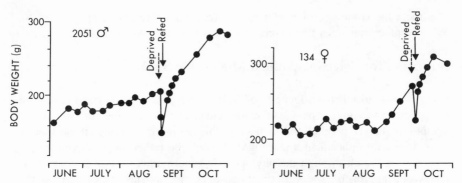

FIGURE 10-4. Body weights of golden-mantled ground squirrels food deprived for a few days during their weight gain phase. The data are from Barnes and Mrosovsky (1974).

(see Mrosovsky and Powley, 1977, for terminology) for body weight (or body fat) climbs steadily, with defense of progressively higher levels. This characterization of the process of fattening arises from experiments where the animals are temporarily forced off their programmed weights by food deprivation. When a period of deprivation occurs during the weight gain phase, then on the return of food the animals gain weight at greater rates than before the deprivation (Fig. 10-4). They were not, therefore, gaining weight at maximal rates previously. Moreover, on refeeding, they catch up to weights that would have been expected at that time had no manipulation been introduced; this suggests that there is a programmed increase in set point. Similar types of experiments demonstrate that during phases of spontaneous anorexia and weight loss, animals regulate weight around set points that slide progressively lower (for review, see Mrosovsky and Sherry, 1980).

Both eating and energy expenditure are considered as effectors available for defense of body weight (Keesey and Powley, 1986). Hibernators, unlike rats, eat more when in a warm room than in a cold room over the winter. This occurs because reductions in energy expenditure through torpor cannot be as successful in the warm room; another effector, eating, takes over the defense of weight. Individual ground squirrels that for some reason stop hibernating in a cold room in midseason start to eat much more, while their weight loss continues in a progressive way according to the dictates of the sliding set point. Weight gain of golden hamsters in short photoperiods does not necessarily require increased caloric intake (Bartness and Wade, 1984). By accounting for changes in energy intake and expenditure, set point interpretations introduce some economy into explanations of body weight cycles.

Defense of climbing set points is not confined to hibernators. It has been demonstrated in warblers prior to their migration (for review, see Gwinner, 1986) and also in the Svalbard ptarmigan (Mortensen and Blix, 1985; Fig. 10-5). Defense of declining body weight occurs when voles are transferred to short photoperiods (Dark and Zucker, 1986). Seasonal weight change in many other species, although not tested experimentally for changes in defended levels, probably also depends on such processes.

Do these same processes underlie the weight changes seen in SAD? The body weight regulatory system is not the only factor determining food intake, as anyone who has been to a good dinner party knows. It might be that regulatory systems remain unchanged physiologically in SAD but that people become more responsive to external cues coming from the food, or that homeostatic signals from the body are overriden in some way by stress. However, it is also plausible that, just as in animals, the essential process underlying the increased weight is a resetting of the defended weight. It is possible to look into this matter in relatively simple ways.

One method that could be used, if manipulations of weight itself were not feasible, would be Cabanac's (1971) alliesthesia method. "Alliesthesia" refers to the fact that an external stimulus, such as a sweet taste, can be perceived as either pleasant or unpleasant, depending on the signals coming from inside the body. For instance, the subjective pleasantness or hedonic value of the taste of a given concentration of sucrose solution is reduced after 50 g of glucose has been introduced into the stomach (i.e., there is negative alliesthesia). However, if the person receiving the stomach load has previously been dieting and is well below normal weight, then the glucose load does not affect the hedonic rating of the sucrose; the negative alliesthesia is abolished or much attenuated by the discrepancy between actual and normally defended body weight (Cabanac *et al.*, 1971).

The alliesthesia method has been used to study anorexia nervosa. It has been argued that the body weight set point is not reduced in this condition, in that the hedonic ratings of patients were much less affected by a 400-kcal meal than were those of normal-weight control subjects (Garfinkel *et al.*, 1978). Although some additional controls would have been desirable (see Mrosovsky,

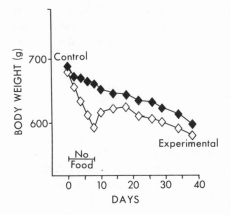

FIGURE 10-5. Body weights of Svalbard ptarmigans. The experimental group was deprived of food for 8 days in early December. The control group was fed *ad libitum;* their loss of weight is normal for this species at this time of year. The data are from Mortensen and Blix (1985).

1983), the anorexic group behaved like the dieting subjects in the Cabanac *et al.* (1971) study.

Longitudinal studies of alliesthesia in SAD as a function of season and body weight should be feasible. The baselines, prior to the stomach load, might also help quantify and illuminate the matter of carbohydrate cravings. Tests could be made before and after light therapy.

Discovery and Throwaway Theories

The word *constellation* has been used deliberately in this chapter. The ancients gazed into the night sky and saw clusters in the bewildering multiplicity of stars. And they peopled the sky with the animals and gods of their imagination. The stars in the north became the Great Bear. Rosenthal and his colleagues have looked into the darker inner sky of the despairing human mind and wondered whether they could see there, if not a bear, at least a hamster or a chipmunk. Are they attempting to join things that are as far apart as the stars in a constellation? For the reasons given, especially the variety of seasonal changes and combinations of changes in animals, I believe that there is no unitary system underlying human seasonal pathology. Nevertheless, in their search for order, especially temporal order, Rosenthal and his colleagues have brought the question of seasonality in affective state into sharper focus than ever before; their bold analogies are a way of breaking new ground, of breaking out of the constraints of hypothetico-deductive reasoning. And it should be noted that even if speculation has been uninhibited, ideas have also been abandoned with equal alacrity in the face of contrary evidence. For instance, on the basis of their recent experiments, Wehr *et al.* (1986) no longer consider the time of day as being critical for light therapy, thus undermining explanations of SAD based on changes in photoperiod and melatonin: "[I]t is ironic that the well-studied animal model involving photoperiodically driven seasonal rhythms has led to a new antidepressant treatment modality for which the model may no longer be valid." Such ironies are the fabric of science. Columbus thought he had reached Asia, but he brought back corn. It does not matter if a theory is wrong so long as it serves its purpose of leading to new discoveries, so long as the data are sound.

Questions about the Data Base for SAD

How solid are the data provided by the proponents of SAD? It is here that I enter some reservations about this field, while recognizing that some of these may be dispelled by new data presented in this issue or in the near future. One may wonder about the reliability of an instrument with a name like the Clinical Global Impressions Scale, employed by Wehr *et al.* (1986), but it is evidently an accepted tool (Guy, 1976). Other procedures, however, may need some attention.

1. Seven supplementary questions have been tacked onto the Hamilton Depression Rating Scale (Rosenthal *et al.*, 1987b). Data on their reliability and validity are not presented. One of the items refers to increased eating (e.g., "0 = is not eating more than usual," "1 = is eating a little more than usual," etc.). How is "usual" defined? How do those filling out the scales become familiar with the usual (summer?) eating habits of their patients? Self-reports of eating behavior are controversial.

Another question refers to appetite increases. Objective rating of an actual behavior such as eating can be difficult enough. Assessing appetite is presumably harder still. How does one obtain knowledge of a patient's appetite to answer a question such as "2 = wants to eat somewhat more than usual"?

2. Weight gain given for SAD patients seems to be based on self-reports. I do not imply that it is impossible for people to know when their weight changes, but quantification would be useful for learning how similar the changes were from year to year and for assessing the effects of therapy. Simple indices of obesity such as weight/height^2 could be employed (Garrow and Webster, 1985). Suarez and Barrett-Connor (1982), in a cross-sectional population study in California, found that weight/height^2 increased over the winter. They also found elevations in fasting plasma glucose in this season. Others have reported increased incidence of insulin-dependent diabetes in the young in the winter (Gleason *et al.*, 1982) and poorer tolerance after a 50-g glucose load in the winter in middle-aged men (Jarrett *et al.*, 1984). Slimming treatment consisting of diets with low caloric totals, in an inpatient setting with ambient temperature controlled, is more effective in the spring and summer than in the autumn and winter (Zahorska-Markiewicz, 1980). Seasonal weight change in man appears to be a real phenomenon. In this context, weight change, and perhaps also glucose dynamics in SAD, merit study by more objective methods.

Another quantitative tool that could be useful in the study of SAD is the Restraint Scale (Polivy *et al.*, 1988). This scale identifies people who are weight-conscious and trying to diet. It has reliability and also validity, in that those with high restraint scores eat less in baseline testing conditions. Of particular interest is that both restrained eaters and SAD patients tend to show atypical depression—that is, depression with weight gain. Depressed patients who score high on the scale tend to gain weight, whereas those who score low tend to lose weight. It has been suggested that unpleasant emotional states present during depression disrupt the self-control needed for successful dieting (Polivy and Herman, 1976). These considerations lead to the thought that weight gain in SAD may be secondary to depression. Perhaps depression in the winter disrupts restraint and so allows weight to rise toward the set point. This interpretation is consistent with the higher incidence of SAD in females; in the summer, social pressure to demonstrate thinness of body may be greater for this sex, leaving more weight to be restored when dieting fails in the winter.

The predictions about seasonal changes in alliesthesia deriving from this account are different from those derived from the suggestion that set point rises in the winter (but see Esses and Herman, 1984, for some complications).

3. It is said that cloudy weather exacerbates the symptoms of SAD (Rosenthal et al., 1987b). What is the empirical support for this statement? Were hours of cloud cover measured? What time of day were measurements of SAD symptoms made? To develop explanations of SAD based on photoperiodism, it would also be interesting to learn how quickly mood changes in response to weather. Does one cloud passing over the sun precipitate depression, or must overcast persist for hours or even days? Some seasonal responses require the photoperiodic conditions to persist for a number of days, and it has been argued that integration of information over a number of days may help prevent animals from mistaking cloudy for short days (Gwinner and Dittami, in press).

4. Lack of sufficient controls for the specificity of light therapy remains a problem. It has been suggested that white noise may be an appropriate control (Hallonquist, personal communication).

5. Let me take a devil's advocate position to the problem of defining SAD by considering a spatial analogy. Suppose that the distribution of moles on the body is random or relatively so. We then define anyone with three or more moles in a row as having mole alignment disorder (MAD). We then advertise for people who have this problem. After excluding some respondents (moles too small, not perfectly aligned), we have a sample. We can then study the physiological and psychological concomitants of MAD.

For an individual to qualify as having SAD, there have to be at least two consecutive years in which depression has developed during the fall or winter and remitted during the following spring or summer (Rosenthal et al., 1984). To boost confidence that SAD is a distinct entity, it would be desirable to have more information about the temporal distribution of recurrent bouts of affective disorder in a population not screened for seasonal incidence. Suppose, to take an extreme case, that bouts of depression and remission were distributed in a random way; then, out of a large sample, some cases would be found with repeated disorder in the winter and remission in the summer. SAD would then arise as a result of the screening technique used to define it.

To counter this problem, we need evidence that recurrent bouts of depression are not randomly distributed. If we look first at the information from Rosenthal et al.'s (1984) group of SAD patients, there are some indications (though not perhaps proof) of nonrandomness. The mean number of annual cycles was 9.5. That such frequently repeated winter depression should arise by chance seems unlikely; yet this does depend on the characteristics of the population from which the sample is drawn. It is possible, even if the distribution of depression bouts is not totally random, that at least some cases were defined as SAD because they happened to occur at certain times of year, and not because of any seasonal factors. If a statistically higher percentage of a group of SAD patients continued to show episodes at the same time of year after they had been diagnosed, this would enhance the validity of SAD. However, there might be ethical constraints on withholding treatment in order to follow the time course of the disorder.

Another indication of nonrandomness in Rosenthal et al.'s (1984) sample is that onset of depression was more frequent in November and December than in adjacent months, and remission was far more common in March than any other month. This suggests some nonrandom element, but the matter is complicated by variation in the length of bouts of depression. The mean bout length was 3.9 months (Rosenthal et al., 1984). An average-length bout starting in April cannot meet the criterion for SAD. Therefore, resulting from the exclusion of bouts with late winter onset that do not remit by the spring, there will be a tendency for fewer onsets in the late winter in a SAD group selected according to Rosenthal et al.'s (1984) qualifying criteria, unless bout length is also seasonal. To guide one through these complexities, it might be helpful if figures including data for all individuals were given; horizontal bars showing onset and duration of depression, just like horizontal bars for hibernation bouts (e.g., Pengelley and Fisher, 1966), would not take too much space.

These concerns are not entirely unreasonable as, waiting in the wings, there is a reverse SAD, with spring–summer depression and fall–winter hypomania (Wehr et al., 1987). Cold comfort instead of "light relief" (King, 1986) has already been tried as a therapy, and estivation has been proposed as an animal model (Wehr et al., 1987). Should we be looking forward to the discovery of "semireverse SAD"?

The basic problem is that if episodes are totally or even largely randomly distributed, then the qualifying temporal criteria for SAD are inappropriate for characterizing a distinct entity. But it is not valid to take seasonality of recurrence of depressive episodes in SAD as showing a distinct disorder, because the patients were selected by advertisements. Paradoxically then, one has to look outside of the data on SAD itself for evidence of its reality.

There are numerous reports, dating back at least to Kraepelin (1921), describing seasonal patterns of affective disorders. In fact, the data presented by Kraepelin in his book do little to demonstrate seasonality, nor is it clear what he himself thought about this matter. His remarks about repeatedly seeing "moodiness set in in the autumn and pass over in the spring," and about the sap rising in the spring, have been quoted in papers on SAD. A few pages later, though, he also wrote that "the multiplicity of the courses taken by manic–depressive insanity . . . is absolutely inexhaustible. The cases reported only show that there can be no talk of even an approximate regularity in the course" (p. 149). He continued, "It is this experience which makes all delimitations and classifications futile, which are grounded on definite varieties of the course."

However, more recently an increasing mass of data from records of admissions to hospitals has shown seasonal variations (e.g., Eastwood and Stiasny, 1978). Rosenthal et al. (1983) provide an enlightening summary and review of these studies. Many of the studies show peaks in the fall; additional peaks in the spring are also common. Peaks of incidence of suicide—often a manifestation of extreme depression—have also been discovered to occur in May in the Northern Hemisphere (for review, see Aschoff, 1981). But there are some problems in bringing such data to bear on the issue of SAD. One is that the diagnostic entities may not be the same. Patients with SAD usually exhibit relatively mild forms of depression. Some have not sought help previously. Abnormalities of dexamethasone suppression are absent (Rosenthal *et al.*, 1984). When people are admitted to a hospital, one can assume that there is a relatively serious disturbance. It is a reasonable assumption that mild forms of depression would have seasonal patterns similar to those of severe cases, but it does remain to be proven. Admissions for endogenous depressions are as common in the spring as in the fall, or more so (Eastwood and Stiasny, 1978). Would one expect the incidence of reverse SAD to be as high as that of SAD? Or does SAD resemble more the kinds of neurotic depression presenting often in the fall (Eastwood and Stiasny, 1978)?

A more difficult problem, perhaps, is that demonstrations of seasonality from hospital admissions include first-time admissions, readmissions, and (one hopes) episodes with no recurrence. Without further analysis of the data from individuals contributing two or more admissions to the sample, the seasonality of recurrence of episodes within patients can only be guessed at. Such further analysis is usually lacking. However, the data of Kraepelin have been restudied by Slater (1938). He found that individuals were more likely to have episodes at the same time of year than at other times; that is, within-subject variability for month of onset of depression was less than the population variability (quoted from Rosenthal *et al.*'s 1983 account). Rosenthal *et al.* (1983) note in their review that "This potentially fruitful line of investigation has been largely neglected in the decades which have elapsed since Slater published this work." Alas!

Animal Models for the Temporal Aspects of SAD

Without more information on some of these matters, it remains unclear what type of animal model would be suitable for the temporal aspects of SAD. Three possibilities are considered here.

1. If there are many different types of seasonal disturbances (SAD, reverse SAD, semireverse SAD, etc.), it suggests the possibility of endogenous circannual rhythms. Such rhythms may have become more or less emancipated from external synchronizers or become resynchronized at unusual phase angles. Studies of zeitgebers in species with robust circannual cycles, such as ground squirrels or some birds (Mrosovsky, 1978; Gwinner, 1986), might be appropriate.

The existence of endogenous circannual rhythms in people is problematical, as they have not yet lived in constant conditions for more than a year. A less dull way to address the question might be for psychiatrists and their patients to fly from North America to Australia and study the time course of SAD. If synchronization to the austral winter were to take several years, just as synchronization of the circadian system takes several days after time zones are crossed, then it would indicate the presence of an endogenous rhythm with inherent circannual periodicity. The animal experiments of Davis and Finnie (1975) might be appropriate models. They reported that woodchucks flown from Pennsylvania to Australia took several years to adjust their circannual body weight cycles (but see Mrosovsky, 1976, for a critique). If SAD were to shift instantly to the new environmental conditions, it would indicate that winter conditions have direct inducing effects, rather than synchronizing an internal rhythmic process.

2. If a distinct seasonal entity with predictable winter onset can be better established, then it suggests that the periodicity of SAD arises because particular cues are present at this time each year. However, if this is the case, at least two different approaches could be taken in the selection of animal models. If SAD patients are thought of as overreacting to seasonal events, then a species especially sensitive to external cues might be studied. An alternative is that SAD arises because of insensitivity to signals (e.g., artificial lighting) that in most of the population are sufficient to counteract the external cues present in fall and winter. Appropriate animal work in this case might include investigations of within-species individual differences in reactions to photoperiod. When white-footed mice or hamsters are kept in short days, most animals show testicular regression, but there are usually a few individuals who march to a different drummer (Johnston and Zucker, 1980; Puchalski and Lynch, 1986).

3. Yet another possibility is that the temporal mechanisms are unimpaired, and are the same in SAD and normal subjects, but that what is different is the degree of response. Detailed comparisons of the time course of seasonal changes in SAD to those lesser changes in normal groups, or in SAD patients in remission, would bear on this possibility. If excessive responsiveness to seasonal cues is the problem, then an analogy, though not necessarily a model, might be the exaggerated amplitude of weight cycles in ground squirrels with ventromedial hypothalamic lesions (Mrosovsky, 1975).

To produce appropriate animal models of psychiatric disturbance, we need to know better what it is that we are modeling.

An Upbeat Conclusion

Demand for more rigorous methods runs the risk of throwing out the baby of psychiatric insight with the bathwater of clinical constraints and the very real difficulties in maintaining measurements over long periods. This is not intended. All the same, perhaps just a little more of the bathwater could be siphoned off without loss of the baby. It is worth trying, because surely there is an infant here worth nurturing. If we shun meretricious resemblances like the inertness and withdrawn posture of hibernation, work with animals may indeed be quite productive. For the temporal aspects of SAD, it may not matter much what seasonal variables are studied in animals. These are like pictures on a calendar, which can be selected according to taste. The temporal information resides in the numbers and the monthly structure. If we wish to study the manifestations of SAD, such as weight gain and inactivity, examples of seasonal changes in these processes (except perhaps for mood itself) can be found in animals. They can be studied separately, in convenient preparations. We may then look for similar mechanisms in SAD. One thing that emerges with absolute certainty from the study of seasonality in animals is the impressive capacity for change: from thin to fat, from dark coat to white, from sexually motivated to disinterested, from active to lethargic. The enormous and widespread capacity for seasonal change in mammalian physiology is unlikely either to be absent in our own species or to be unsusceptible to pathological manifestation.

Acknowledgements

I thank Norman Rosenthal for providing unpublished information, and especially for his enthusiasm and colleagueship. I am also grateful to J. D. Hallonquist, P. Herman, and I. Zucker for comments. Support came from the Natural Sciences and Engineering Research Council of Canada.

This chapter originally appeared in *Journal of Biological Rhythms*, Volume 3, Number 2, pp. 189–207, 1988. Reprinted by permission of The Guilford Press.

References

Ambid, L., and R. Berges (1986) Testicular activity and hibernation in a seasonal hibernating animal, the ground squirrel *(Citellus tridecemlineatus)*. In *Behavioural Rhythms*, Y. Quéinnec and N. Delvolvé, eds., pp. 83–92, Privat, I.E.C., Toulouse, France.

Aschoff, J. (1981). Annual rhythms in man. In *Handbook of Behavioral Neurobiology*, Vol 4, *Biological Rhythms*, J. Aschoff, ed., pp. 475–487, Plenum Press, New York.

Barnes, D. S., and N. Mrosovsky (1974) Body weight regulation in ground squirrels and hypothalamically lesioned rats: Slow and sudden set point changes. Physiol. Behav. *12:* 251–258.

Bartholomew, G. A. (1986) The diversity of temporal heterothermy. In *Living in the Cold: Physiological and Biochemical Adaptations*, H. C. Heller, X. J. Musacchia, and L. C. H. Wang, eds., pp. 1–9, Elsevier, New York.

Bartness, T. J., and G. N. Wade (1984) Photoperiodic control of body weight and energy metabolism in Syrian hamsters *(Mesocricetus auratus):* Role of pineal gland, melatonin, gonads, and diet. Endocrinology *114:* 492–498.

Berthold, P. (1976) Animalische und vegetabilische ernährung omnivorer singvogelarten: Nahrungsbevorzugung, jahresperiodik der nahrungswahl, physiologische und okologische bedeutung. J. für Ornithol. *117:* 145–209.

Cabanac, M. (1971) Physiological role of pleasure. Science *173:* 1103–1107.

Cabanac, M., R. Duclaux, and N. H. Spector (1971) Sensory feedback in regulation of body weight: Is there a ponderostat? Nature 229: 125–127.

Dark, J., and I. Zucker (1983) Short photoperiods reduce winter energy requirements of the meadow vole (Microtus pennsylvanicus). Physiol. Behav. 31: 699–702.

Dark, J., and I. Zucker (1986) Photoperiod regulation of body mass and fat reserves in the meadow vole. Physiol. Behav. 38: 851–854.

Davis, D. E., and E. P. Finnie (1975) Entrainment of circannual rhythm in weight of woodchucks. J. Mammal. 56: 199–203.

Davis, D. E., and R. H. Swade (1983) Circannual rhythm of torpor and molt in the ground squirrel, Spermophilus beecheyi. Comp. Biochem. Physiol. 76A: 183–187.

Eastwood, M. R., and S. Stiasny (1978) Psychiatric disorder, hospital admission, and season. Arch. Gen. Psychiat. 35: 769–771.

Esses, V. M., and P. Herman (1984) Palatability of sucrose before and after glucose ingestion in dieters and nondieters. Physiol. Behav. 32: 711–715.

Feierman, J. R., E. T. Pengelley, A. J. Mandell, and S. Knapp (1978) Hibernation as a biological model for manic–depressive illness: Pilot studies. J. Therm. Biol. 3: 100.

Fisher, K. C. (1964). On the mechanism of periodic arousal in the hibernating ground squirrel. Ann. Acad. Sci. Fenn. A.IV. 71/10: 143–156.

Fisher, K. C., and N. Mrosovsky (1970) Effectiveness of KCl and NaCl injections in arousing 13-lined ground squirrels from hibernation. Canad. J. Zool. 48: 595–596.

French, A. R. (1986) Patterns of thermoregulation during hibernation. In Living in the Cold: Physiological and Biochemical Adaptations, H. C. Heller, X. J. Musacchia, and L. C. H. Wang, eds., pp. 393–402, Elsevier, New York.

Garfinkel, P. E., H. Moldofsky, D. M. Garner, H. C. Stancer, and D. V. Coscina (1978) Body awareness in anorexia nervosa: Disturbances in "body image" and "satiety." Psychosom. Med. 40: 487–498.

Garrow, J. S., and J. Webster (1985) Quetelet's index (W/H^2) as a measure of fatness. Int. J. Obesity 9: 147–153.

Giedke, H., and H. Pohl (1985) Lithium suppresses hibernation in the Turkish hamster. Experientia 41: 1391–1392.

Gleason, R. E., C. B. Kahn, I. B. Funk, and J. E. Craighead (1982) Seasonal incidence of insulin-dependent diabetes (IDDM) in Massachusetts, 1964–1973. Int. J. Epidemiol. 11: 39–45.

Guy, W. (1976) ECDEU Assessment Manual for Psychopharmacology, National Institute of Mental Health, Rockville, MD.

Gwinner, E. (1986) Circannual Rhythms, Springer-Verlag, Berlin.

Gwinner, E., and J. Dittami (in press) Adaptive functions of circannual clocks. In Endocrine Regulations as Adaptive Mechanisms to the Environment, I. Assenmacher and J. Boissin, ed., Editions du CNRS, Paris.

Haberey, P., C. Dantlo, and C. Kayser (1966) Méthode d'exploration du comportement alimentaire d'un hibernant, le Lérot Eliomys quercinus. C. R. Soc. Biol. 160: 655–659.

Heller, H. C., and S. F. Glotzbach (1977) Thermoregulation during sleep and hibernation. In International Review of Physiology: Environmental Physiology II, Vol. 15, D. Robertshaw, ed., pp. 147–188, University Park Press, Baltimore.

Hock, R. J. (1960) Seasonal variations in physiological functions of arctic ground squirrels and black bears. In Mammalian Hibernation, Bulletin of the Museum of Comparative Zoology, Harvard, Vol. 124, C. P. Lyman and A. R. Dawe, eds., pp. 155–171, Harvard University, Cambridge, MA.

Hoffman, K. (1973) The influence of photoperiod and melatonin on testis size, body weight, and pelage colour in the Djungarian hamster (Phodopus sungorus). J. Comp Physiol. 85: 267–282.

Jarrett, R. J., T. J. Murrells, M. J. Shipley, and T. Hall (1984) Screening blood glucose values: Effects of season and time of day. Diabetologia 27: 574–577.

Johnston, P. G., and I. Zucker (1980) Photoperiodic regulation of the testes of adult white-footed mice *(Peromyscus leucopus)*. Biol. Reprod. *23:* 859–866.

Joy, J. E., and N. Mrosovsky (1982) Circannual cycles of molt in ground squirrels. Canad. J. Zool. *60:* 3227–3231.

Karsch, F. J., and D. L. Foster (1981) Environmental control of seasonal breeding: A common final mechanism governing seasonal breeding and sexual maturation. In *Environmental Factors in Mammal Reproduction,* D. Gilmore and B. Cook, eds., pp. 30–53, Macmillan, Hong Kong.

Kayser, C. (1961) *The Physiology of Natural Hibernation,* Pergamon Press, Oxford.

Keesey, R. E., and T. L. Powley (1986) The regulation of body weight. Ann. Rev. Psychol. *37:* 109–133.

King, J. R. (1986) Seasonal affective disorder. Brit. J. Psychiat. *148:* 478.

Kraepelin, E. (1921) *Manic–Depressive Insanity and Paranoia,* E. & S. Livingstone, Edinburgh.

Kripke, D. F. (1981) Photoperiodic mechanisms for depression and its treatment. In *Biological Psychiatry 1981,* C. Perris, G. Struwe, and B. Jansson, eds., pp. 1249–1252, Elsevier/North-Holland Biomedical Press, Amsterdam.

Lange, J. (1928) Die endogenen und reaktiven Gemütserkrankungen und die manisch–depressive konstitution. In *Handbuch der Geisteskrankheiten,* O. Bumke, ed., pp. 1–231, Springer-Verlag, Berlin.

Licht, P., I. Zucker, G. Hubbard, and M. Boshes (1982) Circannual rhythms of plasma testosterone and luteinizing hormone levels in golden-mantled ground squirrels *(Spermophilus lateralis).* Biol. Reprod. *27:* 411–418.

Lincoln, G. A., and R. V. Short (1980) Seasonal breeding: Nature's contraceptive. Rec. Prog. Horm. Res. *36:* 1–52.

Luecke, R. H., and F. E. South (1972) A possible model for thermoregulation during deep hibernation. In *Hibernation and Hypothermia: Perspectives and Challenges,* F. E. South, J. P. Hannon, J. R. Willis, E. T. Pengelley, and N. R. Alpert, eds., pp. 577–604, Elsevier, Amsterdam.

Morin, L. P., and I. Zucker (1978) Photoperiodic regulation of copulatory behaviour in the male hamster. J. Endocrinol. *77:* 249–258.

Morrison, P. (1960) Some interrelations between weight and hibernation function. In *Mammalian Hibernation,* Bulletin of the Museum of Comparative Zoology, Harvard, Vol. 124, C. P. Lyman and A. R. Dawe, eds., pp. 75–91, Harvard University, Cambridge, MA.

Mortensen, A., and A. S. Blix (1985) Seasonal changes in the effects of starvation on metabolic rate and regulation of body weight in Svalbard ptarmigan. Ornis Scand. *16:* 20–24.

Mrosovsky, N. (1966) Self-stimulation in hypothermic hibernators. Cryobiology *2:* 229–239.

Mrosovsky, N. (1971) *Hibernation and the Hypothalamus,* Appleton-Century-Crofts, New York.

Mrosovsky, N. (1975) The amplitude and period of circannual cycles of body weight in golden-mantled ground squirrels with medial hypothalamic lesions. Brain Res. *99:* 97–116.

Mrosovsky, N. (1976) Lipid programmes and life strategies in hibernators. Amer. Zool. *16:* 685–697.

Mrosovsky, N. (1978) Circannual cycles in hibernators. In *Strategies in Cold: Natural Torpidity and Thermogenesis,* L. C. H. Wang and J. W. Hudson, eds., pp. 21–65, Academic Press, New York.

Mrosovsky, N. (1983) Animal anorexias, starvation, and anorexia nervosa: Are animal models of anorexia nervosa possible? In *Anorexia Nervosa: Recent Developments in Research,* P. L. Darby *et al.,* eds., pp. 199–205, Alan R. Liss, New York.

Mrosovsky, N. (1985) Cyclical obesity in hibernators: The search for the adjustable regulator. In *Recent Advances in Obesity Research,* Vol. 4, J. Hirsch and T. B. Van Itallie, eds., pp. 45–56, J. Libbey, London.

Mrosovsky, N. (1986) Thermal effects on the periodicity, phasing, and persistence of circannual cycles. In *Living in the Cold: Physiological and Biochemical Adaptations,* H. C. Heller, X. J. Musacchia, and L. C. H. Wang, eds., pp. 403–410, Elsevier, New York.

Mrosovsky, N., R. B. Melnyk, K. Lang, J. D. Hallonquist, M. Boshes, and J. E. Joy (1980) Infradian cycles in dormice *(Glis glis)*. J. Comp. Physiol. *137:* 315–339.

Mrosovsky, N., and T. L. Powley (1977) Set points for body weight and fat. Behav. Biol. *20:* 205–223.

Mrosovsky, N., and D. F. Sherry (1980) Animal anorexias. Science *207:* 837–842.

Pengelley, E. T., and K. C. Fisher (1966) Locomotor activity patterns and their relation to hibernation in the golden-mantled ground squirrel. J. Mammal. *47:* 63–73.

Polivy, J. and C. P. Herman (1976) Clinical depression and weight change: A complex relation. J. Abnorm. Pysychol. *85:* 338–340.

Polivy, J., C. P. Herman, and K. I. Howard (1988) The Restraint Scale: Assessment of dieting. In *Dictionary of Behavioral Assessment Techniques,* M. Hersen and A. S. Bellack, eds., pp. 377–380, Pergamon Press, New York.

Puchalski, W., and G. R. Lynch (1986) Evidence for differences in the circadian organization of hamsters exposed to short day photoperiod. J. Comp. Physiol. *159:* 7–11.

Raeside, J. I., and M. F. McDonald (1959) Seasonal changes in the oestrous response by the ovariectomized ewe to progesterone and oestrogen. Nature *184:* 458–459.

Rosenthal, N. E., M. Genhart, F. M. Jacobsen, R. G. Skwerer, and T. A. Wehr (1987a) Disturbances of appetite and weight regulation in seasonal affective disorder. Ann. NY Acad. Sci. *499:* 216–230.

Rosenthal, N.E., M. Genhart, D. A. Sack, R. G. Skwerer, and T. A. Wehr (1987b) Seasonal affective disorder: Relevance for the treatment and research of bulimia. In *Psychobiology of Bulimia,* J. I. Hudson and H. G. Pope, Jr., eds., American Psychiatric Press, Washington, DC.

Rosenthal, N. E., D. A. Sack, J. C. Gillin, A. J. Lewy, F. K. Goodwin, Y. Davenport, P. S. Mueller, D. A. Newsome, and T. A. Wehr (1984) Seasonal affective disorder: A description of the syndrome and preliminary findings with light therapy. Arch. Gen. Psychiat. *41:* 72–80.

Rosenthal, N.E., D. A. Sack, and T. A. Wehr (1983) Seasonal variation in affective disorders. In *Circadian Rhythms in Psychiatry,* T. A. Wehr and F. K. Goodwin, eds., pp. 185–201, Boxwood Press, Pacific Grove, CA.

Sisk, C. L., and F. W. Turek (1983) Developmental time course of pubertal and photoperiodic changes in testosterone negative feedback on gonadotropin secretion in the golden hamster. Endocrinology *112:* 1208–1216.

Slater, E. (1938) Zur periodik des manisch–depressiven irreseins. Zeit. Ges. Neurol. Psychiat. *162:* 794–801.

Smale, L., K. Pelz, I. Zucker, and P. Licht (1986) Neonatal androgenization in ground squirrels: Influence on sex differences in body mass and luteinizing hormone levels. Biol. Reprod. *34:* 507–511.

Strumwasser, F. (1959) Regulatory mechanisms, brain activity and behavior during deep hibernation in the squirrel, *Citellus beecheyi.* Amer. J. Physiol. *196:* 23–30.

Suarez, L., and E. Barrett-Connor (1982) Seasonal variation in fasting plasma glucose levels in man. Diabetologia *22:* 250–253.

Walker, J. M., A. Garber, R. J. Berger, and H. C. Heller (1979) Sleep and estivation (shallow torpor): continuous processes of energy conservation. Science *204:* 1098–1100.

Walker, J. M., E. H. Haskell, R. J. Berger, and H. C. Heller (1980) Hibernation and circannual rhythms of sleep. Physiol. Zool. *53:* 8–11.

Wehr, T. A., F. M. Jacobsen, D. A. Sack, J. Arendt, L. Tamarkin, and N. E. Rosenthal (1986) Phototherapy of seasonal affective disorder: Time of day and suppression of melatonin are not critical for antidepressant effects. Arch. Gen. Psychiat. *43:* 870–875.

Wehr, T. A., D. A. Sack, and N. E. Rosenthal (1987) Seasonal affective disorder with summer depression and winter hypomania. Amer. J. Psychiat. *144:* 1602–1603.

Wirz-Justice, A., C. Bucheli, P. Graw, P. Kielholz, H.-U. Fisch, and B. Weggon (1986) Light treatment of seasonal affective disorders in Switzerland. Acta Psychiat. Scand. *74:* 193–204.

Zahorska-Markiewicz, B. (1980) Weight reduction and seasonal variation. Int. J. Obesity *4:* 139–143.
Zucker, I., and J. Dark (1986) Neuroendocrine substrates of circannual rhythms in ground squirrels. In *Living in the Cold: Physiological and Biochemical Adaptations,* H. C. Heller, X. J. Musacchia, and L. C. H. Wang, eds., pp. 351–358, Elsevier, New York.
Zvolsky, P., L. Jansky, J. Vyskocilova, and P. Grof (1981) Effects of psychotropic drugs on hamster hibernation—pilot study. Prog. Neuro-Psychopharmacol. *5:* 599–602.

11

Seasonal Affective Disorders: Animal Models Non Fingo

Irving Zucker

Public support for biological research on animals, financed in the United States by the National Institutes of Health, is predicated on the assumption of ultimate direct benefit to people. In the present climate of animal rights activism, research that does not deal with disease states, but that nevertheless has clinical significance, reaffirms the value of basic scientific inquiry (cf. Comroe, 1978). Because behavioral and psychological research on animals has been attacked as useless or without scientific merit by several groups (e.g., the Human/Animal Liberation Front and the Medical Research Modernization Committee), I was gratified to learn that winter depression could be alleviated by extending natural winter daylengths with bright artificial light (Rosenthal *et al.*, 1985); animal research played an important role in the development of this treatment (see, e.g., Wehr *et al.*, 1986). The interplay between basic (i.e., non-mission-oriented) scientific research and clinical advances has been documented many times (e.g., Comroe, 1978), but animal researchers would do well to relate their activities wherever possible to clinical concerns.

In this chapter, I evaluate the utility of animal models in the study of seasonal affective disorder (SAD). Although I conclude that there are no adequate animal models of SAD, it nevertheless is clear that animal research in chronobiology can continue to play an important role in understanding normal and aberrant seasonal rhythms of humans. Moreover, the development of pharmacological and photic interventions for treating seasonal affective disorders is likely to benefit from insights generated by animal research.

SAD Phenomenology in Comparative Perspective

Ordinary room lighting (200 lux) is a potent zeitgeber for biological rhythms of many animals, but much brighter illumination (2500 lux) is needed to entrain

This chapter is dedicated to the memory of Frank A. Beach.

Irving Zucker. Department of Psychology, University of California, Berkeley, California.

human circadian rhythms, or to suppress nighttime melatonin levels (reviewed in Lewy and Sack, 1986). Prior to 1980, humans were viewed as differing from all other creatures in their lack of susceptibility to photic entrainment of circadian rhythms (Wever, 1979), but animal research provided part of the impetus for the re-examination that established photic entrainment in humans (Czeisler et al., 1981).

The common chronobiological heritage of humans and other animals was extended with the description of the SAD syndrome; lethargy, sleep distur-bance, carbohydrate craving, weight gain, and clinical depression are among symptoms that recur in certain individuals during the winter months each year (Rosenthal et al., 1985). The amelioration of SAD symptoms with supplemen-tary bright-light treatment in winter, while exciting in its own right, was remi-niscent of photoperiodic effects on seasonal behavioral rhythms in many other animals; extension of daylength in winter prematurely instates springtime phys-iological relations and transforms winter responses to those typical of spring and summer (e.g., Zucker et al., 1980).

Clinical researchers charged with the daunting task of caring for the sea-sonally depressed seek understanding, inspiration, and guidance from animal research. Though the current fashion is to study animal models rather than animals, processes (e.g., circadian organization, photoperiodism, phase re-sponse curves) rather than disease states are usually modeled. Chronobiologists have clarified the nature of temporal organization by elucidating formal prop-erties (Pittendrigh and Daan, 1976) and mechanisms for generation and entrain-ment (Rusak and Zucker, 1979) of biological rhythms.

Chronobiological principles derived from animal research have been ap-plied in developing therapies for-several human temporal dysfunctions, includ-ing those manifested by shift workers and jet-lagged travelers (Czeisler et al., 1983) and the affectively disordered (Wehr et al., 1979).

Animal models of depression are evaluated on the basis of several criteria, including face validity, or the extent to which the model resembles human depression in terms of etiology, biochemistry, symptomatology, and treatment (McKinney and Bunney, 1969); they are also evaluated on the basis of predic-tive validity, or the success enjoyed by the model in developing antidepressant treatments, and the frequency with which the model makes errors of commis-sion or omission. Finally, construct validity is assessed by whether behavior of the model and the feature of depression it models can be unambiguously inter-preted and are homologous (Willner, 1984). Having reviewed animal research in chronobiology that influenced the development of phototherapy for depres-sion, I am convinced that sensu strictu there are no acceptable animal models of SAD, although some of the models have limited face and predictive validity. Despite this negative conclusion, the heuristic value of the animal research in guiding and stimulating innovative approaches to the study of SADs cannot be denied. Information in support of these conclusions is presented below.

Models as Nonmodels

According to one dictionary definition, a "model" is a standard, pattern, example, or ideal to be imitated, or in comparison with which anything is to be judged. Investigators of SAD will be frustrated if they attempt to imitate animal research; comparison of human and animal studies with respect to robustness, reliability, and presumed function of the phenomena under study serves little or no useful purpose and slights the far greater complexity of the human syndrome, as well as the difficulties inherent in clinical research. Hence the title of my chapter (with apologies to Isaac Newton). Animal studies in chronobiology aid SAD researchers by describing a conceptual framework for biological time measurement (see Pittendrigh, Chapter 8, this volume) and by providing paradigms for manipulating rhythmic functions and elaborating their physiological basis. But I fail to see that the animal investigations have furnished surrogates for human seasonal depression, and think that they are unlikely to do so. This failure does not, in my view, detract seriously from the utility of animal research for those who would understand SADs.

The biological psychiatrist perusing physiology journals for a viable animal model of SAD, like the reader of fashion ads, is in danger of buying a bill of goods. The animal physiologist has available several thousand species for chronobiological investigation and can turn up specimens that manifest virtually any trait in exaggerated or muted form. Laboratory settings can be structured to produce uniform conditions and to yield reliable data that are simply unattainable in most human experimentation. The descendants of animals that respond in other than the normative fashion can be eliminated from subsequent studies, thereby creating a subject pool that shares many features with modal animals, but, like fashion models in advertisements, shows none of the scars associated with life in the woods. The animal researcher has access to airbrushes denied the clinician. It is unrealistic and ultimately defeating to expect studies of SAD in the outpatient or psychiatric ward to achieve results as pristine as those from the laboratory.

Benefits of Animal Behavioral Research

If viable animal models are not likely to materialize, what benefits can animal research provide for SAD investigation? Traditionally, animal experimentation has been the most efficient route for developing methods to describe and classify behavior for subsequent application to human studies. The function of a particular behavior in a given species can be appreciated more fully if the behavior has been investigated in a number of species (Hinde, 1974), and animal experiments provide perspective on the uniqueness of human behavior. For example, documentation that free-living female baboons withdraw from the social group and are more prone to negative or agonistic encounters during the premenstruum (Hausfater and Skoblick, 1985) is valuable in dismissing claims that the premenstrual syndrome in humans is exclusively a product of our unique psyches, expectations, and cognition.

Beach (1979) argues that meaningful comparisons between animal and human data must be based on functional outcomes and not on formal characteristics of the behavior under study. Thus, it is not valid *a priori* to use male–male mounting behavior of rats as a model of homosexuality in humans, despite obvious similarities in the behavior patterns. Nor is it legitimate to use winter weight gain of Syrian hamsters *(Mesocricetus auratus)* as a model of seasonal weight increases of SAD patients, unless the functions of weight gain are similar for each species. Confidence also increases if the animal behavior in question shares a common mechanism with the human behavior being modeled. It is difficult to satisfy these criteria.

Scientifically valid comparisons between species require the use of common analytic procedures and similar dimensions, and the validity of interspecific generalization cannot exceed the reliability of intraspecific analysis (Beach, 1979). Pains should be taken to make subject selection and statistical treatment in SAD research conform to standards common in other research. The monitoring of similar endpoints (e.g., serum melatonin levels, body weight, sleep onset and end, etc.) in animal and human studies is a positive feature to be retained in future SAD investigations.

Having enumerated some of the difficulties involved in modeling human disorders, I still maintain that *principles* emerging from animal studies are germane to SAD research. Several chronobiological themes relevant to SADs are developed in what follows.

Seasonal Rhythms: How Endogenous Are They?

Circannual Rhythms

Completely endogenous annual rhythms (labeled "circannual," Gwinner, 1986), recur at intervals of approximately 12 months in the absence of periodic changes in the external environment. Mammals known to manifest such rhythms include monkeys, bats, ground squirrels, chipmunks, marmots, dormice, jumping mice, deer, goats, and sheep (Gwinner, 1986, pp. 15–16). Figure 11-1 illustrates circannual body weight cycles of individual golden-mantled ground squirrels maintained for several years in an unvarying photoperiod of 10 hr light per day and a constant temperature of 23°C. The period of the rhythm, measured peak to peak, was on average 336 ± 5 and 356 ± 9 days, respectively, during the first and second cycles for sham-operated animals (Zucker, 1985); pinealectomy shortened the period of the circannual rhythm by 27 and 58 days in the

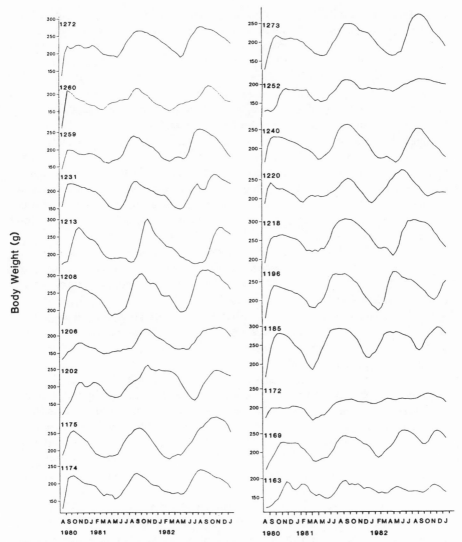

FIGURE 11-1. Body weights of individual pinealectomized (right panel) and sham-pinealectom-
ized (left panel) squirrels over 29 consecutive months. Body weight measures (except for the first
in each record) represent 3-point moving means. Note discontinuities in the ordinate scale. From
Zucker (1985). Reprinted by permission of the American Physiological Society.

first and second cycle, respectively. The results are perhaps most relevant to the SAD phenomenon in demonstrating that seasonal cycles can persist in pinealectomized mammals in a constant environment (Fig. 11-1, right panel). In this species, seasonal variations in pineal melatonin secretion are not necessary for generation of circannual rhythms of body weight or reproduction.

In human studies, it is not possible to provide constant environmental conditions over an interval of 2 or more years; therefore, determination of whether SADs or other human seasonal rhythms are "circannual" in the sense in which Gwinner (1986) uses the term is not possible. Given the robust circannual rhythms shown by rhesus monkeys (Michael and Bonsall, 1977), and the seeming entrainment of such cycles by photoperiod (Bielert and Vandenbergh, 1981), some, if not many, human seasonal rhythms are probably generated by a circannual mechanism. In particular, seasonal variations in human brain chemistry and in reactivity to environmental stimuli may predispose some people to depression or other behavioral sequelae at certain times of year.

The neural pathways and circuits involved in the generation of circannual rhythms are not known for any species (Zucker and Dark, 1986). Integrity of the suprachiasmatic nuclei (SCN), which is essential for normal expression of many circadian rhythms (Rusak and Zucker, 1979; Moore, 1983), is not required for generation of circannual rhythms in most golden-mantled ground squirrels (Zucker et al., 1983; Dark et al., 1985). Nor are circannual rhythms derived by frequency demultiplication (a form of counting) of circadian rhythms (Carmichael and Zucker, 1986).

The range of environmental conditions under which circannual rhythms are expressed is relatively narrow in comparison with circadian rhythms (Gwinner, 1986). In some species (e.g., the European starling, *Sturnus vulgaris*), circannual rhythms persist in an LD 12:12 photoperiod but not in photoperiods shorter than 11 hr or longer than 13 hr per day (see Gwinner, 1986). Of potential interest to SAD researchers, the annual rhythms of one behavior may persist, whereas another may dampen or not be expressed at all under different test conditions.

The period of the free-running circannual rhythm deviates markedly from 12 months; it is not uncommon for ground squirrels to have cycles 9 months in duration. This deviation from the matched geophysical cycle is much larger than is observed for circadian rhythms. Circannual rhythms, in contrast to circadian rhythms, also can be entrained to a much broader range of environmental cycles. For example, the circannual antler cycle of Sika deer can be driven with an accelerated photoperiod regimen to express periods of 4 months (Goss, 1969).

In the golden-mantled ground squirrel, circadian rhythms vary on a circannual basis, *even when animals are maintained under unvarying conditions over the course of several years*. This is shown in Figures 11-2 and 11-3 for squirrels housed in an LD 14:10 photoperiod or in constant light. In the LD cycle, squirrels remain entrained to the photoperiod all year; however, the phase angle

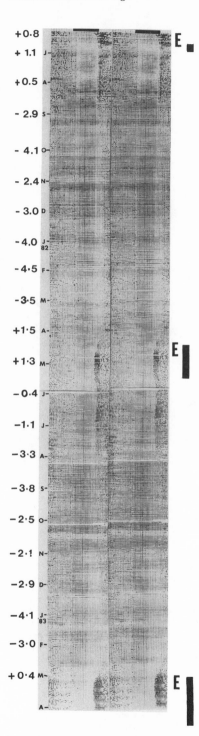

FIGURE 11-2. Continuous double-plotted record of wheel-running activity of a squirrel maintained in an LD 14:10 photoperiod from June 1981 through April 1983. The daily dark phase (2100–0700 hr) is designated by the horizontal bar at the top of the record. Numbers along the left margin indicate mean time of activity onset for each month relative to 0700 hr; onsets before and after 0700 hr were assigned positive and negative values, respectively. Transitions from negative to positive values occurred between March and April in 1982 and between February and March in 1983; circannual period for the transition was therefore 11 months. Duration of estrus (E) each year is indicated by vertical bars along the right margin; the period between onsets of estrus in 1982–1983 was 10.7 months. From Lee *et al.* (1986). Reprinted by permission of the American Physiological Society.

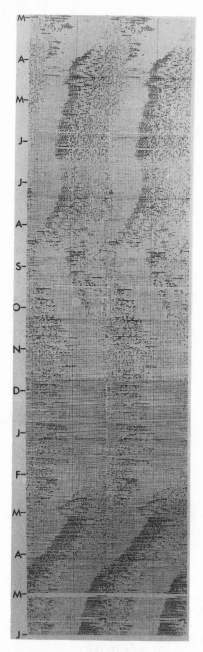

FIGURE 11-3. Continuous activity record of a squirrel, beginning 133 days after the animal was placed in constant light. From Zucker *et al.* (1983). Reprinted by permission of the American Physiological Society.

of activity onset and end (Fig. 11-2), as well as the amount of activity, vary markedly over the course of each circannual cycle (Lee *et al.*, 1986). Changes in phase angles of activity onset correspond to, and probably are caused by, circannual variations in the period of the circadian oscillator(s) for locomotor activity (Fig. 11-3). Although humans undergo seasonal cycles in the period of their free-running circadian temperature rhythms and in the sleep fraction (Wirz-Justice *et al.*, 1984), these differences seem to disappear when subjects are entrained by environmental zeitgebers.

Seasonal Rhythms Dependent on Environmental Input

Most seasonal rhythms do not persist for more than one cycle in the absence of periodic environmental input. A "typical" long-day mammal (e.g., the Syrian hamster, *Mesocricetus auratus*) will maintain reproductive activity when housed in a fixed long-day photoperiod (>14 hr of light/day) or in constant light, and will not undergo reproductive involution or manifest reproductive cycles. In a fixed short-day photoperiod or in constant darkness, hamsters undergo regression of the reproductive system, including loss of spermatogenesis and ovulation. Reproductive quiescence endures approximately 4 months, after which the reproductive system undergoes "spontaneous" recrudescence and full reproductive activity is regained and maintained thereafter. In no instance do hamsters kept in any fixed daylength manifest recurrent reproductive cycles (Reiter, 1978). However, recurrent cycles are observed under natural photoperiods or when long and short daylengths are alternated over the course of a year, to simulate the natural illumination cycle (Reiter, 1978). Thus, many species require seasonal variations in daylength to accomplish what is achieved in others by the endogenous circannual mechanism.

I have emphasized body weight and reproductive rhythms in but two species to illustrate different time measurement systems, but the description also applies to other seasonal rhythms and to a number of mammals (Dark and Zucker, 1985; Stetson and Watson-Whitmyre, 1984). If SAD is mediated by a circannual pacemaker, one would expect eventual remission of winter depression and associated symptoms, *even in the absence of changes in daylength*. A similar prediction applies if SAD is a photoperiodically regulated seasonal rhythm; that is, when the neuroendocrine axis becomes refractory to the prevailing photoperiod, as it does for all known photoperiodic traits, symptoms ought to abate.

Individual Differences

To most biologists, individual differences are a bugbear; after all, high variances obscure effects of experimental treatments. It is a rare investigator who has not at times felt that compelling evidence in support of a pet hypothesis would have materialized, had it not been for the few individuals intuition dictated should have been excluded from the study in the first place. The need for statistical analysis arises in large part because of individual differences in response to treatment. The pervasiveness of individual differences in nonhuman populations, and their functional meaning, are underappreciated (see Slater, 1981). In clinical studies, it is not uncommon for interventions that are generally ineffective to help some proportion of the test population. Rosenthal *et al.* (1986 and personal communication) found that the mood of 3 of 19 SAD patients administered the beta-adrenergic blocker atenolol markedly improved during drug treatment, but not otherwise. For other patients, the treatment was no better than a placebo. How does one interpret such findings?

Several examples from animal chronobiology illustrate the significance and pervasiveness of individual differences. Only 3 of 26 pinealectomized European starlings became permanently arrhythmic; 6 others manifested arrhythmicity for at least 4 weeks after they were pinealectomized; and the remaining 17 pinealectomized birds retained normal circadian rhythms (Gwinner, 1978). Since pineal gland removal was confirmed for each of these animals, and since incidental damage to nearby structures presumably did not compromise the outcome, the disparate intraspecific response is puzzling. Moreover, in several other avian species, pinealectomy consistently abolishes circadian rhythmicity (Menaker and Zimmerman, 1976). Gwinner attempts to reconcile these findings by proposing that the pineal gland is a self-sustained circadian oscillator in each of the individual birds considered above, and that other self-sustained oscillators ("slaves"), weakly coupled to each other and strongly linked to the pineal pacemaker, constitute the network responsible for generating the circadian rhythm in locomotion. In individual birds (or species), in the absence of the pineal, the coupling among the slave oscillators may be too weak to keep them synchronized with each other, and they free-run with their own natural frequencies, eventually resulting in arrhythmicity. In other individuals, coupling among the slave oscillators is stronger, and rhythmicity is retained in the absence of the driving pineal pacemaker.

This example illustrates the principle that natural selection is concerned with a particular outcome (in this case, circadian rhythmicity of the birds' locomotor activity) and not with the specific mechanisms by which this end is achieved. Although the proposition cannot be proven, it seems plausible. Variation in coupling strength between oscillators in individual animals can be viewed as "noise" that can be tolerated because it does not affect the important outcome. Situations may exist in which there is no selective basis for differences among adaptations; consequently, different adaptations can be adopted by individuals from the same population (cf. Gould and Lewontin, 1979). The tasks of the comparative physiologist include elaboration of constraints on the number and nature of mechanisms that yield a particular form of temporal organization.

A second possibility, suggested by studies of photoperiodism and reproduction in white-footed mice (Johnston and Zucker, 1980), is that selection favors the adoption of different strategies by different individuals, reflecting exploitation of different aspects of the environment (Bock, 1980). First-generation offspring of wild-caught mice were maintained in the laboratory from birth to adulthood in an LD 14:10 photoperiod and then transferred to a 10:14 (short-day) photocycle. Approximately 70–80% of the short-day animals in different experiments underwent gonadal involution, the remainder showing no signs of regression during extended short-day treatment. Variants of this finding have been reported for several rodent species (Desjardins and Lopez, 1983; Eskes and Zucker, 1978) and for different photoperiodic traits. In natural populations of small rodents, some percentage of the animals are not obligatorily photoperiodic and therefore not compelled to regress their gonads with the advent of short daylengths. Such individuals retain the capability of breeding in winter (e.g., Christian, 1980), under unpredictably favorable environmental circumstances (a warm spell or availability of a rich food source). This trait presumably was selected for and retained in some individuals because it increased their fitness. It is to be expected that physiological mechanisms that mediate responsiveness to short daylengths (potentially involving the circadian system, patterns and amounts of melatonin secretion, sensitivity of target tissues to hormones, etc.) will differ among individuals that do or do not retain the ability to breed in winter.

Feral mice, like SAD patients, are a more heterogeneous lot than some laboratory studies of inbred strains have indicated; response variability to intero- and exteroceptive stimuli may be noise to be filtered and eliminated, or part of an adaptive program established through natural selection.

Adaptive Significance

Rosenthal and Wehr (1987) imply that seasonal depression in humans may have evolved in the service of energy conservation. This is unlikely on allometric grounds (Mrosovsky, Chapter 10, this volume). We need to recall that not all phenotypic traits are adaptations. Some organismal features undoubtedly are functionless, and others that may now enhance fitness were not built by selection for their current use (Gould and Vrba, 1982; Olding-Smee, 1983).

Traits, Not Individuals, Are Photoperiodic

Species as well as individuals have been characterized as photoperiodic or nonphotoperiodic, respectively. This classification is based on one or at most a few traits that vary or remain unchanged in the face of seasonal changes in daylength. Laboratory rats and mice are considered nonphotoperiodic (Bronson, 1979; Nelson and Zucker, 1981), because their gonads do not involute in short

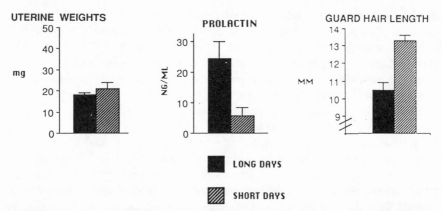

FIGURE 11-4. Uterine weights, plasma prolactin levels, and guard hair length in female voles maintained in long (LD 16:8) or short (LD 8:16) daylengths from birth and sampled at 47 days of age. Adapted from Smale *et al.* (1988). Used by permission.

daylengths; Syrian hamsters and meadow voles epitomize photoperiodic rodents, because exposure to short days produces gonadal involution (Reiter, 1980; Dark and Zucker, 1985). This oversimplified classification requires revision, as exemplified by responses of the prairie vole, *Microtus ochrogaster*. In the field in south central Illinois, this species is highly seasonal, with reproduction curtailed during most winters. Laboratory descendants of these animals are, in adulthood, minimally responsive to variations in daylength *vis-à-vis* reproduction (Nelson, 1985), and thus were labeled "nonphotoperiodic." Subsequently, other traits of these voles were found to be highly responsive to photoperiod. Fur is thicker and guard hairs longer in short daylengths, and plasma levels of prolactin are lower (Fig. 11-4). The same voles whose pelage and prolactin levels are regulated by daylength harbor a reproductive system completely indifferent to photoperiod (Smale *et al.,* 1988; Fig. 11-4). Depending on the trait chosen, these animals could just as legitimately be labeled photoperiodic or nonphotoperiodic. Classification along the photoperiodic dimension must be restricted to particular traits, not extended to whole animals.

The circadian mechanism used to measure daylength appears to exist even in species in which certain key traits (e.g., reproduction) are nonphotoperiodic (e.g., rats; Nelson *et al.,* 1982). Since variations in daylength are, for the most part, transduced by the pineal gland, through variation in the duration of elevated nighttime melatonin secretion (Goldman and Darrow, 1983; Bittman, 1985), coexistence of nonphotoperiodic and photoperiodic traits in an individual animal is most likely attributable to postpineal factors. Selective target tissue sensitivity, or masking by hormones, may permit one trait to be unaffected by photoperiod while another remains responsive. Alternatively, some effects of daylength may be mediated by pineal-independent processes (Bartness and Wade, 1985). The implications for the multifaceted SAD syndrome are apparent.

Interspecific Constancy: Joys of the Black Box

The emphasis heretofore on differences between and within species reflects the diverse mechanisms that subserve the same phenomenon (seasonality) in several mammalian species. Nevertheless, many relations between biological clocks and behavior have been preserved in the course of evolution. With few exceptions, animals and plants have not adopted hourglass mechanisms for measurement of daylength (Elliott, 1976), and instead make use of their circadian rhythms to distinguish long from short days (Elliott and Goldman, 1981). Whether they do so through internal or external coincidence mechanisms (Pittendrigh, 1981) is a separate issue, but deployment of circadian machinery to chart the passage of the seasons is firmly established. We can therefore confidently assume that any human seasonal rhythm based on photoperiodic time measurement is mediated by the circadian system. This extrapolation from animal to human systems well exemplifies the utility of animal research for understanding human seasonal rhythms.

The entrainment of free-running circadian (and circannual) rhythms by the light–dark cycle is nearly universal and implies, as an analytic necessity, the existence of phase response curves (PRCs) to light. This feature has been confirmed in many species of plants and animals. The exact shape of the PRC differs between species; however, in virtually all cases, light exposure early in the subjective night delays, and light late in the subjective night advances, circadian rhythms. Although we do not have a PRC for human circadian rhythms, it again seems safe to assume that its general features will correspond to those described for other mammals.

Research on reptiles, birds, and mammals, involving either manipulation of light cycles or perturbation of the neuroendocrine system, indicates that vertebrate circadian systems are composed of driving pacemakers that synchronize slave oscillators in other tissues and organs. The complete temporal program emerges when the driving pacemaker is entrained by external zeitgebers and in turn synchronizes slave oscillators (Pittendrigh, 1981).

Some relations, to date established for one or a few species, probably apply generally. It is commonplace that after a phase shift in the illumination cycle, resynchronization of rhythms occurs gradually over the course of several days. This does not accurately reflect the pacemaker's resetting, which occurs much more rapidly (Pittendrigh, 1981). During the interval characterized by transients between the old and new steady state, the relation between the pacemaker and its rhythms is disrupted.

It is hard to conceive how these and other relations could have been realized except through studies of nonhuman organisms. Research directed at understanding temporal organization in animals has led to paradigms for manipulating and conceptualizing human biological rhythms, as is made abundantly clear in a volume titled *Circadian Rhythms in Psychiatry* (Wehr and Goodwin, 1983).

The relation between animal and clinical researchers in understanding SADs is illustrated by the tale of the leek farmer who was invited by a group of chefs to pass judgment on several varieties of vichyssoise. He addressed his hosts as follows: "Leeks are beautiful to contemplate, and growing them is rewarding, especially when chefs use them in soups to good advantage. Some of you have doctored the leeks to such an extent I can't even detect them in the soup, but for the most part I like what you have done with my produce. I understand the pressures of keeping a restaurant open every week of the year, with customers seeking the ultimate vichyssoise. So I'll try to grow new and better leeks. But please remember, the quality of your soup will depend at least as much on your skill in selecting and blending other ingredients as on the leeks themselves. Ultimately, chefs and restaurant patrons, not farmers, must judge whether the soup is good."

Acknowledgments

Preparation of this chapter was supported in part by Grant No. HD-14595 from the National Institute of Child Health and Human Development. I am grateful to Warren Holmes, Frank Beach, Norman Rosenthal, Theresa Lee, and John Dark for comments on an earlier version of this chapter.

This chapter originally appeared in *Journal of Biological Rhythms,* Volume 3, Number 2, pp. 209–223, 1988. Reprinted by permission of The Guilford Press.

References

Bartness, T. J., and G. N. Wade (1985) Photoperiodic control of seasonal body weight cycles in hamsters. Neurosci. Biobehav. Rev. *9:* 599–612.

Beach, F. A. (1979) Animal models for human sexuality. Ciba Found. Symp. *62:* 113–143.

Bielert, C., and J. G. Vandenbergh (1981) Seasonal influences on births and male sex skin coloration in rhesus monkeys *(Macaca mulatta)* in the Southern Hemisphere. J. Reprod. Fert. *62:* 229–233.

Bittman, E. L. (1985) The role of rhythms in the response to melatonin. Ciba Found. Symp. *117:* 149–164.

Bock, W. J. (1980) The definition and recognition of biological adaptation. Amer. Zool. *20:* 217–227.

Bronson, F. H. (1979) Light intensity and reproduction in wild and domestic house mice. Biol. Reprod. *15:* 94–97.

Carmichael, M. S., and I. Zucker (1986) Circannual rhythms of ground squirrels: A test of the frequency demultiplication hypothesis. J. Biol. Rhythms *1:* 277–284.

Christian, J. J. (1980) Regulation of annual rhythms of reproduction in temperate small rodents. In *Testicular Development, Structure, and Function,* A. Steinberger and E. Steinberger, eds., pp. 367–380, Raven Press, New York.

Comroe, J. H., Jr. (1978) The road from research to new diagnosis and therapy. Science *200:* 931–937.

Czeisler, C. A., M. C. Moore-Ede, and R. M. Coleman (1983) Resetting circadian clocks: Applications to sleep disorders medicine and occupational health. In *Sleep/Wake Disorders: Natural History, Epidemiology, and Long Term Evolution,* C. Guilleminault and E. Lugaresi, eds., pp. 243–260, Raven Press, New York.

Czeisler, C. A., G. S. Richardson, J. C. Zimmerman, M. C. Moore-Ede, and E. Weitzman (1981) Entrainment of human circadian rhythms by light–dark cycles: A reassessment. Photochem. Photobiol. *34:* 239–247.

Dark, J., G. E. Pickard, and I. Zucker (1985) Persistence of circannual rhythms in ground squirrels with lesions of the suprachiasmatic nuclei. Brain Res. *332:* 201–207.

Dark, J., and I. Zucker (1985) Seasonal cycles in energy balance: Regulation by light. Ann. NY Acad. Sci. *453:* 170–181.

Desjardins, C., and M. J. Lopez (1983) Environmental cues evoke differential responses in pituitary–testicular function in deer mice. Endocrinology *112:* 1398–1406.

Elliott, J. A. (1976) Circadian rhythms and photoperiodic time measurement in mammals. Fed. Proc. *35:* 2339–2346.

Elliott, J. A., and B. D. Goldman (1981) Seasonal reproduction: photoperiodism and biological clocks. In *Neuroendocrinology of Reproduction,* N. T. Adler, ed., pp. 377–426, Plenum Press, New York.

Eskes, G. A., and I. Zucker (1978) Photoperiodic control of hamster testis: Dependence on circadian rhythms. Proc. Natl. Acad. Sci. *75:* 1034–1038.

Goldman, B. D., and J. M. Darrow (1983) The pineal gland and mammalian photoperiodism. Neuroendocrinology *37:* 386–396.

Goss, R. J. (1969) Photoperiodic control of antler cycles in deer: I. Phase shift and frequency changes. J. Exp. Zool. *170:* 311–324.

Gould, S. J., and R. C. Lewontin (1979) The spandrels of San Marco and the Panglossian paradigm: A critique of the adaptationist programme. Proc. Roy. Soc. Lond. B. *205:* 581–598.

Gould, S. J., and E. S. Vrba (1982) Exaptation–a missing term in the science of form. Paleobiology *8:* 4–15.

Gwinner, E. (1978) Effects of pinealectomy on circadian locomotor activity rhythms in European starlings *(Sturnus vulgaris).* J. Comp. Physiol. *126:* 123–129.

Gwinner, E. (1986) *Circannual Rhythms,* Springer-Verlag, Berlin.

Hausfater, G., and B. Skoblick (1985) Perimenstrual behavior changes among female yellow baboons: Some similarities to premenstrual syndrome (PMS) in women. Amer. J. Primat. *9:* 165–172.

Hinde, R. A. (1974) *The Biological Basis of Human Social Behavior,* McGraw-Hill, New York.

Johnston, P. G., and I. Zucker (1980) Photoperiodic regulation of the testes of adult white-footed mice *(Peromyscus leucopus).* Biol. Reprod. *23:* 859–866.

Lee, T. M., M. S. Carmichael, and I. Zucker (1986) Circannual variations in circadian rhythms of ground squirrels. Amer. J. Physiol. *250:* R831–R836.

Lewy, A. J., and R. L. Sack (1986) Light therapy and psychiatry. Proc. Soc. Exp. Biol. Med. *183:* 11–18.

McKinney, W. T., and W. E. Bunney (1969) Animal model of depression: Review of evidence and implications for research. Arch. Gen. Psychiat. *21:* 240–248.

Menaker, M., and N. Zimmerman (1976) Role of the pineal in the circadian system of birds. Amer. Zool. *16:* 45–55.

Michael, R. P., and R. W. Bonsall (1977) A 3-year study of an annual rhythm in plasma androgen levels in male rhesus monkeys *(Macaca mulatta)* in a constant laboratory environment. J. Reprod. Fert. *49:* 129–131.

Moore, R. Y. (1983) Organization and function of a central nervous system circadian oscillator: The suprachiasmatic hypothalamic nucleus. Fed. Proc. *42:* 2783–2789.

Nelson, R. J. (1985) Photoperiod influences reproduction in the prairie vole *(Microtus ochrogaster).* Biol. Reprod. *33:* 596–602.

Nelson, R. J., M. K. Bamat, and I. Zucker (1982) Photoperiodic regulation of testis function in rats: Mediation by a circadian mechanism. Biol. Reprod. *26:* 329–335.

Nelson, R. J., and I. Zucker (1981) Photoperiodic control of reproduction on olfactory-bulbectomized rats. Neuroendocrinology *32:* 266–271.

Olding-Smee, F. J. (1983) Multiple levels in evolution: An approach to the nature–nurture issue via "applied epistemology." In *Animal Models of Human Behavior*, G. C. L. Davey, ed., pp. 135–158, Wiley, Chichester, England.

Pittendrigh, C. S. (1981) Circadian organization and the photoperiodic phenomena. In *Biological Clocks in Seasonal Reproductive Cycles*, B. K. Follett and D. E. Follett, eds., pp 1–35, John Wright & Sons, Bristol, England.

Pittendrigh, C. S., and S. Daan (1976) A functional analysis of circadian pacemakers in nocturnal rodents: V. Pacemaker structure: A clock for all seasons. J. Comp. Physiol. *106:* 333–355.

Reiter, R. J. (1978) Interaction of photoperiod, pineal and seasonal reproduction as exemplified by findings in the hamster. Prog. Reprod. Biol. *4:* 169–190.

Reiter, R. J. (1980) The pineal and its hormones in the control of reproduction in mammals. Endocrinol. Rev. *1:* 109–131.

Rosenthal, N. E., D. A. Sack, F. M. Jacobsen, S. P. James, B. L. Parry, J. Arendt, L. Tamarkin, and T. A. Wehr (1986) Melatonin in seasonal affective disorder and phototherapy. J Neural Trans. *21*(Suppl.): 257–267.

Rosenthal, N. E., D. A. Sack, S. P. James, B. L. Parry, W. B. Mendelson, L. Tamarkin, and T. A. Wehr (1985) Seasonal affective disorder and phototherapy. Ann. NY Acad. Sci. *453:* 260–269.

Rosenthal, N. E., and T. A. Wehr (1987) Seasonal affective disorders. Psychiat. Ann. *17*(10): 670–674.

Rusak, B., and I. Zucker (1979) Neural regulation of circadian rhythms. Physiol. Rev. *59:* 449–526.

Slater, P. J. B. (1981) Individual differences in animal behavior. In *Perspectives in Ethology*, P. P. G. Bateson and P. H. Klopfer, eds., pp. 35–49, Plenum Press, New York.

Smale, L., R. J. Nelson, and I. Zucker (1988) Daylength influences pelage and plasma prolactin concentrations but not reproduction in the prairie vole, *Microtus ochrogaster*. J. Reprod. Fert. *83:* 99–106.

Stetson, M. H., and M. Watson-Whitmyre (1984) Physiology of the pineal and its hormone melatonin in annual reproduction in rodents. In *The Pineal Gland*, R. J. Reiter, ed., pp. 109–153, Raven Press, New York.

Wehr, T. A., and F. K. Goodwin, eds. (1983) *Circadian Rhythms in Psychiatry*, Boxwood Press, Pacific Grove, CA.

Wehr, T. A., F. M. Jacobsen, D. A. Sack, J. Arendt, L. Tamarkin, and N. E. Rosenthal (1986) Phototherapy of seasonal affective disorder. Time of day and suppression of melatonin are not critical for antidepressant effects. Arch. Gen. Psychiat. *43:* 870–875.

Wehr, T. A., A. Wirz-Justice, F. K. Goodwin, W. Duncan, and J. C. Gillin (1979) Phase advance of the circadian sleep–wake cycle as an anti-depressant. Science *206:* 710–713.

Wever, R. (1979) *The Circadian System of Man*, Springer-Verlag, Berlin.

Willner, P. (1984) The validity of animal models of depression. Psychopharmacology *83:* 1–16.

Wirz-Justice, A., R. A. Wever, and J. Aschoff (1984) Seasonality in free-running circadian rhythms in man. Naturwissenschaften *71:* 316–319.

Zucker, I. (1985) Pineal gland influences period of circannual rhythms of ground squirrels. Amer. J. Physiol. *249:* R111–R115.

Zucker, I., M. Boshes, and J. Dark (1983) Suprachiasmatic nuclei influence circannual and circadian rhythms of ground squirrels. Amer. J. Physiol. *244:* R472–R480.

Zucker, I., and J. Dark (1986) Neuroendocrine substrates of circannual rhythms in ground squirrels. In *Living in the Cold*, H. C. Heller, X. J. Musacchia, and L. C. H. Wang, eds., pp. 351–358, Elsevier, New York.

Zucker, I., P. G. Johnston, and D. Frost (1980) Comparative, physiological and biochronometric analyses of rodent seasonal reproductive cycles. Prog. Reprod. Biol. *5:* 102–133.

Seasonal Changes in the Normal Population

Seasonal Variation in Normal Subjects: An Update of Variables Current in Depression Research

Verena Lacoste and Anna Wirz-Justice

Temporal order in living systems becomes evident in biological rhythms, especially in those rhythms which correspond to temporal structures in the environment. There are four of them: the tides, day and night, the phases of the moon, and the seasons.

—Aschoff and Pohl (1970)

The study of seasonal rhythms in humans is of respectable lineage. Although periodic phenomena often become more evident in pathological states, an overview of the literature in the past shows large diversity in the biological functions and behavioral patterns that, in healthy subjects, vary with time of year (summarized, e.g., in Reinberg, 1974, 1979; Aschoff, 1981; Halberg *et al.*, 1983).

Among the diseases with a seasonal course (reviewed in De Rudder, 1952; Faust and Sarreither, 1975; Faust, 1976; Reinberg and Smolensky, 1983b; Abel *et al.*, 1986), affective disorder is perhaps the earliest studied in detail with respect to periodicity (Menninger-Lerchenthal, 1960; Papousek, 1976). Recent reawakened interest in temporal organization and disorganization in depression has led to modifications of old concepts such as the monoamine hypothesis (Halbreich, 1985; Siever and Kenneth, 1985), and to formulation of new ones such as the phase-advance hypothesis (Wehr *et al.*, 1979) and the "Process S" hypothesis (Borbély and Wirz-Justice, 1982). In particular, the description of seasonal affective disorder (SAD)—the periodic recurrence of a major depressive disorder in consecutive autumn or winter months, with remission in summer—requires a reconsideration of the possible physiological basis of susceptibility to a depressive episode in winter.

The aim of this chapter is not to review the literature on seasonal effects

Verena Lacoste and Anna Wirz-Justice. Psychiatric University Clinic, CH-4025 Basel, Switzerland.

in healthy subjects extensively; rather, we have selected those behavioral, physiological, and biochemical measures that have been considered important in the pathophysiology of affective disorders, particularly SAD. The chronobiological principles implicit in such a perspective have been elucidated in detail elsewhere (Randall, 1970; Pengelley, 1974; Scheving *et al.*, 1974; Rusak and Zucker, 1975; Pittendrigh and Daan, 1976; Gwinner, 1981, 1986; Farner, 1985; Hastings *et al.*, 1985).

Two problems have been encountered in preparing this review: that of the variability in the design of a seasonal study, so that comparison is difficult; and that of the unfortunate variability in quality of the studies, precluding definitive statements in many cases.

Psychological Variables

Are long-term changes in psychobehavioral assessments characteristic only for disease states with seasonal mood swings, or are they present also in normal subjects? If seasonality is not restricted to a subjective "preferential time of year," but is reflected in consistent changes in measurable variables in a healthy population, this would have widespread impact. It would lead to a more differentiated insight into the role of the environment in modifying, to a greater or lesser extent, our behavior—from the integration of seasonal affective disease states on a continuum, to a detail such as seasonal standardization of rating scales.

Mood and Related States

To our knowledge, there are few long-term studies of mood states and related variables. Reports of depressed mood, sleep disturbances, and anergia during winters in high northern latitudes are somewhat anecdotal. Our transverse study of self-rated "fatigue" and "depressed mood" revealed a bimodal pattern of highest values in early winter and late spring (see Fig. 12-6, below; Lacoste *et al.*, 1987a).

By far the most extensive longitudinal study published (another study, that of Whybrow *et al.* [1985], is available only in an abstract to date) is that of Eastwood *et al.* (1985). In this project, control subjects and depressed patients (age- and sex-matched) carried out daily self-ratings of mood, anxiety, energy level, and sleep duration for 14 months. Spectral analysis revealed significant infradian rhythms of period lengths ranging from 1 week to 4 months. Patients showed sustained cyclicity in mood and energy more often than controls, as well as a larger amplitude of such cycles, a third of which could be considered seasonal (>85 days). These results confirm the hypothesis put forward by the investigators (and applicable to a large number of variables in our review):

> Affective symptoms, principally mood, are continuously distributed variables with a periodic component. That is, individuals with affective disorders and healthy control subjects both have cycles. . . . The significant difference between disorder and normality in the analysis of these periodicities is in amplitude. (Eastwood *et al.*, 1985, p. 295)

Evidence for such a continuum comes from a recent random-sample survey in New York City (see Terman, Chapter 20, this volume), using the Seasonal Pattern Assessment Questionnaire (SPAQ; Rosenthal *et al.*, 1984). An unexpectedly large number (25%) reported mood, sleep, and appetite aggravation in winter (of these, perhaps 2–3% reached SAD severity), with another 35% noting symptoms but not complaining. Thus the "winter blahs" are apparently widespread at this latitude, resulting in some impairment of function. A smaller survey (nonrandom) in England revealed a similar pattern (Thompson *et al.*, 1988).

A detail in the New York survey is perhaps of interest. Although SAD patients showed a large-amplitude, unimodel seasonal rhythm of symptoms, the random sample showed a tendency to biomodality—a major peak in winter, but also a small group with symptoms peaking in summer. In our study of self-rated mood (not retrospective, as the SPAQ is), there was also a bimodal pattern of subjective "depressivity" and "fatigue" in early winter and in late spring. Since this was a transverse study, the bimodality may result from two populations with differential seasonal susceptibility. Both surveys suggest a possible relationship between this minor summer peak of symptoms and the summer depression shown by a small group ("summer SAD") (see Wehr *et al.*, Chapter 5, this volume).

Performance

Early studies of performance have been extensively reviewed (Hildebrandt and Strempel, 1975). One psychophysiological variable of particular interest, critical flicker–fusion frequency, indicated minimal stress-bearing capacity in spring both in hospitalized patients with different diseases and in older healthy subjects (Drietosomsky, cited in Akos and Akos, 1973). Worst results for mental performance have been obtained in winter (Klinker and Schrader, 1984). The apparently widespread winter "anergy" present in a random population (Terman, Chapter 20, this volume), and our own observations of a "seasonal anergy syndrome" in winter without depressive concomitants (Wark, Wirz-Justice, and Graw, unpublished data), indicate that a proportion of healthy subjects may suffer from reduced performance in winter.

Personality Profiles

A classical tool in the psychologist's armamentarium is the personality inventory. Multivariate analysis yields a profile characteristic for the individual, considered to be a description of trait and not of state. But what if these so-called stable personality characteristics in healthy subjects are dependent upon the season in which the inventory was administered?

A standard, validated self-rating instrument used in German-speaking countries, the Freiburger Personality Inventory (Fahrenberg *et al.*, 1978), has been analyzed with respect to season. Healthy volunteers were administered the inventory in balanced sex- and age-matched groups in each month of an entire year (a transverse study; Lacoste *et al.*, 1987). Three dimensions showed significant seasonal variation within this range (Lacoste and Wirz-Justice, 1987) and are of interest because their seasonal patterns surprisingly resemble parallel phenomena in the seasonality of affective disorders.

The dimension "nervosity—psychosomatic symptoms," which also contains items regarding sleep disturbances, was highly correlated with depressiv-

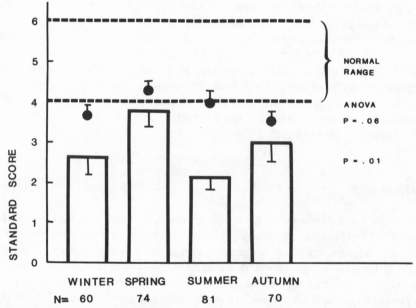

FIGURE 12-1. Seasonal changes on the dimension "depressivity—psychosomatic symptoms" of the Freiburger Personality Inventory (filled circles). The dotted lines indicate the normal range for this dimension, indicating that the sample was at the lower limit (i.e., the subjects were "supernormals" with respect to this mood dimension). In parallel, the Beck Depression Inventory scores in these subjects are indicated by the open bars ($\pm$ *SEM*)—again, very low depressivity ratings. Transverse study ($n = 285$, Basel, Switzerland, 48°N). The data are from Lacoste and Wirz-Justice (1987) and Lacoste *et al.* (1987).

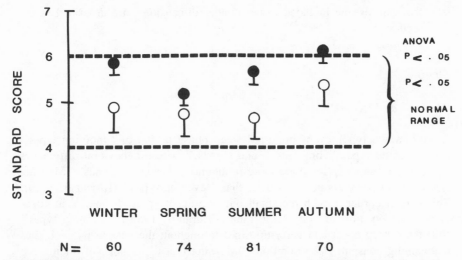

FIGURE 12-2. Seasonal changes on the dimensions "aggressivity" (filled circles) and "masculinity" (open circles) of the Freiburger Personality Inventory. The dotted lines indicate the normal range for these dimensions, indicating that the sample showed seasonal changes within these limits. Transverse study ($n = 285$, Basel, Switzerland, 48°N). The data are from Lacoste and Wirz-Justice (1987) and Lacoste et al. (1987a).

ity. Highest values were found in spring (Fig. 12-1). In addition, the Beck Depression Inventory (Beck et al., 1961), which was used to screen subjects for the study, also showed highest values in spring with a lesser peak in autumn (Fig. 12-1), although it is emphasized that absolute scores were far below levels for psychopathology. These slight but significant increases in "depressivity" in normal subjects in spring have a parallel in the spring peak in the incidence of depression or suicide (for reviews, see Eastwood and Peacocke, 1976; Aschoff, 1981; Rosenthal et al., 1983).

Two other, interrelated dimensions showed significant seasonal peaks in autumn: "spontaneous aggressivity" and "masculinity" (Fig. 12-2). This time of year is that previously reported for maximal aggressivity (Michael and Zumpe, 1983). A number of studies indicate the existence of seasonal change in testicular activity of the human male, with a peak in late autumn and early winter and a trough in spring (Reinberg, 1974; Smals et al., 1976; Reinberg and Lagoguey, 1978).

We thus need to ask how the conventional personality profiles (containing dimensions related to state) are standardized with respect to time of year, if at all. Even though the seasonal variations we observed in this population are within the normal range, their very existence indicates an effect of time of year on personality dimensions.

Seasonal changes in subjective "morningness–eveningness," a character-

istic that can also be included in personality dimensions, are described in the
next section.

Sleep

"Larks" and "Owls"

A well-known typology of preferred sleep phase is that of "morning types"
and "evening types," or "larks" and "owls," whose behavioral differences
(as registered in sleep logs) are more pronounced during weekends. "Morning
types" go to sleep about 1 hr earlier than "evening types" (Kloeppel, 1980).
This is in accordance with the small but significant group difference in circadian phase position of body temperature (Kerkhof, 1985). "Evening types"
shift their sleep onset and wake-up times throughout the year in parallel, thus
maintaining constant sleep duration. "Morning types" do not shift their sleep
onset times throughout the year, but change duration through altered wake-up
times (Kloeppel, 1980).

Three of the rating scales developed for morningness–eveningness have
been tested for their reliability throughout the year in a longitudinal study
(Kloeppel, 1980, 1982). Only one fulfills the criterion of being independent of
seasonal influence. Conversely, it is of interest that the same subjects can rate
themselves as being more "morning types" in spring and more "evening types"
in winter (Fig. 12-3A). An early subjective phase position might be considered
related to the early phase position of the circadian temperature rhythm in spring
(Wirz-Justice *et al.*, 1984).

A simplified morningness–eveningness scale derived from the Horne–Östberg questionnaire (Horne and Östberg, 1976) was administered to a large number of healthy volunteers in a transverse study (Lacoste *et al.*, 1987a). Surprisingly, nearly twice as many subjects considered themselves to be "morning
types" as believed themselves to be "evening types" in spring. An equal distribution was found in the other seasons (Fig. 12-3B).

Using both the Horne–Östberg (1976) and the Torsvall–Akerstedt (1980)

FIGURE 12-3. Seasonal changes in the subjective estimation of "morningness–eveningness." (A)
Longitudinal study: Mean monthly changes in the degree of morningness–eveningness in eight
healthy men and women (Marburg, West Germany, 50°N). The seasonal patterns from three different questionnaires are compared; only the Horne–Östberg scale and that of Wendt showed susceptibility to seasonal shifts. Adapted from Kloeppel (1980). Used by permission. (B) Transverse
study: Distribution of self-estimated "morning types," "evening types," and "intermediate types"
(using a modified Horne–Östberg questionnaire) in healthy men and women across the four seasons
($n = 285$; Basel, Switzerland, 48°N). The shift to "morning types" in spring occurred at the cost
of the "intermediate types" and not the "evening types." The data are from Lacoste and Wirz-
Justice (1987) and Lacoste *et al.* (1987).

(A)

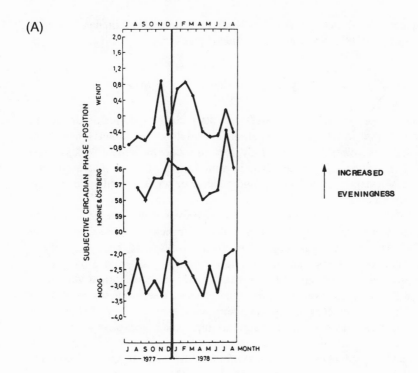

(B)

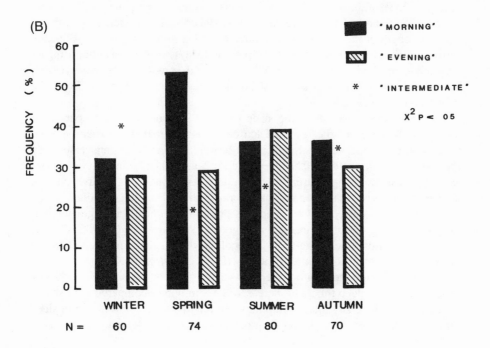

questionnaires, SAD patients ($n = 99$) tended to more "eveningness" than a control group ($n = 78$) (Wirz-Justice, Kräuchi, and Graw, unpublished data).

Sleep Architecture and Duration

One of the primary complaints of SAD patients is the continuous tiredness and the increased need for sleep they experience throughout the winter. Their sleep is, however, not refreshing (one study has also documented 50% less delta sleep in SAD patients in winter than in summer, in spite of increased total sleep time; Mendelson et al., 1985), and patients experience difficulties in getting up in the morning.

The few studies of seasonality in electroencephalographic (EEG) sleep measures and rest–activity cycles from subjective protocols are summarized in Table 12-1. Healthy, normal subjects are likely to be so highly synchronized to their social obligations that there is little room—apart from Sundays—to express variations in sleep need. A remarkable early study of normal volunteers sleeping under controlled conditions for many days or weeks investigated "depth of sleep" by random interpolation of nights with arousal stimuli (Michelson, 1891). Sleep was "deeper" in late autumn and winter than at other times of year.

In a study by Mendelson et al. (1985), healthy subjects showed little differences in sleep profiles in summer and winter. However, a transverse study of sleep EEG parameters in healthy subjects and depressed patients (Rosenthal et al., 1982) showed rapid eye movement (REM) latency increases with increasing length of the photoperiod, with a slight lag in the longest REM latency between controls (July) and depressive patients (May). In the Antarctic, a higher percentage of slow-wave sleep (SWS) was found in winter (Paterson, 1975), but no seasonal differences in any sleep measure were found in a study in the Arctic (Weitzman et al., 1975).

Retrospective analysis of the sleep fraction (percentage of sleep per circadian period) under another kind of extreme condition, that of isolation from time cues, did reveal seasonal changes in healthy subjects in a transverse study (Wirz-Justice et al., 1984). The sleep fraction was greatest in autumn and winter, and least in spring. Furthermore, under these conditions of free choice, women slept longer than men (on the average, about 1 hr longer) (Fig. 12-4).

Other data, derived from sleep log protocols, indicate a lengthening of sleep time during winter compared with summer (Whybrow et al., 1985; Giedke, 1987). In addition, such long-term protocols have revealed periodicities in the infradian range from 1 week to 4 months (Eastwood et al., 1985).

Thus, although the data on sleep are scanty, there appears to be a tendency toward increased sleep time and increased SWS in winter compared with spring or summer. Is there any relationship between the marked sex difference in sleep time noted in temporal isolation (Wirz-Justice et al., 1984) and the unusually

TABLE 12-1. Seasonal Variation of Sleep Parameters

Variable	Subjects			Sampling interval[a]	Rhythm detection method	p	Trough	Peak	Location	Latitude	Reference
	n	Sex	Age								
Total sleep time; sleep stages in percentage of total sleep time (1–4, REM)	7	M	22–40	Four seasons	—	n.s.	—	—	Tromsø (Norway)	69°N	Weitzman et al. (1975)
Percentage of sleep per circadian period[b]	96 40	M F	—	Bimonthly (15 years)	ANOVA	<0.01	May–June	September–October	Andechs (West Germany)	48°N	Wirz-Justice et al. (1984)
Total sleep time	45 18	F M	20–82	—	—	—	Summer	Winter	New England (United States)	46°N	Whybrow et al. (1985)
SWS, REM latency, REM density, total sleep time	—	M,F	—	Two seasons—summer, winter	—	n.s.	—	—	Bethesda, MD (United States)	39°N	Mendelson et al. (1985)
Sleep onset, sleep latency, length of the first REM period, time of waking, delta sleep, REM latency	40	M,F	—	Monthly (10 years)	—	n.s. <0.01 (trend)	January	July	Bethesda, MD (United States)	39°N	Rosenthal et al. (1982)
SWS (in percentage of total sleep time)	10	—	$\bar{x}=25$	Monthly	t test	<0.01	October–November (spring)	June (winter)	Antarctica	75°S	Paterson (1975)

Note. REM, rapid eye movement sleep; SWS, slow-wave sleep; ANOVA, analysis of variance; n.s. nonsignificant.
[a]Durations, where applicable, are given in parentheses.
[b]Transverse study. Subjects isolated from time cues.

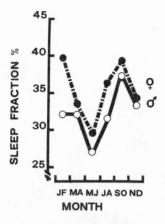

FIGURE 12-4. Seasonal changes in the fraction of sleep per circadian period under conditions of isolation from external time cues. The figure shows a retrospective analysis of data collected over 15 years in normal subjects living on an endogenously generated and self-sustaining activity-rest cycle. The bimonthly mean sleep fraction (without *SEM*, for clarity) was calculated separately for women (filled circles; $n = 32$) and for men (open circles; $n = 68$) (transverse study). Least sleep occurred in spring and most sleep in autumn and winter (analysis of variance; $p < 0.01$); women slept longer than men (average: 54 min longer). Adapted from Wirz-Justice *et al.* (1984). Used by permission.

high proportion of women in the SAD population? Even though the extensive sleep EEG studies of Williams and Spiegel do not have any data on seasonality, they do indicate that after middle age, women tend to sleep longer than men (Spiegel, 1981). This sex difference has recently been confirmed in a multivariate analysis (Kerkhofs *et al.*, 1988).

Feeding and Metabolic Functions

The study of metabolic functions, for many years displaced from depression research by more sophisticated biochemical measures and techniques, is experiencing a revival of interest among psychiatrists, in large measure due to the description of SAD symptomatology (Rosenthal *et al.*, 1984). In healthy subjects, there are hints for seasonality in metabolism, less on the behavioral than on the physiological level.

Adult populations do not manifest significant seasonal modification of total energy intake (Zifferblatt *et al.*, 1980; Behall *et al.*, 1984; Van Staveren *et al.*, 1986; Kräuchi and Wirz-Justice, 1988). As to the seasonal variation of macronutrients and specific foods, both positive (Sargent, 1954; Debry *et al.*, 1975; Räsänen, 1979; Zifferblatt *et al.*, 1980; Van Staveren *et al.*, 1986) and negative findings exist (Suarez and Barrett-Connor, 1982; Kräuchi and Wirz-Justice, 1988). Female SAD patients did show a seasonal rhythm in carbohydrate-rich food intake that a comparable control group of women did not. Neither SAD patients nor controls showed seasonality in protein consumption (Kräuchi and Wirz-Justice, 1988; Fig. 12-5).

The obesity index (weight/height^2) had highest levels in winter in a transverse study of a large population (Suarez and Barrett-Connor, 1982). A longitudinal study did not find body weight change with season, but the percentage

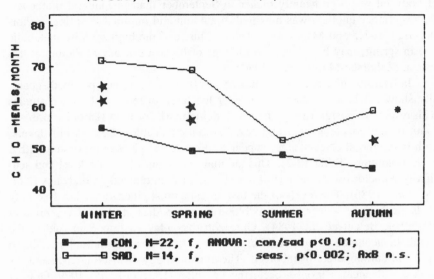

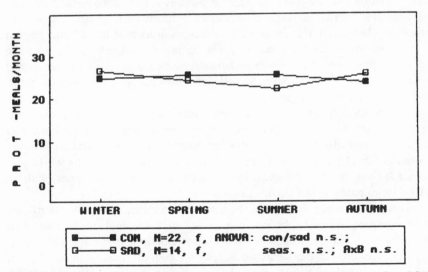

FIGURE 12-5. Seasonal patterns of macronutrient intake in a group of female controls and SAD patients. The number of carbohydrate-rich meals per month was calculated from the sum of intake of bread, potatoes, rice, and pasta; the number of protein-rich meals per month was calculated from the sum of intake of meat, fish, sausages, and innards (animal entrails). Statistics as shown. Only SAD patients showed a seasonal rhythm of carbohydrate-rich intake, and significantly higher intake than controls in winter and spring. Adapted from Kräuchi and Wirz-Justice (1988). Used by permission.

of body fat was significantly higher in September than in January; moreover, the respiratory quotient was maximal in autumn and minimal in spring (Zahorska-Markiewicz and Markiewicz, 1984). This, and the high exercise metabolic rate in spring, may be relevant to findings of highest efficacy of dieting at this season (Zahorska-Markiewicz, 1980).

In healthy subjects, blood glucose levels, both basal and postload, generally show a winter increase, in spite of the large differences between studies with respect to design (transverse vs. longitudinal), location (latitude north vs. south of the equator), age, and sex distribution (Table 12-2). Insulin levels, both basal and after challenge, appear to precede the glucose maximum with a peak in autumn (Table 12-2). This autumn maximum of insulin level and sensitivity coincides with the peak time of insulin requirements in diabetics (Kollop et al., 1986). The levels of the insulin antagonist glucagon and of free fatty acids are high in winter, whereas blood ketone bodies are low (Kuroshima et al., 1979; Behall et al., 1984). Glucagon may play an important role in the metabolic acclimatization to cold as well as to heat, possibly through regulating lipid and carbohydrate metabolism. The epidemiology of insulin-dependent diabetes, with increased onset occurring in winter (Durruty et al., 1979; Gray et al., 1979), corresponds with the maxima of plasma glucose levels, of tolerance to glucose load, and of plasma glucagon.

More than 40 years ago, the observation of a summer trough and winter peak in fasting glucose levels in diabetic patients led to subsequent systematic and carefully controlled single-case studies (Chrometzka, 1940). These confirmed the clinical observation of a clear-cut amplification of the seasonal rhythm in this pathophysiological condition. The author considered that lack of the regulatory influence of insulin in diabetics renders the system more labile and sensitive to environmental stimuli, and thus particularly apt for studying seasonal modification of metabolism.

An elevated metabolic rate in winter, replicably observed by a long-term Japanese study but not by American investigators (discussed in Yoshimura et al., 1966), may also be considered as an adaptive strategy to the cold winter season. A recent reappraisal of metabolic rate data from around the world provides a striking pattern of highest values in winter in temperate zones, with no definite seasonality in the tropics (Sasaki, 1987).

However, earlier findings summarized by Aschoff and Pohl (1970) are rather controversial as to the presence or not of a seasonal trend in standard metabolic rate. For these authors, such nonsystematic findings are not surprising: "If it is correct that seasonal adaptation consists mainly in changes in insulation, seasonal variations are to be expected in the lower critical temperature and in reactions to cold rather than in standard metabolic rate" (1970, p. 1549). Indeed, all measurements made in the cold, according to Aschoff and Pohl's summary, show a higher increase in metabolism in summer than in winter.

TABLE 12-2. Seasonal Variation in Metabolic Functions

Variable	Subjects			Sampling interval[a]	Rhythm detection method	p	Trough	Peak or acrophase[b]	Location	Latitude	Reference
	n	Sex	Age								
Glucose											
At least 2 hr postprandial[c]	2473 / 873	M / F	≥45	Four seasons	t test	<0.05–0.001	Spring	Winter	London (England)	52°N	Jarrett et al. (1984)
Postload	60	M	20–30	Monthly (2 years)	Cosinor	s.	—	September	Nancy (France)	49°N	Mejean et al. (1977)
Fasting (A.M.)	11	M,F	26–60	Four seasons	ANOVA	<0.05	Autumn	Spring	Basel (Switzerland)	48°N	Lacoste et al. (1988)
At least 2 hr postprandial (P.M.)	11	M,F	26–60	Four seasons	ANOVA	<0.001	Autumn	Winter	Basel (Switzerland)	48°N	Lacoste et al. (1988)
Fasting[c]	2600	F	30–39	Monthly	t test	n.s.	—	—	Montreal (Canada)	46°N	Letellier and Desjarlais (1982)
Clearance rate	4	F	—	Four seasons	ANOVA	n.s.	—	—	Winston-Salem, NC (United States)	36°N	Meis et al. (1984)
Lowering effect of insulin (i.v.)	4	F	—	Four seasons	ANOVA	n.s.	—	—	Winston-Salem, NC (United States)	36°N	Meis et al. (1984)
Fasting[c]	2040 / 2501	M / F	20–79	Four seasons	ANOVA	<0.0001	Spring	Winter	San Diego, CA (United States)	33°N	Suarez and Barrett-Connor (1982)
Postload	22	M	22–30	Four seasons	Factor analysis	<0.05	December (midsummer)	June (midwinter)	Antarctica	75°S	Campbell et al. (1975a)
Insulin											
Basal	60	M	20–30	Monthly (2 years)	Cosinor	n.s.	—	—	Nancy (France)	49°N	Mejean et al. (1977)
Response to 50 g glucose (p.o.) (peak height)	60	M	20–30	Monthly (2 years)	Cosinor	s.	April	October	Nancy (France)	49°N	Mejean et al. (1977)

(continued)

TABLE 12-2. (Continued)

Variable	Subjects n	Sex	Age	Sampling interval[a]	Rhythm detection method	p	Trough	Peak or acrophase[b]	Location	Latitude	Reference
Basal	17	F	15–50	Four seasons	Cosinor	s.	—	*Winter*	Minnesota (United States)	46°N	Haus et al. (1983)
Basal	18	F	Elderly	Four seasons	Cosinor	n.s.	—	—	Bucharest (Rumania)	44°N	Haus et al. (1983)
Basal	14	M	Elderly	Four seasons	Cosinor	s.	—	*Autumn, winter*	Bucharest (Rumania)	44°N	Haus et al. (1983)
Response to 250 mg tolbutamide (i.v.)	4	M	25–28	Bimonthly	Cosinor	s.	—	*January*	Chieti (Italy)	42°N	Guagnano et al. (1983a)
Basal (P.M., fasting)	13 16	M F	22–49 20–53	Two seasons	ANOVA	<0.0001	Spring	Autumn	Beltsville, MD (United States)	39°N	Behall et al. (1984)
Response to 1 g glucose/kg body weight (p.o.)	13 16	M F	22–49 20–53	Two seasons	ANOVA	<0.01	Spring	Autumn	Beltsville, MD (United States)	39°N	Behall et al. (1984)
Glucose–insulin ratio after glucose load	12	M	Young	Four seasons	t test	<0.001	March (autumn)	All other seasons	Antarctica	75°S	Behall et al. (1984)
Glucagon	13 8	M F	20–42	Monthly	ANOVA	<0.001	Autumn	Winter	Asahikawa (northern Japan)	44°N	Kuroshima et al. (1979)
Glucagon	13 16	M F	22–49 20–53	Four seasons	ANOVA	<0.01	Spring	Winter	Beltsville, MD (United States)	39°N	Behall et al. (1984)
Free fatty acids	13 8	M F	20–42	Monthly	ANOVA	<0.01	Summer	Winter	Asahikawa (northern Japan)	44°N	Kuroshima et al. (1979)

	n, sex	Age	Sampling	Statistical test	p			Location	Latitude	Reference
Ketone bodies	13 M, 8 F	20–42	Monthly	ANOVA	<0.001	Winter	Summer	Asahikawa (northern Japan)	44°N	Kuroshima et al. (1979)
Metabolic rate										
Basal[c]	119 M	—	Two seasons	Rank–sum test (Mann–Whitney)	<0.05[d]	Summer	Winter	Copenhagen (Denmark)	56°N	Ingemann-Hansen and Halkjaer-Kristensen (1982)
Basal	6 M, 4 F	20–43	Four seasons	t test	<0.01–0.001	Autumn	Winter	Tokyo (Japan)	36°N	Tanaka et al. (1984)
Basal	13 M	$\bar{x}=26$	Monthly	—	n.s.	—	—	Nagoya (Japan)	35°N	Matsui et al. (1978)
Basal	15 M,F	Students	Weekly (2 years)	Cosinor	<0.05–0.001	—	*Winter*	Kumamoto (Japan)	33°N	Sasaki and Halberg (1979)
Exercise[c]	119 M	—	Two seasons	Rank–sum test (Mann–Whitney)	<0.01	Winter	Summer	Copenhagen (Denmark)	56°N	Ingemann-Hansen and Halkjaer-Kristensen (1982)
Exercise	18 M,F	21–30	Monthly	Cosinor	<0.001	December	*April*	Katowice (Poland)	50°N	Zahorska-Markiewicz and Markiewicz (1984)
Respiratory quotient	18 M,F	21–30	Monthly	Cosinor	<0.001	May	*October*	Katowice (Poland)	50°N	Zahorska-Markiewicz and Markiewicz (1984)

Note. ANOVA, analysis of variance; n.s., nonsignificant; s., significant (not otherwise specified).
[a] Durations, where applicable, are given in parentheses.
[b] Acrophases, where applicable, are given in italics.
[c] Transverse study.
[d] For basal metabolic rate when expressed relative to lean body mass and body surface area (but not relative to weight).

TABLE 12-3. Seasonal Variation in Thermoregulation

Variable	Subjects n	Sex	Age	Sampling interval	Rhythm detection method	p	Trough	Peak or acrophase[a]	Location	Latitude	Reference
Body temperature (mean)											
Rectal	1	M	—	Monthly	—	n.s.	—	—	Manchester (England)	53°N	Mills and Waterhouse (1973)
Rectal[b]	8	M,F	11–52	Monthly	Cosinor	<0.001	October	*August*	Marburg (West Germany)	51°N	Kloeppel (1980)
Oral[b]	8	M,F	11–52	Monthly	Cosinor	<0.001	February	*June*	Marburg (West Germany)	51°N	Kloeppel (1980)
Oral	9 / 9	M / F	21–30	Monthly	Cosinor	n.s.	—	—	Katowice (Poland)	50°N	Zahorska-Markiewicz and Markiewicz (1984)
Rectal	6	M	Elderly	Four seasons; circadian, 4-hr interval	t test	<0.001	June	January	Paris (France)	49°N	Touitou et al. (1986)
Rectal	6	F	Elderly	Four seasons; circadian, 4-hr interval	Cosinor	<0.001	June	*February*	Paris (France)	49°N	Touitou et al. (1986)
Oral[c,d]	147 / 138	M / F	20–71	Monthly	ANOVA	=0.057	November	June	Basel (Switzerland)	48°N	Lacoste et al. (1987a)
Rectal	6	M	—	Four seasons—May, September, December, February	—	n.s.	—	—	Toyohashi (Japan)	34°N	Yasuda and Miyamura (1983)
Rectal (τ)[c,e]	96 / 40	M / F	—	Bimonthly	ANOVA	<0.05	March–April	July–August	Andechs (West Germany)	48°N	Wirz-Justice et al. (1984)

	Sex	n	Age	Sampling	Statistic	p			Location	Latitude	Reference
Skin temperature											
Basal	M / F	9 / 9	21–30	Monthly	Cosinor	n.s.	—	—	Katowice (Poland)	50°N	Zahorska-Markiewicz and Markiewicz (1984)
Basal[c,d]	M / F	147 / 138	20–71	Monthly	ANOVA	n.s.	—	—	Basel (Switzerland)	48°N	Lacoste et al. (1987a)
Basal[d]	M / F	12 / 12	—	Four seasons	t test	<0.001	January	July	Kanagawa (Japan)	35°N	Takahashi et al. (1980)
After local cooling (rate of rewarming)[c,d]	M / F	147 / 138	20–71	Monthly	ANOVA	<0.001	October	May	Basel (Switzerland)	48°N	Lacoste et al. (1987a)
After local cooling (rate of rewarming)[b]	M / F	6 / 4	20–43	Four seasons—April, July, October, January	t test (autumn vs. other seasons)	<0.05	Autumn	Spring	Tokyo (Japan)	36°N	Tanaka et al. (1984)
Thermal perception											
Subjective cold sensitivity[c,d]	M / F	147 / 138	20–71	Monthly	ANOVA	=0.034	May	November	Basel (Switzerland)	48°N	Lacoste et al. (1987a)

Note. Abbreviations as in Table 12-2.
[a] Acrophases are given in italics.
[b] Thermostatically controlled chamber.
[c] Transverse study.
[d] Room conditions not standardized.
[e] Free-running period (τ) of circadian rhythm, under temporal isolation.

Thermoregulation

The presence of seasonal rhythms in basal skin temperature as well as in body temperature is controversial (Table 12-3), partially due to the different environmental thermal recording conditions. The response to cold, however, seems to provide more replicable seasonal patterns. This can be illustrated by changes in vasomotor tone, whose dependence on season was suggested 40 years ago by the observation of greater periodic dilation of the skin vessels in ice water (the "Lewis reaction") in summer compared with winter (Kramer and Schulze, 1948).

Skin Temperature and Thermal Perception

Highly significant and comparable seasonal differences in rewarming rates of finger temperature after local cooling have been established in both a transverse study (Lacoste and Spiegel, 1985; Lacoste et al., 1987a) and a longitudinal study (Tanaka et al., 1984). The mean rate of rewarming was slowest in autumn and fastest in spring (Fig. 12-6). A Baltic study demonstrated an earlier seasonal rhythm in rewarming rates, slowest in summer and fastest in winter (Klinker, 1968); this difference may be attributable to the coastal climate.

Parallel to these findings of maximal constrictory response in autumn, a maximal increase in shivering in naked subjects after 1 hr of exposure to 14°C was reported to occur in autumn (Davis and Johnston, 1961) whereas in clothed subjects outdoors, subjective cold sensation occurred at about 14°C lower in winter than in summer (Schulz, 1960). Subjective cold sensation during local cooling was most sensitive in November, when oral temperature was minimal (Fig. 12-6; Lacoste et al., 1987a), and women were more sensitive to cold than men. All measures in this study, combined for both men and women, showed a striking overlap of seasonal patterns in thermoregulatory variables (Fig. 12-6). Thus there is evidence that the body's insulation increases across the transition from summer to winter.

Core Body Temperature

Core body temperature is not only the first variable for which a circadian rhythm was described (Davy, 1845), but is also the most extensively studied and replicable circadian measure (Aschoff and Wever, 1980; Reinberg and Smolensky, 1983a). Thus it is not surprising that in the few seasonal studies available, the emphasis is put on the circadian aspect of the seasonal changes rather than on the mean level of body temperature.

Three studies indicate that the circadian temperature maximum is later in spring–summer than in autumn–winter (Horne and Coyne, 1975; Touitou *et*

Seasonal course of monthly means (healthy subjects)   N = 20–35/month

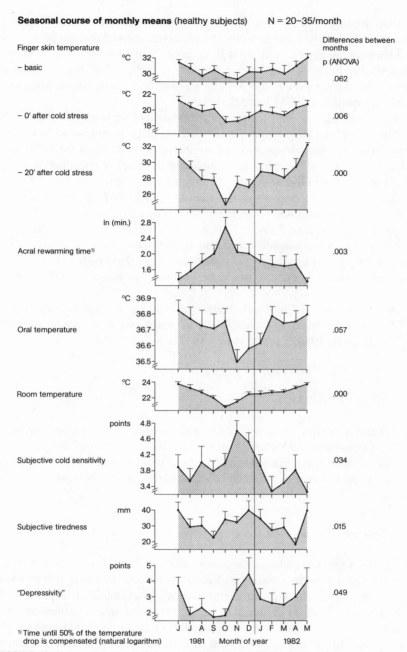

Finger skin temperature

– basic

– 0′ after cold stress

– 20′ after cold stress

Acral rewarming time[1]

Oral temperature

Room temperature

Subjective cold sensitivity

Subjective tiredness

"Depressivity"

Differences between months
p (ANOVA)

.062
.006
.000
.003
.057
.000
.034
.015
.049

[1] Time until 50% of the temperature drop is compensated (natural logarithm)

J J A S O N D J F M A M
1981   Month of year   1982

FIGURE 12-6. Seasonal course of the monthly means ($\pm$ *SEM*) of selected thermoregulatory and subjective mood parameters in a transverse study in healthy men and women (Basel, Switzerland, 48°N, $n = 285$). Adapted from Lacoste *et al.* (1987). Used by permission.

al., 1986; Maruta *et al.*, 1987). However, the most carefully controlled study, under conditions of bed rest in a climatic chamber, showed that the peak of the rectal temperature rhythm was latest in winter compared to spring and autumn, with a smaller delay in acrophase in summer (see Fig. 12-8, below). Furthermore, a less steep morning rise in both oral and rectal temperature was noted during the winter months (Kloeppel, 1980).

An earlier study of oral temperature rhythms in Eskimos in Alaska (71°N) had also suggested a bimodal pattern in circadian phase position—a phase delay at both summer and winter solstices compared with the equinoces (Bohlen, 1971). A decrease in the circadian amplitude of rectal temperature with age was documented for all four seasons (Touitou *et al.*, 1986).

In a retrospective analysis of the circadian period of core temperature under free-running conditions, shorter periods were found in spring and longer periods in autumn–winter (Wirz-Justice *et al.*, 1984). Given that the phase angle between the endogenous circadian period and the external zeitgeber is determined by period length (provided that the zeitgeber strength does not vary), a later temperature acrophase would be predicted in autumn–winter than in spring.

As to the results of seasonal changes in body temperature levels, the positive ones show a trend to higher levels in spring–summer than in autumn–winter (Kloeppel, 1980; Lacoste *et al.*, 1987a).

Vegetative Functions

The autonomic nervous system occupies a key position in reconciling the needs of the organism with the demands of the environment to maintain equilibrium. Thus we would expect many vegetative functions to be involved in seasonal adaptation and to undergo pronounced changes throughout the year.

Cardiovascular System

Arterial blood pressure undergoes seasonal variation (Table 12-4), whereas resting heart rate, studied under similar or identical protocols, does not, at least not in the general population. Individuals may do so, as exemplified in perhaps the first report (Coste, 1891) of annual curves derived from self-measurements over a period of 5 years. Each year, the pulse fell in spring until midsummer, and then rose steadily in autumn to a peak in midwinter. In contrast to the resting heart rate, the exercise-induced increase has been shown, both in a population study (Erikssen and Rodahl, 1979) and in a longitudinal study (Zahorska-Markiewicz and Markiewicz, 1984), to vary significantly over the year, with greater increases in autumn–winter compared to summer.

In reports of blood pressure, a winter elevation and a summer trough are dominant. Age and pathophysiological states (Rose, 1961) may modify the seasonal timing and also the extent of the seasonal variation. In advanced age, and in borderline and untreated established hypertension, the seasonal amplitude is found to be augmented (Brennan et al., 1982; Hata et al., 1982). This is confirmed by our own data: No significant seasonal differences in blood pressure were found in normotensives, but there was higher autumn and winter blood pressure in the hypertensive group (Wirz-Justice, 1979). A corresponding winter elevation was reported for plasma norepinephrine (NE) in both controls and hypertensive patients, reflecting the degree of sympathetic neuronal activity (Lake, 1979; Fig. 12-7). Another study found higher serum NE levels and blood pressure in winter in hypertensive patients only (Hata et al., 1982). Also, plasma dopamine-β-hydroxylase (DBH), which reflects longer-term sympathetic nerve activity over hours or days, was highest in winter and spring in normotensive subjects, and high in winter but low in spring in hypertensives (Wirz-Justice, 1979 and unpublished data). A longitudinal study of serum DBH in healthy men showed slight but significant changes throughout the year, with maximal values in winter (Markianos and Wirz-Justice, 1978).

It is not yet clear to what extent the seasonal variations in cardiovascular functions contribute to the seasonal variation in susceptibility to cardiovascular and cerebrovascular morbidity and mortality. However, there is an impressive concordance of the seasonal timing of these diseases around the world (Smolensky, 1983). With few exceptions, maximal mortality occurs in the winter of

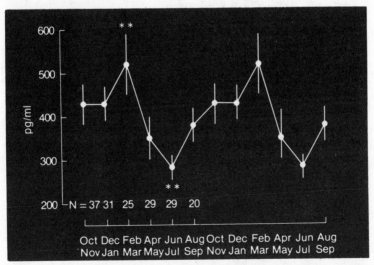

FIGURE 12-7. Seasonal rhythm in resting plasma norepinephrine in normotensive subjects, studied from 1974 to 1979 as healthy controls for a number of investigations (Lake, 1979; Wirz-Justice, Lake, and Ziegler, unpublished data). Two monthly averages (mean ± SEM) are double-plotted to facilitate examination of the data.

TABLE 12-4. Seasonal Variation in Arterial Blood Pressure (Systolic and Diastolic)

Variable	Subjects			Sampling interval[a]	Rhythm detection method	p	Trough	Peak	Location	Latitude	Reference
	n	Sex	Age								
Baseline blood pressure[b,c]	17,000	M,F	35–64	Monthly	Method not described	Trend in all age, sex, and medication groups	Summer	Winter	United Kingdom	50–57°N	Brennan et al. (1982)
Baseline blood pressure[d]	56	M	Middle-aged	Monthly (1–3 years)	—	—	Late summer	Spring	London (England)	52°N	Rose and Murphy (1987)
Baseline blood pressure[e]	274 / 557	M / F	Different ages	Two seasons (4 years)	—	s.	Summer	Winter	Northeastern Japan	40–45°N	Sasaki et al. (1969)
Baseline blood pressure[b]	87 / 107	M / F	11 ± 1.5	Four seasons, circadian, 4-hour interval	ANOVA	<0.001	—	Winter	Tirgoviste (Rumania)	45°N	Haus et al. (1985)
Baseline blood pressure[b]	153	M,F	77 ± 8	Four seasons; circadian, 4-hour interval	ANOVA	Syst. <0.001 Diast. =0.02	—	Spring–summer	Bucharest (Rumania)	44°N	Nicolau et al. (1986)
Baseline blood pressure[f]	39	M	29–71	Four seasons (6 years)	t test	n.s.	—	—	Milwaukee, WI (United States)	44°N	Kochar et al. (1985)

	N	Sex	Age		Test	Trend			Location	Latitude	Reference
Supine and upright blood pressure[e]	84	M,F	12–80	Four seasons	t test		Summer	Winter–Spring	Washington, DC (United States)	39°N	Lake (1979)
Supine and upright blood pressure[e,g]	67	M,F	12–80	Four seasons	—	s.	Spring	Autumn	Arkansas (United States)	35°N	Wirz-Justice (1979)
Supine and upright blood pressure	14	M	41±8	Two seasons	t test	n.s.	—	—	Osaka (Japan)	35°N	Hata et al. (1982)
Supine and upright blood pressure[h]	9	M	42±1	Two seasons	t test	<0.05	Summer	Winter	Osaka (Japan)	35°N	Hata et al. (1982)
Supine and upright blood pressure[i]	11	M	45±6	Two seasons	t test	<0.05	Summer	Winter	Osaka (Japan)	35°N	Hata et al. (1982)

Note. Abbreviations as in Table 12-2.
[a]Durations, where appropriate, are given in parentheses.
[b]Longitudinal and transverse study.
[c]Patients with borderline hypertension, receiving medication.
[d]Patients with ischemic heart disease.
[e]Transverse study.
[f]Patients with established hypertension, receiving hypertension drugs.
[g]Patients with established hypertension.
[h]Patients with borderline hypertension, no medication.
[i]Patients with established hypertension, antihypertensive drugs discontinued at least 3 weeks prior to the study.

both the Northern and the Southern Hemispheres. Since quite prominent circannual variations in cardiovascular risk occur in very temperate climes, environmental temperature is obviously not the only important factor.

Pupil Size

A vegetative function related to the visual system, and thus intimately involved in adaptation to lighting change, is pupil size. Pupillary diameter measured under constant illumination has been shown to be maximally dilated in summer and contracted in winter, in both the Northern and the Southern Hemispheres (Klinker and Spangenberg, 1985). Furthermore, in the more extreme latitude of the Antarctic, the annual amplitude of pupil diameter changes was larger. In a study of pupil diameter under dark adaptation and during bright illumination (2500 lux), we observed a similar annual course (Lacoste *et al.*, 1988). Parallel findings have been reported for visual scotopic sensitivitiy, which is lowest in summer and highest in winter (Sweeney *et al.*, 1960; Barris *et al.*, 1980).

Circadian Phase Position

An extensive investigation of circadian rhythms in a large number of physiological and behavioral functions (Kloeppel, 1980) provides the best illustration of vegetative changes with season. The measurements in this longitudinal study of eight healthy younger subjects each month for an entire year were taken under conditions of bed rest and controlled diet in a climatic chamber.

In 17 out of the 21 vegetative functions investigated, significant circadian rhythms were detected. Among these, eight exhibited highly significant seasonal changes of the circadian acrophase (oral and rectal temperature, pulse rate, pulse-to-respiration ratio, urinary potassium and sodium excretion rates, urine volume, sleep times); 6 showed significant seasonal changes (respiration rate, urinary cortisol, potassium and sodium concentrations, activation, and deactivation); and 3 showed no seasonal changes (urinary calcium concentration, high activation, and appetite).

The acrophases of the 14 significant seasonal rhythms were strikingly concentrated in the winter months: 21% in December, 43% in January, and 29% in February. As examples of this acrophase delay in winter, rectal temperature, pulse, and respiratory rate are depicted in Figure 12-8. Interindividual differences in the circadian phase position were relatively small and deviated little from the group mean. The annual course of the circadian acrophase changes in vegetative functions summarized here shows a parallel to the subjective morningness–eveningness phase position, where maximal eveningness occurs in winter (see Fig. 12-3A).

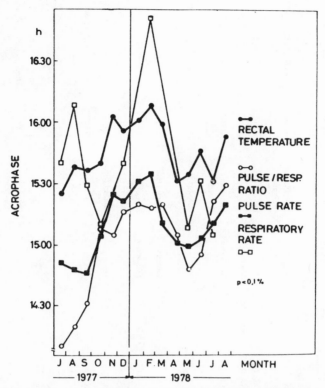

FIGURE 12-8. Annual course of circadian acrophases derived from 24-hr profiles of rectal temperature, pulse–respiration ratio, pulse rate, and respiration rate, carried out under controlled bed rest and dietary conditions (longitudinal study, $n = 8$; Marburg, West Germany, 50°N). Later acrophases are in the positive direction of the y-axis. Adapted from Kloeppel (1980). Used by permission.

The Neuroendocrine Axis

The measurement of plasma hormones, their circadian profile, and their response to stimulation tests is an established strategy in depression research ("the window to the brain"). Some data on seasonal modifications of normal values are available.

Thyroid Function

Table 12-5 shows that significant seasonal variations in thyroid hormones are apparent in 8 out of 12 studies, with 3-iodothyronine (T_3) and thyroxine (T_4) levels tending to be highest in autumn and winter and lowest in summer. There

TABLE 12-5. Seasonal Variation in Thyroid Function

| Variable | Subjects | | Sampling interval[a] | Rhythm detection method | p | Trough | Peak or acrophase[b] | Location | Latitude | Reference |
	n	Sex	Age								
TSH											
Basal	6	M	24–26	Two seasons	Spectral analysis	n.s.	—	—	Brussels (Belgium)	51°N	Copinschi et al. (1977)
Basal	5	M	26–31	Bimonthly	{ Cosinor { t test	= 0.02 <0.0005	— November	April May	Paris (France)	49°N	Hugues et al. (1983)
Basal	17	F	—	Four seasons	Cosinor	<0.05	—	November	Minnesota (United States)	46°N	Halberg et al. (1980)
Basal	14 10	M F	24–48	Bimonthly	Cosinor	n.s.	—	—	Bologna (Italy)	44°N	Pasquali et al. (1984)
Basal	4	M	25–28	Bimonthly	—	s.	—	January	Chieti (Italy)	42°N	Guagnano et al. (1984)
Basal[c]	150	M,F	6–10	Monthly (4 years)	Cosinor	= 0.02	—	December	Naples (Italy)	41°N	Bellastella et al. (1984)
Basal	40	M,F	—	Two seasons	t test	n.s.	—	—	Madrid (Spain)	40°N	Perez et al. (1980)
Basal	11	F	—	Four seasons	Cosinor	n.s.	—	—	Kyushu (Japan)	33°N	Halberg et al. (1980)
Response to TRH (i.v.)											
200 µg	3 3	M F	—	Four seasons	t test	<0.01	July	January	Derby (England)	53°N	Harrop et al. (1985)
500 µg	7 3	M F	21–64	Two seasons	t test	n.s.	—	—	Sapporo (Japan)	43°N	Konno and Morikawa (1982)
500 µg	4	M,F	24–34	Two seasons	t test	n.s.	—	—	Osaka (Japan)	35°N	Hamada et al. (1984)

Thyroid hormones

Hormone	N	Sex	Duration[a]	Sampling	Method	p			Location	Latitude	Reference
T$_3$, T$_4$	6	M,F	—	Monthly	t test	<0.01	June–August	September–February	Derby (England)	53°N	Harrop et al. (1985)
T$_3$, T$_4$	13	M	24–45	Four seasons	ANOVA	=0.02	July	April	Nimeguen (Netherlands)	52°N	Smals et al. (1977)
T$_4$	5	M	26–31	Bimonthly	t test	<0.01	March	September	Paris (France)	49°N	Reinberg et al. (1978)
T$_3$, T$_4$	17	F	—	Four seasons	Cosinor	n.s.	—	—	Minnesota (United States)	46°N	Halberg et al. (1980)
T$_3$	24	M,F	24–48	Monthly	Cosinor	<0.05	January	September	Bologna (Italy)	44°N	Pasquali et al. (1984)
T$_4$					Cosinor	<0.05	March	August			
T$_3$	4	F	25–28	Bimonthly	t test	<0.05	July	October	Chieti (Italy)	42°N	Guagnano et al. (1983b)
T$_4$					t test	n.s.	—	—			
T$_3$, T$_4$[c]	150	M,F	6–10	—	Cosinor	n.s.	—	—	Naples (Italy)	41°N	Bellastella et al. (1984)
T$_3$	40	M,F	—	Two seasons	t test	<0.005	Summer	Winter	Madrid (Spain)	40°N	Perez et al. (1980)
T$_4$					t test	<0.05	Summer	Winter			
T$_3$	13 / 16	M / F	20–49 / 20–53	Four seasons	ANOVA	<0.001	Summer	Winter	Beltsville, MD	39°N	Behall et al. (1984)
T$_4$	13 / 16	M / F	20–49 / 20–53	Four seasons	ANOVA	<0.0001	Winter	Summer	Beltsville, MD (United States)	39°N	Behall et al. (1984)
T$_3$, T$_4$	8	M,F	24–34	Two seasons	t test	n.s.	—	—	Osaka (Japan)	35°N	Hamada et al. (1984)
T$_3$, T$_4$	11	F	—	Four seasons	Cosinor	n.s.	—	—	Kyushu (Japan)	33°N	Halberg et al. (1980)
T$_4$[c]	212	M,F	40–65	Two seasons	t test	<0.0001	December (summer)	May (winter)	Perth (Australia)	32°S	McLellan et al. (1979)

Note. TSH, thyrotropin; TRH, thyrotropin-releasing hormone; T$_3$, 3-iodothyronine; T$_4$, thyroxine. Other abbreviations as in Table 12-2.
[a] Durations, where applicable, are in parentheses.
[b] Acrophases, where applicable, are in italics.
[c] Transverse study.

may also be a difference in these patterns between men and women (Behall *et al.*, 1984).

Another factor of importance is individual constancy of thyroid function. In spite of the group finding of seasonal variations in thyroid hormone concentrations, individuals maintain both T_3 and T_4 within narrow limits (Harrop *et al.*, 1985). This high degree of individuality implies that rigorous comparison of thyroid hormone results against a population-based "normal range" can be potentially misleading.

Basal thyrotropin (TSH) values are also usually highest in winter (Table 12-5). The circadian rhythm of TSH shows seasonal shifts (Copinschi *et al.*, 1977), as does that of thyroid hormones (Reinberg *et al.*, 1978; Guagnano *et al.*, 1983b). There may be a seasonal variation in the thyrotropin-releasing hormone (TRH) stimulation of TSH that is dose-dependent. The dose of TRH generally used in depression research (500 μg i.v.; Loosen, 1985) did not reveal a summer–winter difference (Konno, 1978; Konno and Morikawa, 1982; Hamada *et al.*, 1984), whereas a lower dose of 200 μg TRH did (Harrop *et al.*, 1985; Fig. 12-9).

Hypothyroid patients showed lower T_3 levels, together with higher TSH levels and TSH response to TRH, in winter (Hamada *et al.*, 1984). This led to the suggestion that the dose required for replacement thyroid hormone may be higher in winter than in summer. Another observation in this study is of interest: Although in normal subjects the basal metabolic rate was higher in winter than in summer, the opposite tendency occurred in hypothyroid subjects.

Thus thyroid function is a primary candidate in mechanisms of seasonal adaptation: Seasonal changes in thyroid function may reflect a centrally mediated response of the hypothalamic–pituitary–thyroid axis to long-term changes in environmental temperature.

Growth Hormone

Seasonal studies of growth hormone (GH) are few, and have produced only marginally significant findings (Table 12-6). A careful study of 24-hr profiles of GH carried out in Norway showed no difference in the circadian timing or mean secretion according to season (Weitzman *et al.*, 1975). Since GH secretion is closely linked to sleep, a tendency toward higher values in autumn and winter might be expected. Further seasonal studies of GH should include response paradigms (e.g., to clonidine), which might reveal seasonal differences in GH, such as may underlie the circannual growth rates of children (Aschoff, 1981; Reinberg *et al.*, 1984).

Prolactin

There is little evidence for a seasonal rhythm in prolactin (Table 12-6), and few studies have measured the circadian rhythm (Van Cauter *et al.*, 1981a).

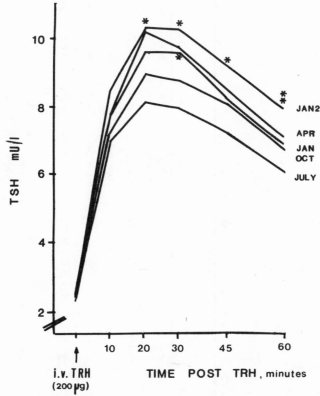

FIGURE 12-9. Mean serum TSH response to 200 μg TRH (i.v.) in six normal subjects at four different seasons (July, October, January, and April). An additional TRH test was carried out in the following years (January 2) when outside temperature was particularly cold. Significant differences from July levels: *$p < 0.05$; **$p < 0.01$. Adapted from Harrop *et al.* (1985). Used by permission.

Daytime prolactin may be higher in winter and spring only in women. Circadian profiles of prolactin show that seasonal shifts occur in the nighttime values, being higher in winter in two different populations (Haus *et al.,* 1980).

Adrenocortical Function

Most seasonal investigations into cortisol (Table 12-7) show highest values in winter. Early studies also reported increased adrenocortical activity in winter with a smaller second peak in summer, as measured by urinary 17-hydroxycorticosteroids (17-OHCS) (Watanabe, 1964). A single-case study of urinary 17-OHCS excretion over 16 years revealed a yearly rhythm with a trough in spring and a peak in late autumn–early winter, together with several other infradian frequencies (Halberg *et al.,* 1965). In addition, the response of 17-OHCS to

TABLE 12-6. Seasonal Variation in Growth Hormone (GH) and Prolactin

Variable	Subjects			Sampling interval[a]	Rhythm detection method	p	Trough	Peak or acrophase[b]	Location	Latitude	Reference
	n	Sex	Age								
GH	10	M	22–40	Four seasons	—	n.s.	—	—	Tromsø (Norway)	69°N	Weitzman et al. (1975)
GH	5	M	26–32	Bimonthly	Cosinor	= 0.03	—	*September*	Paris (France)	49°N	Pansu et al. (1979)
GH	4	M	25–28	Bimonthly	t test	<0.05	December	April	Chieti (Italy)	42°N	Guagnano et al. (1983b)
GH[c]	150	M,F	6–10	Monthly	Cosinor	n.s.	—	—	Naples (Italy)	41°N	Bellastella et al. (1984)
Prolactin	24	M	21–41	Monthly	Duncan's new multiple-range test	s.[d]	August	January	Oulu (Finland)	65°N	Martikainen et al. (1985)
Prolactin	10	M	21–29	Three seasons	—	n.s.	—	—	Brussels (Belgium)	51°N	Van Cauter et al. (1981a)
Prolactin	5	M	26–31	Bimonthly	Cosinor	n.s.	—	—	Paris (France)	49°N	Reinberg et al. (1978)
Prolactin	7	M	Young	Four seasons	Cosinor	n.s.	—	—	Paris (France)	49°N	Touitou et al. (1983a)
Prolactin	6	M	Elderly	Four seasons	Cosinor	n.s.	—	—	Paris (France)	49°N	Touitou et al. (1983a)

Hormone	n	Sex	Age/Duration	Sampling	Method	p		Acrophase	Location	Latitude	Reference
Prolactin	6	F	Elderly	Four seasons	Cosinor	<0.01	—	*May*	Paris (France)	49°N	Touitou et al. (1983a)
Prolactin	5 / 1	M / F	33 ± 1	Monthly	ANOVA	n.s.	—	—	Basel (Switzerland)	48°N	Wirz-Justice and Richter (1979)
Prolactin	17	F	Adults	Four seasons	Cosinor	n.s.	—	—	Minnesota (United States)	46°N	Haus et al. (1980)
Prolactin	4	M	25–28	Bimonthly	Cosinor	n.s.	—	—	Chieti (Italy)	42°N	Guagnano et al. (1984)
Prolactin	6 / 1	M / F	26–40	Biweekly (13 months)	Power spectrum	n.s.	—	—	Wayne, MI (United States)	41°N	Gala et al. (1977)
Prolactin	122	M,F	6–10	Monthly	Zero-amplitude test	=0.003	—	March	Naples (Italy)	41°N	Bellastella et al. (1983)
					Sinusoidality test	<0.01	—	—			
Prolactin	11	F	Adults	Four seasons	Cosinor	<0.05	—	*November*	Kyushu (Japan)	33°N	Haus et al. (1980)

Note. Abbreviations as in Table 12-2.
[a]Durations, where applicable, are in parentheses.
[b]Acrophases, where applicable, are in italics.
[c]Transverse study.
[d]Only when values are converted to percentage of the individual annual mean.

TABLE 12-7. Seasonal Variation in Adrenocortical Function

Variable	Subjects			Sampling interval[a]	Rhythm detection method	p	Trough	Peak or acrophase[b]	Location	Latitude	Reference
	n	Sex	Age								
Cortisol											
Plasma	7	M	22–40	Four seasons	—	s.	Spring–summer	Autumn–winter	Tromsø (Norway)	69°N	Weitzman et al. (1975)
Plasma	6	M	21–26	Two seasons	—	n.s.	—	—	Brussels (Belgium)	51°N	Van Cauter et al. (1981b)
Plasma	7	M	Young	Four seasons	Cosinor	s.	—	May	Paris (France)	49°N	Touitou et al. (1983b)
Plasma	6	M	Elderly	Four seasons	Cosinor	n.s.	—	—	Paris (France)	49°N	Touitou et al. (1983b)
Plasma	6	F	Elderly	Four seasons	Cosinor	n.s.	—	—	Paris (France)	49°N	Touitou et al. (1983b)
Plasma	5	M	26–31	Bimonthly	t test	<0.05	September	February	Paris (France)	49°N	Reinberg et al. (1978)
Plasma[c]	71 120	M F	20–54	Four seasons (7 years)	—	Trend	—	Winter	Turin (Italy)	45°N	Agrimonti et al. (1982)

	n	Sex	Age	Duration	Test	Significance			Location	Latitude	Reference
Plasma	4	M	25–28	Bimonthly	t test	<0.05	October	December	Chieti (Italy)	42°N	Guagnano et al. (1983b)
Plasma[c]	62 66	M F	—	Monthly	Cosinor	n.s.	—	—	Naples (Italy)	41°N	Bellastella et al. (1983)
Urinary	8	M	27–49	Weekly/biweekly	Cosinor	<0.001	August	*February*	Iowa City, IA (United States)	41°N	Kathol (1985)
Urinary	30	M,F	31±1	Two seasons—summer and winter solstices	—	<0.05	—	Winter	Adelaide (Australia)	35°S	Kennaway and Royles (1986)
ACTH	6	M	21–26	Two seasons	—	n.s.	—	—	Brussels (Belgium)	51°N	Van Cauter et al. (1981b)
β-MSH	6	M	21–26	Two seasons	—	=0.03	—	Winter	Brussels (Belgium)	51°N	Van Cauter et al. (1981b)

Note. ACTH, adrenocorticotropic hormone; β-MSH, β-melanocyte-stimulating hormone. Other abbreviations as in Table 12-2.
[a] Durations, where applicable, are in parentheses.
[b] Acrophases, where applicable, are in italics.
[c] Transverse study.

adrenocorticotropic hormone (ACTH 1–17 injections) varies with both time of day and time of year (Reinberg, 1983; Reinberg et al., 1983).

Studies that investigated the circadian profile of cortisol indicate that the rhythm is delayed in winter (Reinberg et al., 1978; Kennaway and Royles, 1986). In an antarctic study (Griffiths et al., 1986), the circadian rhythm of cortisol showed low amplitude and a phase advance in summer compared with other seasons. In a transverse study (Agrimonti et al., 1982) where no change in mean values with season was discernible, 5 years out of 7 showed the same pattern, with the most delayed acrophase and reduced amplitude in autumn.

The dexamethasone suppression test (DST), consisting of ACTH suppression by a synthetic corticosteriod, has not been applied on a large scale to normal subjects. However, a World Health Organization (WHO) multicenter diagnostic study of the usefulness of the DST in depressive patients prompted further analysis of the DST results with respect to seasonality and latitude (for an overview, see WHO Collaborative Study Group, 1987). The highest percentage of nonsuppression occurred in summer and the lowest in winter (Arato et al., 1986; Swade et al., 1987). Furthermore, a meta-analysis of all the data from the WHO study—averaged for each center across the entire year—showed a noticeable "cline" with latitude (Northern Hemisphere only). The highest percentage of nonsuppression occurred in the north and the lowest in the south (Rihmer, 1987). Thus caution is required in defining a "normal" rate of percentage of nonsuppression, since findings may be masked by time of year or the geographical location of the study, independent of differences in clinical populations investigated.

Adrenocortical activity is known to suppress cellular immune function and seems to be more effective against T-suppressor cells. One consequence of seasonal variation in corticosteriods might be a seasonal pattern in immune function. The following findings support a winter trough in immune function: Maximal depression of T-cell function, accompanied by elevated B-cell function occurs in winter with a reversed pattern in summer (MacMurray et al., 1983). Among the T-cells, the highest inducer-to-suppressor ratio was obtained in summer (Canon et al., 1986).

Melatonin

In Table 12-8, seasonal studies of plasma and urinary melatonin are summarized. Three show a bimodal pattern, with high values in summer and winter (Wirz-Justice and Richter, 1979; Birau, 1981; Martikainen et al., 1985). Postmortem human pineal hydroxyindole-*O*-methyltransferase (HIOMT) activity also shows a bimodal pattern, with peak enzyme activity in January and July (Smith et al., 1981). These studies only measured samples once or twice daily. How-

TABLE 12-8. Seasonal Variation in Melatonin and Its Metabolites

| Variable | Subjects | | | Sampling interval[a] | Rhythm detection method | p | Trough | Peak or acrophase[b] | Location | Latitude | Reference |
	n	Sex	Age								
Melatonin Plasma	11	M	21–41	Monthly; 10–12 hr	Duncan multiple-range test	<0.05	August	December and May	Oulu (Finland)	65°N	Martikainen et al. (1985)
Plasma[c]	174	M,F	—	Monthly (2 years)	—	s.	April	January and June	Bremen (West Germany)	53°N	Birau (1981)
Plasma	6	M	27–50	Two seasons—July/January; circadian, 2-hr interval	—	n.s.	—	—	Prague (Czechoslovakia)	50°N	Illnerová et al. (1985)
Plasma	7	M	24±4	Four seasons; circadian, 4-hr interval	—	s.	January	June	Paris (France)	49°N	Touitou et al. (1984)
Plasma	6	M	75±7	Four seasons; circadian, 4-hr interval	—	s.	October	January, March	Paris (France)	49°N	Touitou et al. (1984)
Plasma	6	F	78±9	Four seasons; circadian, 4-hr interval	—	n.s.	—	—	Paris (France)	49°N	Touitou et al. (1984)
Plasma	5	M	33±1	Monthly; 0800 hr	ANOVA	<0.01	May and October	January and July	Basel (Switzerland)	48°N	Wirz-Justice and Richter (1979)
Plasma	12	F	—	Two seasons—summer, April–September; winter, October–March	—	—	Summer	Winter	Vienna (Austria)	48°N	Dietzel et al. (1986)
Plasma[d]	15	F	—	Two seasons—summer, April–September; winter, October–March	—	—	Winter	Summer	Vienna (Austria)	48°N	Dietzel et al. (1986)

(continued)

TABLE 12-8. (Continued)

| Variable | Subjects | | | Sampling interval[a] | Rhythm detection method | p | Trough | Peak or acrophase[b] | Location | Latitude | Reference |
	n	Sex	Age								
Plasma	11	M,F	25–46	Monthly 0800 hr	Cosinor (6-month rhythm)	<0.05	May and October	*January and July*	Geneva (Switzerland)	46°N	Arendt *et al.* (1979)
				1200 hr	Cosinor	n.s.	—	—			
				2400 hr	t test	<0.05–0.005	May and November	*February and August*			
Urinary	—	—	—	Four seasons	—	n.s.	—	—	Kyushu (Japan)	33°N	Wetterberg *et al.* (1981)
Urinary	30	M,F	—	Two seasons—winter vs. summer; circadian, 4-hr interval	Cosinor	n.s.	—	—	Adelaide (Australia)	35°S	Kennaway and Royles (1986)
Urinary	4	M	—	Monthly (March–December); morning	No statistics	—	August (winter)	March (autumn)	Antarctica	70°S	Dubbels and Khoory (1986)
aMT6S Urinary	7	M	23–33	Four seasons; circadian, 6-hr interval	ANOVA	n.s.	—	—	Antarctica	67°S	Griffiths *et al.* (1986)
HIOMT Pineal, postmortem brain[e,f]	40	M,F	69 ± 8	Monthly	t test	<0.05	March and October	*January and July*	London (England)	51°N	Smith *et al.* (1981)

Note. aMT6S, 6-hydroxymelatonin sulfate; HIOMT, hydroxyindole-*O*-methyltransferase. Other abbreviations as in Table 12-2.
[a]Durations, where applicable, are given in parentheses.
[b]Acrophases, where applicable, are given in italics.
[c]Transverse and longitudinal study.
[d]Depressed patients.
[e]Transverse study.
[f]Healthy subjects and schizophrenics.

ever, these seasonal variations are small in comparison with the amplitude of the circadian rhythm.

A few studies have measured circadian profiles of plasma melatonin. Although no differences in mean values between summer and winter were found, a number of studies have found a delayed winter rhythm (Illnerová et al., 1985; Dietzel et al., 1986; Kennaway and Royles, 1986; Broadway et al., 1987). An antarctic study of the urinary metabolite 6-hydroxymelatonin sulfate (aMT6S) found no statistically significant difference over four seasons; however, the resolution of urine samples taken every 6 hr cannot be compared with that of plasma samples taken every hour, which shows a phase advance in summer of the order of magnitude of 1 hr (Arendt, 1986; Griffiths et al., 1986). In addition, even in the absence of a strong light–dark cycle in the polar winter, the melatonin rhythm is not free-running and must therefore be entrained by other factors (Arendt, 1986; Griffiths et al., 1986). The seasonal shifts in these few subjects in Antarctica resemble, however, the seasonal shifts in normal subjects in England (Bojkowski and Arendt, 1987) and SAD patients in Switzerland (Wirz-Justice et al., 1988). In both groups, the circadian rhythm of aMT6S is delayed in winter compared with summer.

It is surprising, in view of the interest in melatonin as a marker of circadian phase and in its role in seasonal rhythms in certain species, that a detailed study of the intraindividual course of the circadian rhythm throughout the year has taken so long to be carried out. In normal subjects in England, the circadian rhythm of plasma melatonin was delayed in winter compared with summer (Bojkowski and Arendt, 1987). A further step in this direction is the international collaborative study at present under way, measuring nocturnal excretion of melatonin at different times of the year at different latitudes (Wetterberg, in preparation).

An unusual finding in a completely different field, that of polymorphisms in enzyme function, indicates that melatonin synthesis may have indeed been selected for with respect to photoperiod: There is a ''cline'' in the allele for two isomorphic forms of N-acetyltransferase activity with latitude (Evans, 1985).

Central Nervous System Monoamines

The monoamines (NE, dopamine (DA), and serotonin (5-HT); acetylcholine; and a number of neuropeptides are important hypothalamic and limbic system neurotransmitters and neuromodulators that show not only circadian but also seasonal rhythmicity. The scattered and incomplete literature on neurotransmitters is not reviewed here (peripheral measures of NE metabolism have been described above; see "Cardiovascular System"). We focus here only on one neurotransmitter, 5-HT, which may be of particular interest in SAD.

Serotonin

Both circadian and seasonal variations in monoamines have been documented in postmortem brain (Carlsson *et al.*, 1980). 5-HT in the hypothalamus decreases abruptly in winter after highest values in autumn.

Baseline values of cerebrospinal fluid (CSF) 5-hydroxyindoleacetic acid (5-HIAA) in healthy subjects and probenecid values in untreated depressives showed lowest values in spring and highest in summer and autumn (Wirz-Justice, 1979; Brewerton *et al.*, 1988) (Fig. 12-10). CSF 5-HIAA from both Alzheimer patients and schizophrenic patients also showed lowest levels in spring (Losonczy *et al.*, 1984). Further north, baseline CSF 5-HIAA in healthy subjects and depressive patients showed lowest values in autumn and highest values in summer (Asberg *et al.*, 1981), and chronic pain patients had lowest CSF 5-HIAA values in winter and highest in summer (von Knorring *et al.*, 1982).

Thus, although CSF 5-HIAA shows significant seasonal variation in a number of studies, the actual times of peak and trough vary with latitude and the population studied, and thus cannot be directly compared.

Imipramine Binding

In the human platelet, regarded as a model 5-HT system that reflects many characteristics of cerebral 5-HT (Wirz-Justice, 1988), seasonal rhythms have been found in 5-HT uptake (e.g., Fig. 12-10, Table 12-9) and in [^{3}H]imipramine binding (Table 12-10), but no consensus as to the pattern has been attained. This may reflect physiological variability (i.e., it may be related to photoperiodicity and/or hours of sunshine at a given geographical location, demographic factors, or constitutional factors), or it may be a methodological artifact (e.g., the result of diet or of assay technique).

There are few comparable seasonal studies of the human serotonergic system. However, the large-amplitude seasonal change in serotonergic function that has been found thus far may be important in considering serotonergic dysfunction in SAD patients (Jacobsen *et al.*, 1987). Additional evidence for serotonergic involvement comes from the successful treatment of SAD with L-tryptophan (Buckwald, McGrath, and Resnick, unpublished data) or a 5-HT agonist drug, fenfluramine (O'Rourke *et al.*, 1987).

Conclusions

The seasonal rhythm studies reported in this review concern mainly the temperate climes and the Northern Hemisphere. Studies at or near the equator are

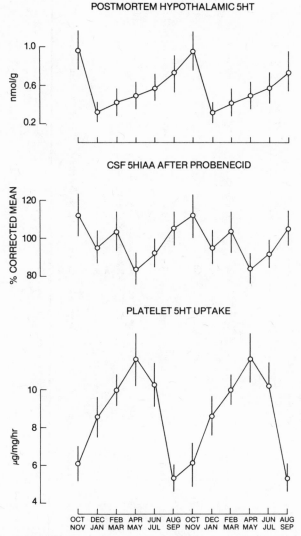

FIGURE 12-10. Three measures of serotonergic function in humans are shown as seasonal rhythms. To facilitate examination of the data, the data have been double-plotted on a 24-month scale (i.e., the same data are repeated over 2 years as bimonthly averages ($\pm$ *SEM*). The values for postmortem hypothalamic 5-HT are from Carlsson *et al.* (1980); the unpublished CSF 5-HIAA data are from Wirz-Justice (1979); and the platelet 5-HT uptake data (a longitudinal study) are from Wirz-Justice and Richter (1979). Redrawn from raw data.

TABLE 12-9. Seasonal Variation of Serotonin (5-HT) Uptake

| Variable | Subjects | | | Sampling interval[a] | Rhythm detection method | p | Trough | Peak or acrophase[b] | Location | Latitude | Reference |
	n	Sex	Age								
5-HT uptake in platelets											
V_{max}[c]	43 29	M F	10–60	Monthly (6 years)	ANOVA	n.s.	—	—	Tromsø (Norway)	69°N	Lingjaerde (1984)
V_{max}	7 2	M F	32±7	Monthly	t test	<0.001	March	July	Brussels (Belgium)	51°N	Egrise et al. (1986)
$[1 \times 10^{-8}$ M]	6	M,F	33±1	Monthly	ANOVA Cosinor	<0.001 <0.05	August —	Late spring *April*	Basel (Switzerland)	48°N	Wirz-Justice and Richter (1979)
V_{max}[c]	104	M,F	26±8	Monthly	ANOVA	=0.004	April–June	January– February and September	Chicago, IL (United States)	42°N	Arora et al. (1984)
5-HT in postmortem brain[c,d]	32 24	M F	26–91	Bimonthly (14 months)	t test	<0.001	December– January	October– November	Umea (Sweden)	63°N	Carlsson et al. (1980)

Note. V_{max}, maximal uptake rate. Other abbreviations as in Table 12-2. Affinity constant (K_m) did not change in any study.
[a]Durations, where appropriate, are given in parentheses.
[b]Acrophases, where appropriate, are given in italics.
[c]Transverse study.
[d]Subjects without any known psychiatric or neurological disorder.

rare, as are those from the Southern Hemisphere. These concluding statements must therefore be considered within this limiting factor.

Whether the measures are of behavior, physiology, hormones or neurochemistry, our review emphasizes their relatedness with respect to season. Occasionally, it has been debated that biological oscillations (at whatever time scale) defy the concept of homeostasis. Yet oscillatory behavior is not pathological, but constitutes a functional advantage (Rapp, 1987). For seasonal rhythms, as for circadian rhythms, the ability to predict repetitive events with the appropriate physiological responses is of evolutionary significance (Farner, 1985; Rapp, 1987; Gwinner and Dittami, 1987).

In attempting to summarize these seasonal rhythms in amplitude and timing, some tendencies emerge (Table 12-11). This review suggests that thermoregulatory and metabolic functions are of particular interest, with a crucial role for thyroid function in seasonal cold acclimatization. Although humans are usually able to avoid excessive exposure to cold and its accompanying stress by changing behavior and insulation, adaptive strategies have necessarily been evolved for coping with environmental changes throughout the year. It has furthermore been demonstrated that T_3 is the most responsive hormone to environmental cold, and is increased in winter in men living in a cold environment but not living in centrally heated rooms (Nagata et al., 1976). In view of the evolution of human beings in tropical latitudes, it may be important to consider that humans have moved into cooler climes for which they may have insufficient thermoregulatory buffers, because their thermoregulatory system is close to that of tropical species (Aschoff, 1971).

One recent review of basic metabolic rate throughout the world illustrates this complexity (Sasaki, 1987). First, climate is a major factor, yet is dependent on the long- and short-term adaptiveness of the population. Basal metabolism in the indigenous population living in arctic or highland regions is high, that of nonindigenous populations less so; those indigenous to the tropics have lower basal metabolism, whereas the metabolism of nonindigenous populations is also low, but to a lesser extent. The pattern of the "cline" in metabolic rate with latitude manifests a "biological equator" north of the geographical equator, as is proposed by Aschoff (1981). In addition, basal metabolism shows a winter peak in temperate zones, but no such peak in the tropics.

In numerous measures, a unimodal seasonal rhythm is apparent (blood pressure, body temperature, glucose, glucagon, etc); in others, a bimodal seasonal rhythm is suggested (melatonin, fatigue, depressivity, circadian phase position of vegetative functions, etc.). It has also been observed that a given rhythm may show a monophasic course in men and a biphasic one in women (e.g., acral rewarming; see Fig. 12-11). The significance of these two patterns has not yet been adequately addressed. For changes in mean values, a unimodal rhythm would be explicable in terms of change in temperature or photoperiod, whereas a bimodal rhythm requires a threshold response to extremes (such as heat and cold, short and long days) or the rate of change of daylength.

TABLE 12-11. Summary of the Times of Year When Psychobiological Functions Are at Their Maximum

Variable	Seasonal rhythmicity[a]	Maximum
Monoaminergic		
Platelet imipramine binding	Yes	Autumn[b]
Platelet 5-HT uptake	Yes	No consistent pattern
Endocrinological		
Thyroid function		
TSH basal	Yes	Winter[b]
TRH response	(Trend)	Winter[b]
T_3, T_4	Yes	Winter[b]
GH	(Trend)	No consistent pattern
Prolactin	M no, F yes	No consistent pattern
Cortisol	Yes	Winter[b]
Melatonin	(Trend) Bimodal	Summer and winter[b]
Metabolic		
Glucose		
Basal ⎱ Load ⎰	Yes	Winter[c]
Insulin		
Basal ⎱ Response ⎰	Yes	Autumn[b]
Glucagon	(Trend)	Winter[c]
Metabolic rate (basal)	(Yes)	Winter[c]
Physiological		
Blood pressure	Yes	Winter[c]
Heart rate	(No)	
Pupil diameter	(Trend)	Summer[b]
Body temperature	Trend	Summer[b]
Skin temperature		
Basal	No	
Rewarming after cold	(Trend)	Spring[b]
Sleep		
SWS	(Trend)	Winter[b]
Sleep time	(Trend)	Winter[b]
Maximal circadian phase delay of most functions	Yes	Winter[b]
Psychological		
Subjective fatigue	(Trend) Bimodal	Early summer and early winter[b]
Depressed mood	(Trend) Bimodal	Early summer and early winter[b]

(continued)

TABLE 12-11. (Continued)

Variable	Seasonal rhythmicity[a]	Maximum
Morning/evening type (movement toward greater eveningness)	(Trend)	Winter[b]
Epidemiological[d]		
Diabetes mellitus (onset)	Yes	Winter

Cardiovascular
  Morbidity ⎫
  Mortality ⎭
	Yes	Winter

Affective disorder (incidence)	Yes	Spring and autumn
Mania (incidence)	Yes	Summer
SAD (incidence)	Yes	Autumn and winter
Suicide rate	Yes	Spring and summer

[a] For rhythmicity, "yes" means 50% or more significant reports; "no" means fewer than 50% significant reports; entries in parentheses mean that four or fewer studies were available.
[b] 50% or more of the studies show a peak at the same time of year.
[c] 75% or more of the studies show a peak at the same time of year.
[d] According to clinical review articles and not separate analysis.

For changes in circadian phase position, a possible model for light dependency of seasonal rhythms has been discussed by Kloeppel (1980). According to Aschoff's rule for circadian period, light as zeitgeber determines phase position not only through daylength, but also through the length of the dawn and dusk transitions (Pittendrigh, 1960). With respect to the former, the day–night ratio is greatest in summer and smallest in winter. Therefore, the circadian phase position of day-active mammals should be earlier in summer than in winter (unimodal seasonal rhythm). With respect to the latter, the length of the dawn and dusk transitions is longer at the solstices than at the equinoces, so that the phase position in both summer and winter should be earlier than in spring and autumn (bimodal seasonal rhythm). In addition, dusk and dawn are effectively much longer in temperate zones than the astronomical calculation would suggest, as meteorological factors play an important role. Thus cloud conditions lead to longest transition times in the months of November to February (Klinker and Zenker, 1969, 1972). The findings that most unimodal rhythms measured showed their latest phase position in January and February, and not in December when the day–night ratio is minimal, suggest that both influences—photoperiod *and* length of dawn and dusk—are superimposed. Thus both factors are important to a different extent in determining the seasonal patterns and shifts of different physiological and hormonal systems. More also

needs to be known as to whether the "biological equator" postulated by Aschoff (1981) for epidemiological variables, and the amplitude of a seasonal
oscillation that is maximum in temperate zones, are also applicable to biological variables, as the data for basal metabolism indicate (Sasaki, 1987).

Methodology

We emphasize the methodological shortcomings present in many of the studies
reviewed. Careful reading indicates that discrepancies in seemingly similar protocols may be due to small but important methodological differences. Too few
of these studies were carried out under controlled conditions of bed rest, vigilance state, diet, temperature, and light synchronization.

Future research requires awareness of the extent of compromise between
theoretical designs for data collection and analysis, and the limitations that
reality imposes. The importance of better circadian rhythm measures needs to
be stressed. Ideally, a circadian rhythm should be measured at each month of
an entire year, under controlled external and behavioral conditions, in an adequately large and representative sample. More than 1 year's data would add to
the requirement of replicability of seasonal patterns. There are important modifying factors that need to be taken into account in the design of the study,
such as subjects' sex, subjects' age, and geographical location; there are other
factors that need to be taken into account in its analysis, such as the real weather
conditions in the year that the study is carried out (e.g., cloud cover, hours of
sunshine and rain, and temperature).

The choice of methods of analysis (e.g., cosinor, periodogram, analysis
of variance) depends on the number of time points studied. Cosinor analysis
has the disadvantage of masking relevant details of nonsinusoidal wave forms,
in particular bimodal seasonal rhythms. Visual inspection reveals patterns that
may differ according to definitions of season (e.g., meteorological vs. calendar
season).

The most common—because easiest—sampling procedure is transverse
collection of data, but this requires a large number of subjects. For circadian
rhythms, comparison of transverse with longitudinal studies (using comparable
subjects and experimental conditions) reveals similar results (Reinberg, 1974).
This statement may be extended to seasonal rhythms, as some of our examples
(morningness–eveningness, blood glucose, acral rewarming) and previous analyses show (Reinberg, 1974).

With respect to methodology, two factors are discussed in detail here,
since they are of utmost importance in defining the sample of "normal" values
with respect to seasonality: sex and age. In addition, it is important in future
studies that certain aspects of personality or typology (such as morningness–
eveningness) be included in the description of the subjects.

Seasonal Modification: Sex Differences

Since more than 80% of patients with SAD and more than 60% of depressive patients are female, it is perhaps significant how many of the variables summarized show clear sex differences, either averaged throughout the whole year or manifested as a different seasonal profile. Women sleep longer under conditions of temporal isolation (Wirz-Justice et al., 1984); older women tend to sleep longer than men and have more SWS (Spiegel, 1981); and midwinter insomnia occurs more often in women (Lingjaerde et al., 1985). In addition, both healthy and depressed women have a different seasonal rhythm of cold sensitivity and acral rewarming than men (Lacoste et al., 1987a, 1987b); their thermal response to infusion of a 5-HT precursor, 5-hydroxytryptophan, is opposite (Lacoste et al., 1976); their fasting glucose and basal metabolism rate are lower; and their hormonal patterns and responses, such as those for prolactin (Touitou et al., 1983a) or cortisol suppression (De Vigne et al., 1985), are different. Finally, females of hibernating species hibernate more often and for longer periods than males (Stephan, 1983; Giedke, 1986).

As an example of important physiological differences between men and women throughout the year, and of their relevance to depression research, we briefly summarize our long-term studies on vasomotor tone after cold exposure. Among the various thermoregulatory functions reported to be disturbed in affective illness, vasomotor tone is impaired in depression. Rewarming rates of acral temperature after cooling are delayed (Beck, 1962; Michalik et al., 1979; Lacoste et al., 1987b). This delayed rewarming time is not specific for depression, since it is found in other pathophysiological states. Moreover, since vasomotor tone represents an important heat conservation mechanism in the defense against cold, it is not surprising that control values are extremely dependent on time of year.

The results of a transverse, parallel study of healthy control subjects and depressed patients throughout an entire year are summarized in Figure 12-11. There were marked sex differences in vasomotor tone, as well as significant seasonal changes. The amplitude of the seasonal rhythm was greater in the patient group. Furthermore, in the patient group significant seasonality was detected even in baseline, prestimulus measures.

The remarkable March and October troughs in rewarming rate observed in depressed women correspond with our previous findings in a retrospective analysis on more than 1000 depressed patients (1978–1980). Each year, depressed women had lowest acral temperatures and slowest rewarming rates in March and November, with a marked peak in May. In contrast, values in male patients followed the seasonal gradations in environmental temperature (Lacoste, 1982). A second collective of depressed patients also showed the same seasonal pattern, with greater amplitude for women (Lacoste, 1986). In addition, 90% of the female patients did not mobilize glucose after local cooling in winter, compared with 55% in spring and summer and 66% in autumn.

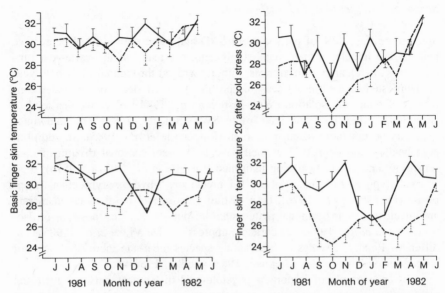

FIGURE 12-11. Seasonal variation in acral temperature in baseline conditions (left) and after local cooling (right) in the course of a year. The upper graphs document healthy subjects; the lower graphs document a sample of depressed patients. The temperature values are separately documented for men (continuous line) and women (dashed lines), as mean ± *SEM* for 10–12 healthy subjects per month and sex, and 3–12 depressed patients per month and sex. Transverse study, Basel, Switzerland, 48°N. Adapted from Lacoste *et al.* (1987). Used by permission.

In these patient studies, we cannot exclude an effect of antidepressant drug treatment, even though medication was qualitatively and quantitatively similar throughout the year. Most centrally active drugs impair thermoregulatory responses, not at thermoneutral ambient temperatures but at the extremes (Weihe, 1986).

In conclusion, these aspects of thermoregulatory responses suggest that any study of normative values requires not only inclusion of seasonal characteristics, but also separation by sex. Both men and women show seasonal rhythms, but with a different annual course. The results with a large, diagnostically diverse group of depressive patients suggest that adaptation to environmental changes is impaired to a different extent, and at a different time of year, in men and women.

Seasonal Modification: Age Differences

As is often the case for circadian rhythms, where the amplitude is decreased with increasing age, so a few studies of seasonal rhythms (e.g., cortisol; Touitou *et al.*, 1984) indicate that this amplitude is also lower in older subjects.

Since there have been attempts to describe depression as a "premature aging" with respect to biological variables, where the amplitude of rhythms is also decreased (as for cortisol), it is a fascinating further analogy to consider that the seasonal cortisol rhythm also appears dampened in depressed patients compared with age-matched controls (Kathol, 1985). On the other hand, it has also been observed that certain seasonal rhythms are actually accentuated with increasing age, such as that of blood pressure (Brennan et al., 1982).

Clinical Implications

Our review substantiates the assumption, explicitly expressed by Eastwood et al. (1985), that physiological variation can shade into pathological variants. This is recognized for hypertension and diabetes mellitus, both with highest incidence in winter, when normal values are also highest. Such accentuation of a pre-existing seasonal "predisposition" can be extended to other pathophysiological states, such as thyroid dysfunction and several immunological diseases. It may also be valid at the behavioral level. As has been shown previously, affective symptoms are universal, with a periodic component that differs in degree rather than in kind (Eastwood et al., 1985). Thus subgroups of affective disorders may be considered as variants of normal hedonic states as well. An example is the representative epidemiological study in New York of seasonal mood changes (see Terman, Chapter 20, this volume). In this sample a remarkably concurrent pattern of winter exacerbation has been observed, varying from mimimal dysphoria (no marked effect on quality of life), through subsyndromal dysphoria (significant impairment), to the complete clinical picture of SAD.

It is necessary to remember that the epidemiology of depression and suicide as a whole shows that the incidence of depression is actually minimal in winter (Eastwood and Peacocke, 1976; Aschoff, 1981; Rosenthal et al., 1983), and that SAD is a very specific form of periodic depression. Thus care needs to be taken in applying the analogies presented in this chapter for SAD pathophysiology to affective illness in general.

The therapeutic effects of light in winter depression; the prevalence of winter depression, which decreases toward the tropics (Potkin et al., 1986); and the therapeutic effect of cold exposure in summer depression indicate that external zeitgebers are intimately involved in both timing of these illnesses and their treatment. The nature of the beneficial effect of light and environmental temperature in these syndromes, whether achieved naturally (by moving to regions with more favorable climatic conditions) or artificially (by light or thermic exposure), is unknown. Yet a similar therapeutic procedure—artificial heat acclimatization in winter—has been found to remove clinical symptoms of a winter disease, cholinergic urticaria (Udassin et al., 1981).

SAD in the Light of Normal Winter Physiology

SAD is characterized by recurring cycles of depression in autumn or winter and remission in summer, with atypical symptoms of hypersomnia, anergia, fatigue, carbohydrate craving, and weight gain. The syndrome occurs predominantly in women and responds well to phototherapy (Rosenthal *et al.,* 1984; Terman, Chapter 20, this volume).

Our summary of changes in healthy subjects with season may contribute to an understanding of the present state of research into the pathophysiology of SAD. Skwerer *et al.,* (Chapter 17, this volume) have emphasized the large number of negative findings; however, these need to be viewed in the light of normal winter physiology, which may mask any effects of time of year.

Two of these negative findings can be discussed in detail. The response of SAD patients to 500 μg TRH was the same in winter as in summer. Although this is the standard dose in testing depressive patients (Loosen, 1985), it is a dose that overrides seasonal sensitivity (Konno, 1978; Hamada *et al.,* 1984). With a lower dose of 200 μg TRH, a higher TSH response was found in winter than in summer in healthy subjects (Harrop *et al.,* 1986; Fig. 12-9). Thus further studies in SAD are required to discriminate between possible masking effects of dose and clinical state, since depressed patients show a blunted response to TRH, and SAD patients are depressed in winter and euthymic in summer.

Second, SAD patients show normal suppression of cortisol after dexamethasone challenge (James *et al.,* 1986). This normal hormonal status may indeed be a specific feature of SAD. It may also be an example of seasonal and latitude masking: Lower abnormal responses to dexamethasone have been shown in winter, and at southern latitudes equivalent to that of Washington, D.C. In addition, age and sex modification of the dexamethasone suppression test must be taken into account. SAD patients are mostly middle-aged women, and there is no correlation between the diagnosis of depression and abnormal dexamethasone suppression in this age group (De Vigne *et al.,* 1985). Finally, the finding that abnormal dexamethasone suppression is correlated with weight loss (Berger *et al.,* 1982; Edelstein *et al.,* 1983) needs to be considered, since this is a symptom generally absent in SAD—if anything, a weight gain is noted in many individual patients.

SAD patients appear to have an inappropriate response to winter onset, and this may be a key to their pathophysiology. For example, SAD patients have low plasma NE and inadequate orthostatic challenge response (Skwerer *et al.,* Chapter 17, this volume) at a time of year when normals show highest values. In addition, SAD patients, but not controls, sleep significantly more in winter than in summer (Rosenthal *et al.,* 1984), but have 50% less delta sleep in winter, when controls have more (Skwerer *et al.,* Chapter 17, this volume). Thus the natural tendency to sleep more in winter, as expressed by healthy subjects under temporal isolation (Wirz-Justice *et al.,* 1984) is exaggerated in

SAD patients; yet the quality of sleep—as reflected in delta sleep—is dramatically reduced. Since most SAD patients are women, who maintain delta sleep longer than men, this decrease of delta sleep in SAD is even more striking. Furthermore, the significant seasonal rhythms in carbohydrate-rich food intake, without marked increase in body weight, suggest a generally modified metabolic response in SAD patients in winter.

Healthy women, but not men, show a striking vasoconstrictory response to a cold challenge in autumn and winter (Fig. 12-11). It has recently been shown that in winter, female SAD patients have a less efficient heat loss mechanism than control subjects, as measured by a slower recovery rate after temperature elevation by exercise. Light therapy normalizes the recovery rate, which in summer is even more efficient than that of controls (Depue et al., Chapter 13, this volume).

The fascination with, and limitations of, animal models for SAD are discussed at length elsewhere in this volume (Mrosovsky, Chapter 10; Zucker, Chapter 11). We thus explicitly limit our seasonal model to the "atypical symptoms" of SAD, since parallels can be drawn at the behavioral level without any assumptions as to the psychological and cognitive concomitants of depression (Kräuchi et al., 1987).

Animals with lesions in or intracerebral application of neurotransmitters to the "medial hypothalamus," particularly the paraventricular nucleus (PVN) and ventromedial hypothalamus (VMH), show the following behaviors (detailed in Kräuchi and Wirz-Justice, 1988): carbohydrate preference, mediated by α_2-noradrenergic (stimulatory) and serotonergic (inhibitory) mechanisms in the PVN; body weight increase (via NE in the VMH); increased amplitude of the seasonal rhythm of body weight in a hibernating animal; inhibition and activation of sympathetic and parasympathetic nervous systems, respectively; and circadian rhythm disturbances of food intake (via NE in the VMH), sleep parameters, and melatonin secretion. Furthermore, seasonal rhythms such as metabolism, reproduction, and melatonin secretion are mediated by the photoperiod acting via the medial hypothalamus (in particular, the PVN).

Taken together, many of the behavioral and physiological parameters described above result from enhanced α_2-noradrenergic and/or reduced serotonergic mechanisms in the medial hypothalamic "satiety system." These neurotransmitters are therefore putative candidates for induction of the atypical symptoms in SAD.

Other Clinical Phenomena

Latitude and season effects are not limited to SAD. In the far north, a form of sleep onset insomnia appears to reflect a phase delay during the long dark winter days without sufficient light as zeitgeber, and this insomnia has been treated with light (Lingjaerde et al., 1985). A somewhat different study showed that the number of self-reported sleep disturbances in a large population of patients undergoing a cure was minimal in summer and maximal in winter. Furthermore, there was a modification by sunlight itself, in that more sleep disturbances were noted on dark days compared with bright days (Klinker and Zenker, 1972).

A different example, of a so-called "biological marker" for depression, shows that nonsuppression of cortisol by dexamethasone is more prevalent in summer than in winter and at higher latitudes in depressed patients (Arato *et al.*, 1986; Rihmer, 1987). Another relationship between the dexamethasone suppression test and season is found when separating the abnormal from normal responses in a depressed population (Beck-Friis *et al.*, 1985). The normal-responder group undergo seasonal rhythmicity in the incidence of depression, and, in addition, are those patients with high melatonin. The abnormal-re-sponder group are more uniformly distributed throughout the year, and have low melatonin levels.

A recent analysis of initiation of antidepressant treatment in a large gen-eral-practice population (Skegg *et al.*, 1986) provides epidemiological evidence for seasonality in men, with peaks in June and December, but not, unexpect-edly, in women. Another study of antidepressant prescriptions (which was not, however, analyzed separately for men and women) showed a spring peak in each of 3 years, with a lesser winter peak (Harris, 1986). This bimodal pattern of drug prescriptions is similar to that reported for general-practice consulta-tions for depression (Harris, 1984).

Finally, there are very few studies considering the therapeutic issue of whether response to treatment varies with time of year. In a study of amitrip-tyline treatment, the greatest reduction in Hamilton Depression Rating Scale scores after 3 weeks occurred when treatment was initiated in autumn (Swade and Coppen, 1980). However, it has also been shown that placebo response follows a seasonal course, being minimal in winter (Rabkin *et al.*, 1987). The antidepressant response to a single night's sleep deprivation did not vary with season either in Berlin (53°N, $n = 217$) or in Basel (47°N, $n = 153$) (Fähndrich and Wirz-Justice, unpublished data).

Perspectives

Our review raises more questions than it answers. For example:

1. How reproducible is a given seasonal rhythm in an individual over several years? Are there stable, individual, genetically determined patterns?

2. How important are which environmental geophysical zeitgebers for hu-mans, and to what extent are social zeitgebers sufficient for synchronization? Can we categorize humans as a photoperiodic species?

3. What relevance is attributable to which factors in modifying seasonal rhythm parameters?

4. What is the significance of increased or reduced amplitude of a seasonal rhythm? What is the importance of timing of the seasonal peak or shifts in the circadian acrophase? And what are the consequences, if any, associated with deviations in such timing?

5. What models are applicable to seasonal rhythms in humans? Where is the cutoff between physiological and pathological rhythm characteristics?

The circadian basis of seasonal rhythms ("a clock for all seasons"; Pittendrigh and Daan, 1976), and the role of zeitgebers such as light, temperature, weak electromagnetic fields, modifications by the weather itself, and social cues, all need to be incorporated into a comprehensive framework of seasonal physiology. Knowledge of the regulation of seasonal rhythms in humans by external and internal factors still remains fragmentary. For example, it appears that different organ systems and different variables within the same organ system show specificity in the presence of and/or the pattern of seasonal variation, and perhaps are synchronized by (or are sensitive to) different zeitgebers.

Although as biologists we have emphasized the season-dependent alterations in light and temperature as explicatory constructs, winter is also associated with subtle but persistent reinforcement schedule shifts. A conditioned behavioral response of season ("winter blahs and spring irritability"), particularly in northern climates, may overlie the original physiological changes initiated by light duration and heat and cold (Persinger, 1983).

The gradual recognition of the importance of seasonal rhythms in humans should not be related to the category of "methodological problems to be controlled for," but used for a deeper and differentiated understanding of seasonal susceptibility to affective illness per se. Further research in healthy subjects may differentiate the characteristics of those individuals with susceptibility to seasonal change. In addition, a better elucidation of seasonal rhythms in patients with specific defects in particular functions (e.g., the thyroid or adrenocorticoid axis) may provide insight into the diversity of rhythmic phenomena and the specificity of their change in depressive states. The importance of the transition from "inside to outside" (Aschoff, 1960) is perhaps more relevant in the study of depression than previously thought.

Acknowledgments

We thank A. Schudel for assistance, C. Mahler for providing literature, and J. Aschoff and K. Kräuchi for helpful discussions. Our research with SAD patients was supported by Swiss National Science Foundation Grant Nos. 3.879-0.85 and 3.821-0.86.

References

Abel, H., A. Baumgartner, and W. Donle (1986) Jahresgänge der Saisonkrankheiten. In *Wetter-Klima-Menschliche Gesundheit,* V. Faust, ed., pp. 33–52, Hippokrates Verlag, Stuttgart.

Agrimonti, F., A. Angeli, R. Frairia, A. Fazzari, C. Tamagnone, D. Fornaro, and F. Ceresa

(1982) Circannual rhythmicities of cortisol levels in the peripheral plasma of healthy subjects. Chronobiologia 9: 107–114.

Akos, K., and M. Akos (1973) Pseudo-seasonal rhythm of human cerebral stress bearing capacity in the psychochronographic (PCG) test. Acta Med. Acad. Sci. Hung. 30: 127–137.

Arato, M., Z. Rihmer, and E. Szadoczky (1986) Seasonal influence on the dexamethasone suppression test. Arch. Gen. Psychiat. 43: 813–816.

Arendt, J. (1986) Assay of melatonin and its metabolities: results in normal and unusual environments. J. Neural Trans. (Suppl.) 21: 11–33.

Arendt, J., and J. Broadway (1986) Phase response of human melatonin rhythms to bright light in Antarctica. J. Physiol. 377: 68.

Arendt, J., A. Wirz-Justice, J. Bradtke, and M. Kornemark (1979) Long-term studies on immunoreactive human melatonin. Ann. Clin. Biochem. 16: 307–312.

Arora, R., L. Kregel, and H. Y. Meltzer (1984) Seasonal variation of serotonin uptake in normal controls and depressed patients. Biol. Psychiat. 19: 795–804.

Asberg, M., L. Bertlisson, and E. Rydin (1981) Monoamine metabolites in cerebrospinal fluid in relation to depressive illness, suicidal behavior and personality. In Recent Advances in Neuropharmacology, B. Agrist, G. D. Burrows, and M. Lader, eds., pp. 257–271, Pergamon Press, Oxford.

Aschoff, J. (1960) Exogenous and endogeneous components in circadian rhythms. Cold Spring Harbor Symp. Quant Biol. 25: 11–28.

Aschoff, J. (1971) Temperaturregulation. In Physiologie des Menschen, Vol. 2, O. H. Gauer, K. Kramer, and R. Jung, eds., pp. 102–107, Urban & Schwarzenberg, Munich.

Aschoff, J. (1981) Annual rhythms in man. In Handbook of Behavioral Neurobiology, Vol. 4, Biological Rhythms, J. Aschoff, ed., pp. 475–487, Plenum, New York.

Aschoff, J., and H. Pohl (1970) Rhythmic variations in energy metabolism. Fed. Proc. 29: 1541–1552.

Aschoff, J., and R. Wever (1980) Ueber die Reproduzierbarkeit circadianer Rhythmen beim Menschen. Klin. Wochenschr. 58: 325–335.

Barris, M. C., W. W. Dawson, and C. L. Theiss (1980) The visual sensitivity of women during the menstrual cycle. Doc. Ophthalmol. 49: 293–301.

Beck, A. T., C. H. Ward, M. Mendelson, J. E. Mock, and J. Erbauch (1961) An inventory for measuring depression. Arch. Gen. Psychiat. 4: 561–571.

Beck, D. (1962) Vegetative Untersuchungen: Therapie und Prognose der Erschöpfungsdepression. Schweiz. Arch. Neurol. Psychiat. 90: 371–391.

Beck-Friis, J., B. F. Kjellman, B. Aperia, F. Unden, D. von Rosen, J. G. Ljunggren, and L. Wetterberg (1985) Serum melatonin in relation to clinical variables in patients with major depressive disorder and a hypothesis of a low melatonin syndrome. Acta Psychiat. Scand. 71: 319–330.

Behall, K. M., D. Scholfield, J. G. Hallfrisch, J. L. Kelsay, and S. Reiser (1984) Seasonal variatoin in plasma glucose and hormone levels in adult men and women. Amer. J. Clin. Nutr. 40: 1352–1356.

Bellastella, A., T. Criscuolo, A. Mango, L. Perrone, A. A. Sinisi, and M. Faggiano (1983) Circannual rhythms of plasma luteinizing hormone, follicle-stimulating hormone, testosterone, prolactin and cortisol in prepuberty. Clin. Endocrinol. 19: 453–459.

Bellastella, A., T. Criscuolo, A. Mango, L. Perrone, A. A. Sinisi, and M. Faggiano (1984) Circannual rhythms of plasma growth hormone, thyreotropin and thyroid hormones in prepuberty. Clin. Endocrinol. 20: 531–537.

Berger, M., P. Doerr, R. Lund, T. Bonisch, and D. von Zerssen (1982) Neuroendocrinological and neurophysiological studies in major depressive disorders: Are there biological markers for the endogenous subtype? Biol. Psychiat. 17: 1217–1242.

Birau, W. (1981) Melatonin in human serum: Progress in screening and clinic. In Melatonin: Current Status and Perspectives, N. Birau and W. Schloot, eds., pp. 287–295, Pergamon Press, Oxford.

Bohlen, J. G. (1971) *Circumpolar Chronobiology,* PhD dissertation, University of Wisconsin.

Bojkowski, C., and J. Arendt (1987) Circannual changes in 6-sulfatoxy-melatonin excretion in man. J. Endocrinol. *115:* (Suppl.) 116. (Abstract)

Borbély, A. A., and A. Wirz-Justice (1982) Sleep, sleep deprivation and depression: A hypothesis derived from a model of sleep regulation. Hum. Neurobiol. *1:* 205–210.

Brennan, P. J., G. Greenberg, W. E. Miall, and S. G. Thompson (1982) Seasonal variation in arterial blood pressure. Brit. Med. J. *285:* 919–923.

Brewerton, T., W. H. Berrettini, J. I. Nurnberger, M. Linnoila (1988) An analysis of seasonal fluctuations of CSF monoamine metabolites and neuropeptides in normal controls: Findings with 5-HIAA and HVA. Psychiat. Res *23:* 257–265.

Broadway, J., J. Arendt, and S. Folkard (1987) Bright light phase shifts the human melatonin rhythm during the antarctic winter. Neurosci. Lett. *79:* 185–189.

Campbell, I. T., R. J. Jarrett, and H. Keen (1975a) Diurnal and seasonal variation in oral glucose tolerance: Studies in the Antarctic. Diabetologia *11:* 139–145.

Campbell, I. T., R. J. Jarrett, P. Rutland, and L. Stimmler (1975b) The plasma insulin and growth hormone response to oral glucose: Diurnal and seasonal observations in the Antarctic. Diabetologia *11:* 147–150.

Canon, C., F. Levi, Y. Touitou J. Sulon, E. Demey-Ponsart, A. Reinberg, and G. Mathe (1986) Circadian and seasonal changes of the inducer: suppressor ratio (OKT4+:OKT8+) in venous blood of healthy adults. C. R. Acad. Sci. (III) *302:* 519–524.

Carlsson, A., L. Svennerholm, and B. Winblad (1980) Seasonal and circadian monoamine variations in human brains examined post mortem. Acta Psychiat. Scand. *61*(Suppl. 280): 75–85.

Carstens, M. E., A. H. Engelbrecht, V. A. Russell, C. Aalbers, C. Gagiano, D. O. Chalton, and J. F. Taljaard (1986) Imipramine binding sites on platelets of patients with major depressive disorder. Psychiat. Res. *18:* 333–342.

Chrometzka, F. (1940) Sommer–Winterrhythmus im menschlichen Stoffwechsel. Klin. Wochenschr. *19:* 972–976.

Copinschi, G., R. Leclerq, J. Goldstein, C. Robyn, M. De Laet, E. Virasoro, L. Vanhaelst, M. L'Hermite, and E. van Cauter (1977) Seasonal modification of circadian and ultradian variations of ACTH, cortisol, Beta-MSH, hPrl and TSH in normal man. Chronobiologia *4:* 106.

Coste, F. H. P. (1891) Five years pulse curve. Nature *44:* 35–37.

Davis, T. R. A., and D. R. Johnston (1961) Seasonal acclimatization to cold in man. J. Appl. Physiol. *16:* 231–234.

Davy, J. (1845) On the temperature of man. Phil. Trans. Roy. Soc. 319–333.

De Rudder, B. (1952) *Grundriss einer Meteorobiologie des Menschen,* Springer-Verlag, Berlin.

De Vigne, J. F., W. Depauw, M. Ansseau, P. Castro, H. D'Haenen, A. Doumont, P. Hubain, J. Mendlewicz, I. Pelc, A. Toscano, and G. Charles (1985) Age and sex effects on the diagnostic power of the DST. In *Abstracts of the IV World Congress of Biological Psychiatry, Philadelphia,* p. 93.

Debry, G., R. Bleyer, and A. Reinberg (1975) Circadian, circannual and other rhythms in spontaneous nutrient and caloric intake of healthy four year olds. Diabet. Metab. *1:* 91–99.

Dietzel, M., O. M. Lesch, and F. Reschenhofer (1986) Seasonal variation of melatonin differs in depressed patients and healthy controls. In *Proceedings of the 15th CINP Congress, Puerto Rico,* Vol. 9, Suppl. 4, pp. 199–201, Raven Press, New York.

Dubbels, R., and R. Khoory (1986) Circannual changes of melatonin excretion in an Antarctic station. J. Neural Trans. (Suppl.) *21:* 483–484.

Durruty, P., F. Ruiz, and M. Garcia de los Rios (1979) Age at diagnosis and seasonal variation in the onset of insulin-dependent diabetes in Chile (Southern Hemisphere). Diabetologia *17:* 357–360.

Eastwood, M. R., and J. Peacocke (1976) Seasonal patterns of suicide, depression and electroconvulsive therapy. Brit. J. Psychiat. *129:* 472–475.

Eastwood, M. R., J. L. Whitton, P. M. Kramer, and A. M. Peter (1985) Infradian rhythms: A comparison of affective disorders and normal persons. Arch. Gen. Psychiat. *42:* 295–299.

Edelstein, C. K., P. Roy-Byrne, F. I. Fawzy, and X. Dornfeld (1983) Effects of weight loss on dexamethasone suppression test. Amer. J. Psychiat. *140:* 338–341.

Egrise, D., D. Desmets, A. Schoutens, and J. Mendlewica (1983) Circannual variations in the density of tritiated imipramine binding sites on blood platelets in man. Neuropsychobiology *10:* 101–102.

Egrise, D., M. Rubinstein, A. Schoutens, F. Cantraine, and J. Mendlewicz (1986) Seasonal variation of platelet serotonin uptake and 3H-imipramine binding in normal and depressed subjects. Biol. Psychiat. *21:* 283–292.

Erikssen, J., and K. Rodahl (1979) Seasonal variation in work performance and heart rate response to exercise. Eur. J. Appl. Physiol. *42:* 133–140.

Evans, D. A. P. (1985) Acetylation. In *Ethnic Differences in Reactions to Drugs and Xenobiotics.* W. Kalow, H. W. Goedde, and D. Agarwal, eds., pp. 209–241, Alan R. Liss, New York.

Fahrenberg, J., H. Selg, and R. Hampel (1978) *Das Freiburger Persönlichkeitsinventar (FPI),* Verlag für Psychologie, Dr. C. J. Hogrefe, Göttingen.

Farner, D. S. (1985) Annual rhythms. Ann. Rev. Physiol. *47:* 65–82.

Faust, V. (1976) *Biometerologie: Der Einfluss von Wetter und Klima auf Gesunde und Kranke.* Hippokrates Verlag, Stuttgart.

Faust, V., and P. Sarreither (1975) jahreszeit und psychische Krankheit. Med. Klin. *70:* 467–473.

Gala, R. R., C. Van de Walle, W. H. Hoffman, D. M. Lawson, D. R. Pieper, S. W. Smith, and M. G. Subramanian (1977) Lack of circannual cycle of daytime prolactin in man and monkey. Acta Endocrinol. *86:* 257–262.

Galzin, A., H. Loo, D. Sechter, and S. Z. Langer (1986) Lack of seasonal variation in platelet ^{3}H-imipramine binding in humans. Biol. Psychiat. *21:* 876–882.

Giedke, H. (1986) Hibernation as a model of endogenous depression. Pharmacopsychiatry *19:* 192–193.

Giedke, H. (1987) Schlaf, Winterschlaf und Depression. In *Schlaf–Wach Funktionen,* H. Hippius, E. Rüther, and M. Schmauss, eds., pp. 55–76, Springer-Verlag, Berlin.

Gray, R. S., L. J. P. Duncan, and B. F. Clarke (1979) Seasonal onset of insulin dependent diabetes in relation to sex and age at onset. Diabetologia *17:* 29–32.

Griffiths, P. A., S. Folkard, C. Boijkowski, J. English, and J. Arendt (1986) Persistent 24-h variations of urinary 6-hydroxy melatonin sulphate and cortisol in Antarctica. Experientia *42:* 430–432.

Guagnano, M. T. E. Angelucci, A. Del Ponte, R. Boni, and S. Sensi (1984) Variazioni circadiane e circannuali del livelli del TSH e della protattina plasmatica in adulti sani di sesso maschile. Boll. Soc. Ital. Biol. Sper. *60:* 2039–2045.

Guagnano, M. T., A. Del Ponte, L. Cervone, S. Basile, E. Angelucci, E. Vitacolonna, A. Nuzzo, P. Menduni, and S. Sensi (1983a) Struttura temporale della secretione endocrina: variazione circannuale della responsivita insulinica alla tolbutamide nell'uomo. Boll. Soc. Ital. Biol. Sper. *59:* 1076–1081.

Guagnano, M. T., A. Del Ponte, P. Menduni, A. Nuzzo, E. Palummeri, E. Angelucci, E. Vitacolonna, and S. Sensi (1983b) La struttura temporale della secrezione endocrina: Il variazioni circannuali delle frazioni libere della tri-tetraiodiotironina, del cortisole, del l'human growth hormone e dell' insulina plasmatica in soggetti sani. Boll. Soc. Ital. Biol. Sper. *59:* 1243–1247.

Gwinner, E. (1981) Circannuale Rhythmen bei Tieren und ihre photoperiodische Synchronisation. Naturwissenschaften *68:* 542–551.

Gwinner, E. (1986) *Circannual Rhythms,* Springer-Verlag, Berlin.

Gwinner, E., and J. Dittami (1987) Adaptive functions of circannual clocks. In *Endocrine Regulations as Adaptive Mechanisms to the Environment,* I. Assenmacher and J. Boissin, eds., pp. 115–123, Centre National de Recherche Scientifique, Paris.

Halberg, F., M. Engeli, C. Hamburger, and D. Hillman (1965) Spectral resolution of low frequency small-amplitude rhythms in excreted 17-ketosteroids: Probable androgen induced circaseptan desynchronisation. Acta Endocrinol. *50*(Suppl. 103): 405–417.

Halberg, F., E. Haus, B. Tarquini, M. Cagnoni, G. Cornelissen, D. Lakatua, T. Kawasaki, L. A. Wallach, E. Halberg, and T. Omeae (1980) Circannual and circadian variations in some blood hormones, notably prolactin. In *Proceedings of the XIV International Congress of Internal Medicine (ISIM), Rome, 1978*, L. Condorelli, U. Teodori, A. Baretta Anguissola, and M. Sangiorgi, eds., pp. 1090–1104, Excerpta Medica, Amsterdam.

Halberg, F., M. Lagoguey, and A. Reinberg (1983) Human circannual rhythms over a broad spectrum of physiological processes. Int. J. Chronobiol. *8:* 225–268.

Halbreich, U. (1985) Hormones and depression—conceptual transitions. Psychopharmacol. Bull. *21:* 568–573.

Hamada, N., M. Ohno, H. Morii, N. Jaeduk, J. Yamakawa, M. Jnaba, S. Jkeda, and M. Wada (1984) Is it necessary to adjust the replacement dose of thyroid hormone to the season in patients with hypothyroidism? Metabolism *33:* 215–218.

Harris, C. M. (1984) Seasonal variations in depression and osteoarthritis. J. Coll. Gen. Pract. *34:* 436–439.

Harris, C. M. (1986) Further observation on seasonal variation: 2. Depression. J. Coll. Gen. Pract. *36:* 319–321.

Harrop, J.-S., K. Ashwell, and M.-R. Hopton (1985) Circannual and within-individual variations of thyroid function tests in normal subjects. Ann. Clin. Biochem. *22:* 371–375.

Hastings, M. H., J. Herbert, N. D. Martensz, and A. C. Roberts (1985) Annual reproductive rhythms in mammals: Mechanisms of light synchronization. Ann. NY Acad. Sci. *453:* 182–204.

Hata, T., T. Ogihara, A. Maruyama, H. Mikami, M. Nakamura, T. Naka, Y. Kumahara, and C. A. Nugent (1982) The seasonal variation of blood pressure in patients with essential hypertension. Clin. Exp. Hyper.—Theory and Prac. *A4*(3): 341–354.

Haus, E., D. J. Lakatua, F. Halberg, G. Cornelissen, L. Sackett, H. G. Berg, T. Kawasaki, K. Uezono, M. Matsuoka, and T. Omae (1980) Chronobiological studies of plasma prolactin in women in Kyushu, Japan and Minnesota, USA. Clin. Endocrinol. Metabol. *51:* 632–640.

Haus, E., G. Nicolau, F. Halberg, D. Lakatua, and L. Sackett-Lundeen (1983) Circannual variations in plasma insulin and C-peptide in clinically healthy subjects. Chronobiologia *10:* 132.

Haus, E., G. Y. Nicolav, D. J. La Kuta, A. Jachimowitz, L. Plinga, L. Sackett-Lundeen, E. Petrescu, and E. Ungureanu (1985) Circannual variation in blood pressure, urinary catecholamine excretion and serum sodium, potassium, calcium and magnesium. Chronobiologia *12:* 250.

Hildebrandt, G., and H. Strempel (1975) Chronobiological problems of performance and adaptation capacity. In *International Society for Chronobiology: Proceedings of XIIth International Conference*, pp. 103–115, Il Ponte, Milan.

Horne, J. A., and I. Coyne (1975) Seasonal changes in the circadian variation of oral temperature during wakefulness. Experientia *31:* 1296–1297.

Horne, J. A., and O. Östberg (1976) A self-assessment questionnaire to determine morningness–eveningness in human circadian rhythms. Int. J. Chronobiol. *4:* 97–110.

Hrdina, P. D., V. D. Lapierre, E. R. Horn, and D. Bakish (1985) Platelet 3H-imipramine binding: A possible predictor of response to antidepressant treatment. Prog. Neuropsychopharmacol. Biol. Psychiat. *9:* 619–622.

Hugues, J. N. A. Reinberg, M. Lagoguey, E. Modigliani, and J. Saboun (1983) Les rythmes biologiques de la sécrétion thyréotrope. Ann. Med. Interne *134:* 84–94.

Illnerová, H., P. Zvolsky, and J. Vaněček (1985) The circadian rhythm in plasma melatonin concentration of the urbanized man: The effect of winter and summer. Brain Res. *328:* 186–189.

Ingemann-Hansen, T., and J. Halkjaer-Kristensen (1982) Seasonal variation of maximal oxygen consumption rate in humans. Eur. J. Appl. Physiol. *49:* 151–157.

Jacobsen, F. M., D. A. Sack, T. A. Wehr, S. Rogers, and N. E. Rosenthal (1987) Neuroendocrine response to 5-hydroxytryptophan in seasonal affective disorder. Arch. Gen. Psychiat. *44:* 1086–1091.

James, S. P., T. A. Wehr, D. A. Sack, B. L. Parry, S. Rogers, and N. E. Rosenthal (1986) The dexamethasone suppression test in seasonal affective disorder. Comp. Psychiat. *127:* 224–226.

Jarrett, R. J., T. J. Murrells, M. J. Shipley, and T. Hall (1984) Screening blood glucose values: Effects of season and time of day. Diabetologia *27:* 574–577.

Kathol, R. G. (1985) Persistent elevation of urinary free cortisol and loss of circannual periodicity in recovered depressive patients: A trait finding. J. Affect. Dis. *8:* 137–145.

Kennaway, D. J., and P. Royles (1986) Circadian rhythms of 6-sulphatoxy melatonin, cortisol and electrolyte excreption at the summer and winter solstices in normal men and women. Acta Endocrinol. *113:* 450–456.

Kerkhof, G. A. (1985) Interindividual differences in the human circadian system: A review. Biol Psychiat. *20:* 83–112.

Kerkhofs, M., C. Kempenaers, P. Linkowski, V. de Maerteler, and J. Mendlewica (1988) Multivariate study of sleep EEG in depression. Acta Psychiat. Scand. *77:* 463–468.

Klinker, L. (1968) Modellvorstellung über Regulationsprinzipien des menschlichen Organismus: Versuch einer einheitlichen Deutung von biologischer Tages-und Jahresrhythmik. In *Abhandlungen des Meteorologischen Dienstes der Deutschen Demokratischen Republik,* Vol. 11, No. 87, pp. 1–19, Akademie-Verlag, Berlin.

Klinker, L., and G. Schrader (1984) Langzeitstudie zum rhythmischen Verhalten von geistigen Leistunger Z. Ges. Hyg. *30:* 661–663.

Klinker, L., and W. Spangenberg (1985) Zum Finfluss des Lichtes auf die menschliche Regulation-Ergebnisse über jahreszeitliche Variationen der Pupillenweite. Z. Ges. Hyg. *31:* 88–90.

Klinker, L., and H. Zenker (1969) Biologischer Jahresrhythmus und meteoro-pathologische Erscheinungen. Deut. Gesundh.-Wesen *24:* 1527–1528.

Klinker, L., and H. Zenker (1972) Der Einfluss von Jahreszeit und Wetter auf den menschlichen Organisums. Z. Physiother. *2:* 143–151.

Kloeppel, H.-B (1980)) *Circannuale Aenderungen der circadianen Phasenlage des Menschen,* PhD dissertation, University of Marburg/Lahn.

Kloeppel, H.-B (1982) Circannual changes of the circadian phase position in man. In *Biological Adaptation: International Symposium at the University of Larburg/Lahn,* G. Hildebrandt and H. Hankel, eds., pp. 137–145, Georg Thieme, Stuttgart.

Kochar, M. S., S. Ristow, and J. H. Kalbfleisch (1985) Effect of seasonal temperature change on blood pressure in a treated hypertensive population. J. Clin. Hypertens. *1:* 49–52.

Kollop, M. A., A. Bicakova-Rocher, P. Drouin, L. Mejean, and G. Deebry (1986) Ultradian, circadian and circannual rhythms of blood glucose and injected insulin documented in six self-controlled diabetics. Ann. Rev. Chronopharmacol. *43:* 389–390.

Konno, N. (1978) Comparison between the thyrotropin response to thyrotropin-releasing hormone in summer and that in winter in normal subjects. Endocrinol. Jap. *25:* 635–639.

Konno, N., and K. Morikawa (1982) Seasonal variation of serum thyrotropic concentration and thyrotropic response to thyrotropin releasing hormone in patients with primary hypothyroidism on constant replacement of thyroxine. J. Clin. Endocrinol. Metab. *54:* 1118–1124.

Kramer, K., and W. Schulze (1948) Die Kältedilatation der Hautgefässe. Pflügers Arch. *250:* 141–170.

Kräuchi, K., and A. Wirz-Justice (1988) The four seasons food intake frequency in seasonal affective disorder in the course of a year. Psychiat. Res. *25:* 323–338.

Kräuchi, K., A. Wirz-Justice, and H. Feer (1987) "Medial hypothalamus-syndrome" as a model of atypical symptoms in seasonal affective disorders (SAD). Experientia *43:* 715.

Kuroshima, A., K. Doi, and T. Ohno (1979) Seasonal variation of plasma glucagon concentration in men. Jap. J. Physiol. *29:* 661–668.

Lacoste, V. (1982) Seasonality in autonomous nervous functions of depressed patients. Experientia *38:* 716

Lacoste, V. (1986) Effects of local cooling on acral rewarming and glucose response in depression. Experientia *42:* 707.

Lacoste, V., A. Schudel, K. Kräuchi, and A. Wirz-Justice (1988) Seasonal rhythms in blood pressure, blood glucose and pupil size in healthy subjects. Experientia *44:* A 34.

Lacoste, V., and R. Spiegel (1985) Seasonal variation in thermoregulatory and psychometric parameters in healthy subjects. Experientia *41:* 831.

Lacoste, V., R. Spiegel, H. Amsler, U. Ferner, and W. Maurer (1987a) Untersuchungen zur akralen Wiedererwärmung. Teil I: "Normdaten" einer gesunden Erwachsenenpopulation. Schweiz. Arch. Neurol. Psychiat. *138:* 51–71.

Lacoste, V., R. Spiegel, and M. Schweingruber (1987b) Untersuchungen zur akralen Wiedererwärmung. Teil II: Vergleich von Gesunden und Depressiven. Schweiz. Arch. Neurol. Psychiat. *138:* 73–86.

Lacoste, V., and A. Wirz-Justice (1987) Seasonality in personality dimensions. Psychiat. Res. *21:* 181–183.

Lacoste, V., A. Wirz-Justice, P. Graw, W. Pühringer, and M. Gastpar (1976) Intravenous L-5-hydroxytryptophan in normal subjects: An interdisciplinary precursor loading study. Part IV: Effects on body temperature and cardiovascular functions. Pharmakopsychiatrie *9:* 289–294.

Lake, R. (1979) Relationship of sympathetic nervous system tone and blood pressure. Nephron *23:* 84–90.

Letellier, G., and F. Desjarlais (1982) Study of seasonal variations for eighteen biochemical parameters over a four-year period. Clin. Biochem. *15:* 206–211.

Lingjaerde, O. (1984) Blood platelets as a model system for studying the biochemistry of depression. In *Frontiers in Biochemical and Pharmacological Research in Depression,* F. Sjöquist, ed., pp. 99–111, Raven Press, New York.

Lingjaerde, O., O. Bratlid, T. Hansen (1985) Insomnia during the "dark period" in northern Norway. Acta Psychiat. Scand. *71:* 506–512.

Loosen, P. T. (1985) The TRH test in psychiatric disorders. In *Directions in Psychiatry,* F. Flach, ed., Vol. 5, Lesson 9, Hatherleigh, New York.

Losonczy, M. F., R. C. Mohs, and K. L. Davis (1984) Seasonal variations of human lumbar CSF Neurotransmitter metabolite concentrations. Psychiat. Res. *12:* 79–87.

MacMurray, J. P., J. P. Barker, J. D. Armstrong, L. P. Bozetti, and I. N. Kuhn (1983) Circannual changes in immune function. Life Sci. *32:* 2363–2370.

Markianos, E., and A. Wirz-Justice (1978) Annual rhythms of serum DBH in man. In *Abstracts of the 4th International Catecholamine Congress, Asilomar, CA.*

Martikainen, H., J. Tapanainen, O. Vakkuri, J. Leppaluoto, and I. Huhtamiemi (1985) Circannual concentrations of melatonin, gonadotrophins, prolactin and gonadal steroids in a geographical area with large variations in daylight. Acta Endocrinol. *109:* 446–450.

Maruta, N., K. Natsume, H. Tokura, K. Kawakami, and N. Isoda (1987) Seasonality of circadian pattern in human rectal temperature rhythm under semi-natural conditions. Experientia *43:* 294–296.

Matsui, H., K. Shimaoka, M. Miyamura, and K. Kobayashi (1978) Seasonal variation of aerobic work capacity. In *Environmental Stress: Individual Human Adaptations,* L. J. Folinsbee and J. L. Wagner, eds., pp. 279–291, Academic Press, New York.

McLellan, G. H., W. J. Riley, and C. P. Davies (1979) Season variation in serum thyroxine. Lancet *i:* 883–884.

Meis, P. J., J. S. Rose, and M. Swain (1984) Pregnancy alters diurnal variation of plasma glucose concentrations. Chronobiol. Int. *1:* 145–149.

Mejean, L., A. Reinberg, G. Gay, and G. Debry (1977) Circannual changes of the plasma insulin in response to glucose tolerance test of healthy young human males. In *Proceedings of the XXVII International Congress of Physiology Paris,* Vol. 13, p. 498.

Mendelson, W. B., N. E. Rosenthal, D. A. Sack, S. P. James, J. I. Nurnberger, and T. A. Wehr (1985) Experimental modalities in the treatment of seasonal and non-seasonal affective disorders. In *Abstracts of the IV World Congress of Biological Psychiatry, Philadelphia,* p. 30.

Menninger-Lerchenthal, E. (1960) *Periodizität in der Psychopathologie,* Wilhelm Maudrich Verlag, Vienna.

Michael, R. P., and D. Zumpe (1983) Sexual violence in the United States and the role of season. Amer. J. Psychiat. *140:* 883.

Michalik, M., R. Uebelhak, I. Grote, H. Meffert, and K. Seidel (1979) Das Verhalten vegetativer Parameter unter Anwendung von Ouabain: Akrale Wiedererwärmung. Schweiz. Arch. Neurol Psychiat. *125:* 171–178.

Michelson, E. (1891) Einfluss der Jahreszeit auf den Verlauf der Schlaftiefe. In *Untersuchung über die Tiefe des Schlafs,* Inaugural Dissertation, Dorpat.

Mills, J. N., and J. M. Waterhouse (1973) Circadian rhythms over the course of a year in a man living alone. Int. J. Chronobiol. *1:* 73–79.

H. Nagata, T. Izumiyama, K. Kamata, S. Kono, Y. Yukimura, M. Tawata, T. Aizawa, and T. Yamada (1976) An increase of plasma triiodothyronine concentration in man in a cold environment. J. Clin. Endocrinol. Metab. *43:* 1153–1156.

Nicolau, G. Y., E. Haus, C. Bogdan, L. Plinga, L. Robu, E. Ungureanu, L. Sackett-Lundeen, and E. Petrescu (1986) Circannual rhythms of systolic and diastolic blood pressure in relation to plasma aldosterone and urinary norepinephrine in elderly subjects and children. Rev. Rouman. Med. Endocrinol. *24:* 97–107.

O'Rourke, D., D. Wurtman, J. Brzesinski, A. Abou-Nader, P. Marchant, and R. J. Wurtman (1987) Treatment of seasonal affective disorder with d-fenfluramine. Ann. NY Acad. Sci. *499:* 329–330.

Pansu, D., A. Reinberg, M. Lagoguey, P. Guillet, and A. Prader (1979) Circannual changes in plasma growth hormone (GH) of healthy adults and in effectiveness of HGH injections in a case of isolated GH deficiency. In *Chronopharmacology,* A. Reinberg and F. Halberg, eds., pp. 75–76, Pergamon Press, Oxford.

Papousek, M. (1975) Chronobiologische Aspekte der Zyklothymie. Fortschr. Neurol. Psychiat. *43:* 381–440.

Pasquali, R., G. Baraldi, F. Casimirri, L. Mattioloi, M. Capelli, N. Melchionda, F. Capani, and G. Labo (1984) Seasonal variations of total and free thyroid hormones in healthy men: A chronobiological study. Acta Endocrinol. *107:* 42–48.

Paterson, R. A. H. (1975) Seasonal induction of slow-wave sleep at an Antarctic coastal station. Lancet *i:* 468–469.

Pengelley, E. T., ed. (1974) *Circannual Clocks: Annual Biological Rhythms,* Academic Press, New York.

Perez, P. R., J. G. Lopez, I. P. Mateos, A. D. Escribano, and M. L. S. Sanchez (1980) Seasonal variations in thyroid hormones in plasma. Rev. Clin. Espan. *156:* 245–247.

Persinger, M. A. (1983) Winter blahs and spring irritability: The chronic but subtle behavioral operations. Percept. Mot. Skills. *57:* 494–496.

Pittendrigh, C. S. (1960) Circadian rhythms and the circadian organization of living systems. Cold Spring Harbor Symp. Quant. Biol. *25:* 159–184.

Pittendrigh, C. S., and S. Daan (1976) A functional analysis of circadian pacemakers in nocturnal rodents: V. Pacemaker structure: A clock for all seasons. J. Comp. Physiol. *106:* 333–355.

Potkin, S. G., M. Zetin, V. Stamenkovic, D. Kripke, and W. E. Bunney, Jr. (1986) Seasonal affective disorder: Prevalence varies with latitude and climate. Clin. Neuropharmacol. *9*(Suppl. 4): 74.

Rabkin, J. G., J. W. Stewart, P. J. McGrath, J. S. Markowitz, W. Harrison, and F. M. Quitkin (1987) Baseline characteristics of 10-day placebo washout responders in antidepressant trials. Psychiat. Res. *21:* 9–22.

Randall, W. (1970) Sunshine, a possible zeitgeber for multiphasic biological rhythms during a year. J. interdiscipl. Cycle Res. *1:* 389–404.

Rapp, P. E. (1987) Why are so many biological systems periodic? Prog Neurobiol. *29:* 261–273.

Räsänen, L. (1979) Nutrition survey of Finnish rural children: VI. Methodological study comparing 24-hour recall and the dietary history interview. Amer. J. Clin. Nutr. *32:* 2560–2567.

Reinberg, A. (1974) Aspects of circannual rhythms in man. In *Circannual Clocks: Annual Biological Rhythms,* E. T. Pengelley, ed., pp. 423–509, Academic Press, New York.

Reinberg, A. (1979) Circadian and circannual rhythms in healthy adults: sleep, wakefulness and circadian rhythm. In *Sleep, Wakefulness and Circadian Rhythms,* NATO Agard Lecture Series 105, pp. 1–27.

Reinberg, A. (1983) Clinical chronopharmacology: An experimental basis for chronotherapy. In *Biological Rhythms and Medicine,* A. Reinberg and M. H. Smolensky, eds., pp. 211–263, Springer-Verlag, Berlin.

Reinberg, A., and M. Lagoguey (1978) Circadian and circannual rhythms in sexual activity and plasma hormones (FSH, LH, testosterone) of five human males. Arch. Sex. Behav. *7:* 13–30.

Reinberg, A., M. Lagoguey, F. Cesselin, Y. Touitou, J.-C. Legrand, A. Delasalle, J. Antreassian, and A. Lagoguey (1978) Circadian and circannual rhythms in plasma hormones and other variables of five healthy young human males. Acta Endocrinol. *88:* 417–427.

Reinberg, A., F. Levi, and G. Depry (1984) Chronobiologie et nutrition. Encycl. Med. Chir. Glandes Endocrines–Nutrition A 10, 1–10.

Reinberg, A., and M. H. Smolensky (1983a) Chronobiology and thermoregulation. Pharmacol. Ther. *22:* 425–464.

Reinberg, A., and M. H. Smolensky, eds. (1983b) *Biological Rhythms and Medicine,* Springer-Verlag, Berlin.

Reinberg, A., Y. Touitou, F. Levi, and A. Nicolai (1983) Circadian and seasonal changes in ACTH-induced effects in healthy young men. Eur. J. Clin. Pharmacol. *25:* 657–665.

Rihmer, Z. (1987) The geography of DST. Biol. Psychiat. *22:* 1044–1045.

Rose, G. (1961) Seasonal variation in blood pressure in man. Nature *189:* 235.

Rose, S. P. R., and S. Murphy (1987) Psychotherapy and imipramine binding to blood platelets. In *Abstracts of the IBRO Conference, Budapest, August 1987.*

Rosenthal, N. E., W. J. Duncan, T. A. Wehr, A. J. Lewy, and J. C. Gillin (1982) Seasonal variation in REM latency in depressives and normals. Unpublished manuscript.

Rosenthal, N. E, D. A. Sack, J. C. Gillin, A. J. Lewy, F. K. Goodwin, P. S. Mueller, D. A. Newsome, and T. A. Wehr (1984) Seasonal affective disorder: A description of the syndrome and preliminary findings. Arch. Gen. Psychiat. *41:* 72–80.

Rosenthal, N. E., D. A. and T. A. Wehr (1983) Seasonal variations in affective disorders. In *Circadian Rhythms in Psychiatry,* T. A. Wehr and F. K. Goodwin, eds., pp. 185–201, Boxwood Press, Pacific Grove, CA.

Rusak, B., and I. Zucker (1975) Biological rhythms and animal behavior. Ann. Rev. Psychol. *26:* 137–171.

Sargent, F. (1954) Season and the metabolism of fat and carbohydrate: A study of vestigial physiology. Meteorol. Monogr. *2:* 68–80.

Sasaki, T. (1987) Geographical distribution of basal metabolic rate with remarks to biological equator and circannual peak. Chronobiologia *14:* 232.

Sasaki, T., and F. Halberg (1979) Reproducibility during decades and individualisation of circannual rhythmic metabolic rate in Japanese men and women. In *Advances in Bioscience,* Vol. 19, *Chronopharmacology,* A. Reinberg and F. Halberg, eds., pp. 247–254, Pergamon Press, Oxford.

Sasaki, N., J. Takeda, S. Fukushi, M. Hasunuma, H. Ichikawa, M. Ichinohe, K. Tanaka, I. Sasaki, T. Takei, K. Sugita, K. Takemori, and N. Yamada (1969) Seasonal variation in the blood pressure of the inhabitants in the northeastern parts of Japan. Hirosaki Med. J. *21:* 202–211.

Scheving, L. E., D. F. Halberg, and J. E. Pauly (1974) *Chronobiology,* Georg Thieme Verlag, Stuttgart.

Schneider, L. S., D. Munjack, J. A. Severson, and R. Palmer (1987) Platelet 3H-imipramine binding in generalized anxiety disorder, and agoraphobia with panic attacks. Biol. Psychiat. 22: 59–66.

Schulz, L. (1960) Der jahreszeitliche Gang der Temperaturempfindung des Menschen anhand einer zehnjährigen Beobachtungsreihe. Arch. Phys. Therapie (Leipzig) 11/12: 245–255.

Siever, L. J., and L. D. Kenneth (1985) Overview: Toward a dysregulation hypothesis of depression. Amer. J. Psychiat. 142: 1017–1031.

Skegg, K., D. Skegg, and B. W. McDonald (1986) Is there seasonal variation in the prescribing of antidepressants in the community? J. Epidem. Commun. Health 40: 285–288.

Smals, A. G. H., P. W. C. Kloppenberg, and T. J. Benraad (1976) Circannual cycle in plasma testosterone levels in man. J. Clin. Endocrinol. Metab. 42: 979–982.

Smals, A. G. H., H. A. Ross, and P. W. C. Kloppenberg (1977) Seasonal variation in serum T3 and T4 levels in man. J. Clin. Endocrinol. Metab. 44: 998–1001.

Smith, J. A., T. J. X. Mee, D. J. Padwick, and G. Spokes (1981) Human post-mortem pineal enzyme activity. Clin. Edocrinol. 14: 75–81.

Smolensky, M. H. (1983) Aspects of human chronopathology. In Biological Rhythms and Medicine, A. Reinberg and M. H. Smolensky, eds., pp. 131–209, Springer-Verlag, Berlin.

Spiegel, R. (1981) Sleep and Sleeplessness in Advanced Age, MTP Press, Lancaster, England.

Stephan, J. (1983) Die endogene Depression als phylogenetisches Relikt des Winterschlafs? MD thesis, University of Tübingen.

Suarez, L., and E. Barrett- Connor (1982) Seasonal variation in fasting plasma glucose levels in man. Diabetologia 22: 250–253.

Swade, C., and A. Coppen (1980) Seasonal variations in biochemical factors related to depressive illness. J. Affect. Dis. 2: 249–255.

Swade, C., M. Metcalfe, A. Coppen, J. Mendlewicz, and P. Linkowski (1987) Seasonal variations in the dexamethasone suppression test. J. Affect. Dis. 13: 9–11.

Sweeney, E. J., J. A. S. Kinney, and A. Ryan (1960) Seasonal changes in scotopic sensitivity. J. Opt. Soc. Amer. 50: 237–240.

Takashi, A., J. Mayuzumi, N. Kiruchi, and S. Arai (1980) Seasonal variations in skin temperature, skin pH, evaporative water loss and skin surface lipid values on human skin. Chem. Pharm. Bull. 28: 387–392.

Tanaka, M., Y. Harimura, Y. Tochihara, S. Yamazaki, T. Ohnaka, J. Matsui, and K. Yoshida (1984) Effect of season on peripheral resistance to localised cold stress. Int. J. Biometerol 28: 39–45.

Tang, S. W., and J. M. Morris (1985) Variation in human platelet 3H-imipramine binding. Psychiat. Res. 16: 141–146.

Thompson, C., D. Stinson, M. Fernandez, J. Fine, and G. Isaacs (1988) The seasonal pattern assessment questionnaire: A validation study and a comparison of normal, bipolar, and seasonal affective disorder patients. J. Affect. Disord. 14: 257–264.

Torsvall, L., and T. Akerstedt (1980) A diurnal type scale: Construction, consistency and validation in shift work. Scand. J. Work Environ. Health 6: 283–290.

Touitou, Y., A. Carayon, A. Reinberg, A. Bogdan, and H. Beck (1983a) Differences in the seasonal rhythmicity of plasma prolactin in elderly human subjects: Detection in women but not in men. J. Endocrinol. 96: 65–71.

Touitou, Y., M. Fevre, A. Bogdan, A. Reinberg, J. De Prins, H. Beck, and C. Touitou (1984) Patterns of plasma melatonin with ageing and mental condition: Stability of nyctohemeral rhythms and differences in seasonal variations. Acta Endocrinol. 106: 145–151.

Touitou, Y., A. Reinberg, A. Bogdan, A. Auzeby, H. Beck, and C. Touitou (1986) Age related changes in both circadian and seasonal rhythms of rectal temperature with special reference to senile dementia of Alzheimer type. Gerontology 32: 110–118.

Touitou, Y., J. Sulon, A. Bogdan, A. Reinberg, J.-C. Sodoyez, and E. Demey-Ponsart (1983b) Adrenocortical hormones, aging and mental condition: Seasonal and circadian rhythms of plasma 18-hydroxy-11-dehydroxy-corticosterone, total and free cortisol and urinary corticosteroids. J. Endocrinol. 96: 53–64.

Udassin, R., Z. Harari, Y. Shoenfeld, and G. Keren (1981) Cholinergic urticaria: A seasonal disease. Arch. Intern. Med. *141:* 1029–1030.

Van Cauter, E., M. L'Hermite, G. Copinschi, S. Refetoff, D. Desir, and C. Robyn (1981a) Quantitative analysis of spontaneous variations of plasma prolactin in normal man. Amer. J. Physiol. *241:* 355–363.

Van Cauter, E., E. Virasoro, R. Leclerg, and G. Copinischi (1981b) Seasonal, circadian and episodic variations of human immunoreactive beta-MSH, ACTH and cortisol. Int. J. Peptide Protein Res. *17:* 3–13.

Van Staveren, W. A. P. Deurenberg, J. Burema, L. P. G. M. De Groot, and J. G. A. J. Hautvast (1986) Seasonal variation in food intake pattern of physical activity and change in body weight in a group of young adult Dutch women consuming self-selected diet. Int. J. Obesity *10:* 133–145.

von Knorring, L., B. G. L. Almay, F. Johansson, and A. Wahlströhm (1982) Circannual variation in concentrations of endorphines in cerebrospinal fluid. Pain *12:* 265–272.

Watanabe, G. (1964) Seasonal variation of adrenal cortex activity. Arch Envir. Health *9:* 192–200.

Wehr, T. A., A. Wirz-Justice F. K. Goodwin, W. Duncan, and J. C. Gillin (1979) Phase advance of the sleep–wake cycle as an antidepressant. Science *206:* 710–713.

Weihe, W. H. (1986) Klima-Wetter-Pharmaka. In *Wetter-Klima-Menschliche Gesundheit,* V. Faust, ed., pp. 151–164, Hippokrates Verlag, Stuttgart.

Weitzman, E. D., A. S. de Graaf, J. F. Sassin, T. Hansen, O. B. Godtlibsen, M. Perlow, and L. Hellman (1975) Seasonal patterns of sleep stages and secretion of cortisol, and growth hormone during 24 hour periods in northern Norway. Acta Endocrinol. *78:* 65–76.

Wetterberg, L., F. Halberg, E. Haus, T. Kawasaki, K. Uezono, M. Ueno, and T. Omae (1981) Circadian rhythmic urinary Melatonin excretion in four seasons by clinically healthy Japanese subjects in Kyushu. Chronobiologia *8:* 188–194.

Whitaker, P. M., J. J. Warsh, H. C. Stancer, E. Persad, and C. K. Vint (1984) Seasonal variation in platelet 3H-imipramine binding: Comparable values in control and depressed populations. Psychiat. Res. *11:* 127–141.

Whybrow, P. C., P. Graf, and J. Schiffman (1985) Seasonal changes in behavior and affect in a northern New England population. In *Abstracts of the IV World Congress of Biological Psychiatry, Philadelphia,* p. 327.

Wirz-Justice, A. (1979) Seasonality in affective illness. In *Abstracts of the 132nd Annual Meeting of the American Psychiatry Association, Chicago.*

Wirz-Justice, A. (1988) Platelet research in psychiatry. Experientia *44:* 145–152.

Wirz-Justice A., and R. Richter (1979) Seasonality in biochemical determinations: A source of variance and a clue to the temporal incidence of affective illness. Psychiat. Res. *1:* 53–60.

Wirz-Justice, A., R. A. Wever, and J. Aschoff (1984) Seasonality in freerunning circadian rhythms in man. Naturwissenschaften *71:* 316–319.

Wirz-Justice, A., P. Graw, A. Jochum, B. Gisin, J. Arendt, M. Aldhous, K. Kräuchi, and W. Pöldinger (1988) Light at night is as good as in the morning in SAD patients. In *Abstracts of the XVI CINP Congress, Munich.*

World Health Organization (WHO) Collaborative Study Group (1987) The dexamethasone suppression test in depression. Brit. J. Psychiat. *150:* 459–462.

Yasuda, Y., and M. Miyamura (1983) Seasonal variation of forearm blood flow at rest and during exercise. J. Physiol. Soc. Japan *45:* 640–643.

Yoshimura, M., K. Yukiyoshi, T. Yoshioka, and H. Takeda (1966) Climatic adaptation of basal metabolism. Fed. Proc. *25:* 1169–1174.

Zahorska-Markiewicz, B. (1980) Weight reduction and seasonal variation. Int. J. Obesity *4:* 139–143.

Zahorska-Markiewicz, B., and A. Markiewicz (1984) Circannual rhythm of exercise metabolic rate in humans. Eur. J. Appl. Physiol. *52:* 328–330.

Zifferblatt, S. M., C. S. Wilbur, and J. L. Pisky (1980) Understanding food habits. J. Amer. Diet. Assoc. *76:* 9–14.

13

Dopamine Functioning in the Behavioral Facilitation System and Seasonal Variation in Behavior: Normal Population and Clinical Studies

Richard A. Depue, Paul Arbisi, Michele R. Spoont, Arthur Leon, and Barbara Ainsworth

The most frequently observed form of seasonal affective disorder (SAD) is manifested as a set of covarying depressive symptoms that occur during winter, but not during summer, months (Rosenthal *et al.*, 1984). Thus far, symptoms have been viewed solely as a means of defining SAD for diagnostic purposes and as indicators of treatment efficacy. It is possible, however, to view the symptoms of SAD from the perspective of major behavioral systems—that is, to ask whether this covarying set of symptoms represents an alteration in an integrated behavioral system. It is, indeed, possible to view many forms of psychopathology within this framework, the benefit being that the neurobiology of behavioral systems is extensively addressed in animal work (Depue, in press; Depue and Iacono, in press), and thereby provides guidelines for neurobiological hypotheses of psychopathology.

If the symptoms of SAD can be validly understood within such a framework, then a series of research questions arises: (1) Does the behavioral system affected in SAD manifest seasonal variation naturally in the normal population? (2) If so, is this form of seasonal variation dimensional in nature? (3) If it is dimensional, do SAD cases represent the extreme tail of this seasonality dimension? and (4) If the neurobiology of this behavioral system were to be defined, is seasonal variation in this behavioral system, and particularly the extreme variation that occurs in SAD, related to functional characteristics of this neurobiology?

Richard A. Depue, Paul Arbisi, and Michele R. Spoont. Department of Psychology, University of Minnesota, Minneapolis, Minnesota.

Arthur Leon and Barbara Ainsworth. Departments of Physiology and Epidemiology, School of Medicine, University of Minnesota, Minneapolis, Minnesota.

In the discussion that follows, we outline the neurobehavioral system within which we believe SAD is manifested. We then describe several of our studies, on both normal and SAD populations, that begin to explore the research questions arising from this framework.

The Behavioral Facilitation System

A large body of animal and human research indicates that behavior is organized into several major systems that direct and motivate behavior in response to classes of significant environmental stimuli (Schneirla, 1959; Gray, 1982; Depue and Spoont, 1986; Depue, in press;). The most relevant of these to the current focus is the behavioral facilitation system (BFS), which is a very basic behavioral system that has been described in all animals across phylogenetic levels. The BFS functions to mobilize behavior so that active engagement with the environment occurs under appropriate stimulus conditions. The BFS is thought to be activated mainly by inherently rewarding stimuli (food, social, sexual, novelty, and achievement-related patterns) or conditioned signals of these stimuli (Schneirla, 1959; Gray, 1982). Behavioral facilitation is achieved through stimulus elicitation of what are believed to be the two major components of the BFS, initiation of locomotor activity (LA) and incentive–reward motivation. Moreover, recent reviews of human research (Tellegen, 1985; Depue *et al.,* 1987; Depue, in press) indicate that the specific *mood* associated with behavioral engagement, and presumably BFS activity, is positive mood, which accompanies the process of reward acquisition. Conversely, an *absence* of positive mood (a nonreactive, low-incentive depressed mood), rather than negative mood, accompanies low levels of engagement. Thus, overall, the BFS provides a motor–affective (motivational) contribution to the process of active environmental engagement.

Neurobiology of the Behavioral Facilitation System

The construct of the BFS as a generalized system that facilitates behavioral engagement is supported by neurobiological research on the two major components of the BFS: LA and incentive–reward motivation. In particular, investigation of the process of LA *initiation* has led to a general model of BFS facilitation of behavioral engagement. Therefore, the neurobiology of the two major BFS components is briefly outlined first, followed by more general modeling of behavioral engagement.

Initiation of Locomotor Activity

Processes involved in the generation of volitional locomotion can be divided into three useful, albeit oversimplified, phases: initiation, programming, and execution (Mogenson *et al.*, 1980). It is specifically the initiation phase of locomotor generation that relates to the facilitation construct of the BFS, because the initiation process is closely tied to affective–motivational input to the motor system.

There is a vast literature demonstrating that dopamine (DA) is the primary neurotransmitter in the initiation of LA (see comprehensive reviews by Fishman *et al.*, 1983; Oades, 1985). Importantly, LA initiation occurs via the action of DA and its agonists in the mesolimbic DA system in general, and in the well-established ventral tegmental area of Tsai (VTA, specifically the A10 DA cell group) projection to the nucleus accumbens (NAS, also referred to as the ventral striatum) in particular (Fishman *et al.*, 1983; Oades, 1985). The quantity of spontaneous exploratory LA and magnitude of amphetamine-induced LA are both positively related to number of DA neurons (including those of the A10 cell group), to the relative density of innervation of DA terminals in target fields, and to DA content in the NAS in inbred mouse strains (Fink and Reis, 1981; Sved *et al.*, 1984, 1985; Oades, 1985)—effects perhaps related to the proportionately greater synthesis and release of DA in high-DA neuron strains (Sved *et al.*, 1984).

DA is the primary neurotransmitter involved in LA initiation, inasmuch as, in the absence of any central DA receptor arousal, LA will not occur to any significant extent (Fishman *et al.*, 1983; Oades, 1985). Although this cannot be said for the receptors of any other neurotransmitter system (Fishman *et al.*, 1983), LA is nevertheless the product of the mutual interaction of a number of neurotransmitter systems. Much of this interaction is unknown, but a recent neurobiological model of NAS circuitry illustrates current concepts; the interested reader is referred to this work (Jones *et al.*, 1981).

Incentive–Reward Motivation

Because LA represents the strongest indicator of an incentive motivational state (Iversen, 1978), the second component of the BFS—incentive–reward motivation—may have a neurobiology linked to LA. Data indicate that LA and incentive–reward motivation are integrated within VTA A10 DA pathways (Iversen, 1978; Kelly, 1978; Mogenson *et al.*, 1980; Oades, 1985). Recent reviews have concluded that DA, but not unequivocally NE, plays a critical role in mediating the effects of reward on behavior (Beninger, 1983; Stein, 1983; Mason, 1984), one of the strongest lines of evidence being DA agonist self-administration. For instance, amphetamine, cocaine (which acts strongly on the DA system), and selective DA receptor agonists piribedil and apomorphine are avidly self-administered by rats, even under conditions of catecholamine depletion (if depletion is >90%; Freed and Yamamoto, 1985).

That VTA (and nigrostriatal) DA pathways mediate reward is supported by reviews (Beninger, 1983); by self-administration of cocaine in the NAS and the medial prefrontal cortex (Goeders and Smith, 1983; Goeders *et al.*, 1986); and by the fact that the distribution of intracranial self-stimulation reward points, even with micromapping techniques, coincides with that of DA terminals in the NAS and frontal cortex (Routtenberg and Sloan, 1972; Mason, 1984). Recent work suggests that self-administration of cocaine is greatest in, or perhaps largely accounted for by, some VTA DA projections to the medial prefrontal cortex (Goeders and Smith, 1983; Goeders *et al.*, 1986). This suggests that the BFS construct encompasses some of the VTA A10 DA projections to prefrontal cortex as well as those to the NAS.

Although it is not certain that the same reward systems are involved in drug and electrical self-administration as in natural reward (however, recent findings indicate that they are similar; Goeders and Smith, 1983; Porrino *et al.*, 1984), on the basis of these findings, Stein (1983) and others (Hoffman and Beninger, 1985) have concluded that DA activity mediates the incentive type of reward that activates goal acquistion, rather than the gratifying type of reward that brings behavior to a satisfying termination.

Nucleus Accumbens: Interface between Limbic and Motor Systems

Because LA and incentive–reward motivation represent fundamental components of goal-directed behaviors (Mogenson *et al.*, 1980), a central role for some A10 DA projections to the NAS and prefrontal cortex in the initiation of behavioral engagement is suggested. Thus, these pathways may be viewed conceptually as a generalized system of behavioral facilitation (i.e., the BFS). Research particularly supports a generalized facilitation role of the A10-to-NAS DA pathway, in that, depending on the sum total effects of all inputs to the VTA A10 DA enurons (including those from limbic–hypothalamic structures, from arousal integrative centers such as the locus ceruleus, from prefrontal cortex, and from the dorsal raphe nuclei; Glowinski, 1981), DA may modulate the response of NAS neurons to limbic input (Yim and Mogenson, 1983). The NAS is thereby placed in a central position to modulate the extent to which *some* limbic projections influence the motor system, and presumably the initiation of LA and goal-directed behavior. The significance of this is that limbic forebrain structures, in interaction with hypothalamic nuclei, are implicated as integrative centers for innate drives and motivational and emotional processes that are prerequisites for the initiation of various goal-directed behaviors, including attack, sexual, social, drinking, feeding, and other behaviors (MacLean, 1975; Mogenson *et al.*, 1980; Nauta and Domesick, 1981).

Central placement of the NAS in facilitating behavioral engagement suggests that DA activity in the NAS serves as a gating mechanism that influences whether some signals from limbic structures reach the motor system. This is concordant with the evolving functional principle of DA activity as a switching–initiation mechanism, where DA promotes the switching between alternative sources of information (see review by Oades, 1985). Importantly, a *generalized* switching–initiation function for DA is consistent with behavioral data. On the basis of studies on behavioral consequences of selective lesions of A10 DA neurons at the level of cell bodies, and at the level of terminals in the prefrontal cortex, in the NAS, and in the lateral septum, the A10 DA neurons do not appear to have a specific behavioral role; rather, they seem to facilitate or initiate processes in regions that they innervate (Taghzouti *et al.*, 1986).

Implications for SAD

The relevance of the BFS to SAD is suggested by the nature of the affected behaviors in SAD and by their contrasted manifestation in the summer. This is particularly clear in SAD patients who become hypomanic in the summer (i.e., who manifest bipolar II disorder), but it may be equally applicable to unipolar SAD cases who describe the occurrence of hyperthymic periods (hypomanic-like periods without the impairment associated with hypomania) during the summer. As illustrated in Figure 13-1, SAD behavioral characteristics of winter retarded depression (at the bottom of the figure) and summer hypomania (at the top) appear to represent opposite extremes of normal behavioral dimensions. Inspection of the extremes of these dimensions indicates that the winter and summer behavioral manifestations of SAD appear to represent extreme states of engagement with the interpersonal and achievement-related environment—characterized by excessively low behavioral engagement in the winter and by normal or at times excessive engagement in the summer. *Such pervasive alterations in behavioral engagement raise the possibility that SAD may involve extreme seasonal alternations in BFS functioning.*

It is proposed that the winter depressive and summer hyperthymic/hypomanic phases of SAD represent opposite extreme manifestations of a single dimension of BFS *functional* activity, being deficient in depression, high in hyperthymia/hypomania. The power of this formulation is that these divergent symptom patterns are parsimoniously explained by the switching–initiation–incentive principle of DA activity—a principle that must exert its influence on behavior if A10 DA pathways are dysfunctional (for whatever reasons). From the standpoint of this principle, the dimension of BFS functional activity may be viewed as a dimension of the probability that relevant external and internal (including cognitive) eliciting stimuli will switch on, initiate, or facilitate motor and affective responses—or, put differently, as a dimension of the propensity to behavioral and affective reactivity to eliciting stimuli.

Although our goal is not to account for each specific symptom, if BFS dysfunction underlies SAD symptom patterns, then the BFS major components of motor and incentive–reward motivation should represent core features of both the depressive and hyperthymic/hypomanic phases. In winter depression, motor retardation (where motor and speech responsiveness is delayed and slowed)

MOTOR			INCENTIVE-REWARD ACTIVATION		MOOD	NONSPECIFIC AROUSAL						COGNITIVE	
Locomotion	Speech	Facies	Hedonia (Social, Sex, Food)	Desire for Excitement		Appetite	Energy	Sleep/Wake	Thought	Attention	Sensory Vividness	Optimism	Self-Worth
hyperactivity	rapid, pressured	expressive	excessive interest and pleasure	excessive, creates new activities	elation, euphoria, reactive	decreased	excessive, boundless	↓ need for sleep	sharper, flight of ideas, witty, > decisional power	distractible	extremely vivid	> self-confidence, < estimation of negative outcomes, grandiosity	increased worth, grandiosity
retardation, slowed, delayed, stupor	retardation, slowed, delayed, mute	unchanging, unexpressive	no interest or pleasure (pervasive anhedonia)	avoidance of stimulation	devoid of emotion, depression, lack reactivity	> carbohydrate intake	easily fatigued, devoid of energy	hypersomnia, naps	< decisional power, thoughts "dead", mind dull	poor concentration	senses dull, food tastes bland	pessimistic, persistent gloom, brood about past, hopeless about future outcomes, suicidal ideation	totally worthless, delusional

FIGURE 13-1. Symptoms of the winter depressive (bottom) and summer hyperthymic/hypomanic (top) phases of SAD. Symptoms form extreme ends of normal behavioral dimensions and may be viewed as representing low (bottom) and high (top) behavioral engagement with rewarding stimuli in the environment.

and a lack of incentive–reward motivation (subjectively, a lack of interest and excitement) to engage with social, sexual, vocational, or recreational stimuli form highly prominent features (Rosenthal et al., 1983, 1984). Furthermore, the depression in SAD is characterized by a *lack of affective reactivity* to positive stimuli, even stimuli that are highly rewarding—where the depression has a quality distinct from a reactive form of depressed affect found, for instance, in a bereaved state. The human literature on the structure of behavioral states is concordant with this view: The ''low'' extreme of the major positive-engagement dimension is characterized by an absence of positive affect rather than by negative affect (Tellegen, 1985; Depue et al., 1987). All of these symptoms may be interpreted from the standpoint of the functional principle of DA as a state in which the normal eliciting stimuli of behavioral engagement do not activate BFS function, and hence do not initiate LA, incentive–reward motivation, and positive mood.

The summer hyperthymic/hypomanic phase of SAD also manifests the BFS core components, but the opposite extreme exists. There is a heightened probability that signals of reward and novelty (including those that are cognitively generated; Milner, 1977) ''switch on'' motor behavior (hyperactivity) and initiate a subjective state of increased incentive–reward motivation and pleasurable excitement.

Thus, it may be fruitful to view the depressive and hyperhymic/hypomanic phases of SAD as related to divergent states of BFS activity, and, at a more global level, to divergent states of behavioral engagement with the environment. Although this model may be equally applicable, for different etiological reasons, to the symptoms of nonseasonal bipolar affective disorders, *it is the fact that these divergent BFS states are temporally associated with the seasons that would provide the unique feature of SAD.* It is important to note that primary support for the notion that BFS activity shows naturally occurring seasonal variation would derive from evidence indicating that there is seasonal variation in DA functioning. Significantly, indices of DA functioning do exhibit a circadian rhythm in primates (Perlow et al., 1977), and one index of this rhythm in rodents appears to show seasonal variation in absolute peak, in level and duration of values during the animal's active period, and in amplitude—all values being highest in summer, lowest in winter (Kafka et al., 1983). Thus, to the extent that altered DA function is involved in SAD, this model suggests that analysis of seasonal effects on DA function may provide guidelines for understanding the excessive seasonal variation in behavioral engagement in SAD.

Dimensionality of Seasonal Variation in Behavioral Engagement in the Normal Population

The proposal that SAD is characterized by extreme seasonal variation in BFS activity and, accordingly, in more global patterns of behavioral engagement raises a preliminary question as to whether mean level of behavioral engagement manifests seasonal variation naturally in the normal population. If it does, this would raise the possibility that the seasonal variation manifested in behavioral engagement in SAD represents an extreme case of a normal process of seasonal variation in behavior. To assess this issue, the Inventory of Seasonal Variation (ISV) was constructed. The ISV was developed within a construct validation framework. The construct of seasonality underlying the ISV is defined as changes in level of behavioral engagement that occur as a function of season, where the minimum level occurs in winter and the maximum level occurs in one of the other seasons. Although other seasonal patterns may exist, our data suggest that they are rare in the general population, and therefore they are not the focus of the ISV.

Item Content

Substantive validity of the ISV (i.e., transformation of the definition of the construct into manifest inventory content) had been achieved by developing items that represent the major behavioral areas of engagement shown in Figure 13-1 above. The ISV is comprised of 15 items; the 13 substantive items are shown in Table 13-1. Eleven items are direct representatives of behavioral engagement areas, whereas two additional items are of theoretical interest (level of food consumption, changeability). The changeability item is meant to assess the extent of variability (or instability) in mood and energy within a day as a function of season. Finally, two bogus items—not related to behavioral engagement and not expected to have seasonal variation—have been included in the ISV to detect random or perseverative response biases: entertainment preference (for violent TV programs), and interactional opportunity (or the extent to which one takes advantage of others).

TABLE 13-1. The 13 Substantive Items of the Inventory of Seasonal Variation (ISV)

Energy (physiological activation)
Sleep (amount)
Pleasure (hedonia)
Elevated mood (frequency)
Depressed mood (frequency)
Sociability (enjoyment of, *not* need for)
Sensation seeking (desire for exciting, rewarding stimuli)
Sensory vividness (physiological activation)
Physical movements (amount and speed)
Interest in sex (hedonia)
Optimism (cognitive)
Changeability (frequency of mood and energy fluctuations per day)
Level of food consumption

TABLE 13-2. Item Example from the ISV

Energy
   A. Very large increase—almost never fatigued, sometimes feels like too much energy
   B. Large increase—more often active throughout the day with no fatigue
   C. Moderate increase—more often feel energetic
   D. Slight increase—less likely to be fatigued
   E. About average for me
   F. Slight decrease—more often feel *slightly* tired
   G. Moderate decrease—more often feel *very* tired
   H. Large decrease—more often fatigued from everyday activities
   I. Very large decrease—more often too tired to do *some* everyday activities

Rating Scale

Each ISV item is rated on a 9-point scale, once for each season. A sample item
tapping energy is represented in Table 13-2. As shown in Table 13-2, each of
the 9 points has a weighted verbal label ranging from "very large increase" to
"very large decrease," and each of these labels is accompanied in most items
by a descriptive statement. In each item, the central position on the scale is
labeled "About average for me." Thus, the subject's task is (1) to consider his
or her average level across the year for the behavior in question, and (2) to rate
each season on the 9-point scale relative to his or her personal yearly average.

As is clear from the description above, the rating scale format for the ISV
is not based on absolute levels of behaviors. Pilot interviews with respondents
on earlier versions of the ISV indicated that absolute-level assessment was not
possible for two main reasons. First, there was great variation between subjects
in their level on the item behaviors, so an impossibly large assortment of descriptive statements would have been required. More importantly, because a
season is 3 months in duration, absolute levels do not apply very well to such
long periods; subjects were confused as to which descriptor to select. Therefore, a relative-level assessment has been chosen for rating scales, in which all
items are rated relative to the subject's personal yearly average level. To provide a guide for the selection of levels, the descriptive statement accompanying
each weighted label describes general absolute levels of the behavior in question, but the main difference between levels is in the frequency with which that
level is experienced within a season. This connotes that one is more or less
frequently at a certain level within a season, which is more in keeping with the
natural phenomenology of behavior over time.

Scoring Procedure

All of our data on the ISV indicate that a very simple scoring procedure may
be employed. Individual examination of the seasonal patterns of over 457 uni-

versity subjects showed the frequency of patterns displayed in Table 13-3. From these data, it is clear that 94% of the subjects reported a seasonal pattern consistent with the ISV construct definition of seasonality, and another 5% simply fell at the very low end of the seasonality dimension. Only 1% of the subjects showed reverse seasonality according to the ISV construct definition of seasonality. Hence, for 99% of subjects, the following deviation score accurately dimensionalizes their seasonality:

Level of highest season − Level of winter = Seasonal deviation score

This scoring procedure would misclassify only 1% of subjects with reverse seasonality; these subjects would receive a negative score, which would be converted to 0 and treated as representing zero seasonality (as defined by the ISV construct of seasonality).

Internal Structural Validity

After two pilot studies with the ISV, each of which resulted in refinement of the ISV item content and rating scales, the internal structural validity of the ISV was assessed on 457 university subjects, ranging in age from 18 to 35 years and of about equal sex ratio. Calendrical time of taking the ISV for the 457 subjects was evenly distributed across the four seasons. Internal consistency was excellent: Coefficient alpha was 0.87, indicating that the ISV items tap the construct of seasonality in a homogeneous manner. Each item also related well to the total seasonal deviation score, as shown in Table 13-4. As shown in the table, all items performed quite well, with physical movements, energy, and depressed mood relating to total score highest, and sex the lowest. The sex item has been revised and will be retested. Note also that the bogus items bore no relation to total seasonal deviation score, indicating that subjects were not rating items in a biased manner.

The factorial structure of the ISV has been explored with a common factor procedure, using a principal-factor solution with communalities estimated from

TABLE 13-3. Types of Seasonal Patterns Reported on the ISV

Seasonal pattern	%
Winter lowest, spring or summer highest	82
Winter lowest, fall–spring or –summer highest	8
Winter–fall lowest, spring or summer highest	4
Total for winter lowest	94
Minimal difference across all seasons (minimal seasonality)	5
Winter–fall highest, spring or summer lowest (reverse seasonality)	1

TABLE 13-4. Item–Total Score Correlations for the ISV

Item	r
Energy	0.69
Sleep	0.56
Pleasure	0.63
Food consumption	0.63
Elevated mood	0.67
Depressed mood	0.69
Sociability	0.59
Sensation seeking	0.58
Sensory vividness	0.57
Physical movements	0.73
Interest in sex	0.31
Optimism	0.65
Changeability	0.50
Entertainment preference (bogus item)	0.04
Interactional opportunity (bogus item)	0.09

multiple R^2 and then iteration, and varimax rotation. The optimal structure is a four-factor solution, shown in Table 13-5 with underlined item loadings indicating the item's highest loading.

Because the behaviors included in the ISV would be expected to covary, due to the common action of the BFS on a host of behavioral engagement patterns, many ISV items do not load highly solely on one factor. However, the patterning of the loadings suggests that three of the behavioral engagement

TABLE 13-5. Factor Loadings of ISV Items in a Four-Factor Solution

Item	Factor			
	1	2	3	4
Energy	<u>0.62</u>	0.21	0.19	0.33
Sleep	<u>0.58</u>	0.09	0.06	0.22
Pleasure	<u>0.64</u>	0.33	0.15	0.09
Food consumption	0.21	0.10	0.21	<u>0.71</u>
Elevated mood	0.42	<u>0.60</u>	0.25	0.06
Depressed mood	0.39	<u>0.59</u>	0.23	0.18
Sociability	0.25	<u>0.41</u>	0.37	0.07
Sensation seeking	0.16	0.14	<u>0.67</u>	0.16
Sensory vividness	0.22	0.25	<u>0.56</u>	0.06
Physical movements	0.36	0.29	<u>0.54</u>	0.28
Optimism	0.32	0.37	<u>0.42</u>	0.17
Entertainment preference (bogus item)	−0.03	0.08	0.19	0.05
Interactional opportunity (bogus item)	0.04	0.03	0.06	0.08

areas shown in Figure 13-1 are represented most predominantly in the ISV. Factor 1 appears to be an Activation factor, with heaviest loadings by energy and sleep, while moderate loadings (>0.30) occur for physical movement, the mood items, and optimism. Pleasure also loads highly on this factor, indicating that the rewarding value of life's experiences is closely related to a state of activation. This is consistent with the human literature on the structure of behavioral states discussed above. Factor 2 appears to be most strongly a Mood factor, while pleasure, sociability, and optimism have moderate loadings. Factor 3 appears to be a Locomotor/Incentive–Reward factor, in that the highest loadings are those for sensation seeking (desire for exciting, rewarding stimulation) and physical movements, as well as sensory vividness. Moderate loadings occur for optimism and sociability. Interestingly, the cognitive component of behavioral engagement does not emerge by itself, but rather has moderately high loadings on all three of the engagement-related factors. Finally, Factor 4 is defined solely by food consumption, and thus may be interpreted as a Metabolic Function factor. Metabolic function appears not to be a tightly coupled component of engagement (since it has relatively low loadings on all three other factors), but it is related to the ISV seasonal deviation score, as indicated by its having obtained one of the highest item–total correlations (0.63). Thus, overall, the factor analysis of the ISV confirms that the inventory is comprised of the different components of behavioral engagement, and in that sense supports the substantive validity of the ISV. Finally, in all of the internal structure analyses, no significant sex differences were observed.

Retest Stability

Over a 2-week period, ISV retest stability measured in the summer months was 0.77 ($p < 0.01$, $n = 175$), with no significant mean or *SD* differences occurring.

Separation of Seasonal Distributions

Since the efficacy of the ISV seasonal deviation score in detecting individual differences in seasonality is dependent on the degree of separation between the frequency distributions of the seasons on the 9-point rating scale, these distributions are plotted on a standard 9-point rating scale (horizontal axis) in Figure 13-2. This 9-point scale may be viewed as a dimension of behavioral engagement, where lower numbers represent decreases in engagement, higher numbers represent increases, and the scale point of 5 is "above average." As may be seen in the figure, there is little overlap of the frequency distributions for winter, on the one hand, and for spring or summer, on the other hand. The distribution for winter falls mainly below the average point, while those for

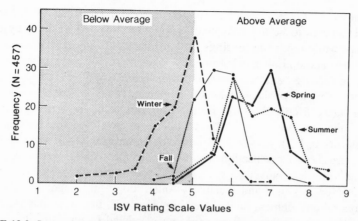

FIGURE 13-2. Seasonal separation of the frequency distributions of ISV rating scale values in the normal population. The 9-point ISV rating scale is shown on the horizontal axis, where point 5 represents an average level of behavioral engagement across the year. The distribution for winter scores is mainly below average, indicating low behavioral engagement, whereas the distributions for spring and summer scores fall almost entirely above average, indicating high levels of engagement.

spring and summer fall almost entirely above the average point. The fall distribution lies in between the other distributions.

Dimensional Qualities of the Seasonal Deviation Score

As Figure 13-3 shows, the frequency distribution of ISV seasonal deviation scores for the sample of 457 subjects was quite broad, providing seasonal deviations ranging from 0 to 5.9 rating scale points, and was finely graded across the full range. To obtain a behavioral sense of the magnitude of a 5- or 6-point deviation score, the sample ISV item tapping energy provided in Table 13-2 above may be observed. These subjects reported large changes across the seasons, indeed. And it will be recalled that subjects were administered the ISV evenly across the seasons, so extreme scores did not occur as a function of winter testing only. Finally, the distribution of ISV scores approached a normal distribution, with a long, thin tail toward high scores. All of these features are promising indicators of the ISV's potential to provide a sensitive dimensional index of seasonality.

Importantly, 15 SAD subjects who had participated in our winter studies all received ISV seasonal deviation scores above 4.5, indicating that they fell in the upper 3% of the ISV distribution of deviation scores. All of the SAD subjects took the ISV after marked antidepressant responses to phototherapy, so their high ISV scores were not unduly influenced by a depressed state. However, the manner in which SAD subjects rate themselves on the ISV during summer months is an important question, which we are currently assessing.

In conclusion, the ISV is based on a theoretical construct of seasonality in behavioral engagement; it appears to have good psychometric properties; and initial data indicate that SAD subjects fall within the upper 3% of the ISV distribution of seasonal deviation scores. After additional validation work, large-scale studies of the nature of seasonal variation in behavior may become feasible through the use of the ISV. In this work, it will be most interesting to determine which biological and behavioral variables are related to seasonal variation in behavioral engagement, as indexed dimensionally by the ISV.

Indicators of Dopamine Functioning in SAD

On the basis of the neurobiology of the BFS, the proposal that the winter depressive and summer hyperthymic/hypomanic phases of SAD represent decreased and increased states of BFS activity, respectively, suggests that DA functioning may show similar seasonal alterations in SAD subjects. We recently began to test this hypothesis by assessing several indicators of DA functioning in SAD and control subjects. Three indicators were selected: prolactin (PRL) secretion, hypothermic response to heat challenge, and the frequency of spontaneous eye blinking. Although each of these indicators is an imperfect reflection of DA functioning, the strategy was to select indicators that (1) are strongly influenced by DA functioning, and (2) involve the functioning of different DA cell groups. The latter guideline was followed because, if functional alteration is found across several DA indicators reflecting the activity of different DA cell groups, a more general role for DA in SAD may be posited.

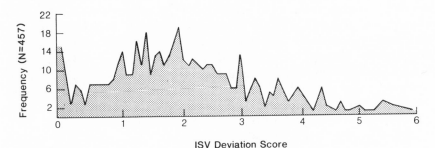

FIGURE 13-3. Frequency distribution of ISV seasonal deviation scores (highest seasonal level of engagement minus winter level of engagement) for the normal population. There is a broad and finely graded distribution of deviation scores, which are basically normally distributed. SAD subjects fall above 4.5 on the horizontal axis, representing the upper 3% of the distribution.

Study 1A. Winter and Summer Basal Prolactin Secretion in SAD

DA is the major neurotransmitter involved in tonic inhibitory modulation of PRL secretion (Jimerson and Post, 1984). The source of this DA influence is the tuberoinfundibular DA pathway, receptors for which are the D_2 type, the same receptor type believed to mediate DA's facilitatory effects on LA, incentive–reward, and irritative aggression (Fluckiger et al., 1985; Oades, 1985). If DA functional activity is deficient in the winter phase of SAD, two possible findings for basal PRL secretion are possible: (1) On average, PRL levels will be higher than normal due to deficient tonic inhibitory modulation by DA; or (2) the functionally deficient DA state will result in up-regulation of the D_2 receptors, and accordingly, very low basal PRL levels will result due to increased inhibitory modulation. This second possibility is similar to the DA receptor supersensitivity hypothesis proposed to explain the rapid behavioral switches from bipolar depression to hypomania/mania (Bunney et al., 1977).

SUBJECTS AND METHODS

Participating in the study were 8 SAD and 14 control premenopausal females matched for age in years (SAD, $M \pm SD = 29.6 \pm 4.3$, range 21–34; control, $M \pm SD = 27.9 \pm 5.2$, range 20–34; $p = 0.25$) and weight in kilograms (winter, $M \pm SEM$: SAD $= 60.8 \pm 1.7$, control $= 62.4 + 2.1$, $p = 0.30$; summer, $M \pm SEM$: SAD $= 58.9 \pm 1.3$, control $= 61.4 \pm 1.9$, $p = 0.30$). Subjects were obtained by media advertisements, and respondents were interviewed by use of a modified Schedule for Affective Disorders and Schizophrenia, Lifetime Version (SADS-L) interview. SAD subjects met *Diagnostic and Statistical Manual of Mental Disorders,* third edition (DSM-III) criteria for a major depression that developed during the fall, was continuous during the winter, and remitted the following spring, for at least the last 3 consecutive years; the SAD subjects also met the newly developed DSM-III, revised (DSM-III-R) criteria for a seasonal pattern to the major depression. The winter depressions were not in reaction to seasonally varying psychosocial stressors. SAD subjects also had to be free of depressed periods during the last 3 consecutive summers. Interview report of SAD subjects concerning their behavior during the summer satisfied the hypomania criteria included in the DSM-III criteria for cyclothymic disorder. Controls were free of psychiatric disorder as determined by the same structured interview. Subjects (SAD and control) reporting postmenopausal status, pregnancy, use of birth control pills during the previous 4 months, any prescribed medication during the past 6 months, any form of substance abuse, menstrual cycle irregularities, endocrinopathies or other relevant medical conditions, an eating disorder, or epilepsy were excluded from the study.

Basal serum PRL was assessed in winter between January 5 to 21 and in summer between July 9 and August 21. PRL secretion was assessed over a 45-min period by averaging the value of three blood samples, each separated by a

15-min interval. Timing of PRL sampling was controlled: (1) Blood samples were collected in the early to middle follicular phase of the menstrual cycle (between 2 and 7 days), and number of days into the follicular period of winter and summer sampling occasions was not significantly different between groups ($p = 0.80$), seasons ($p = 0.15$), or groups × seasons ($p = 0.77$); and (2) to control for circadian variation, and because SAD is associated with a marked symptomatic worsening in late afternoon, blood samples were collected at 1530, 1545, and 1600 hr.

On blood sampling days, subjects consumed the same liquid protein drink at noon, before and after which they fasted except for water. They had abstained from caffeine and alcoholic beverages for no less than 24 hr. Subjects sat for 40 min prior to blood sampling to control activity level in a temperature-controlled room with overhead illumination of 300 lux measured at eye level.

Blood samples were spun down immediately, and serum samples were assayed in duplicate within 1–2 days using a double-antibody radioimmunoassay. Sensitivity of the assay was 1.0 ng/ml, with an interassay coefficient of variation (CV) of 7.1% and an intraassay CV of 6.3%

Six SAD and five control subjects from the current sample were also assayed for PRL 2 weeks later in winter (between January 19 and February 7) during the middle to late luteal phase of the menstrual cycle (between 19 and 25 days). Number of days into the menstrual cycle at this assessment time did not differ significantly between the groups.

Depression for the preceding 1-week period was blindly assessed in SAD and control subjects on the day of PRL assessment by use of the 21-item Hamilton Depression Rating Scale (HDRS). To further assess the stability of depression, all SAD and control subjects were also administered a second HDRS approximately 2 weeks later (which was the time of luteal PRL assessment for those subjects participating in this analysis), also covering a 1-week period. Thus, for all subjects, level of depression was assessed over 2 of the 3 weeks surrounding the PRL assessment times. In summer, the HDRS assessment also covered a 1-week period. Also in summer, periods of depression of any length over the month prior to PRL assessment were to be rated on the HDRS, but no ratable periods of depression were reported by SAD or control subjects for that month. Thus, in both winter and summer, mood at the time of PRL assessment represented a relatively stable state.

RESULTS

HDRS scores for controls at the two winter and one summer assessments did not exceed the range of 0–4. HDRS scores ($M \pm SEM$) for SAD subjects at these three assessments, respectively, were as follows: 22.8 ± 1.45, range 17–29; 21.1 ± 1.3, range 15–27; 1.8 ± 0.5, range 0–4. One-way analysis of variance (ANOVA) with repeated measures on the SAD HDRS scores was highly significant ($F = 328.20$, p < 0.0001). Whereas the two winter HDRS scores did not differ significantly for SAD subjects, both of the latter scores differed significantly from the summer HDRS score (Newman–Keuls, p's<0.0001). For the subgroup of six SAD and five control subjects assessed for luteal PRL, HDRS assessment indicated significant depression at the luteal assessment for the SAD subjects ($M \pm SEM = 20.8 \pm 1.2$, range 15–27).

An ANOVA with repeated measures revealed no significant differences for basal serum PRL as a function of season ($p = 069$) or of group × season interaction ($p = 0.89$), but SAD subjects had highly significantly lower PRL values than controls overall ($p < 0.001$, $F = 18.2$) (Fig. 13-4). Post hoc Newman–Keuls analysis showed that the lower PRL values in SAD subjects were highly significantly different from those of controls in both seasons (winter PRL (ng/ml), $M + SEM$: SAD $= 4.33 \pm 0.78$, control $= 10.57 \pm 0.98$, $p < 0.0001$; summer PRL (ng/ml), $M \pm SEM$: SAD $= 4.13 \pm 0.72$, control $= 10.14 \pm 1.30$, $p < 0.003$).

Luteal PRL assessment revealed that both groups showed the increase in basal PRL secretion associated with the luteal phase (Djursing *et. al.*, 1981), and the magnitude of this increase did not differ significantly between the groups ($p = 0.11$), but the PRL of SAD subjects remained significantly lower than that

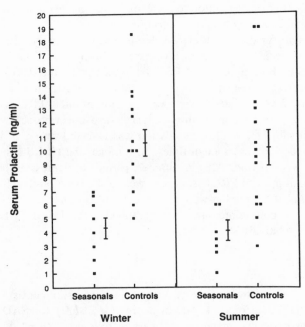

FIGURE 13-4. Late afternoon basal serum prolactin values for normal control and seasonal subjects during the winter (left) and summer (right). All subjects were premenopausal and in the early to middle follicular phase of the menstrual cycle. Seasonal subjects were significantly lower in prolactin secretion than controls in both seasons.

of controls (SAD $M \pm SEM = 8.83 \pm 1.30$ ng/ml, control $M \pm SEM = 13.60 \pm 0.73$ ng/ml; Student's $t = 3.20$, $p = 0.01$).

Study 1B. Effects of Phototherapy on Basal Prolactin Secretion in SAD

METHODS

During the months of January and February, five of the SAD and five of the control subjects who participated in Study 1A (matched for age and weight) had an additional PRL assay, under the same procedures, after a 2-week exposure to bright full-spectrum artificial light (Vitalite, Durotest Co.) of 2500-lux intensity during 0600–0800 hr and 1800–2000 hr daily. In all cases, the post-bright-light PRL sampling occurred 28–30 days after the original follicular sampling, so pre- and postphototherapy samplings fell within the early to middle follicular phase of the menstrual cycle.

To control for expectation effects from phototherapy, subjects were also exposed at the same daily light exposure times to a dim-light placebo (300 lux, achieved by use of brown paper over the Vitalite screen) for 1 week prior to bright-light treatment. To counter differential expectation effects of the two light conditions, the dim light was described to subjects in scientific jargon as a condition of "diffuse" (as opposed to "direct, bright") light, and the special "structure" of the brown paper was shown to subjects. Moreover, subjects were told that both diffuse and direct light have resulted in clinical changes in past work. The study was described as further testing the efficacy of these two types of light. Subjects' ratings of expectations for clinical improvement prior to the study and prior to each light condition did not differ significantly between the bright- and dim-light conditions.

HDRS scores were derived at the time of the first (baseline) and second (end of 2 weeks of bright light) prolactin samplings, as well as at the end of the week of the dim-light placebo condition. HDRS scores for SAD subjects for the three assessment times were as follows: baseline, $M \pm SEM = 22.4 \pm 1.4$, range 17–29; dim light, $M \pm SEM = 20.3 \pm 1.3$, range 15–27; and bright light, $M \pm SEM = 2.9 \pm 0.7$, range 0–6. The univariate ANOVA was highly significant ($p < 0.001$), and post hoc Newman–Keuls testing showed that, whereas the baseline and dim-light HDRS scores did not differ significantly, both of these scores differed significantly from bright-light scores (p's < 0.01). Across all three conditions, the five normal control subjects had HDRS scores that did not exceed the range of 0–4.

RESULTS

Figure 13-5 shows the prolactin values of the SAD and normal control subjects who had PRL assayed both at baseline and after bright-light therapy. A two-

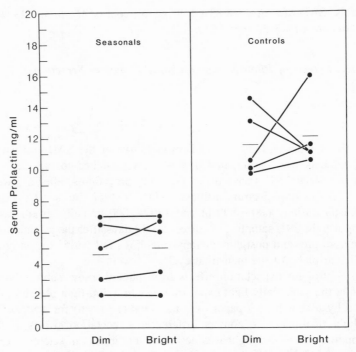

FIGURE 13-5. Late afternoon basal serum prolactin values for normal control and seasonal subjects after 1 week of exposure to dim placebo light (300 lux) and 2 weeks of exposure to bright light (2500 lux) (0600–0800 hr and 1800–2000 hr daily). All subjects were premenopausal and in the early to middle follicular phase of the menstrual cycle at both prolactin samples times. The seasonal subjects were significantly lower in prolactin secretion than controls, and this difference was not altered, as was clinical state, by bright-light therapy.

factor ANOVA with repeated measures showed that the two groups were significantly different in PRL secretion ($p < 0.01$), but there were no significant treatment or interaction effects on prolactin values. Therefore, despite the fact that these five SAD subjects showed significant clinical improvement in depression with the use of bright-light therapy, PRL values changed very little as a function of treatment.

COMMENTS

Results suggest that SAD is characterized by very low basal PRL secretion in the late afternoon during the early follicular phase. There is no consistent finding of reduced basal PRL secretion in women with other psychiatric disorders, including schizophrenia, bipolar affective disorder, nonseasonal major unipolar depression, schizoaffective disorder, mania, and various personality disorders (Meltzer *et al.*, 1984; Siever *et al.*, 1984; Cookson, 1985). The difference in

PRL values between SAD subjects and controls in this study cannot be accounted for by nonspecific factors, such as diet, activity prior to PRL assessment, weight, age, menopausal status, medications, circadian rhythm, or phase of menstrual cycle. It is also unlikely that personal history of stress or experimental procedural stress contributed to the low values in SAD subjects, since stress has a stimulatory effect on PRL secretion, and none of the SAD or control subjects reported fear of venous puncture on questioning. Similarly, the effect of daytime naps and perhaps sleepiness, which are characteristics of SAD during the winter, is not likely to be relevant to the low PRL results found here, because the effect of these factors is to stimulate PRL secretion and daytime naps are not characteristic of SAD in the summer, a time when we found equally low PRL values in euthymic SAD subjects.

Importantly, the low PRL values in our SAD subjects were not due to unrepresentatively high PRL values in the control subjects. The largest published study of basal PRL secretion, controlling for circadian variation, in healthy premenopausal women ($n = 75$) of similar age and phase of the menstrual cycle as controls in this study found the following: (1) The lowest PRL value was 5 ng/ml (the same value for controls in this study in winter and similar in summer), and (2) 95% of the women had values of 8 ng/ml or greater (80% in the current study (Djursing et al., 1981).

Low basal PRL secretion in the SAD subjects appeared to have trait status, in that it did not vary significantly as a function of season or of marked changes in mood state. Two additional findings are relevant. First, in the winter luteal PRL assessment in the six SAD and five control subjects from the current sample, both groups showed the increase in PRL secretion associated with the luteal phase (Djursing et al., 1981), and the magnitude of this increase did not differ significantly between the groups; however, SAD subjects remained significantly lower in basal PRL secretion than controls. Because the increase in PRL secretion during the luteal phase is thought to be due, in part, to an inhibitory influence of some ovarian steroids on DA inhibition of PRL secretion (Ben-Jonathan, 1985), the apparently normal increase in PRL secretion during the luteal phase found here raises the possibility that the generally low PRL values in SAD are not due to a markedly aberrant ovarian steroid–DA interaction. Second, low early follicular PRL values in five of the current SAD subjects remained low when ressessed in the early follicular phase after a marked antidepressant response to 2 weeks of phototherapy (2500 lux at 0600–0800 hr and 1800–2000 hr daily). Thus, in five of the eight SAD subjects in this study, low PRL secretion was found on four occasions (in six of the eight, on three occasions): in the early folllicular phase during winter, summer, and after successful phototherapy, and in the luteal phase during the winter.

If the current results are not specific to the pituitary control system, but rather reflect a more generalized, central neurochemical problem in SAD, the findings raise two hypotheses. First, low basal PRL secretion may result from compensatory up-regulation of D_2 receptors in the anterior pituitary, due to reduced functional activity of DA. A reduction in DA reaching the anterior pituitary can result in an up-regulation of D_2 binding sites and an enhanced pituitary responsiveness of DA inhibition (Ben-Jonathan, 1985), but whether pituitary D_2 receptors are regulated in a manner similar to the D_2 brain receptors thought to mediate behaviors relevant to SAD is uncertain (Jimerson and Post, 1984). Factors that significantly affect the functional influence of DA in controlling PRL secretion and behavior, such as opiates and gonadal hormones (Ben-Jonathan, 1985), will require consideration in testing this hypothesis. Increased DA functional activity could also account for low PRL secretion, but such a DA condition, if generalized to other central DA systems, is not consistent with the joint observations that DA strongly facilitates locomotion and affective behavior, but that SAD is characterized by a marked reduction in the facilitation of behavior during the winter. Second, low PRL secretion raises the possibility of reduced serotonin (5-HT) stimulatory action (Siever *et al.*, 1984; Ben-Jonathan, 1985). 5-HT may stimulate PRL-releasing hormone, but evidence also exists for interposing DA and opiate mechanisms (Ben-Johnathan, 1985). Studies incorporating specific pharmacological challenges are now required to assess these hypotheses.

Study 2. Hypothermic Response to Heat Challenge in SAD in Winter, after Phototherapy, and in Summer

The mechanisms responsible for heat loss are closely dependent on the adequate functioning of DA (see review by Lee *et al.*, 1985). This DA influence arises mainly from DA cell groups located in the hypothalamus and preoptic area, which project short local fibers within these same areas (Fluckiger *et al.*, 1985); however, it may also arise from DA activity in the caudate nucleus, perhaps facilitating behavioral responses that functionally reduce heat. These findings suggest that one strategy for testing a DA hypothesis of SAD is to experimentally induce a heat challenge for SAD subjects, and then assess the temporal and stability features of the heat loss process—a process that is dependent on the functional integrity of DA neurotransmission.

Our approach employed a 1-hr treadmill task to generate heat, and then bed rest for an additional hour to assess the heat loss process. The treadmill test was selected because it provides the most accurate and highest estimate of maximum oxygen uptake (and, thereby, the best estimate of an individual's maximum workload or energy expenditure, and consequently increased temperature—the $\dot{V}O_{2max}$ procedure) and is least subject to the influence of individual differences in exercise skill and efficiency (Shaw, 1986). Moreover, since subjects differ mainly in their maximum level of workload (i.e., in the $\dot{V}O_{2max}$ achieved), and would thereby differ in temperature generated at this level, having all subjects exercise at a set percentage of their $\dot{V}O_{2max}$ results in practically the same amount of energy expenditure, and consequently temperature gain, across subjects.

SUBJECTS AND METHODS

Four of the SAD patients and four of the control subjects who participated in the PRL and phototherapy studies described above comprised the subjects for this study. The two groups were matched on fitness, and neither group included extremely sedentary or fit subjects, since their $\dot{V}O_{2max}$ values may have differed significantly from other normally fit subjects. Moreover, extremely fit subjects have a faster temperature recovery slope than normally fit subjects (Shaw, 1986).

All eight subjects were tested during the early to middle follicular period of the menstrual cycle under three conditions: in winter, prior to phototherapy; in winter, after bright-light therapy; and in summer. Winter and summer dates of testing were the same as those given in the PRL study.

Heat Challenge Protocol. The heat challenge protocol consisted of walking subjects on a motorized treadmill for 1 hr at two-thirds of their $\dot{V}O_{2max}$ value (i.e., at a treadmill speed and grade that was two-thirds of the value at which the subject reached $\dot{V}O_{2max}$). $\dot{V}O_{2max}$ was determined prior to the study twice for each subject using a graded exercise procedure following the Bruce protocol, where the first determination served as a habituation run, the second as the usable value. To determine $\dot{V}O_{2max}$, individuals were exercised on a motorized treadmill until increases in exercise intensity resulted in no further increase in $\dot{V}O_{2max}$. Target heart rate corresponding to two-thirds of $\dot{V}O_{2max}$ was determined and used to assure maintenance of that effort during the treadmill task. Resultant values for maximal O_2 consumption were broadly within age expectations. In normally fit subjects, the heat challenge protocol used in this study creates an average increase in core body temperature of $>1°C$ within 45 min (Shaw, 1986).

Hypothermic Response. Immediately at the end of the treadmill task, subjects were placed in bed in a dimly lit room for 1 hr to measure temperature recovery. A 1-hr recovery period was chosen because previous research has shown that most subjects recover fully to pretreadmill temperature within 1 hr using the heat challenge protocol employed in this study (Shaw, 1986). Subjects were covered with a blanket during recovery to prevent heat generation as a result of shivering.

Temperature Measurement. Core body temperature was recorded every 60 sec by use of Vitalog monitors (Vitalog Corp.) and a rectal thermistor for 1 hr prior to the treadmill task, and during the 2 hr of the treadmill task and recovery period.

Controlled Variables. Subjects were kept in a temperature- and humidity-controlled environment of approximately 300-lux illumination for 1.5 hr prior to the treadmill task, and during the treadmill task and recovery period. Moreover, subjects were kept in bed or seated for 1 hr prior to the treadmill task to control activity level. Subjects consumed the same protein drink for lunch 4 hr prior to the treadmill task. To control circadian factors and to have the task coincide with the symptomatically worst time of the day for SAD subjects (see discussion in Study 1A, above), the treadmill task occurred from 1600 to 1700 hr, and the recovery period lasted from 1700 to 1800 hr.

RESULTS AND COMMENTS

The major dependent variable was the absolute temperature recovery that occurred over the 1-hr rest period, expressed in ratio to absolute temperature gained in the treadmill task. This ratio allowed an estimate of heat loss as a function of the individual's actual heat gain. This variable is shown as a function of group and light condition in Figure 13-6. Importantly, a 2×2 repeated-measures ANOVA showed that heat gain during exercise was not significantly different for groups or light conditions.

A 2×2 ANOVA with repeated measures on the temperature ratio variable revealed that the group $\times$ condition interaction was significant ($F = 4.99$, $p < 0.006$). Post hoc Newman–Keuls testing showed that, whereas controls did not change significantly in heat loss characteristics as a function of condition, relative to winter temperature recovery, SAD subjects showed a significant increase in temperature recovery both after 2 weeks of bright-light treatment ($p < 0.05$) and during the summer ($p < 0.01$). Because DA is the major hypothermic mechanism for meeting a heat challenge, the slower recovery of SAD subjects relative to controls in winter is consistent with the possibility that DA functioning is not adequate within this thermoregulation system. Moreover, the hypothermic response of SAD subjects was responsive to bright light, being indiscriminable from the recovery rate of normal controls by the end of phototherapy. Interestingly, heat loss mechanisms in summer appeared to be more efficient in SAD subjects than controls (Arbisi *et al.*, in press).

Study 3. Effects of Phototherapy on Spontaneous Eye-Blinking Rates in SAD

Central DA activity appears to modulate the rate of spontaneous, as opposed to reflex, eye blinking in nonhuman primates and humans (Karson, 1983). For instance, the DA agonists apomorphine and bromocriptine effected a dose-related increase in the spontaneous blink rates of nonhuman primates, whereas sulpiride, a D_2 receptor blocker, obliterated the apomorphine-included increase when administered prior to apomorphine injection (Casey *et al.*, 1980; Karson *et al.*, 1981; Karson, 1983). Dose-related effects were not found for α-adrenergic agonists, the sedative action of diazepam, or DA (which does not cross

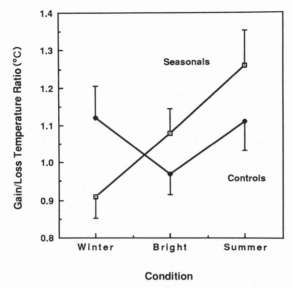

FIGURE 13-6. Temperature reduction (in ratio with temperature gain) during recovery from a treadmill heat challenge task for normal control and seasonal subjects after 1 week of exposure to dim placebo light (300 lux) and 2 weeks of exposure to bright light (2500 lux) (0600–0800 hr and 1800–2000 hr daily) and during the summer. The group × light condition interaction is significant, indicating that seasonal subjects recovered in temperature more slowly than controls in the dim-light condition, no differently than controls in the bright-light condition, but more efficiently than controls in the summer.

the blood–brain barrier); the last finding suggests that the DA effect on blinking is of central origin (Karson, 1983).

Human studies are consistent with animal work. Spontaneous blink rates are reduced in patients with Parkinson disease, a disease thought to be strongly related to DA deficiency in the neostriatum and perhaps the NAS (Hornykiewicz, 1974), and this reduction is correlated with the stage of disability of the disease (Karson, 1983). When such patients experience levodopa-induced dyskinetic periods, blink rate is roughly double that of nondyskinetic periods. Conversely, in schizophrenia (with normal cerebral ventricles), a disorder hypothesized to be related to DA overactivity in some forms (Stevens, 1978), spontaneous blink rates have been found to be higher than those of controls (Stevens, 1978; Karson, 1983), but show a decrease on neuroleptic medications that correlates with a reduction in positive symptoms (Karson *et al.*, 1982; Karson, 1983). Spontaneous blink rate, therefore, appears to serve as another indicator of central DA activity; accordingly, we assessed it in SAD patients prior to and after successful phototherapy (Depue *et al.*, 1988).

SUBJECTS AND METHODS

The four SAD patients and four controls who participated in Study 2 described above comprised the subjects for this study. The phototherapy protocol, and HDRS scores were exactly the same as described in Study 2.

The vertical electro-oculogram (EOG; eye blinks), as well as the horizontal EOG, were recorded on a Beckman R612 Dynograph in a sound-deadened, dimly lit room. Silver/silver chloride electrodes were attached at the superior and inferior orbital rims of the left eye to record blinks, and to the outer canthi for horizontal recording. A ground electrode was attached to the right earlobe. Alternating current (AC) coupling with a 3-sec time constant was used.

A blink was operationally defined as a sharp high-amplitude wave greater than 50 μV and less than 1000 msec in duration, consistent with past studies of human blink rates (Karson, 1983). High-amplitude waves temporally coincident with horizontal eye movements were not counted as blinks.

To control circadian factors, and to measure blinks during the symptomatically worst time of the day for SAD subjects, blink recordings occurred between 1500 and 1800 hr. After a 10-min period of accommodation to the recording room, blinks were recorded for a 3-min period while the subject sat silent. No subject wore contact lenses during the recordings, and none of the subjects fell asleep. The dependent variable was the total number of blinks occurring in the 3-min period.

RESULTS AND COMMENTS

A 2×2 ANOVA with repeated measures revealed no significant group ($p < 0.41$) or light condition ($p < 0.71$) main effects, but the group $\times$ light condition interaction was significant ($F = 6.39$, $p < 0.04$). As shown in Figure 13-7, and confirmed by post hoc Newman–Keuls testing, SAD subjects had a significantly higher blink rate than controls in the dim-light condition ($M \pm SEM$: SAD $= 69.25 \pm 14.1$, control $= 31.25 \pm 11.9$; $p < 0.01$), but were not significantly different from controls after 2 weeks of successful bright-light therapy ($M \pm SEM$: SAD $= 44.75 \pm 10.4$, control $= 49.25 \pm 20$). Minute-by-minute analysis of the variation in blink rate across the 3-min period revealed no significant differences between groups, light conditions, or their interaction, indicating that blink rate was stable across the 3-min recording period in both groups and in both light conditions.

To the extent that spontaneous eye-blinking rate reflects the influence of central DA activity, the elevated blink rate in the current SAD subjects during a winter photoperiod—a rate that was more than twice the rate of controls—may be interpreted in the same way as the low PRL secretion findings of Studies 1A and 1B. This is, low DA functioning in SAD may have resulted in an up-regulation of the D_2 receptors involved in the modulation of eye blinking. Unlike the PRL results, where low PRL secretion appears to be a trait and

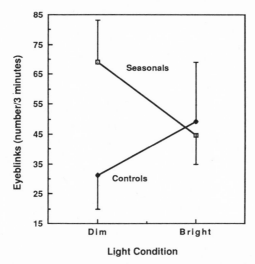

FIGURE 13-7. Number of spontaneous eye blinks for normal controls and seasonal subjects after 1 week of exposure to dim placebo light (300 lux) and 2 weeks of exposure to bright light (2500 lux) (0600–0800 hr and 1800–2000 hr daily). The group × light condition interaction is significant, indicating that SAD subjects blinked at over twice the rate of controls during dim-light placebo, but no differently from controls after bright-light therapy. Adapted from Depue *et al.* (1988). Used by permission.

would lead to the expectation that D_2 receptors are traitwise up-regulated, the elevated blink rate appears to be a state-related phenomenon, having been eliminated by bright-light treatment. Not all DA pathways are regulated in a similar manner, so it is possible that the host of factors operating in the neural systems influencing blink rate and PRL secretion are differentially responsive to light effects.

Concluding Remarks

Our research program has focused on determining the extent to which seasonal variation occurs in the BFS, as manifested in more global patterns of behavioral engagement with the environment; on determining the dimensional nature of this variation; and on establishing the extent to which DA functioning appears to be altered in SAD subjects. Our initial data on the first issue, using the ISV, suggest that seasonal variation in behavioral engagement does exist, with winter months being associated with the lowest levels of engagement. Moreover, the ISV data indicate that seasonal variation in engagement is dimensional in nature, and the retest data indicate that the dimension of seasonal variation in engagement is stable and may be a trait. The extent to which DA functioning per se contributes to seasonal variation in behavioral engagement via a BFS effect in unknown, but seasonal variation in DA functioning has been observed (Kafka *et al.*, 1983).

Our initial attempts to test the hypothesis that DA may be involved in SAD have focused on variables that are strongly influenced by DA functioning, including PRL secretion, hypothermic response to heat challenge, and the frequency of eye blinking. Findings from these three variables are complex and do not lend themselves to one clear interpretation. During the winter, the eye-blinking and PRL results suggest the possibility that low DA functioning results in a compensatory up-regulation of D_2 postsynaptic receptors, but the significantly slower temperature recovery of SAD subjects to heat challenge is not consistent with this interpretation. It is not known, however, whether D_2 receptors are involved in the hypothermic response system, so the hypothesis of low DA functioning and D_2 up-regulation remains a possibility. Since D_2 receptors are thought to mediate the *behavioral* effects of DA agonists (Fishman *et al.*, 1983; Oades, 1985; Taghzouti *et al.*, 1986), an important test of the D_2 up-regulation hypothesis in SAD is a behavioral analysis of a DA agonist challenge. At this time, perhaps the strongest statement concerning our results is that each DA-relevant variable appears to be altered in SAD during the winter. Since these variables involve DA pathways originating from three different DA cell groups, the possibility of a generalized DA problem in SAD is raised.

No consistent effect of bright-light therapy or summer photoperiod was discernible in these three DA-relevant variables in SAD subjects: PRL secretion remained low, whereas hypothermic response and eye-blinking rate were both strongly affected, as were behavior and mood. Without additional data, a clear interpretation of these differences is not possible. One possible factor concerns the functional role of DA in modulating these variables. In the case of PRL, DA plays a dominant, tonic inhibitory role; in eye blinking, hypothermic response, and behavior, DA plays a dynamic, interactive role with a host of other factors in determining the level of the outcome variable. It is possible that light-induced changes in DA functioning, or some moderator of DA, are reflected more markedly in a dynamic than in a dominant, tonic system.

One interesting effect of bright light on blink rate and summer photoperiod on hypothermic response in SAD subjects is that these variables exceed normal values in these light conditions. Hypothermic response efficiency is better than that of controls in summer, and blink rates decrease from twice the normal rate to below the normal rate after bright-light exposure. We have found a similar result in behavioral response to bright-light therapy. Bipolar II SAD subjects are characterized by marked afternoon troughs in level of mood and energy; although controls also show this trough, it is much less marked. After 2 weeks of phototherapy, controls maintain the afternoon trough, whereas the trough virtually disappears in SAD subjects. It is as if SAD subjects are hyperresponsive to light conditions in these variables.

Our initial work suggests that further studies of DA functioning in SAD may be fruitful. Thus, far, our studies have been limited to the BP 2 form of

SAD, and so extension of the studies to seasonal unipolar subjects is an important step. Also, the extent to which DA functioning in behaviorally relevant pathways, such as mesolimbic and mesocortical DA pathways, is involved in SAD is virtually untested. Therefore, particularly informative would be *behavioral* analyses of DA postsynaptic receptor agonists conducted across the seasons.

Acknowledgment

The work reported herein was supported in part by National Institute of Mental Health Research Grant No. MH 37195 awarded to Richard A. Depue.

References

Arbisi, P., R. Depue, M. Spoont, A. Leon, and B. Ainsworth (in press) Thermoregulatory response to a thermal challenge in seasonal affective disorder. Psychiat. Res.

Beninger, R. (1983) The role of dopamine in locomotor activity and learning. Brain Res. Rev. *6:* 173–196.

Ben-Jonathan, N. (1985) Dopamine: A prolactin-inhibiting hormone. Endocrinol. Rev. *6:* 564–589.

Bunney, W., R. Kopanda, and D. Murphy (1977) Sleep and behavioral changes possibly reflecting central receptor hypersensitivity following catecholamine synthesis inhibition in man. Acta Psychiat. Scand. *56:* 189–203.

Casey, D. E., J. Gerlach, and E. Christenson (1980) Behavioral aspects of GABA–dopamine interrelationships in the monkey. Brain Res. Bull. 5(Suppl. 2): 269–273.

Cookson, J. C. (1985) The neuroendocrinology of mania. J. Affect. Dis. *8:* 233–241.

Depue, R. (in press) *Neurobehavioral Systems, Personality, and Psychopathology,* Springer-Verlag, New York.

Depue, R., and W. G. Iacono (in press) Neurobehavioral aspects of artective disorders. Ann. Rev. Psychol.

Depue, R., W. G. Iacono, R. Muir, and R. Arbisi (1988) Effect of phototherapy on spontaneous eye-blink rate in seasonal affective disorder. Amer. J. Psychiat. *145:* 1457–1459.

Depue, R., S. Krauss, and M. Spoont (1987) A two-dimensional threshold model of seasonal bipolar affective disorder. In *Psychopathology: An Interactionist Perspective,* D. Magnuson and A. Ohman, eds., pp. 31–62, Academic Press, New York.

Depue, R., and M. Spoont (1986) Conceptualizing a serotonin trait: A behavioral dimension of constraint. Ann. NY Acad. Sci. *487:* 47–62.

Djursing, H., C. Hagen, J. Moller, and C. Christiansen (1981) Short- and long-term fluctuations in plasma prolactin concentration in normal subjects. Acta Endocrinol. *96:* 1–6.

Fink, J., and D. Reis (1981) Genetic variations in midbrain dopamine cell number: Parallel with differences in responses to dopaminergic agonists and in naturalistic behaviors mediated by central dopaminergic systems. Brain Res. *222:* 335–349.

Fishman, R., J. Feigenbaum, J. Yanai, and H. Klawans (1983) The relative importance of dopamine and norepinephrine in mediating locomotor activity. Prog. Neurobiol. *20:* 55–88.

Fluckiger, E., E. Muller, and M. Thorner, eds. (1985) *The Dopaminergic System,* Springer-Verlag, New York.

Freed, C., and B. Yamamoto (1985) Regional brain dopamine metabolism: A marker for speed, direction, and posture of moving animals. Science *229:* 62–65.

Glowinski, J. (1981) Present knowledge on the properties of the mesocortico-frontal dopaminergic neurons. In *Psychiatry and the Biology of the Human Brain*, S. Matthysse, ed., pp. 15–28, Elsevier/North-Holland, New York.

Goeders, N., S. Dworkin, and J. Smith (1986) Neuropharmacological assessment of cocaine self-administration into the medial prefrontal cortex. Pharmacol. Biochem. Behav. *24:* 1429–1440.

Goeders, N., and J. Smith (1983) Cortical dopaminergic involvement in cocaine reinforcement. Science *221:* 773–775.

Gray, J. (1982) *The Neuropsychology of Anxiety*, Oxford University Press, New York.

Hoffman, D., and R. Beninger (1985) The effects of pimozide on the establishment of conditioned reinforcement as a function of the amount of conditioning. Psychopharmacology *87:* 454–460.

Hornykiewicz, O. (1974) The mechanisms of action of L-DOPA in Parkinson's disease. Life Sci. *15:* 1249–1259.

Iversen, S. (1978) Brain dopamine systems and behavior. In *Handbook of Psychopharmacology*, Vol. 8, L. Iversen, S. Iversen, and S. Snyder, eds., pp. 333–384, Plenum, New York.

Jimerson, D., and R. Post (1984) Psychomotor stimulants and dopamine agonists in depression. In *Neurobiology of Mood Disorders*, R. Post and J. Ballenger, eds., pp. 619–628, Williams & Wilkins, Baltimore.

Jones, D., G. Mogenson, and M. Wu (1981) Injections of dopaminergic, cholinergic, serotonergic and GABAergic drugs into the nucleus accumbens: Effects on locomotor activity of the rat. Neuropharmacology *20:* 29–38.

Kafka, M., A. Wirz-Justice, D. Naber, R. Moore, and M. Benedito (1983) Circadian rhythms in rat brain neurotransmitter receptors. Fed. Proc. *42:* 2796–2801.

Karson, C. N. (1983) Spontaneous eye-blink rates and dopaminergic systems. Brain *106:* 643–653.

Karson, C. N., J. E. Kleinman, W. J. Freed, L. B. Bigelow, D. R. Weinberger, and R. J. Wyatt (1982) Blink rates in schizophrenia. In *Biological Markers in Psychiatry and Neurology*, E. Usdin and I. Hanin, eds., pp. 339–345, Pergamon Press, New York.

Karson, C. N., R. A. Staub, J. E. Keinman, and R. J. Wyatt (1981) Drug effect on blink rates in rhesus monkeys: Preliminary studies. Biol. Psychiat. *16:* 249–254.

Kelly, P. (1978) Drug-induced motor behavior. In *Handbook of Psychopharmacology*, Vol. 8, L. Iversen, S. Iversen, and S. Snyder, eds., pp. 295–332, Plenum, New York.

Lee, T., F. Mora, and R. Myers (1985) Dopamine and thermoregulation: An evaluation with special reference to dopaminergic pathways. Neurosci. Biobehay. Rev. *9:* 589–598.

MacLean, P. (1975) Sensory and perceptive factors in emotional functions of the triune brain. In *Emotions: Their Parameters and Measurement*, L. Levi, ed., pp. 71–92, Raven Press, New York.

Mason, S. (1984) *Catecholamines and Behavior*, Cambridge University Press, New York.

Meltzer, H. Y., T. Kolakowska, V. Fang, L. Fogg, A. Robertson, R. Lewine, M. Strahievitz, and D. Bush (1984) Growth hormone and prolactin response to apomorphine in schizophrenia and the major affective disorders. Arch. Gen. Psychiatr. *41:* 512–519.

Milner, P. (1977) Theories of reinforcement, drive, and motivation. In *Handbook of Psychopharmacology*, Vol. 7, L. Iversen, S. Iversen, and S. Snyder, eds., pp. 181–200, Plenum, New York.

Mogenson, G., D. Jones, and C. Yim (1980) From motivation to action: Functional interface between the limbic system and the motor system. Prog. Neurobiol. *14:* 69–97.

Nauta, W., and V. Domesick (1981) Ramifications of the limbic system. In *Psychiatry and the Biology of the Human Brain*, S. Matthysse, ed., pp. 165–188, Elsevier/North-Holland, New York.

Oades, R. (1985) The role of noradrenaline in tuning and dopamine in switching between signals in the CNS. Neurosci. Biobehav. Rev. *9:* 261–282.

Perlow, M., E. Gordon, M. Ebert, H. Hoffman, and T. Chase (1977) The circadian variation in dopamine metabolism in the subhuman primate. J. Neurochem. *28:* 1381–1383.

Phillipson, O., and A. Griffiths (1985) The topographic order of inputs to nucleus accumbens in the rat. Neuroscience *16:* 275–296.

Porrino, L., R. Esposito, T. Seeger, A. Crane, A. Pert, and L. Sokoloff (1984) Metabolic mapping of the brain during rewarding self-stimulation. Science *224:* 306–309.

Rosenthal, N., D. Sack, J. Gillin, A. Lewy, F. Goodwin, Y. Davenport, P. Mueller, D. Newsome, and T. Wehr (1984) Seasonal affective disorder: A description of the syndrome and preliminary findings with light therapy. Arch. Gen. Psychiat. *41:* 72–84.

Rosenthal, N., D. Sack, and T. Wehr (1983) Seasonal variation in affective disorders. In *Circadian Rhythms in Psychiatry,* T. Wehr and F. Goodwin, eds., pp. 185–202, Boxwood Press, Pacific Grove, CA.

Routtenberg, A., and M. Sloan (1972) Self-stimulation in the frontal cortex of *Rattus norvegicus.* Behav. Biol. *7:* 567–572.

Schneirla, T. (1959) An evolutionary and developmental theory of biphasic processes underlying approach and withdrawal. In *Nebraska Symposium on Motivation,* Vol. 7, M. Jones, ed., pp. 71–88, University of Nebraska Press, Lincoln.

Shaw, D. (1986) *Thermoregulation under Heat Challenge Conditions,* doctoral dissertation, University of Minnesota.

Siever, L. J., L. B. Guttmacher, and D. L. Murphy (1984) Serotonergic receptors: Evaluation of their possible role in the affective disorders. In *Neurobiology of Mood Disorders,* R. C. Post and J. C. Ballenger, eds., pp. 587–600, Williams & Wilkins, Baltimore.

Stein, L. The chemistry of reward. In *Biological Bases of Sensation Seeking, Impulsivity, and Anxiety,* M. Zuckerman, ed., pp. 151–176, L. Erlbaum, Hillsdale, NJ.

Stevens, J. R. (1978) Eye blink and schizophrenia: Psychosis or tardive dyskinesia? Amer. J. Psychiat. *135:* 223–226.

Sved, A., H. Baker, and D. Reis (1984) Dopamine synthesis in inbred mouse strains which differ in numbers of dopamine neurons. Brain Res. *303:* 261–266.

Sved, A., H. Baker, and D. Reis (1985) Number of dopamine neurons predicts prolactin levels in two inbred mouse strains. Experientia *41:* 644–646.

Taghzouti, K., H. Simon, and M. Le Moal (1986) Disturbances in exploratory behavior and functional recovery in the Y and radial mazes following dopamine depletion of the lateral septum. Behav. Neural. Biol. *45:* 48–56.

Tellegen, A. (1985) Structures of mood and personality and their relevance to assessing anxiety, with an emphasis on self-report. In *Anxiety and the Anxiety Disorders,* A. Tuma and J. Maser, eds., pp. 681–716, Erlbaum, Hillsdale, NJ.

Yim, C., and G. Mogenson (1983) Response of ventral pallidal neurons to amygdala stimulation and its modulation by dopamine projections to nucleus accumbens. J. Neurophysiol. *50:* 148–161.

14

Psychological Effects of Light Therapy in Normals

Siegfried Kasper, Susan L. B. Rogers, Angela Yancey, Robert G. Skwerer, Patricia M. Schulz, and Norman E. Rosenthal

Kraepelin (1921) first noted that manic–depressive patients with winter depressions and spring hypomanias show mood swings that "correspond in a certain sense to the emotional changes which come over even healthy individuals at the change of the seasons." Two recent independent epidemiological surveys conducted in New York City (Terman, Chapter 20, this volume) and in Montgomery County, Maryland (Kasper *et al.*, in press-b) found that people generally feel worst during January, February, and March and best during April, May, and June. In the past several years, a group of patients with marked seasonal mood changes has been described and studied. The characteristic syndrome that has emerged has been called seasonal affective disorder (SAD) by Rosenthal *et al.* (1984). Following the consistently reported success of light therapy in SAD patients (Lewy *et al.*, 1982, 1983, 1987; Rosenthal *et al.*, 1984, 1985; James *et al.*, 1985; Hellekson *et al.*, 1986; Terman *et al.*, 1986; Wirz-Justice *et al.*, 1986; Thompson and Isaacs, 1988), we have now questioned whether other segments of the population might also benefit from this treatment.

Observations such as those of Kraepelin, and the results of the above-mentioned surveys (Terman, Chapter 20, this volume; Kasper *et al.*, in press-b), are compatible with the idea that the seasonal changes found in SAD patients may be the extreme end of a behavioral spectrum, which can also be observed in normals to a lesser extent. These findings also demonstrate that during the wintertime there are many normal individuals who complain of symptoms that resemble but are less intense than those of patients with SAD. On the other hand, there are also people who have noted no such changes. If seasonality is a behavioral dimension that spans both normal and affectively

Siegfried Kasper, Susan L. B. Rogers, Angela Yancey, Robert G. Skwerer, Patricia M. Schulz, and Norman E. Rosenthal. Clinical Psychobiology Branch, National Institute of Mental Health, Bethesda, Maryland.

disturbed individuals, does bright-light exposure have a mood-enhancing and energizing effect in some normal subjects?

To explore whether the mood-enhancing effect of phototherapy, given in a manner that has produced antidepressant effects in SAD patients, is also present in other segments of the population, we have previously studied the effects of bright-light exposure in normal subjects (Rosenthal et al., 1987a). In that study, 2 hr of bright artificial light administered for 1 week did not alter mood in 11 normal subjects (see Study 1, below). Although some subjects reported a history of seasonal behavioral changes, there was no overall mood response to light. However, these normal subjects did not in general have a history of symptomatic seasonal changes. Following this study, we sought to determine whether normal individuals with mild winter symptoms might show a response to light treatment and whether longer durations of exposure would enhance their response. In a follow-up study, we therefore examined two populations of normal individuals: one group with a history of mild SAD-type symptoms, and one group without these symptom features. In order to evaluate the importance of duration of light treatment, we further subdivided these two groups into two different phototherapy schedule regimens. We have thus attempted to address the question of whether the propensity to respond to light and the duration of treatment required to induce such a response are associated with the extent to which an individual is affected by the changing seasons.

Study 1: Bright versus Dim Light

Subjects and Methods

A total of 22 normal subjects (20 women and 2 men; mean age $= 35.46 \pm 10.25$) were recruited by means of an advertisement in a newsletter. Exclusion criteria were (1) a personal or family history (first-degree relatives only) of psychiatric illness or psychological counseling; (2) significant medical illness; and (3) inability or unwillingness to adhere to the conditions of the experiment. Subjects were assigned by a process of balanced randomization to either a bright-light (2500-lux) or a dim-light (300-lux) condition. Light treatment was administered during wintertime and took place in the subjects' own homes or offices. They were asked to sit 3 feet from the light for 2 hr between 0630 and 0930 hr for 7 days. Similar light treatments have been reported to produce significant antidepressant effects in patients with SAD (for review, see Rosenthal et al., 1987b).

Before starting the study, subjects completed a questionnaire designed to assess the extent to which they had previously been affected by seasonal changes (the Seasonal Pattern Assessment Questionnaire, or SPAQ; Rosenthal et al., 1987b). In addition, their expectations of the treatment's effects on their moods (Rosenthal and Heffernan, 1986) were assessed prospectively by a scale derived from that of Borkovec and Nau (1972).

TABLE 14-1. Hamilton Depression Rating Scale (HDRS) Total Scores ($M \pm SD$) for Normals Exposed to Bright or Dim Light

Group	Baseline	Treatment	Withdrawal
Bright light (2500 lux) ($n = 11$)	4.6 ± 4.5	6.4 ± 7.2	2.9 ± 4.2
Dim light (300 lux) ($n = 11$)	3.7 ± 2.4	4.2 ± 2.9	2.9 ± 2.3

Clinical state was evaluated "blind" to treatment conditions before and after treatment, and after withdrawal of treatment, by means of the Hamilton Depression Rating Scale (HDRS; Hamilton, 1967), together with a 7-item supplement (Rosenthal *et al.*, 1987b). Subjects were further asked to complete twice daily a visual analogue-type mood rating and a sleep log.

Results

The mean ($\pm SD$) HDRS total scores before and after treatment and after withdrawal of bright-light treatment are shown in Table 14-1. The slight increase in the HDRS scores after both treatments was not statistically significant. Analysis of daily rating forms, which included measures of mood, energy, anxiety, fatigue, and general well-being, showed no change after either the bright- or dim-light condition. There was no consistent relationship between pretreatment expectations and outcome.

Questionnaires examining retrospectively the extent to which the participants had been affected by seasonal changes showed that most subjects noted some change in mood, energy, sleep, and eating patterns with the seasons. Of the 22 subjects, 9 reported clear trends toward winter behavior changes during 2 or more winter months, but there was no evidence that these seasonal changes ever reached symptomatic proportions. There was also no consistent relationship between the response to light treatment and the reported seasonality in this relatively small sample of 11 subjects exposed to 2 hr of full-spectrum light in the morning.

Study 2: Normals with and without Mild SAD-Type Symptoms

Subjects and Methods

RECRUITMENT

We recruited 20 normal individuals with no reported seasonal difficulties (non-S-SAD) and 20 normals with mild SAD-type symptoms (subsyndromal SAD, or S-SAD) by means of two different advertisements in a newsletter. Inclusion criteria for S-SAD subjects were these:

1. Subjects had a history of some difficulty during the winter months that had occurred on a regular basis (at least two consecutive winters) and that had lasted for a sustained period of time (at least 4 weeks). Examples of these difficulties were decreased energy, efficiency at work (e.g., concentration, completing tasks), creativity, or interest in socializing, change in eating habits (e.g., eating more carbohydrates), weight (gaining weight), or sleep patterns (more sleep).

2. Subjects regarded themselves as "normal" (i.e., not suffering from an illness or disorder).

3. They had not sought medical or psychological help specifically for their winter difficulties, nor had anyone else suggested that they should do so.

4. People who did not know them well did not recognize that they had a problem, or if they did, easily attributed it to circumstances such as "flu" or "overwork."

5. The symptoms experienced by the subjects had not disrupted their functioning to a major degree (e.g., calling in sick several times per winter, or severe marital discord).

6. Subjects had no history of major affective disorder in wintertime.

Exclusion criteria for the normal control group (non-S-SAD) were (1) reported difficulties related to seasonal changes; (2) personal history of psychiatric illness or psychological counseling; (3) serious medical illness; and (4) inability or unwillingness to adhere to the conditions of the experiment.

RESEARCH DESIGN

The two groups were further subdivided into groups of 10, and these subgroups were exposed during wintertime to either 5 hr of bright artificial full-spectrum light per day (2.5 hr in the morning between 0630 and 0930 hr, and 2.5 hr in the evening between 1830 and 2130 hr) or 2 hr per day (1 hr in the morning between 0630 and 0800 hr, and 1 hr in the evening between 1830 and 2000 hr) of the same light source. The probands randomly assigned to the four groups were age- and sex-matched (32 women, 8 men; ages 23–58 years; mean age, 39.5 ± 9.1) All were medically healthy.

The psychometric assessment was similar to that of Study 1, but in addition, a clinician-rated hypomania scale (see Fig. 14-1) and a self-rating scale, the Profile of Mood States (POMS; McNair et al., 1981), were completed each week.

Results

As we would have predicted on the basis of our screening criteria, S-SAD probands demonstrated a significantly ($p < 0.001$) higher score of seasonality

HYPOMANIA RATING SCALE

1. Expansive Mood
   0 = Absent
   1 = Indicates only on questioning
   2 = Spontaneously reports verbally
   3 = Communicates nonverbally (i.e., through facial expression, posture, voice, laughter, etc.)

2. Irritable Mood
   0 = Absent
   1 = Indicates only on questioning
   2 = Spontaneously reports verbally
   3 = Communicates nonverbally (i.e., through facial expression, posture, voice)

3. Decreased Need for Sleep (compared with euthymic state)
   0 = None
   1 = Less than 1 hr/night
   2 = 1–2 hr/night
   3 = 2–3 hr/night
   4 = 3–4 hr/night
   5 = >4 hr less sleep per night

4. Work and Activity
   0 = No change
   1 = Mild energy increase, more efficient at work
   2 = Marked energy increase or efficiency
   3 = Increased energy or speed begins to interfere with efficiency
   4 = Considerable impairment in quality of work as a result of increased distractibility or difficulty in focusing

5. Activation
   0 = No increase in energy or activity reported
   1 = Increase in energy or activity reported
   2 = Increase in energy or activity seen at interview
   3 = Interview difficult

6. Insight
   0 = Acknowledges being "high"
   1 = Acknowledges being "high," but attributes state to external circumstances
   2 = Denies being "high"

7. Speech
   0 = No increase in speech rate
   1 = Slight pressure of speech
   2 = Moderate pressure of speech
   3 = Marked pressure of speech *or* interrupts interviewer

8. Flight of Ideas
   0 = Absent
   1 = Mild
   2 = Moderate
   3 = Marked

9. Creativity
   0 = No increase
   1 = Mild increase
   2 = Moderate increase
   3 = Marked increase

10. Impulsive Behavior (spending, sexual, work-related, decision-making)
    0 = No change
    1 = Wishes to behave impulsively, but not acted upon
    2 = Minor acting out of impulses
    3 = Acting out which has mildly impaired some aspect of the patient's functioning (social, domestic, work)
    4 = Acting out which has markedly impaired some aspect of the patient's functioning (social, domestic, work)

11. Libido
    0 = No change
    1 = Mild increase
    2 = Moderate increase
    3 = Marked increase

12. Social Activities
    0 = No increase
    1 = Increased wish to socialize
    2 = Has been socializing considerably more than before
    3 = Indiscriminate socializing (e.g., continually striking up conversation with strangers)

FIGURE 14-1. The clinician-rated hypomania scale used in Study 2.

TABLE 14-2. HDRS Total Scores ($M \pm SD$) for Normals with (S-SAD) and without (Non-S-SAD) Mild SAD-Type Symptoms, Exposed to 2-Hr or 5-Hr Light Treatment

Group	Baseline	Treatment	Withdrawal
S-SAD, 2-hr treatment ($n = 10$)	5.4 ± 4.1	3.3 ± 5.0	4.7 ± 6.7
S-SAD, 5-hr treatment ($n = 10$)	7.6 ± 4.1	2.1 ± 1.4	4.5 ± 3.8
Non-S-SAD, 2-hr treatment ($n = 10$)	1.6 ± 1.7	1.5 ± 2.8	0.9 ± 1.7
Non-S-SAD, 5-hr treatment ($n = 10$)	0.9 ± 1.6	2.2 ± 3.6	0.5 ± 1.1

Note. For statistical information, see text.

($\bar{x} = 11.1 \pm 2.1$) compared to the non-S-SAD group ($\bar{x} = 2.7 \pm 2.3$), as measured by an index of seasonal change derived from the SPAQ.

The statistical evaluation (three-way analysis of variance) of baseline corrected values revealed that the response to light therapy was significantly different (group $\times$ time interaction; group, S-SAD vs. non-S-SAD; time, baseline corrected treatment and withdrawal value), as measured by the HDRS ($F = 4.0$, $p < 0.05$) and the 7-item supplement ($F = 9.4$, $p < 0.01$). Post hoc multiple t tests and simple effects (Winer, 1971) indicated no change in the non-S-SAD groups. In the S-SAD group there was a statistically significant ($p < 0.05$) difference between the 2-hr and 5-hr conditions, with a higher drop in HDRS total scores after the 5-hr condition (see Table 14-2).

Although the group $\times$ time interaction did not reach statistical significance for hypomania ratings ($F = 3.5$, $p = 0.06$), the more pronounced increase was seen in the S-SAD group after either the 5-hr or the 2-hr light treatment; in the non-S-SAD group, light treatment raised the values just slightly. There was a significant correlation between the change of hypomania ratings following treatment and retrospectively reported seasonality in the total group of 40 subjects ($r = 0.42$, $p < 0.01$) and the non-S-SAD group ($r = 0.67$; $p < 0.001$). The lack of correlation in the S-SAD group can be explained by the more homogenous distribution of seasonality, in contrast to the more heterogeneous non-S-SAD group.

The POMS results were similar to those of the observer ratings. The following factors showed significant differences (group $\times$ time interaction) between the groups studied, with the greatest change in the S-SAD probands treated with 5 hr of light treatment and the second greatest change in the S-SAD probands treated with 2 hr of light; depression ($F = 4.3$, $p < 0.05$), fatigue ($F = 4.1$, $p < 0.05$), and a tendency for tension ($F = 3.6$, $p < 0.06$).

There were no correlations between pretreatment expectations and improvement or worsening in the S-SAD group and in controls.

Discussion

The results for the groups of normals studied under different durations of phototherapy suggest that bright light is only beneficial in subjects who report a history of symptomatic seasonal changes. The effect of this treatment is thus not generalizable to other segments of the population. Furthermore, it can be shown that in individuals with symptomatic seasonal changes, 5 hr of phototherapy per day are more effective than 2 hr.

Besides the two studies reported above, two other papers have addressed the question of whether psychological changes after phototherapy can be observed in normals. Using a research design in which 10 normals were exposed to 2 hr of bright light treatment per day for 1 week (1 hr in the morning and 1 hr in the evening), Wirz-Justice et al. (1986) found that mood improved approximately 30%, as measured by a visual analogue-type scale. Dietzel et al. (1986) reported a significant increase in general well-being (according to the subjective well-being scale, Bf-S; von Zerssen et al., 1970) when 10 normal subjects were exposed to 7 hr of light in one 24-hr period. This mood-enhancing effect of light therapy in the subjects of these two studies is comparable to the effect we have observed in our S-SAD groups, but not in the subjects without mild SAD-like symptoms. The discrepancy between the results of these investigations and ours could be explained by the different methods of selection and screening used. Based on our findings, we would conclude that individuals who have a history of symptomatic seasonal changes, and who are generally regarded as "normal," respond to treatment with bright light, whereas normal individuals without such a history do not. Furthermore, even in this latter group, there was a correlation between the degree of seasonal changes reported on history and the change in hypomania ratings. It is possible that the normal volunteers studied by Wirz-Justice et al. and Dietzel et al. may have had histories of symptomatic seasonal changes, in which case their findings would be compatible with ours.

It is important to note that the HDRS total scores were quite low in the groups investigated. Whereas HDRS values are generally above 20 in patients with SAD (Kasper and Rosenthal, 1989), the average HDRS score in our S-SAD group was 6.8 ± 5.3, and in the group without seasonal difficulties it was 1.4 ± 2.3. It is obvious that no decrease in HDRS values could have been expected in the nonseasonal normals, since their baseline HDRS scores were so low. For this reason, we included the POMS in Study 2; the POMS is a standardized self-report inventory that has proved to be a sensitive measure of the effects of various experimental manipulations upon normal subjects and other nonpsychiatric populations (McNair et al., 1981). Among the six clearly defined POMS factors, depression and fatigue exhibited a significant difference between the groups studied, with an improvement in the S-SAD probands, but no change in the controls with either 2 or 5 hr of light treatment.

There are only a few reports in the literature about the effects of bright light on mood, vigilance, and performance in normal subjects. Chaves and Delay (1982) found that increasing the intensity of ambient illumination improved vigilance performance in 36 college students. Maas et al. (1974) reported that 29 students revealed less perceptual fatigue under lighting that closely approximated the spectral quality of natural sunlight. Whiting *et al.* (1972) demonstrated that the ability to concentrate was significantly superior at the illumination of 2100 lux, compared to intensities of 200–600 lux. It is possible that the favorable effects of light in these studies might have been due to the inclusion of S-SAD subjects in the study populations.

The finding that certain individuals generally regarded as "normal" respond favorably to enhanced environmental lighting, while others do not, has both practical and theoretical implications. On the practical side, this implies that individuals who would not seek medical help might nonetheless benefit from it. Enhancing environmental light exposure in such individuals should thus be considered a public health issue (Jacobsen *et al.*, 1987). The significant correlation between retrospectively reported seasonal changes in behavior and energy level, as measured by the SPAQ, and subsequent response to light implies that it is possible to predict to some degree those individuals who stand to benefit by environmental lighting manipulations. If this finding, which was true for individuals who answered a newspaper advertisement, is generalizable to other populations, it should be possible to evaluate target populations by means of the SPAQ and to improve the quality of life of those who show high seasonality scores by enhancing their light exposure during the winter. It would appear logical and worthwhile to pursue this direction in future studies.

The susceptibility of certain individuals to having their mood and behavior modified by enhancing their environmental light exposure raises certain theoretical questions as well. Figure 14-2 summarizes the relationship between a given vulnerability to develop SAD symptoms and the amount of lack of light. From this model, it can be deduced that individuals with a low degree of vul-

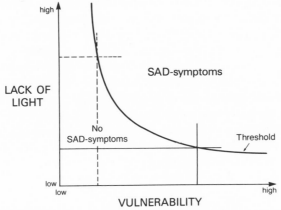

FIGURE 14-2. Relationships between the degree of vulnerability to develop SAD symptoms and the amount of lack of light. The dotted lines represent the possible relationships in S-SAD individuals, and the solid lines represent the relationships in SAD patients. Vertical lines indicate the development and involution of SAD symptoms with the amount of lack of light.

nerability might reach the threshold to develop SAD symptoms after experiencing a high degree of lack of light. On the other hand, individuals with a high vulnerability might suffer from SAD symptoms after only a low degree of lack of light. The former might represent the group of S-SAD individuals, and the latter the more severely affected SAD patients. The vertical lines in this graph demonstrate the influence of light therapy, which reduces the amount of lack of light and therefore also the possibility of presenting SAD symptoms. As the amount of lack of light can be corrected by environmental factors and light therapy, the question of what physiological and biochemical processes underlie such a susceptibility to develop SAD symptoms is of further interest. Is the susceptibility a marker of vulnerability to affective episodes in general, or the partial expression of some genetic trait expressed more fully in patients with full-blown SAD? It is noteworthy that another marker of affective vulnerability involving the processing of visual information has been described—namely, the supersensitivity of bipolar patients to the suppressing effects of light on nocturnal melatonin secretion (Lewy et al., 1980). This biological effect may indeed represent a genetic marker for the condition, since children of patients with bipolar affective disorder show greater sensitivity to the suppressing effects of light on melatonin secretion than matched controls (Nurnberger et al., 1988).

Our growing understanding of the biological abnormalities in patients with SAD and the effects of bright light on these patients may also be relevant to subjects with S-SAD. Thus patients with SAD have been shown to have abnormally low plasma norepinephrine levels and abnormally elevated lymphocyte transformation in response to mitogen stimulation in vitro (Skwerer et al., Chapter 17, this volume). Both of these abnormalities can be reversed by exposing subjects to bright artificial light. Similarly, in SAD patients the P300 component of the event-related brain potential response to visual stimuli is increased in amplitude by exposing subjects to bright light, and the increase is directly proportional to the improvement in mood (Duncan and Rosenthal, 1986). This relationship between mood improvement and increased P300 amplitude is not apparent following auditory stimuli. This implies another specific abnormality in visual information processing in patients with SAD.

The SPAQ seasonality score for subjects with S-SAD, is intermediate between that for non-S-SAD normals and that for SAD patients, yet significantly different from both of these other groups (Kasper et al., in press-a). If the biological markers described above are abnormal in proportion to the abnormality in seasonal behavior changes, one would predict values for the S-SAD population intermediate between those of normals and those of SAD patients.

Conclusion

In conclusion, exposure of normal individuals to bright environmental light appears to alter mood and behavior only in those individuals with a history of seasonal changes in these variables. Such a history can be elicited by the administration of a simple standardized self-administered questionnaire, the SPAQ. The effect of light appears to depend on the duration of light exposure, insofar as the 5-hr treatment condition showed a greater effect than the 2-hr condition. Since these normal individuals are unlikely to present to health care professionals, this finding is of public health importance. The behavioral changes in subjects with S-SAD are intermediate between those of non-S-SAD normals and patients with SAD. It would be worthwhile investigating whether their biological profile also occupies such an intermediate position, and whether they are genetically related to individuals with a more florid affective presentation.

Acknowledgment

Siegfried Kasper is supported by the German Research Foundation (DFG).

References

Chaves, M. E., and E. R. Delay (1982) Effects of ambient illumination over days on human vigilance performance. Percept. Mot. Skills *55:* 667–672.

Borkovec, T. D., and S. D. Nau (1972) Credibility of analogue therapy rationales. J. Behav. Ther. Exp. Res. *3:* 257–260.

Dietzel, M., F. Waldhauser, O. M. Lesch, M. Musalek, and H. Walter (1986) Bright light treatment success not explained by melatonin. J. Interdiscip. Cycle Res. *16:* 165.

Duncan, C. C., and N. E. Rosenthal (1986) Effects of phototherapy on brain potentials in patients with seasonal affective disorder: A pilot study. Paper presented at the 26th Annual Meeting of the Society for Psychophysiological Research, Montreal, October 16–19.

Hamilton, M. (1967) Developement of a rating scale for primary depressive illness. Brit. J. Soc. Clin. Psychol. *6:* 278–296.

Hellekson, C. J., J. A. Kline, and N. E. Rosenthal (1986) Phototherapy for seasonal affective disorder in Alaska. Amer. J. Psychiat. *143:* 1035–1037.

James, S. P., T. A. Wehr, D. A. Sack, B. L. Parry, and N. E. Rosenthal (1985) Treatment of seasonal affective disorder in children and adolescents. Amer. J. Psychiat. *147;* 424–428.

Jacobsen, F. M., T. A. Wehr, D. A. Sack, S. P. James, and N. E. Rosenthal (1987) Seasonal affective disorder: A review of the syndrome and its public health implications. Amer. J. Pub. Health *77:* 57–60.

Kasper, S., S. Rogers, A. Yancey, P. M. Schulz, R. G. Skwerer, and N. E. Rosenthal (in press-a) Phototherapy in individuals with subsyndromal seasonal affective disorder. Arch. Gen. Psychiat.

Kasper, S., and N. E. Rosenthal (1989) Anxiety and depression in seasonal affective disorders. In *Anxiety and Depression: Distinctive and Overlapping Features,* P. C. Kendall and D. Watson, eds., Academic Press, New York.

Kasper, S., T. A. Wehr, J. J. Bartko, P. A. Gaist, and N. E. Rosenthal (in press-b) Epidemiological findings of seasonal changes in mood and behavior. A telephone survey of the Montgomery county population. Arch. Gen. Psychiat.

Kraepelin, E. (1921) *Manic–Depressive Insanity and Paranoia,* R. M. Barclay, trans., G. M. Robertson, ed., E. and S. Livingstone, Edinburgh.

Lewy, A. J., H. A. Kern, N. E. Rosenthal and T. A. Wehr (1982) Bright artificial light treatment of a manic–depressive patient with a seasonal mood cycle. Amer. J. Psychiat. *139:* 1496–1498.

Lewy, A. J., R. L. Sack, R. H. Frederickson, M. Reaves, D. D. Denney, and D. R. Zielske (1983) The use of bright light in treatment of chronobiologic sleep and mood disorders: The phase-response curve. Psychopharmacol. Bull. *19:* 523–525.

Lewy, A. J., R. L. Sack, L. S. Miller, and T. M. Hoban (1987) Antidepressant and circadian phase-shifting effects of light. Science *235:* 352–354.

Lewy, A. J., T. A. Wehr, F. K. Goodwin, D. A. Newsome, and S. P. Markey (1980) Light suppresses melatonin secretion in humans. Science *210:* 1267.

Maas, J. B., J. K. Jayson, and D. A. Kleiber (1974) Effects of spectral differences in illumination on fatigue. J. Appl. Psychol. *59:* 524–526.

McNair, D. M., M. Lorr, and L. F. Droppelmann (1981) *Profile of Mood States,* Educational and Industrial Testing Service, San Diego.

Nurnberger, J., W. Berretini, L. Tamarkin, J. Hamovit, J. Norton, and E. Gershon (1988) Supersensitivity to melatonin suppression by light in young people at risk for affective disorder. Neuropsychopharmacology *1:* 217–223.

Rosenthal, N. E., M. Genhardt, D. A. Sack, R. G. Skwerer, and T. A. Wehr (1987b) Seasonal affective disorder: Relevance for treatment and research of bulimia. In *Psychobiology of Bulimia,* J. I Hudson and H. G. Pope, Jr., eds, American Psychiatric Press, Washington, DC.

Rosenthal, N. E., and M. M. Heffernan (1986) Bulimia, carbohydrate craving, and depression: A central connection? In *Nutrition and the Brain,* Vol. 7, R. J. Wurtman and J. J. Wurtman, eds., pp. 139–166, Raven Press, New York.

Rosenthal, N. E., A. Rotter F. M. Jacobsen, and R. G. Skwerer (1987a) No mood-altering effects found following treatment of normal subjects with bright light in the morning. Psychiat. Res. *22:* 1–9.

Rosenthal, N. E., D. A. Sack, C. J. Carpenter, B. L. Parry, W. B. Mendelson, and T. A. Wehr (1985) Antidepressant effects of light in seasonal affective disorder. Amer. J. Psychiat. *142:* 606–608.

Rosenthal, N. E., D. A. Sack, J. C. Gillin, A. J. Lewy, F. K. Goodwin, Y. Davenport, P. S. Mueller, D. A. Newsome, and T. A. Wehr (1984) Seasonal affective disorder: A description of the syndrome and preliminary findings with light therapy. Arch. Gen. Psychiat. *41:* 72–80.

Terman, M., F. M. Quitkin, and J. S. Terman (1986) Light therapy for SAD: Dosing regimens. In *New Research Abstracts of the Annual Meeting of the American Psychiatric Association,* No. 121, p. 77, American Psychiatric Association, Washington, DC.

Thompson, C., and G. Isaacs (1988) Seasonal affective disorder—a British sample. Symptomatology in relation to mode of referral and diagnostic subtype. J. Affect. Disord. *14:* 1–11.

von Zerssen, V. D., D. M. Koeller, and E. R. Rey (1970) Die Befindlichkeitsskala (Bf-S)—ein einfaches Instrument zur Objektivierung von Befindlichkeitsstörungen, insbesondere im Rahmen von Längsschnittuntersuchungen. Arzn. Forsch. (Drug Res.) *20:* 915–918.

Wehr, T. A., F. M. Jacobsen, D. A. Sack, J. Arendt, L. Tamarkin, and N. E. Rosenthal (1986) Phototherapy of seasonal affective disorder: Time of day and suppression of melatonin are not critical for antidepressant effects. Arch. Gen. Psychiat. *43:* 870–875.

Whiting, H. T. A., G. J. K. Alderson, D. Cocup, J. W. R. Hutt, and T. B. Renfrew (1972) Level of illumination and performance in a simulated table-tennis task. Int. J. Sport Psychol. *3:* 32–41.

Winer, B. J. (1971) *Statistical Principles in Experimental Design,* McGraw-Hill, New York.

Wirz-Justice, A., C. Bucheli, P. Graw, P. Kielholz, H.-U. Fisch, and B. Woggon (1986) Light treatment of seasonal affective disorder in Switzerland. Acta Psychiat. Scand. *74:* 193–204.

Phototherapy for Winter Seasonal Affective Disorder and Nonseasonal Depression: Clinical and Theoretical Considerations

Phototherapy for Seasonal Affective Disorder

Norman E. Rosenthal, David A. Sack, Robert G. Skwerer,
Frederick M. Jacobsen, and Thomas A. Wehr

In the past 6 years our knowledge of phototherapy, the newest form of treatment for an affective disorder, has moved rapidly from anecdotal observations and a single case report (Lewy *et al.*, 1982) to an established and accepted treatment (Rosenthal and Wehr, 1987). In this chapter we discuss several aspects of this development, summarize what is known about phototherapy for seasonal affective disorder (SAD), and outline the areas of uncertainty and critical questions for future research.

Historical Note

The concept of exposing patients to artificial light sources for therapeutic purposes is not a new one. Indeed, books were written on the subject in the early decades of this century (Humphris, 1924; Kovacs, 1932). However, there are important distinctions between the treatments outlined in these earlier texts and the phototherapy currently in use. These earlier clinicians regarded phototherapy as a broad-spectrum treatment for a wide variety of ills. Ultraviolet light was considered an important component of the treatments, and the entire body was exposed to the light. The emphasis was thus on exposing the skin to light, and special "light baths" were designed to maximize skin exposure and to shield the eyes from toxic ultraviolet rays. In contrast, phototherapy is currently regarded as helpful only with certain specific types of patients; the light sources used have contained relatively little ultraviolet light; and emphasis has been placed on the eyes rather than the skin as the portal of entry of the therapeutic effect.

Norman E. Rosenthal, David A. Sack, Robert G. Skwerer, and Thomas A. Wehr. Clinical Psychobiology Branch, National Institute of Mental Health, Bethesda, Maryland.

Frederick M. Jacobsen. Clinical Psychobiology Branch and Laboratory of Clinical Science, National Institute of Mental Health, Bethesda, Maryland.

The majority of phototherapy studies conducted in the past few years have involved patients with SAD, a condition characterized by regular winter depressions alternating with nondepressed periods in the spring and summer (Rosenthal *et al.*, 1984). There are a few recorded historical examples of manipulations of lighting and climate specifically aimed at reversing certain winter difficulties such as depression and lethargy. Esquirol (1845) reported a case of a man with symptoms remarkably similar to those of SAD, whom he treated successfully by advising him to move from overcast Belgium to sunny Italy for the duration of the winter. In a later report, an insightful ship's doctor used bright artificial light to combat the languor and malaise experienced by his crew when they sailed through the dark days of an Arctic winter (Jefferson, 1986).

It was not, however, until the 1980s that the modern era of phototherapy began, inspired by the finding of Lewy *et al.* (1980) that bright light was capable of suppressing the nocturnal secretion of human melatonin, whereas ordinary room light was not. The importance of melatonin as a chemical mediator of the effects of light on seasonal rhythms in animals, and the knowledge that the neural pathways involved in its suppression by light traverse the hypothalamus (Tamarkin *et al.*, 1985), both suggested its possible therapeutic value in the treatment of seasonal depressions. However, the existence and, indeed, widespread prevalence of such seasonal depressions had not as yet been appreciated by many clinicians. A critical step in achieving this end was accomplished by H. E. Kern, himself a scientist, who had carefully charted his circannual mood cycles over a 15-year period and had independently concluded that changes in environmental light might be the cause of these regularly occurring mood cycles (Lewy *et al.*, 1982; Rosenthal *et al.*, 1983). Kern brought his observations to the attention of Peter S. Mueller, MD, as well as to the group at the National Institute of Mental Health (NIMH). Mueller subsequently referred another patient with SAD to the NIMH, and her case history was used to recruit the first series of SAD patients to be treated with light (Rosenthal *et al.*, 1984).

It should be noted that at the same time as the treatment of SAD with light was evolving, Kripke (1981) proposed that nonseasonal depression might result from inadequate light exposure at critical times of the day. Kripke *et al.* (1983, 1985) subsequently went on to test this hypothesis in a series of studies on nonseasonal depression, a subject that falls outside the scope of this paper.

Methodology of Phototherapy Studies of SAD

Discussion of the different phototherapy studies of SAD is made considerably easier because of the similar ways in which the populations were recruited and selected and the similarities in study design. Important common elements in study methodology are discussed below.

Recruitment

Patients have generally been recruited via the media, usually the press. Typically, a newspaper article will describe a patient with SAD, briefly discuss prevailing ideas about the condition, and provide referral information for people who believe they may be suffering from the condition. There may be some conflict between the reporter, who would like to provide as much information as possible about existing knowledge on the subject, and the investigator, who wishes to conceal the critical hypotheses to be tested in forthcoming studies. However, it has generally been possible to reach a compromise, and critical experimental details have not been revealed. Responders to the newspaper article have generally been screened, initially by means of a questionnaire[1] and later by means of a clinical interview. In most studies, criteria for the diagnosis of SAD and admission to protocols have been similar to those used by Rosenthal *et al.* (1984).

The use of media recruitment has resulted in criticism of the final sample obtained. A common criticism has been that such patients do not, in fact, have SAD but misrepresent their histories, perhaps even unintentionally, in order to be included in a research program. A more troublesome extension of this criticism is that such individuals are highly suggestible, come into the program with high treatment expectations, and are therefore especially susceptible to placebo responses. The former criticism has been easier to address than the latter. By now, hundreds of SAD patients have been studied by several different groups of investigators, who have prospectively observed their regular seasonal changes in mood, behavior, and vegetative symptoms. In more recent years, an increasing number of patients has been referred by other health care professionals, and there is no evidence of any difference in the symptom profiles of these two groups except that the physician referrals tend to be more severely affected (Thompson and Isaacs, 1988). The second criticism, concerning a possible placebo effect, has been more difficult to address and is discussed below.

Measurement of Mood

Once admitted into research programs, patients are generally followed until they become depressed. Such depression has generally been measured by the 21-item Hamilton Depression Rating Scale (HDRS). It should be noted, however, that this scale underestimates the severity of symptoms in this condition, as many of the characteristic symptoms (notably increased appetite, carbohy-

---

1. A copy of our standardized screening questionnaire can be obtained by writing to Norman E. Rosenthal.

drate craving, and weight gain) are either not represented on the standard HDRS or are represented only in their opposite form. Thus the presence of decreased appetite and sleep, and weight loss, often signs of overall improvement, will increase the HDRS severity score. In order to measure changes in the behaviors characteristic of SAD more fully, we have adopted a supplement to the HDRS (Rosenthal and Heffernan, 1986) as well as a Hypomania Scale (Rosenthal and Wehr, unpublished); we have found both of these to be quite useful clinically, although they have not as yet been formally validated. In one study of light therapy, Wirz-Justice *et al.* (1986) were able to demonstrate a significant difference between active and control lighting conditions by means of the atypical supplementary items, but not the standard HDRS. However, notwithstanding its deficiencies, the typical HDRS has been surprisingly reliable and sensitive in many phototherapy studies, and we still use it in its original form together with the extra scales mentioned above. The usual severity threshold for initial inclusion in our treatment studies has been a score of 14 on the HDRS, and others have used a similar threshold for entry.

Use of a Crossover Design

Almost all studies of phototherapy for SAD have employed a crossover design. In general, two different treatments have been administered for 1 week each, separated from each other by a week of withdrawal from light treatment. Such a design works well, as the response to phototherapy can often be detected by the fourth treatment day, and relapse following withdrawal of light treatment is generally apparent by the fourth day of withdrawal (Rosenthal *et al.*, 1985b). In some studies patients were not withdrawn following light treatment (Lewy *et al.*, 1987a) or were withdrawn only if a clinical response occurred (Rosenthal *et al.*, 1984; Isaacs *et al.*, 1988; Checkley *et al.*, in press). There are problems in evaluating data when these strategies are adopted. In studies where there is no withdrawal between treatments, the baseline for the second treatment is the posttreatment score of the first. If the first treatment is more effective than the second, this may create the impression that the second treatment is making the patient worse. There can also be difficulties if the first treatment is partially effective but less so than the second treatment. In this situation, the second treatment does not receive a fair trial, and the chances of distinguishing between the efficacy of the two treatments is diminished. In studies where individuals are withdrawn only if they have responded clinically, statistical problems arise. The usual analysis of variance with repeated measures cannot be performed, as the posttreatment scores for the first treatment and baseline scores for the second treatment represent the same measurements in certain cases. One strategy that has been used to overcome this problem has been to compare the change scores of the two types of treatment.

We should note that even in the standard type of crossover, some problems have arisen. Most notable of these is the ordering effect. Even though relapse is generally detectable to some degree by the fourth day following withdrawal of light treatment, complete relapse to pretreatment levels is often not apparent within a week. The ordering effect has not reached statistical significance in most studies, probably because the sample sizes have not been large enough. However, in most crossover studies the baseline score for the less effective treatment has been somewhat lower than for the more effective treatment (see Tables 15-1–15-14, below). Statistically significant ordering effects occurred in the studies of Hellekson *et al.* (1986) and Wirz-Justice *et al.* (1987). The former study involved a crossover between three treatment conditions—a type of design that is most likely to succeed in places such as Alaska, where the winter is very long. However, Hellekson *et al.* studied all subjects after the winter solstice, and by the time the third treatment was reached, the days were rapidly getting longer, thus attenuating the treatment effect.

In order to minimize the likelihood of an ordering effect, it is important to try to run subjects through the crossover study evenly throughout the winter; not to admit them into the second treatment condition unless relapse has occurred to a certain predetermined degree (we have arbitrarily chosen an HDRS score of 10 for this purpose); and to take the ordering effect into account in the statistical analysis. An ordering effect may also result from different expectations of the two treatments, in that a patient's expectations of the second treatment may be influenced by the results of the first treatment.

Despite the problem of the ordering effect, crossover studies have been extremely useful in studying the effects of phototherapy in SAD, as they have enabled researchers to show differences between different types of treatment with sample sizes that would have been too small to demonstrate such differences if parallel treatment designs had been employed. In addition, the design offers the opportunity of comparing different interventions in the same individual, thus minimizing the statistical noise created by interindividual differences. It is also conceivable that subsets of patients may respond differently to different types of treatment. If such subsets do exist, the use of a crossover design may be helpful in clarifying such differences.

Minimizing the Placebo Effect

In this chapter, the "placebo effect" is defined as the psychological effect of the experimental intervention. As in drug studies, it is important to control for the placebo effect. However, phototherapy falls into that category of interventions—which includes psychotherapy, electroconvulsive therapy, and sleep deprivation—where the nature of the treatment intervention cannot generally be concealed from the patient. Thus it may never be possible to control for the placebo effect; however, much can be done to minimize its impact on the outcome of the study and the conclusions drawn. The use of a suitable control treatment is clearly important in order to control, at least in part, for the placebo effect among other factors. The design of a suitable control treatment and other considerations for minimizing the impact of the placebo effect are prerequisites for an adequate study and are outlined below. In addition, raters should be blind to the treatment condition to avoid rater bias. In the case of drug studies, the double-blind design is regarded as necessary to avoid a placebo effect. The following guidelines may be useful in controlling for and minimizing the placebo effect.

THE DEVELOPMENT OF A SUITABLE CONTROL TREATMENT

One major element in the placebo effect is the expectation of the patient prior to treatment. It is therefore important that a plausible control treatment be devised in order for expectations of the control treatment to be approximately equal to those of the active treatment. Control treatments have included light sources of different intensities and spectra; light administered at different times of the day and for different durations; and different ways of presenting light to the patient—for example, to the skin as opposed to the eyes (Wehr *et al.*, 1987). In addition to being plausible, a control treatment should be ineffective if the efficacy of the "active" treatment is the focus of the study. However, in certain studies, where the treatment is presumed to be somewhat effective, the hypothesis being tested may involve the relative efficacy of different control treatments.

PRESENTATION OF EXPERIMENTAL CONDITIONS

In order to prevent unintentional communication of researcher bias, which may enhance or reduce the placebo effect, the conditions of the experiments should be presented to the subjects in a standardized way, preferably by reading written instructions to them. Similarly, written responses to the more commonly asked questions should be prepared. If the study has crossover design, the different conditions should be presented in a balanced fashion, which does not promote differential expectations.

EVALUATION OF PATIENT EXPECTATIONS

One means of evaluating the extent to which a placebo effect may be at work is to test the patient's expectations of treatment (Jacobson and Baucom, 1977; Kazdin, 1979; Kazdin and Krouse, 1983). In order to test for plausibility in phototherapy studies, expectations of both active and control treatments have been elicited from patients retrospectively (Lewy *et al.*, 1987a) or prospectively (Rosenthal *et al.*, 1984; Wehr *et al.*, 1987; Wirz-Justice *et al.*, 1987). In the latter two studies, the researchers used a questionnaire modified from that of Borkovec and Nau (1972) and visual analogue scales, respectively. More recently, the NIMH group has used the questionnaire of Kazdin and Krouse (1983) as well. It is probably best to elicit expectations prospectively, with or without retrospective inquiry (Jacobson and Baucom, 1977). Retrospective reporting suffers from distortion based on the individual's actual experience with the treatment modality. For example, in the study by Wirz-Justice *et al.* (1987), in which 2 hr and 30 min of morning light were compared, prospective ratings of expectations did not correlate with outcome, whereas retrospective evaluations did.

Even if expectations of active and control treatments are equal at the beginning of a study, they may diverge during the study. Such a divergence may be due to the different behavioral effects of the two interventions or to differences in plausibility that develop after the study has started. The latter situation is particularly difficult to evaluate, but can be minimized by having the nonblind clinicians interact in a standardized way with subjects. Expectations could be measured repeatedly, but this would not distinguish between the two possibilities mentioned above. In addition, there is always the risk that measuring expectations will actually influence them. There is no evidence that this has been the case in phototherapy studies. We have routinely emphasized to each subject, following evaluation of expectations, that our intention is to measure the actual effect of the treatment rather than the accuracy of the subject's predictions, in an attempt to minimize the impact of the evaluation on outcome. It is unclear, however, whether such a clarification has any beneficial effect. Some students of the placebo effect have advocated the use of suggestions to modify subject expectations, at times even in a direction opposite to that predicted by the researcher (Kazdin, 1979). Thus far, such a strategy has not been adopted in phototherapy studies.

Minimizing Other Unintended Effects

Apart from the placebo effect, other factors need to be considered in designing an adequate phototherapy study, including the ordering effect (mentioned above), sleep deprivation, and unintended light exposure. If the control treatment is not equivalent to the treatment being studied in all respects, it is harder to draw a clear conclusion. For example, sleep deprivation was not adequately controlled in the first treatment study by Rosenthal *et al.* (1984), and patients probably slept less during the active than during the control treatment. It took this group two further studies to rule out sleep deprivation as a necessary element in the antidepressant effect of light treatment (James *et al.*, 1985; Rosenthal *et al.*, 1985b). Lewy *et al.* (1987b) have emphasized the importance of controlling lighting conditions when patients are not intended to be receiving treatment. This is especially important in treatment studies where timing of treatment is being investigated.

Results of Phototherapy Studies in SAD

The results of 19 controlled phototherapy studies of SAD available at the time of writing of this chapter are shown in Tables 15-1–15-4. The one conclusion on which all researchers agree is that bright-light treatment is an effective antidepressant in SAD. Areas of uncertainty or disagreement concern specific parameters of light treatment that are necessary or optimal for producing this response. A study of these areas is of clear importance, both in establishing optimal guidelines for phototherapy administration and in attempting to understand the physiological mechanisms involved in phototherapy. These parameters of phototherapy are discussed below.

Intensity

In phototherapy studies, intensity has been measured as illuminance—that is, the amount of light incident on the patient, as opposed to the amount of light leaving the light source or the perceived brightness of the source. Illuminance has generally been reported in lux. Intensity of the light source was the first parameter to be studied systematically, its importance having been suggested by the finding that suppression of nocturnal melatonin secretion required high-intensity light (2500 lux), which is far brighter than ordinary room light (500 lux or less) (Lewy et al., 1980). It seemed self-evident that ordinary room light could not be curative, since patients developed symptoms during the winter despite continued use of ordinary room light.

A series of studies conducted at the NIMH on 33 SAD patients established that bright-light treatment was significantly superior to dim-light treatment (Rosenthal et al., 1984, 1985a; James et al., 1985; see Table 15-1). The superiority of bright over dim light was replicated by Checkley et al. (in press) and Isaacs et al. (1988). Wirz-Justice et al. (1986) compared bright to dim light in 11 subjects, only 4 of whom were completely crossed over between conditions, and found no significant difference between the two treatments, as measured by the standard HDRS. However, when they examined the atypical symptoms (Rosenthal and Heffernan, 1986), they found bright light to be superior. The bright-light sources used in the studies above were full-spectrum fluorescent lights (2500 lux); the dim-light sources (400 lux or less) were either full-spectrum, yellow, or red.

It seems reasonable to conclude, on the basis of most studies, that intensity of the light source is an important parameter in achieving an antidepressant effect. The exact threshold probably varies from patient to patient, and, in our experience, some subjects appear to benefit even from using lights of intensities somewhat lower than 2500 lux. A few subjects preferred the dimmer light and appeared to derive sustained benefit from 300-lux light treaments. On the other hand, preliminary reports by Terman (Chapter 20, this volume) suggest that for

TABLE 15-1. Controlled Studies of Phototherapy: Intensity of Light

Authors	Years of study	n	Patient status	Active/control[a]	Spectrum	Intensity	Timing	Results Baseline	Results Treatment	Percentage decrease	Conclusion
Rosenthal et al. (1984)	1981–1982	9	Outpatient	Active	Full-spectrum light	2500 lux	0530–0830 hr and 1800–2000 hr	17.7	6.2	62[b]	Bright > dim
				Control	Yellow	100 lux	As above	15.1	13.2	13	
Rosenthal et al. (1985b)	1982–1983	6	Inpatient	Active	Full-spectrum	2500 lux	0600–0900 hr and 1800–2100 hr	30.1	17.8	41[b]	Bright > dim
				Control	Incandescent	<5 lux	As above	27.1	25.7	5	
		7	Outpatient	Active	Full-spectrum	2500 lux	As above	22.9	9.5	59[b]	
				Control	As above	300 lux	As above	21.9	20.5	5	
James et al. (1985)	1983–1984	9	Outpatient	Active	Full-spectrum	2500 lux	1800–2300 hr	24.3	13.4	45[c]	Bright > dim
				Control	As above	300 lux	As above	23.0	18.4	20	
Wirz-Justice et al. (1986)	1984–1985	9	Outpatient	Active	Full-spectrum	2500 lux	0600–0800 hr and 1800–2000 hr	30.0	11.2	63[c]	Bright = dim; both effective
		6		Control	Yellow	300 lux		26.3	13.5	49[c]	Bright > dim on supplementary HDRS items
Checkley et al. (in press)	1985–1986	10	Outpatient	Active	Full-spectrum	2500 lux	0700–1000 hr and 2000–2300 hr	18.5	10.3	44[b]	Bright > dim
				Control	Red	400 lux	As above	17.3	13.7	21	
Isaacs et al. (1988)	1985–1986	11	Outpatient	Active	Full-spectrum	2500 lux	0700–0900 hr and 1800–2000 hr	13.9	9.5	32	4 hr bright at midday > 2 hr in morning + 2 hr in evening
				Control	As above	300 lux	As above	16.3	11.7	28	
Wehr et al. (1987)	1985–1986	10	Outpatient	Active	Full-spectrum	2500 lux to eyes	1830–2230 hr	25.6	10.3	20.5	Eye exposure (bright light) > skin exposure (dim light)
				Control	As above	100 lux to eyes	As above	23.4	20.3	23.9	

Note. All light used were fluorescent unless otherwise stated.

[a] "Active" signifies the treatment predicted by investigators to be active; "control" signifies the treatment predicted to be inactive. If there was no specific prediction, all treatments are designated as active.

[b] A significant difference between treatments.

[c] A significance difference from baseline, but not between treatments.

some people light intensities of up to 10,000 lux may be superior to the conventional bright light. In all studies of intensity performed to date, only two different intensities have been used. It would be useful to determine dose–response curves for the antidepressant effects of light for different individuals over a wider range of intensities.

Timing

There has been considerable interest in whether timing of light treatment is important or even critical for achieving an antidepressant response to phototherapy, and several research groups have investigated this question. These investigations have been approached from two separate theoretical orientations. The first was derived from studies of photoperiodic control of seasonal rhythms in animals, where the modulatory effects of light on behavior have depended on exposure to light at certain critical times of day outside of the usual winter photoperiod (Hoffmann, 1981; Wehr et al., 1986). The second approach, advanced by Lewy et al. (1987a), was based on the hypothesis that patients with SAD become depressed during the winter because the timing of their circadian rhythms is abnormal. According to this theory, light exposure at certain critical times of the day may correct this abnormality, thereby exerting its antidepressant affect.

Lewy et al. (1987a) showed that 2 hr of bright-light treatment in the early morning were superior to 2 hr of evening light treatment (see Table 15-2)—a finding that was replicated by Terman et al. (1987), Avery, Kham, and Dunner (personal communication), and Lewy et al. (1987b). However, in several studies researchers failed to show a significantly superior effect of morning versus evening light exposure (Hellekson et al., 1986; Yerevanian et al., 1986; Terman et al., in press; Wirz-Justice et al., in press; Yerevanian and Grota, personal communication). The reasons for these discrepant findings are unclear. One possible reason is that in both studies by Lewy et al. and in the study by Avery et al., a very strict protocol was maintained. Light treatments were given early in the mornings (0600–0800 hr), at times when patients in other, less stringent studies were still asleep (Hellekson et al., 1986; Wirz-Justice et al., in press). However, in some studies that showed no difference between morning and evening light, the morning light was administered early (Terman et al., in press; Yerevanian and Grota, personal communication).

There were other methodological differences between studies that may have accounted for differences in outcome. For example, the study by Wirz-Justice et al. (in press) followed a trial of melatonin administration, which, though it did not alter mood status significantly, may nonetheless have influenced outcome. Special circumstances prevailing in the Hellekson et al. (1986) study were the very long nights of the Alaskan winter, which might conceivably modify responsivity to light. The studies of Yerevanian *et al.* (1986; Yerevanian and Grota, personal communication) differed from the other studies in that these researchers used incandescent light.

A meta-analysis of light treatment data from different centers (Terman *et al.*, in press) suggests that some individuals may respond exclusively to morning light, whereas very few individuals seem to respond exclusively to evening light. It is possible that those studies that demonstrated superiority of morning light might have included a greater number of the former type of patients.

Although time of day appears to be an influence on sensitivity to phototherapy—an influence that may be critical in certain SAD patients—it does not appear to be critical for most SAD patients to receive light treatment at a specific time of day. Several studies, apart from those mentioned above, have shown significant antidepressant effects of phototherapy administered at times other than the early morning hours. Such times include the evening (James *et al.*, 1985; Wehr *et al.*, 1987; Doghramji, Gaddy, Stewart, Rosenthal, and Brainard, personal communication) and during daylight hours (Wehr *et al.*, 1986; Jacobson *et al.*, 1987; Isaacs *et al.*, 1988). Even those researchers who have found morning light to be superior to evening light have found this latter treatment to be somewhat effective in their more recent studies (Lewy *et al.*, 1987b; Avery *et al.*, personal communication), though a placebo effect cannot be ruled out in these cases.

Despite the studies that have failed to confirm a superiority of morning light, the observation that some patients are differentially sensitive to phototherapy at different times of the day may have important practical implications in the light treatment of certain patients and may be a clue to the mechanisms underlying its efficacy. In addition, the possible existence of such a circadian pattern of phototherapy response would be a powerful argument against a placebo effect as the sole determinant of the antidepressant response.

Duration

Several groups have studied the importance of duration of light treatment in influencing the outcome of phototherapy (Terman *et al.*, 1987; Wirz-Justice *et al.*, 1987; Lewy *et al.*, 1987b; Hellekson and Woodward, personal communication; see Table 15-3). In evaluating their experience with a variety of durations of light treatment administered at different times of the day, Terman *et al.* (1987) found that duration of light treatment did influence outcome. Wirz-Justice *et al.* (1987) and Lewy *et al.* (1987b), using similar study designs, both compared 2 hr with 30 min of bright-light treatment in the morning. Wirz-Justice *et al.* found 2 hr to be significantly superior to 30 min, whereas Lewy *et al.* found no difference between the two treatment conditions. It should be noted that Wirz-Justice and colleagues only noted the effect of duration after

TABLE 15-2. Controlled Studies of Phototherapy: Timing

Authors	Years of study	n	Patient status	Active/control[a]	Treatment Spectrum	Treatment Intensity	Treatment Timing	Results Baseline	Results Treatment	Percentage decrease	Conclusion
					Studies exploring periodicity						
Wehr et al. (1986)	1984–1985	7	Inpatient	Active	Full-spectrum	2500 lux	0730–1030 hr and 2000–2300 hr (long skeleton photoperiod, or LSP)	29.1	14.7	50[c]	LSP = SSP; antidepressant effects of light do not depend on extending photoperiod
				Control	As above	As above	0900–1200 hr and 1400–1700 hr (short skeleton photoperiod, or SSP)	26.0	15.7	40[c]	
Isaacs et al. (1988)	1985–1986	11	Outpatient	Active #1	Full-spectrum	2500 lux	0700–0900 hr and 1800–2000 hr	13.9	9.5	32	4 hr bright at midday > 2 hr in morning + 2 hr in evening
				Active #2	As above	2500 lux	1000–1400 hr	16.1	7.6	53[b]	
				Control	As above	300 lux	0700–0900 hr and 1800–2000 hr	16.3	11.7	28	
					Studies exploring phase-shifting effects						
Lewy et al. (1987a)	1983–1984	8	Outpatient	Active	Full-spectrum or cool white	2500 lux	0600–0800 hr	15.4	6.6	57[b]	Morning > evening
				Control	As above	2500 lux	2000–2200 hr	15.4	15.2	1	
Hellekson et al. (1986)	1983–1984	6	Outpatient	Active #1	Full-spectrum	2500 lux	2 hr on rising	16.1	4.4	73[c]	Morning = evening = morning + evening

Study	Year	n	Setting	Condition	Light	Intensity	Timing				Outcome
Yerevanian et al. (1986)	1985–1986	6	Outpatient	Active #2	As above	2500 lux	1 hr on rising + 1 hr in evening	14.4	6.0	58[c]	
		5		Active #3	As above	2500 lux	2 hr in evening	15.0	4.0	53[c]	Morning = evening
Terman et al. (1987)	1985–1986	17	Outpatient	Active #1	Incandescent	2500 lux	0530–0730 hr	16.7	4.3	74[c]	
		12		Active #2	As above	2500 lux	2000–2200 hr	16.4	7.4	55[c]	Morning > evening
Jacobsen et al. (1987)	1985–1986	16	Outpatient	Active #1	Full-spectrum	2500 lux	0600–0800 hr	15.4	5.9	61[b]	
				Active #2	As above	2500 lux	1800–2000 hr	16.8	13.5	20	Morning > evening
Avery et al. (personal communication)	1986–1987	7	Outpatient	Active	Full-spectrum	2500 lux	0700–0900 hr	22.4	16.3	27[c]	
				Control	As above	2500 lux	1200–1400 hr	21.6	13.9	36[c]	Morning = midday
Wirz-Justice et al. (in press)	1986–1987	8	Outpatient	Active #1	Full-spectrum	2500 lux	0600–0800 hr	18.4	5.0	73[b]	
				Active #2	As above	2500 lux	2000–2200 hr	19.4	11.0	43	
				Active #1	Full-spectrum	2500 lux	1 hr between 0600 and 0800 hr	17.5	6.9	62[c]	
				Active #2	As above	2500 lux	1 hr between 2130 and 2330 hr	16.0	6.7	57[c]	Morning = evening
Terman et al. (in press)	1986–1987	13	Outpatient	Active #1	Full-spectrum	2500 lux	0600–0800 hr	17.8	4.8	73[c]	
		10		Active #2	As above	As above	1900–2100 hr	17.3	6.4	63[c]	Morning = evening
Yerevanian & Grota (personal communication)	1986–1987	8	Outpatient	Active #1	Incandescent	2500 lux	0530–0730 hr	15.4	8.6	44[c]	
		10		Active #2	As above	As above	2000–2200 hr	18.4	6.7	67[c]	Morning = evening

Note. All footnotes in Table 15-1 apply here.

TABLE 15-3. Controlled Studies of Phototherapy: Duration

Authors	Years of study	n	Patient status	Active/control[a]	Spectrum	Treatment Intensity	Timing	Results Baseline	Treatment	Percentage decrease	Conclusion
Checkley et al. (in press)	1985–1986	10	Outpatient	Active	Full-spectrum	2500 lux	0700–1000 hr and 2000–2100 hr	18.5	10.3	44[b]	Bright > dim and 6 hr > 2 hr
				Control	As above	2500 lux	0700–0800 hr and 2200–2300 hr	17.8	13.2	26	
Lewy et al. (1987b)	1985–1986	19	Outpatient	Active	Full-spectrum or cool-white	2500 lux	0600–0800 hr	N.A.	N.A.[c]		2 hr = 30 min of light morning
				Control	As above	2500 lux	0600–0630 hr	N.A.	N.A.[c]		
Terman et al. (1987)	1985–1986	25	Outpatient	Active #1	Full-spectrum	2500 lux	0600–0800 hr and 1800–2000 hr	16.2	4.7	71	2 hr twice a day > 1 hr twice a day > 30 min twice a day
		6		Active #2	As above	2500 lux	0630–0730 hr and 1830–1930 hr	15.7	6.5	59	
		20		Active #3	As above	2500 lux	0730–0800 hr and 1800–1830 hr	15.5	8.7	44	
Jacobsen et al. (1987)	1985–1986	16	Outpatient	Active	Full-spectrum	2500 lux	0700–0900 hr	22.4	16.3	27	Morning = midday
				Control	As above	2500 lux	1200–1400 hr	21.6	13.9	36	
Wirz-Justice et al. (1987)	1985–1986	14	Outpatient	Active	Full-spectrum	2500 lux	0600–0800 hr	20.5	11.6	43[b]	2 hr > 30 min (allowing for ordering effect)
				Control	As above	2500 lux	0600–0630 hr	21.6	14.8	31	
Hellekson & Woodward (personal communication)	1986–1987	7	Outpatient	Active #1	Full-spectrum	2500 lux	Upon rising for 30 min	27.9	23.6	15	2 hr = 1 hr in morning but both 1 and 2 hr in morning > 30 min
				Active #2	As above	2500 lux	Upon rising for 1 hr	27.7	14.9	4.6[b]	
				Active #3	As above	2500 lux	Upon rising for 2 hr	25.1	14.7	41[b]	
Doghramji et al. (personal communication)	1986–1987	6	Outpatient	Active #1	Full-spectrum	2500 lux	1800–2200 hr	20.3	9.3	54[c]	4 hr = 2 hr in evening
				Active #2	As above	2500 lux	1800–2000 hr	21.0	9.8	53[c]	

Note. All footnotes in Table 15-1 apply here. N.A., not available.

taking into account a significant ordering effect. Hellekson and Woodward (personal communication), taking advantage of the long Alaskan winter, performed a three-way crossover among 30 min, 1 hr, and 2 hr in seven SAD patients. They found a poor response to the 30-min treatment, but marked and equally significant responses to the other two conditions. Hellekson and Woodward's patients differed from those of Lewy *et al.* and Wirz-Justice *et al.* in that they were more severely depressed.

To our knowledge, only one group has investigated the effects of different durations of light during the evening. Doghramji *et al.* (personal communication) have compared 2 hr and 4 hr of evening light treatment in a small number of subjects; they have found both treatments to be effective, with no difference in efficacy between them. An inspection of different studies where evening light was used does not show a clear distinction between those studies in which 2 hr and 4–5 hr of light were used. Although studies in which the longer duration was used (James *et al.*, 1985; Wehr *et al.*, 1987) showed robust improvements in mood, studies using only 2 hr in the evening showed a range of responses from negligible (Lewy *et al.*, 1987a; Terman *et al.*, 1987) to robust (Hellekson *et al.*, 1986; Terman *et al.*, in press; Wirz-Justice *et al.*, in press). The importance of duration in evening light treatment of SAD is unclear at this time.

Terman *et al.* (1987) evaluated the relative effects of morning plus evening light, using total durations of treatment of 1, 2, and 4 hr, and concluded that rate of improvement increased with increasing duration.

In summary, there have been too few studies of duration of light therapy for firm conclusions to be reached. However, it is highly likely that duration is an important parameter of treatment. The duration necessary to achieve an antidepressant effect probably varies from individual to individual, according to the time of day, time of year, amount of ambient light, and intensity of the light source. Preliminary evidence for this last point has been presented by Terman (Chapter 20, this volume), who found that when light intensities four times as high as the conventional bright light were used, the duration of treatment could be shortened without loss of efficacy.

Spectrum

Most investigators have used full-spectrum fluorescent light in their phototherapy studies. The initial rationale for using this light source was its strong resemblance to the spectrum of sunlight emitted from the sky. If summer sunlight is indeed responsible for reversing the symptoms of SAD, it was conceivable that there may be something special about the spectrum of the light that is critical for its antidepressant effects. Full-spectrum fluorescent lights resemble other fluorescent lights in many ways, but have more blue light and near-ultraviolet light, and less yellow and green light. It would be of interest for both practical and theoretical reasons to know what part of the visual spectrum is responsible for the antidepressant effect. Practical reasons involve the potentially toxic effects of the ultraviolet light to eyes and skin. From a theoretical point of view, it would be of interest to know what photopigments and photoreceptors are involved in the original transduction of light into nerve impulses in the retina, the presumptive neuroanatomical gateway for the antidepressant response.

A few studies with small sample sizes have compared full-spectrum fluorescent lights with fluorescent lights containing few or no ultraviolet rays (Lewy *et al.*, 1987a; Docherty, Welch, and Rosenthal, unpublished observation; see Table 15-4). In both studies, the different light sources have been equally effective. However, in the study of Docherty *et al.*, both treatments resulted in relatively small changes in the HDRS (see Table 15-4). Yerevanian *et al.* (1986) treated nine SAD patients with incandescent light and found it to be an effective antidepressant. In this study, however, there was no control condition, but rather a control population of nonseasonal depressives, who did not respond to the same light treatment. In a more recent study, Yerevanian and Grota (personal communication) again reported significant antidepressant effects with incandescent light. Although more studies of alternative light sources are clearly indicated, those already performed suggest that full-spectrum lights and the ultraviolet part of the spectrum are probably not necessary for a treatment response. However, until the efficacy and safety of alternative light sources have been properly demonstrated, clinicians should continue to use light sources and treatment regimens that have been most thoroughly evaluated.

Brainard, Sherry, Kelly, Skwerer, Schulz, Waxler, and Rosenthal (unpublished observation) have compared 2500 lux of full-spectrum light with two different-colored fluorescent lights, red and blue, controlling for intensity as measured by the number of photons per unit area. They found that the full-spectrum light had a superior antidepressant effect to the colored lights, but this difference did not reach statistical significance. However, when the strict response criteria suggested by Terman *et al.* (1987) were used—namely, a reduction in HDRS score to less than 8 and to less than 50% of baseline—the full-spectrum light was far superior to the blue and red, which yielded results similar to those of dim-light control treatments from other studies. Further studies of this kind would clearly expand our understanding of the retinal receptors involved in the antidepressant response to light.

Presentation of Light

One might consider the presentation of light to the individual in a number of ways. For example, the lighting may be direct or indirect; at eye level or above eye level; and in front of the individual or to the side. Light exposure may be to the skin or the eye, or to the macula or the periphery of the retina. These

TABLE 15-4. Controlled Studies of Phototherapy: Spectrum

Authors	Years of study	n	Patient status	Active/control[a]	Treatment Spectrum	Treatment Intensity	Treatment Timing	Results Baseline	Results Treatment	Percentage decrease	Conclusion
Docherty et al. (unpublished observation)	1986–1987	6	Outpatient	Active #1	Vitalite® full-spectrum	2500 lux	4 hr/day; mostly morning	20.6	15.6	24	Presence of ultraviolet light does not affect outcome
				Active #2	Design 50 full-spectrum; no ultraviolet	2500 lux	As above	15.0	10.4	31	
Brainard et al. (unpublished observation)	1986–1987	12	Outpatient	Active #1	Full-spectrum	2500 lux	2 hr in morning + 2 hr in evening	17.8	9.0	49	Full-spectrum superior to both red and blue
				Active #2	Blue	Photon equivalent to 2500 lux	As above	20.8	14.3	31	
				Active #3	Red	As above	As above	19.3	14.8	23	
Lewy et al. (1987a; personal communication)	1985–1987	14	Outpatient	Active #1	Vitalite®	2500 lux	0600–0800 hr	N.A.	N.A.	N.A.	Vitalite® = Cool White®
				Active #2	Cool White®	2500 lux	As above				

Note. All footnotes in Table 15-1 apply here. N.A., not available.

considerations have both theoretical and practical implications, as they concern the precise neuroanatomical pathways involved in the antidepressant response and determine the optimal way of administering light treatment.

Only one controlled study has specifically addressed this issue. Wehr *et al.* (1987) compared the effects of skin versus eye exposure to 11 SAD patients and found the eye exposure to be significantly superior. In our controlled studies of phototherapy, we have asked our subjects not to stare at the lights, but to glance at them for a few seconds every minute. We do not know whether it is even necessary for subjects to glance directly at the light periodically, or whether it would be just as effective for them to be exposed constantly to indirect light. If the latter is true, it would imply that the effects of light are mediated via the periphery of the retina and therefore, presumably, via the rods. Yerevanian *et al.* (1986) reported that indirect light was an effective antidepressant in nine SAD patients, which would appear to corroborate the importance of a peripheral retinal mechanism.

Phototherapy, as it is has been most commonly practiced, involves cumbersome and expensive light fixtures. It would be useful to find cheaper, more portable, and more convenient light sources. This is likely to be an area of future research.

Side Effects of Phototherapy

Phototherapy is generally a benign form of treatment. Most patients tolerate it well, and it is rather unusual for someone to need to discontinue treatment because of side effects. It is perhaps for this reason that there have not as yet been any systematic surveys of side effects. Those side effects about which patients most commonly complain are eyestrain, headaches, and irritability. Fatigue and nausea have also been reported by some. Eyestrain and headaches often decrease after a few days of treatment and may be minimized by decreasing duration or proximity to the light source for several days and then gradually increasing them again. When irritability occurs, it resembles the hypomanic symptoms seen in spring and summer, and generally responds well to decreasing the duration of treatment. We have not to date encountered any manic episodes among typical SAD patients, though we did observe one such episode in a patient with several atypical features, and a few other cases observed by other researchers have come to our attention. Fatigue may be related to modification of sleep–wake schedules that may be necessary to accommodate the light treatment. After a week of treatment, if it is effective, the need for sleep generally decreases, and patients frequently report less fatigue than at baseline. We have also not encountered any problems with the eyes or skin even after chronic use of light for several years. However, there is a possibility that the use of light sources emitting ultraviolet radiation could pose a hazard to the skin or the eyes with long-term use. If light sources that are free of ultraviolet radiation prove to be as effective as those with such radiation, it would seem prudent to switch over to the former lights, especially for long-term usage.

Prediction of Response to Phototherapy

There is currently no consensus as to how response to phototherapy should be defined, what instruments should be used, and what parameters should be set. Since improvements may occur as a result of placebo and nonspecific factors, it would be useful to find a definition that is not so sensitive as to include the majority of placebo responses. However, too strict a definition risks missing partial responses that surely occur in many cases. The definition reached by Terman *et al.* (in press) has proven useful in analyzing results from studies across centers. It would be worthwhile to find other strategies for discriminating between specific and placebo responses.

Regardless of how one defines and measures response to phototherapy, it would be useful to know what factors predict a favorable response. In a multiple-regression analysis of 47 patients with SAD who had been treated with at least 4 hr of bright light per day, we found that the symptoms of hypersomnia, severity of diurnal variation, reverse diurnal variation (mood and energy worst later in the day), and anxiety were all favorable predictors of response (Jacobsen *et al.*, 1986). On an anecdotal level, those relatively rare SAD patients afflicted with a severe endogenous depressive picture have appeared to respond worst to treatment.

The Use of Phototherapy for Variants of SAD

Phototherapy may be of use in clinical situations that deviate from the strict criteria for SAD that have been set down for research purposes (Rosenthal *et al.*, 1984). For example, chronically depressed patients with fall–winter exacerbations, or patients with another major psychiatric syndrome (e.g., alcohol abuse or bulimia) with or without concomitant major depression but with regular winter exacerbations, may benefit from phototherapy. A light-responsive variant of SAD has been described in children and adolescents (Rosenthal *et al.*, 1986; Sonis *et al.*, 1987). Phototherapy also appears to be helpful in mild forms of SAD without marked affective symptoms but with prominent anergy. Such cases have been termed "atypical SAD" (Rosenthal *et al.*, 1985b), "seasonal energy syndrome" (Mueller and Davies, 1986), or "subsyndromal SAD" (Kasper *et al.*, Chapter 14, this volume). The condition of midwinter insomnia has been described in Norway (Lingjaerde *et al.*, 1986) and apparently responds to bright-light exposure in the early morning. One common element in all of these conditions is that they are seasonal. Although Kripke and colleagues have performed several studies of phototherapy in nonseasonal depressives, its antidepressant efficacy in this group has not yet been convincingly demonstrated. However, it clearly warrants further study.

Conclusions

In conclusion, the efficacy of phototherapy for SAD has by now been widely demonstrated and generally acknowledged. Several factors appear to influence efficacy, including the intensity, duration, and timing of light. The initial receptors for the antidepressant response appear to be in the eye rather than the skin. No doubt there will be further formal studies of those parameters of phototherapy that are important for determining outcome.

An antidepressant effect is usually observed within a few days of starting treatment, and relapse generally occurs within a week of stopping treatment. The mechanism of action of phototherapy is not as yet known (Skwerer *et al.*, Chapter 17, this volume; Terman, Chapter 20, this volume), but certain biological effects of light have been described (Rosenthal *et al.*, 1987; Skwerer *et al.*, Chapter 17, this volume). This will surely be a fertile area for future exploration. Research into this question should be facilitated by a number of factors: Patients with SAD are an unusually homogeneous population; the rapid onset and offset of the effects of light therapy allow for random ordering of "lights-on" and "lights-off" conditions; and the absence of medication eliminates a variable that complicates other antidepressant studies.

The full scope of the therapeutic effects of phototherapy has yet to be determined. For example, it may be helpful in other seasonal syndromes affecting mood, energy, and sleep. Its value in the treatment of nonseasonal syndromes has also not as yet been explored thoroughly. A great deal has been learned about this new antidepressant modality in the 7 years since the first patient was treated. There is no reason to believe that the rapid accumulation of knowledge in this area is likely to slow down.

Acknowledgments

This chapter originally appeared in *Journal of Biological Rhythms,* Volume 3, Number 2, pp. 101–120, 1988. Reprinted by permission of The Guilford Press.

References

Borkovec, T. D., and S. D. Nau (1972) Credibility of analogue therapy rationales. J. Behav. Ther. Exp. Psychiat. *3:* 257–260.
Checkley, S., F. Winton, C. Franey, and T. Korn (in press) Antidepressant effects of light in seasonal affective disorder. In *Seasonal Affective Disorders,* C. Thompson and T. Silverstone, eds., CNS Clinical Neuroscience, London.

Esquirol, E. (1845) *Mental Maladies: Treatise on Insanity*, E. K. Hunt, ed., Lea & Blanchard, Philadelphia.

Hellekson, C. J., J. A., Kline, and N. E. Rosenthal (1986) Phototherapy for seasonal affective disorder in Alaska. Amer. J. Psychiat. *143*(8): 1035–1037.

Hoffmann, K. (1981) Photoperiodism in vertebrates. In *Handbook of Behavioral Neurobiology*, Vol. 4, J. Aschoff, ed., pp. 449–473, Plenum Press, New York.

Humphris, F. H. (1924) *Artificial Sunlight and Its Therapeutic Uses*, Humphrey Milford Oxford Press, London.

Isaacs, G., D. S. Stainer, T. E. Sensky, S. Moor, and C. Thompson (1988) Phototherapy and its mechanism of action in seasonal affective disorder. J. Affect. Dis. *14:* 13–19.

Jacobsen, F. M., D. A. Sack, T. A. Wehr, S. P. James and N. E. Rosenthal (1986) Prediction of treatment response in seasonal affective disorder. Paper presented at the 140th American Psychiatric Association Meeting, Washington, DC.

Jacobsen, F. M., T. A. Wehr, R. A. Skwerer, D. A. Sack, and N. E. Rosenthal (1987) Morning versus midday phototherapy of seasonal affective disorder. Amer. J. Psychiat. *144*(10): 1301–1305.

Jacobson, N. S., and D. H. Baucom (1977) Design and assessment of nonspecific control groups in behavior modification research. Behav. Ther. *3:* 709–719.

James, S. P., T. A. Wehr, D. A. Sack, B. L. Parry, and N. E. Rosenthal (1985) Treatment of seasonal affective disorder with light in the evening. Brit. J. Psychiat. *147:* 424–428.

Jefferson, J. W. (1986) An early study of seasonal depression. Amer. J. Psychiat. *143*(2): 261–262.

Kazdin, A. E. (1979) Therapy outcome questions requiring control of credibility and treatment-generated expectancies. Behav. Ther. *10:* 81–93.

Kazdin, A. E., and R. Krouse (1983) The impact of variations in treatment rationales on expectancies for therapeutic change. Behav. Ther. *14:* 657–671.

Kovacs, R. (1932) *Electrotherapy and the Elements of Light Therapy*, Lea & Febiger, Philadelphia.

Kripke, D. F. (1981) Photoperiodic mechanisms for depression and its treatment. In *Biological Psychiatry 1981*, C. Perris, G. Struwe, and B. Jansson, eds., pp. 1249–1252, Elsevier/North-Holland Biomedical Press, Amsterdam.

Kripke, D. F., S. C. Risch, and D. Janowsky (1983) Bright white light alleviates depression. Psychiat. Res. *10:* 105–112.

Kripke, D. F., D. J. Mullaney, J. C. Gillin, S. C. Risch, and D. S. Janowsky (1985) Phototherapy of non-seasonal depression. In *Biological Psychiatry 1985*, C. Shagass, R. C. Josiassen, W. H. Bridger, K. J. Weiss, D. Stoff, and G. M. Simpson, eds., pp. 993–995, Elsevier, New York.

Lewy, A. J., H. E. Kern, N. E. Rosenthal, and T. A. Wehr (1982) Bright artificial light treatment of a manic–depressive patient with a seasonal mood cycle. Amer. J. Psychiat. *139:* 1496–1498.

Lewy, A. J., R. L. Sack, S. Miller, and T. M. Hoban (1987a) Antidepressant and circadian phase-shifting effects of light. Science *235:* 352–354.

Lewy, A. J., R. L. Sack, C. M. Singer, and D. M. White (1987b) The phase shift hypothesis for bright light's therapeutic mechanism of action: Theoretical considerations and experimental evidence. Psychopharmacol. Bull. *23*(3): 349–353.

Lewy, A. J., T. A. Wehr, F. K. Goodwin, D. A. Newsome, and S. P. Markey (1980) Light suppresses melatonin secretion in humans. Science *210:* 1267–1269.

Lingjaerde, O., T. Bradlid, T. Hansen, and K. G. Gotestam (1986) Seasonal affective disorder and midwinter insomnia in the Far North: Studies on two related chronobiological disorders in Norway. Clin. Neuropharmacol. *9*(Suppl. 4): 187–189.

Mueller, P. S., and R. K. Davies (1986) Seasonal affective disorders: Seasonal energy syndrome? Arch. Gen. Psychiat. *43:* 188–189.

Rosenthal, N. E., C. J. Carpenter, S. P. James, B. L. Parry, S. L. B. Rogers, and T. A. Wehr

(1986) Seasonal affective disorder in children and adolescents. Amer. J. Psychiat. *143*(3): 356–358.

Rosenthal, N. E., and M. M. Heffernan (1986) Bulimia, carbohydrate craving, and depression: A central connection? In *Nutrition and the Brain,* Vol. 7, R. J. Wurtman, and J. J. Wurtman, pp. 139–165, Raven Press, New York.

Rosenthal, N. E., A. J. Lewy, T. A. Wehr, H. E. Kern, and F. K. Goodwin (1983) Seasonal cycling in a bipolar patient. Psychiat. Res. *8:* 25–31.

Rosenthal, N. E., D. A. Sack, C. J. Carpenter, B. L. Parry, W. B. Mendelson, and T. A. Wehr (1985a) Antidepressant effects of light in seasonal affective disorder. Amer. J. Psychiat. *142:* 606–608.

Rosenthal, N. E., D. A. Sack, J. C. Gillin, A. J. Lewy, F. K. Goodwin, Y. Davenport, P. S. Mueller, D. A. Newsome, and T. A. Wehr (1984) Seasonal affective disorder: A description of the syndrome and preliminary findings with light therapy. Arch. Gen. Psychiat. *41:* 72–80.

Rosenthal, N. E., D. A. Sack, S. P. James, B. L. Parry, W. B. Mendelson, L. Tamarkin, and T. A. Wehr (1985b) Seasonal affective disorder and phototherapy. Ann. NY Acad. Sci. *453:* 260–269.

Rosenthal, N. E., R. G. Skwerer, D. A. Sack, C. C. Duncan, F. M. Jacobsen, L. Tamarkin, and T. A. Wehr (1987) Biological effects of morning-plus-evening bright light treatment of seasonal affective disorder. Psychopharmacol. Bull. *23*(3): 364–369.

Rosenthal, N. E., and T. A. Wehr (1987) Seasonal affective disorders. Psychiat. Ann. *17*(10): 670–674.

Sonis, W. A., A. M. Yellin, B. D. Garfinkel, and H. H. Hoberman (1987) The antidepressant effect of light in seasonal affective disorder in childhood and adolescence. Psychopharmacol. Bull. *23*(3): 360–363.

Tamarkin, L., C. J. Baird, and O. F. X. Almeida (1985) Melatonin: A coordinating signal for mammalian reproduction? Science *227:* 714–720.

Terman, M., F. M. Quitkin, J. S. Terman, J. W. Stewart, and P. J. McGrath (1987) The timing of phototherapy: Effects on clinical response and the melatonin cycle. Psychopharmacol. Bull. *23*(3): 354–357.

Terman, M., J. S. Terman, F. M. Quitkin, P. J. McGrath, J. W. Stewart, and B. Rafferty (in press) Light therapy for seasonal affective disorder: A review of efficacy. Neuropsychopharmacology.

Thompson, C., and G. Isaacs (1988) Seasonal affective disorder—a British sample: Symptomatology in relation to mode of referral and diagnostic subtype. J. Affect. Dis. *14:* 1–11.

Wehr, T. A., F. M. Jacobsen, D. A. Sack, J. Arendt, L. Tamarkin, and N. E. Rosenthal (1986) Phototherapy of seasonal affective disorder: Time of day and suppression of melatonin are not critical for antidepressant effects. Arch. Gen. Psychiat. *43:* 870–875.

Wehr, T. A., R. G. Skwerer, F. M. Jacobsen, D. A. Sack, and N. E. Rosenthal (1987) Eye- versus skin-phototherapy of seasonal affective disorder. Amer. J. Psychiat. *144*(6): 753–757.

Wirz-Justice, A., C. Buchelli, P. Graw, P. Kielholz, H.-U. Fisch, and B. Woggan (1986) Light treatment of seasonal affective disorder in Switzerland. Acta. Psychiat. Scand. *74:* 193–204.

Wirz-Justice, A., P. Graw, C. Bucheli, A. C. Schmid, B. Gisin, A. Jochum, and W. Poldinger (in press) Seasonal affective disorder in Switzerland: A clinical perspective. In *Seasonal Affective Disorders,* C. Thompson and T. Silverstone, eds., CNS Clinical Neuroscience, London.

Wirz-Justice, A., A. C. Schmid, P. Graw, K. Krauechi, P. Kielholz, W. Poldinger, H.-U., Fisch, and C. Buddenberg (1987) Dose relationships of morning bright white light in seasonal affective disorders (SAD). Experientia *43:* 574–576.

Yerevanian, B. I., J. L. Anderson, L. J. Grota, and M. Bray (1986) Effects of bright incandescent light on seasonal and non-seasonal major depressive disorder. Psychiat. Res. *18:* 355–364.

16

Winter Depression and the Phase-Shift Hypothesis for Bright Light's Therapeutic Effects: History, Theory, and Experimental Evidence

Alfred J. Lewy, Robert L. Sack, Clifford M. Singer, David M. White, and Tana M. Hoban

In both diurnal and nocturnal animals, melatonin production is quiescent during the day (Quay, 1964; Lynch and Ralph, 1970). Production of melatonin by the pineal gland begins after dusk and ends at or before dawn (Goldman and Darrow, 1983). Exposure to light during the night causes abrupt cessation of melatonin production (Minneman et al., 1974). For many years, it was generally accepted that human melatonin production was not affected by light (Vaughan et al., 1976; Jimerson et al., 1977; Lynch et al., 1977; Arendt, 1978; Weitzman et al., 1978; Wetterberg, 1978; Akerstedt et al., 1979; Vaughan et al., 1979; Perlow et al., 1980). However, a few years ago we showed that human melatonin production can be suppressed by light, providing it is sufficiently intense (Lewy et al., 1980).

This finding had at least two potentially important implications. First, humans had biological rhythms that were cued to sunlight and that would not be confounded by the use of ordinary indoor light (which is not sufficiently bright to be effective). Two, bright artificial light could be used to experimentally, and perhaps therapeutically, manipulate these rhythms.

In 1980, we first tested these implications in a patient who regularly became depressed each year as daylength shortened (Lewy et al., 1982). We

Alfred J. Lewy, Robert L. Sack, Clifford M. Singer, David M. White, and Tana M. Hoban. Departments of Psychiatry, Ophthalmology, and Pharmacology, Sleep and Mood Disorders Laboratory, Oregon Health Sciences University, Portland, Oregon. (Current address for David M. White: Psychology Laboratory, Harbt view Medical Center, Seattle, Washington. Current address for Tana M. Hoban: Department of Animal Physiology, University of California at Davis, Davis, California.)

hypothesized that he had a seasonal rhythm that, like the rhythms of other animals, was regulated by photoperiod. We further hypothesized that by exposing him to bright artificial light between 0600 and 0900 hr and between 1600 and 1900 hr, we could bring him out of his winter depression, similar to what normally happened to him in the spring. After 4 days of exposure to 2000-lux light scheduled so as to extend daylength, our patient began to emerge from his depression.

Since then, many such patients have been similarly treated; dim-light exposure at these times is not effective (Rosenthal *et al.*, 1984, 1985). Investigators most experienced in treating this disorder agree that extending daylength is not critical (Wehr *et al.*, 1986). We have proposed that the antidepressant effect of light in this and other disorders depends on correcting abnormally phased circadian rhythms—the phase-shift hypothesis (Lewy *et al.*, 1983, 1984).

The Phase Response Curve

Our hypothesis is grounded in animal studies (DeCoursey, 1964; Pittendrigh and Daan, 1976; Binkley *et al.*, 1981) that have demonstrated the common features of phase response curves (PRCs). In constant dark (free-running) conditions, a short pulse of light will shift the phase of circadian rhythms, depending on when the light is scheduled. Exposure to light during the subjective day has relatively little effect. Exposure to light during the subjective night causes a phase delay (shift to a later time) if it occurs during the first part of the night, and causes a phase advance (shift to an earlier time) if it occurs during the later part of the night. In the middle of the night, there is an inflection point that separates phase delays from phase advances. For many PRCs, the closer to the middle of the night the light pulse occurs, the greater the magnitude of the phase shift.

Based on these animal studies, we hypothesized that humans had similarly shaped PRCs, except that humans would require bright light for these responses (Lewy *et al.*, 1983). We first tested this hypothesis when we advanced "dusk" for a week and then delayed "dawn" for a week, holding sleep time constant in four healthy volunteers (Lewy *et al.*, 1984, 1985a). At the end of the first week, there was an advance in the timing of the circadian melatonin production rhythm. At the end of the second week, there was a delay in the melatonin rhythm. Thus, the first of our implications seemed to be supported: Contrary to what was previously thought, human circadian rhthyms can be shifted by the light–dark cycle independent of the sleep–wake rhythm. Our study further suggested that humans have PRCs that are essentially similar in shape to those of other animals. Other studies in our own lab (Lewy *et al.*, 1985b, 1987a; Sack *et al.*, 1986), and also by Wever *et al.* (1983), Eastman (1986), and Czeisler *et al.* (1986), have substantiated this conclusion.

"Phase-Typing" Chronobiological
Sleep and Mood Disorders

In applying the phase-shifting properties of appropriately timed bright-light exposure to the treatment of certain types of sleep and mood disorders, we have
built upon the work of Papousek (1975), Kripke *et al.* (1978), and Wehr *et al.*
(1979), who proposed a "phase-advance hypothesis" for affective disorders.
They thought that depression could result from circadian rhythms that were
abnormally advanced (shifted earlier) with respect to real time and to sleep.
We (Lewy *et al.*, 1984, 1985b) have expanded this thinking by proposing "phase
typing." This is, we think that there is also a phase-delay type of depression.
According to our phase-shift hypothesis, endogenous circadian rhythms in
chronobiological mood disorders can be either abnormally phase-advanced or
abnormally phase-delayed with respect to real time and to sleep. (We have also
hypothesized that in chronobiological *sleep* disorders, all circadian rhythms—
including sleep—are phase-shifted to the same extent, or sleep is shifted more
than the other circadian rhythms; see Lewy *et al.*, 1987b.) Not every sleep or
mood disorder will have a chronobiological component. However, appropriately timed bright light should correct whatever phase disturbance is present,
and should be therapeutic to the extent that this component accounts for the
pathology.

Winter Depression: Light Treatment Studies

In the area of light therapy, the most light-responsive and most frequently studied disorder identified to date is winter depression, or "seasonal affective disorder" (SAD) as it is sometimes called. As mentioned above, we originally
conceptualized this disorder as relating primarily to seasonal rhythms, and consequently treated this disorder with bright-light exposure to extend dawn and
dusk (Lewy *et al.*, 1982). We and others (Wehr *et al.*, 1986) no longer think
that extending both dawn and dusk is critical. We now think that this disorder
relates more to circadian rhythms than to seasonal rhythms (Lewy *et al.*, 1987a).
Specifically, we have hypothesized that most winter depressives have abnormally delayed circadian rhythms (Lewy *et al.*, 1984). Because most humans
(having intrinsic periods greater than 24 hr; Wever, 1979) should cue relatively
more to morning light than to evening light, human circadian rhythms should
delay in the winter relative to the summer (Lewy, 1983). We think that the
delay of endogenous circadian rhythms relative to sleep results in winter
depressions in some individuals. Therefore, we have hypothesized that these
patients should preferentially respond to morning bright light compared to bright-
light exposure in the evening (particularly late evening), because the morning

light should provide a corrective phase advance, whereas the evening light may exacerbate the phase delay.

In the winter of 1985, we tested these hypotheses in eight patients and seven healthy volunteers (Lewy et al., 1987a). Subjects participated in a 4-week protocol. Throughout the study, they were permitted to sleep only between 2200 and 0600 hr. This sleep schedule, which involved a phase advance in sleep time of 1–2 hr for most subjects, was chosen in order to accommodate light exposure between 0600 and 0800 hr. The first week was a baseline week. Subjects avoided bright light between 1700 and 0800 hr. The second week, patients were randomly assigned to a week of morning bright light (2500 lux; 0600–0800 hr) or a week of evening bright light (2000–2200 hr) and were crossed over during the third week. The fourth week, subjects were exposed to bright light at both times. Patients were informed that they might have an antidepressant response on any week of the study.

During continuous dim light (so as not to suppress the onset of melatonin production), blood was drawn every 30 min between 1800 and 2300 hr on the first day of the study and on the last day of each week. Plasma melatonin levels were measured using the gas chromatographic–negative chemical ionization mass spectrometric technique of Lewy and Markey (1978). The Hamilton Depression Rating Scale (21 items; Hamilton, 1960, 1969) was administered on each blood-drawing night by a rater who was blind to the light exposure schedule for weeks 2–4.

The behavioral results are shown in Figure 16-1. Hamilton ratings were significantly decreased after the week of morning light compared to the baseline week ($p \leqslant 0.004$)[1] and compared to the week of evening light ($p \leqslant 0.045$). There were no other significant differences. Hamilton ratings after the week of evening light (15.2 ± 1.8 [SEM]) were higher than those after the week of morning light (6.6 ± 1.8) and were similar to those of the baseline week (15.4 ± 2.3). Ratings after the week of combined morning plus evening light (8.6 ± 2.7) were not significantly different from those of the other weeks, which we have interpreted to mean that light exposures scheduled at these times counteract each other to some extent. Of the eight patients, only one responded better to evening light than to morning light. All four patients who were first treated with morning light became more depressed when switched to evening light.

Morning light advanced the melatonin onsets and evening light delayed them (Fig. 16-2). Patients appeared to advance significantly ($p \leqslant 0.01$) more in response to morning light compared to control subjects, which is consistent with phase-delayed circadian rhythms in the patients compared to the controls: Compared to the PRCs of the controls, perhaps the patients' PRCs were either phase-delayed or had more area under the advance portion.

With regard to the behavioral data, the amount of placebo effect was presumably the same for both the morning and evening light exposures, since

---

1. Unless otherwise specified, all probabilities were calculated from either two-tailed paired t tests or Student's t tests, depending on whether or not individuals were compared to themselves.

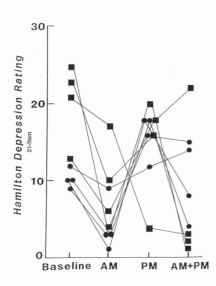

FIGURE 16-1. Individual and average 21-item Hamilton depression ratings *(±SEM)* for eight patients with winter depression for each of the 4 weeks of the first morning versus evening light study. Half of the patients were exposed to morning light on week 2 and to evening light on week 3 (filled circles). Half of the patients were exposed to evening light on week 2 and to morning light on week 3 (filled squares). An analysis of variance for repeated measures indicated a significant ($p \leqslant 0.026$) difference between treatments. Only the paired t tests comparing the week of morning (AM) light and the baseline week ($p \leqslant 0.004$) and comparing the week of morning light and the week of evening (PM) light ($p \leqslant 0.045$) were significant. Average depression ratings ($\pm SEM$) for the seven normal control subjects were 3.0 ± 0.9 at baseline, 2.4 ± 0.3 (morning light), 6.1 ± 1.6 (evening light), and 4.3 ± 0.9 (morning plus evening light, or AM + PM). Adapted from Lewy *et al.* (1987a). Copyright 1987 by the American Association for the Advancement of Science. Used by permission.

these exposures were of equal duration. As assessed by posttreatment questionnaires, patients did not think that morning light would be more antidepressant than evening light, but they did think that light of greater duration would be.

These data suggest that the antidepressant response of these patients was related to a corrective phase advance in their circadian rhythms. Furthermore, compared to the melatonin onsets of the normal control subjects, those of the patients were significantly delayed on the first day of the study ($p \leqslant 0.02$) and after a week of baseline conditions ($p \leqslant 0.05$). We conclude, therefore, that most winter-depressive patients should first be treated with morning light. (However, we recommend that patients who are suspected of having abnormally phase-advanced circadian rhythms should first be treated with evening bright light.)

During the winter of 1987, nine patients[2] were compared to five normal controls in a similar study, except that evening light was scheduled 1 hr earlier (1900–2100 hr) and there was no week of combined morning plus evening light. Similar to our 1985 study, Hamilton depression ratings after the week of morning light (4.5 ± 1.1) were statistically significantly lower compared to those after the baseline week (14.0 ± 1.1; $p \leqslant 0.01$) and compared to those after the week of evening light (7.8 ± 1.4; $p \leqslant 0.05$). Also similar to our 1985 study, patients who were first treated with morning light became more depressed when switched to evening light.

2. Melatonin onset data were obtained on only eight patients.

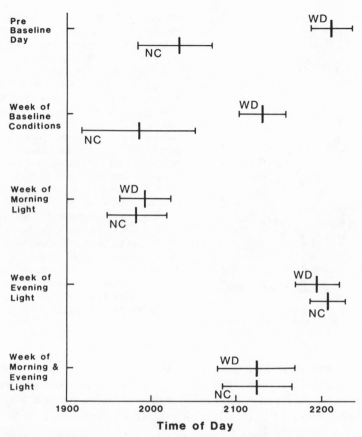

FIGURE 16-2. Average melatonin onset times (±*SEM*) for normal controls (NC) and patients with winter depression (WD) (*n*'s = 6 to 8, except *n* = 4 for the prebaseline melatonin values) in the first study of morning versus evening light. An analysis of variance with repeated measures indicated a significant difference between treatments for both patients ($p \leq 0.001$) and normal controls ($p \leq 0.009$). Significant paired *t* tests for the patients were baseline versus morning light ($p \leq 0.001$), baseline versus evening light ($p \leq 0.012$), and morning versus evening light ($p \leq 0.001$). Significant paired *t* tests for the normal controls were baseline versus morning plus evening light ($p \leq 0.039$), morning versus evening light ($p \leq 0.004$), and morning versus morning plus evening light ($p \leq 0.003$). Melatonin onset times of the patients were delayed compared to those of the normal controls at both prebaseline ($p \leq 0.02$) and baseline ($p \leq 0.05$) (Student's *t* test). From Lewy *et al.* (1987a). Copyright 1987 by the American Association for the Advancement of Science. Reprinted by permission.

Although in this study there was only a trend ($p \leq 0.1$) for a phase delay in the baseline melatonin onsets of the patients compared to the controls, combined data from the 1985 and 1987 studies demonstrated a significant difference ($p \leq 0.01$) in this measure. Similar to our 1985 study, patients advanced significantly ($p \leq 0.05$) more than did controls in response to morning light. Indeed, combined data from these two studies demonstrated that patients advanced significantly ($p \leq 0.001$) more in response to morning light and delayed significantly ($p \leq 0.02$) less in response to evening light, compared to controls. These data are consistent with phase-delayed circadian rhythms in the patients compared to the controls.

In our 1987 study, Hamilton depression ratings were statistically significantly lower after the week of evening light compared to the baseline week ($p \leq 0.05$, Student's t test). How do we explain this? We had previously hypothesized that there may be two antidepressant effects of light (Lewy and Sack, 1986). One effect seems to be related to correcting abnormally phased circadian rhythms. A second effect may be an "energizing effect." (Whether or not there is a specific physiological substrate for this effect or whether it is a nonspecific placebo effect remains to be determined. If and when an energizing effect can be operationally distinguished from a nonspecific placebo effect, we will stop using these two terms interchangeably.) When we scheduled evening light between 2000 and 2200 hr in our 1985 study, its phase-delay effect might have been of sufficient magnitude to completely neutralize the energizing effect. According to our hypothesized PRC, the earlier the evening light is scheduled, the less its phase-delay effect will be, and therefore the less the opposition to its energizing effect will be. This might have been the case when evening light was scheduled between 1900 and 2100 hr.

In the winter of 1986, we compared phase-advancing and antidepressant effects of different light schedules in 14 winter-depressive patients and 5 normal control subjects. Specifically, we compared 2 hr of morning light exposure (0600–0800 hr) to 0.5 hr (0600–0630 hr) in the treatment of winter depression, in a study that was otherwise similar in design to our studies of morning versus evening light. However, in this study, in order to increase the effectiveness of our raters' being blind even to the baseline weeks, we randomly assigned half of the subjects to a baseline week and half of the subjects to a light treatment week for the first week of a 5-week protocol. These two groups were then alternated between light treatment weeks and baseline weeks for the first 4 weeks of the study, one group beginning with a baseline week and the other with a light treatment week. Subjects were randomly assigned and crossed over, so that half were exposed to 2 hr of morning light during their first light treatment week and half were exposed to 0.5 hr of morning light. During the fifth week of both protocols, subjects were exposed to the same duration of light they received during their first light treatment week, in order to test for an order effect.

Overall, in the 14 patients, we found no statistically significant difference in depression ratings after 0.5 hr of light (8.4 ± 1.6) compared to ratings after 2 hr of light (6.6 ± 1.1); both sets of ratings were significantly ($p \leqslant 0.001$) lower than those of the first day of the study (18.3 ± 1.6). However, there was a clear relationship between the average Hamilton rating and the average time of the melatonin onset for the prebaseline day and the four light conditions of the study (first baseline week, second baseline week, week of 2 hr morning light, and week of 0.5 hr morning light): The earlier the melatonin onset, the lower the depression rating (Fig. 16-3).

The melatonin onsets of this group of patients were not significantly delayed, compared to those for this group of control subjects. However, the n was very small in this study for such a comparison, because only half of the subjects could be used for this comparison (those for whom the first week of the protocol was a baseline week). Although pooling baseline melatonin onset data for all three winter depression studies failed to show more than a trend ($p \leqslant 0.1$) for a phase delay in the patients compared to controls, combined data from all three studies demonstrated that patients significantly ($p \leqslant 0.001$) ad-

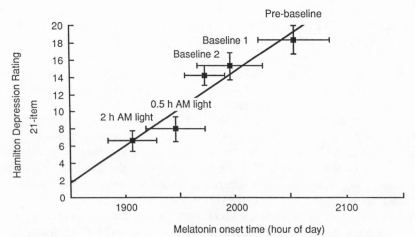

FIGURE 16-3. Correlation between melatonin onset and Hamilton depression ratings in the study of 0.5 hr versus 2 hr of light. Patients received either 0.5 hr or 2 hr morning light immediately upon awakening at 0600 hr or awoke into dim light during the baseline weeks in a randomized crossover design. The average melatonin onsets are plotted on the abscissa, and the average Hamilton depression ratings are plotted on the ordinate. The five plotted points are as follows (from right to left): first day of the study, first baseline week, second baseline week, week of 0.5 hr of morning light, and week of 2 hr of morning light. A linear regression, fitted for the five data points obtained for each of the 12 subjects for whom we had complete data, had a significant correlation coefficient ($r = 0.95$, $df = 4$, $p \leqslant 0.01$). When the slopes were calculated for each subject individually, the mean was also significantly different from zero ($p \leqslant 0.006$, $df = 11$, Student's t test). These data indicate that clinical improvement is highly correlated with a phase advance in the melatonin onset.

vanced more in response to morning light compared to controls. This latter finding suggests that winter-depressive patients may be distinguished from controls more reliably by their phase-shift responses to light rather than by their baseline melatonin onsets. Indeed, as mentioned earlier, combined data from the 1985 and 1987 morning versus evening light studies demonstrated that patients delayed significantly ($p \leq 0.02$) less than controls in response to evening light. These findings are consistent with phase-delayed circadian rhythms in the patients compared to controls.

There also seemed to be an order effect, in that bright light was significantly more antidepressant at the end of the study than at the beginning of the study ($p \leq 0.003$). The order effect was significant ($p \leq 0.01$) for the group that began the protocol with a light treatment week, but was not significant for the group that began the protocol with a baseline week. Of the various possible explanations for such an order effect, we hypothesized that 1 week of morning light is not sufficient to reduce the phase angle between sleep and the other circadian rhythms, particularly if sleep is also being advanced that week. Thus, this finding is consistent with our hypothesis that the phase angle between sleep and the other circadian rhythms is pathogenic for winter depression.

Winter Depression: An Internal Phase Angle Disturbance

It has been hypothesized by others (Papousek, 1975; Kripke *et al.*, 1978; Wehr *et al.*, 1979) that in major depression sleep is not as advanced as the other circadian rhythms. We have proposed that sleep is not as delayed as the other circadian rhythms in winter depression (a phase-delay mood disorder). In our studies of morning versus evening light (as well as in half of the patients in our 0.5-hr vs. 2-hr morning light study), sleep had to be advanced in order to accommodate the morning light exposure schedule. If sleep is advanced at the initiation of morning light exposure, then an antidepressant response may not be observed for several days.

To test our phase angle hypothesis further, we did two pilot studies. In these studies, we delayed, and then advanced, sleep relative to a 2-hr pulse of bright light. Only after several days of waking up into bright light was a sustained antidepressant response observed.

In our morning light exposure studies, sleep was held constant. Thus, we reduced the phase angle between sleep and the other circadian rhythms that are cued to light. In our shifting-sleep studies, we reduced this phase angle by delaying sleep, which also may prove to be an effective antidepressant intervention. Consequently, for optimal antidepressent effects of bright light, we recommend that sleep be held constant after it achieves a normal phase position. If sleep time has to be advanced to accommodate morning light exposure, the antidepressant response may be retarded.

Two Antidepressant Effects of Light: Phase Shifting and "Energizing"

Morning light appears to be antidepressant in winter depression because it is correcting abnormally phase-delayed circadian rhythms. In addition, an as yet incompletely identified energizing affect (which may partly or wholly be a non-specific placebo effect) may be a component in the antidepressant response. To be conservative, we must assume that the energizing effect is present to some extent whenever bright light is scheduled. According to our hypothesis, the energizing effect is additive to the antidepressant (phase-advancing) effect of morning light. When light is scheduled so that no phase advance occurs, there is only the energizing effect. When light is scheduled sufficiently late, the energizing effect opposes the phase-delaying effect that we have hypothesized to be depressant; the net effect on depression ratings depends on the relative strengths of these two effects.

In addition to evening light's being antidepressant through an energizing effect, evening light may appear to be antidepressant by another mechanism. If patients become sufficiently aroused by evening light so that they delay their sleep time, and if light is scheduled so that there is relatively little delay in their other circadian rhythms, the patients could be reducing the phase angle between sleep and the other circadian rhythms in the same way as in our shifting-sleep studies, particularly if patients are not instructed to avoid bright sunlight exposure in the morning. Consequently, we recommend that exposure to bright light around twilight be controlled.

We have reviewed the literature elsewhere (Lewy and Sack, 1986). In the studies we reviewed at that time and in all subsequent studies to date, we have not found results that cannot be explained by our phase-shift hypothesis. Indeed, for the general population of winter-depressive patients, no study has been done to date that has convincingly demonstrated equal or superior efficacy of a light exposure schedule that does not include morning light exposure. In the studies that claim (some) antidepressant efficacy for evening light, sleep was not held constant and/or patients were not kept in dim light around twilight (Hellekson et al., 1985; James et al., 1985); furthermore, depression ratings did not decline to those of normal controls. In the Bethesda group's "skeleton photoperiod" study (Wehr et al., 1986), in which sleep was held constant and light exposure was controlled, depression ratings also did not decline to what we consider to be in the normal range (in our experience, the Hamilton depression ratings of normal controls are always less than 5). This was because the evening light of the longer photoperiod probably caused a phase delay that partially counteracted the phase advance of the morning light.

In a study in which morning light was shown to be no more effective than light scheduled at noon (Jacobsen et al., 1987), many of these patients did not receive morning light until an hour or more after they had awakened (F. Jacobsen, personal communication). According to our hypothesized PRC, morning light may not have a maximal antidepressant effect if it is not scheduled immediately upon awakening. Furthermore, midmorning or early afternoon light may be antidepressant, in that light scheduled at these times may still be advancing circadian rhythms (we do not know the boundaries of the "dead zone," or even whether one exists for the human PRC). Moreover, the PRCs of winter-depressive patients may be delayed, as we have already suggested. Consequently, we think that it is critical to measure circadian phase position in studies that attempt to determine the mechanism of action for the therapeutic effects of bright-light exposure.

The Dim-Light Melatonin Onset as a Marker for Circadian Phase Position

Measurement of melatonin production is useful for marking circadian phase position. If melatonin levels are obtained under continuous dim light after 1700 or 1800 hr, there do not appear to be any "masking effects." Although cortisol levels and core temperature are also good markers, their amplitude is masked by stress and locomotor activity, respectively. Measurement of melatonin levels is particularly important when the phase angle between sleep and the other circadian rhythms is crucial.

Our melatonin findings have to a considerable extent been replicated by Terman et al. (1987). Although they did not measure melatonin levels in normal subjects, they did find that the melatonin onsets of their winter-depressive patients were quite late (around midnight). Under their light treatment schedule (0600–0800 hr and 1800–2000 hr), the melatonin onsets advanced 2–3 hr. As we would predict from our data, light exposure at 1800–2000 hr would not be expected to cause much, if any, phase delay in winter-depressive patients, whereas light exposure at 0600–0800 hr would be expected to cause a significant phase advance. We should also note that Avery (1987) has replicated our behavioral findings when comparing morning versus evening light. Furthermore, he observed a phase advance in the temperature circadian rhythm after bright-light exposure in the morning.

When testing hypotheses other than the phase-shift hypothesis, measurement of circadian phase position is still important to insure that a light exposure schedule does not shift circadian phase position. For example, Rosenthal et al. (1987) have recently reported on several possible physiological mechanisms of action: effects of light on the immune system, plasma norepinephrine levels, and P300 component of the visual evoked potential. Among other variables, they measured melatonin levels to determine circadian phase position. They chose a light exposure shedule (0630–0900 hr and 1800–2100 hr) that they thought would not cause a phase (advance) shift, so as to avoid confounding their study. Unfortunately, melatonin levels following light treatment were obtained during bright-light exposure, so it was not possible to determine whether the exposure schedule (which was antidepressant) caused a phase shift in the melatonin onset. However, our data and data from Terman's group suggest that this light exposure schedule probably causes a phase advance in the melatonin onset (providing the melatonin levels are obtained under the appropriate dim-light conditions).

Although it appears that the melatonin circadian rhythm may be a very useful marker for phase position, the relative phase shifts after morning compared to after evening bright light may be even more useful for marking phase position. We have indicated that patients show larger phase advances to morning light and smaller delays to evening light than controls. These findings are consistent with phase-delayed circadian rhythms in patients compared to controls and suggest that winter-depressive patients may be distinguished from controls more reliably by their phase-shift responses to light than by their baseline melatonin onsets.

By obtaining melatonin onsets at baseline, after a week of morning light and after a week of evening light, one can calculate an A-D differential. (The A-D differential is the advance response to morning light minus the delay response to evening light; a relatively greater—i.e., more positive—A-D differential is consistent with relatively more phase-delayed circadian rhythms.) In our two studies of morning versus evening light (in which A-D differentials could be calculated), patients had significantly ($p \leq 0.001$) greater (more positive) A-D differentials than normal controls. We also found that our one patient who responded best to evening light and worst to morning light in our 1985 study (Lewy $et\ al.$, 1987a) did not have the most phase-advanced baseline melatonin onset of the patients. However, of all of the patients, she had the only negative A-D differential (i.e., showed larger delays than advances to our light pulses).

We have also found in our two studies of morning versus evening light that the baseline melatonin onset predicts the A-D differential (Fig. 16-4), which is consistent with the hypothesis that the baseline melatonin onset marks the phase of its PRC. However, as mentioned above, it seems that the A-D differential may be better able to distinguish patients from controls than the baseline melatonin onset. Perhaps this is because the baseline melatonin onset does not take into account interindividual differences in pineal physiology, such as the biochemical lag time between the onset of sympathetic stimulation of the pineal and the appearance of melatonin in the plasma (Lewy, 1983). Consequently, it may turn out that the A-D differential may be a useful way to "phase-type" patients.

Conclusion

Obviously, not every patient's sleep or mood disorder has a chronobiological component. But to the extent that a phase angle abnormality is a component,

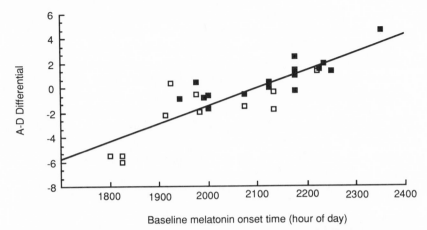

Baseline melatonin onset time (hour of day)

FIGURE 16-4. Data from the two studies of morning versus evening light were combined. The A-D differential was calculated for both patients ($n = 16$) and controls ($n = 11$). The A-D differential is calculated by subtracting the evening light delay shift relative to baseline from the morning light advance shift relative to baseline. The A-D differential may possibly indicate that phase of the PRC, in that a greater (more positive) A-D differential would be consistent with a relatively phase-advanced PRC and a lesser (more negative) A-D differential would be consistent with a relatively phase-delayed PRC. The good correlation shown here ($r = 0.86$, $df = 25$, $p \leq 0.0001$) indicates that the baseline melatonin onset (dim-light melatonin onset) predicts the A-D differential, as if the baseline melatonin onset were marking the phase of its PRC.

the disorder should respond to appropriately timed bright-light exposure. It may turn out that many patients are not abnormally advanced or delayed with respect to a normal control population. However, the phase marker may be ipsative. (We are indebted to Richard I. Shader, MD, for suggesting this term.) In other words, winter depressives may be phase-delayed when depressed compared to when they are euthymic, without being delayed in comparison to a normal control population.

When doing studies on the mechanism of action for bright light's therapeutic effects, we think that the following points should be considered:

1. In order to avoid a Type II error, at least one treatment group should manifest a maximally effective response for comparison. Studies that show equal efficacy among treatment groups are problematic, especially if neither group is completely treated. A complete remission is possible with most winter-depressive patients, who usually experience this in the spring or summer. Although a complete remission may take longer than 1 week in some cases, one week is usually sufficient for Hamilton ratings to decline to within the range of normal subjects.

2. In order to minimize nonspecific placebo responses, it is optimal to achieve the maximum antidepressant effect using the minimum amount of light

exposure. This is also important when trying to minimize potential complications and when trying to maximize compliance.

3. After sleep phase normalizes, sleep time should be held constant.

4. Bright light around twilight should be controlled.

5. If sleep time has to be advanced to accommodate morning light exposure, 1 week may not be sufficient to obtain the antidepressant response.

6. Too much light exposure can overly phase-shift some individuals.

We hope that the guidelines that have resulted from the clinical and physiological responses of winter-depressive patients to appropriately timed bright-light exposure will be of use in the design and interpretation of future studies. These guidelines may also be useful in helping clinicians to optimize treatment efficacy, maximize compliance, and minimize unwanted side effects.

Acknowledgments

We are grateful for the technical assistance of Greg Clark, Lisa Weix, Danna Jennings, and Mary McReynolds. We thank Carol Simonton and Mary Blood for assistance in manuscript preparation. The research was supported by National Institutes of Health Grant Nos. MH-40161 and MH-00703 to Alfred J. Lewy.

This chapter originally appeared in *Journal of Biological Rhythms,* Volume 3, Number 2, pp. 121–134, 1988. Reprinted by permission of The Guilford Press.

References

Akerstedt, T., J. E. Froberg, Y. Friberg, and L. Wetterberg (1979) Melatonin secretion, body temperature and subjective arousal during 64 hours of sleep deprivation. Psychoneuroendocrinology *4:* 219–225.

Arendt, J. (1978) Melatonin assays in body fluids. J. Neural Trans. (Suppl.) *13:* 265–278.

Avery, D. (1987) Morning versus evening bright light treatment of winter depression: Effects on circadian temperature phase. Paper presented at the annual meeting of the West Coast College of Biological Psychiatry, La Jolla, CA, March 28.

Binkley, S., G. Muller, and T. Hernandez (1981) Circadian rhythm in pineal N-acetyltransferase activity: Phase-shifting by light pulses (1). J. Neurochem. *37:* 798–800.

Czeisler, C. A., J. S. Allan, S. H. Strogatz, J. M. Ronda, R. Sanchez, C. D. Rios, W. O. Freitag, G. S. Richardson, and R. E. Kronauer (1986) Bright light resets the human circadian pacemaker independent of the timing of the sleep–wake cycle. Science *233:* 667–671.

DeCoursey, P. J. (1964) Function of a light rhythm in hamsters. J. Cell. Comp. Physiol. *63:* 189–196.

Eastman, C. I. (1986) Bright light improves the entrainment of the circadian rhythm of body temperature to a 26-hr. Sleep–wake schedule in humans. Sleep Res. *15:* 271.

Goldman, B., and J. Darrow (1983) The pineal gland and mammalian photoperiodism. Neuroendocrinology *37:* 386–396.

Hamilton, M. (1960) A rating scale for depression. J. Neurol. Neurosurg. Psychiat. *26:* 56–62.

Hamilton, M. (1969) Standardized assessments and recording of depressive symptoms. Psychiat. Neurol. Neurochir. *72:* 201–205.

Hellekson, C. J., J. A. Kline, and N. E. Rosenthal (1985) Phototherapy for seasonal affective disorder in Alaska. Amer. J. Psychiat. *143:* 1035–1037.

Jacobsen, F. M., T. A. Wehr, R. A. Skwerer, D. A. Sack, and N. E. Rosenthal (1987) Morning versus midday phototherapy of seasonal affective disorder. Amer. J. Psychiat. *144:* 1301–1305.

James, S. P., T. A. Wehr, D. A. Sack, B. L. Parry, and N. E. Rosenthal (1985) Treatment of seasonal affective disorder with evening light. Brit. J. Psychiat. *147:* 424–428.

Jimerson, D. C., H. J. Lynch, R. M. Post, R. J. Wurtman, and W. E. Bunney (1977) Urinary melatonin rhythms during sleep deprivation in depressed patients and normals. Life Sci. *20:* 1501–1508.

Kripke, D. F., D. T. Mullaney, M. L. Atkinson, and S. Wolf (1978) Circadian rhythm disorders in manic–depressives. Biol. Psychiat. *13:* 335–351.

Lewy, A. J. (1983) Biochemistry and regulation of mammalian melatonin production. In *The Pineal Gland,* R. M. Relkin, ed., pp. 77–128, Elsevier/North-Holland, New York.

Lewy, A. J., H. E. Kern, N. E. Rosenthal, and T. A. Wehr (1982) Bright artificial light treatment of a manic–depressive patient with a seasonal mood cycle. Amer. J. Psychiat. *139:* 1496–1498.

Lewy, A. J., and S. M. Markey (1978) Analysis of melatonin in human plasma by gas chromatography negative chemical ionization mass spectrometry. Science *201:* 741–743.

Lewy, A. J., and R. L. Sack (1986) Minireview: Light therapy and psychiatry. Proc. Soc. Exp. Biol. Med. *183:* 11–18.

Lewy, A. J., R. L. Sack, R. H. Fredrickson, M. Reaves, D. D. Denney, and D. R. Zielske (1983) The use of bright light in the treatment of chronobiologic sleep and mood disorders: The phase-responsive curve. Psychopharmacol. Bull. *19:* 523–525.

Lewy, A. J., R. L. Sack, L. S. Miller, and T. M. Hoban (1987a) Antidepressant and circadian phase shifting effects of light. Science *235:* 352–354.

Lewy, A. J., R. L. Sack, and C. M. Singer (1984) Assessment and treatment of chronobiologic disorders using plasma melatonin levels and bright light exposure: The clock-gate model and the phase response curve. Psychopharmacol. Bull. *20:* 561–565.

Lewy, A. J., R. L. Sack, and C. M. Singer (1985a) Immediate and delayed effects of bright light on human melatonin production: Shifting "dawn" and "dusk" shifts the dim light melatonin onset (DLMO). Ann. NY Acad. Sci. *453:* 253–259.

Lewy, A. J., R. L. Sack, and C. M. Singer (1985b) Treating phase typed chronobiologic sleep and mood disorders using appropriately timed bright artificial light. Psychopharmacol. Bull. *21:* 368–372.

Lewy, A. J., R. L. Sack, C. M. Singer, and D. M. White (1987b) The phase shift hypothesis for bright light's therapeutic mechanism of action: Theoretical considerations and experimental evidence. Psychopharmacol. Bull. *23:* 349–353.

Lewy, A. J., T. A. Wehr, F. K. Goodwin, D. A. Newsome, and S. P. Markey (1980) Light suppresses melatonin secretion in humans. Science *210:* 1267–1269.

Lynch, H. J., D. C. Jimerson, Y. Ozaki, R. M. Post, W. E. Bunney, and R. J. Wurtman (1977) Entrainment of rhythmic melatonin secretion in man to a 12-hour phase shift in the light dark cycle. Life Sci. *23:* 1557–2564.

Lynch, H. J., and C. L. Ralph (1970) Diurnal variation in pineal melatonin and its nonrelationship to HIOMT activity. Amer. Zool. *10:* 300.

Minneman, K. P., H. J. Lynch, and R. J. Wurtman (1974) Relationship between environmental light intensity and retina-mediated suppression of rat pineal serotin-*N*-acetyltransferase. Life Sci. *15:* 1791–1796.

Papousek, M. (1975) Chronobiological aspects of cyclothymia. Fortschr. Neurol. Psychiat. *43:* 381–440.

Perlow, M. J., S. M. Reppert, L. Tamarkin, R. J. Wyatt, and D. C. Klein (1980) Photic regulation of the melatonin rhythm: Monkey and man are not the same. Brain Res. *182:* 211–216.

Pittendrigh, C. S., and S. Daan (1976) A functional analysis of circadian pacemakers in nocturnal rodents. IV. Entrainment: Pacemaker as clock. J. Comp. Physiol. A *106:* 291–331.

Quay, W. F. (1964) Circadian and estrous rhythms in pineal melatonin and 5-OH indole-3-acetic acid. Proc. Soc. Exp. Biol. Med. *115:* 710–713.

Rosenthal, N. E., D. A. Sack, J. C. Gillin, A. J. Lewy, F. K. Goodwin, Y. Davenport, P. S. Mueller, D. A. Newsome, and T. A. Wehr (1984) Seasonal affective disorder: A description of the syndrome and preliminary findings with light therapy. Arch. Gen. Psychiat. *41:* 72–80.

Rosenthal, N. E., D. A. Sack, S. P. James, B. L. Parry, W. B. Mendelson, L. Tamarkin, and T. A. Wehr (1985) Seasonal affective disorder and phototherapy. Ann. NY Acad. Sci. *453:* 260–269.

Rosenthal, N. E., R. G. Skwerer, D. A. Sack, C. C. Duncan, F. Jacobsen, L. Tamarkin, and T. A. Wehr (1987) Biological effects of morning plus evening light treatment of seasonal affective disorder. Psychopharmcol. Bull. *23*(3): 364–369.

Sack, R. L., A. J. Lewy, L. S. Miller, and C. M. Singer (1986) Effects of morning versus evening bright light exposure on REM latency. Biol. Psychiat. *21:* 410–413.

Terman, M., F. M. Quitkin, J. S. Terman, J. Stewart, and P. McGrath (1987) The timing of phototherapy: Effects on clinical response and the melatonin cycle. Psychopharmacol. Bull. *23*(3): 354–357.

Vaughan, G. M., R. Bell, and A. De La Pena (1979) Nocturnal plasma melatonin in humans: Episodic pattern and influence of light. Neurosci. Lett. *14:* 81–84.

Vaughan, G. M., R. W. Pelman, S. F. Pang, L. L. Loughlin, K. M. Wilson, K. L. Sandock, M. K. Vaughan, S. H. Koslow, and R. J. Reiter (1976) Nocturnal elevation of plasma melatonin and urinary 5-hydroxy-indoleacetic acid: Attempts at modification by brief changes in environmental lighting and sleep and by autonomic drugs. J. Clin. Endocrinol. Metabol. *42:* 752–754.

Wehr, T. A., F. M. Jacobsen, D. A. Sack, J. Arendt, L. Tamarkin, and N. E. Rosenthal (1986) Phototherapy of seasonal affective disorder: Time of day and suppression of melatonin are not critical for antidepressant effects. Arch. Gen. Psychiat. *43:* 870–875.

Wehr, T. A., A. Wirz-Justice, F. K. Goodwin, W. Duncan, and J. C. Gillin (1979) Phase advance of the circadian sleep–wake cycle as an antidepressant. Science *206:* 710–713.

Weitzman, E. D., U. Weinberg, R. D'Eletto, H. J. Lynch, R. J. Wurtman, C. A. Czeisler, and S. Erlich (1978) Studies of the 24 hour rhythm of melatonin in man. J. Neural Trans. (Suppl.) *13:* 325–377.

Wetterberg, L. (1978) Melatonin in humans: Physiological and clinical studies. J. Neural Trans. (Suppl.) *13:* 289–310.

Wever, R. A. (1979) *The Circadian Systems of Man,* Springer-Verlag, New York.

Wever, R. A., J. Polasek, and C. Wildgruber (1983) Bright light affects human circadian rhythms. Pflügers Arch. *396:* 85–87.

17

Neurobiology of Seasonal Affective Disorder and Phototherapy

Robert G. Skwerer, Frederick M. Jacobsen, Connie C. Duncan,
Karen A. Kelly, David A. Sack, Lawrence Tamarkin, Paul A. Gaist,
Siegfried Kasper, and Norman E. Rosenthal

The investigation of the biochemical basis of seasonal affective disorder (SAD) and light therapy is a new field. As with any body of knowledge undergoing rapid expansion, the data, though interesting, are incomplete and at times even conflicting. In this chapter, we attempt to organize and synthesize the information currently available into a coherent and understandable form.

The syndrome of SAD has been described elsewhere (Rosenthal *et al.*, 1984; Terman, Chapter 20, this volume). Features of SAD include marked changes in energy level, appetite, activity, sleep, weight, and mood. Its response to bright light has been extensively documented (Rosenthal *et al.*, 1984, Chapter 15, this volume). However, the biological basis for these diverse psychological and biological changes remains unclear, as does the mechanism of the antidepressant effects of light. Theories have been advanced to explain the dramatic effects of phototherapy, most notably the "melatonin hypothesis" of Rosenthal *et al.* (1986) and the "phase-shift hypothesis" of Lewy *et al.* (1987a, b, Chapter 16, this volume). Neither of these theories has been fully supported by experimental testing, as is discussed below. Alternative approaches to the mechanisms of SAD and phototherapy are also discussed. Table 17-1 contains a summary of the biological findings in SAD.

Chronobiology

The treatment of SAD patients with bright light in the past decade was influenced by the finding of Lewy *et al.* (1980) that nocturnal melatonin secretion

Robert G. Skwerer, Karen A. Kelly, David A. Sack, Lawrence Tamarkin, Paul A. Gaist, Siegfried Kasper, and Norman E. Rosenthal. Clinical Psychobiology Branch, National Institute of Mental Health, Bethesda, Maryland.

Frederick M. Jacobsen. Clinical Psychobiology Branch and Laboratory of Clinical Science, National Institute of Mental Health, Bethesda, Maryland.

Connie C. Duncan. Laboratory of Psychology and Psychopathology, National Institute of Mental Health, Bethesda, Maryland.

TABLE 17-1. Summary of Biological Findings in Seasonal Affective Disorder (SAD)

Authors	Study	Subjects (n)	Conclusion
	Catecholamines		
Skwerer, Jacobsen, Sack, and Rosenthal (unpublished observation)	Resting plasma norepinephrine (NE)	SAD depressed (14) SAD treated (13) Controls untreated (11)	• Significant negative correlation between baseline Hamilton Depression Rating Scale (HDRS) and NE level • Significant positive correlation between change (increase) in NE after light treatment and decrease in HDRS
Rosenthal, Rudorfer, Skwerer, Jacobsen, and Wehr (unpublished observation)	Cerebrospinal fluid (CSF) 3-methoxy-4-hydroxyphenylglycol (MHPG)	SAD treated (10) SAD untreated (10) Controls untreated (9)	• No difference between groups or conditions
Rosenthal, Skwerer, Jacobsen, Kasper, Duncan, Sack, and Wehr (unpublished observation)	24-hr plasma melatonin profile	SAD depressed (15) SAD treated (15) Controls untreated (11)	• Low in depressed SAD patients • Light had no effect on profile
	Serotonin and dopamine		
Rosenthal, Skwerer, Jacobsen, Duncan, Kasper, Sack, and Wehr (unpublished observation)	24-hr plasma prolactin profile	SAD depressed (15) SAD treated (15) Controls untreated (10)	• Lower at night • Light had no effect on profile
Rosenthal, Rudorfer, Skwerer, Jacobsen, Sack, and Wehr (unpublished observation)	CSF 5-hydroxyindoleacetic acid (5-HIAA)	SAD depressed (10) SAD treated (10) Controls untreated (9)	• No difference between groups or conditions
Rosenthal et al. (1987)	Administered carbohydrate-rich meals	SAD depressed (16) Controls untreated (16)	• Decreased sedation in patients • Increased sedation in controls
Jacobsen et al. (1987c)	Serum prolactin and cortisol	SAD depressed (10) Controls untreated (10)	• Prolactin significantly higher in patients in the morning • Cortisol significantly increased and prolactin significantly decreased in both groups
Jacobsen et al. (1987b)	5-hydroxytryptophan(5-HTP)-stimulated serum prolactin and cortisol (placebo-controlled) Serum prolactin and cortisol	SAD depressed (10) SAD treated (10)	• No difference between groups or conditions for unstimulated prolactin, and significantly higher in treated SAD than controls
	m-Chlorophenylpiperazine(m-CPP)-stimulated serum	Controls untreated (11) Controls treated (11)	• Stimulated prolactin and cortisol significantly greater in patients both before and after treatment
Depue et al. (Chapter 13, this volume)	Serum prolactin	SAD depressed (8) SAD treated (8) Controls untreated (16)	• Significantly lower in patients in the afternoon; treatment had no effect

Reference	Measure	Subjects (n)	Results
Buckwald, McGrath, and Resnick (personal communication, 1987)	L-Tryptophan	SAD depressed (13) SAD treated (13)	• L-Tryptophan significantly superior to placebo
Rosenthal, Rudorfer, Skwerer, Jacobsen, and Wehr (unpublished observation)	CSF homovanillic acid (HVA)	SAD depressed (10) SAD treated (10) Controls (9)	• No difference between groups or conditions
Rosenthal, Skwerer, Kasper, Jacobsen, Gaist, Hardin, Schultz, Sack, and Wehr (unpublished observation)	24-hr plasma melatonin profile	SAD depressed (15) SAD treated (15) Controls untreated (10)	• Low in depressed SAD patients • Light had no effect
Lewy et al. (1987a,b)	Plasma melatonin	SAD depressed (8) SAD treated (8) Controls untreated (7) SAD depressed (11) SAD treated (11)	• Delayed melatonin onset in depressed patients compared to controls • Light treatment in the morning advanced the timing of melatonin secretion in proportion to antidepressant effects
		Cortisol	
Rosenthal, Skwerer, Kasper, Jacobsen, Gaist, Hardin, Schultz, Sack, and Wehr (unpublished observation)	24-hr plasma cortisol profile	SAD depressed (15) SAD treated (15) Controls untreated (9)	• No difference in depressed patients compared to controls • No effect of light on profile
Jacobsen et al. (1987b)	m-CPP serum cortisol	SAD depressed (10) SAD treated (10) Controls untreated (11) Controls treated (11)	• Stimulated rise in cortisol significantly greater in patients than controls in both conditions
James et al. (1986)	Dexamethasone suppression test (DST)	SAD depressed (20) Controls untreated (7)	• Patients suppressed normally
		Thyroid hormones	
Rosenthal, Skwerer, Jacobsen, Duncan, Sack, Kasper, and Wehr (unpublished observation)	24-hr thyroid-stimulating hormone (TSH) profile	SAD depressed (7) SAD treated (7)	• Light treatment significantly suppressed TSH levels
Rosenthal et al. (1984)	TSH response to thyrotropin-releasing hormone (TRH)	SAD depressed in the winter (8) SAD remitted in the summer (8)	• No differences between conditions
		Metabolic rate	
Rosenthal (unpublished observation)	Resting metabolic rate (RMR)	SAD depressed (10) SAD treated (10) Controls untreated (9) Controls treated (9)	• Trend for patients to have higher baseline values • RMR decreased significantly in treated patients • Light treatment had no effect on controls

(continued)

TABLE 17-1. (*Continued*)

Authors	Study	Subjects (*n*)	Conclusion
	Electroencephalographic		
Duncan, Deldin, Skwerer, Jacobsen, Wehr, and Rosenthal (unpublished observation)	P300 component of event-related potential (ERP)	SAD depressed (9) SAD treated (9)	• Light treatment enhanced the P300 in the visual mode in direct proportion to its antidepressant effect
Rosenthal, Sack, Mendelson, James, Jacobsen, and Wehr (unpublished observation)	Sleep	SAD depressed in the winter (15) SAD remitted in the summer (15) Controls in the winter (9) Controls in the summer (9)	• Patients had increased sleep length in the winter • Patients had increased delta sleep in the winter • Patients had higher rapid-eye-movement (REM) density than controls in both seasons
Rosenthal, Skwerer, Jacobsen, Kasper, Duncan, Sack, and Wehr (unpublished observation)	Sleep	SAD depressed (17) SAD treated (17) Controls untreated (7) Controls treated (7)	• Light treatment increased delta sleep and sleep efficiency in patients but decreased these in controls • REM time, REM percentage, and movement time were greater in patients than controls • No differences in REM latency between groups
	Immune function		
Skwerer, Tamarkin, Jacobsen, Sack, and Rosenthal (unpublished observation)	Mitogen stimulation with phytohemagglutinin (PHA) and Concanavalin A (Con A)	SAD depressed (18) SAD treated (18) Controls untreated in the winter (18) Controls treated through their eyes only in the winter (7) Controls untreated in the summer (9) Controls treated in the summer (9)	• Patients' stimulation greater than controls' for PHA and Con A in the winter and for Con A in the summer • Light treatment of patients reduced mitogen stimulation to a level comparable to controls • Light treatment of controls in the summer and winter increased mitogen stimulation; this appeared to be mediated through the eyes

314

in humans could be suppressed by bright environmental light but not by ordinary room light. When it later emerged that the antidepressant effects of light also occurred after exposure to bright light but not to ordinary room light (Rosenthal *et al.*, 1984, 1985; James *et al.*, 1985, 1986), these coupled observations served as a basis for the melatonin hypothesis — the theory that bright-light treatment exerts its antidepressant effects by modifying the pattern of melatonin secretion, which is responsible for the symptoms of SAD (Rosenthal *et al.*, 1986).

Lewy *et al.* (1987a, b) observed that the onset of melatonin secretion is a useful marker of the timing of circadian rhythms. They showed that the timing of bright-light exposure was capable of influencing the timing of the onset of melatonin secretion under dim-light conditions. This finding led these researchers to hypothesize that an abnormality of circadian rhythms is the basis for the seasonal changes in mood and behavior found in SAD patients and that light therapy exerts its antidepressant effects by correcting these abnormal rhythms.

Both of these theories of the mechanism of phototherapy depend upon the importance of its timing in determining antidepressant effects. All animal studies in which melatonin secretion has been manipulated as an important intervening variable in mediating seasonal rhythms have depended upon light exposure occurring during the subjective night (Tamarkin *et al.*, 1985). However, available evidence suggests that the antidepressant effects of light in SAD do not depend on interruption of the dark phase (Wehr *et al.*, 1986; Jacobsen *et al.*, 1987d; Isaacs *et al.*, 1988). The melatonin hypothesis has been explored in several studies. Wehr *et al.* (1986) showed that SAD patients responded equally well when treated with bright light administered in patterns that mimicked the ''skeleton'' of short and long photoperiods (Hoffmann, 1981). This was true regardless of whether these pulses extended the normal photoperiod or suppressed melatonin secretion. Oral administration of melatonin reversed the antidepressant effects of light on the atypical symptoms (overeating, carbohydrate craving, and oversleeping), but not the typical symptoms of depression in SAD patients (Rosenthal *et al.*, 1986). The beta-adrenergic blocking agent atenolol, which has been shown to suppress melatonin secretion, administered to 19 patients with SAD, was no more effective as an antidepressant than placebo for the population as a whole, However, a subgroup of three patients appeared to respond very well to the drug for three consecutive winters, suggesting that melatonin may play an important role in certain individuals with SAD (Rosenthal *et al.*, 1988).

Several studies of nonseasonal depressives have shown abnormally low nocturnal melatonin secretion (Wetterberg *et al.*, 1979; Lewy, 1984; Brown *et al.*, 1985). We have recently shown a similar profile of low plasma melatonin ($p < 0.0001$, t test) in 15 SAD patients (mean $\pm$ *SEM:* 45.5 $\pm$ 4.3 pg/ml) compared with 11 normal controls (71.1 $\pm$ 4.3 pg/ml), studied under conditions of ordinary room light (Rosenthal, Skwerer, Jacobsen, Kasper, Duncan, Sack, and Wehr, unpublished observation). Bright-light treatment had no effect on the mean nocturnal secretion or on the timing of its onset or offset. There was no correlation between severity of depression and baseline plasma melatonin levels, but a high correlation for mean nocturnal melatonin secretion within individuals across conditions ($r = 0.79$, $p < 0.001$). This is supportive of the findings of Dietzel et al. (1986).

Lewy et al. (1987a) have reported delayed onset of melatonin secretion in dim-light conditions in SAD patients. They have found that light treatment in the morning advances the timing of onset of secretion in direct proportion to its antidepressant effect in most SAD patients. More recently, they have suggested that the relative degree to which SAD patients show phase advances to morning light and phase delays to evening light may be a meaningful biological marker and may predict treatment response (Lewy et al., 1987b).

The importance of timing of light in determining outcome in phototherapy remains controversial. Some studies have shown bright-light treatment in the morning to be superior to treatment at other times of day (Avery et al., personal communication, 1987; Lewy et al., 1987a, b; Terman et al., 1987). Other studies have shown no difference between light treatment in the morning and at other times of day (Hellekson et al., 1986; Wehr et al., 1986; Wirz-Justice et al., 1986; Jacobsen et al., 1987d; Yerevanian and Grota, personal communication, 1987; Isaacs et al., 1988; Terman, Chapter 20, this volume). Whereas a proportion of SAD patients may respond best to light treatment in the morning, for many the timing of treatment does not appear to be critical.

Terman and colleagues (see Terman, Chapter 20, this volume) undertook a meta-analysis of all treatment studies performed through the winter of 1986–1987 and showed that, if stringent response criteria were applied, some patients from almost all studies appear to respond only to morning light. Although several patients also appear to respond to evening light when the same criteria are used, it is unusual to find a patient who responds only to evening light. Although it is conceivable that, in those patients who respond selectively to morning light, the mechanism of response is the correction of abnormal circadian phases (as suggested by Lewy et al., 1987a, b), it is also possible that increased therapeutic effects of morning light change a diurnal rhythm based on factors other than phase correction of abnormal entrainment.

Sleep

Patients with SAD frequently complain of sleep abnormalities during the winter months (Rosenthal et al., 1984). Sleep is generally increased in length but disrupted, and patients often report that they do not feel well rested during the daytime. A minority of patients complain of reduced sleep length. Rosenthal et al. (1984) confirmed that sleep length was increased in the winter compared to the summer in nine patients with SAD by means of electroencephalographically (EEG) recorded sleep. In addition, the delta sleep length was decreased in the winter. Scoring techniques used in all sleep studies are as described by Rechschaffen and Kales (1968).

We recently increased the total number of SAD subjects to 15 and studied 9 normal volunteers in summer and winter (Rosenthal, Sack, Mendelson, James, Jacobsen, and Wehr, unpublished observation). SAD patients showed increased sleep length (mean ± SEM: 409.7 ± 23.5 min) in winter compared to summer (348.4 ± 10.3 min) (group × season interaction: $F = 4.6$, $p < 0.05$), but no such increase occurred in normal controls. Delta sleep measurements differed significantly across seasons between patients and normals, with patients showing decreased delta sleep in the winter (36.5 ± 6.0) compared to the summer (47.5 ± 8.0) and normal subjects showing the opposite effect (group × season interaction: $F = 4.2$, $p = 0.05$). Patients showed significantly higher rapid eye movement (REM) densities in both summer (1.7 ± 0.1) and winter (1.9 ± 0.2) than did normals, whose corresponding values were 1.1 ± 0.1 and 1.3 ± 0.1 ($F = 8.6$, $p < 0.008$ for both seasons).

A study of diurnal variation of sleepiness, mood, energy, and anxiety was performed in 12 patients with SAD and 12 controls during the summer (Jacobsen et al., 1987a). Subjects completed self-rating scales every 2 hr from 0700 hr to 2300 hr for 3 consecutive days. Patients scored significantly higher in sleepiness (on the Stanford Sleepiness Scale; $p < 0.001$), depression ($p < 0.005$), fatigue ($p = 0.001$), and anxiety ($p < 0.005$) than controls in the winter, but failed to show these differences from controls in the summer. Both groups showed similar diurnal variations in mood, energy, and sleepiness in winter and summer. These results were interpreted as providing evidence against a circadian rhythm phase disturbance in SAD.

We evaluated the effects of bright-light treatment (2500 lux, 2.5 hr in both the morning and evening) in 17 SAD patients and 7 normals. Significant interactions between subject group and light condition were found for sleep efficiency, delta sleep, and delta percentage ($F = 4.6$, $p = 0.05$; $F = 4.4$, $p < 0.05$; and $F = 4.3$, $p = 0.05$, for these three variables, respectively) (Rosenthal, Skwerer, Jacobsen, Kasper, Duncan, Sack, and Wehr, unpublished observation). Delta sleep (52.9 ± 9.8 min), delta percentage (13.8% ± 2.5%), and sleep efficiency (89.2 ± 1.4) were increased in patients after light treatment compared to untreated values (35.1 ± 7.1 min, 9.2% ± 1.9%, and 84.7 ± 2.5, for delta sleep, delta percentage, and sleep efficiency, respectively). The opposite was true in control subjects.

REM time (95.5 ± 6.5 min) and REM percentage (26.1% ± 2.2%) were significantly greater in patients than in normals (67.3 ± 9.3 min and 16.9% ± 2.2%, for REM time and REM percentage, respectively) during the ordinary light condition ($p < 0.03$ for both variables). Light treatment had no effect on either variable in patients but increased both REM time and REM percentage in normals, thereby eradicating patient–normal differences. There were no differences in REM latency in depressed patients compared with normals. These findings do not support the hypothesis that circadian rhythms are abnormal in SAD, since the timing of REM sleep onset has been taken as a marker of circadian phase position (Gillin *et al.,* 1984).

Vogel (1975) has suggested that alterations in REM sleep induced by antidepressant drugs are causally related to their antidepressant properties. Most heterocyclic antidepressants and monoamine oxidase inhibitors suppress REM sleep. We found no evidence that light had this effect in depressed patients with SAD.

None of the sleep abnormalities described in patients with SAD in the winter is specific for this group of depressives. Increased REM density and decreased delta sleep have been observed in nonseasonally depressed subjects (Gillin *et al.,* 1984). It is interesting that the shortened REM latency, which is one of the most frequently noted abnormalities in the sleep profiles of depressives (Gillin *et al.,* 1984), is not present in SAD. However, shortened REM latency may be absent in certain mildly to moderately depressed nonseasonal patients (Gillin *et al.,* 1984; Wehr and Sack, 1988). Thus, its absence in SAD patients may be a function of severity of depression, which may be less marked in the SAD patient population than in nonseasonal depressives, or it may be associated with an "atypical" symptom pattern (overeating, oversleeping, weight gain). Thase, Himmelhoch, Mallinger, Jarrett, and Kupfer (unpublished observation) have reported similarly normal REM latency measurements in atypical depressive patients recruited without regard to their seasonality. The difference in REM latency between SAD patients and nonseasonal depressives may also reflect a fundamental difference in underlying pathological processes.

The differences in delta sleep between patients and normals across the seasons, and in both delta sleep and sleep efficiency under different lighting conditions, suggest that bright light may have different biological effects on these two populations. Winter sleep abnormalities appear to be normalized by bright light in patients with SAD. The effects of light on sleep may prove to be a useful marker for SAD.

Event-Related Brain Potentials

Patients with SAD frequently complain of difficulty in attending, concentrating, and processing information. The event-related brain potential (ERP) has been established as a dynamic measure of brain function, and the amplitude of the P300 component of the ERP reflects the amount of attentional or processing resources committed to a stimulus (Duncan-Johnson and Donchin, 1982). Subjects were tested with auditory and visual versions of three reaction time tasks (Duncan, Deldin, Skwerer, Jacobsen, Wehr, and Rosenthal, unpublished observation). ERPs were measured in response to visual and auditory stimuli in nine SAD patients both off and on light treatment (2.5 hr of light in both morning and evening). Testing was done within 1 hr after the end of the morning light treatment. Phototherapy enhanced the P300 in the visual but not the auditory modality, in direct proportion to its antidepressant effects ($r = -0.85$, $p < 0.001$). These results suggest that the response to phototherapy in SAD patients may involve an improvement in the processing of visually guided information. The change in amplitude of the P300 appears to be an early, objective, semiquantitative measure of antidepressant response to light therapy. As such, it may prove to be a valuable predictor of treatment response.

Neurotransmitters and Neurohormones

A variety of neurotransmitters and neurohormones have been the focus of investigations of the pathogenesis and pathophysiology of affective disorders (reviewed by Sachar, 1981). Even though there may be no direct causal association between neurotransmitter abnormalities and depression, such biochemical abnormalities or differences may be markers of disease state or of vulnerability to illness (trait markers).

Catecholamines

Plasma norepinephrine (NE) measurements have been advocated as a useful reflection of central noradrenergic functioning by some researchers (Schildkraut, 1978; Roy *et al.*, 1984). We found (Skwerer, Jacobsen, Sack, and Rosenthal, unpublished observation) that resting plasma NE levels in depressed patients with SAD were inversely related to their level of depression ($n = 14$; $r = -0.75$; $p < 0.05$) as measured by the Hamilton Depression Rating Scale (HDRS; Hamilton, 1967). After at least 9 days of phototherapy (2500 lux; 2.5 hr in both morning and evening), resting NE levels increased in direct proportion to improvement in mood ($n = 13$; $r = 0.59$; $p < 0.05$). Although NE levels were not low in untreated SAD patients compared with normals, it is conceivable that levels in SAD patients in the winter are suboptimal for those individuals. The increase in plasma NE following light treatment may be causally related to, or a result of, the antidepressant response.

Baseline plasma NE studies have yielded mixed results in populations of nonseasonally depressed patients. In general, lower plasma NE levels have been reported in bipolar depressives, whereas elevated levels have been reported in unipolar subjects (Potter *et al.*, 1987). The population of SAD patients we studied was predominantly bipolar.

Cerebrospinal fluid (CSF) 3-methoxy-4-hydroxyphenylglycol (MHPG), a major metabolite of NE, was measured in depressed and light-treated patients with SAD ($n = 10$) and in untreated normal control subjects ($n = 9$) (Rosenthal, Rudorfer, Skwerer, Jacobsen, and Wehr, unpublished observation). No significant differences between groups or conditions were observed.

Serotonin

Abnormalities in serotonergic functioning have been postulated to be part of the pathophysiology of nonseasonal depression (reviewed by Sachar, 1981). There are additional reasons for considering the potential importance of such abnormalities in the etiology of SAD and the mechanism of action of phototherapy. Seasonal variations in several aspects of serotonin metabolism in normal human subjects have been documented in numerous studies (Lacoste and Wirz-Justice, Chapter 12, this volume). For example, Carlsson *et al.* (1980) found significantly reduced serotonin concentrations in the hypothalamus during the winter compared to the summer in human postmortem specimens. The prominent symptoms of carbohydrate craving and overeating of carbohydrates seen in SAD may constitute behavioral attempts to regulate brain serotonin concentration, since dietary carbohydrates have been shown to increase brain serotonin in experimental animals under certain circumstances (Fernstrom and Wurtman, 1972), and similar effects on brain serotonin may occur in humans as well (Wurtman and Wurtman, 1988). However, this theory has recently been called into question (Fernstrom, 1987), and its validity has yet to be demonstrated.

CSF levels of 5-hydroxyindoleacetic acid (5-HIAA), a major serotonin metabolite, did not differ between patients and normals, nor did the levels of this metabolite differ between on-light and off-light conditions (Rosenthal, Rudorfer, Skwerer, Jacobsen, Sack, and Wehr, unpublished observation).

Low plasma levels of prolactin in SAD patients found by Rosenthal *et al.* (see "Dopamine," below) and Depue *et al.* (Chapter 13, this volume) are compatible with decreased serotonin function in SAD, since serotonin is one of the stimulatory neurotransmitters involved in the regulation of prolactin secretion (Reichlin, 1981). In contrast to this, Jacobsen *et al.* (1987c) have reported high plasma prolactin in the morning in SAD. However, the results of this study are called into question by a subsequent study in which baseline prolactin levels, drawn at the same time of day, were no different from those of controls (Jacobsen *et al.*, 1987b).

Several paradigms that challenge the serotonin system in SAD have been explored. Jacobsen *et al.* (1987c) administered the serotonin precursor 5-hydroxytrytophan (5-HTP; 200 mg orally) to 10 depressed patients with SAD and 10 matched controls in a double-blind placebo-controlled crossover study. No differences between patients and controls were found in the 5-HTP-stimulated secretion of either cortisol or prolactin. This result contrasts with that of Meltzer *et al.* (1984), who have reported greater 5-HTP-stimulated cortisol response in patients with major affective disorder than in controls.

A subsequent study used a more selective serotonergic drug, the serotonin postsynaptic agonist m-chlorophenylpiperazine (m-CPP), in 10 depressed patients with SAD and 11 matched controls (Jacobsen *et al.*, 1987b). Subjects were given infusions of m-CPP (0.1 mg/kg) before and after exposure to a week of phototherapy and rated on numerous physiological and subjective measures. Both patients and controls showed robust stimulation of cortisol and prolactin in response to intravenous m-CPP. This serotonergically mediated hormonal rise was significantly greater over time in patients than in controls for both cortisol ($F = 4.06$, $p = 0.0005$) and prolactin ($F = 5.59$, $p < 0.005$), an effect that occurred both before and after light treatment.

Prior to treatment with light, depressed SAD patients also differed markedly from normals with regard to feelings experienced following infusion of m-CPP. For example, depressed SAD patients reported dramatic feelings of euphoria following infusion of m-CPP, whereas controls did not report euphoria (visual analogue scale) following m-CPP (mean m-CPP-stimulated peak-minus-baseline rating for "euphoria": delta max for SAD patients = 27.0 vs. 2.2 for controls; $t = 2.28$, $p < 0.05$). The patients also reported being significantly *less* "slowed down" following the infusion of m-CPP than controls (slowed-down delta max for SAD patients = 0.3 vs. 1.6 for controls; $t = -2.58$, $p < 0.05$). This latter difference is reminiscent of the different responses to high-carbohydrate meals seen in patients with SAD and in normals (Rosenthal *et al.*, 1987). In that study, depressed SAD patients reported decreased drowsiness in the hour following the carbohydrate-rich meal, whereas normal subjects felt drowsier. Following treatment with phototherapy and associated resolution of depressive symptoms, the patient's subjective responses to m-CPP tended to normalize.

Taken together, the difference between SAD patients and controls in serotonergically mediated hormonal and subjective responses imply that SAD patients may have an underlying dysregulation in brain serotonergic function. Moreover, the normalization of serotonergically stimulated subjective responses in SAD patients following effective phototherapy suggests that exposure to bright light or change in mood state (or both) results in changes in serotonergic function in SAD patients.

Apart from the above-mentioned psychobiological studies of serotonergic functioning in SAD, at least one research group has attempted to manipulate serotonergic function in the treatment of SAD. Buckwald and colleagues (Buckwald, McGrath, and Resnick, personal communication, 1987) have used dietary L-tryptophan in 13 SAD patients and reported it to be somewhat effective (mean $\pm$ *SEM* improvement on the 17-item HDRS was 6.9 ± 1.92 and 1.3 ± 1.78 for treatment with L-tryptophan compared to placebo, respectively; $F = 5.31$, $p < 0.04$).

Although there are some inconsistencies, serotonergic function seems to be altered in SAD, and this dysregulation seems to be normalized by both phototherapeutic intervention and by an agent that is known to affect serotonergic functioning.

Dopamine

Dopamine in the hypothalamic–hypophyseal portal circulation results in tonic inhibition of prolactin secretion (Gudelsky, 1981). Thus prolactin secretion may be a useful measure of dopaminergic function and has been studied in nonseasonal affective disorder (Jimerson and Post, 1984).

Depue *et al.* (Chapter 13, this volume) found decreased basal plasma prolactin levels in the afternoon in depressed SAD patients compared with normals. Light treatment had no effect on prolactin levels. On the other hand, Jacobsen *et al.*, in two separate studies (1987b, 1987c), showed an increase or no difference in basal prolactin secretion in SAD patients compared with controls. Both Jacobsen *et al.* (1987c) and Depue *et al.* (Chapter 13, this volume) have interpreted their observed prolactin abnormalities as evidence of dopamine deficiency, even though the prolactin findings were in opposite directions.

We found low nocturnal plasma prolactin values in 15 SAD patients compared with 10 normal controls (mean $\pm$ *SEM*: 8.1 ± 0.3 and 11.7 ± 0.8 ng/ml for patients and controls, respectively; $p < 0.0001$, t test) (Rosenthal, Skwerer, Jacobsen, Duncan, Kasper, Sack, and Wehr, unpublished observation). Neither we nor Depue *et al.* found any effect of light treatment on prolactin levels in patients. We also found that the levels of the dopamine metabolite homovanillic acid (HVA) were no different in the CSF of depressed patients and 9 controls. Light therapy (2500 lux, 2.5 hr in both morning and evening) had no effect on HVA levels in patients (Rosenthal, Rudorfer, Skwerer, Jacobsen, and Wehr, unpublished observation).

Thus, most of the evidence points to decreased prolactin secretion in SAD in the winter. Whether this reduction in prolactin secretion in SAD is of any causal significance or simply an epiphenomenon of the condition is unknown.

Hypothalamic–Pituitary–Adrenal Axis

Abnormalities of the hypothalamic–pituitary–adrenal (HPA) axis have been particularly well studied in nonseasonal affective disorder (reviewed by Gold *et al.*, 1987; Potter *et al.*, 1987). It is not surprising that this axis has been a focus of interest in SAD as well. James *et al.* (1986) performed the dexamethasone suppression test (DST) on 20 depressed SAD patients and 7 normal control subjects. Nineteen of the patients and all controls showed normal suppression of serum cortisol (less than 5.0 μg/dl). We measured plasma cortisol over a 24-hr period and found no differences in either mean plasma cortisol levels or timing of the cortisol rhythm in depressed SAD patients ($n = 15$) compared with controls ($n = 11$) (mean $\pm$ *SEM*: 6.96 ± 0.25 μg/dl and 6.82 ± 0.25 μg/dl for patients and controls, respectively) (Rosenthal, Skwerer, Jacobsen, Duncan, Kasper, Sack, and Wehr, unpublished observation). Light treatment of patients (2.5 hr in both the morning and evening) had no effect on the timing of cortisol secretion.

As noted above, infusion of the specific serotonin agonist m-CPP was followed by a significantly greater rise in cortisol in the patients than in controls in both untreated and light-treated conditions (Jacobsen *et al.*, 1987b). This finding may be due to increased sensitivity of the pituitary adrenocorticotrophic hormone (ACTH) receptors in patients with SAD, which would be consistent with normal DST suppression. Despite normal plasma cortisol levels, it is conceivable that SAD patients may be functionally hypocortisolemic, leading to an increased activity of ACTH receptors. This hypothesis could be tested by stimulating the pituitary with corticotropin-releasing hormone, such as has been done in nonseasonal depression (Gold et al., 1987), and measuring the resulting ACTH and cortisol responses.

Thyroid

Thyroid-stimulating hormone (TSH) levels were significantly lower in seven SAD patients in both untreated (mean $\pm$ SEM: 1.9 ± 0.2 μU/liter, $p < 0.01$) and light-treated (2.0 ± 0.2 μU/liter, $p = 0.01$) (2500 lux, 2.5 hr in both the morning and evening) states compared to five untreated control subjects (2.7 ± 0.2 μU/liter) (Rosenthal, Skwerer, Jacobsen, Duncan, Sack, Kasper, and Wehr, unpublished observation).

Studies of normal subjects (reviewed by Lacoste and Wirz-Justice, Chapter 12, this volume) have shown TSH, T_3, and T_4 to be elevated in the winter compared with the summer. Rosenthal et al. (1984) found no seasonal differences in the TSH response to thyrotropin-releasing hormone (TRH) (500 μg i.v.) in seven depressed patients with SAD in the winter compared with the same remitted patients in the summer (all stimulated values exceeded 5 IU/dl). In normal subjects there is usually a winter increase in the TSH response to TRH (Lacoste and Wirz-Justice, Chapter 12, this volume). Eliciting such seasonal variation in the TSH response appears to depend on the dose of TRH administered (Lacoste and Wirz-Justice, Chapter 12, this volume). The common dose of 500 μg shows no differences in TSH response, but the lower dose of 200 μg reveals an increased response in the winter. Presumably the 500-μg dose stimulated normal subjects maximally both in summer and winter. It is conceivable that no difference in response to TRH was noted in SAD patients across the seasons by Rosenthal et al. (1984) because the dose of the TRH used was too high. Alternatively, it is possible that the normal summer–winter differences seen in the pituitary response to TRH are decreased in SAD patients.

Metabolism

Since many of the winter symptoms of SAD could be construed as having an energy-conserving function (Rosenthal et al., 1987) — for example, overeating, oversleeping, and weight gain — we hypothesized that resting metabolic rate (RMR) might also be reduced. The weight loss seen in some SAD patients treated with bright light might be a result of decreased appetite, which is often reported by patients, or, perhaps, a consequence of increased RMR. In order to test this hypothesis, we compared RMR in 10 SAD patients and 9 age- and sex-matched normal volunteers during conditions of bright light (2500 lux, 2.5 hr in both the morning and evening) and ordinary room light (Rosenthal, Obarzanek, Gaist, Skwerer, Jacobsen, Duncan, and Wehr, unpublished observation). Over the 10-day period between the two conditions, SAD patients lost an average of 1 kg body weight. There was no average body weight change in the normals. Contrary to our prediction, RMR decreased significantly in SAD patients treated with bright light: baseline (mean $\pm$ SEM kcal), 1648 ± 84; treated; 1497 ± 118 ($p < 0.04$, t test). There were no significant baseline differences in RMR between patients and normals, though patients had somewhat higher values than the controls (1648 ± 84 kcal and 1357 ± 126 kcal for patients and controls, respectively; $p = 0.07$). Bright light had no effect on RMR in normal volunteers. The reduction in RMR during the light treatment could not be explained by changes in plasma norepinephrine or thyroid hormones, both of which are known to increase rate of metabolism. It is interesting to note that Frenstrom et al. (1985) reported decreased RMR in nonseasonal depressives treated with antidepressants.

One possible explanation for our finding is that RMR decreased secondarily to decreased appetite, food intake, and weight loss. Such decreases in RMR have been well documented in other weight loss situations (Keys et al., 1950).

Immune Function

Cellular immune function has been shown to be altered in depression (Kronfol et al., 1983; Schleifer et al., 1984, 1985; Calabrese et al., 1985). For example, the response of peripheral blood lymphocytes to mitogen stimulation is reduced in some depressed patients compared to normal subjects. In addition, Albrecht et al. (1985) have shown that treatment of unipolar and bipolar depressed patients with tricyclic antidepressants, lithium, or electroconvulsive therapy seems to reduce the blastogenic response of their peripheral blood lymphocytes to mitogen stimulation. SAD patients provide an ideal cohort in which to assess cellular immune function before and after antidepressant therapy without the confounding variable of pharmacological treatment.

Using mitogen-induced lymphocyte blastogenesis of peripheral blood lymphocytes (PBLs) as an in vitro measure of cellular immunity, we compared immune function of both nine untreated depressed and nine light-treated SAD patients with the immune function of nine normal healthy volunteers (Skwerer, Tamarkin, Jacobsen, Sack, and Rosenthal, unpublished observation; see Table 17-2). The doses of mitogens used were as follows: 0.63, 1.25, 2.5, 5.0, and 10.0 μg/ml of media. At baseline, the PBLs of the depressed patients had

TABLE 17-2. Mitogen-Induced Lymphocyte Blastogenesis

	Mitogen dose (PHA or Con A) (µg/ml)				
	0.63	1.25	2.5	5.0	10.0
Winter study, PHA					
Depressed patients	9286 (3565)	18,537 (7399)	33,331 (12,041)	39,831 (13,703)	35,732 (11,740)
Treated patients	1141 (612)	3463 (1321)	6153 (2230)	8678 (3159)	10,959 (2892)
Untreated controls	3048 (1202)	6329 (2078)	8023 (2644)	12,373 (3458)	9648 (3175)
Summer study, Con A					
Untreated controls	12,812 (5314)	17,641 (8261)	25,996 (8777)	38,100 (16,242)	56,466 (25,447)
Untreated patients	48,264 (26,128)	77,557 (33,171)	98,890 (35,985)	139,357 (36,895)	204,726 (71,480)
Light treatment (summer), PHA					
Untreated controls	59,295 (7641)	100,452 (10,235)	121,671 (11,675)	114,428 (11,273)	97,693 (11,049)
Treated controls	63,818 (14,195)	109,446 (15,547)	142,340 (25,907)	159,856 (20,182)	140,562 (21,159)
Eye study, PHA					
Untreated controls	64,702 (12,240)	93,470 (14,398)	124,645 (21,718)	127,734 (24,664)	115,049 (21,928)
Treated controls	117,057 (26,539)	154,384 (25,849)	203,799 (31,808)	205,916 (31,520)	182,654 (27,352)
Eye study, Con A					
Untreated controls	23,715 (9896)	28,592 (6621)	51,532 (12,897)	68,181 (15,332)	67,113 (14,711)
Treated controls	34,982 (7975)	65,752 (12,287)	80,577 (17,649)	123,624 (23,339)	118,522 (18,039)

Note. The data are expressed in disintegrations per minute.

significantly greater response to the mitogen phytohemagglutinin (PHA), compared to those of the untreated normals ($F = 4.4$, $p = 0.05$ for effect of condition and $F = 4.4$, $p < 0.004$ for condition $\times$ dose of mitogen interaction; analysis of variance). After approximately 1 week of light treatment (2500 lux, 2.5 hr in both the morning and evening), the mitogen-stimulated responses of the patients' cells were significantly reduced in amplitude, with a flattening of the dose–response curve compared to pretreatment curves ($F = 5.3$, $p = 0.05$ for treatment effect and $F = 4.8$, $p < 0.004$ for treatment $\times$ dose of mitogen interaction); these values were comparable to those of the untreated controls. This finding was replicated the following winter in a study that was identical except for the use of an additional mitogen, concanavalin A (Con A).

We also compared the immune function of 9 untreated, euthymic SAD patients to that of 9 normal controls in the summer (see Table 17-2). As in the winter, the mitogen-stimulated responses of the patients' lymphocytes to Con A were significantly greater than those of the normal controls ($F = 6.8$, $p < 0.02$ for treatment effect). However, the PBL response to PHA did not differ between groups. In summer, the mitogen-induced lymphocyte blastogenesis of the PBLs of normal subjects ($n = 9$) exposed to bright light (2500 lux, 2.5 hr in both the morning and evening) was signficantly increased compared to baseline (for PHA, $F = 3.9$, $p = 0.01$ for treatment $\times$ dose interaction, and for Con A, $F = 7.9$, $p < 0.03$ for treatment effect) (see Table 17-2).

In a separate study, in winter, normal subjects were exposed to either bright light ($n = 9$; 2500 lux, 2.5 hr in both the morning and evening) or ordinary room light ($n = 7$; less than 300 lux, 2.5 hr in both the morning and evening) in a parallel design (see Table 17-2). The volunteers were masked and gowned, allowing only their eyes to be exposed to light. After exposure to ordinary room light, there was no significant change in PBL response to mitogens compared to baseline. However, as in the summer study, the PBLs of the bright-light group showed increased lymphocyte proliferation after 1 week of exposure compared to baseline (for PHA, $F = 7.4$, $p < 0.03$ for treatment effect; for Con A, $F = 12.4$, $p < 0.008$ for treatment effect). This study demonstrated that the photoimmune effect was an eye-mediated phenomenon that, at least in normal controls, did not seem to be seasonal, insofar as the normal controls had increased proliferation both in summer and winter. There were no significant correlations between any of these immunological findings and any of the other biological variables mentioned above.

The baseline differences between SAD patients and normal volunteers noted for PHA and Con A in winter and for Con A in summer are opposite to those some researchers have observed in nonseasonal depression (Schleifer *et al.*, 1984, 1985; Calabrese *et al.*, 1985). The difference in the results with PHA and Con A in the summer may be related to the ability of PHA to stimulate helper cells more than suppressor cells; the opposite is true for Con A (Roitt, 1977).

The persistence, regardless of mood, of the baseline differences between patients and normals in the mitogen response to Con A, and the opposite response of the patients and normal volunteers to light exposure of the patients and normal volunteers to light exposure, suggest that this test of cellular immune function may be a trait marker for SAD. If this is true, the study of immune function in SAD may provide valuable insights into the pathophysiology of this disorder, especially since abnormalities in the direction of enhanced PBL response have not been documented in nonseasonal depression. These immunological abnormalities in SAD may also have clinical significance. However, no conclusions about clinical implications of the immune function in SAD can be drawn from the data given above, since mitogen stimulation is not necessarily a good reflection of *in vivo* immune function. *In vivo* testing will need to be done in order to understand the clinical relevance of these *in vitro* immunological findings.

Conclusion

The broad similarities between the symptoms of SAD and the seasonal changes in behavior seen in many species initially suggested to researchers that the experience of basic scientists could be helpful in understanding the biological mechanisms underlying the phenomena of SAD and phototherapy. This line of reasoning inspired the melatonin hypothesis and the phase-shift hypothesis, both of which are based on our understanding of the circadian system and its entrainment by light (Pittendrigh, 1981; Tamarkin *et al.*, 1985). Although neither of these models has left researchers empty-handed, neither is strongly supported by the data. Both theories may yet have some applicability, albeit perhaps in only a small subset of patients.

The light sensitivity that is a clinical hallmark of SAD patients may also emerge as a useful biological marker. Lewy *et al.* (1987b) have used the response of circadian rhythms to light as a means of subtyping SAD patients and suggest that such subtyping may have predictive value in determining the optimal timing of treatment. This hypothesis awaits thorough testing, but is of interest even if the phase response curve and circadian pattern of sensitivity to the antidepressant effects of light turn out to covary and not to be causally associated. Sensitivity to suppression of melatonin by light, which has been shown to be increased in bipolar patients and children at risk for bipolar disorder, should also be tested in SAD patients. Other light-sensitive markers would also seem worth exploring.

Apart from melatonin, other hormones that have been shown in animals to vary seasonally and to be responsible for behaviors that vary seasonally may be worth studying. Prolactin and thyroid hormones fall into this category, and it is interesting that several studies have reported abnormal prolactin levels in

SAD. It appears that the thyroid axis may also be abnormal, but, if this is the case, the abnormality may be a more subtle one than has been reported in other studies in depressed populations.

The extensive neuroendocrine studies in nonseasonal depressives have inspired similar approaches in SAD populations. However, the HPA axis, found to be hyperactive in endogenous depressives, has not as yet shown any abnormalities in SAD. The opposite nature of many of the vegetative symptoms seen in SAD (overeating, weight gain, and oversleeping) to those seen in more classical depressives (undereating, weight loss, and insomnia) have led us to speculate that the HPA axis might be *underactive* in SAD in a manner too subtle to be detected by methods used thus far.

Classical biological studies of depression have focused on the monoamine neurotransmitters. It was logical that these should be examined in SAD patients as well. Of the neurotransmitter systems examined thus far, the serotonin system appears most likely to be dysregulated. Such dysregulation could account for (1) the low plasma prolactin levels reported by both Depue *et al.* (Chapter 13, this volume) and our group (Rosenthal, Skwerer, Jacobsen, Duncan, Kasper, Sack, and Wehr, unpublished observation); (2) the abnormal psychological and hormonal responses to m-CPP reported by Jacobsen *et al.* (1987b); (3) the abnormal response to carbohydrate-rich meals (Rosenthal *et al.*, 1987); and (4) the beneficial effects of d-fenfluramine (O'Rourke *et al.*, 1987) and L-tryptophan (Buckwald, McGrath, and Resnick, personal communication, 1987).

A case can be made for dysregulation of noradrenergic systems, since (1) plasma NE levels appear to be inversely related to the level of depression in SAD patients; (2) these levels appear to increase, following light treatment in direct proportion to its efficacy (Skwerer, Jacobsen, Sack, and Rosenthal, unpublished observation); and (3) melatonin levels, a function of noradrenergic activity, are reduced in SAD patients (Rosenthal, Skwerer, Jacobsen, Kasper, Duncan, Sack, and Wehr, unpublished observation). The case for abnormal dopaminergic functioning in SAD appears to be less well founded at this time.

An extremely useful clue to the understanding of the biological abnormalities in SAD patients resides in their responsiveness to light. Which biological measures change following light treatment, and how do these changes correlate with the clinical effects and differ between patients and normal subjects and across the seasons? Thus delta sleep and sleep efficiency decrease in SAD patients but increase in normal subjects in winter. Conversely, bright-light treatment increases delta sleep and sleep efficiency in paitents but decreases it in normal subjects. Similarly, bright-light treatment increases the amplitude of the P300 component of the ERP in SAD patients but not in normals. These changes seen in SAD patients may prove to be useful biological markers, assisting clinicians in subdividing patients into meaningful subtypes and helping predict clinical response. Their values as clues to the underlying psychobiology of SAD is diminished by our lack of understanding of the neurophysiological mechanisms underlying the brain wave changes.

It is difficult to determine which biological effects of light are relevant to the clinical changes seen in patients. A surprisingly large range of biological effects of light has been found in the past few years. We suspect that many of these effects may not be directly related to the mechanism of action of phototherapy, but may be of considerable interest in their own right. Our photoimmune findings (Skwerer, Tamarkin, Jacobsen, Sack, and Rosenthal, unpublished observation) may fall into this category. So it may be that just as the discovery that bright light was capable of suppressing human melatonin secretion (Lewy *et al.*, 1980) led to the use of bright light in phototherapy, so this latter effect may lead us to understanding other effects of light.

In conclusion, it is apparent that simple theoretical models of the pathophysiology of SAD and the mechanism of action of phototherapy have rapidly proven inadequate. It is far more likely that the changing seasons exert their effects in a more complex manner, with different behavioral outputs being modulated by different mechanisms. Similarly, phototherapy may work by multiple mechanisms, which may differ in different individuals.

Acknowledgments

This chapter originally appeared in *Journal of Biological Rhythms,* Volume 3, Number 2, pp. 135–154, 1988. Reprinted by permission of The Guilford Press.

References

Albrecht, J. J., J. H. Helderman, M. A. Schlesser, and A. J. Rush (1985) A controlled study of cellular immune function in affective disorders before and during somatic therapy. Psychiat. Res. *15:* 185.

Brown, R., J. H. Kocsis, S. Caroff, J. Amsterdam, A. Winokur, P. E. Stokes, and A. Frazer (1985) Differences in nocturnal melatonin secretion between melancholic depressed patients and control subjects. Amer. J. Psychiat. *142:* 811–816.

Calabrese, J. R., R. G. Skwerer, B. Barna, A. D. Gulledge, R. Valenzuela, A. Butkus, S. Subichin, and N. E. Krupp (1985) Depression, immunocompetence, and prostaglandins of the E series. Psychiat. Res. *7:* 41.

Carlsson, A., L. Svennerholm, and B. Winblad (1980) Seasonal and circadian monoamine variation in human brain examined post-mortem. Acta Psychiat. Scand. *61*(Suppl. 280): 75–78.

Dietzel, M., F. Waldhauser, O. M. Lesch, M. Musalek, and H. Walter (1986) Bright light treatment success not explained by melatonin. Paper presented at the IV World Congress of Biological Psychiatry, Philadelphia, September.

Duncan-Johnson, C. C. and E. Donchin (1982) The P300 component of the event-related potential as an index of information processing. Biol. Psychol. *14:* 1–52.

Fernstrom, J. D. (1987) Food-induced changes in brain serotonin synthesis: Is there a relationship to appetite for specific macronutrients? Appetite *8:* 163–182.

Fernstrom, J. D., and R. J. Wurtman (1972) Brain serotonin content: Physiological regulation by plasma neutral amino acids. Science *178:* 414–416.

Fernstrom, M. H., L. H. Epstein, D. G. Spiker, and D. J. Kupfer (1985) Resting metabolic rate is reduced in patients treated with antidepressants. Biol. Psychiat. *20:* 688–692.

Gillin, J. C., N. Sitaram, T. A. Wehr, W. Duncan, R. Post, D. L. Murphy, W. B. Mendelson, R. J. Wyatt, and W. E. Bunney (1984) Sleep and affective illness. In *Neurobiology of Mood Disorders*, R. M. Post and J. C. Ballenger, eds., pp. 175–180, Williams & Wilkins, Baltimore.

Gold, P. W., M. A. Kling, I. Khan, J. R. Calabrese, K. Kalogresas, R. M. Post, P. C. Averinos, D. L. Loriaux, and G. P. Chrousos. Corticotropin releasing hormone: Relevance to normal physiology and the pathophysiology and differential diagnosis of hypercortisolism and adrenal insufficiency. In *Hypothalamic Dysfunction in Neuropsychiatric Disorders*, D. Nerozzi, F. K. Goodwin, and E. Costa, eds., pp. 183–200, Raven Press, New York.

Gudelsky, G. A. (1981) Tuberoinfundibular dopamine neurons and the regulation of prolactin secretion. Psychoneuroendocrinology *6:* 3–16.

Hamilton, M. (1967) Development of a rating scale for primary depressive illness. Brit. J. Soc. Clin. Psychol. *6:* 278–296.

Hellekson, C. J., J. A. Kline, and N. E. Rosenthal (1986) Phototherapy for seasonal affective disorder in Alaska. Amer. J. Psychiat. *143*(8): 1035–1037.

Hoffman, K. (1981) Photoperiodism in vertebrates. In *Handbook of Behavioral Neurobiology*, Vol. 4, *Biological Rhythms*, J. Aschoff, ed., pp. 449–473, Plenum, New York.

Isaacs, G., D. S. Stainer, T. E. Sensky, S. Moor, and C. Thompson (1988) Phototherapy and its mechanism of action in seasonal affective disorder. J. Affect. Dis. *14:* 13–19.

Jacobsen, F. M., A. Dreizzen, N. E. Rosenthal, and T. A. Wehr (1987a) Diurnal variation in seasonal affective disorder. Presented at the 140th annual meeting of the American Psychiatric Association, Chicago, May.

Jacobsen, F. M., E. A. Mueller, D. A. Sack, and N. E. Rosenthal (1987b) Subjective and physiological responses of SAD patients and controls to intravenous m-CPP. Paper presented at the 42nd annual meeting of the Society of Biological Psychiatry, Chicago, May.

Jacobsen, F. M., D. A. Sack, T. A. Wehr, S. Rogers, and N. E. Rosenthal (1987c) Neuroendocrine responses to 5-hydroxytrytophan in seasonal affective disorder. Arch. Gen. Psychiat. *44*(12): 1086–1091.

Jacobsen, F. M., T. A. Wehr, R. G. Skwerer, D. A. Sack, and N. E. Rosenthal (1987d) Morning versus midday phototherapy of seasonal affective disorder. Amer. J. Psychiat. *144:* 1301–1305.

James, S. P., T. A. Wehr, D. A. Sack, B. L. Parry, S. Rogers, and N. E. Rosenthal (1986) The dexamethasone suppression test in seasonal affective disorder. Comp. Psychiat. *127*(3): 224–226.

James, S. P., T. A. Wehr, D. A. Sack, B. L. Parry, and N. E. Rosenthal (1985) Evening light treatment of seasonal affective disorder. Brit. J. Psychiat. *147:* 424–428.

Jimerson, D. C., and R. M. Post (1984) Psychomotor stimulants and dopamine agonists in depression. In *Neurobiology of Mood Disorders*, R. M. Post and J. C. Ballenger, eds., pp. 619–620, Williams & Wilkins, Baltimore.

Keys, A., J. Brozek, A. Henschel, O. Mickelsen, and H. L. Taylor (1950) *The Biology of Human Starvation*, Vol. 1, University of Minnesota Press, Minneapolis.

Kronfol, Z., J. Silva, J. Greden, S. Demginski, R. Gardner, and B. J. Carroll (1983) Impaired lymphocyte function in depressive illness. Life Sci. *33:* 241.

Lewy, A. J. (1984) Human melatonin secretion (I): A marker for adrenergic function. In *Neurobiology of Mood Disorders*, R. M. Post and J. C. Ballenger, eds., pp. 207–214, Williams & Wilkins, Baltimore.

Lewy, A. J., R. L. Sack, S. Miller, and T. M. Hoban (1987a) Antidepressant and circadian phase-shifting effects of light. Science *235:* 352–354.

Lewy, A. J., R. L. Sack, C. M. Singer, and D. M. White (1987b) The phase shift hypothesis for bright light's therapeutic mechanism of action: Theoretical considerations and experimental evidence. Psychopharmacol. Bull. *23*(3): 349–353.

Lewy, A. J., T. A. Wehr, F. K. Goodwin, D. A. Newsome, and S. P. Markey (1980) Light suppresses melatonin secretion in humans. Science *210:* 1267–1269.

Meltzer, H. Y., B. Umberkoman-Wiita, A. Robertson, B. J. Tricou, M. Lowry, and R. Perline (1984) Effect of 5-hydroxytrypophan on serum cortisol levels in major affective disorders. Arch. Gen. Psychiat. *41:* 366–374.

O'Rourke, D. A., J. J. Wurtman, A. Brzezinski, T. A. Nader, and B. Chew (1987) Serotonin implicated in the etiology of seasonal affective disorder. Psychopharmacol. Bull. *23*(3): 358–360.

Pittendrigh, C. S. (1981) Circadian systems: Entrainment. In *Handbook of Behavioral Neurobiology*, Vol. 4, *Biological Rhythms*, J. Aschoff, eds., pp. 95–124, Plenum, New York.

Potter, W. Z., M. V. Rudorfer, F. K. Goodwin (1987) Biological findings in bipolar disorders. In *Psychiatric Update: American Psychiatric Association, Annual Review*, Vol. 6, R. E. Hales and A. F. Frances, eds., pp. 32–60, American Psychiatric Press, Washington, DC.

Rechtschaffen, A., and A. Kales, eds. (1968) *A Manual of Standardized Terminology, Techniques and Scoring System for Sleep Stages of Human Subjects*, Publication NIH 204, Neurological Information Network, Bethesda, MD.

Reichlin, S. (1981) Neuroendocrinology. In *Textbook of Endocrinology*, R. H. Williams, ed., pp. 616–617, W. B. Saunders, Philadelphia.

Roitt, I. (1977) *Essential Immunology*, 3rd ed., Blackwell Scientific Publications, Oxford.

Rosenthal, N. E., M. Genhart, F. M. Jacobsen, R. G. Skwerer, and T. A. Wehr (1987) Disturbances of appetite and weight regulation in seasonal affective disorder. Ann. NY Acad. Sci. *499:* 216–230.

Rosenthal, N. E., F. M. Jacobsen, D. A. Sack, J. Arendt, S. P. James, B. L. Parry, and T. A. Wehr (1988) Atenolol in seasonal affective disorder: A test of the melatonin hypothesis. Amer. J. Psychiat. *145*(1): 52–56.

Rosenthal, N. E., D. A. Sack, C. J. Carpenter, B. L. Parry, W. B. Mendelson, and T. A. Wehr (1985) Antidepressant effects of light in seasonal affective disorder. Amer. J. Psychiat. *142:* 606.

Rosenthal, N. A., D. A. Sack, J. C. Gillin, A. J. Lewy, F. K. Goodwin, Y. Davenport, P. S. Mueller, D. A. Newsome, and T. A. Wehr (1984) Seasonal affective disorder: A description of the syndrome and preliminary findings with light therapy. Arch. Gen. Psychiat. *41:* 72–80.

Rosenthal, N. E., D. A. Sack, F. M. Jacobsen, S. P. James, B. L. Parry, J. Arendt, L. Tamarkin, and T. A. Wehr (1986) Melatonin in seasonal affective disorder and phototherapy. J. Neural Trans. (Suppl.) *21:* 257–267.

Roy, A., D. Pickar, M. Linnoila, and W. Z. Potter (1984) Plasma norepinephrine levels in affective disorder. Arch. Gen. Psychiat. *41:* 72.

Sachar, E. J. (1981) Psychobiology of affective disorders. In *Principles of Neural Science*, E. R. Kandel and J. H. Schwartz, eds., pp. 611–619, Elsevier/North-Holland, New York.

Schildkraut, J. J. (1978). Current status of the catecholamine hypothesis of affective disorders. In *Psychopharmacology: A Generation of Progress*, M. A. Lipton, A. DiMascio, and K. F. Killam, eds., pp. 1223–1234, Raven Press, New York.

Schleifer, S. J., S. E. Keller, A. T. Meyerson, M. J. Raskin, K. L. Davis, and M. Stein (1984) Lymphocyte function in major depressive disorder. Arch. Gen. Psychiat. *41:* 484.

Schleifer, S. J., S. E. Keller, S. G. Siris, K. L. Davis, and M. Stein (1985) Depression and immunity: Lymphocyte function in ambulatory depressed patients, hospitalized schizophrenic patients, and patients hospitalized for herniorrhaphy. Arch. Gen. Psychiat. *42:* 129.

Tamarkin, L. C., C. J. Baird, and O. F. X. Almeida (1985) Melatonin: A coordinating signal for mammalian reproduction? Science *227:* 714–720.

Terman, M., F. M. Quitkin, J. S. Terman, and P. J. McGrath (1987) The timing of phototherapy: Effects on clinical response and the melatonin cycle. Psychopharmacol. Bull. *23*(3): 354–357.

Vogel, G. S. (1975) A review of REM sleep deprivation. Arch. Gen. Psychiat. *32:* 749–761.

Wehr, T. A., F. M. Jacobsen, D. A. Sack, J. Arendt, L. Tamarkin, and N. E. Rosenthal (1986)

Phototherapy of seasonal affective disorder: Time of day and suppression of melatonin are not critical for antidepressant effects. Arch. Gen. Psychiat. *43:* 870–875.

Wehr, T. A., and D. A. Sack (1988) The relevance of sleep research to affective illness. In *Sleep 1986: Proceedings of the 8th European Congress on Sleep Research, Szeged, Hungary,* W. P. Koella, F. Obal, H. Schulz, and P. Visser, eds., pp. 207–211, Karger, Basel.

Wetterberg, L., J. Beck-Friis, B. Aperia, and U. Petterson (1979) Melatonin/cortisol ratio in depression. Lancet *ii:* 2361.

Wirz-Justice, A., C. Buchelli, P. Graw, P. Kielholz, H.-V. Fisch, and B. Weggon (1986) Light treatment of seasonal affective disorder in Switzerland. Acta Psychiat. Scand. *74:* 193–204.

Wurtman, R. J., and J. J. Wurtman (1988) Nutritional control of central neurotransmitters. In *Psychobiology of Anorexia Nervosa,* K. M. Dirke, W. Vendereyken, and D. Ploog, eds., pp. 4–11, Springer-Verlag, Heidelberg.

18

The Role of Serotonin in Seasonal Affective Disorder and the Antidepressant Response to Phototherapy

Frederick M. Jacobsen, Dennis L. Murphy, and Norman E. Rosenthal

The idea that the neurotransmitter serotonin might be involved in the pathogenesis of affective disorders and in the therapeutic effects of antidepressants is a long-standing one (Coppen, 1967; Lapin and Oxenkrug, 1969). In the last decade, electrophysiological, biochemical, and clinical psychopharmacological studies of the serotonergic system have provided increasing evidence that alteration of serotonergic neurotransmission may play an important role in mediating the therapeutic effects of antidepressant drugs (Murphy et al., 1978; Green, 1985). Our recent description of a seasonally based mood disturbance, seasonal affective disorder (SAD), which is alleviated by treatment with a novel antidepressant modality, bright artificial light (Rosenthal et al., 1984), has opened new areas for investigation and has raised questions as to how this illness and exposure to bright light might relate physiologically to other forms of affective illness and their treatments.

In this chapter, we first review the lines of empirical evidence that suggest a potential role for serotonin in SAD. We then summarize the studies specifically relating to the serotonergic system both in patients with SAD and in the antidepressant response to phototherapy. Finally, we comment on our clinical experience with serotonergic agents in SAD and on potential avenues for further investigation.

Frederick M. Jacobsen. Clinical Psychobiology Branch and Laboratory of Clinical Science, National Institute of Mental Health, Bethesda, Maryland.

Dennis L. Murphy. Laboratory of Clinical Science, National Institute of Mental Health, Bethesda, Maryland.

Norman E. Rosenthal. Clinical Psychobiology Branch, National Institute of Mental Health, Bethesda, Maryland.

Seasonal Changes in Serotonin and Mood

Seasonal rhythms in lower mammals are often induced by changes in the amount of daily sunlight (photoperiod) and mediated by changes in the secretion of hormones (cf. Aschoff, 1981), many of which are known to be influenced by changes in serotonergic function. Photoperiodically induced seasonal rhythms of reproduction and coat coloration, for example, have been shown to be mediated by changes in the secretion of the serotonergically influenced hormones melatonin (Tamarkin *et al.*, 1985) and prolactin (Duncan and Goldman, 1985) in some mammals.

Evidence directly relating the changes of the seasons to alterations in serotonergic function is abundant. In humans, Carlsson *et al.* (1980) have demonstrated that levels of serotonin in the hypothalamus tend to drop from the fall to the winter, and Wirz-Justice and Richter (1979) have demonstrated a circannual rhythm of serotonin in blood platelets. These seasonal fluctuations in serotonin levels may be related to frequently observed patterns of seasonal changes in mood. For example, the peak incidence of suicides in the early spring of the Northern Hemisphere may be correlated with the nadir of central nervous system (CNS) serotonin. This follows from the demonstration by Asberg *et al.* (1976) of dramatic correlations between decreased levels of the serotonin metabolite 5-hydroxyindoleacetic acid (5-HIAA) in the cerebrospinal fluid (CSF) and aggressive suicide attempts, and the recent observation that CSF 5-HIAA may reach a nadir in the early spring (T. D. Brewerton, personal communication, 1987).

SAD Symptoms and Serotonin

SAD is a cyclic illness characterized by recurrent episodes of fall–winter depression alternating with periods of spring–summer euthymia or hypomania (Rosenthal *et al.*, 1984). SAD patients typically fulfill the diagnostic criteria for bipolar II affective disorder, and most complain of "atypical" depressive symptoms such as hypersomnia, hyperphagia, carbohydrate craving, and weight gain during the winter, which then resolve during the spring or summer. The predominance of these atypical symptoms in SAD depressions has necessitated the construction of a separate rating scale for SAD-related symptoms (Rosenthal and Heffernan, 1986), since research instruments focusing on classical "endogenomorphic" symptoms fail to track SAD complaints adequately.

Many of the vegetative functions that are disturbed in SAD have been shown to have important relationships to serotonergic functioning in normals. For example, serotonergic mechanisms have long been known to play pivotal roles in the initiation of sleep (Jouvet, 1969). Hypersomnia is a frequent complaint of SAD patients, with over 80% reporting daytime drowsiness and a similar percentage complaining of increased nocturnal sleep duration (Jacobsen *et al.*, 1987c). Nocturnal sleep, daytime naps, and possibly sleepiness are associated with hormonal changes indicative of increases in serotonergic neurotransmission (Parker *et al.*, 1973).

Serotonergic mechanisms are also involved in appetite and weight regulation (cf. Stunkard, 1980). Disturbance of appetite and weight regulation is a frequent complaint of SAD patients, with over 65% reporting increases in appetite and carbohydrate craving and nearly 75% complaining of increased weight during winter depressive episodes (Rosenthal *et al.*, 1987). Wurtman *et al.* (1985) have presented evidence that serotonin may be involved in both carbohydrate craving and in weight gain, particularly in obese individuals, although these data have recently been questioned (Fernstrom, 1987).

Because of the dual association between depression and SAD-like symptoms and alterations in serotonergic function, several research groups have begun investigating the potential role of serotonin in SAD.

Studies Investigating the Role of Serotonin in SAD

A Study of 5-Hydroxytryptophan in SAD

Serotonin is formed in the brain and CNS from the precursor 5-hydroxytryptophan (5-HTP) by the action of an amino acid decarboxylase enzyme. As direct measurement of serotonin in the CNS can only be accomplished in postmortem brain samples, changes in CNS serotonergic activity have been inferred from the effects of serotonergic agents such as 5-HTP on the secretion of certain hormones (e.g., prolactin, cortisol), the regulation of body temperature, and other psychobiological responses. Administration of 5-HTP has been demonstrated to lead to an increase in serotonergic activity when given orally in humans, as indicated by increases in serum cortisol and prolactin (Mashchak *et al.*, 1983). Using a 5-HTP challenge paradigm, Meltzer *et al.* (1984) have reported that patients with major affective disorders have exaggerated secretion of cortisol in response to 5-HTP when compared with controls. On the basis of this information, we hypothesized that if an abnormality exists in the functional regulation of cortisol or prolactin secretion in SAD patients, then this might become evident following stimulation with 5-HTP (Jacobsen *et al.*, 1987b). Since serotonin is converted to melatonin in the pineal gland, we were also interested in the potential effects that 5-HTP might have on melatonin secretion in SAD patients because of the role melatonin plays in the circadian rhythms and seasonal behavioral changes of lower mammals (Rosenthal *et al.*, 1986).

A double-blind random-ordered comparison of the effects of placebo and 5-HTP (200 mg, orally) in 10 depressed SAD patients and 10 matched controls revealed slightly higher basal levels of serum cortisol and prolactin in the patients than in the controls. After administration of 5-HTP, serum cortisol significantly increased in both patients and controls, while serum prolactin significantly decreased. No differences in serum melatonin were noted between patients and controls, except in a single SAD patient who was a melatonin hypersecreter and who showed a dramatic rise in serum melatonin following 5-HTP. No differences in growth hormone, blood pressure, pulse, or side effects were noted between patients and controls during either the placebo or 5-HTP conditions, and the timing of hormonal secretions was also similar for patients and controls. The subjective responses to 5-HTP did not differ between patients and controls: Neither group was noted to have affective responses, and both groups reported increased sleepiness following 5-HTP.

Fasting daytime cortisol levels in both unipolar and bipolar patients are frequently increased during depressive episodes (Sachar et al., 1973, Carroll et al., 1976)—a phenomenon that is thought to indicate dysfunction of the hypothalamic–pituitary–adrenal axis (Rubinow et al., 1984). Although we have previously reported that most SAD patients have normal plasma cortisol responses to the dexamethasone suppression test during their winter depressive episodes (James et al., 1986), the basal cortisol levels of patients in those studies were not compared with the basal cortisol levels of normal controls. The trend toward elevated basal cortisol levels seen in SAD patients in the 5-HTP study is consistent with the cortisol elevations seen in other groups of affectively disturbed patients. The suppression of prolactin following 5-HTP was unexpected and was unlikely to have been a serotonergic effect. However, 5-HTP-induced prolactin suppression has been previously reported by van Praag et al. (1976); it is presumably a result of dopaminergic stimulation, since 5-HTP is capable of releasing central neuronal stores of dopamine (Ng et al., 1972).

Although the 5-HTP study failed to demonstrate direct evidence of an abnormal sensitivity to serotonergic stimulation in most of the SAD patients, the enhanced melatonin secretory response to 5-HTP in a hypermelatonemic patient could indicate an enhanced sensitivity to the serotonin precursor in that individual. Because the administration of 5-HTP gave the mixed effects of cortisol stimulation and prolactin suppression, which could not be solely accounted for by serotonergic stimulation, we decided to use a more selective serotonergic agent in a further attempt to clarify potential serotonergically related neuroendocrine changes in SAD patients.

A Study of m-Chlorophenylpiperazine in SAD

Following the release of the antidepressant trazodone (Desyrel®), one of our groups pioneered the use of the drug's active metabolite, the serotonin₁ postsynaptic agonist m-chlorophenylpiperazine (m-CPP), as a selective serotonergic agent for neuroendocrine studies (Mueller et al., 1985). m-CPP has now been demonstrated to reliably stimulate the secretion of cortisol, prolactin, adrenocorticotropic hormone (ACTH), and also body temperature when given both orally and intravenously to normal volunteers (Murphy et al., in press). These responses were blocked by the serotonin antagonist metergoline (Mueller *et al.*, 1986). Subsequently, we conducted a study in which 10 depressed patients with SAD and 11 matched controls were given infusions of m-CPP (0.1 mg/kg) before and after exposure to a week of phototherapy and tested on numerous physiological and subjective measures (Jacobsen *et al.*, 1987a).

Prior to administration of m-CPP, SAD patients had higher basal levels of cortisol than controls, whereas resting prolactin levels did not differ significantly between the two groups. Both patients and controls showed robust stimulation of cortisol and prolactin in response to i.v. m-CPP. This serotonergically mediated hormonal rise was significantly greater over time in patients than in controls for both cortisol and prolactin. Moreover, compared with controls, patients demonstrated exaggerated serotonergically mediated cortisol and prolactin secretory responses both before and after treatment with phototherapy (Jacobsen *et al.*, 1987a). This finding could indicate that SAD patients are supersensitive to selective serotonergic stimulation. However, although the exaggerated m-CPP-stimulated cortisol rise may be somewhat analogous to the Meltzer *et al.* (1984) finding of exaggerated 5-HTP-stimulated cortisol secretion in patients with major affective disorder, the exaggerated m-CPP-stimulated prolactin rise in SAD patients is strikingly different from our report of blunted prolactin responses to another serotonin agonist, fenfluramine, in depressed patients (Siever *et al.*, 1984) and a similar finding by Heninger *et al.* (1984) using i.v. tryptophan. It remains to be seen whether these differences may be related to the greater selectivity of m-CPP compared with other serotonergic challenge agents or to different types of serotonergic abnormalities in our SAD patients and the depressives in these other studies.

Prior to treatment with phototherapy, depressed SAD patients also differed markedly from controls on some subjective responses to m-CPP. For example, depressed SAD patients reported dramatic feelings of euphoria following infusion of m-CPP, whereas controls did not. The patients also reported feeling significantly less "slowed down" following the m-CPP infusion than the controls. Interestingly, following treatment with phototherapy and associated resolution of depressive symptoms, the patients' subjective responses to m-CPP tended to resemble those of the normal controls more closely.

Taken together, the differences between SAD patients and controls in serotonergically mediated physiological and subjective responses imply that SAD patients may have an underlying dysregulation in brain serotonergic function. The higher serotonergically stimulated cortisol and prolactin levels of patients were present in both depressed and remitted states, suggesting the possibility that SAD patients may have a trait of heightened sensitivity to changes in serotonergic function. To test this hypothesis further, patients could be studied under a similar paradigm during the summer, when they are naturally euthymic or hypomanic. However, the normalization of m-CPP-induced subjective responses in SAD patients following phototherapy and alleviation of depression (or, in some patients, an actual switch into hypomania) appears to indicate that exposure to phototherapy or change in mood state (or both) may result in changes in serotonergic function in SAD patients.

A Study of d-Fenfluramine in SAD

d-Fenfluramine is a serotonergic agent that has the dual activity of both releasing serotonin and also blocking its reuptake. Wurtman et al. (1985) have demonstrated that d-fenfluramine is effective in reducing carbohydrate craving in obese subjects. Although obesity per se is not a primary characteristic of SAD patients, over 70% of patients with SAD report increased appetite with carbohydrate craving and accompanying weight gain during winter depressive episodes (Rosenthal et al., 1987). On the basis of this evidence, O'Rourke et al. (1987) gave d-fenfluramine (15 mg orally, twice daily) in a placebo-controlled double-blind crossover study to seven depressed patients with SAD. Four of the seven patients went into remission with the d-fenfluramine, and a fifth had resolution of hyperphagia (but not depression). These results appear to provide further evidence to support the hypothesis that serotonin plays a role in the symptomatology of SAD.

A Study of L-Tryptophan in SAD

Tryptophan is the precursor of 5-HTP, which, as previously noted, is the immediate precursor of serotonin in the brain. Numerous groups have used the administration of tryptophan as a neuroendocrine challenge to the serotonergic system (Charney et al., 1984) or as a treatment for depression (van Praag, 1981). Buckwald, McGrath, and Resnick (submitted) compared the antidepressant effects of L-tryptophan (1.5 g + pyridoxine 50 mg + ascorbic acid 300 mg), placebo (+ pyridoxine 50 mg + ascorbic acid 300 mg), and phototherapy (2 hr each evening) in nine depressed subjects diagnosed as suffering from SAD. Each treatment lasted for 1 week and was followed by a 1-week washout period. Although results were mixed, possibly due to the complexity of the study design, the SAD patients appeared to benefit approximately equally from the L-tryptophan and the phototherapy (both of which were superior to placebo).

Dietary Serotonin in SAD Patients

Based on the theory that dietary carbohydrates regulate central serotonin metabolism under certain dietary conditions (cf. Wurtman and Wurtman, 1987), Rosenthal, Genhart, Caballero, Jacobsen, Skwerer, Rogers, Coursey, and Spring (unpublished data) compared two isocaloric meals in a crossover design (one high in carbohydrates, one high in proteins) in 16 depressed patients with SAD and in 16 matched controls. Fatigue and numerous other subjective items were measured using the Profile of Mood States (McNair and Lorr, 1964). A major finding was that SAD patients reported decreased drowsiness in the hour following the carbohydrate-rich meal, whereas normal subjects reported increased drowsiness after the meal. These differences are reminiscent of the different subjective responses to m-CPP seen in depressed SAD patients and controls, and would be consistent with an alteration in serotonergic functioning in SAD patients.

Clinical Experience with Other Serotonergic Agents

Working from the hypothesis of a serotonergic dyregulation in SAD, we have had encouraging results in treating small numbers of depressed SAD patients in open trials with antidepressants known to have mainly serotonergic activity. One of us (Rosenthal, unpublished observation) has noted robust antidepressant responses in a few SAD patients treated with as little as 25–50 mg of the triazolopryridine compound trazodone. Another of us (Jacobsen, unpublished observation) has observed dramatic antidepressant responses in three SAD patients treated with low doses (20 mg) of the serotonin reuptake blocker fluoxetine. Although these observations may be further evidence of altered serotonergic sensitivity in SAD, it is premature to draw such conclusions until controlled trials can be conducted; the number of patients studied to date has been very small, and SAD patients not infrequently also respond to standard antidepressants (Jacobsen and Rosenthal, 1986).

Conclusions

The recent description of SAD and the use of bright lights as an antidepressant have raised intriguing questions regarding the physiology of these novel entities. With the bulk of evidence now weighing against a dysregulation of melatonin as the key physiological abnormality in most patients with SAD, new hypotheses have been generated. Viewed as a whole, the studies described in this chapter appear to provide a substantial base for continuing to explore a hypothesis of serotonergic dysregulation in SAD. Moreover, the dramatic change of serotonergically stimulated subjective responses in SAD patients, but not in normals, following a week of phototherapy in the m-CPP study appears to indicate that exposure to bright light or remission of depression (or both) may also be associated with changes in serotonergic function in seasonal depressives.

References

Asberg, M., L. Traskman, and P. Thorén (1976) 5-HIAA in the cerebrospinal fluid—a biochemical suicide predictor? Arch. Gen. Psychiat. *33:* 1193–1197.

Aschoff, J., ed. (1981) *Handbook of Behavioral Neurobiology,* Vol. 4, *Biological Rhythms,* Plenum, New York.

Carlsson, A., L. Svennerholm, and B. Winblad (1980) Seasonal and circadian monoamine variations in human brains examined post-mortem. Acta Psychiat. Scand. *61:* 75–85.

Carroll, B. J., G. C. Curtis, and J. Mendels (1976) Neuroendocrine regulation in depression: I. Limbic system–adrenocortical dysfunction. Arch. Gen. Psychiat. *33:* 1039–1044.

Charney, D. S., G. R. Heninger, J. F. Teinhard, D. E. Steinberg, and K. M. Hafstead (1982) The effects of intravenous L-tryptophan on prolactin and growth hormone and mood in healthy subjects. Psychopharmacology *77:* 217–222.

Coppen, A. (1967) Biochemistry of affective disorders. Brit. J. Psychiat. *112:* 1237–1264.

Duncan, M. J., and B. D. Goldman (1985) Physiological doses of prolactin stimulate pelage pigmentation in Djungarian hamster. Amer. J. Physiol. *248:* R664–R667.

Fernstrom, J. D. (1987) Food-induced changes in brain serotonin synthesis: Is there a relationship to appetite for specific macronutrients? Appetite *8:* 163–182.

Green, A. R. (1985) *Neuropharmacology of Serotonin,* Oxford University Press, London.

Heninger, G. R., D. S. Chaney, and D. E. Sternberg (1984) Serotonergic function in depression. Prolactin response to intravenous tryptophan in depressed patients and healthy subjects. Arch. Gen. Psychiat. *41:* 398–402.

Jacobsen, F. M., E. A. Mueller, D. A. Sack, N. E. Rosenthal, R. G. Skwerer, S. Rogers, and D. L. Murphy (1987a) Subjective and physiological responses of patients with seasonal affective disorder and controls to intravenous m-CPP. Soc. Biol. Psychiat. Abstr. *42:* 236.

Jacobsen, F. M., and N. E. Rosenthal (1986) Seasonal affective disorder and the use of light as an antidepressant. Direc. Psychiat. *6:* 1–7.

Jacobsen, F. M., D. A. Sack, T. A. Wehr, S. Rogers, and N. E. Rosenthal (1987b) Neuroendocrine responses to 5-hydroxytryptophan in seasonal affective disorder (SAD). Arch. Gen. Psychiat. *44:* 1086–1091.

Jacobsen, F. M., T. A. Wehr, D. A. Sack, S. P. James, and N. E. Rosenthal (1987c) Seasonal affective disorder: A review of the syndrome with implications for public health. Amer. J. Pub. Health *77:* 57–60.

James, S. P., T. A. Wehr, D. A. Sack, B. L. Parry, S. Rogers, and N. E. Rosenthal (1986) The dexamethasone suppression test in seasonal affective disorder. Comp. Psychiat. *27:* 224–226.

Jouvet, M. (1969) Biogenic amines and the states of sleep. Science *163:* 32–41.

Lapin, I. P., and G. F. Oxenkrug (1969) Intensification of the central serotonergic process as a possible determinant of the thymoleptic effect. Lancet *i:* 132–136.

Mashchak, C. A., O. A. Kletzky, C. Spencer, and R. Artal (1983) Transient effect of L-5-hydroxytryptophan on pituitary function in men and women. J. Clin. Endocrinol. Metab. *56:* 170–176.

McNair, D. M., and M. Lorr (1964) An analysis of mood in neurotics. J. Abnorm. Soc. Psychol. *69:* 620–627.

Meltzer, H. Y., B. Umberkoman-Wiita, A. Robertson, B. J. Tricou, M. Lowy, and R. Perline (1984) Effect of 5-hydroxytryptophan on serum cortisol levels in major affective disorders. Arch. Gen. Psychiat. *41:* 366–374.

Mueller, E. A., D. L. Murphy, and T. Sunderland (1985) Neuroendocrine effects of m-chlorophenylpiperazine, a serotonin agonist, in humans. J. Clin. Endocrinol. Metab. *61:* 1179–1184.

Mueller, E. A., D. L. Murphy, and T. Sunderland (1986) Further studies of the putative serotonin agonist, m-chlorophenylpiperazine: Evidence for a serotonin receptor mediated mechanism of action in humans. Psychopharmacology *89:* 1179–1184.

Murphy, D. L., I. Campbell, and J. L. Costa (1978) Current status of the indoleamine hypothesis of the affective disorders. In *Psychopharmacology: A Generation of Progress,* M. A. Lipton, A. D. Mascio, and K. F. Killian, eds., pp. 1235–1247, Raven Press, New York.

Murphy, D. L., E. A. Mueller, J. L. Hill, T. Tolliver, and F. M. Jacobsen (in press) Comparative anxiogenic, neuroendocrine, and other physiologic effects on m-chlorophenylpiperazine given intravenously and orally to healthy volunteers. Psychopharmacology.

Ng, L. K. Y., T. N. Chase, R. W. Colburn, and I. J. Kopin (1972) Release of ³H-dopamine by L-5-hydroxytryptophan. Brain Res. *45:* 400–505.

O'Rourke, D. A., J. J. Wurtman, A. Brzezinski, T. A. Nader, and B. Chew (1987) Serotonin implicated in the etiology of seasonal affective disorder. Psychopharmacol. Bull. *23:* 358–359.

Parker, D. C., L. G. Rossman, and E. F. VanderLaan (1973) Sleep-related nychthemeral and briefly episodic variation in human plasma prolactin concentrations. J. Clin. Endocrinol. Metab. *36:* 1119–1124.

Rosenthal, N. E., M. Genhart, F. M. Jacobsen, R. G. Skwerer, and T. A. Wehr (1987) Disturbances of appetite and weight regulation in seasonal affective disorder. Ann. NY Acad. Sci. *499:* 216–230.

Rosenthal, N. E., and M. M. Heffernan (1986) Bulimia, carbohydrate craving, and depression. A central connection? In *Nutrition and the Brain,* Vol. 7, R. J. Wurtman and J. J. Wurtman, eds., pp. 139–166, Raven Press, New York.

Rosenthal, N. E., D. A. Sack, J. C. Gillin, A. J. Lewy, F. K. Goodwin, Y. Davenport, P. S. Mueller, D. A. Newsome, and T. A. Wehr (1984) Seasonal affective disorder: A description of the syndrome and preliminary findings with light therapy. Arch. Gen. Psychiat. *41:* 72–80.

Rosenthal, N. E., D. A. Sack, F. M. Jacobsen, S. P. James, B. L. Parry, J. Arendt, L. Tamarkin, and T. A. Wehr (1986) The role of melatonin in seasonal affective disorder. J. Neural Trans. (Suppl. 21): 257–267.

Rubinow, D. R., R. M. Post, P. W. Gold, J. C. Ballenger, and E. A. Wolff (1984) The relationship between cortisol and clinical phenomenology of affective illness. In *Neurobiology of Mood Disorders,* R. M. Post and H. C. Ballenger, eds., pp. 271–289, Williams & Wilkins, Baltimore.

Sachar, E. J., L. Hellman, H. P. Roffwarg, H. P. Halpern, D. K. Fukushima, and T. F. Gallagher (1973) Disrupted 24-hour patterns of cortisol secretion in psychotic depression. Arch. Gen. Psychiat. *28:* 19–24.

Siever, L. J., D. L. Murphy, S. Slater, E. de la Vega, and S. Lipper (1984) Plasma prolactin changes following fenfluramine in depressed patients compared to controls: An evaluation of central serotonergic responsivity in depression. Life Sci. *34:* 1029–1039.

Stunkard, A. J., ed. (1980) *Obesity,* W. B. Saunders, Philadelphia.

Tamarkin, L., C. J. Baird, and O. F. X. Almeida (1985) Melatonin: A coordinating signal for mammalian reproduction? Science *227:* 714–720.

van Praag, H. M. (1981) Management of depression with serotonin precursors. Biol. Psychiat. *16:* 291–309.

van Praag, H. M., J. Korf, and R. M. Lequin (1976) An unexpected effect of L-5-hydroxytryptophan-ethylester combined with a peripheral decarboxylase inhibitor on human prolactin secretion. Psychopharm. Comm. *2:* 369–378.

Wirz-Justice, A., and R. Richter (1979) Seasonality in biochemical determinations: A source of variance and a clue to the temporal incidence of affective illness. Psychiat. Res. *1:* 53–60.

Wurtman, J., and R. Wurtman, eds. (1987) Human obesity. Ann. NY Acad. Sci. *499:* 343–348.

Wurtman, J., R. Wurtman, S. Mark, R. Tsay, W. Gilbert, and J. Growden (1985) d-Fenfluramine selectively suppresses carbohydrate snacking by obese subjects. Int. J. Eat. Dis. *4:* 89–99.

19

Phototherapy for Nonseasonal Major Depressive Disorders

D. F. Kripke, D. J. Mullaney, T. J. Savides, and J. C. Gillin

In 1910, Dr. J. H. Kellogg, superintendent of the Battle Creek, Michigan Sanitarium, published *Light Therapeutics: A Practical Manual of Phototherapy for the Student and Practitioner*. Light treatment was provided at the Battle Creek Sanitarium to 4000–5000 invalids yearly for conditions such as malarial cachexia, diabetes, gangrene, obesity, chronic gastritis, cirrhosis, hysteria, and writer's cramp. For melancholia, Kellogg recommended arc lights and buttermilk. Unfortunately, Kellogg's therapeutic program seems to have died out along with house calls and the bedside manner.

Today's physicians, having treated fewer patients with light, are more skeptical of the wide applicability of light treatments than our hero of old. Modern interest in bright-light treatment has focused mainly on that minority of depressed patients whose depression recurs each winter (Lewy *et al.*, 1982, 1987; Rosenthal *et al.*, 1984, 1985a,b). Let us examine whether it is theoretically plausible that light benefits are restricted to winter depressives, and then review the experimental evidence.

Photoperiodic Theories

We had first thought that depression might be a vestigial remnant of hibernation—that, is a photoperiodic phenomenon (Kripke *et al.*, 1978; Kripke, 1984). An intriguing model was presented by the Syrian hamster, which displays a critical photosensitive interval about 12 hr in duration during the night (Elliott, 1976; Elliott and Goldman, 1981). If light falls on any portion of this critical photosensitive interval, as must occur during the long days of summer, the hamster's gonads tend to grow, and reproduction occurs. In the short photoper-

D. F. Kripke, D. J. Mullaney, T. J. Savides, and J. C. Gillin. San Diego Veterans Administration Medical Center, San Diego, California; Department of Psychiatry, University of California at San Diego, La Jolla, California.

iod (and long nights) of winter, gonadal regression occurs, which might seem analogous to the reduced libido and reduced gonadotropins found in depression.

In Siberian hamsters, evidence suggests that the duration of the nocturnal melatonin elevation controls the photoperiodic seasonal response (Carter and Goldman, 1983; Yellon and Goldman, 1984; Hoffmann et al., 1986). Long melatonin elevations, as occur in winter, suppress the gonads, whereas short elevations are inductive. The length of the melatonin elevation, in turn, seems to be determined by the phase angle between the evening and morning oscillators, theoretical constructs that are synchronized by dusk and dawn (Illnerová and Vaněček, 1982, 1986).

Perhaps this model has some attractiveness for winter depressives, who both seem behaviorally suppressed in the winter and seem to have an accentuated seasonality of conception. Unfortunately for the model, their fertility seems to peak in August or September, which is somewhat later than would be expected if a long photoperiod were to heighten their gonadal function. The Syrian hamster model also seems inadequate for the bulk of humanity, both because human fertility may tend to display two peaks per year (Aschoff, 1981; Shimura et al., 1981; Mathers and Harris, 1983), and because the most common depressive illnesses seem to peak both in spring and fall—not in the winter at all, and not even at a single time of year (Aschoff, 1981; Rosenthal et al., 1983).

A third model has been offered by the Turkish hamster, which displays gonadal growth only in a moderate window of photoperiods. In the laboratory, this species displays functional testes only in photoperiods from 15 to 17 hr (Hong et al., 1986). Photoperiods of less than 15 hr or more than 17 hr tend to cause gonadal regression. As Figures 19-1 and 19-2 suggest, a model with a limited window of progonadal photoperiods could produce two intervals of reproductive induction per year, both in the spring and in the fall, which may perhaps be analogous to epidemiological data for humans. The human species is thought to have evolved in equatorial latitudes, where photoperiods would be moderate.

A model with a photoperiod window might fit the phenomenology of depression as follows. The winter depressives might be seen as patients who receive light equivalent to a photoperiod of insufficient duration. Other depressives, either summer or nonseasonal, might be seen as patients who respond to an excessive photoperiod. This would be consistent with evidence that the nocturnal melatonin elevation is abnormally low among many melancholics (Mendlewicz et al., 1980; Beck-Friis and Wetterberg, 1984; Claustrat et al., 1984; Steiner and Brown, 1984; Beck-Friis et al., 1985b; Brown et al., 1985), as it is low in Turkish hamsters exposed to photoperiods exceeding 17 hr (Hong et al., 1986). Nonseasonal depressives might respond as if exposed to an excessive photoperiod—not because actual daylight exposure has an excessive duration, but rather because of excessive sensitivity to light (Lewy et al., 1981, 1985a), leading to sensitivity to indoor lighting. This is supported by data sug-

FIGURE 19-1. In the Turkish hamster, only a narrow band of photoperiods promotes testicular function and reproduction (Hong *et al.*, 1986).

gesting increased melatonin sensitivity to light suppression among nonseasonal depressives.

Following the Turkish hamster model, for bright light to be therapeutic, we might have to hypothesize that light exposures can cause *increased* melatonin elevations among depressed patients whose response to light is excessive. One possible mechanism would be a melatonin rebound phenomenon, described by Beck-Friis *et al.* (1985a) among healthy subjects (but, unfortunately for this theory, not among depressives). Another possible mechanism would be that bright-light exposures produce tolerance to dimmer indoor lighting. Such tolerance to dim-light suppression of melatonin has been described in rodents (Lynch *et al.*, 1985). These models suffer from a lack of evidence that winter depressives have excess melatonin or that the duration of the melatonin elevation is abnormal in either winter or nonseasonal depressives.

To summarize, whether based on Syrian or Siberian or Turkish hamsters or whatever, the photoperiodic models suffer from various logical weaknesses. Such models do not provide clear guidance as to what light effects might be in nonseasonal depressions. The various hamster models remind us that human groups also may have different photoperiod responses, depending on their geographic origin.

Circadian Phase Theories

Several investigators have hypothesized that depression might be caused by abnormalities in the phase of certain circadian rhythms. About 10 years ago, we noted that some rapidly cycling bipolar patients in San Diego had displayed evidence of phase advances (Kripke *et al.*, 1978). A simple phase-advance theory of depression could not be proposed, because two of the original patients studied seemed to display phase delays. It was suggested that the trigger for depression might not be a single oscillator phase, but, rather, an altered or abnormal phase-angle relationship between two circadian oscillators. Perhaps either relative advances or relative delays of the strong oscillator in reference to the weak oscillator might be pathological (Kripke, 1983). Note that these oscillators are probably not analogues of the morning and evening oscillators described in the rodent literature (Illnerová and Vaněček, 1986).

Lewy *et al.* (1985b,c, 1987) have similarly suggested that there are de-

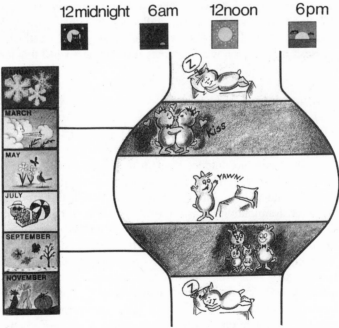

FIGURE 19-2. To show the annual pattern of photoperiodism, the seasons of the year are plotted on the ordinate with the hours of the day on the abscissa. The photoperiod (outlined) is broader in summer. The shaded areas suggest the range of photoinduction in a species responding to intermediate photoperiods. A species with gonadal induction in an intermediate photoperiod could experience two peaks of fertility per year, although this may not occur in the Turkish hamster in its normal habitat (Hong *et al.*, 1986).

pressed patients with both phase-advance and phase-delay syndromes. This group proposed that melancholics tend to display phase advances and winter depressives tend to display phase delays, with some overlap between the groups. Lewy and colleagues further hypothesized that light treatments work by correcting abnormal circadian phase angles. The data from Oregon seemed convincing, both in showing a phase delay among winter depressives and in showing that they responded better to morning than to evening light (Lewy et al., 1987). Nevertheless, the Oregon patients were not made worse by evening light (as a phase-delay theory would suggest). Moreover, in Bethesda, Maryland, and Alaska, evening light was shown to be therapeutic for winter depressives (James et al., 1985; Hellekson et al., 1986). Furthermore, we found small but significant benefit among nonseasonal depressives with morning light exposures, which should be harmful to patients with phase-advance syndromes, according to Lewy's theory (Kripke et al., 1983a,b). It is not yet clear whether these contradictions arise from heterogeneity of patient samples or from a deficiency in the phase-disorder theories.

Neither a critical photosensitive interval theory nor a phase theory would predict that midday bright light would have an antidepressant effect, but Wehr et al. (1986) have presented some data indicating that this is the case. More subjects need to be studied before the value of midday light treatments can be adequately assessed. Our own recent studies add perspective to this theory.

Studies of Illumination Exposure

Photoperiodic models of the birds and the bees, the flowers and the trees, have generally described species that are outdoors most or all of the day, or at least receiving brief exposures to outdoor light in the case of burrowing nocturnal rodents (Lynch et al., 1985). These images may be misleading, for the crucial reason that modern humans in our society spend relatively little time outdoors. In general, indoor illumination is insufficiently bright to suppress melatonin or to alter the phase of circadian rhythms, because humans require very bright light (exceeding 500–2000 lux) for these effects. Indeed, photoperiodic models related to daylight duration may be rather irrelevant to contemporary human experience.

To assess the light exposure that humans actually experience, over a period of years our group has developed a measurement system to monitor biologically effective illumination (Savides et al., 1986). First, we sought a broad range of measurement, to mirror the enormous range of illuminations that humans experience. With careful balancing of photocell sensitivity with a neutral density filter, we achieved a transducer capable of registering a range of illuminations from 10 to 50,000 lux—that is, from dim twilight to a brightness only experienced when looking toward the sun.

Next, the spectral sensitivity was adjusted. It is not entirely clear what sensitivity spectrum is most desirable to measure illumination relevant to affective syndromes. There has been controversy over the best spectral properties for therapeutic lights (Mueller and Davies, 1986). A manufacturer promoted the notion that "full-spectrum" lighting was advantageous for enhancing sexual potency, reducing dental caries, fighting winter blues, and so on, until the Food and Drug Administration ruled that this was "health fraud" (Duarte, 1986). To the contrary, there have been no reliable data on the antidepressant efficiency of different light wavelengths; however, both incandescent and ordinary fluorescent bulbs seem to be effective (Yerevanian *et al.*, 1986; Lewy *et al.*, 1987). We can only guess that antidepressant effects are likely to have a similar action spectrum to melatonin-suppressing effects, which seem to be strongest in the green portion of the spectrum (Brainard *et al.*, 1985). Indeed, antidepressant effects might well be mediated by the rods and thus by rhodopsin. Following this reasoning, we mounted a green filter over our photocell to obtain a transducer with spectral properties relatively similar to those of rhodopsin (Fig. 19-3). The transducer response thus corresponds relatively closely to the subjective sensations of brightness produced by different mixtures of light colors.

The visual cortex responds to a narrow angle of foveal vision combined with a much wider circular angle of peripheral vision. It seems likely that both melatonin suppression and circadian rhythm synchronization are mediated largely through the retinohypothalamic tract to the suprachiasmatic nucleus. Mammalian data suggest that suprachiasmatic nucleus cells have very broad receptive fields (Groos and Mason, 1980). Thus, we allowed our neutral density filter to broaden the transducer receptive angle to approximately 180° (Fig. 19-4). This had the advantage that the transducer did not have to be mounted exactly with the orientation of the eyes. To demonstrate this, 10 subjects were recorded for 24 hr each, wearing similar transducers on the forehead above the eyes and on the wrist. Minute-by-minute measurements of log lux correlated on average

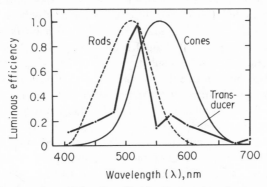

FIGURE 19-3. The spectral sensitivity of our illumination transducer is compared to the sensitivity of rods and cones in the human eye.

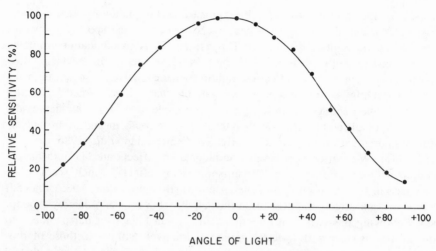

FIGURE 19-4. The relative sensitivity of our transducer to light falling from different angles is shown. The transducer responds to light over a circular angle of about 180°.

0.90 between the two transducers. Furthermore, there was no significant bias in illumination measured at the forehead or wrist. Thus, a wrist placement quite adequately reflects illumination reaching the eyes.

We have developed a new software system in conjunction with the Vitalog PMS-8 computer in order to monitor light continuously for up to a week. The system samples our transducers once per second, converts the analog signal to calibrated log lux, and stores the mean log lux (the geometric mean) once per minute.

We have now measured the illumination experience of over 100 subjects in the San Diego region. We have generally summarized results in terms of the total duration per 24 hr that subjects experienced illumination exceeding 2000 lux, reasoning that 2000 lux is roughly the threshold both for melatonin suppression and for light synchronization of circadian rhythms. Savides *et al.* (1986) studied 10 healthy young adults in their usual habitats, and found that the average subject experienced about 1.5 hr per day of illumination exceeding 2000 lux. Nevertheless, half the subjects (who were medical researchers) experienced less than 30 min of bright-light exposure per 24 hr. Campbell *et al.* (1988) studied groups of patients with Alzheimer disease and age-matched healthy elderly controls. The healthy elderly averaged 1.0 hr per day of light exceeding 2000 lux, whereas the Alzheimer patients averaged only 37 min of bright-light exposure. Furthermore, in both groups, males experienced more than three times as much bright-light exposure duration as females, presumably because they spent more time outdoors. This may be relevant to the higher prevalence of depression among females. Loving and Kripke (unpublished data) studied 10 patients hospitalized on an acute psychiatric ward in a Veterans Administration

Medical Center. The average patient experienced about 42 min per day of illumination exceeding 2000 lux. Greg and Kripke (unpublished data) studied the illumination exposure of a medical student spending the summer near Waikiki Beach. Even in this tropical environment, exposures to bright light were relatively brief; this was attributable to the medical student's devotion to studies.

To summarize these varied results, many adults in contemporary society have only very short exposures to illumination exceeding 2000 lux. Their experiences with bright light are fragmentary and rather scattered throughout the daylight hours. It is likely that in most urban centers, people experience even less illumination than in San Diego, a city renowned for its broad vistas and excellent weather. Therapeutic bright-light treatments of 1–3 hr per day could increase the patients' total daily bright-light exposure by several-fold. Thus, Wehr et al.'s (1986) argument that the quantity rather than the timing of bright light is critical to the antidepressant effects is plausible. If so, the antidepressant benefits of bright light may be similar in winter depressives and those with nonseasonal depressions, although the environmental reasons for inadequate light exposure may differ.

Bright-Light Treatment of Nonseasonal Major Depressions

Several investigators have described bright-light treatments of patients with nonseasonal major depressions. Dietzel et al. (1986) found that single bright-light treatments at 1700–2100 hr and 0600–0900 hr significantly improved the mood and sleep of 10 females with major depressive disorders. It is not certain that winter depressives were excluded from this group, and there was no placebo group or counterbalancing of baseline and treatment order. Yerevanian et al. (1986) reported that bright-light treatments had no significant effect among nonseasonal depressives, whereas similar treatments produced dramatic and significant benefits among seasonal depressives. All subjects in each group except one were female. Bright (>2000 lux) incandescent light was used either from 2000 to 2200 hr or from 0530 to 0730 hr. However, their statistical treatment of nonseasonal patients was distorted by dropouts. In fact, four of the six patients who were administered the Hamilton Depression Rating Scale (HDRS) at day 7 showed improvement, whereas the two others were unchanged ($p = .036$). The seasonal group was larger, which might have contributed to the greater statistical significance of its response. This was an open trial without randomization.

In San Diego, we have now completed five controlled bright-light studies of patients with major depressive disorders, and a sixth study is in progress, comprising over 100 patients (Table 19-1). None of our volunteers have had classic winter depressions. Our patients are veterans hospitalized on a Veterans

TABLE 19-1. Studies of Bright Light in the Treatment of Patients with Major Depressive Disorders: Summary of Results

Year	n	Timing of light	No. days treatment	No. of items	Hamilton Depression Rating Scale results					Reference
					Baseline	After dim red	After bright white	Baseline vs. white	Red vs. white	
1981	12	0500–0600 hr	1	24	16.2	12.8	10.8	$p < 0.01$	$p < 0.025$	Kripke (1981), Kripke et al. (1983a)
1982	12	0500–0600 hr	1	24	18.3	17.9	17.1	NS	NS	Kripke et al. (1983b)
		0200–0300 hr (red only)	1	24	—	17.5	—	NA	$p < 0.05$	
1983	6	0500–0600 hr	5 ⎫	21	19.1	18.2	15.9	$p < 0.05$	NS	Kripke et al. (1987)
	8	2100–2200 hr and 0500–0600 hr	5 ⎭							
1984–1985	16	0500–0600 hr	1	17	—	10.9	12.1	NA	NS	
		2100–2200 hr	1	17	—	—	12.2	NA	NS	
		2100–2200 hr and 0500–0600 hr	1	17	—	—	11.6	NA	NS	
1984–1985	7	2100–2200 hr and 0500–0600 hr	5	17	21.6	19.7	—	NS	NS	
	5	2100–2200 hr and 0500–0600 hr	5	17	14.1	—	13.5			
1985–present	14	1900–2200 hr	7	17	19.2	—	15.2	NT	NT	
	12	1900–2200 hr	7	17	14.7	14.8	—	NT	NT	

Note. NS, not significant; NA, not applicable; NT; not tested.

Administration psychiatric unit with a research milieu. Unlike the subjects in most other studies of bright-light treatment, almost all subjects in our series are male. Patients are not admitted specifically for light studies, so they are not selected for high expectations. They are usually depressives who are willing to spend time on an inpatient unit without standard somatic treatments, either because their illnesses have been refractory to standard therapies or because, frankly, they are in no great hurry to be discharged. Not all of our subjects have primary depressions; indeed, about half have histories of significant alcohol or drug abuse. Consequently, our patients may be more treatment-refractory than subjects recruited by some other investigators.

All of our studies have compared treatments with bright white fluorescent light (1500–2500 lux) to randomized control treatments with dim red light. In all studies, the patients have been blind to the expectation that bright white light will be superior to dim red light, and in all studies, the person doing HDRS ratings is blind to the type of treatment.

Results have been quite encouraging. The first two studies compared a single hour of bright white light given from about 0500 to 0600 hr with a similar hour of dim red light, administered on a separate day in a counterbalanced crossover design (Kripke *et al.*, 1983a,b). Both studies showed a significant advantage for the bright white light over the dim red light. The benefits were small (about 5–15% on HDRS and Beck Depression Inventory [BDI] ratings); nevertheless, one certainly could not obtain similar benefits with a single hour's treatment with imipramine or psychotherapy. These subjects were not drug-free, which implies that bright-light treatments may be additive to pharmacological antidepressant effects.

To extend these results, we compared 5 days of treatment with bright white light to 5 days of treatment with dim red light, again using a counterbalanced crossover design with each patient (Kripke *et al.*, 1987). Six patients received treatment for only 1 hr per day, from 0500 to 0600 hr, but eight received treatment both from 0500 to 0600 hr and from 2100 to 2200 hr. Both HDRS and BDI ratings showed significant improvement with the bright white light after 5 days, although there was little improvement on the first day. The group receiving dim red light did not significantly improve, but none of the contrasts between the bright-light and the dim-light conditions achieved significance. These subjects were free of psychotropic drugs.

Following this somewhat equivocal result, we completed two other inconclusive studies. In the fourth study, 16 subjects received four light treatments given on consecutive nights in counterbalanced orders: bright light from 2100 to 2200 hr, bright light from 0500 to 0600, bright light both from 2100 to 2200 hr and from 0500 to 0600 hr, and dim red light from 0500 to 0600 hr. Perhaps because of the brevity of these treatments and possible carryover affects from one treatment to another, or because these subjects were not drug-free, analyses of variance showed no significant treatment effects. In the fifth study, five subjects received 7 days of treatment from 2100 to 2200 hr and from 0500 to

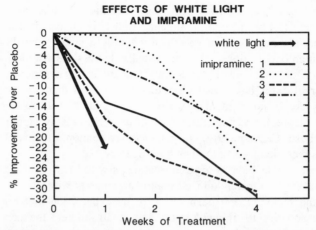

FIGURE 19-5. The relative benefit of five active treatments is plotted as the percentage of decrease in Hamilton Depression Rating Scale scores with active treatment minus the percentage of decrease with placebo. The bold arrow shows the benefit with 1 week of bright white light (see text). Data from four studies of imipramine are plotted for comparison: (1) Feighner *et al.* (1983), (2) Cohn *et al.* (1984), (3) Merideth *et al.* (1984), and (4) Feighner (1980).

0600 hr with bright light, and seven were randomly assigned to dim light in a parallel design. This study was discontinued because the effects seemed too weak to justify continuation, and there were no significant results.

Our current, ongoing study examines effects of light treatments from 2000 to 2300 hr for 1 week. After a 2-day baseline, patients with major depressive disorders are randomly assigned to bright white light (>2000 lux) or dim red light. It is interesting that there has been a slight (not significant) trend for patients to expect more benefit from the red light, both before and after participating in the study; furthermore, actual antidepressant effects have been uncorrelated with expectations. Accordingly, suggestion has been excluded as a factor. The HDRS rater is blind to the random treatment assignment. Because this study will not be completed for over a year, it would be wrong to hazard an interim statistical assessment; however, results for 26 subjects are summarized in Figure 19-5. The patients treated with bright white light are showing about a 20% decrease in HDRS and BDI ratings as compared to the group receiving dim red light, which has not improved. Thus far, we have found no differential response between subjects with melancholia and those with secondary depressions. Both groups seem to respond.

To provide a perspective on these interim results, Figure 19-5 also displays the relative benefits over placebo achieved in four studies of imipramine, a standard antidepressant drug (Feighner, 1980; Feighner *et al.*, 1983; Cohn *et al.*, 1984; Merideth *et al.*, 1984). In none of these studies did imipramine produce as much benefit within 1 week as bright white light; however, impramine benefits after 4 weeks were somewhat better in some studies than bright-light benefits after 1 week. Can we conclude that bright-light treatment is better than imipramine for patients with nonseasonal major depressive disorders? We must reserve our opinion. First, our study is unfinished. We do not have statistical confidence in the results. Second, we have not yet studied bright-light treatments for longer than 1 week to see whether the benefits progress from week to week. Finally, the contrast between bright light and imipramine treatments in Figure 19-5 is obviously not based on any randomized comparison.

In summary, we cannot yet have Kellogg's confidence in bright-light treatment of melancholia. We have studied fewer patients than Kellogg and reserve our judgment, but the preponderance of evidence points to a beneficial effect. Our ongoing study suggests that bright-light treatments may ultimately compare favorably with alternative treatments of major depressive disorders, when such comparisons are completed. Evidence is not yet sufficient to permit us to endorse bright light for clinical treatment of patients with nonseasonal depressions. The available results do justify further testing, in which we hope our colleagues will join us.

Acknowledgments

The research reported here was supported by grants from the following: the National Institute of Mental Health (Nos. MH38822 and MH00117, to D. F. Kripke), the National Heart, Lung, and Blood Institute (No. HL07491-05), the National Institute on Aging (Nos. AG05131 and AG02711), and the Veterans Administration. S. Messin and C. Senger assisted with electronic design.

References

Aschoff, J. (1981) Annual rhythms in man. In *Handbook of Behavioral Neurobiology*, Vol. 4, *Biological Rhythms*, J. Aschoff, ed., pp. 475–487, Plenum, New York.

Beck-Friis, J., G. Borg, and L. Wetterberg (1982) Rebound increase of nocturnal serum melatonin levels following evening suppression by bright light exposure in healthy men: Relation to cortisol levels and morning exposure. Ann. NY Acad. Sci. *453:* 371–375.

Beck-Friis, J., B. F. Kjellman, B. Aperia, F. Unden, D. von Rosen, J.-G. Ljunggren, and L. Wetterberg (1985b) Serum melatonin in relation to clinical variables in patients with major depressive disorder and a hypothesis of a low melatonin syndrome. Acta Psychiat. Scand. *71:* 319–330.

Beck-Friis, J., and L. Wetterberg (1984) A possible low melatonin syndrome in depressed patients. Ann. Clin. Res. *24–25:* 319–330.

Brainard, G. C., A. J. Lewy, M. Menaker, R. H. Fredrickson, L. S. Miller, R. G. Weleber, V. Cassone, and D. Hudson (1985) Effects of light wavelength on the suppression of nocturnal plasma melatonin in normal volunteers. Ann. NY Acad. Sci. *453:* 376–378.

Brainard, G. C., B. A. Richardson, T. S. King, and R. J. Reiter (1984) The influence of different light spectra on the suppression of pineal melatonin content in the Syrian hamster. Brain Res. *294:* 333–339.

Brown, R., J. H. Kocsis, S. Caroff, J. Amsterdam, A. Winokur, P. E. Stokes, and A. Frazer

(1985) Differences in nocturnal melatonin secretion between melancholic depressed patients and control subjects. Amer. J. Psychiat. *142:* 811–816.

Campbell, S. S., D. F. Kripke, J. C. Gillin, and J. C. Hrubovcak (1988) Exposure to light in healthy elderly subjects and Alzheimer's patients. Physiol. Behav. *42:* 141–144.

Carter, D. S., and B. D. Goldman (1983) Antigonadal effects of timed melatonin infusion in pinealectomized male Djungarian hamsters: Duration is the critical parameter. Endocrinology *113:* 1261–1267.

Claustrat, B., G. Chazot, J. Brun, D. Jordan, and G. Sassolas (1984) A chronobiological study of melatonin and cortisol secretion in depressed subjects: Plasma melatonin, a biochemical marker in major depression. Biol. Psychiat. *19:* 1215–1228.

Cohn, J. B., L. Varga, and A. Lyford (1984) A two-center double-blind study of nomifensine, imipramine, and placebo in depressed geriatric outpatients. J. Clin. Psychiat. *45:* 68–72.

Dietzel, M., B. Saletu, O. M. Leusch, W. Sieghart, and M. Schjerve (1986) Light treatment in depressive illness: Polysomnographic, psychometric and neuroendocrinological findings. Eur. Neurol. *25:* 93–103.

Duarte, D. (1986) *Lamp's Labeling Found to be Fraudulent,* Food and Drug Administration Talk Paper T86-69, Rockville, MD.

Elliott, J. A. (1976) Circadian rhythms and photoperiodic time measurement in mammals. Fed. Proc. *35:* 2339–2346.

Elliott, J. A., and B. D. Goldman (1981) Seasonal reproduction: Photoperiodism and biological clocks. In *Neuroendocrinology of Reproduction,* N. T. Adler, ed., pp. 377–423, Plenum, New York.

Feighner, J. P. (1980) Trazodone, a triazolopyridine derivative, in primary depressive disorder, J. Clin. Psychiat. *41:* 250–255.

Feighner, J. P., C. H. Merideth, N. R. Frost, S. Chammas, and G. Hendrickson (1983) A double-blind comparison of alprazolam versus imipramine and placebo in the treatment of major depressive disorder. Acta Psychiat. Scand. *68:* 223–233.

Groos, G. A., and Mason, R. (1980) The visual properties of rat and cat suprachiasmatic neurones. J. Comp. Physiol. *135:* 349–356.

Hellekson, C. J., J. A. Kline, and N. E. Rosenthal (1986) Phototherapy for seasonal affective disorder in Alaska. Amer. J. Psychiat. *143:* 1035–1037.

Hoffmann, K., H. Illnerová, and J. Vaněček (1986) Change in duration of the nighttime melatonin peak may be a signal driving photoperiodic responses in the Djungarian hamster *(Phodopus sungorus).* Neurosci. Lett. *67:* 68–72.

Hong, S. M., M. D. Rollag, and M. H. Stetston (1986) Maintenance of testicular function in Turkish hamsters: Interaction of photoperiod and the pineal gland. Biol. Reprod. *34:* 527–531.

Illnerová, H., and J. Vaněček (1982) Two-oscillator structure of the pacemaker controlling the circadian rhythm of N-acetyltransferase in the rat pineal gland. J. Comp. Physiol. *145:* 539–548.

Illnerová, H., and J. Vaněček (1986) Effect of light on the N-acetyltransferase rhythm in the rat pineal gland. Adv. Pineal Res. *1:* 69–76.

James, S. P., T. A. Wehr, D. A. Sack, B. L. Parry, and N. E. Rosenthal (1985) Treatment of seasonal affective disorder with light in the evening. Brit. J. Psychiat. *147:* 424–428.

Kellogg, J. H. (1910) *Light Therapeutics: A Practical Manual of Phototherapy for the Student and Practitioner,* Good Health, Battle Creek, MI.

Kripke, D. F. (1981) Photoperiodic mechanisms for depression and its treatment. In *Biological Psychiatry 1981.* C. Perris, G. Struwe, and B. Jansson, eds., pp. 1249–1252, Elsevier/North-Holland, Amsterdam.

Kripke, D. F. (1983) Phase advance theories for affective ilnesses. In *Circadian Rhythms in Psychiatry: Basic and Clinical Studies,* T. A. Wehr and F. W. Goodwin, eds., pp. 41–69, Boxwood Press, Pacific Grove, CA.

Kripke, D. F. (1984) Critical interval hypotheses for depression. Chronobiol. Int. *1:* 73–80.

Kripke, D. F., J. C. Gillin, D. J. Mullaney, S. C. Risch, and D. S. Janowsky (1987) Treatment of major depressive disorders by bright white light for five days. In *Chronobiology and Neuropsychiatric Disorders*, A. Halaris, ed., pp. 207–218, Elsevier, New York.

Kripke, D. F., D. J. Mullaney, M. Atkinson, and S. Wolf (1978) Circadian rhythm disorders in manic–depressives. Biol. Psychiat. *13:* 335–351.

Kripke, D. F., S. C. Risch, and D. Janowsky (1983a) Bright white light alleviates depression. Psychiat. Res. *10:* 105–112.

Kripke, D. F., S. C. Risch, and D. S. Janowksy (1983b) Lighting up depression. Psychopharmacol. Bull. *19:* 525–530.

Lewy, A. J., H. A. Kern, N. E. Rosenthal, and T. A. Wehr (1982) Bright artificial light treatment of a manic–depressive patient with a seasonal mood cycle. Amer. J. Psychiat. *139:* 1496–1498.

Lewy, A. J., J. I. Nurnberger, T. A. Wehr, D. Pack, L. E. Becker, R. Powell, and D. A. Newsome (1985a) Supersensitivity to light: Possible trait marker for manic–depressive illness. Amer. J. Psychiat. *142:* 725–728.

Lewy, A. J., R. L. Sack, L. S. Miller, and T. M. Hoban (1987) Antidepressant and circadian phase-shifting effects of light. Science *235:* 352–354.

Lewy, A. J., R. L. Sack, L. S. Miller, T. M. Hoban, C. M. Singer, J. R. Samples, and G. L. Krauss (1985b) The use of plasma melatonin levels and light in the assessment and treatment of chronobiologic sleep and mood disorders. In *Melatonin in Humans*, R. J. Wurtman and F. Waldhauser, eds., pp. 279–289, Center for Brain Sciences and Metabolism Charitable Trust, Cambridge, MA.

Lewy, A. J., R. L. Sack, and C. M. Singer (1985c) Bright light, melatonin, and biological rhythms: Implications for the effective disorders. Psychopharmacol. Bull. *21:* 368–372.

Lewy, A. J., T. A. Wehr, F. K. Goodwin, D. A. Newsome, and N. E. Rosenthal (1981) Manic–depressive patients may be supersensitive to light (Letter to the editor). Lancet *i:* 383–384.

Lynch, H. J., M. H. Deng, and R. J. Wurtman (1985) Indirect effects of light: Ecological and ethological considerations. Ann. NY Acad. Sci. *453:* 231–241.

Mathers, C. D., and R. S. Harris (1983) Seasonal distribution of births in Australia. Int. J. Epidemiol. *12*(3): 326–331.

Mendlewicz, J., L. Branchey, U. Weinberg, N. Branchey, P. Linkowski, and E. D. Weitzman (1980) The 24 hour pattern of plasma melatonin in depressed patients before and after treatment. Comm. Psychopharmacol. *4:* 49–55.

Merideth, C. H., J. P. Feighner, and G. Hendrickson (1984) A double-blind comparative evaluation of the efficacy and safety of nomifensine, imipramine, and placebo in depressed geriatric outpatients. J. Clin. Psychiat. *45:* 73–77.

Mueller, P. S., and R. K. Davies (1986) Seasonal affective disorders: Seasonal energy syndrome? Arch. Gen. Psychiat. *43:* 188–189.

Rosenthal, N. E., D. A. Sack, C. J. Carpenter, B. L. Parry, W. B. Mendelson, and T. A. Wehr (1985a) Antidepressant effects of light in seasonal affective disorder. Amer. J. Psychiat. *142:* 163–170.

Rosenthal, N. E., D. A. Sack, J. C. Gillin, A. J. Lewy, F. K. Goodwin, Y. Davenport, P. S. Mueller, D. A. Newsome, and T. A. Wehr (1984) Seasonal affective disorder: A description of the syndrome and preliminary findings with light therapy. Arch. Gen. Psychiat. *41:* 72–80.

Rosenthal, N. E., D. A. Sack, S. P. James, B. L. Parry, W. B. Mendelson, L. Tamarkin, and T. A. Wehr (1985b) Seasonal affective disorder and phototherapy. Ann. NY Acad. Sci. *453:* 260–269.

Rosenthal, N. E., D. A. Sack, and T. A. Wehr (1983) Seasonal variation in affective disorders. In *Circadian Rhythms in Psychiatry: Basic and Clinical Studies*, T. A. Wehr and F. K. Goodwin, eds., pp. 185–201, Boxwood Press, Pacific Grove, CA.

Savides, T. J., S. Messin, C. Senger, and D. F. Kripke (1986) Natural light exposure of young adults. Psychol. Behav. *38:* 571–574.

Shimura, M., J. Richter, and T. Miura (1981) Geographical and secular changes in the seasonal distribution of births. Soc. Sci. Med. *15D:* 103–109.

Steiner, M., and G. M. Brown (1984) Melatonin/cortisol ratio: A biological marker? In *New Research Abstracts of the Annual Meeting of the American Psychiatric Association,* No. 54, American Psychiatric Association, Washington, DC.

Wehr, T. A., F. M. Jacobsen, D. A. Sack, J. Arendt, L. Tamarkin, and N. E. Rosenthal (1986) Phototherapy of seasonal affective disorder: Time of day and suppression of melatonin are not critical for antidepressant effects. Arch. Gen Psychiat. *43:* 870–875.

Yellon, S. M., and B. D. Goldman (1984) Photoperiodic control of reproductive development in the male Djungarian hamster. Endocrinology *114:* 664–670.

Yerevanian, B. I., J. L. Anderson, L. J. Grota, and M. Bray (1986) Effects of bright incandescent light on seasonal and nonseasonal major depressive disorder. Psychiat. Res. *18:* 355–364.

20

On the Question of Mechanism in Phototherapy for Seasonal Affective Disorder: Considerations of Clinical Efficacy and Epidemiology

Michael Terman

When an antidepressant manipulation—in this case, phototherapy—is able to induce complete remissions in a recurrent major depression within a few days, the discovery of mechanism would appear close at hand. By contrast, medications require weeks or months to exert their effects, and the clinical results are often not so dramatically straightforward. We may guess that bright light to the retina, in light-starved patients suffering from seasonal affective disorder (SAD), excites central responses through direct connections to the hypothalamus, where aberrant vegetative sleep and feeding patterns can be brought under control and the mood can be elevated. Indeed, given preliminary evidence that antidepressant medications may change the retina's sensitivity to light (Terman, Remé, and Wirz-Justice, in preparation), the primary locus may be peripheral.

But we are far from fleshing out such scenarios with convincing data, and there are more negative than positive results as the likely biochemical substrates are investigated. Skwerer *et al.* (Chapter 17, this volume) have considered a range of biochemical factors implicated in depressive disorders—growth hormone; thyrotropin and the thyroid hormones; prolactin; cortisol; melatonin—as substrates that would distinguish normals from SAD patients when depressed (winter), under phototherapy (winter), or in spontaneous remission (summer). SAD-specific functions have been elusive. There are a few encouraging leads, such as potentiated plasma norephinephrine in patients under phototherapy (Skwerer *et al.*, Chapter 17, this volume), and a strong positive therapeutic response using the anorectic serotoninergic drug *d*-fenfluramine (O'Rourke *et al.*, 1987, 1988) without lights. Serotonin dysregulation, while not unique to

Michael Terman. New York State Psychiatric Institute, New York, New York; Department of Psychiatry, Columbia University, New York, New York.

SAD in the scope of depressive disorders, provides an integrative framework for current investigations of both SAD and nonseasonal carbohydrate craving and weight gain (Wurtman and Wurtman, 1989). Skwerer *et al.* point further to increases in an evoked-potential measure of visual alertness with phototherapy, and to a differential immune response between patients and normals. But the mechanism of light's action remains a puzzle.

Much attention has been given to circadian effects of light exposure that may correct abnormally phased daily cycles during winter. Lewy *et al.* (Chapter 16, this volume) have phase-shifted patients' melatonin cycles relative to sleep by selective morning and evening light exposures, with superior therapeutic benefit for early morning light accompanied by a melatonin phase advance. They have shown in several patients that the baseline nocturnal melatonin phase is delayed in winter, relative to that of normals. We (Terman *et al.*, 1988a) have given phase-delayed patients a combination of early morning and early evening light, and obtained normalizing phase advances of the melatonin cycle of up to 3 hr, accompanied by remissions. Whether melatonin per se is a biochemical substrate of phototherapeutic action is a separate question; both pineal and retinal melatonin have been interpreted as physiological signals of darkness (Terman, Remé, and Wirz-Justice, in preparation). However, individual depressed SAD patients may show either high or low melatonin in the circulation (Brzezinski, Lynch, and Wurtman, in progress). The nocturnal secretion pattern appears highly individualistic, boding ill for group-average comparisons of patients and normals.

The circadian scenario uses melatonin or body temperature measures as a marker for circadian phase, and deals with mechanism without positing specific biochemical substrates. As Pittendrigh (Chapter 8, this volume) points out, functionally similar circadian responses can be subserved by a variety of mechanisms. This system might first be understood at the level of formal chronobiological properties. Yet, as investigators posit benefits for phototherapy regardless of time of day, or point to patients who appear not to be phase-delayed when depressed, the circadian scenario seems incomplete. To what extent, for example, is bright light a nonspecific "activator," exclusive of its chronobiological properties? Direct effects of light and passive masking effects often exist side by side with chronobiological phase-shifting effects, as has been shown repeatedly in the animal literature (cf. Moore-Ede *et al.*, 1982), but these have not yet been sorted out in the context of antidepressant phototherapy.

There is little doubt that light can influence the timing of daily physiological cycles, including hormones, temperature, and sleep, in humans. Current investigations will clarify the circadian mechanism by measuring bright-light effects against a baseline without external day–night cues (e.g., Honma *et al.*, 1987; Minors, Waterhouse, Wirz-Justice, Aschoff, and Daan, in progress). Sleep in SAD patients merits further analysis as a regulated depletion process whose time course is modulated by circadian phase, but not locked to it (Daan *et al.*, 1984). Skwerer *et al.* (Chapter 17, this volume) report that hypersomnic SAD patients show reduced delta sleep in winter; delta is a major contributor toward the depletion process, which may therefore be slowed, with a hypersomnic result. Without any shift in circadian phase, sleep phase and duration may vary through the positioning of rhythmic circadian "thresholds" that trigger daily reversals in sleep–wake states. Lewy et al. (Chapter 16, this volume) have shown a therapeutic effect in SAD delaying the sleep episode through instructions, and then stabilizing a delayed circadian phase through light presentations upon awakening at midday.

The sleep cycle is not a simple circadian function, and its hypersomnic manifestation in SAD may provide some indirect clues to the mechanism of phototherapy. The winter months—with later dawn, earlier dusk, and shortened photoperiod—may result in an expanded nighttime interval ("rho") for the underlying circadian cycle, at the expense of daytime "alpha," an effect reflected in animals' melatonin cycles (Illnerová and Vaněček, 1985). Though humans often show phase delays of the melatonin cycle in winter, Illnerová and Vaněček found the alpha–rho ratio to be remarkably constant across the seasons. They hypothesized that the indoor urban lifestyle, with minimal exposure to bright light outdoors (cf. Kripke et al., Chapter 19, this volume), fosters a lengthy nocturnal secretion interval that might otherwise contract naturally in summer. Broadway and Arendt (1985) did observe an apparent winter increase in the duration of nocturnal melatonin secretion in normal volunteers living under dim light in Antartica, concurrent with the morning phase delay, and Broadway et al. (1987) obtained corrective phase advances with bright-light exposures in early morning and evening, with a result indistinguishable from the melatonin pattern in summer.

The sleep-dependent function ("Process S"; Daan et al., 1984) can be construed to detect rho–alpha transitions, triggering awakening. An extended rho, or a phase-delayed rho–alpha transition, may result in hypersomnia. Taken against the baseline of relative light deprivation in winter, phototherapy may have multiple effects that indirectly influence the time course of sleep by changing circadian amplitude, phase, and alpha–rho ratio. A nonspecific energizing effect of light may set the difference between upper and lower threshold levels of the circadian system, irrespective of phase shifts, and may determine when an individual decides to go to sleep and awaken. Finally, phototherapy may directly affect the time course of Process S itself, exclusive of circadian system involvement. Dijk et al. (1987), however, found that integrated electroencephalographic energy, which is considered to directly reflect Process S, was unaffected by morning light exposure in normal subjects. They concluded that shortened sleep duration resulted from a change in the wake-up threshold—the most straightforward interpretation for which is a circadian phase advance.

Depression has multifarious facets, and it is simplistic to imagine that, given the array of dissociable symptoms in SAD, there will be a unitary key to the phototherapeutic mechanism, such as an effect on sleep. Patients may present without hypersomnia, for example, and still respond well to light. Hypersomnics may show reduced sleep and elevated mood under phototherapy, but lingering carbohydrate craving and weight gain. Some patients respond equally well to morning or evening light exposures, while others require morning exposure. So, despite the fact that phototherapy can act quickly and unambiguously, resolving questions of mechanism will entail sorting out variations of both symptomatology and clinical response. Jacobsen *et al.* (1986) have pointed to fatigability, anxiety, and diurnal mood variation as symptoms that best predict successful response to phototherapy. New York SAD patients show greater relative severity of fatigability than of depressed mood at baseline. Furthermore, a group of nonseasonal atypical depressives—with vegetative symptoms similar to those of SAD patients—have not shown convincing phototherapeutic responses (Stewart, Quitkin, Terman, and Terman, in preparation).

Twenty years of biological research in depression have had equivocal success in finding state or trait markers for the illness, or predictors for therapeutic success. Thus it would be surprising to find a single biochemical factor that responds to light and induces remissions in SAD. Furthermore, there are many open questions concerning the clinical efficacy of various treatment regimens and the epidemiology of the disorder. We still do not have comprehensive answers to fundamental questions, such as "Who beyond diagnosed SAD patients might respond to phototherapy?" or even "Who shows seasonality?" Evidence is mounting that seasonal variations in mood, sleep, weight, and energy are widespread as we move away from the Equator, and that large numbers of people who are not necessarily clinically depressed may respond to phototherapy. If so, how do we construe the "normal control group" in studies of clinical efficacy and mechanism?

Although Rosenthal *et al.* (Chapter 15, this volume) state conservatively that phototherapy has been convincingly demonstrated only for people showing a seasonal symptom pattern—a conclusion supported by the equivocal response of nonseasonal atypical depressives—work in progress indicates that chronic melancholic depression (Kripke *et al.*, Chapter 19, this volume), chronic anergia (Terman and Wirz-Justice, in preparation), and nonseasonal circadian disorders such as delayed sleep phase syndrome (Lewy and Sack, 1986), jet lag (Daan and Lewy, 1984; Czeisler and Allan, 1987), and shift work difficulties (Eastman, 1987) may also respond to light.

Although Kripke *et al.* (Chapter 19, this volume) note that SAD patients comprise but a small minority of depressives, and Mrosovsky (Chapter 10, this volume) muses that the syndrome may be a self-fulfilling prophecy resulting from selective clinical screening, Kasper *et al.* (Chapter 14, this volume) point to a potentially large group of subsyndromal seasonal types who respond well to light. Furthermore, within the clinical spectrum, we (Terman *et al.*, in press-b) have shown phototherapy to eliminate SAD symptoms in minor depressives whose lower severity, as assessed in a lifetime diagnosis, distinguishes them from patients with major affective disorder. From this expanded vantage point,

SAD may be seen as an extreme on a continuum of adversity born of life in the temperate zones.

Wehr *et al.* (1987) complicate matters in their diagnosis of patients with reliable summer depressions who are well in winter, as well as summer–winter types who are well only in spring and fall. Do such proliferating diagnoses confirm Mrosovsky's (Chapter 10, this volume) suspicion that recurrent depressions may be linked to any season if patients are selectively screened? Assuming that this is not the case, are winter and summer syndromes flip-side cases of a common disorder? Or does the symptom picture differ?

The new DSM-III-R diagnosis of seasonal pattern (American Psychiatric Association, 1987; Spitzer and Williams, Chapter 7, this volume) is neutral with respect to which season causes problems, and merely provides criteria for identifying the consistent annual recurrence of symptoms. A specific diagnosis of winter depression with tighter timing constraints based on analyses of incidence seems a worthy goal for a future edition of the DSM, given that phototherapy has become widely available to clinicians.

Although the designation of SAD primarily connotes winter depression, bipolar swings to hypomania (or, rarely, mania) in late spring and summer can spell trouble all year. Several research centers have found a dominant unipolar pattern, with mood in spring and summer best described as euthymic or hyperthymic (Depue *et al.*, Chapter 13, this volume), without behavioral impairment or pathology. Thus the designation of SAD has begun to fuzz (winter or summer depressions, or both; bipolar or unipolar patterning) into a set of disorders for which etiology, symptomatology, and treatment approach may vary. Given the DSM-III-R designation of "mood" (vs. "affective") disorders, the clever "SAD" acronym may be dated only shortly after its birth. Furthermore, as broader sets of patients are considered, seasonal variation of mood may prove secondary to that of the atypical vegetative symptoms. The global SAD rubric has become a bit confusing.

Questions about Clinical Efficacy

The clinical chapters in this volume are unanimous in asserting that phototherapy effectively alleviates the winter symptoms of SAD, which is probably correct. However, in comparison to standard clinical trials of antidepressant medications, fairly few patients have received phototherapy; most studies have included small sample sizes (e.g., 10), which are extremely vulnerable to spurious statistical outcomes. Most studies have identified a positive outcome in terms of statistically significant reductions in Hamilton Depression Rating Scale (HDRS) scores between pretreatment baseline and a posttreatment assessment usually only 1 week later. In several cases the magnitude of the score improvement has not been great—indeed, many studies have considered a positive response to have occurred if the HDRS scores decrease by only 4 points—and it would be incorrect to judge the patients as clinically significantly improved.

Mrosovsky (Chapter 10, this volume) questions the patient's ability to answer HDRS questions accurately (i.e., to report on his or her behavior without direct measurements). A related issue is that of the criteria used by the clinician in making severity ratings during the HDRS interview. It should be pointed out that the clinician, not the patient, determines the severity ratings, and the HDRS item set is meant to guide detailed, spontaneous questioning about each symptom. Experienced HDRS raters make confident ratings, and those working within a group can achieve high reliability. Across groups the issue is more troublesome, with substantial variations in baseline scores from study to study despite ostensibly similar screening criteria, and the opportunity to gauge improvement or exacerbation idiosyncratically. Future clinical trials might benefit by use of structured interview guides for the HDRS, including supplementary atypical/ vegetative items and a separate scale for hyperthymia/hypomania for use in spring and summer (Williams *et al.*, 1988a, b).

A worrisome factor is the impossibility of double-blind testing (the treatment must be visible to the patient) with a conventional placebo control. Placebo response rates in the range of 20–40% are common in antidepressant medication studies (Rabkin *et al.*, 1983)—a level of improvement also typical under phototherapy. A dim-light control has produced fewer remissions than bright light, but patients' expectations for dim light are lower (Rosenthal *et al.*, 1984b), which may lead to an underestimate of the true placebo response rate. Several studies have obtained score improvement under lights without deterioration or relapse when the lights are withdrawn; is this *prima facie* evidence of placebo response? Or may some patients learn to seek additional outdoor or indoor light during withdrawals, confounding clinical assessments within a protocol?

Pooling the Data

An ongoing project is codifying the clinical results across research centers by applying a common set of measures of improvement under contrasting phototherapy regimens, and pooling the data of individual patients, in order to accumulate a larger sample size that will allow more confident assessment of treatment effects (Terman *et al.*, in press-c). This work benefits by the collaboration of a large group of investigators who have developed sufficiently similar protocols and screening and assessment methods to enable integration of the data set.

Initial results of the pooling exercise are shown in Table 20-1, for studies carried out through the winter of 1986–1987 in Alaska (C. Hellekson), England (S. Checkley, C. Thompson), Illinois (C. Eastman), Minnesota (R. Depue), New Hampshire (J. Docherty), New Jersey (R. McGrath), New York

TABLE 20-1. Treatment Outcome across Light Therapy Studies (through Winter 1986–1987)

Light exposure condition[a]	n	Baseline HDRS[b]	Treatment HDRS	Proportion showing HDRS decrements posttreatment		
				−50%	<8	−50%, <8
Morning light alone[c]	172	17.77	8.10**	0.66	0.56	0.53
Midday light alone[c]	34	21.22	12.39**	0.50	0.32	0.32
Evening light alone[c]	143	17.97	10.13**	0.50	0.43	0.38
Morning + evening light[c]	136	21.14	9.20**	0.68	0.52	0.51
Dim-light control[d]	77	23.41	19.98*	0.21	0.13	0.11

Note. From Terman *et al.* (in press-c).

[a] All studies considered presented lights for at least 2 hr per day.

[b] Mean 21-item Hamilton Depression Rating Scale (HDRS) scores are based on computations of individual data shown in published tables or graphics, or from unpublished original data provided by the investigators. When possible within a crossover design, withdrawal scores immediately preceding a light treatment condition are used as baseline; given successive treatments without withdrawals, the pretreatment score is used. Scores for several studies using 17- or 23-item HDRS scales are omitted from the means, but are considered in the proportion measures of improvement.

[c] Illuminance approximately 2500 lux at the level of the eyes.

[d] Illuminance ≤300 lux.

*$p < 10^{-3}$ (Wilcoxon signed-ranks test).

**$p < 10^{-4}$ (Wilcoxon signed-ranks test).

City (F. Quitkin and myself), Oregon (A. Lewy, R. Sack), Pennsylvania (G. Brainard, K. Doghramji, J. Gaddy), Rochester, NY (B. Yerevanian), Switzerland (A. Wirz-Justice), and Washington, DC (F. Jacobsen, N. Rosenthal, D. Sack, T. Wehr). Because a sample size much larger than that of any individual study has been accumulated, some broad generalizations emerge about the relative efficacy of various phototherapy schedules, against which specific experiments may be interpreted. First, we are finding that all exposure regimens, including the dim-light "placebo" control, yield statistically significant reductions in HDRS scores. Second, all bright-light exposure regimens yield similar mean posttreatment scores, ranging from 8.10 (morning light alone) to 12.39 (midday light alone). These measures do not suggest any substantial differences between bright-light treatment regimens.

A more detailed picture is gained by analyzing the magnitude of HDRS score reduction of individual patients. Table 20-1 shows three measures of improvement, relative and absolute, that do suggest differential responsivity. The proportion of patients showing at least 50% score reduction—a reasonable goal for an effective treatment—is ≥0.66 when morning light is presented by itself or in combination with evening light, and is 0.50 when midday or evening light is presented alone. Similarly, the proportion of patients achieving posttreatment scores <8 (minimal residual symptomatology, within the normal range) is ≥0.52 when morning light is presented by itself or in combination with evening light, and ≤0.43 when midday or evening light is presented alone.

The most stringent measure of improvement combines both relative and absolute criteria (50% score reduction accompanied by a posttreatment score <8), and indicates remission rates ≥0.51 when morning light is presented by itself or in combination with evening light, and ≤0.38 when midday or evening light is presented alone. A hypothesis test of proportions confirms the morning–evening difference to be statistically significant ($p < 0.01$). It seems clear that there is no increased benefit from evening light when added to the morning exposure. Although individual patients may respond nondifferentially to morning light alone and evening light alone, as tested in crossover designs, only 2 of 71 cases have responded exclusively to evening light.

Skeptics may question whether remission rates in the 30–40% range, for midday and evening light, exceed expected placebo response rates for depressed patients. The dim-light control yields only 11% remissions, significantly smaller than those for evening alone ($p < 0.0001$), and if this were a valid placebo test we would conclude that evening bright light does offer a degree of efficacy. Lewy et al. (Chapter 16, this volume) argue that evening light may work by delaying the sleep episode, so that upon awakening it is already bright outdoors and the patient inadvertently experiences effective morning light—a confound that might be controlled by wearing goggles in the morning. However, we have seen cases in which the sleep episode is not delayed, awakening occurs before sunrise, and evening light is still effective; perhaps these are the true placebo responders.

The 10-day placebo response rate for antidepressant medications—measured within a time span that closely matches the acute treatment phase in most phototherapy studies—is apparently itself a seasonal variable. Rabkin et al. (1987) have documented this trend, month by month, for medication trials at the New York State Psychiatric Institute. Figure 20-1 shows that the placebo response reaches its nadir in winter and its peak in summer. That depressed patients in general are least likely to respond to placebo between the fall and spring equinoxes lends some additional credence to the phototherapeutic responses of SAD patients in winter, regardless of the time of day of light exposure. Thase (Chapter 6, this volume) points to a seasonal pattern among approximately 15% of patients at the Western Psychiatric Institute depression clinic, which suggests that the winter reduction in placebo responses reflects an increase in SAD symptoms unmasked by the use of an ineffective treatment.

Dose–Response

Although several individual studies have achieved >80% remission rates using phototherapy with SAD patients, the general finding of approximately 50% given morning light indicates that half of the patients failed to achieve posttreatment HDRS scores within the normal range. Not surprisingly, data for individual patients show fewer remissions as the baseline severity becomes higher.

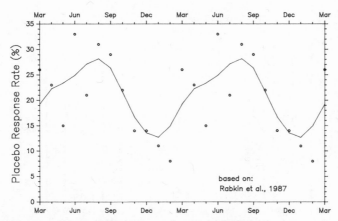

FIGURE 20-1. Seasonal variation in the 10-day placebo response rate for patients in antidepressant medication trials. Double-plot facilitates examination of all seasonal transitions. Curve fit is based on a repeated running median that filters out random fluctuations within a 3-month moving window. Adapted from Rabkin *et al.* (1987). Used by permission.

It would be nice to be able to show that enhanced phototherapeutic regimens would bring greater benefit to severely depressed patients, without leaving a need for supplementary medication. Checkley *et al.* (1986), for example, obtained no remissions among severely depressed SAD inpatients using two 1-hr sessions of light per day, but approximately 50% remissions when exposure was increased to two 3-hr sessions.

Several other studies have shown increasing benefits as a function of duration within the 30-min to 2-hr range (Hellekson, Chapter 3, this volume; Terman *et al.*, in press-b; Wirz-Justice *et al.*, 1987), which suggests a dose–response function for light. But our survey of studies using 2500-lux illumination (the standard) indicates minimal additional benefit with durations of >2 hr. Lewy *et al.* (Chapter 16, this volume) point out that a given patient may respond best to either short or long durations. Standard durations administered to a group are thus likely to yield nonoptimum results.

Intensity offers an additional approach. Current work in New York City (Terman *et al.*, 1988b) and Switzerland (that of Wirz-Justice) indicates increased efficacy of 10,000 lux, a level of light reached outdoors within half an hour of sunrise. Patients who respond to 2 hr at 2500 lux, but relapse under 30 min at 2500 lux, show quick and enduring remissions under 30 min at 10,000 lux. A case study illustrates this effect (Fig. 20-2). The patient failed to respond to 2 hr of evening light at 1900–2100 hr (Vita-Lite at 2500 lux), but showed a remission (with residual atypical symptoms) under 2 hr of morning light at 0600–0800 hr. When morning light duration was reduced to 1 hr at 0600–0700 hr, symptoms increased slightly, but a relapse occurred under 30 min of exposure at 0630–0700 hr. With intensity increased to 10,000 lux (ob-

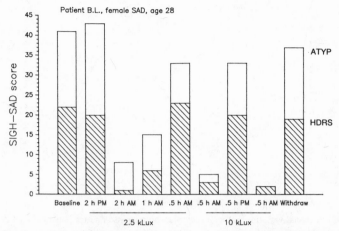

FIGURE 20-2. Depression rating scale scores based on the Structured Interview Guide for the Hamilton Depression Rating Scale (HDRS)—Seasonal Affective Disorder version (SIGH-SAD; Williams *et al.*, 1988a). Striped bars show the HDRS subset. Open bars (ATYP) show supplementary scores for atypical/vegetative symptoms of social withdrawal, weight gain, appetite increase, increased eating, carbohydrate craving, hypersomnia, fatigability, and late-afternoon slump.

tained by concatenating three standard light boxes in a "booth" arrangement), however, remission recurred. The following season, we tested this level of light for 30 min in the evening at 1900–1930 hr (Color-Gard lamps in the Medic-Light Model 10K work station), and the patient failed to respond. Return to morning exposure was successful, however, with complete elimination of the atypical symptoms and an HDRS score of 2.

Pending the outcome of systematic clinical trials of such high-intensity illumination, in progress, this treatment approach may offer several benefits: It may increase remission rates across the board, given relatively weak results at 2500 lux, and strengthen the data base in support of clinical efficacy; it compresses the treatment session to a duration that is more convenient for patients who must leave home for a normal workday; and it increases the specificity of the circadian phase being illuminated, which could result in more clear-cut contrasts in scheduling studies, as well as the opportunity for finer phase adjustments in individual patients. Finally, it raises the question about the mechanism—retinal or central—that integrates bright light over the time range in a reciprocal relation with intensity.

Who Shows Seasonality?

The mechanism of the phototherapeutic response may be clarified by knowledge of the population vulnerable to SAD. If it were only the rare patient who responded to light, the mechanism might be quite specialized. Prevalence estimates of SAD have been lacking, although national newspaper surveys indicate a latitude dependency within the north temperate zone (Potkin *et al.*, 1986), extending to within the Arctic zone (Lingjaerde *et al.*, 1986). Epidemiological studies of the syndrome will require extensive random sampling with detailed clinical evaluations. A related question is the prevalence of SAD symptoms in the population at large, whether or not these are clinically severe. Is SAD a discrete illness, or are its troublesome manifestations seen in normals, too?

Seasonality in a General Population Sample

We have conducted a population survey in New York City (Terman *et al.*, in press-a), and preliminary results indicate widespread occurrence of seasonal mood swings and associated vegetative symptoms. Subjects were selected at random from the telephone book and sent the Seasonal Pattern Assessment Questionnaire (Rosenthal *et al.*, 1984a), which asks for judgments of SAD symptom severity and temporal pattern. They rated the degree of seasonal change in sleep length, social activity, mood, weight, appetite, and energy; identified the months of the year (if any) in which they slept most and least, socialized most and least, felt best and worst, gained and lost most weight, and ate most and least; and rated the degree to which seasonal changes presented a personal problem in their lives.

Of more than 200 respondents, 50% reported lowered energy, 47% reported increased weight, 42% reported increased sleep, 31% reported decreased social activity, and 31% reported feeling worst in late fall and throughout the winter. Twenty-five percent (the "complainers") stated that such seasonal variations posed a personal problem—a finding that can be extrapolated to describe approximately 2 million people in the New York City area alone. Of these complainers, 80% reported lowered energy, 61% reported increased weight, 53% reported increased sleep, 53% reported decreased social activity, and 41% reported feeling worst in the winter season. It is apparent that seasonal variations of vegetative symptoms are more prevalent than variation of mood disturbance in the population at large. This result might be explained by the normal seasonality of thermoregulation, metabolic and thyroid function, sleep, and peripheral adrenergic measures, summarized by Lacoste and Wirz-Justice (Chapter 12, this volume).

By our rules for random sampling, half the inquiries were addressed to males and females, with nearly equal returns. There were no significant sex differences for the group reporting winter problems, regardless of the level of severity. This is a surprising result, given the strong preponderance of females—approximately 74–94% (cf. Hellekson, Chapter 3, this volume)—who have been diagnosed with SAD at research clinics. One would expect random sampling to reflect this sex bias, assuming that the questionnaire is valid. On

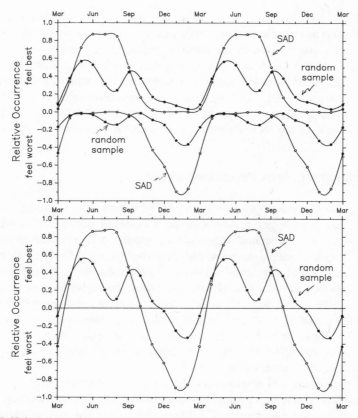

FIGURE 20-3. Relative frequency distributions of seasonal mood changes, as reported on the Seasonal Pattern Assessment Questionnaire by diagnosed SAD patients and respondents to a random-sample population survey. Top panel shows relative frequencies of response to separate questions, in which the months of feeling worst and feeling best are identified. The responses of feeling worst are given negative values. Bottom panel meshes these separate questions into a continuous metric in which the proportion feeling worst is subtracted from the proportion feeling best, in order to derive a continuous bipolar function.

the other hand, the survey guaranteed respondents' anonymity and avoided any mention of psychiatry or mental health per se, which might have encouraged males, who would otherwise keep their silence and suffer, to come forward.

Figure 20-3 compares the seasonal mood swing in the random sample with the reports of 86 SAD patients diagnosed at the New York State Psychiatric Institute. The upper panel presents relative frequency distributions of month-by-month responses to the items "feel best" and "feel worst." The patients reported feeling best with increasing frequency beginning in April, and a symmetrical decrease began in September. By comparison, reports of feeling worst began more gradually in October, and reached a discrete wintertime peak in

January and February before abating in March. New patients tended to seek phototherapy after the winter solstice, when symptom severity was highest, and they often continued treatment into April. In subsequent years, with apparatus already on hand, they could allay development of the symptoms by resuming treatments earlier in the fall.

The population at large showed a more complex seasonal pattern. Reports of feeling best increased in early spring, reached a peak in May and June, decreased in July and August, increased again in September and October, and thereafter declined gradually toward zero frequency in February. The reports of feeling worst conformed by showing an increase in July and August, albeit of lower magnitude than the decrease in feeling best, and a winter negative peak like that of the SAD patients, but at lower amplitude.

These data confirm the recent identification of a clinically depressed summer subgroup (Wehr et al., 1987). We scanned the questionnaires for cases that could be clearly categorized as unimodal or bimodal in their seasonal mood slumps. Of our respondents, 49.8% fell into the winter-only group, 12.3% into the summer-only group, and 6.6% into the winter-and-summer group; 28.0% reported no months worst, while 3.3% indicated months with no identifiable seasonal pattern. Mrosovsky (Chapter 10, this volume) wonders whether there would be equal numbers of summer-only and winter-only subtypes, given aggressive patient screening. Our data indicate that the summer slump, while clearly present in New Yorkers, falls far short of the winter slump.

The lower panel of Figure 20-3 treats the binary "feel best–worst" judgments as quantitatively interrelated, by subtracting the relative frequency of negative reports from that of positive reports. In any given month, subsets of the population might provide split judgments; if half felt best while half felt worst, the mean population response would be neutral. SAD patients showed little such division of opinion except at the transition points around the equinoxes. For the population at large, divided opinion applied in varying degrees throughout the year except in late spring and late summer, when there were few reports of feeling worst. The subtraction procedure provides a continuous picture of seasonal bipolarity among the SAD patients, with the general population showing a lower-amplitude oscillation with a prominent summer slump. There was a phase delay of approximately 1.5 months, relative to the SAD patients, in the swing toward depressed mood in late fall.

Figure 20-4 compares bipolar representations of four seasonal symptom trends in SAD patients and the population at large. In the patients, mood, social activity, sleep, and weight covaried tightly, with similar phase-locked waveforms. The general population showed varying seasonal patterns, symptom by symptom, within the framework of winter exacerbation and summer alleviation, as well as the midsummer mood slump in which approximately 15% of respondents reported feeling worst. The social activity pattern did not strictly mirror mood: After a springtime increase, there was a gradual decline across the summer and fall (with no discrete summer slump), and a marked transient

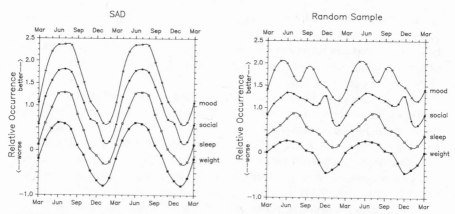

FIGURE 20-4. Seasonal trends in mood, social activity, sleep, and weight, as reported on the Seasonal Pattern Assessment Questionnaire. Diagnosed SAD patients are compared with respondents to a random-sample population survey. In each panel the bottom curve, for weight, is positioned on a scale of −1 (maximum winter exacerbation) to +1 (maximum summer alleviation); successive curves are displaced upward by 0.5 units on the ordinate.

increase during the winter holidays, followed by a precipitous social withdrawal.

Weight and sleep behaved in the simplest manner, like low-amplitude reflections of the patients' trends. There was no evidence of summertime exacerbation of vegetative sleep and weight symptoms concurrent with the mood slump. Wehr *et al.* (1987) report that patients with "reverse SAD" tend to show summer hypersomnia and fatigability, as well as winter hypomania—a cohesive pattern that would indicate an alternate manifestation of the same illness as SAD. Conceivably, evidence for increased atypical/vegetative symptoms in midsummer was washed out in the pooled population result. We identifed 26 individuals in the random sample who reported feeling worst exclusively in summer. Of these potential "reverse SAD" types, only 3 reported sleeping most or gaining most weight at the same time of year. By contrast, 15 reported sleeping most in winter, and 13 reported gaining most weight, following the general population trends. Only 2 reported feeling best in winter, lending minimal evidence for the seasonal bipolar pattern seen so clearly in SAD patients and the population as a whole. These self-report data suggest that summer depression may present a functionally different clinical picture from that of SAD, with a unipolar mood shift occurring independently of vegetative sleep and weight patterns, which show winter exacerbations. Diagnosed "reverse SAD" patients may represent special cases in which all the symptoms of SAD are seasonally shifted as an ensemble—but, unlike the pattern for winter depression, this is not reflected in a general population trend.

The population as a whole resembles SAD patients most closely in the seasonal oscillation of vegetative symptoms, which appear to run their course regardless of transient fluctuations in mood and social activity. One might posit that these aspects of seasonality are a general characteristic of human physiology in the temperate zones (cf. Lacoste and Wirz-Justice, Chapter 12, this volume), without an intimate connection to mood. An extension of the random-sample survey to communities from Florida to New Hampshire (Rosen, Rosenthal, Targum, Hoffman, Kasper, Docherty, Terman, and colleagues, in preparation) will permit quantitative comparisons of these functions across latitudes that vary in the prevalence of the clinical disorder.

Season, of course, is a complex variable, encompassing changes in daylight availability, temperature, and other climatic factors. Zucker (Chapter 11, this volume) draws a distinction between circannual physiology, in which seasonal changes are internally programmed and would persist under constant conditions, and annual cycles that are driven by environmental signals. In the case of SAD, one might posit the latter function, given that phototherapy quickly reverses the wintertime symptoms with minimal transient adjustment.

In order to illustrate the possible dependence of vegetative symptoms on the external lighting environment, Figure 20-5 presents proportional transforms of sleep length data superimposed on the sunrise curve for 41° north latitude (the latitude of New York City). Both patients and random-sample respondents reported proportional seasonal oscillations in sleep length, in tight concordance with the changing time of sunrise. The curves are symmetrical about the equinoces, at which time reports of sleeping most or least averaged out to zero, and reach their maxima and minima near the solstices. Given the tight correlation between sleep and sunrise functions (patients, $r = 0.99$; general population, $r = 0.97$), one could posit that the behavior tracks this signal even if it is sam-

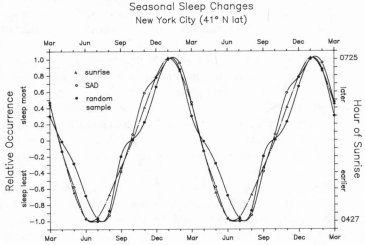

FIGURE 20-5. Scaled seasonal sleep trends for diagnosed SAD patients and respondents to a random-sample population survey, superimposed on the seasonal sunrise function.

pled only imperfectly from within the bedroom. Such results do not demonstrate that sunrise is a direct wake-up signal; winter hypersomnic bouts can extend well past noon. It is possible also that sunrise may be missed entirely and that photic information at midday and evening may supply essential cues to the season, and good correlations with the sleep data. These questions can be resolved experimentally. Simulated spring or summer sunrise in the bedroom, from newly designed computerized lighting apparatus that accurately mimics the dawn twilight transition (Terman, in press, Terman *et al.*, in press-d), may provide a naturalistic wake-up signal with phototherapeutic benefit in winter.

Severity of Seasonality in Patients and Normals

A Global Seasonality Score (GSS) can be derived from the Seasonal Pattern Assessment Questionnaire by adding self-rating points from the severity scales for changing sleep length, social activity, mood, weight, appetite, and energy level. Figure 20-6 (top panel) shows GSS distributions for diagnosed SAD cases, the random sample, and the subset of respondents who indicated feeling worst exclusively in late fall and winter. Although SAD patients showed generally higher scores than the population-at-large, there was considerable overlap among the distributions. More than half of the winter-only subset showed a GSS within the range of the SAD distribution. Clinical interviews would be needed to determine the proportion of SAD diagnoses in the winter-only group. A conservative guess, based on the proportion of winter-only respondents with a GSS greater than the mean SAD GSS (16.7), is 2.4% of the population. The proportion of males and females in this most severely affected subset of the random sample was nearly equal. Furthermore, despite the large preponderance of females among diagnosed SAD patients, the level of severity, as reflected by the mean female GSS (16.7), did not differ statistically from that of males (16.9).

Kasper *et al.* (Chapter 14, this volume) reported that subsyndromal SAD patients, who were responsive to phototherapy, showed a mean GSS of 11.1 in comparison to 2.7 for a control group without seasonal variation. In Figure 20-6 (lower panel), these ratings are put into the context of diagnosed SAD cases and subsets of the random sample, including winter-only respondents who reported that seasonal changes caused a personal problem in their lives ("complainers"); winter-only noncomplainers; the total random sample; and nonseasonals.

The complainers, comprising 14% of the random sample, closely matched diagnosed subsyndromal SAD patients in severity. It can be surmised that this fraction of the general population would be responsive to phototherapy. Noncomplainers, who nonetheless showed seasonal variation, barely exceeded the general population in GSS; perhaps this level of severity should be considered the norm. Nonseasonals, who comprised 31% of the random sample, showed

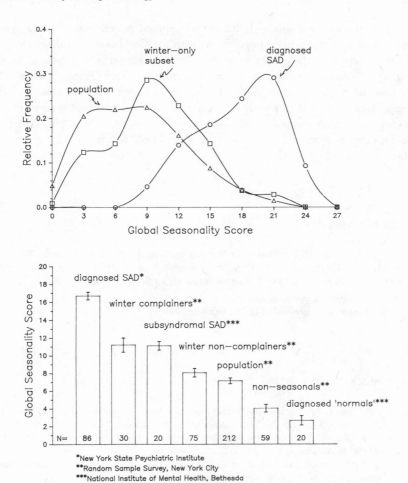

FIGURE 20-6. Top panel: The distribution of Global Seasonality Scores (GSS) from the Seasonal Assessment Pattern Questionnaire, for diagnosed SAD cases ($n = 86$), a random sample taken in New York City ($n = 212$), and a population subset that reported lowered mood exclusively in the late fall and winter ($n = 105$). Bottom panel: Comparisons of the mean GSS ($\pm SEM$) of SAD patients, subsets of the population in a random-sample survey, diagnosed subsyndromal SAD patients who received phototherapy, and trouble-free controls ("diagnosed 'normals' ").

approximately half the severity of the noncomplainers. Finally, the nonseasonal "diagnosed 'normals,' " who received phototherapy without effect (Kasper *et al.*, Chapter 14, this volume), showed the lowest GSS of any group; these people might more appropriately be considered highly selected "supernormals." Future studies may show that the noncomplainers, who comprised 35% of the general population sample, would also respond to phototherapy, with alleviation of their vegetative sleeping and eating patterns and excessive fatigue.

In summary, our survey indicates widespread prevalence of SAD symptoms throughout the general population, with the likelihood of widespread sensitivity to supplementary light in winter. The conclusion is underscored by the ubiquity of seasonal variations in normals, with an exacerbation of vegetative functions in winter (Lacoste and Wirz-Justice, Chapter 12, this volume). The mechanisms of phototherapy, once discovered, will enhance our general understanding of human physiological functioning in relation to sunlight. Our conceptual emphasis on pathology must be questioned, in view of the normative data.

Acknowledgments

Research reported here was supported by National Institute of Mental Health Grant Nos. K02 MH00461, RO1 42931, and MHCRC 30906. I wish to thank Carla Hellekson, Alfred Lewy, Norman Rosenthal, and Anna Wirz-Justice for comments on the manuscript.

This chapter originally appeared in *Journal of Biological Rhythms,* Volume 3, Number 2, pp. 155–172, 1988. Reprinted by permission of The Guilford Press.

References

American Psychiatric Association (1987) *Diagnostic and Statistical Manual of Mental Disorders,* 3rd ed., rev., American Psychiatric Association, Washington, DC.

Broadway, J. W., and J. Arendt (1985) 24-hour rhythms of human 6-hydroxymelatonin sulfate (aMT6s) in Antarctica. J. Endocrinol. *107:* Abstr. 96.

Broadway, J., J. Arendt, and S. Folkard (1987) Bright light phase shifts the human melatonin rhythm during the Antarctic winter. Neurosci. Lett. *79:* 185–189.

Checkley, S., F. Winton, C. Franey, and J. Arendt (1986) Effects of phototherapy upon mood and melatonin in seasonal affective disorder. Paper presented at the Royal College of Psychiatry, London.

Czeisler, C. A. and J. S. Allan (1987) Acute circadian phase reversal in man via bright light exposure: Application to jet-lag. Sleep Res. *16:* 605.

Daan, S., D. G. M. Beersma, and A. A. Borbély (1984) Timing of human sleep: recovery process gated by a circadian pacemaker. Amer. J. Physiol. *246:* R161–R178.

Daan, S., and A. J. Lewy (1984) Scheduled exposure to daylight: A potential strategy to reduce "jet lag" following transmeridian flight. Psychopharmacol. Bull. *20:* 566–568.

Dijk, D. J., C. A. Visscher, G. M. Bloem, D. G. M. Beersma, and S. Daan (1987) Reduction in human sleep duration after bright light exposure in the morning. Neurosci. Lett. *73:* 181–186.

Eastman, C. I. (1987) Bright light in work–sleep schedules for shift workers: Application of circadian rhythm principles. In *Temporal Disorder in Human Oscillatory Systems,* L. Rensing, U. van der Heiden, and M. C. Mackey, eds., pp. 176–185, Springer-Verlag, Berlin.

Honma, K., S. Honma, and T. Wada (1987) Phase dependent phase shift of free-running human circadian rhythms in response to a single bright light pulse. Experientia 43: 1205–1207.

Illnerová, H., and J. Vaněček (1985) Complex control of the circadian rhythm in pineal melatonin production. In *The Pineal Gland: Current State of Pineal Research,* B. Mess, C. Rúzsás, L. Tima, and P. Pévet, eds., pp. 137–153, Elsevier, Amsterdam.

Jacobsen, F. M., T. A. Wehr, D. A. Sack, and N. E. Rosenthal (1986) Predictors of response to phototherapy in seasonal affective disorder. Paper presented at American Psychiatric Association meetings, Washington, DC.

Lewy, A. J., and R. L. Sack (1986) Melatonin physiology and light therapy. Clin. Neuropharmacol. *9:* 196–198.

Lingjaerde, O., T. Bratlid, T. Hansen, and K. G. Gøtestam (1986) Seasonal affective disorder and midwinter insomnia in the Far North: Studies on two related chronobiological disorders in Norway. Proc. Coll. Inter. Neuro-Psychopharmacol. *15:* 187–189.

Moore-Ede, M. C., F. M. Sulzman, and C. A. Fuller (1982) *The Clocks That Time Us: Physiology of the Circadian Timing System,* Harvard University Press, Cambridge, MA.

O'Rourke, D., A. Brzezinski, T. A. Nader, and B. Chew (1987) Serotonin implicated in etiology of seasonal affective disorder. Psychopharmacol. Bull. *23:* 358–360.

O'Rourke, D., J. J. Wurtman, and R. J. Wurtman (1988) Serotonin implicated in etiology of seasonal affective disorder with carbohydrate craving. In *Psychobiology of Bulimia Nervosa,* K. M. Dirke, W. Vendereyken, and D. Ploog, eds., pp. 13–17, Springer-Verlag, Heidelberg.

Potkin, S., M. Zetin, V. Stamenkovic, D. F. Kripke, and W. E. Bunney, Jr. (1986) Seasonal affective disorder: Prevalence varies with latitude and climate. Clin. Neuropharmacol. *9*(Suppl. 4): 181–183.

Rabkin, J. G., D. F. Klein, and F. M. Quitkin (1983) Somatic treatment of acute depression. In *Schizophrenia and Affective Disorders: Biology and Drug Treatment,* A. Rifkin, ed., pp. 35–78, Wright–PSG, Boston.

Rabkin, J. G., J. W. Stewart, P. J. McGrath, J. S. Markowitz, W. Harrison, and F. M. Quitkin (1987) Baseline characteristics of ten-day placebo washout responders in antidepressant trials. Psychiat. Res. *21:* 9–22.

Rosenthal, N. E., G. H. Bradt, and T. A. Wehr (1984a) *Seasonal Pattern Assessment Questionnaire,* National Institute of Mental Health, Bethesda, MD.

Rosenthal, N. E., D. A. Sack, J. C. Gillin, A. J. Lewy, F. K. Goodwin, Y. Davenport, P. S. Mueller, D. A. Newsome, and T. A. Wehr (1984b) Seasonal affective disorder: A description of the syndrome and preliminary findings with light therapy. Arch. Gen. Psychiat. *41:* 72–80.

Terman, M. (in press) Daylight deprivation and replenishment: A psychobiological problem with a naturalistic solution. In *Proceedings of the Second International Daylighting Conference: Architecture and Natural Light,* E. Bales and R. McCluney, eds., American Society of Heating, Refrigeration, and Air Conditioning Engineers, Atlanta, GA.

Terman, M., J. S. Terman, F. M. Quitkin, T. B. Cooper, E. S. Lo, J. M. Gorman, J. W. Stewart, and P. J. McGrath (1988a) Response of the melatonin cycle to phototherapy for seasonal affective disorder. J. Neural Trans. *72:* 147–165.

Terman, M., J. S. Terman, D. Schlager, and F. M. Quitkin (1988b) Efficacy of 10,000 lux light therapy. Paper presented at World Psychiatric Association meetings, Washington, DC.

Terman, M., S. R. Botticelli, B. G. Link, M. J. Link, F. M. Quitkin, T. E. Hardin, and N. E. Rosenthal (in press-a) Seasonal symptom patterns in New York: Patients and population. In *Seasonal Affective Disorder,* C. Thompson and T. Silverstone, eds., CRC Clinical Neuroscience, London.

Terman, M., J. S. Terman, F. M. Quitkin, J. W. Stewart, P. J. McGrath, E. V. Nunes, S. G. Wager, and E. Tricamo (in press-b) Dosing dimensions of light therapy: Duration and time of day. In *Seasonal Affective Disorder,* C. Thompson and T. Silverstone, eds., CRC Clinical Neuroscience, London.

Terman, M., J. S. Terman, F. M. Quitkin, P. J. McGrath, J. W. Stewart, and B. Rafferty (in press-c) Light therapy for seasonal affective disorder: A review of efficacy. Neuropsychopharmacology.

Terman, M., D. Schlager, S. Fairhurst, and B. Perlman (in press-d) Dawn and dusk simulation as a therapeutic intervention. Biol. Psychiat.

Wehr, T. A., D. A. Sack, and N. E. Rosenthal (1987) Seasonal affective disorder with summer depression and winter hypomania. Amer. J. Psychiat. *144*: 1602–1603.

Williams, J. B. W., M. Link, N. E. Rosenthal, and M. Terman (1988a) *Structured Interview Guide for the Hamilton Depression Scale—Seasonal Affective Disorder Version* (SIGH-SAD), New York State Psychiatric Institute, New York.

Williams, J. B. W., M. Link, N. E. Rosenthal and M. Terman (1988b) *Hypomania Interview Guide, with Hyperthymia* (HIGH-SAD), New York State Psychiatric Institute, New York.

Wirz-Justice, A., A. C. Schmid, P. Graw, K. Krauechi, P. Kielholz, W. Poeldinger, H. U. Fisch, and C. Buddeberg (1987) Dose relationships of morning bright white light in seasonal affective disorders. Experientia *43*: 574–576.

Wurtman, R. J., and J. J. Wurtman (1989) Carbohydrates and depression. Sci. Amer. (Jan.): 68–75.

Index

A10 DA cell group, 232, 233
N-Acetyltransferase activity, 203
ACTH
  receptor sensitivity, 323
  seasonal variation, 199, 200
A-D differential, 306
Adipocytes, 117
Adipose tissue, hamsters, 115–118
Adolescents, 46–53
  diagnosis and treatment, 49, 50
  etiology and phenomenology, 46–49
  phototherapy, 47, 48
  SAD natural history, 70
Adrenal glucocorticoids
  body weight, hamsters, 119, 120
  seasonal variation, normals, 195
Affective symptoms, normals, 169
Age differences
  dexamethasone suppression test, 216
  seasonal patterns, 214, 215
Age of onset, 35, 36, 48, 70
Aggressivity dimension, 171
Alaska, 33–43
Alcoholism
  family history, 73
  seasonal variation, 34
Alliesthesia method, 137, 138
Alpha–rho ratio, 359
Amitriptyline, 218
Anergic depression, 65
Anergy syndrome
  in normals, 169
  phototherapy, 291, 360
Animal models, 4, 5, 27, 135, 149–162
Anopheles, 93
Anorexia nervosa, 137, 138
Antidepressant drugs
  versus bright light, 352, 353
  placebo response rate, seasons, 364
  recurrent depressions, 72
  response to, 218

Anxiety
  disorders, 57
  in normals, 168
  phototherapy response, 360
Aphid, photoperiodicity, 91
Appetite changes (see also Weight changes)
  children and adolescents, 49
  measurement, 139
  summer depression, 57, 58
  winter symptoms, 37, 42, 58
Aristotle, 14
Arterial blood pressure, 186–189
Aschoff's rule, 97
Atenolol, 315
Attention deficit disorder, 49, 50
Atypical depression
  versus endogenous depression, 56–61
  seasonal patterns, 61
  winter symptoms, 37, 38, 42, 56–61
Atypical SAD, 291
Auditory evoked potentials, 318, 319
August onset, Alaskan study, 38
Autonomic nervous system, 118

B-cell function, 200
Baillarger, J., 18
Basal metabolic rate, 178, 181, 209, 213
Bat, phase response curve, 93
Beck Depression Inventory
  adolescents, 51, 52
  seasonal variation, scores, 170, 171
Behavioral facilitation system
  characteristics, 231
  and dopamine, 231–257
  seasonal variation, 234–236
Biological equator, 209, 211
Bipolar disorder (see also Recurrent depression)
  bipolar I disorder, 40, 41

Bipolar disorder (*continued*)
  bipolar II disorder
    SAD natural history, 68, 69
    volunteer subjects, survey, 40, 41
  seasonal variation, 34
Birth rhythms, 130
Birthrate, 38
Blood glucose, 178, 179
Blood pressure, 186–189, 210
Blue fluorescent light, 288, 289
Body fat, 108, 109, 178
Body temperature
  hibernation model, 131
  in normals, 182–186, 210
Body weight
  bright light effects, 324
  circannual rhythm, squirrels, 152–157
  diet effects, hamsters, 110, 111
  hamsters, 105–122
  in normals, 176
  reversibility, hamsters, 110
  set points, hibernation, 135–138
  sex differences, hamsters, 111
Breeding, hamsters, 107, 108
Bright light conditions
  versus dim light, 71, 261, 262, 280, 281,
    351, 352
  normals, 261–269
  timing, 282, 316
Brown adipose tissue, 115–117
Burton, Robert, 24

Californian ground squirrels, 133
Carbohydrate craving
  alliesthesia method, 138
  fenfluramine effect, 338
  hibernation model, 131, 138
  in normals, 176, 177
  serotonin, 335, 338
  winter symptoms, 37, 42, 50
Carbohydrate-rich meal, 338, 339
Cardiovascular system, 186–191, 211
Catecholamines, 319
Children, 46–53
  diagnosis and treatment, 49, 50
  etiology and phenomenology, 46–49
  phototherapy, 47–50, 291
  SAD natural history, 70
Children's Depression Rating Scale, 48
m-Chlorophenylpiperazine, 312, 320–323,
    328, 336, 337
Chloroplasts, 88

Cholinergic urticaria, 215
Circadian phase position, 211
Circadian rhythms (*see also* Phase shift)
  animal models, 142, 143
  versus circannual rhythms, 154
  depression theories, 345, 346
  hamsters, 113, 114
  and hibernation, 128, 129
  in house mouse, 90
  individual differences, 158
  light-coupled pacemakers, 101
  methodology, 212
  nightlength importance, 99–103
  phase disturbances, 75, 345, 346, 358, 359
  photoperiod control, 95–103, 358, 359
  programming of, animals, 88–103
  vegetative functions, 190, 191
Circannual rhythms
  characteristics, animals, 152–157
  versus circadian rhythms, 154
  melatonin secretion, 154
Climatotherapy, 25
Clinical Global Impressions Scale, 138
Cloudy weather, 140
Cold manipulation, 25, 26
Cold sensitivity
  in normals, 183–185
  sex differences, 213
Cold treatment, 60
Coleus (green plant), 93
Concanavalin A, 314, 325, 326
Conception rates, 130
Construct validity
  animal models, 150
  SAD, 81
Control treatments, 278, 279, 363, 364
Core body temperature, 184–186
Cortisol
  body weight regulation, 120
  m-CPP effect, 337
  5-hydroxytryptophan effect, 335, 336
  phototherapy effect, 322
  seasonal variation, 195, 198–200, 210, 313, 322
Cosinor analysis, 212
Critical flicker–fusion, 169
Crossover design, 276, 277
Cytochrome oxidase, 116

Dark treatment, 60
Dawn–dusk transitions, 211
"Day within," 87–103
Daylength, 211

Deer mouse, 93
Delta sleep
  normals, 175
  phototherapy, 317, 318
  recurrent depression, 74
  sex differences, 217
  winter depression, 38, 73, 316, 317
Descriptive validity, 80, 81
Dexamethasone suppression test
  methodology, 216
  phototherapy effect, 322
  recurrent depressions, 73, 74
  seasonal variation, 200, 216, 218
  winter depression, 38, 313
Diabetes, 139, 178, 211
Diet effects, hamsters, 110, 111
Dim-light conditions
  versus bright light, 71, 261, 262, 280, 281,
    351, 352
  as control, 362, 363
  melatonin onset, marker, 306, 306
  in normals, 261, 262
Diurnal variation
  and phototherapy response, 291, 360
  sleep, 317
Djungarian hamsters, 121
Dopamine
  and heat challenge, hypothermia, 250–252,
    256
  incentive–reward motivation, 232–234
  locomotion initiation, 232
  in normals, behavior, 230–257
  prolactin effects, 243–250, 256, 312, 321,
    322
  spontaneous eye blinking, 252–256
Dopamine-β-hydroxylase, 187
Dopamine receptor supersensitivity, 244, 249,
  250
Dose–response, 280–282, 364–366
Double-blind testing, 362
Drosophila auraria
  light cycle entrainment, 99, 100
  phase response curve, 93, 94
Drosophila pseudoobscura, 91, 93–96
Drug prescriptions, 218
DSM-III, 81–83
DSM-III-R, 81–83, 361
Duration of phototherapy
  and intensity of exposure, 287, 365
  and outcome, 283, 286, 287, 364–366

Electroencephalography
  normals, 174–176

recurrent depression, 73–75
Emperor penguins, 134
Endogenous features
  phototherapy, 71, 291
  seasonal patterns, 61
  summer depression, 56–61
Energizing effect, 301, 304, 305
Energy balance, 115–120
Energy intake, 176
Energy level
  children and adolescents, 50–52
  in normals, 168, 169
Environmental lighting, 267
Environmental treatments, 25
Epidemiology, 357–374
  overview, 2–4
  recurrent depression, 67, 68
  seasonal affective disorder, 67, 68, 357–374
Esquirol, Julien, 16–18, 56
Euglena, 93
European starling, 154, 158
Evening light
  effectiveness, 282, 283, 316, 363, 364
  energizing effect, 304, 305
  and morning light, 363, 364
  phase-shift hypothesis, 295–305
Event-related potentials, 268, 318, 319
Exercise-induced heart rate, 187
Expectations of treatment, 278, 279
Eye blink (*see* Spontaneous eye blinking)
Eye exposure, phototherapy, 290
Eye strain, 290

Face validity
  animal models, 150
  seasonal affective disorder, 80
Fall-onset depression, 11, 12, 367–370
Family history
  recurrent depression, 73
  survey data, 39, 40
Fasting glucose levels, 178, 179
Fatigue
  in normals, 168, 169, 210, 266
  phototherapy response, 360
  phototherapy side effect, 290
Females (*see* Sex differences)
Fenfluramine, 204, 338
Fertility, 38, 43
Finger temperature, 184–186
Flicker–fusion, 169
Flowering time, photoperiodicity, 91
Fluorescent light, 287, 288, 347

Fluoxetine, 339
Food intake
  normals, 176–183
  set points, hibernation, 137, 138
Free fatty acids, 178, 180
Freiburger Personality Inventory, 170, 171
Full-spectrum light, 287, 289

Galen, 25, 27
Global Seasonality Score, 372
Glucagon levels, 178, 180, 210
Glucocorticoids, 119, 120
Glucose levels
  in normals, 178, 179, 210
  sex differences, 213
Glucose tolerance, 38
Goal-directed behavior, 233, 234
Golden hamsters, 105–122, 132, 133
Golden-mantled ground squirrels, 152–157
Gonad size
  hamster model, 342, 343
  hibernation model, 132
Gonadal steroids, 135
Gonadostat resetting, 135
Gonadotropins
  body weight influence, hamsters, 119
  and feedback changes, 135
Gonyaulax, 93
Greek physicians, 26
Grenville, Ann, 14
Griesinger, W., 18
Ground squirrels
  body fat regulation, 109
  circannual rhythms, 152–157
  hibernation, 131, 132
Growth hormone, 194, 196, 210
Guanosine diphosphate binding, 116

Hamilton Rating Scale for Depression, 27, 28,
    275
  evaluation, 361, 362
  supplement, 276
Hamsters, 105–122
  adipose tissue changes, 115–118
  body weight variations, 105–122
  circannual rhythms, 157
  depression model, 342, 343
  hibernation, 132, 133
  light-coupled oscillators, 101, 157
  metabolism variations, 105–122
  nonphotoperiodic responses, 160

phase response curve, 93
  seasonal reproduction, 107, 108, 342, 343
Headaches, 290
Heart disease, 187
Heart rate, 186, 210
Heat challenge, 243, 250–252, 256
Heat manipulation, 25, 26
Hibernation, 127–144
  depression model, 27, 128
  Galen's theory, 25
  periodic events model, 128, 129
  SAD dissimilarities, 130–132
  set points, body weight, 135–138
  sex differences, 213
  species diversity, 134
  synchronizing agents, diversity, 132–134
High-fat diet, 110, 111
Hippocrates, 13, 14, 26
Hokkaido pacemaker, 93, 94
Holidays, depression, 34
Homovanillic acid
  phototherapy effect, 322
  seasonal variation, 313, 322
Horne–Östberg questionnaire, 172, 174
Hospital admissions, 141, 142
House mouse
  circadian rhythms, 90
  phase response curve, 93
17-Hydroxycorticosteroids, 195
5-Hydroxyindoleacetic acid
  phototherapy effect, 320
  seasonal variation, 205, 312, 320, 334
  and suicide, 334
Hydroxyindole-O-methyltransferase, 200, 203
6-Hydroxymelatonin sulfate, 202, 203
5-Hydroxytryptophan, 312, 320, 335, 336
Hypersomnia, 291, 359
Hypertension, 187
Hyperthymia, 42
Hypocortisolemia, 323
Hypomania
  differentiation, 42
  natural history, SAD, 68, 69
  phototherapy, 265
  summer symptom spectrum, 38, 42
Hypomania Scale, 276
Hypothalamic paraventricular nucleus (see Para-
    ventricular nucleus)
Hypothalamic–pituitary–adrenal axis, 322,
    323, 328
Hypothermia
  dopamine indicator, challenge, 243, 250–
    252, 256

Hypothermia (*continued*)
    heat challenge, 243, 250–252
    phototherapy, 252
Hypothyroidism, 194

Illuminance, 280–282
Illumination exposure, 346–349
Imipramine
    binding, 204, 208–210
    versus bright light, 352, 353
    recurrent depression, 72
    torpor reduction, animals, 128, 129
Immune function
    and corticosteroids, 200
    seasonal depression, 314, 324–327
Incandescent light, 288, 347
Incentive–reward motivation, 231–234
    behavioral facilitation system, 231–234
    neurobiology, dopamine, 232–234
    seasonal variation, 235
Indirect light, 290
Individual differences, 157–159
Insomnia, 217, 128
Insulin
    body weight role, 120
    in normals, 178–180, 210
Insulin-dependent diabetes, 139, 178
Intensity of light
    antidepressant effect, 280–282, 364, 365
    and light duration, 287
Inventory of Seasonal Variation, 237–241
Involutional melancholia, 79, 80
3-Iodothyronine (T_3), 191–194, 209, 210, 323

Japanese fruit fly, 93
Jet-lag
    and animal research, 150
    phototherapy, 360

Kellogg, J. H., 342
Kern, Herbert, 26, 27
Ketone bodies, 178, 181
Kraepelin, Emil, 18, 21, 24–26
Kraines, S., 18, 56

"Larks," 173, 174
Latitude, 24, 25, 34, 36
Leucophaea (cockroach), 93
Lewis reaction, 184

Libido
    hibernation model, 130, 132
    winter symptoms, survey, 37, 38, 57
Light cycles, 91–103
Light-sensitive markers, 327
Light supersensitivity, 75
Light therapy (*see* Phototherapy)
Limbic system, 233, 234
Lipoprotein lipase activity, 117, 118
Lithium, 128, 129
Lizard, photoperiodicity, 91
Locomotion
    behavioral facilitation system, 231
    neurobiology, dopamine, 231, 232
    seasonal variation, 235
Longitudinal studies, 212
Lunar–tidal programming, 88
Lux, 280–282, 346–348
Lymphocytes, 314, 324–327

Mania, 34
Masculinity dimension, 171
m-CPP (*see* m-Chlorophenylpiperazine)
Meadow voles, 160
Media recruitment, 275
Medial hypothalamus, 217
Melancholia
    phototherapy response, 342–353, 360
    validity, 80
Melanocyte-stimulating hormone, 199
Melatonin
    body weight regulation, hamsters, 111–122
    circannual rhythms, squirrels, 154
    duration of secretion, 107, 121
    energy balance regulation, 119
    evaluation, 315, 316
    graded responses, hamsters, 112
    5-hydroxytryptophan effect, 335, 336
    hypothesis, 6, 7, 75, 315
    -independent mechanisms, 114, 115
    light supersensitivity, 75
    light suppression, marker, 268
    as marker, circadian phase, 305, 306
    morning light influence, 299–301
    nonseasonal depression, 343, 344
    onset, 299–303
    phase-shift hypothesis, 299–308
    phototherapy response, 75, 268
    rebound, 344
    reproduction regulation, hamsters, 107, 108
    seasonal variation, normals, 200–203, 210
    timing of signal, 111, 112

Menstrual cycle, 249
Menstrual difficulties, 38, 43
Mesocricetus, 93, 105–122
Meta-analysis, 283
Metabolic rate
  and adaptation, 207
  in normals, 178, 181, 210
Metabolism
  bright light conditions, 324
  hamsters, 105–122
  in normals, 176–183, 209, 210
  seasonal depression, 313, 323, 324
  sex differences, 213
Methodology
  data base, 138–142
  phototherapy, 274–279, 361–364
  seasonal change measurement, 212–215
3-Methoxy-4-hydroxyphenylglycol
  phototherapy effect, 319
  seasonal variation, 312
Microtus ochrogaster, 160
Midday light, 102, 103, 363, 364
Milton, John, 14, 56 ·
Mitogen-induced lymphocyte blastogenesis,
      324–327
Miyake pacemaker, 93, 94
Monoamines, 201–204
Mood
  behavioral facilitation system, 231
  children and adolescents, 50–52
  measurement of, 275, 276
  New York City survey, 369–372
  in normals, 168, 169, 266
  phototherapy, normals, 266
  recurrent patterns, 76
  seasonal variation, 235
  serotonin levels, 334
Morning light
  controversy, 316
  dose–response, 365, 366
  effectiveness, 282, 283, 304, 305, 363, 364
  and evening light, 363, 364
  melatonin onset, 299–303
  phase-shift hypothesis, 399–305
Morningness–eveningness dimension, 172,
      174, 211
Mosquito, 93
Motivation (*see* Incentive–reward motivation)
aMT6S (*see* 6-Hydroxymelatonin sulfate)
Mus musculus, 90, 93

Natural history studies, 24, 68–70
Natural selection, 158, 159

Neurotransmitters
  phototherapy effect, 319–322
  seasonal variation, normals, 201–204
New York City survey, 367
Newspaper recruitment, 275
Nightlength signal
  circadian system entrainment, 99–103
  seasonality, 91
Nonseasonal depression
  phototherapy, 342–353, 360
  symptom severity, 372, 373
Norepinephrine
  phototherapy effect, 319
  seasonal variation, 186, 312, 328
  Syrian hamster, 116, 118
Normals, 167–219
  children and adolescents, 50–52
  dopamine, 230–257
  metabolism and feeding, 176–183
  phototherapy effect, 260–269
  seasonal changes, 5, 6, 33, 34, 167–219
  sleep, 173–176
  thermoregulation, 183–186
  vegetative functions, 187–191
Norwegian study, 34
November onset, 38
Nucleus accumbens
  dopamine, locomotion, 232
  incentive–reward motivation, 232, 233
  limbic–motor system interface, 233, 234

Obesity, 106
  index, 176
Oral temperature, 182, 185, 186
Ordering effect, 277, 303
Oscillating systems
  circadian rhythms, 88
  control of, 91–103
  individual differences, 158
"Owls," 173, 174

P*300,* 268, 318, 319
Pacemakers, 161
Parasympathetic nerves, 118
Paraventricular nucleus
  energy balance, 188
  lesions, 217
Passerine birds, 88
Patient expectations, 278, 279
Performance
  in normals, 169
  phototherapy effect, normals, 266
Periodicity, animal models, 87–103

Peripheral blood lymphocytes, 324–327
Peromyscus leucopus, 93
Peromyscus maniculatus, 93
Personality, 170–173
Phase angle hypothesis, 303, 345
Phase response curve
  animal models, 161, 296
  circadian pacemakers, 91–103
Phase shift, 295–308
  controversy, 6, 345, 346
  depression theory, evaluation, 345, 346
  phototherapy effect, 285, 358, 359
Phase typing, 297
Photoperiod window, 343, 344
Photoperiodic phenomona
  animal models, 87–103, 142, 143
  circannual rhythms, 152–157
  depression theories, 342–344
  diet interactions, hamsters, 110, 111
  graded responses, hamsters, 112
  hibernation, 132–134
  individual differences, 158, 159
  sensing of, 91–103
  trait response, 159, 160
Phototherapy
  Alaskan study, 41
  animal models, 102
  children and adolescents, 47–50
  circadian basis, 102, 297–308
  dopamine function, 247–257
  duration, 283, 286, 287
  effectiveness, 273–292, 357–374
  epidemiology, 357–374
  history, 26, 27, 273, 274
  hypothermic response, 250–252
  methodology, 274–279, 361–364
  nightlength shortening principle, 102
  nonseasonal depression, 342–353
  overview, 6, 7
  prediction of response, 291
  prolactin secretion, 247–250
  psychological effects, normals, 260–269
  recurrent depression, response, 70, 71
  and relapse, 71
  risk factors, 40
  serotonin role, 333–339
  side effects, 290, 291
  spontaneous eye blinking, 252–255
  timing importance, 102, 103, 138, 282–285
Phytohemagglutinin, 314, 325, 326
Pilcz, A., 18, 56
Pineal-independent mechanisms, 114, 115
Pinealectomy, 158, 159
Pinel, Philippe, 14–16, 25

Placebo response, 277–279, 362, 363
  rate of, 363, 364
  seasonal aspects, 364, 365
Posidonius, 13
Prairie voles, 160
Prediction of phototherapy response, 291
Predictive validity
  animal models, 150
  seasonal affective disorder, 81
Presentation of light, phototherapy, 288–290
Process S, 359
Profile of Mood States, 266
Prolactin
  and body weight, hamsters, 119
  m-CPP effect, 337
  dopamine function indicator, 243–250, 312, 321, 322
  5-hydroxytryptophan effect, 335, 336
  phototherapy effect, 247–250, 322
  seasonal variation, 194–197, 210, 312, 327, 328
  and serotonin, 320, 335
Protein consumption, 176, 177
Psychomotor symptoms, 58
Pulse rate
  circadian rhythms, 190, 191
  seasonal variation, 186
Pupil size, 190, 210

Recruitment of subjects, 275
Rectal temperature
  circadian rhythms, 190, 191
  in normals, 182, 186
Recurrent depression, 64–76
  family history, 73
  laboratory studies, 73–75
  SAD comparison, 64–76
  temporal distribution, 140
  treatment response, 70–72
Red light, 288, 289, 351, 352
Relapse, 176, 277
Relaxation treatment, 50
REM density
  normals, 174–176
  phototherapy, 317, 318
  recurrent depression, 74
REM latency
  normals, 174–176
  phototherapy, 317, 318
  recurrent depression, 73–75
  winter depression, 38
REM sleep
  and hibernation, 131

REM sleep (*continued*)
  normals, 174–176
  phototherapy, 317, 318
Reproduction
  circannual rhythms, 157
  hamsters, regulation, 107, 108, 342, 343
  hibernation model, 130–132, 134
  individual differences, 159
Research Diagnostic Criteria, 34, 35
Respiratory quotient, 178, 181
Respiratory rate, 190, 191
Response to drug treatment, 218
Resting metabolic rate, 313, 323, 324
Restraint Scale, 139
Retinal mechanisms, 290
Retinal melatonin, 358
Reverse diurnal variation, 291
Reverse SAD, 370
Reversed neurovegetative pattern, 72
Reward (*see* Incentive–reward motivation)
Rewarming rates, 183–185, 210, 213
Rhesus monkeys, 154
Rho interval, 359
Rhodopsin, 347
Roman physicians, 26
Running-wheel activity, 88, 89

Sarcophaga, 93
Saturnid moths, 101
Scheduling (*see* Timing of phototherapy)
Screening techniques, 140
Seasonal Pattern Assessment Questionnaire, 56, 57, 169, 261, 367, 372
Seasonal Symptom Checklist for Children, 48, 50, 51
Seasonal Symptom Questionnaire, 57
Serotonergic agents, 339
Serotonin, 333–339
  in diet, 339, 340
  and mood, 334
  and prolactin secretion, 250
  SAD symptoms role, 334, 335
  seasonal variation, 201, 204–206, 210, 334
Set points, 135–138
Sex differences
  body weight, hamsters, 111
  children and adolescents, 48, 51
  dexamethasone suppression test, 216
  hibernation model, 131
  New York City survey, 367, 368
  normals, sleep, 174–176

Shift workers
  and animal research, 150
  phototherapy, 360
Shivering response, 184
Siberian hamsters, 343
Side effects, phototherapy, 290, 291
Skin exposure, phototherapy, 290
Skin temperature, 183, 210
Slave oscillators
  circadian program, 101
  individual differences, 158
  interspecies constancy, 161
Sleep
  children and adolescents, 49
  deprivation
    controlling for, 279
    seasonal response, 218
  fraction, 174
  hibernation model, 131
  length
    New York City survey, 371, 372
    normals, 174–176, 210
    sex differences, 213, 216, 217
    winter depression, 316, 317
  methodological factors, 216, 217
  New York City survey, 369–373
  in normals, 33, 34, 168, 169, 173–176, 210
  and phase-shift studies, 296–308
  phototherapy effect, 316–318, 359
  recurrent depression, 73–75
  serotonin role, 334, 335
  sex differences, 213, 216, 217
  summer depression, 57, 58
  time (*see* Sleep, length)
  winter symptom spectrum, 37, 38, 58, 316–318
Slimming treatments, 139
Slow-wave sleep
  hibernation, 131
  in normals, 174–176, 210
  recurrent depressions, 74
Social activity, 369–372
Sparrows, 101
Spectrum of light
  illuminance exposure, 346, 347
  phototherapy effectiveness, 287–289
Spontaneous eye blinking
  dopamine indicator, 243, 252–256
  phototherapy, 252–256
Spring-onset depression
  course of illness, 22
  incidence, 11, 12, 367–370
Standard metabolic rate, 178
Steroids (*see* Gonadal steroids)

Sturnus vulgaris, 154
Subjective cold sensitivity, 183
Subjective night, 92, 99, 100
Suicide
   risk factors, 40
   seasonal variation, 24, 34, 142, 211
   serotonin levels, 334
   summer depression, 57
Summer depression, 55–61
   environmental factors, 60, 61
   Esquirol's description, 17, 56
   history, 17–23
   incidence, 11, 12, 367–372
   natural history, 24
   New York City survey, 369–372
   reliability, 361
   symptomatology, 56–60
   versus winter depression, 55–61
Summer symptom spectrum, 38
Supersensitivity to light, 75
Suprachiasmatic nuclei
   circannual rhythms, 154
   energy balance, 118
   illuminance exposure, 347, 348
Svalbard ptarmigan, 134, 136, 137
Sympathetic nervous system, 118
Syrian hamsters, 105–122, 157, 160, 342, 343

T-cell function, 200
T experiments, 100, 103
T_3 (*see* 3-Iodothyronine)
T_4 (*see* Thyroxine)
Taphozous, 93
Temperature effects, 103, 134 (*see also* Body
   temperature)
Temperature manipulation, 25, 26
Temporal isolation studies
   normals, 174–176
   sex differences, 174–176, 213
Thermal perception, 183
Thermoregulation
   hamsters, 115–117
   in normals, 183–186
   sex differences, 213, 214
Thyroid function
   acclimatization role, 207
   energy balance, 119
   seasonal variation, 191–194, 210
Thyrotropin (TSH)
   methodological aspects, 216
   seasonal variation, 192, 194, 195, 210, 216,
     313, 323

Thyrotropin-releasing hormone
   recurrent depression, 73, 74
   seasonal variation, 192, 194, 195, 210, 216,
     323
Thyroxine (T_4), 191–194, 210, 323
Tidal programming, 88–90
Timing of phototherapy, 282–285
   animal models, 102, 103
   antidepressant response, 282–285
   controversy, 316
   and illuminance exposure, 349
   morning light, 304, 305
Torpor, 128, 134
Travel, 76
Trazodone, 336, 339
Tratment response, 70–72
Tricyclic antidepressants (*see also* Antidepres-
   sant drugs)
   recurrent depression, 72
Tromsø, Norway, 34
L-Tryptophan
   phototherapy comparison, 338
   SAD treatment, 204, 313, 321, 338
TSH (*see* Thyrotropin)
Turkish hamster, 343, 344

Ultraviolet light, 288

V-type atypical depression, 65
Validity, 79–83, 141, 150
Vasomotor tone, 213
Vegetative symptoms, 360, 367, 370–372
Ventral striatum, 232
Ventral tegmental area of Tsai, 232, 233
Ventromedial hypothalamus, 217
Vigilance, 266
Visual evoked potentials, 318, 319
Voles, 160
Volunteers, bias, 35
Vulnerability, 267, 268

Weight changes (*see also* Body weight)
   bright light conditions, 324
   hibernation model, 131, 132
   methodology, weaknesses, 139
   New York City survey, 369–372
   serotonin, 335
   set points, 135–138
   summer depression, 57, 58
   winter symptoms, 37, 42, 58

Weight/height index, 139, 176
White adipose tissue, 117, 118
White-footed mice, 119
White noise, 140
Willis, Thomas, 26
Winter depression
    DSM-III-R, 361
    Esquirol's description, 17
    history, 17–23
    incidence, 11, 12, 369–372
    natural history, 24

New York City survey, 369–372
    phase-shift hypothesis, 295–308
    versus summer depression, 55–61
    symptoms, 56–60
Women (*see* Sex differences)
Woodchucks
    circadian cycles, experiment, 143
    hibernation, 133

Zeitgebers, 89–103, 161